MANAGERIAL ECONOMICS
Theory and Practice

MANAGERIAL ECONOMICS
Theory and Practice

THOMAS J. WEBSTER

Lubin School of Business
Pace University
New York, NY

ACADEMIC PRESS

An imprint of Elsevier Science

Amsterdam Boston Heidelberg London New York Oxford Paris
San Diego San Francisco Singapore Sydney Tokyo

Academic Press
An imprint of Elsevier Science
525 B Street, Suite 1900, San Diego, California 92101-4495, USA
http://www.academicpress.com

Academic Press
84 Theobald's Road, London WC1X 8RR, UK
http://www.academicpress.com

Library of Congress Catalog Card Number: 2003102999

International Standard Book Number: 0-12-740852-5

PRINTED IN THE UNITED STATES OF AMERICA
03 04 05 06 07   7 6 5 4 3 2 1

To my sons, Adam Thomas and Andrew Nicholas

CONTENTS

1

INTRODUCTION

2

INTRODUCTION TO MATHEMATICAL ECONOMICS

3

THE ESSENTIALS OF DEMAND AND SUPPLY

4

ADDITIONAL TOPICS IN DEMAND THEORY

5

PRODUCTION

6

COST

7

PROFIT AND REVENUE MAXIMIZATION

8

MARKET STRUCTURE: PERFECT COMPETITION AND MONOPOLY

9

MARKET STRUCTURE: MONOPOLISTIC COMPETITION

10

MARKET STRUCTURE: DUOPOLY AND OLIGOPOLY

11

PRICING PRACTICES

12

CAPITAL BUDGETING

13

INTRODUCTION TO GAME THEORY

14

RISK AND UNCERTAINTY

15

MARKET FAILURE AND GOVERNMENT
INTERVENTION

1

INTRODUCTION

WHAT IS ECONOMICS?

Economics is the study of how individuals and societies make choices subject to constraints. The need to make choices arises from *scarcity*. From the perspective of society as a whole, scarcity refers to the limitations placed on the production of goods and services because *factors of production* are finite. From the perspective of the individual, scarcity refers to the limitations on the consumption of goods and services because of limited of personal income and wealth.

Definition: Economics is the study of how individuals and societies choose to utilize scarce resources to satisfy virtually unlimited wants.

Definition: Scarcity describes the condition in which the availability of resources is insufficient to satisfy the wants and needs of individuals and society.

The concepts of scarcity and choice are central to the discipline of economics. Because of scarcity, whenever the decision is made to follow one course of action, a simultaneous decision is made to forgo some other course of action. Thus, any action requires a sacrifice. There is another common admonition that also underscores the all pervasive concept of scarcity: if an offer seems too good to be true, then it probably is.

Individuals and societies cannot have everything that is desired because most goods and services must be produced with scarce productive resources. Because productive resources are scarce, the amounts of goods and services produced from these ingredients must also be finite in supply. The concept of scarcity is summarized in the economic admonition that there is no "free lunch." Goods, services, and productive resources that are scarce have a positive price. Positive prices reflect the competitive interplay between the supply of and demand for scarce resources and commodities. A commodity with a positive price is referred to as an *economic good*. Commodities that have a zero price because they are relatively unlimited in supply are called *free goods*.[1]

What are these scarce *productive resources*? Productive resources, sometimes called *factors of production* or *productive inputs*, are classified into one of four broad categories: *land, labor, capital*, and *entrepreneurial ability*. Land generally refers to all natural resources. Included in this category are wildlife, minerals, timber, water, air, oil and gas deposits, arable land, and mountain scenery.

Labor refers to the physical and intellectual abilities of people to produce goods and services. Of course, not all workers are the same; that is, labor is not homogeneous. Different individuals have different physical and intellectual attributes. These differences may be inherent, or they may be acquired through education and training. Although the Declaration of Independence proclaims that everyone has certain unalienable rights, in an economic sense all people are not created equal. Thus some people will become fashion models, professional athletes, or college professors; others will work as clergymen, cooks, police officers, bus drivers, and so forth. Differences in human talents and abilities in large measure explain why some individuals' labor services are richly rewarded in the market and others, despite their noble calling, such as many public school teachers, are less well compensated.

Capital refers to manufactured commodities that are used to produce goods and services for final consumption. Machinery, office buildings, equipment, warehouse space, tools, roads, bridges, research and development, factories, and so forth are all a part of a nation's capital stock. Economic capital is different from *financial capital*, which refers to such things as stocks, bonds, certificates of deposits, savings accounts, and cash. It should be noted, however, that financial capital is typically used to finance a firm's acquisition of economic capital. Thus, there is an obvious linkage between an investor's return on economic capital and the financial asset used to underwrite it.

In market economies, almost all income generated from productive activity is returned to the owners of factors of production. In politically and economically free societies, the owners of the factors of production are collectively referred to as the household sector. Businesses or firms, on the

[1] Is air a free good? Many students would assert that it is, but what is the price of a clean environment? Inhabitants of most advanced industrialized societies have decided that a cleaner environment is a socially desirable objective. Environmental regulations to control the disposal of industrial waste and higher taxes to finance publicly mandated environmental protection programs, which are passed along to the consumer in the form of higher product prices, make it clear that clean air and clean water are not free.

other hand, are fundamentally activities, and as such have no independent source of income. That activity is to transform inputs into outputs. Even firm owners are members of the household sector. Financial capital is the vehicle by which business acquire economic capital from the household sector. Businesses accomplish this by issuing equity shares and bonds and by borrowing from *financial intermediaries*, such as commercial banks, savings banks, and insurance companies.

Entrepreneurial ability refers to the ability to recognize profitable opportunities, and the willingness and ability to assume the risk associated with marshaling and organizing land, labor, and capital to produce the goods and services that are most in demand by consumers. People who exhibit this ability are called *entrepreneurs*.

In market economies, the value of land, labor, and capital is directly determined through the interaction of supply and demand. This is not the case for *entrepreneurial ability*. The return to the entrepreneur is called *profit*. Profit is defined as the difference between total revenue earned from the production and sale of a good or service and the total cost associated with producing that good or service. Although profit is indirectly determined by the interplay of supply and demand, it is convenient to view the return to the entrepreneur as a residual.

OPPORTUNITY COST

The concepts of scarcity and choice are central to the discipline of economics. These concepts are used to explain the behavior of both producers and consumers. It is important to understand, however, that in the face of scarcity whenever the decision is made to follow one course of action, a simultaneous decision is made to forgo some other course of action. When a high school graduate decides to attend college or university, a simultaneous decision is made to forgo entering the work force and earning an income. Scarcity necessitates trade-offs. That which is forgone whenever a choice is made is referred to by economists as *opportunity cost*. That which is sacrificed when a choice is made is the next best alternative. It is the path that we would have taken had our actual choice not been open to us.

Definition: Opportunity cost is the highest valued alternative forgone whenever a choice is made.

MACROECONOMICS VERSUS MICROECONOMICS

Scarcity, and the manner in which individuals and society make choices, are fundamental to the study of economics. To examine these important issues, the field of economics is divided into two broad subfields: *macro-economics* and *microeconomics*.

As the name implies, macroeconomics looks at the big picture. Macro-economics is the study of entire economies and economic systems and specifically considers such broad economic aggregates as gross domestic product, economic growth, national income, employment, unemployment, inflation, and international trade. In general, the topics covered in macro-economics are concerned with the economic environment within which firm managers operate. For the most part, macroeconomics focuses on the variables over which the managerial decision maker has little or no control but may be of considerable importance in the making of economic decisions at the micro level of the individual, firm, or industry.

Definition: Macroeconomics is the study of aggregate economic behavior. Macroeconomists are concerned with such issues as national income, employment, inflation, national output, economic growth, interest rates, and international trade.

By contrast, microeconomics is the study of the behavior and interaction of individual economic agents. These economic agents represent individual firms, consumers, and governments. Microeconomics deals with such topics as profit maximization, utility maximization, revenue or sales maximization, *production efficiency*, market structure, capital budgeting, environmental protection, and governmental regulation.

Definition: Microeconomics is the study of individual economic behavior. Microeconomists are concerned with output and input markets, product pricing, input utilization, production costs, market structure, capital budgeting, profit maximization, production technology, and so on.

WHAT IS MANAGERIAL ECONOMICS?

Managerial economics is the application of economic theory and quantitative methods (mathematics and statistics) to the managerial decision-making process. Simply stated, managerial economics is applied microeconomics with special emphasis on those topics of greatest interest and importance to managers. The role of managerial economics in the decision-making process is illustrated in Figure 1.1.

Definition: Managerial economics is the synthesis of microeconomic theory and quantitative methods to find optimal solutions to managerial decision-making problems.

To illustrate the scope of managerial economics, consider the case the owner of a company that produces a product. The manner in which the firm owner goes about his or her business will depend on the company's organizational objectives. Is the firm owner a profit maximizer, or is manage-

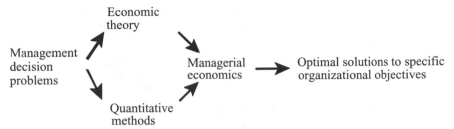

FIGURE 1.1   The role of managerial economics in the decision-making process.

ment more concerned something else, such as maximizing the company's market share? What specific conditions must be satisfied to optimally achieve these objectives? Economic theory attempts to identify the conditions that need to be satisfied to achieve optimal solutions to these and other management decision problems.

As we will see, if the company's organizational objective is profit maximization then, according to economic theory, the firm should continue to produce widgets up to the point at which the additional cost of producing an additional widget (marginal cost) is just equal to the additional revenue earned from its sale (marginal revenue). To apply the "marginal cost equals marginal revenue" rule, however, the firm's management must first be able to estimate the empirical relationships of total cost of widget production and total revenues from widget sales. In other words, the firm's operations must be quantified so that the optimization principles of economic theory may be applied.

THEORIES AND MODELS

The world is a very complicated place. In attempting to understand how markets operate, for example, the economist makes a number of simplifying assumptions. Without these assumptions, the ability to make predictions about cause-and-effect relationships becomes unmanageable. The "law" of demand asserts that the price of a good or service and its quantity demanded are inversely related, *ceteris paribus*. This theory asserts that, other factors remaining unchanged (i.e., *ceteris paribus*), individuals will tend to purchase increasing amounts of a good or service as prices fall and decreasing amounts as the prices rise. Of course, other things do not remain unchanged. Along with changes in the price of the good or service, disposable income, the prices of related commodities, tastes, and so on, may also change. It is difficult, if not impossible, to generalize consumer behavior when multiple demand determinants are simultaneously changing.

Definition: *Ceteris paribus* is an assertion in economic theory that in the analysis of the relationship between two variables, all other variables are assumed to remain unchanged.

It is good to remember that economics is a social, not a physical, science. Economists cannot conduct controlled, laboratory experiments, which makes economic theorizing all the more difficult. It also makes economists vulnerable to ridicule. One economic quip, for example, asserts that if all the economists in the world were laid end to end, they would never reach a conclusion. This is, of course, an unfair criticism. In business, the objective is to reduce uncertainty. The study of economics is an attempt to bring order out of seeming chaos. Are economists sometimes wrong? Certainly. But the alternative for managers would be to make decisions in the dark.

What then are theories? Theories are abstractions that attempt to strip away unnecessary detail to expose only the essential elements of observable behavior. Theories are often expressed in the form of models. A *model* is the formal expression of a theory. In economics, models may take the form of diagrams, graphs, or mathematical statements that summarize the relationship between and among two or more variables. More often than not, there will be more than one theory to explain any given economic phenomenon. When this is the case, which theory should we use?

"GOOD" THEORIES VERSUS "BAD" THEORIES

The ultimate test of a theory is its ability to make predictions. In general, "good" theories predict with greater accuracy than "bad" theories. If one theory is known to predict a particular phenomenon with 95% accuracy, and another theory of the same phenomena is known to predict with 96% accuracy, the former theory is replaced by the latter theory. It is in the nature of scientific progress that "good" theories replace "bad" theories. Of course, "good" and "bad" are relative concepts. If one theory predicts an event with greater accuracy, then it will replace alternative theories, no matter how well those theories may have predicted the same event in the past.

Another important observation in the process of theorizing is that all other factors being equal, simpler models, or theories, tend to predict better than more complicated ones. This principle of parsimony is referred to as *Ockham's razor*, which was named after the fourteenth-century English philosopher William of Ockham.

Definition: Ockham's razor is the principle that, other things being equal, the simplest explanation tends to be the correct explanation.

The category of "bad" theories includes two common errors in economics. The most common error, perhaps, relates to statements or theories regarding cause and effect. It is tempting in economics to look at two sequential events and conclude that the first event caused the second event.

Clearly, this is not always the case, some financial news reports not with standing. For example, a report that the Dow Jones Industrial Average fell 200 points might be attributed to news of increased tensions in the Middle East. Empirical research has demonstrated, however, while specific events may indirectly affect individual stock prices, daily fluctuations in stock market averages tend, on average, to be random. This common error is called the fallacy of *post hoc, ergo propter hoc* (literally, "after this, there-fore because of this").

Related to the pitfall of *post hoc, ergo propter hoc* is the confusion that often arises between correlation and causation. Case and Fair (1999) offer the following illustration. Large cities have many automobiles and also have high crime rates. Thus, there is a high correlation between automobile own-ership and crime. But, does this mean that automobiles cause crime? Obvi-ously not, although many other factors that are highly correlated with a high concentration of automobiles (e.g., population density, poverty, drug abuse) may provide a better explanation of the incidence of crime. Certainly, the presence of automobiles is not one of these factors.

The second common error in economic theorizing is the *fallacy of com-position*. The fallacy of composition is the belief that what is true for a part is necessarily true for the whole. An example of this may be found in the paradox of thrift. The paradox of thrift asserts that while an increase in saving by an individual may be virtuous ("a penny saved is a penny earned"), if all individuals in an economy increase their saving, the result may be no change, or even a decline, in aggregate saving. The reason is that an increase in aggregate saving means a decrease in aggregate spending, resulting in lower national output and income. Since saving depends upon income, increased savings may be less advantageous under certain circum-stances for the economy as a whole. At a more fundamental level, while it may be rational for an individual to run for the exit when he is the only person in a burning theater, for all individuals in a crowded burning theater to decide to run for the exit would not be.

THEORIES VERSUS LAWS

It is important to distinguish between theories and laws. The distinction relates to the ability to make predictions. Laws are statements of fact about the real world. They are statements of relationships that are, as far as is com-monly known, invariant with respect to specified underlying assumptions or preconditions. As such, laws predict with absolute certainty. "The sun rises in the east" is an example of a law. A law in economics is the *law of diminishing marginal returns*. This law asserts that for an efficient produc-tion process, as increasing amounts of a variable input are combined with one or more fixed inputs, at some point the additions to total output will get progressively smaller.

By contrast, a theory is an attempt to explain or predict the behavior of objects or events in the real world. Unlike laws, theories cannot predict events with complete accuracy. There are very few laws in economics, although some economic theories are inappropriately referred to as "laws." This is because economics deals with people, whose behavior is not absolutely predictable.

DESCRIPTIVE VERSUS PRESCRIPTIVE MANAGERIAL ECONOMICS

Managerial economics has both descriptive and prescriptive elements. Managerial economics is descriptive in that it attempts to interpret observed phenomena and to formulate theories about possible cause-and-effect relationships. Managerial economics is prescriptive in that it attempts to predict the outcomes of specific management decisions. Thus, the principles developed in a course in managerial economics may be used to prescribe the most efficient way to achieve an organization's objectives, such as profit maximization, sales (revenue) maximization, and maximizing market share.

Managerial economics can be utilized by goal-oriented managers in two ways. First, given the existing economic environment, the principles of managerial economics may provide a framework for evaluating whether managers are efficiently allocating resources (land, labor, and capital) to produce the firm's output at least cost. If not, the principles of economics may be used as a guide for reallocating the firm's operating budget away from, say, marketing and toward retail sales to achieve the organization's objectives.

Second, the principles of managerial economics can help managers respond to various economic signals. For example, given an increase in the price of output or the development of a new lower cost production technology, the appropriate response generally would be for a firm to increase output.

QUANTITATIVE METHODS

Quantitative methods refer to the tools and techniques of analysis, including optimization analysis, statistical methods, game theory, and capital budgeting. Managerial economics makes special use of mathematical economics and econometrics to derive optimal solutions to managerial decision-making problems. Managerial economics attempts to bring economic theory into the real world. Consider, for example, the formal (mathematical) demand model represented by Equation (1.1).

$$Q_D = f(P, I, P_s, A) \tag{1.1}$$

Equation (1.1) says that the quantity demand of a good or service commodity Q_D is functionally related to its selling price P, per-capita income I, the price of a competitor's product P_s, and advertising expenditures A.[2] By collecting data on Q, P, I, and P_s it should be possible to quantify this relationship. If we assume that this relationship is linear, Equation (1.1) may be specified as

$$Q_D = b_0 + b_1 P + b_2 I + b_3 P_r + b_4 A \tag{1.2}$$

It is possible to estimate the parameters of Equation (1.2) by using the methodology of regression analysis discussed in Green (1997), Gujarati (1995), and Ramanathan (1998). The resulting estimated demand equation, as well as other estimated relationships, may then be used by management to find optimal solutions to managerial decision-making problems. Such decision-making problems may entail optimal product pricing or optimal advertising expenditures to achieve such organizational objectives as revenue maximization or profit maximization.

THREE BASIC ECONOMIC QUESTIONS

Economic theory is concerned with how society answers the basic economic questions of *what* goods and services should be produced, and in what amounts, *how* these goods and services should be produced (i.e., the choice of the appropriate production technology), and *for whom* these goods and services should be produced.

WHAT GOODS AND SERVICES SHOULD BE PRODUCED?

In market economies, *what* goods and services are produced by society is a matter determined not by the producer, but rather by the consumer. Profit-maximizing firms produce only the goods and services that their customers demand. Firms that produce commodities that are not in demand by consumers—manual typewriters to day, for example—will flounder or go out of business entirely. Consumers express their preferences through their purchases of goods and services in the market. The authority of consumers to determine what goods and services are produced is often referred to as *consumer sovereignty*. Woe to the arrogant manager who forgets this fundamental economic fact of life.

Definition: Consumer sovereignty is the authority of consumers to determine what goods and services are produced through their purchases in the market.

***

[2] The mathematical concept of a function will be discussed in greater detail in Chapter 2.

HOW ARE GOODS AND SERVICES PRODUCED?

How goods and services are produced refers to the technology of production, and this is determined by the firm's management. Production technology refers to the types of input used in the production process, the organization of those factors of production, and the proportions in which those inputs are combined to produce goods and services that are most in demand by the consumer.

Throughout this text, we will generally assume that firm owners and managers are profit maximizers. It is the inexorable search for profit that determines the methodology of production. As will be demonstrated in subsequent chapters, a necessary condition for profit maximization is cost minimization. In competitive markets, firms that do not combine productive inputs in the most efficient (least costly) manner possible will quickly be driven out of business.

FOR WHOM ARE GOODS AND SERVICES PRODUCED?

Those who are willing, and able, to pay for the goods and services produced are the direct beneficiaries of the fruits of the production process. While the *what* and the *how* questions lend themselves to objective economic analysis, answers to the *for whom* question are fraught with numerous philosophical and analytical pitfalls. Debates about fairness are inevitable and often revolve around such issues as income distribution and ability to pay.

Income determines an individual's ability to pay, and income is derived from the sale of the services of factors of production. When you sell your labor services, you receive payment. The rental price of labor is referred to as a *wage* or a salary. When you rent the services of capital, you receive payment. Economists refer to the rental price of capital as *interest*. When you sell the services of land, you receive rents. The return to entrepreneurial ability is called profit. Wages, interest, rents, and profits define an individual's income.

In market economies, the returns to the owners of these factors of production are largely determined through the interaction of supply and demand. Thus, an individual's income is a function of the quality and quantity of the factors of production owned. Questions about the distribution of income are ultimately questions about the distribution of the ownership of factors of production and the supply and demand of those factors.

The solutions to the *for whom* questions typically are the domain of politicians, sociologists, theologians, and special-interest economists, indeed, anyone concerned with the highly subjective issues of "fairness." This book eschews such thorny moral debates. What follows will focus on finding objectives answers to the *what* and *how* economic questions.

CHARACTERISTICS OF PURE CAPITALISM

Although there are as many economic systems as there are countries, we will discuss the basic elements of *pure capitalism*. Purely capitalist economies are characterized by exclusive private ownership of productive resources and the use of markets to allocate goods and services. Pure capitalism stands in stark contrast to socialism, which is characterized by partial or total public ownership of productive resources and centralized decision making to allocate resources.

Capitalism in its pure form has probably never existed. In all countries characterized as capitalist, government plays an active role in the promotion of overall economic growth and the allocation of goods and services through its considerable control over resources. The reason we examine capitalism in its pure form is essentially twofold. To begin with, most western, developed, economies fundamentally are capitalist, or market, economies. Moreover, and perhaps more important, understanding capitalism in its pure form will better position the analyst to understand deviations and gradations from this "ideal" state. Economies that are characterized by a blend of public and private ownership is known as *mixed economies*.

Most of the discussion in this text will assume that our prototypical firm operates within a purely capitalist market system. Although the complete set of conditions necessary for pure capitalism is not likely to be found in reality, an understanding of the essential elements of pure capitalism is fundamental to an analysis of subtle and not-so-subtle variations from this extreme case.

PRIVATE PROPERTY

In pure capitalism, all productive resources are owned by private individuals who have the right to dispose of that property as manner they see fit. This institution is maintained over time by the right of an individual to bequeath property to his or her heirs.

FREEDOM OF ENTERPRISE AND CHOICE

Freedom of enterprise is the freedom to obtain and organize productive resources for the purpose of producing goods and services for sale in markets. Freedom of choice is the freedom of resource owners to dispose of their property as they see fit, and the freedom of consumers to purchase whatever goods and services they desire, constrained only by the income derived from the sale or rental of privately owned productive resources.

RATIONAL SELF-INTEREST

Rational self-interest refers to the behavior of individuals in a consistent manner to optimize some objective function. Rational self-interest is also referred to by economists as bounded rationality. In the case of the consumer, the postulate of rationality asserts that an individual attempts to maximize the total satisfaction derived from the consumption of goods and services, subject to his or her wealth, income, product prices, insights, and knowledge of market conditions.

The postulate of rationality also has its counterpart in the theory of the firm. Rational firm owners attempt to maximize some organizational objective, subject resource constraints, input prices, market structure, and so on. Entrepreneurs organize productive resources to produce goods and services for sale in markets to maximize profit or some other, equally rational, objective. While it is may be true that not all consumers seek to maximize their utility from their purchases of goods and services and not all firms attempt to maximize profit from the production and sale of output, these are probably the dominant forms of human behavior.

COMPETITION

There are a number of conditions necessary for pure (perfect) competition to exist. For example, there must be buyers and sellers for any particular good or service. This condition ensures that no single individual economic unit has market power to control prices. Large numbers of buyers and sellers ensure the widespread diffusion of economic power, thereby limiting the potential for abuse of such power.

Another necessary condition for perfect competition to exist is relatively easy entry into and exit from the market. This condition implies that there are no or low economic, legal, or regulatory restrictions on the production, sale, or consumption of goods and services. In other words, individuals may easily enter into the production and sale of economic goods, while individuals may also enter into any market to transact goods and services as they see fit.

MARKETS AND PRICES

Markets are the basic coordinating mechanisms of capitalism. Price is the essential underlying information transmission mechanism. Unless there is deception or misunderstanding of the facts, a voluntary exchange between two parties must benefit both parties to the transaction; otherwise they would not have entered into the transaction in the first place. It is in markets, both for outputs and inputs, that buyers and sellers meet to further their own self-interest, unfettered by artificial impediments.

The price system is an elaborate mechanism through which the free choices of individuals are recorded and communicated. The price system, if allowed to operate freely, informs market participants which goods are in greatest demand, and, consequently, where productive resources are most needed. The price system enables society to collectively register its decisions about how resources ought to be allocated and how the resulting output should be distributed. In general, institutional impediments tend to impair the functioning of the price mechanism. Although government intervention in the marketplace often results in socially efficient outcomes, governments that impose the fewest restrictions on the functioning of the price mechanism tend to be the most efficient. Extensive and intrusive government intervention, characteristic of centrally planned economies, is the least efficient mode: such economies have the slowest growth and generally do the poorest job at raising living standards. It should be noted, however, that while economies with minimal government interference tend to grow rapidly, individuals with the greatest amounts of the most productive resources will receive the greatest proportion of an economy's output. Therefore, there appears to be a significant efficiency–equity trade-off in the case of pure capitalism.

The concept of laissez-faire describes limited government participation in the operation of free markets and free choices. Each of the foregoing characteristics of pure capitalism assumes that there are no outside impediments to the market system. For the most part, the government's role is strictly limited to the provision of "public goods," such as public roads or national defense, and the administration of a judicial system to interpret and enforce contracts and private property rights.

THE ROLE OF GOVERNMENT IN MARKET ECONOMIES

MACROECONOMIC POLICY

Government participates in economic activity at the microeconomic and macroeconomic levels. *Macroeconomic policy* may be divided in *monetary policy* and *fiscal policy*. Monetary policy is concerned with the regulation of the money supply and credit. Monetary policy in the United States is conducted by the Federal Reserve.

The other part of macroeconomic policy is fiscal policy. Fiscal policy deals with government spending and taxation. Fiscal policy in the United States may be initiated by the president or Congress but only Congress has the power to levy taxes. In formulating economic policy proposals, the president relies on advice from members of the cabinet, the Office of Management and Budget, and the Council of Economic Advisers.

In general, the objective of macroeconomic policy, sometimes referred to as *stabilization policy*, is to moderate the negative effects of the *business cycle*, the recurring expansions and contractions in overall economic activity. Periods of economic expansion, or economic "booms," are often accompanied by a general and sustained increase in the prices of goods and services, or inflation. Periods of economic contraction are associated with rising unemployment. Macroeconomic policy is directed toward maintaining full employment and price level stability.

MICROECONOMIC POLICY

Economics is the study of how consumers use their limited incomes to purchase goods and services to maximize their utility (satisfaction or happiness). Consumers are also owners of factors of production (land, labor, and capital), the services of which are offered to the highest bidder to generate the income necessary to purchase goods and services from firms. Finally, firms purchase the services of the factors of production to produce goods and services for sale in the market. The revenues generated from the sale of these goods and services are then returned to the owners of the factors of production in the form of wages, interest, and rents. What remains of total revenue after the services of the factors of production have been paid for is called profits. While the prices of land, labor, and capital are directly determined in the resource market, profits are residual payments to the entrepreneur, which is another source of consumer income.

In 1776 Adam Smith argued in *Wealth of Nations* that the actions of self-interested individuals are driven, as if by an *invisible hand*, to promote the general public welfare. This, Smith wrote, is because the interaction of self-interested buyers and sellers in perfectly competitive markets would tend to promote *economic efficiency*. When economic efficiency is realized, consumers' utility, firms' profits, and the public welfare are maximized.

Since, however, the conditions necessary to achieve economic efficiency are not always present, competitive markets are not always perfect. There are generally two justifications for the government's role in economy. One justification for government intervention is that the market does not always result in economically efficient outcomes. The other is that some people do not like the market outcome and use the government to alter the outcome, often for the benefit of some narrowly defined special interest group. The following discussion will focus on the role of the government to promote efficient economic outcomes.

The concept of economic efficiency is often associated with the term *Pareto efficiency*. An outcome is said to be Pareto efficient if it is not possible to make one person in society better off, say through some resource allocation, without making some other person in society worse off. Two related concepts are *production efficiency* and *consumption efficiency*.

Production efficiency occurs when firms produce given quantities of goods and services at least cost. From society's perspective, production efficiency takes place when society's resources are fully employed and are used in the best, most productive way.

Consumption efficiency occurs when consumers derive the greatest level of happiness, satisfaction, or utility from the purchase of goods and services with their limited income. Consumers, in other words, receive the greatest "bang for the buck."

Efficiency in production and consumption depend on a number of conditions, including *perfect information* and the absence of *externalities*. When information is not perfect, or when externalities exist, market imperfections arise and economic efficiency is not achieved.

The main information transmission mechanism in market economies is the system of prices. A change in the market price is a signal to producers and consumers that more or less of a good or service is desired. When market prices are "right," producers and consumers will make the best possible decisions. When prices are "wrong," producers and consumers will not make the best possible decisions. Producers will not utilize the least-cost combination of factors of production, with resulting resource misallocation and waste, while consumers, by failing to allocate their limited incomes in the most efficient manner possible, will not maximize their satisfaction.

It is often argued that when information is not perfect and market solutions are not optimal, the government should step in and require that a certain amount of information be made available. Government policies pursuant to this viewpoint have resulted in companies printing ingredients on product labels, providing health warnings on cigarettes packages, and so on. In most developed countries, government mandates that new pharmaceuticals be tested and certified before being made available to the public, while members of certain professions, such as lawyers, doctors, nurses, and teachers, must be licensed or certified.

Another justification of government participation in economic activity is the existence of externalities. Economic efficiency requires that the participants in any market transaction fully absorb all the benefits and costs associated with that transaction. If this is the case, the market price of that good or service will fully reflect those benefits and costs. However, if a third party not directly involved in the transactions receives some of the costs or benefits of that transaction, externalities are said to exist. When the third party receives some of the benefits of the transaction, the externalities are said to be positive. If, on the other hand, the third party absorbs some of the costs of the transaction, the externalities are said to be negative.

Education is an example of a service that generates *positive externalities*. Increased literacy and higher levels of education, for example, make workers more productive, and democracies operate more efficiently with a better informed electorate. Unfortunately, if producers of education do not receive all the benefits of their efforts, educational services tend to be under-provided. But if it is agreed that positive externalities exist, then one role of government is to step in and subsidize the production of education to bring the output of these goods and services to more socially optimal levels.

Pollution, which is a by-product of the production process, is an example of *negative externalities*: too much of a good or service is being produced because firms are not absorbing all the costs associated with producing that good or service. When the public is forced to pay higher medical bills because of illnesses associated with air and water pollution, resources are diverted away from more socially desirable ends. When negative external-ities exist, government will often step in and tax production, or, in the case of pollution, force firms to undertake measures to eliminate undesirable by-products. In either case, production costs are raised, and output (and pollution) is reduced to more socially desirable levels.

THE ROLE OF PROFIT

For the most part, we will assume that owners of firms endeavor to maximize *total economic profit*, where economic profit π is defined as the difference between total revenue TR and *total economic cost TC*, that is,

$$\pi = TR - TC \tag{1.3}$$

Profit is the engine of maximum production and efficient resource allo-cation in pure capitalism; its cannot be underestimated. The existence of profit opportunities represents the crucial signaling mechanism for the dynamic reallocation of society's scarce productive resources in purely cap-italistic economies. Rising profits in some industries and declining profits in others reflect changes in societal preferences for goods and services. Rising profits signal existing firms that it is time to expand production and serve as a lure for new firms to enter the industry. Declining profits, on the other hand, a signal producers that society wants less of a particular good or service, presenting existing firms with an incentive to reduce production or to exit the industry entirely. In the process, productive resources move from their lowest to their highest valued use. Moreover, profit maximization not only encourages an efficient allocation of resources, but also implies effi-cient (least-cost) production. Thus, purely capitalist economies are charac-terized by a minimum waste of societys' factors of production.

Problem 1.1. Adam's Food World (AFW) is a large, multinational corporation that specializes in food and health care products. The following production function has been estimated for its new brand of soft drink.[3]

$$Q = 10K^{0.5}L^{0.3}M^{0.2}$$

where Q is total output (millions of gallons), K is capital input (thousands of machine-hours), L is labor input (thousands of labor-hours), and M is land input (thousands of acres). Last year, AFW allocated $2 million in its corporate budget for the production of the new soft drink, which was used to purchase productive inputs (K, L, M). The unit prices of K, L, and M were $100, $25, and $200, respectively.

a. AFW last year used its operating budget to purchase 3,500 machine-hours of capital, 50,000 man-hours of labor, and 2,000 acres of land. How many gallons of the new soft drink did AFW produce?

b. This year, AFW decided to hire 1,500 additional machine-hours of capital, but did not increase its operating budget. The number of acres used remained constant at 2,000. How many man-hours of labor did AFW purchase?

c. How many gallons of the new soft drink will AFW be able to produce with the new input mix? Compare your answer with your answer to part a. What conclusions can you draw regarding AFW's operating efficiency?

d. AFW sells its new soft drink to regional bottlers for $0.05 per gallon. What was the impact of the new input mix on company profits?

Solution

a. Substituting last year's input levels into the production function yields

$$Q = 10(3.5)^{0.5}(50)^{0.3}(2)^{0.2} = 10(1.871)(3.233)(1.149)$$
$$= 69.502 \text{ million gallons}$$

At last year's input levels, AFW produced 69.502 million gallons of the new soft drink.

b. The cost to AFW of purchasing 2,000 acres of land is $400,000 ($200 × 2,000), the cost of 5,000 machine hours of capital is $500,000 ($100 × 5,000), which leaves $1,100,000 available to purchase man-hours of labor. At a price of $25 per man-hour, AFW can hire 44,000 man-hours of labor ($1,100,000/$25).

c. At the new input levels, the total output of the new soft drink is

$$Q = 10(5)^{0.5}(44)^{0.3}(2)^{0.2} = 10(2.236)(3.112)(1.149) = 79.952$$

---

[3] This is an example of a *Cobb–Douglas production function*, discussed at length in Chapter 5.

At the new input levels, AFW can produce 79.952 million gallons of the new soft drink, which represents an increase of 10.450 million-gallons with no increase in the cost of production.

It should be clear from these results that AFW was not operating efficiently at the original input levels. While AFW is operating more efficiently with the new input mix, it remains an open question whether the company is maximizing output with an operating budget of $2 million and prevailing input prices. In other words, we still do not know whether the new input mix is optimal.

d. If AFW sells its output at a fixed price, new input levels clearly will cause the company's total profit to rise. The total cost of producing the new soft drink last year and this year was $2,000,000. If AFW can sell the new soft drink to regional bottlers for $0.05 per gallon, last year's total revenues amounted to $3,475,100 ($0.05 × 69,502,000), for a total profit of $1,475,100 ($3,475,100 − $2,000,000). By reallocating the budget and changing the input mix, AFW total revenues increased to $3,997,600 ($0.05 × 79,952,000) for a total profit of $1,997,600, or an increase in profit of $522,500.

THEORY OF THE FIRM

The concept of the "firm" or the "company" is commonly misunderstood. Too often, the corporate entities are confused with the people who own or operate the organizations. In fact, a firm is an activity that combines scarce productive resources to produce goods and services that are demanded by society. Firms are more appropriately viewed as an activity that transforms productive inputs into outputs of goods and services. The manner in which productive resources are combined and organized will depend of the organizational objective of the owner–operator or, as in the case of publicly owned companies, the decisions of the designated agents of the company's shareholders.

Scarce productive resources are many and varied. Consider, for example, the productive resources that go into the production of something as simple as a chair. First, there are various types of labor employed, such as designers, machine tool operators, carpenters, and sales personnel. If the chair is made of wood, decisions must be made regarding the type or types of wood that will be used. Will the chair have upholstery of some kind? If so, then decisions must be made on material, quality, and patterns. Will the chair have any attachments, such as small wheels on the bottom of the legs for easy moving? Will the wheels be made of metal, plastic, or some composite material?

The point is that even something as relatively simple as a chair may require quite a large number of resources in the production process. It should be clear, therefore, that when one is discussing economic and business relationships in the abstract, making too many allowances for reality has its limitations. To overcome this problem, we will assume that production is functionally related to two broad categories of inputs, labor and capital.

THE OBJECTIVE OF THE FIRM

Economists have traditionally assumed that the goal of the firm is to maximize profit π. This behavioral assumption is central to the neoclassical theory of the firm, which posits the firm as a profit-maximizing "black box" that transforms inputs into outputs for sale in the market. While the precise contents of the "black box" are unknown, it is generally assumed to contain the "secret formula" that gives the firm its competitive advantage. In general, neoclassical theory makes no attempt to explain what actually goes on inside the "black box," although the underlying production function is assumed to exhibit certain desirable mathematical properties, such as a favorable position with respect to the law of diminishing returns, returns to scale, and substitutability between and among productive inputs. The appeal of the neoclassical model is its application to a wide range of profit-maximizing firms and market situations.

Neoclassical theory attempts to explain the behavior of profit-maximizing firms subject to known resource constraints and perfect market information. It is important, however, to distinguish between current period profits and the stream of profits over some period of time. Often, managers are observed making decisions that reduce this year's profit in an effort to boost net income in future. Since both present and future profits are important, one approach is to maximize the present, or discounted, value of the firm's stream of future profits, that is,

$$\text{Maximize: } PV(\pi) = \frac{\pi_1}{(1+i)} + \frac{\pi_2}{(1+i)^2} + \ldots + \frac{\pi_n}{(1+i)^n}$$
$$= \sum \frac{\pi_t}{(1+i)^t} \tag{1.4}$$

where profit is defined in Equation (1.3), t is an index of time, and i the appropriate discount rate.[4] The behavior characterized in Equation (1.4) assumes that the objective of the firm is that of wealth maximization over some arbitrarily determined future time period. Equation (1.4) gives the

[4] The concept of the time value of money is discussed in considerable detail in Chapter 12. The time value of money recognizes that $1 received today does not have the same value as $1 received tomorrow. To see this, suppose that $1 received today were deposited into a savings account paying a certain 5% annual interest rate. The value of that deposit would be worth $1.05 a year later. Thus, receiving $1 today is worth $1.05 a year from now. Stated differently, the future value of $1 received today is $1.05 a year from now. Alternatively, the present value of $1.05 received a year from now is $1 received today. The process of reducing future values to their present values is often referred to as discounting. For this reason, the interest rate used in present value calculations is often referred to as the discount rate.

immediate value of the firm's profit stream, which is expected to grow to a specified value at some time in the future. Discounting is necessary because profits obtained in some future period are less valuable than profits earned today, since profits received today may be reinvested at an interest rate i.

Note that Equation (1.4) may be rewritten as

$$PV(\pi) = \sum \frac{\pi_t}{(1+i)^t} = \sum \frac{(TR_t - TC_t)}{(1+i)^t} \qquad (1.5)$$

Equation (1.5) explicitly recognizes the importance of decisions made in separate divisions of a prototypical business organization. The marketing department, for example, might have primary responsibility for company sales, which are reflected in total revenue (TR). The production department has responsibility for monitoring the firm's costs of production (TC), while corporate finance is responsible for acquiring financing to support the firm's capital investment activities and is therefore keenly interested in the interest rate (i) on acquired investment capital (i.e., the discount rate).

This more complete model of firm behavior also has the advantage of incorporating the important elements of time and uncertainty. Here, the primary goal of the firm is assumed to be expected wealth maximization, and is generally considered to be the primary objective of the firm.

Problem 1.2. The managers of the XYZ Company are in a position to organize production Q in a way that will generate the following two net income streams, where $\pi_{i,j}$ designates the ith production process in the jth production period.

$$\pi_{1,1}(Q) = \$100; \; \pi_{1,2}(Q) = \$330$$

$$\pi_{2,1}(Q) = \$300; \; \pi_{2,2}(Q) = \$121$$

For example, $\pi_{1,2}(Q) = \$330$ indicates that net income from production process 1 in period 2 is \$330. If the anticipated discount rate for both production periods is 10%, which of these two net income streams will generate greater net profit for the company?

Solution. Both profit streams are assumed to be functions of output levels and to represent the results of alternative production schedules. Note that although the first profit stream appears to be preferable to the second, since it yields \$9 more in profit over the two periods, computation of present values (PV) reveals that, in fact, the second π stream is preferable to the first.

$$PV(\pi_1) = \sum \frac{\pi^t}{(1+i)^t} = \frac{\$100}{1.1} + \frac{\$330}{(1.1)^2} = \$363.64$$

$$PV(\pi_2) = \sum \frac{\pi^t}{(1+i)^t} = \frac{\$300}{1.1} + \frac{\$121}{(1.1)^2} = \$372.73$$

HOW REALISTIC IS THE ASSUMPTION OF PROFIT MAXIMIZATION?

The assumption of profit maximization has come under repeated criticism. Many economists have argued that this behavioral assertion is too simplistic to describe the complex nature and managerial thought processes of the modern large corporation. Two distinguishing characteristics of the modern corporation weaken the neoclassical assumption of profit maximization. To begin with, the modern large corporation is generally not owner operated. Responsibility for the day-to-day operations of the firm is delegated to managers who serve as agents for shareholders.

One alternative to neoclassical theory based on the assumption of profit maximization is *transaction cost theory*, which asserts that the goal of the firm is to minimize the sum of external and internal transaction costs subject to a given level of output, which is a first-order condition for profit maximization.[5] According to Ronald Coase (1937), who is regarded as the founder of the transaction cost theory, firms exist because they are excellent resource allocators. Thus, consumers satisfy their demand for goods and services more efficiently by ceding production to firms, rather than producing everything for their own use.

Still another theory of firm behavior, which is attributed to Herbert Simon (1959), asserts that corporate executives exhibit *satisficing behavior*. According to this theory, managers will attempt to maximize some objective, such as executive salaries and perquisites, subject to some minimally acceptable requirement by shareholders, such as an "adequate" rate of return on investment or a minimum rate of return on sales, profit, market share, asset growth, and so on. The assumption of satisficing behavior is predicated on the belief that it is not possible for management to know with certainty when profits are maximized because of the complexity and uncertainties associated with running a large corporation. There are also noneconomic organizational objectives, such as good citizenship, product quality, and employee goodwill.

The closely related theory of manager-utility maximization was put forth by Oliver Williamson (1964). Williamson argued that managers seek to maximize their own utility, which is a function of salaries, perquisites, stock options, and so on. It has been argued, however, that managers who place their own self-interests before the interests of shareholders by failing to exploit profit opportunities may quickly find themselves looking for work. This will come about either because shareholders will rid themselves of

---

[5] Transactions costs refer to costs not directly associated with the actual transaction that enable the transaction to take place. The costs associated with acquiring information about a good or service (e.g., price, availability, durability, servicing, safety) are transaction costs. Other examples of transaction costs include the cost of negotiating, preparing, executing, and enforcing a contract.

managers who fail to maximize earnings and share prices or because the company finds itself the victim of a corporate takeover. William Baumol (1967), on the other hand, has argued that sales or market share maximization after shareholders' earnings expectations have been satisfied more accurately reflects the organizational objectives of the typical large modern corporation.

Marris and Wood (1971) have argued that the objective of management is to maximize the firm's *valuation ratio*, which is related to the growth rate of the firm. The firm's valuation ratio is defined as the ratio of the stock market value of the firm to its highest possible value. The highest possible value of this ratio is 1. According to this view, since managers are primarily motivated by job security, they will attempt to achieve a corporate growth rate that maximizes profits, dividends, and shareholder value. The importance of the valuation ratio is that it may be used as a proxy for a shareholder satisfaction with the performance of management. The higher the firm's valuation ratio, the less likely that managers will be ousted.

Still another important contribution to an understanding of firm behavior is *principal–agent theory* (see, for example, Alchain and Demsetz, 1972; Demsetz and Lehn, 1985; Diamond and Verrecchia, 1982; Fama and Jensen, 1983a, 1983b; Grossman and Hart, 1983; Harris and Raviv, 1978; Holstrom, 1979, 1982; Jensen and Meckling, 1976; MacDonald, 1984; and Shavell, 1979). According to this theory, the firm may be seen as a nexus of contracts between principals and "stakeholders" (agents). The principal–agent relationship may be that between owner and manager or between manager and worker. The principal–agent problem may be summarized as follows: What are the least-cost incentives that principals can offer to induce agents to act in the best interest of the firm? Principal–agent theory views the principal as a kind of "incentive engineer" who relies on "smart" contracts to minimize the opportunistic behavior of agents. Owner–manager and manager–worker principal–agent problems will be examined in greater detail in the next two sections.

Definition: This principal–agent problem arises when there are inadequate incentives for agents (managers or workers) to put forth their best efforts for principals (owners or managers). This incentive problem arises because principals, who have a vested interest in the operations of the firm, benefit from the hard work of their agents, while agents who do not have a vested interest, prefer leisure.

Although these alternative theories of firm behavior stress some relevant aspects of the operation of a modern corporation, they do not provide a satisfactory alternative to the broader assumption of profit maximization. Competitive forces in product and resource markets make it imperative for managers to keep a close watch on profits. Otherwise, the firm may lose market share, or worse yet, go out of business entirely. Moreover, alternative organizational objectives of managers of the modern corporation cannot stray very far from the dividend-maximizing self-interests of the company's shareholders. If they do, such managers will be looking for a new venue within which to ply their trade.

Regardless of the specific firm objective, however, managerial economics is less interested in how decision makers actually behave than in understanding the economic environment within which managers operate and in formulating theories from which hypotheses about cause and effect may be inferred. In general, economists are concerned with developing a framework for predicting managerial responses to changes in the firm's operating environment. Even if the assumption of profit maximization is not literally true, it provides insights into more complex behavior. Departures from these assumptions may thus be analyzed and recommendations made. In fact, many practicing economists earn a living by advising business firms and government agencies on how best to achieve "efficiency" by bringing the "real world" closer to the ideal hypothesized in economic theory. Indeed, the assumption of profit maximization is so useful precisely because this objective is rarely achieved in reality.

OWNER–MANAGER/PRINCIPAL–AGENT PROBLEM

A distinguishing characteristic of the large corporation is that it is not owner operated. The responsibility for day-to-day operations is delegated to managers who serve as agents for shareholders. Since the owners cannot closely monitor the manager's performance, how then shall the manager be compelled to put forth his or her "best" effort on behalf of the owners?

If a manager is paid a fixed salary, a fundamental incentive problem emerges. If the firm performs poorly, there will be uncertainty over whether this was due to circumstances outside the manager's control was the result of poor management. Suppose that company profits are directly related to the manager's efforts. Even if the fault lay with a goldbricking manager, this person can always claim that things would have been worse had it not been for his or her herculean efforts on behalf of the shareholders. With absentee ownership, there is no way to verify this claim. It is simply not possible to know for certain why the company performed poorly. When owners are disconnected from the day-to-day operations of the firm, the result is the *owner–manager/principal–agent problem.*

To understand the essence of the owner–manager/principal–agent problem, suppose that a manager's contract calls for a fixed salary of $200,000 annually. While the manager values income, he or she also values leisure. The more time devoted to working means less time available for leisure activities. A fundamental conflict arises because owners want managers to work, while managers prefer leisure. The problem, of course, is that the manager will receive the same $200,000 income regardless of whether he or she puts in a full day's work or spends the entire day enjoying leisure activity. A fixed salary provides no incentive to work hard, which will adversely affect the firm's profits. Without the appropriate incentive, such as continual monitoring, the manager has an incentive to "goof off."

Definition: The owner–manager/principal–agent problem arises when managers do not share in the success of the day-to-day operations of the firm. When managers do not have a stake in company's performance, some managers will have an incentive to substitute leisure for a diligent work effort.

INCENTIVE CONTRACTS

Will the offer of a higher salary compel the manager to work harder? The answer is no for the same reason that the manager did not work hard in the first place. Since the owners are not present to monitor the manager's performance, there will be no incentive to substitute work for leisure. A fixed-salary contract provides no penalty for goofing off. One solution to the principal–agent problem would be to make the manager a stakeholder by offering the manager an *incentive contract*. An incentive contract links manager compensation to performance. Incentive contracts may include such features as profit sharing, stock options, and performance bonuses, which provide the manager with incentives to perform in the best interest of the owners.

Definition: An incentive contract between owner and manager is one in which the manager is provided with incentives to perform in the best interest of the owner.

Suppose, for example, that in addition to a salary of $200,000 the manager is offered 10% of the firm's profits. The sum of the manager's salary and a percentage of profits is the manager's gross compensation. This profit-sharing contract transforms the manager into a stakeholder. The manager's compensation is directly related to the company's performance. It is in the manager's best interest to work in the best interest of the owners. Exactly how the manager responds to the offer of a share of the firm's profits depends critically on the manager's preferences for income and leisure. But one thing is certain. Unless the marginal utility of an additional dollar of income is zero, it will be in the manager's best interest not to goof off during the entire work day. Making the manager a stakeholder in the company's performance will increase the profits of the owner.

OTHER MANAGEMENT INCENTIVES

The principal–agent problem helps to explain why a manager might not put forth his or her effort on behalf of the owner. There are, however, other reasons why a manager would work in the best interest of the owner that are quite apart from the direct incentives associated with being a stakeholder in the success of the firm. These indirect incentives relate directly to the self-interest of the manager. One of these incentives is the manager's own reputation.

Managers are well aware that their current position may not be their last. The ability of managers to move to other more responsible and lucrative positions depends crucially on demonstrated managerial skills in previous employments. An effective manager invests considerable time, effort, and energy in the supervision of workers and organization of production. The value of this investment will be captured in the manager's reputation, which may ultimately be sold in the market at a premium. Thus, even if the manager is not made a stakeholder in the firm's success through profit sharing, stock options, or performance bonuses, the manager may nonetheless choose to do a good job as a way of laying the groundwork for future rewarding opportunities.

Another incentive, which was discussed earlier, relates to the manager's job security. Shareholders who believe that the firm is not performing up to its potential, or is not earning profits comparable to those of similar firms in the same industry, may then move to oust the incumbent management. Closely related to a shareholder revolt is the threat of a takeover. Sensing that a firm's poor performance may be the result of underachieving or incompetent managers another company might move to wrest control of the business from present shareholders. Once in control, the new owners will install a more effective management team to increase net earnings and raise shareholder value.

MANAGER–WORKER/PRINCIPAL–AGENT PROBLEM

The principal–agent problem also arises in the relationship between management and labor. Suppose that the manager is a stakeholder in the firm's operations. While manager's well-being is now synonymous with that of the owners, there is potentially a principal–agent problem between manager and worker. Without a stake in the company's performance, there will be an incentive for some workers to substitute leisure for hard work. Since it may not be possible to closely and constantly monitor worker performance, the manager is confronted with the principal–agent problem of providing incentives for diligent work. As before, the solution is to transform the worker into a stakeholder.

Definition: The manager–worker/principal–agent problem arises when workers do not have a vested interest in a firm's success. Without a stake in the company's performance, there will be an incentive for some workers not to put forth their best efforts.

PROFIT AND REVENUE SHARING

As in the case of the owner–manager/principale–agent problem, workers can be encouraged to put forth their best efforts by linking their compensation to the firm's profitability. Another way to enhance worker performance is to tie compensation to the firm's revenues. This method of compensation is particularly important when worker performance directly impact revenues rather than operating costs. The most common form of revenue sharing is the sales commission. When we think of sales commissions, we tend to think of insurance agents, real estate brokers, automobile salespersons, and so on. But sales commissions take a variety of forms. The familiar system in which bartenders and waiters earn tips also constitutes a revenue-based incentive scheme.

There are, however, problems associated with revenue-based incentive schemes. One problem is that such compensation mechanisms may lead to unethical behavior toward customers. This is especially true when customer contact is on a one-time or impersonal basis. The negative stereotypes associated with some professions, such as telephone marketers or used-car salespeople, attest to the potential dangers of linking compensation to revenues. Another problem with linking compensation to revenues is that there is generally no incentive for workers to minimize cost. Corporate executives who inflate expense accounts in attempts to curry favor with potential clients and bartenders who give free drinks attest to some of the problems associated with revenue-based incentive schemes.

OTHER WORKER INCENTIVES

Other methods of encouraging workers to put forth their best efforts are piecework, time clocks, and spot checks. Piecework involves payment based on the number of units produced. Sweatshop operations, once common in the textile industry, are examples of this type of revenue-based incentive scheme. Of course, when worker compensation is based on piecework high quantity often comes at the expense of low product quality. Low-quality products may lead to customer dissatisfaction, which in turn results in lower sales, revenues, and profits.

Time clocks indicate whether workers show up for work on time and stay til the ends of their shifts. However, time clocks do not monitor worker performance while at the workplace. Thus, the use of time clocks is an inferior solution to the manager–worker/principal–agent problem. A more effective solution, which verifies that not only the worker is on the job but that the worker is performing up to expectations, is the spot check. To be effective, spot checks must be unpredictable. Otherwise, workers will know when to work hard and when goofing off will not be noticed.

There are two distinct problems with spot checks. To be effective, random spot checks must be frequent enough to raise the expected penalty to the worker who is caught goldbricking. Frequent spot checks, however, are costly and reduce the firm's profitability. In addition, frequent spot checks can have a negative effect on worker morale. Low worker morale will negatively affect productivity and profitability. In general, incentive-based schemes based on threats are inferior to compensation-based solutions, such as revenue or profit sharing, to the principal–agent problem.

CONSTRAINTS ON THE OPERATIONS OF THE FIRM

Suppose that the objective of the firm is to maximize short-run profits (or wealth, or value). In attempting to achieve this objective, the firm faces a number of constraints. These constraints might include a scarcity of essential productive resources, such as a certain type of skilled labor, specific raw materials, as might occur because of labor discontent in the country of a foreign supplier, limitations on factory or warehouse space, and unavailability of credit. Constraints might also take the form of legal restrictions on the operations of the firm, such as minimum wage laws, pollution emission standards, and legal restrictions on certain types of business activity. Such constraints are often imposed by government to achieve perceived social (welfare) goals.

For many business and economic applications, it is necessary to think in terms of the optimizing managerial objectives subject to one or more side constraints. This process is referred to as constrained optimization. For example, it might be the goal of a firm to maximize profits subject to limitations on operating budgets or the level of output. The existence of these constraints usually means that the range of possibilities available to the firm is limited. Thus, profit maximization in the strict sense may not be possible. Put differently, the maximum attainable profits in the presence of such constraints are likely to be less than they would have been in the absence of the restrictions. Although most of this text deals with developing principles of firm behavior based on theories of unconstrained profit maximization, we will also introduce the powerful mathematical techniques of Lagrange multipliers and linear programming for dealing with constrained optimization problems.

ACCOUNTING PROFIT VERSUS ECONOMIC PROFIT

To say that products that can be produced profitably will be, and those that cannot be produced profitably will not begs the question of what we mean by "profit." What is commonly thought of as profit by the accountant may not match the meaning assigned to the term by an economist. An economist's notion of profit goes back to the basic fact that resources are scarce and have alternative uses. To use a certain set of resources to produce a good or service means that certain alternative production possibilities were forgone. Costs in economics have to do with forgoing the opportunity to produce alternative goods and services. The economic, or opportunity, cost of any resource in producing some good or service is its value or worth in its next best alternative use.

Given the notion of opportunity costs, economic costs are the payments a firm must make, or incomes it must provide, to resource suppliers to attract these resources away from alternative lines of production. Economic costs (TC) include all relevant opportunity costs. These payments or incomes may be either explicit, "out-of-pocket" or cash expenditures, or implicit. Implicit costs represent the value of resources used in the production process for which no direct payment is made. This value is generally taken to be the money earnings of resources in their next best alternative employment. When a computer software programmer quits his or her job to open a consulting firm, the forgone salary is an example of an implicit cost. When the owner of an office building decides to open a hobby shop, the forgone rental income from that store is an example of an implicit cost. When a housewife decides to redeem a certificate of deposit to establish a day-care center for children, the forgone interest earnings represent an implicit cost. In short, any sacrifice incurred when the decision is made to produce a good or service must be taken into account if the full impact of that decision is to be correctly assessed. These relationships may be summarized as follows:

$$\text{Accounting profit: } \pi_A = TR - TC_{\text{explicit}} \tag{1.6}$$

$$\text{Economic profit: } \pi = TR - TC = TR - TC_{\text{explicit}} - TC_{\text{implicit}} \tag{1.7}$$

Problem 1.3. Andrew operates a small shop specializing in party favors. He owns the building and supplies all his own labor and money capital. Thus, Andrew incurs no explicit rental or wage costs. Before starting his own business Andrew earned $1,000 per month by renting out the store and earned $2,500 per month as a store manager for a large department store chain. Because Andrew uses his own money capital, he also sacrificed $1,000 per month in interest earned on U.S. Treasury bonds. Andrew's monthly revenues from operating his shop are $10,000 and his total monthly expenses for labor and supplies amounted to $6,000. Calculate Andrew's monthly accounting and economic profits.

Solution. Total accounting profit is calculated as follows:

Total revenue	$10,000
Total explicit costs	6,000
Accounting profit	$4,000

Andrew's accounting profit appears to be a healthy $4,000 per month. However, if we take into account Andrew's implicit costs, the story is quite different. Total economic profit is calculated as follows:

Total revenue	$10,000
Total explicit costs	6,000
Forgone rent	1,000
Forgone salary	2,500
Forgone interest income	1,000
Total implicit costs	4,500
Total economic costs	10,500
Economic profit (loss)	$ (500)

Economic profits are equal to total revenue less total economic costs, which is the sum of explicit and implicit costs. Accounting profits, on the other hand, are equal to total revenue less total explicit costs.

It is, of course, a simple matter to make accounting profit equivalent to economic profit by making explicit all relevant implicit costs. Suppose, for example, that an individual quits a $40,000 per year job as the manager a family restaurant to open a new restaurant. Since this is a sacrifice incurred by the budding restauranteur, the forgone salary is an implicit cost. On the other hand, this implicit cost can easily be made explicit by putting the restaurant owner "on the books" for a salary of $40,000. The somewhat arbitrary distinction between explicit and implicit costs is illustrated in the following problem.

Problem 1.4. Adam is the owner of a small grocery store in a busy section of Boulder, Colorado. Adam's annual revenue is $200,000 and his total explicit cost (Adam pays himself an annual salary of $30,000) is $180,000 per year. A supermarket chain wants to hire Adam as its general manager for $60,000 per year.
a. What is the opportunity cost to Adam of owning and managing the grocery store?
b. What is Adam's accounting profit?
c. What is Adam's economic profit?

Solution
a. Opportunity cost is the $60,000 in forgone salary that Adam might have earned had he decided to work as general manager for the supermarket chain.
b. $\pi_A = TR - TC_{explicit} = \$200,000 - \$180,000 = \$20,000$
c. $\pi = TR - TC_{explicit} - TC_{implicit} = \$200,000 - \$180,000 - \$30,000$
$= -\$10,000$

Another way of looking at this problem is to consider Adam's forgone income following his decision to continue to operate the grocery store. Adam's forgone income may be summarized as follows:

$$\pi_A = \text{grocery store salary} - \text{supermarket salary}$$
$$= \$20,000 + \$30,000 - \$60,000 = -\$10,000$$

This is the same as the result in part b, since the grocery store salary less the supermarket salary is just the opportunity cost as defined.

NORMAL PROFIT

Another important concept in economics is that of *normal profit*. Normal profit, sometimes referred to as *normal rate of return*, is the level of profit required to keep a firm engaged in a particular activity. Alternatively, normal profit represents the rate of return on the next best alternative investment of equivalent risk. It is the level of profit necessary to keep people from pulling their investments in search of higher rates of return. If a firm is well established and has a good earnings record, and if there is little to no possibility of financial loss during a specified period of time, then the normal rate of return is approximately equal to the interest rate on a risk-free government bond. If the firm's earnings are erratic and its future prospects questionable, then the *risk-free rate of return* must be augmented by a *risk premium*. Either way, normal profit is a form of opportunity cost. Viewed in this way, it is easy to see that normal profit represents a component of total economic cost.

Definition: Normal profit refers to the level of profits required to keep a firm engaged in a particular activity. Alternatively, normal profit represents the rate of return on the next best alternative investment of equivalent risk. Normal profits are a kind of opportunity cost.

Normal profit is an implicit cost of doing business. To see the relationship between economic profit and normal profit, let us assume that we have explicitly accounted for all economic costs except for normal profits. Define the firm's total operating costs TC_O as total economic costs TC minus normal profit π_N. This relationship is summarized in Equation (1.8).

$$TC_o = TC - \pi_N \qquad (1.8)$$

Definition: Total operating cost is the difference between total economic cost and normal profit.

From Equation (1.8) we may define the firm's total economic profit as the sum of *total operating profit* and normal profit. This relationship is summarized by the relation.

$$\pi = TR - TC = TR - TC_o - \pi_N = \pi_o - \pi_N \qquad (1.9)$$

where $\pi_O = (TR - TC_O)$ is referred to as the firm's *total operating profit*.

Definition: Operating profit is the sum of economic profit and normal profit.

The important thing to note about Equation (1.9) is that a firm that breaks even in an economic sense in fact is earning an operating profit equal to its normal rate of return. The reason for this, of course, is that normal profits are considered to be an implicit cost. Put differently, a firm that is earning zero economic profit is earning a rate of return that is equal to the rate of return on the next best alternative investment of equivalent risk. A firm that is earning zero economic profit is earning an amount that is just sufficient to keep people from pulling their investments in search of a higher rate of return. When economic profits are positive (i.e., when operating profits are greater than normal profits), the firm is said to be earning an *above-normal rate of return*. When firms are earning above-normal profits, investment capital will be attracted into the business. These distinctions will be discussed in greater detail in Chapter 8 when we consider short-run and long-run competitive equilibrium.

VARIATIONS IN PROFITS ACROSS INDUSTRIES AND FIRMS

It was pointed out earlier that profit is the mechanism whereby society signals resource owners and entrepreneurs where goods and services are in greatest demand. If market economies are dynamic and efficient, this would imply that profits tend to be equal across industries and among firms. Yet, this is hardly the case. Established industries, such as textiles and basic metals, tend to generate a lower rate of return than such high-technology industries as computer hardware and software, telecommunications, health care, and biotechnology. There are several theories that help to explain these profit differences.

Although free-market economies tend to be relatively efficient and dynamic, it is this very dynamism that often gives rise to above-normal and below-normal profits. In general, we would expect risk-adjusted rates of return to be the same across all industries and firms. The *frictional theory of profit*, however, helps explain why this is rarely the case. To see this, we make a distinction between short-run and long-run competitive equilibrium. If we assume that firms are profit maximizers, then a firm is in short-run equilibrium if it is earning an above-normal rate of return. The existence of above-normal rates of return tends to attract investment capital, thereby resulting in an increase in industry output, falling product prices, and lower profits. If a firm is earning below-normal rates of return, then investment capital will tend to exit the industry, resulting in lower output, rising product prices, higher prices, and increased profits.

Firms that are just earning a normal rate of return are said to be in long-run equilibrium. When firms are in long-run equilibrium, investment capital will neither enter nor exit the industry. In this case, output neither expands nor contracts, and product prices and profits remain unchanged. In reality, industries are rarely in long-run competitive equilibrium because of recurring supply-side and demand-side "shocks" to the economic system. Examples of supply-side shocks may result from changes in production technology or changes in resource prices, such as fluctuations in energy prices brought about by recurrent changes in OPEC production policies. On the demand side of the market, these shocks may result from the introduction of new products and changing consumer preferences, such as was the case with the introduction of personal computers in 1980s.

The *risk-bearing theory of profit* suggests that above-normal profits are required to attract productive resources into industries with above-average risk, such as petroleum exploration. This line of reasoning is quite analogous to the idea that the rate of return on corporate equities should be higher than that for corporate bonds to compensate the investor for the increased uncertainty associated with the returns on these financial assets.

Sometimes a firm will earn above-normal profits because it is in a position to exercise *market power*. Market power relates to the ability of a firm or an industry to raise the selling price of its product by restricting output. The degree of a firm's market power is usually related to the level of competition. If a firm has many competitors, each selling essentially the same good or service, then that firm's ability to raise price will be severely limited. To raise prices in the face of stiff competition would result in a dramatic decline in sales. As we will discuss in Chapter 8, this is characteristic of firms operating in perfectly competitive industries. At the other extreme, a firm that produces output for the entire industry has a great deal of discretion over its selling price through adjustments in output. This is the extreme case of a monopoly. Such a dominant position in the market may be achieved through patent protection, government restrictions that limit competition, or through cost advantages associated with large scale production.

An extension to the competitive theory of firm behavior is the *marginal efficiency theory of profit*. According to this theory, the firm's ability to extract above-normal profits in the long-run stems from being a more efficient (least-cost) producer. In this case, a firm is able to generate high profits by staying ahead of the competition by adopting the most efficient methods of production and management techniques. Above-normal profits might also be generated through the introduction of a new product or production technique. The *innovation theory of profit* postulates that above-average profits are the rewards associated with being the first to introduce a new product or technology. Steve Jobs, cofounder of Apple Computer, became a multimillionaire after pioneering the desktop personal computer. Such above-normal profits, however, invite a host of imitators and thus are usually short-lived. Usually within a relative short period of time, above-normal profits will be competed away, and some individual producers may be forced to drop out of the industry.

CHAPTER REVIEW

Managerial economics is the application of economic theory and quantitative methods (mathematics and statistics) to the managerial decision-making process. In general, economic theory is the study of how individuals and societies choose to utilize scarce productive resources (land, labor, capital, and entrepreneurial ability) to satisfy virtually unlimited wants. Quantitative methods refer to the tools and techniques of analysis, which include optimization analysis, statistical methods, forecasting, game theory, linear programming, and capital budgeting.

Economic theory is concerned with how society answers the basic economic questions of *what* goods and services should be produced, and in what amounts, *how* these goods and services should be produced (i.e., the choice of the appropriate production technology), and *for whom* these goods and services should be produced. In market economies, *what* goods and services are produced by society is determined not by the producer, but rather by the consumer. Profit-maximizing firms produce only the goods and services their customers demand. How goods and services are produced refers to the technology of production, and this is determined by the firm's management. Profit maximization implies cost minimization. In competitive markets, firms that do not combine productive inputs in the most efficient (least costly) manner possible will quickly be driven out of business. The *for whom* part of the question designates the individuals who are willing, and able, to pay for the goods and services produced.

The study of economics is divided into two broad subcategories: *macroeconomics* and *microeconomics*. Macroeconomics is the study of entire economies and economic systems and specifically considers such broad economic aggregates as gross domestic product, economic growth, national income, employment, unemployment, inflation, and international trade. In general, the topics covered in macroeconomics are concerned with the economic environment within which firm managers operate. For the most part, macroeconomics focuses on variables over which the managerial decision maker has little or no control, although they may be of considerable importance when economic decisions are mode at the micro level of the individual, firm, or industry. Macroeconomics also examines the role of government in influencing these economic aggregates to achieve socially desirable objectives through the use of monetary and fiscal policies.

Microeconomics, on the other hand, is the study of the behavior and interaction of individual economic agents. These economic agents represent individual firms, consumers, and governments. Microeconomics deals with such topics as profit maximization, utility maximization, revenue or sales maximization, product pricing, input utilization, production efficiency, market structure, capital budgeting, environmental protection, and governmental regulation. Microeconomics is the study of the behavior of individual economic agents, such as individual consumers and firms, and the inter-actions between them.

Unlike macroeconomics, microeconomics is concerned with factors that are directly or indirectly under the control of management, such as product quantity, quality, pricing, input utilization, and advertising expenditures. Managerial economics also explicitly recognizes that a firm's organizational objective, usually profit maximization, is subject to one or more operating constraints (size of firm's operating budget, shareholders' expected rate of return on investment, etc.).

The dominant organizational objective of firms in free-market economies is *profit maximization*. Other important organizational objectives, which may be inconsistent with the goal of profit maximization, include a variety of *noneconomic objectives, satisficing behavior*, and *wealth maximization*.

The assumption of profit maximization has come under repeated criticism. Many economists have argued that this behavioral assertion is too simplistic to describe the complexity of the modern large corporation and the managerial thought processes required. Other theories emphasize different aspects of the operations of the modern, large corporation. Despite these attempts, no other theory of firm behavior has been able to provide a satisfactory alternative to the broader assumption of profit maximization.

Profit maximization (loss minimization) involves maximizing the positive difference (minimizing the negative difference) between *total revenue* and *total economic cost*, that is, *total economic profit*. Total revenue is defined as the price of a product times the number of units sold. Total economic cost includes all relevant costs associated with producing a given amount of output. These costs include both *explicit*, "out-of-pocket" expenses and implicit costs.

Economic profit is distinguished from *accounting profit*, which is the difference between total revenue and total explicit costs. Total economic profit considers all relevant economic costs associated with the production of a good or a service. Another important concept is *normal profit*, which refers to the minimum payment necessary to keep the firm's factors of production from being transferred to some other activity. In other words, normal profit refers to the profit that could be earned by a firm in its next best alternative activity. Economic profit refers to profit in excess of these normal returns.

Noneconomic organizational objectives tend to emphasize such intangibles as good citizenship, product quality, and employee goodwill. The achievement of other organizational objectives, such as earning an "adequate" rate of return on investment, or attaining some minimum acceptable rate of sales, profit, market share, or asset growth, is the result of satisficing behavior on the part of senior management. Satisficing behavior is predicated on the belief that it is not possible for senior management to know when profits are maximized because of the complexities and uncertainties associated with running a large corporation. Finally, maximization of shareholder wealth involves maximizing the value of a company's stock by maximizing the present value of the firm's net cash inflows at the appropriate discount rate.

In summary, managerial economics might best be described as applied microeconomics. As an applied discipline, managerial economics integrates economic theory with the techniques of quantitative analysis, including mathematical economics, optimization analysis, regression analysis, forecasting, linear programming, and risk analysis. Managerial economics attempts to demonstrate how the optimality conditions postulated in economic theory can be applied to real-world business situations to optimize firms' organizational objectives.

KEY TERMS AND CONCEPTS

Above-normal profit   A positive level of economic profits (i.e., operating profits are greater than normal profits).

Accounting profit   The difference between total revenue and total explicit costs.

Business cycle   Recurrent expansions and contractions in overall macroeconomic activity.

Ceteris paribus   The assertion in economic theory that when analyzing the relationship between two variables, all other variables are assumed to remain unchanged.

Consumption efficiency   The state in which consumers derive the greatest level of happiness, satisfaction, or utility from the purchase of goods and services subject to limited income.

Economic efficiency   Also referred to as *Pareto efficiency*. An economic outcome in which it not possible to make one person in society better off without making some other person in society worse off. Two related concepts are production efficiency and consumption efficiency.

Economic good   A good or service not available in sufficient quantity to satisfy everyone's desire for that good or service at a zero price.

Factors of production   Inputs that are used to product goods and services. Also called productive resources, factors of production fall into one of four broad categories: land, labor, capital, and entrepreneurial ability.

Financial intermediaries   Institutions that act as a link between those who have money to lend and those who want to borrow money, such as commercial banks, savings banks, and insurance companies.

Fiscal policy   Government spending and taxing policies.

Incentive contract   A contract between owner and manager in which the manager is provided with incentives to perform in the best interest of the owner.

Macroeconomic policy Monetary and fiscal policy. Sometimes referred to as *stabilization policy*, macroeconomic policy is designed to moderate the negative effects of the business cycle.

Macroeconomics The study of entire economies. Macroeconomics deals with broad economic aggregates, such as national product, employment, unemployment, inflation, interest rates, and international trade. Macroeconomics also examines the role of government in influencing these economic aggregates to achieve some socially desirable objective through the use of monetary and fiscal policies.

Manager–worker/principal–agent problem Arises when workers do not have a vested interest in a firm's success. Without a stake in the company's performance, there will be an incentive for some workers not to put forth their best efforts.

Managerial economics The synthesis of microeconomic theory and quantitative methods to find optimal solutions to managerial decision-making problems.

Market economy An economic system characterized by private ownership of factors of production, private property rights, consumer sovereignty, risk taking, entrepreneurship, and a system of prices to allocate scarce goods, services, and factors of production.

Microeconomic policy Government policies designed to promote production and consumption efficiency.

Microeconomics The study of the behavior of individual economic agents, such as individual consumers and firms, and the interactions between them. Microeconomic theory deals with such topics as product pricing, input utilization, production technology, production costs, market structure, total revenue maximization, unit sales maximization, profit maximization, capital budgeting, environmental protection, and governmental regulation.

Monetary policy The part of macroeconomic policy that deals with the regulation of the money supply and credit.

Negative externalities Costs of a transaction borne by individuals not party to the transaction.

Normal profit The level of profits required to keep a firm engaged in a particular activity. Normal profit represents the rate of return on the next best alternative investment of equivalent risk.

Ockham's razor The principle that, other things being equal, the simplest explanation tends to be the correct explanation.

Opportunity cost The highest valued alternative forgone whenever a choice is made.

Owner–manager/principal–agent problem Arises when managers do not share in the success of the day-to-day operations of the firm. When managers do not have a stake in company's performance, some managers will have an incentive to substitute leisure for a diligent work effort.

Positive externalities   Benefits of a transaction that are borne by an individual not a party to the transaction.

Post hoc, ergo propter hoc   A common error in economic theorizing which asserts that because event *A* preceded event *B*, that event *A* caused event *B*.

Principal–agent problem   Arises when there are inadequate incentives for agents (managers or workers) to put forth their best efforts for principals (owners or managers). This incentive problem arises because principals, who have a vested interest in the operations of the firm, benefit from the hard work of their agents, while agents who do not have a vested interest prefer leisure.

Production efficiency   The production by a firm of goods and services at least cost, or the full and productive employment of society's resources.

Pure capitalism   Describes economic systems that are characterized by the private ownership of productive resources, the use of markets and prices to allocate goods and services, and little or no government intervention in the economy.

Satisficing behavior   An alternative to the assumption of profit maximization, satisficing behavior may include maximizing salaries and benefits, maximizing a market share subject to some minimally acceptable (by shareholders) profit level, earning an "adequate" rate of return on investment, and attaining some minimum rate of return on sales, profit, market share, asset growth, and so on.

Scarcity   Describes the condition in which the availability of resources is insufficient to satisfy the wants and needs of individuals and society.

Total economic cost   Includes all relevant costs associated with producing a given amount of output. Economic costs include both explicit (out-of-pocket) expenses and implicit (opportunity) costs.

Total economic profit   Economic profit is the difference between total revenue and total economic costs.

Total operating cost   Economic cost less normal profit.

Total operating profit   Economic profit plus normal profit.

CHAPTER QUESTIONS

1.1 Define the concept of *scarcity*. Explain the significance of this concept in relation to the concept of *opportunity cost*. Are opportunity cost and sacrifice the same thing? Would you say that a sacrifice represents the cost of a particular decision?

1.2 Explain why the concept of scarcity is central to the study of economics.

1.3 The opportunity cost of any decision includes the value of all relevant sacrifices, both explicit and implicit. Do you agree? Explain.

1.4 In economics there is no "free lunch." What do you believe is the meaning of this statement?

1.5 Explain how managerial economics is similar to and different from microeconomics.

1.6 What is the difference between a theory and a model?

1.7 Bad theories make bad predictions. Do you agree with this statement? Explain.

1.8 The "law of demand" is not a law. Do you agree with this statement? Explain.

1.9 Evaluate the following statement: Theories are only as good as their underlying assumptions.

1.10 Explain the difference between a theory and a law.

1.11 The Museum of Heroic Art (MOHA) is a not-for-profit institution. For nearly a century, the mission of MOHA has been to "extol and lionize the heroic human spirit." MOHA's most recent exhibitions, which have featured larger-than-life renditions of such pulp-fiction super-heros as Superman, Wolverine, Batman, Green Lantern, Flash, Spawn, and Brenda Starr, have proven to be quite popular with the public. Art aficionados who wish to view the exhibit must purchase tickets months in advance. The contract of MOHA's managing director, Dr. Xavier, is currently being considered for renewal by the museum's board of trustees. Should theories of the firm based on the assumption of profit maximization play any role in the board's decision to renew Dr. Xavier's contract?

1.12 Many owners of small businesses do not pay themselves a salary. What effect will this practice have on the calculation of the firm's accounting profit? Economic profit? Explain.

1.13 It has been argued that profit maximization is an unrealistic description of the organizational behavior of large publicly held corporations. The modern corporation, so the argument goes, is too complex to accommodate such a simple explanation of the managerial behavior. One alternative argument depicts the manager as an agent for the corporation's shareholders. Managers, so the argument goes, exhibit "satisficing" behavior; that is, they maximize something other than profit, such as market share or executive perquisites, subject to some minimally acceptable rate of return on the shareholders' investment. Do you believe that this assessment of managerial behavior is realistic? Do you believe that the description of shareholder expectations is essentially correct? If not, then why not?

1.14 Suppose you are attending a shareholder meeting of Blue Globe Corporation. A major shareholder complains that Robert Redtoe, the chief operating officer (COO) of Blue Globe, earned $1,000,000 gross compensation, while Sam Pinkeye, the COO of Blue Globe's chief competitor, Green Ball Company, earned only $500,000. Should you support a motion to cut Redtoe's compensation? Explain your position.

1.15 One solution to the principal–agent problem in restaurants is the system in which waiters and waitresses in restaurants work for tips as well as for a small boss salary. Discuss a potential problem for management with this type of revenue-based incentive scheme.

1.16 Employese of fast-food restaurants who work directly with customers do not earn tips like waiters and waitresses. Discuss possible solutions to the manager–worker/principal–agent problem in fast-food restaurants.

1.17 Explain why frequent spot checks by managers to encourage workers to put forth their best effort may not always be in the best interest of the firm's owners.

1.18 Under what condition is the assumption of profit maximization equivalent to shareholder wealth maximization?

1.19 In practice, what is a good approximation of the risk-free rate of return on an investment?

1.20 As a practical matter, how would you estimate the risk premium on an investment?

1.21 Discuss several reasons why a firm in a competitive industry might earn above-normal profits in the short run. Will these above-normal profits persist in the long run? Explain.

1.22 Firms that earn zero economic profit should close their doors and seek alternative investment opportunities. Do you agree? Explain.

1.23 What is likely to happen to the price, quantity, and quality of products produced by firms in competitive industries earning above normal profits? Explain. Cite an example.

CHAPTER EXERCISES

1.1 Tilly's Trilbies has estimated the following revenues and expenditures for the next fiscal year:

Revenues	$6,800,000
Cost of goods sold	5,000,000
Cost of labor	1,000,000
Advertising	100,000
Insurance	50,000
Rent	350,000
Miscellaneous expenses	100,000

a. Calculate Tilly's accounting profit.
b. Suppose that to open her trilby business, Tilly gave up a $250,000 per year job as a buyer at the exclusive Hammocker Shlumper department store. Calculate Tilly's economic profit.

c. Tilly is considering purchasing a building across the street and moving her company into that new location. The cost of the building is $5,000,000, which will be fully financed at a simple interest rate of 5% per year. Interest payments are due annually on the last day of Tilly's fiscal year. The first interest payment will be due next year. Principal will be repaid in 10 equal installments beginning at the end of the fifth year. Calculate Tilly's accounting profit and economic profit for the next fiscal year.

d. Based upon your answer to part c, should Tilly buy the new building? Explain. (*Hint*: In your answer, ignore the economic impact of principal repayments.)

1.2 Last year Chloe quit her $60,000 per year job as a web-page designer for a leading computer software company to buy a small hotel on Saranac Lake. The purchase price of the hotel was $300,000, which she financed by selling a tax-free municipal bond that earned 5.5% per year. Chloe's total operating expenses and revenues were $100,000 and $200,000, respectively.

a. Calculate Chloe's accounting profit.

b. Calculate Chloe's economic profit.

1.3 In the last fiscal year Neptune Hydroponics generated $150,000 in operating profits. Neptune's total revenues and total economic costs were $200,000 and $75,000, respectively. Calculate Neptune's normal rate of return.

1.4 Andrew Oxnard, chief financial officer, has been asked by Harry Pendel, chief executive officer and cofounder of Pendel & Braithwaite, Ltd. (P&B), to analyze two capital investment projects (projects A and B), which are expected to generate the following profit (π) streams:

Profit Streams for Projects A and B
($ thousands)

Period, t	π_A	π_B
1	$100	$350
2	200	300
3	250	200
4	300	100
5	325	100
	$1,175	$1,050

Profits are realized at the end of each period. Assuming that P&B is a profit maximizer, if the discount rate for both projects is 12%, which of the two projects should be adopted?

SELECTED READINGS

Alchain, A. A., and H. Demsetz. "Production, Information Costs, and Economic Organization," American Economic Review, 57 (December 1972), pp. 777–795.

Baumol, W. J. Business Behavior, Value and Growth. New York: Harcourt Brace Jovanovich, 1967.

Boyes, W., and M. Melvin. Microeconomics, 3rd ed. Boston: Houghton Mifflin, 1996.

Brennan, M. J., and T. M. Carroll. Preface to Quantitative Economics & Econometrics, 4th ed. Cincinnati, OH: South-Western Publishing, 1987.

Case, K. E., and R. C. Fair. Principles of Microeconomics. Upper Saddle River, NJ: Prentice-Hall, 1999.

Glass, J. C. An Introduction to Mathematical Methods in Economics. New York: McGraw-Hill, 1980.

Coase, R. "The Nature of the Firm." Economia, 4 (1937), pp. 386–405.

Demsetz, H., and K. Lehn. "The Structure of Corporate Ownership: Causes and Consequences." Journal of Political Economy, 93 (December 1985), pp. 1155–1177.

Diamond, D. W., and R. E. Verrecchia. "Optimal Managerial Contracts and Equilibrium Security Prices." Journal of Finance, 37 (May 1982), pp. 275–287.

Fama, E. F., and M. C. Jensen. "Separation of Ownership and Control." Journal of Law and Economics, 26 (June 1983), pp. 301–325.

————. "Agency Problems and Residual Claims." Journal of Law and Economics, 26 (June 1983), pp. 327–349.

Green, W. H. Econometric Analysis, 3rd ed. Upper Saddle River, NJ: Prentice-Hall, 1997.

Grossman, S. J., and O. D. Hart. "An Analysis of the Principal-Agent Problem" Econometrica, vol. 51 (January 1983), pp. 7–45.

Gujarati, D. Basic Econometrics, 3rd ed. New York: McGraw-Hill, 1995.

Harris, M., and A. Raviv. "Some Results on Incentive Contracts with Applications to Education and Employment, Health Insurance, and Law Enforcement." American Economic Review, 68 (March 1978), pp. 20–30.

Henderson, J. M., and R. E. Quandt. Microeconomic Theory: A Mathematical Approach, 2nd ed. New York: McGraw-Hill, 1971.

Holstrom, B. "Moral Hazard and Observability." Bell Journal of Economics, 10 (Spring 1979), pp. 74–91.

————. "Moral Hazard in Teams." Bell Journal of Economics, 13 (Spring 1982), pp. 324–340.

Jensen, M. C., and W. H. Meckling. "Theory of the Firm: Managerial Behavior, Agency Costs, and Ownership Structure." Journal of Financial Economics, 3 (October 1976), pp. 305–360.

MacDonald, G. M. "New Directions in the Economic Theory of Agency." Canadian Journal of Economics, 17 (August 1984), pp. 415–440.

Marris, R., and A. Wood, eds. The Corporate Economy: Growth, Competition, and Innovative Potential. Cambridge, MA: Harvard University Press, 1971.

McGuire, J. W., J. S. Y. Chiu, and A. O. Elbing. "Executive Incomes, Sales and Profits." American Economic Review, 52 (September 1962), pp. 753–761.

Ramanathan, R. Introductory Econometrics with Applications, 4th ed. New York: Dryden Press, 1998.

Shavell, S. "Risk Sharing and Incentives in the Principal and Agent Relationship." Bell Journal of Economics, 10 (Spring 1979), pp. 55–73.

Silberberg, E. The Structure of Economics: A Mathematical Analysis. New York: McGraw-Hill, 1978.

Simon, H. "Theories of Decision-Making in Economics and Behavioral Science." American Economic Review, 59 (1959), pp. 253–283.

Smith, A. The Wealth of Nations (1776). Available from Modern Library, New York.

Williamson, O. The Economic Institutions of Capitalism. New York: Free Press, 1985.

————. Markets and Hierarchies: Analysis and Antitrust Implications. New York: Free Press, 1975.

————. The Economics of Discretionary Behavior: Managerial Objectives in a Theory of the Firm. Englewood Cliffs, NJ: Prentice Hall, 1964.

Winn, D. N., and J. D. Shoenhair. "Compensation-Based (Dis)incentives for Revenue Maximizing Behavior: A Test of the 'Revised' Baumol Hypothesis." Review of Economics and Statistics, 70 (February 1988), pp. 154–158.

2

INTRODUCTION TO
MATHEMATICAL
ECONOMICS

Managerial economics was defined in Chapter 1 as the synthesis of microeconomic theory, mathematics, and statistical methods to find optimal solutions to managerial decision-making problems. Yet, many students enrolled in managerial economics courses find that their academic training in one or more of these three disciplines is deficient. In this chapter we review the fundamental mathematical methods that will be used throughout the remainder of this book.

This chapter may not be for everyone. Every student brings something of himself or herself to the study of managerial economics. In many engineering programs, for example, students are required to take finance and economics courses to develop an understanding of the business aspects of research, development, construction, and product development. In general, these students come with rich backgrounds in quantitative methods but perhaps are somewhat deficient in economic principles. For students who fall into this category, a very brief review of the topics presented in this chapter may be all that is necessary before moving to chapters that are more specifically about economics. For many liberal arts student, turned business majors, however, a more thorough examination of mathematical methods may be absolutely essential to mastery of the material presented in subsequent chapters of this text.

This chapter begins with a review of the fundamental mathematical concepts that will be encountered throughout this text. Illustrative examples concern primarily economics to highlight the usefulness of these techniques for understanding fundamental economic principles and to provide the student with an idea of things to come. Much of this chapter

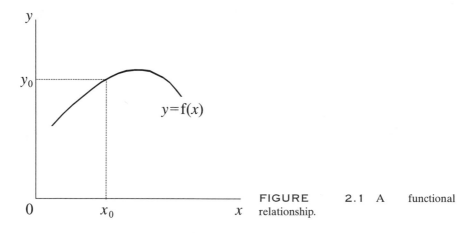

FIGURE 2.1 A functional relationship.

is devoted to the solution of constrained and unconstrained economic optimization problems. In fact, the ability to find solutions to constrained optimization problems is at the very core of the study of economics. After all, economics is the study of how individuals and societies seek to *maximize* virtually unlimited material and spiritual wants and needs *subject to scarce resources.*

FUNCTIONAL RELATIONSHIPS AND ECONOMIC MODELS

In mathematics, a functional relationship of the form

$$y = f(x) \tag{2.1}$$

is read "*y* is a function of *x*." This relationship indicates that the value of *y* depends in a systematic way on the value of *x*. The expression says that there is a unique value for *y* (included in the set of numbers called the *range*) for each value of *x* (drawn from the set of numbers in the *domain*.) The variable *y* is referred to as the *dependent variable*. The variable *x* is referred to as the *independent variable*.

Consider, for example, Figure 2.1.

The functional notation *f* in Equation (2.1) can be regarded as a specific rule that defines the relationship between values of *x* and *y*. When we assert, for example, that $y = f(x) = 3x$, the actual rule has been made explicit. In this case, the rule asserts that when $x = 2$, then $y = 6$, and so on. In this case, the value of *x* has been *transformed*, or *mapped*, into a value of *y*. For this reason, a function is sometimes referred to as a *mapping* or *transformation*. Symbolically, this mapping may be expressed as $f: x \rightarrow y$.

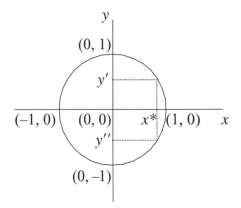

FIGURE 2.2 Correspondences and the unit circle.

Examples
a. $y = f(x) = 4x$
b. $y = f(x) = 4x^2 - 25$
c. $y = f(x) = 25x^2 + 5x + 10$
Assume, for example, that $x = 2$. The foregoing functional relationships become $y = f(2) = 4(2) = 8$, $y = f(2) = 4(2)^2 - 25 = -9$, and $y = f(2) = 25(2)^2 + 5(2) + 10 = 120$.

The value of y may also be expressed as a function of more than one independent variable, that is,

$$y = f(x_1, \ldots, x_n) \tag{2.2}$$

Examples
a. $y = f(x_1, x_2) = 3x_1 + 2x_2$
b. $y = f(x_1, \ldots, x_n) = 3x_1 + 4x_2 + 5x_3 + \ldots + (n + 2)x_n$
Assume, for example, that in the first example $x_1 = 2$ and $x_2 = 3$. The functional relationships become $y = f(2, 3) = 3(2) + 2(3) = 12$.

Functional relationships may be contrasted with the concept of a *correspondence*, where more than one value of y is associated with each value of x. Consider Figure 2.2, which is the diagram of a unit circle.

The equation for the unit circle in Figure 2.2 is $x^2 + y^2 = 1$, which may be solved for y as $y = \pm \sqrt{(1 - x^2)}$. Except for the points $(-1, 0)$ and $(1, 0)$, this expression is not a function, since there are two values of y associated with each value of x. Fortunately, most situations in economics may be expressed as functional relationships.[1]

METHODS OF EXPRESSING ECONOMIC AND BUSINESS RELATIONSHIPS

Economic and business relationships may be represented in a variety of ways, including tables, charts, graphs, and algebraic expressions. Consider,

---

[1] For additional details, see Silberberg (1990), Chapter 5.

TABLE 2.1   Total revenue for output levels
$Q = 0$ to $Q = 6$.

Q	TR
0	0
1	18
2	36
3	54
4	72
5	90
6	108

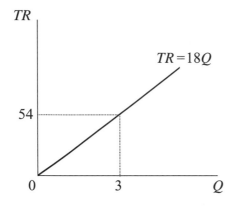

FIGURE 2.3   Constant selling price and linear total revenue.

for example, Equation (2.3), which summarizes total revenue (TR) for a firm operating in a perfectly competitive industry.

$$TR = f(Q) = PQ \qquad (2.3)$$

In Equation (2.3), P represents the market-determined selling price of commodity Q produced and sold within a given period of time (day, week, month, quarter, etc.). Suppose that the selling price is \$18. The total revenue function of the firm may be expressed algebraically as

$$TR = 18Q \qquad (2.4)$$

For the output levels $Q = 0$ to $Q = 6$, this relationship may be expressed in tabular form as shown in Table 2.1.

Total revenue for the output levels $Q = 0$ to $Q = 6$ may also be expressed diagrammatically as in Figure 2.3.

The total revenue (TR) in Figure 2.3 illustrates the general class of mathematical relationships called linear functions, discussed earlier. A linear function may be written in the general form

$$y = f(x) = a + bx \qquad (2.5)$$

where a and b are known constants. The value a is called the *intercept* and the value b is called the *slope*. Mathematically, the intercept is the value of y when $x = 0$. This expression is said to be linear in x and y, where the corresponding graph is represented by a straight line. In the total revenue example just given, $a = 0$ and $b = 18$.

THE SLOPE OF A LINEAR FUNCTION

In Equation (2.5), the parameter b is called the slope, which obtained by dividing the change in the value of the dependent variable (the "rise") by the change in the value of the independent variable (the "run") as we move between two coordinate points. The value of the slope may be calculated by using the equation

$$\text{Slope} = \frac{\Delta y}{\Delta x}$$
$$= \frac{y_2 - y_1}{x_2 - x_1} = \frac{f(x_2) - f(x_1)}{x_2 - x_1} \tag{2.6}$$

where the symbol Δ denotes change. In terms of our total revenue example, consider the quantity—total revenue combinations $(Q_1, TR_1) = (1, 18)$ and $(Q_2, TR_2) = (3, 54)$. We observe that these coordinates lie on the straight line generated by Equation (2.4). In fact, because Equation (2.4) generates a straight line, any two coordinate points along the function will suffice when one is calculating the slope. In this case, a measure of the slope is given by the expression

$$b = \frac{\Delta TR}{\Delta Q}$$
$$= \frac{TR_2 - TR_1}{Q_2 - Q_1} = \frac{f(Q_2) - f(Q_1)}{Q_2 - Q_1} \tag{2.7}$$

After substituting, we obtain

$$b = \frac{54 - 18}{3 - 1} = \frac{36}{2} = 18$$

which, in this case, is the price of the product.

Suppose that we already know the value of the slope. It can easily be demonstrated that the original linear function may be recovered given any single coordinate along the function. The general solution values for Equation (2.5) may be written as

$$b(x_2 - x_1) = (y_2 - y_1)$$

and

$$y_2 = (y_1 - bx_1) + bx_2 \tag{2.8}$$

In Equation (2.8), y_1 and y_2 are solutions to Equation (2.5) given x_1 and x_2, provided $x_1 \neq x_2$. If we are given specific values for y_1, x_1, and b, then Equation (2.8) reduces to Equation (2.5), where $y = y_2$ and $x = x_2$. Equation (2.8) may then be solved for the intercept to yield

$$a = y - bx \tag{2.9}$$

Equation (2.9) is referred to as the slope–intercept form of the linear equation. To illustrate these relationships, consider again the total revenue example. Suppose we know that $b = 18$ and $(Q, TR) = (4, 72)$. What is the total revenue equation? Substituting these values into Equation (2.9), we obtain $a = 72 - 18(4) = 0$. Thus, the total revenue equation is $TR = a + bQ = 0 + 18Q = 18Q$.

AN APPLICATION OF LINEAR FUNCTIONS TO ECONOMICS

Tables, graphs, and equations are often used to explain business and economic relationships. Being abstractions, such models often appear unrealistic. Nevertheless, the models are useful in studying business and economic relationships. Managerial economic decisions should not be made without having first analyzed their possible implications. Economic models help facilitate this process. Consider, for example, the concept of the market in from introductory economics, which is illustrated in Figure 2.4.

In Figure 2.4, the demand curve DD slopes downward to the right, illustrating the inverse relationship between the quantity of output Q that consumers are willing and able to buy at each price P. The supply curve SS

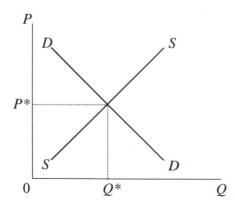

FIGURE 2.4 Demand, supply, and market equilibrium.

illustrates the positive relationship between the quantity of output that suppliers are willing to bring to market at each price. Equilibrium in the market occurs at a price P^*, where the quantity demanded equals the quantity supplied Q^*.

This simple model may also be expressed algebraically as

$$Q_D = f(P) \tag{2.10}$$

$$Q_S = g(P) \tag{2.11}$$

where Q_D represents the quantity demanded and Q_S represents the quantity supplied. Market equilibrium is defined as[2]

$$Q_D = Q_S \tag{2.12}$$

If Q_D and Q_S are linearly related to price, then Equations (2.10) and (2.11) may be written

$$Q_D = a + bP; b < 0 \, (DD \text{ has a negative slope}) \tag{2.13}$$

$$Q_S = c + dP; d > 0 \, (SS \text{ has a positive slope}) \tag{2.14}$$

By equating the quantity supplied and quantity demanded, the equilibrium price P^* may be determined as

$$a + bP = c + dP$$

or

$$P^* = \frac{c - a}{b - d} \tag{2.15}$$

This result may be substituted into either the demand equation or the supply equation to yield Q^*:

$$Q^* = a + b\left(\frac{a - c}{b - d}\right) \tag{2.16}$$

Problem 2.1. The market demand and supply equations for a product are

$$Q_D = 25 - 3P$$

$$Q_S = 10 + 2P$$

---

[2] The reader might have noticed that there is something "wrong" about Figure 2.4. By mathematical convention, the dependent variable is on the vertical axis and the independent (explanatory) variable is on the horizontal axis. Since the publication of Alfred Marshall's (1920) classic nonmathematical analysis of supply, demand, and market equilibrium, the convention in economics has been to put the independent variable P on the vertical axis and the dependent variable Q on the horizontal axis.

where Q is quantity and P is price. Determine the equilibrium price and quantity.

Solution. The equilibrium price and quantity are given as

$$Q_D = Q_S$$

Substituting into this expression we have

$$25 - 3P = 10 + 2P$$

$$P* = \frac{25 - 10}{5} = 3$$

$$Q* = 25 - 3(3) = 16$$

INVERSE FUNCTIONS

Consider, again, the function

$$y = f(x) \tag{2.1}$$

A function $f: x \rightarrow y$ is called *one-to-one* if it is possible to map a given value of x into a unique value of y. This function is also called *onto* if it is possible to map a given value of y onto a unique value of x. If the function $f: x \rightarrow y$ is both one-to-one and onto, then a *one-to-one correspondence* is said to exist between x and y. If a functional relationship is a one-to-one correspondence, then not only will a given value of x correspond to a unique value of y, but a given value of y will correspond to a unique value of x. A nonnumerical example (Chiang, 1984) of a relationship that is one-to-one, but not onto, is the mapping of the set of all sons to the set of all fathers. Each son has one, and only one, father, while each father may have more than one son. By contrast, the mapping of the set of all husbands into all wives in a monogamous society is both one-to-one and onto; that is, it is a one-to-one correspondence because each husband has one, and only one, wife, and each wife has one, and only one, husband.

If Equation (2.1) is a one-to-one correspondence, then the function f has the *inverse function*

$$g(y) = f^{-1}(y) = x \tag{2.17}$$

which is also a one-to-one correspondence.[3] This function, which maps a given value for y into a unique value of x, may be written $f^{-1}: y \rightarrow x$. For example, the function $y = f(x) = 5 - 3x$ has the property that different values

---

[3] In this notation, -1 is not an exponent; that is, f^{-1} does not mean $1/f$. The notation simply means that f^{-1} is the inverse of f.

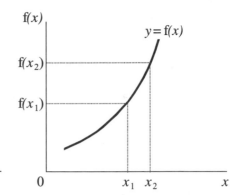

FIGURE 2.5 A monotonically increasing function.

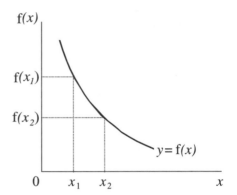

FIGURE 2.6 A monotonically decreasing function.

of x will yield unique values of y. Thus, there exists the inverse function $g(y)$ $= f^{-1}(y) = (5/3) - (1/3)y$ that also has the property that different values of y will yield unique values of x. Figures 2.5 and 2.6 are examples of functions in which a one-to-one correspondence exists between x and y.

Functions for which one-to-one correspondences exist are said to be *monotonically increasing* if $x_2 > x_1 \Rightarrow f(x_2) > f(x_1)$.[4] A monotonically increasing function is depicted in Figure 2.5. Functions for which one-to-one correspondences exist are said to be *monotonically decreasing* if $x_2 > x_1 \Rightarrow f(x_2)$ $< f(x_1)$. A monotonically decreasing function is illustrated in Figure 2.6. In general, for an inverse function to exist, the original function must be monotonic. By contrast, the functional relationship depicted in Figure 2.1 is neither monotonically increasing nor monotonically decreasing, since the value of y first increases with increasing values of x, and then decreases. The functional relationship depicted in Figure 2.1 is not a one-to-one correspondence. The reason is that while this function is "one-to-one," it is not

---

[4] The symbol $\Rightarrow$ denotes "implies."

"onto." The reader should verify that the functional relationship in Figure 2.1 does not have an inverse.

The foregoing discussion suggests that it is not possible to write $x = g(y) = f^{-1}(y)$ until we have determined whether the function $y = f(x)$ is monotonic. Diagrammatically, it is easy to determine whether a function is monotonic by examining its slope. If the slope of the function is positive for all values of x, then the function $y = f(x)$ is monotonically increasing. If the slope of the function is negative for all values of x, then the function $y = f(x)$ is monotonically decreasing. It is easy to see that the linear function $y = f(x) = a + bx$ is a monotonically increasing or decreasing function depending on the value of b. A positive value for b indicates the function is monotonically increasing. A negative value for b indicates that the function is monotonically decreasing.

Because linear functions are monotonic, a one-to-one correspondence must exist between x and y. As a result, all linear functions have a corresponding inverse function. A discussion of the monotonicity of nonlinear functions will be deferred until our discussion of the *inverse-function rule* in connection with the derivative of a function.

> **Example.** Consider the function
>
> $$y = f(x) = 2 - 3x$$
>
> This function is one-to-one because for every value of x there is one, and only one, value for y. When we have solved for x, this function becomes
>
> $$x = g(y) = f^{-1}(y) = 2/3 - (1/3)y$$
>
> This function is also one-to-one, since for each value of y there is one, and only one, value for x. Since the original function is both one-to-one and onto, there is a one-to-one correspondence between x and y. Conversely, since the inverse function is also one-to-one and onto, there is a one-to-one correspondence between y and x. Finally, both the original function and the inverse function are monotonically decreasing, since the slope of each function is negative.

RULES OF EXPONENTS

Before considering nonlinear equations, some students may find it useful to review the rules of exponents. We begin this review by denoting the values of x and y as any two real numbers, and m and n any two positive integers.[5] Consider the following rules of dealing with exponents:

$$\text{Rule 1: } x^m \cdot x^n = x^{m+n} \tag{2.18}$$

> **Examples**
> a. $x^2 \cdot x^3 = x^{2+3} = x^5 = x \cdot x \cdot x \cdot x \cdot x$
> b. $3^2 \cdot 3^4 = 3^{2+4} = 3^6 = 3 \cdot 3 \cdot 3 \cdot 3 \cdot 3 \cdot 3 = 729$
> c. $y^r \cdot y^s = y^{r+s}$

[5] A real number is defined as the ratio of any two integers.

$$\text{Rule 2: } \left(x^m\right)^n = x^{mn} \tag{2.19}$$

Examples
a. $(x^3)^8 = x^3 \cdot x^3 \cdot x^3 \cdot x^3 \cdot x^3 \cdot x^3 \cdot x^3 \cdot x^3 = x^{3+3+3+3+3+3+3+3} = x^{3 \cdot 8} = x^{24}$
b. $(2^2)^3 = 2^2 \cdot 2^2 \cdot 2^2 = 4 \cdot 4 \cdot 4 = 2^{2+2+2} = 2^{2 \cdot 3} = 2^5 = 32$
c. $(y^m)^n = y^{mn}$

$$\text{Rule 3: } (xy)^m = x^m y^m \tag{2.20}$$

Examples
a. $(xy)^2 = xy \cdot xy = xx \cdot yy = x^2 \cdot y^2$
b. $(3 \cdot 2)^3 = (3 \cdot 2)(3 \cdot 2)(3 \cdot 2) = (3 \cdot 3 \cdot 3)(2 \cdot 2 \cdot 2) = 3^3 \cdot 2^3 = 6^3 = 216$

$$\text{Rule 4: } x^0 = 1 \tag{2.21}$$

Examples
a. $10^0 = 1$
b. $y^0 = 1$

$$\text{Rule 5: } x^{-m} = \frac{1}{x^m} \tag{2.22}$$

Examples

a. $x^{-3} = \dfrac{1}{x^3}$

b. $4^{-1} = \dfrac{1}{4^1} = \dfrac{1}{4} = 0.25$

c. $5^{-2} = \dfrac{1}{5^2} = \dfrac{1}{25}$

d. $y^{-n} = \dfrac{1}{y^n}$

$$\text{Rule 6: } x^{1/n} = \sqrt[n]{x} \tag{2.23}$$

Examples
a. $x^{1/2} = \sqrt[2]{x} = \sqrt{x}$
a. $1000^{1/3} = \sqrt[3]{1000} = 10$
c. Combining rules 2 and 6, we have

$$4^{2/3} = \left(4^2\right)^{1/3} \sqrt[3]{4^2} = \sqrt[3]{16} \approx 2.52$$

In general, $x^{m/n} = \sqrt[n]{x^m}$

GRAPHS OF NONLINEAR FUNCTIONS OF ONE INDEPENDENT VARIABLE

As we have seen, the distinguishing characteristic of a linear function is its constant slope. In other words, the ratio of the change in the value of the dependent variable given a change in the value of the independent variable

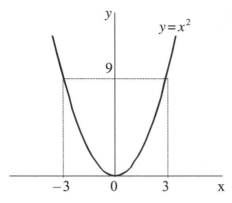

FIGURE 2.7 The quadratic function $y = a + bx + cx^2$, where $a = b = 0$.

is constant. In the case of *nonlinear functions* the slope is variable. In other words, graphs of nonlinear functions are "curved."

Polynomial functions constitute a class of functions that contain an independent variable that is raised to some nonnegative power greater than unity.[6] Two of the most common polynomial functions encountered in economics and business are the *quadratic function* and the *cubic function*.

The general form of a quadratic function is

$$y = a + bx + cx^2 \tag{2.24}$$

where $c \neq 0$.[7] A quadratic function generates a graph known as a *parabola*. The values of the parameters define the shape of the parabola. When $a = b = 0$, the parabola will pass through the origin because $y = 0$ when $x = 0$. Moreover, since $(-x)^2 = x^2$, the parabola will be symmetric about the y axis (see Figure 2.7). If c is positive, the parabola will "open downward." When c is negative, the parabola, will "open upward." The greater the absolute value of c, the narrower the parabola, since y increases more rapidly as x increases.

If $a \neq 0$ and $b = 0$, the parabola will continue to remain symmetrical about the y axis but will no longer pass through the origin. Thus, when $a \neq 0$ and $b = 0$, $y = a + cx^2$, so that when $x = 0$, $y = a$. As in the case of a linear function, the value of a indicates where the function intersects the y axis. If $a = 0$ and $b \neq 0$, the parabola passes through the origin but will no longer be symmetric about the y axis. Thus, when $a = 0$ and $b \neq 0$, then $y = a + cx^2$. Factoring out x yields $y = x(b + cx)$. When $x = -b/c$, then $y = 0$. Thus, the function will cross the x axis twice—once at the origin (when $x = 0$) and once at the point where $x = -b/c$ (Figure 2.8).

---

[6] A linear function is a special case of a polynomial function in which the exponent attached to the independent variable is unity.

[7] In the case of $c = 0$, Equation (2.24) reduces to Equation (2.5).

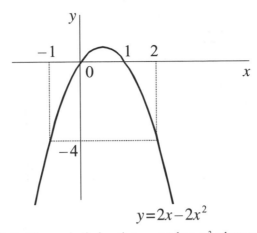

FIGURE 2.8   The quadratic function $y = a + bx + cx^2$, where $a = 0$, and $b \neq 0$.

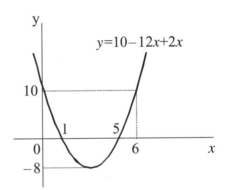

FIGURE 2.9 The quadratic equation $y = a + bx + cx^2$, where $a \neq 0, b = 0$, and $c \neq 0$.

Finally, when $b = 0$, $a \neq 0$, and $c \neq 0$, then $y = a + cx^2$. In this case the parabola will no longer pass through the origin. It may cross the x axis twice, once (a tangency point), or not at all (see Figure 2.9).

Cubic functions are of the general form

$$y = a + bx + cx^2 + dx^3 \tag{2.25}$$

Suppose, for example, that we have the following total cost (TC) equation for a firm producing Q units of a particular good or service:

$$TC = 6 + 33Q - 9Q^2 + Q^3 \tag{2.26}$$

From this equation, consider Table 2.2, which gives the total cost schedule for output values $Q = 0$ to $Q = 6$.

The values in Table 2.2 are plotted in Figure 2.10 as the total cost curve.

TABLE 2.2 Total cost for output levels $Q = 0$ to $Q = 6$.

Q	TC
0	6
1	31
2	44
3	51
4	58
5	71
6	96

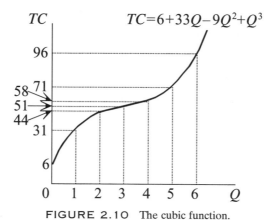

FIGURE 2.10 The cubic function.

SUM OF A GEOMETRIC PROGRESSION

A geometric progression of n terms is a sequence of numbers

$$a_1 = a, \quad a_2 = ar, \quad a_3 = ar^2, \quad a_4 = ar^3, \ldots, a_n = ar^{n-1}$$

The value r is called the *common ratio* of a geometric progression. The sum of a geometric progression may be written as

$$R = a + ar + ar^2 + ar^3 + \ldots + r^{n-1}$$
$$= a(1 + r + r^2 + r^3 + \ldots + r^{n-1}) = a\sum_{k=1\to(n-1)} r^k \tag{2.27}$$

Let

$$S = 1 + r + r^2 + r^3 + \ldots + r^{n-1} = \sum_{k=0\to(n-1)} r^k \tag{2.28}$$

Thus, Equation (2.27) may be rewritten as

$$R = aS \tag{2.29}$$

Multiplying both sides of Equation (2.28) by r yields

$$rS = r + r^2 + r^3 + r^4 + \ldots + r^n = \sum\nolimits_{k=1 \to (n-1)} r^k \tag{2.30}$$

Subtracting Equation (2.30) from Equation (2.28) yields

$$
\begin{aligned}
S - rS &= \sum\nolimits_{k=0 \to (n-1)} r^k - \sum\nolimits_{k=1 \to (n-1)} r^k \\
&= (1 + r + r^2 + r^3 + \ldots + r^{n-1}) - (r + r^2 + r^3 + r^4 + \ldots + r^n) \\
&= 1 + r + r^2 + r^3 + \ldots + r^{n-1} - r - r^2 - r^3 - r^4 + \ldots + r^{n-1} - r^n \\
&= 1 - r^n
\end{aligned}
\tag{2.31}
$$

Equation (2.31) may be rewritten as

$$S(1 - r) = 1 - r^n \tag{2.32}$$

Rearranging Equation (2.32) yields

$$S = \frac{1 - r^n}{1 - r} \tag{2.33}$$

Substituting Equation (2.33) into Equation (2.29) the yields

$$R = a\left(\frac{1 - r^n}{1 - r}\right) \tag{2.34}$$

Problem 2.2. Use Equation (2.34) to compute the sum of the geometric progression

$$R = 2 + 6 + 18 + 54 + 162 + 486$$

Solution. The sum of this geometric progression may be written as

$$
\begin{aligned}
R &= 2 + 6 + 18 + 54 + 162 + 486 \\
&= 2 + 2(3) + 2(9) + 2(27) + 2(81) + 2(243) \\
&= 2 + 2(3) + 2(3)^2 + 2(3)^3 + 2(3)^4 + 2(3)^5 = 728
\end{aligned}
$$

Letting $a = 2$ and $r = 3$, this becomes

$$R = a + ar + ar^2 + ar^3 + ar^4 + ar^5$$

where $r^5 = r^{n-1}$.

From Equation (2.34) the solution to this expression is

$$
\begin{aligned}
R &= a\left(\frac{1 - r^n}{1 - r}\right) = 2\left(\frac{1 - 3^6}{1 - 3}\right) = 1\left(\frac{1 - 729}{1 - 3}\right) \\
&= 2\left(\frac{-728}{-2}\right) = 728
\end{aligned}
$$

Problem 2.3. Use Equation (2.33) to compute the sum of the geometric progression

$$R = 3 + \frac{3}{2} + \frac{3}{4} + \frac{3}{8} + \frac{3}{16} + \frac{3}{32} + \frac{3}{64} + \frac{3}{128}$$

Solution. The sum of this geometric progression may be written as

$$R = 3 + \left(\frac{3}{2}\right) + \left(\frac{3}{4}\right) + \left(\frac{3}{8}\right) + \left(\frac{3}{16}\right) + \left(\frac{3}{32}\right) + \left(\frac{3}{64}\right) + \left(\frac{3}{128}\right)$$

$$= 3 + 3\left(\frac{1}{2}\right) + 3\left(\frac{1}{4}\right) + 3\left(\frac{1}{8}\right) + 3\left(\frac{1}{16}\right) + \left(\frac{3}{32}\right) + 3\left(\frac{1}{64}\right) + 3\left(\frac{1}{128}\right)$$

$$= 3 + 3\left(\frac{1}{2}\right) + 3\left(\frac{1}{2}\right)^2 + 3\left(\frac{1}{2}\right)^3 + 3\left(\frac{1}{2}\right)^4 + 3\left(\frac{1}{2}\right)^5 + 3\left(\frac{1}{2}\right)^6 + 3\left(\frac{1}{2}\right)^7$$

$$= 3 + 1.5 + 0.75 + 0.375 + 0.1875 + 0.0938 + 0.0469 + 0.0234 = 5.9766$$

Letting $a = 3$ and $r = \frac{1}{2}$, this becomes

$$R = a + ar + ar^2 + ar^3 + ar^4 + ar^5 + ar^6 + ar^7$$

where $r^7 = r^{n-1}$.

From Equation (2.34) the solution to this expression is

$$R = a\left(\frac{1-r^n}{1-r}\right) = 3\left(\frac{1-(1/2)^8}{1-(1/2)}\right)$$

$$= 3\left(\frac{1-(1/256)}{1-(0.5)}\right) = 3\left(\frac{1-0.0039}{1-0.5}\right)$$

$$= 2\left(\frac{0.9961}{0.5}\right) = 3(1.9922) = 5.9766$$

SUM OF AN INFINITE GEOMETRIC PROGRESSION

There are a number of situations in economics and business when it is useful to be able to calculate the sum of a geometric progress. Deriving spending multipliers of the Keynesian model macroeconomic theory or calculating the future value of an ordinary annuity, which is discussed in Chapter 12, are just two of the many applications of the sum of a geometric progression. To see what is involved, consider the sum of the infinite geometric progression

$$R = a + ar + ar^2 + ar^3 + \ldots = a(1 + r + r^2 + r^3 + \ldots) = a \sum_{k=0 \to \infty} r^k \qquad (2.35)$$

Clearly, when $r > 1$, $R = \infty$. A special case of Equation (2.35) occurs when $0 < r < 1$. To see this, let

$$S = 1 + r + r^2 + r^3 + \ldots = \sum_{k=0 \to \infty} r^k \tag{2.36}$$

Again, Equation (2.36) may be rewritten as

$$R = aS \tag{2.29}$$

After multiplying both sides of Equation (2.36) by r we get

$$rS = r + r^2 + r^3 + \ldots = \sum_{k=0 \to \infty} r^k \tag{2.37}$$

Subtracting Equation (2.37) from Equation (2.36) yields

$$\begin{aligned} S - rS &= \sum_{k=0 \to \infty} r^k - \sum_{k=1 \to \infty} r^k \\ &= (1 + r + r^2 + r^3 + \ldots) - (r + r^2 + r^3 + r^4 + \ldots) \\ &= 1 + r + r^2 + r^3 - \ldots - r - r^2 - r^3 - r^4 - \ldots = 1 \end{aligned} \tag{2.38}$$

Equation (2.38) may be rewritten as

$$S(1 - r) = 1 \tag{2.39}$$

Rearranging Equation (2.39) yields

$$S = \frac{1}{1 - r} \tag{2.40}$$

Substituting Equation (2.40) into Equation (2.29) yields

$$R = a\left(\frac{1}{1 - r}\right) \tag{2.41}$$

Problem 2.4. Use Equation (2.41) to compute the sum of the geometric progression

$$R = 3 + \left(\frac{3}{2}\right) + \left(\frac{3}{4}\right) + \left(\frac{3}{8}\right) + \left(\frac{3}{16}\right) + \left(\frac{3}{32}\right) + \left(\frac{3}{64}\right) + \left(\frac{3}{128}\right) + \ldots$$

Solution. The sum of this geometric progression may be written

$$\begin{aligned} R &= 3 + \left(\frac{3}{2}\right) + \left(\frac{3}{4}\right) + \left(\frac{3}{8}\right) + \left(\frac{3}{16}\right) + \left(\frac{3}{32}\right) + \left(\frac{3}{64}\right) + \left(\frac{3}{128}\right) + \ldots \\ &= 3 + 3\left(\frac{1}{2}\right) + 3\left(\frac{1}{4}\right) + 3\left(\frac{1}{8}\right) + 3\left(\frac{1}{16}\right) + 3\left(\frac{1}{32}\right) + 3\left(\frac{1}{64}\right) + 3\left(\frac{1}{128}\right) + \ldots \\ &= 3 + 3\left(\frac{1}{2}\right) + 3\left(\frac{1}{2}\right)^2 + 3\left(\frac{1}{2}\right)^3 + 3\left(\frac{1}{2}\right)^4 + 3\left(\frac{1}{2}\right)^5 + 3\left(\frac{1}{2}\right)^6 + 3\left(\frac{1}{2}\right)^7 + \ldots \\ &= 3 + 1.5 + 0.75 + 0.375 + 0.1875 + 0.0938 + 0.0469 + 0.0234 + \ldots \end{aligned}$$

Letting $a = 3$ and $r = \frac{1}{2}$, this becomes

$$R = a + ar + ar^2 + ar^3 + ar^4 + ar^5 + ar^6 + ar^7 + \ldots$$

From Equation (2.41) the solution to this expression is

$$R = a\left(\frac{1}{1-r}\right) = 3\left(\frac{1}{1-(1/2)}\right) = 3\left(\frac{1}{0.5}\right) = 3(2) = 6$$

ECONOMIC OPTIMIZATION

Many problems in economics involve the determination of "optimal" solutions. For example, a decision maker might wish to determine the level of output that would result in maximum profit. The process of economic optimization essentially involve three steps:

1. Defining the goals and objectives of the firm
2. Identifying the firm's constraints
3. Analyzing and evaluating all possible alternatives available to the decision maker

In essence, economic optimization involves maximizing or minimizing some objective function, which may or may not be subject to one or more constraints. Before discussing the process of economic optimization, let us review the various methods of expressing economic and business relationships.

OPTIMIZATION ANALYSIS

The process of economic optimization may be illustrated by considering the firm's profit function π, which is defined as

$$\pi = TR - TC \tag{2.42}$$

where TR represents total revenue and TC represents total economic cost. Substituting Equations (2.4) and (2.26) into Equation (2.42) we get

$$\pi = (18Q) - (6 + 33Q - 9Q^2 + Q^3) = -6 - 15Q + 9Q^2 - Q^3 \tag{2.43}$$

Consider Table 2.3, which combines the data presented in Tables 2.1 and 2.2.

The profit values in Table 2.3 are plotted in Figure 2.11 to yield the total profit curve.

It is evident from Table 2.3 and Figure 2.11 that π reaches a maximum value of $19 at an output level of $Q = 5$. Note also that π attains a minimum (maximum loss) of $-$13$ at an output level of $Q = 1$. While these extreme values can be read directly from Table 2.3 and Figure 2.11, they also may be determined directly from the underlying π function. For a clue to how this might be determined, note that if a smooth curve had been fitted to the data plotted in Figure 2.11, the slope (steepness) of the π curve at both the minimum and maximum output levels would be zero; that is, the curve

TABLE 2.3 Total profit for output levels $Q = 0$ to $Q = 6$.

Q	TR	TC	π
0	0	6	−6
1	18	31	−13
2	36	44	−8
3	54	51	3
4	72	58	14
5	90	71	19
6	108	96	12

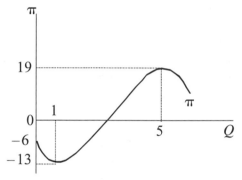

FIGURE 2.11 A cubic total profit function with two optimal solutions: a minimum and a maximum.

would be neither upward sloping nor downward sloping. The significance of this becomes evident when it is pointed out that the slope of any total function at all values of the independent variable is simply the corresponding marginal function. In the case of the total revenue equation, for example, the slope at any output level is defined as the "rise" over the "run," that is, change in total revenue divided by the change in output, $\Delta TR/\Delta Q$. But this is the definition of marginal revenue (MR). If it is possible to efficiently determine the slope of any total function for all values of the independent variables, then the search for extreme values of the dependent variable should be greatly facilitated.

Fortunately, differential calculus offers an easy way to find the marginal function by taking the first derivative of the total function. Taking the first derivative of a total function results in another equation that gives the value of the slope of the function for values of the independent variable. In the case of Equation (2.43), total profit will be maximized or minimized at an output level at which the slope of the profit function is zero. This is accomplished by finding the *first derivative* of the profit function, setting it equal to zero, and solving for the value of the corresponding output level. Before proceeding, however, let us review the rules for taking the first derivative of a function.

DERIVATIVE OF A FUNCTION

Consider, again, the function

$$y = f(x) \tag{2.1}$$

The slope of this function is defined as the change in the value of y divided by a change in the value of x, or the "rise" over the "run." When defining the slope between two discrete points, the formula for the slope may be given as

$$\text{Slope} = \frac{\Delta y}{\Delta x}$$

$$= \frac{y_2 - y_1}{x_2 - x_1} = \frac{f(x_2) - f(x_1)}{x_2 - x_1} \tag{2.6}$$

Consider Figure 2.12, and use the foregoing definition to calculate the value of the slope of the cord AB. As point B is brought arbitrarily closer to point A, however, the value of the slope of AB approaches the value of the slope at the single point A, which would be equivalent to the slope of a tangent to the curve at that point. This procedure is greatly simplified, however, by first taking the derivative of the function and calculating its value, in this case, at x_1.

The first derivative of a function (dy/dx) is simply the slope of the function when the interval along the horizontal axis (between x_1 and x_2) is made infinitesimally small. Technically, the derivative is the *limit* of the ratio $\Delta y / \Delta x$ as Δx approaches zero, that is,

$$\frac{dy}{dx} = \lim_{\Delta x \to 0} \left(\frac{\Delta y}{\Delta x} \right) \tag{2.44}$$

When the limit of a function as $x \to x_0$ equals the value of the function at x_0, the function is said to be *continuous* at x_0, that is, $lim_{x \to x_0} f(x) = f(x_0)$.

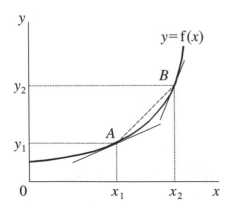

FIGURE 2.12 Discrete versus instantaneous rates of change.

Calculus offers a set of rules for using derivatives (slopes) for making optimizing decisions such as minimizing cost (*TC*) or maximizing total profit (π).

RULES OF DIFFERENTIATION

Having established that the derivative of a function is the limit of the ratio of the change in the dependent variable to the change in the independent variable, we will now enumerate some general rules of differentiation that will be of considerable value throughout the remainder of this course. It should be underscored that for a function to be differentiable at a point, it must be *well defined*; that is it must be continuous or "smooth." It is not possible to find the derivative of a function that is discontinuous (i.e., has a "corner") at that point. The interested student is referred to the selected adings at the end of this chapter for the proofs of these propositions.

POWER-FUNCTION RULE

A power function is of the form

$$y = f(x) = ax^b$$

where *a* and *b* are real numbers. The rule for finding the derivative of a power function is

$$\frac{dy}{dx} = f'(x) = bax^{b-1} \tag{2.45}$$

where $f'(x)$ is an alternative way to denote the first derivative.

Example

$$y = 4x^2$$

$$\frac{dy}{dx} = f'(x) = 2(4)x^{2-1} = 8x$$

A special case of the power-function rule is the identity rule:

$$y = f(x) = x$$

$$\frac{dy}{dx} = f'(x) = 1(1)x^{1-1} = 1x^0 = 1$$

Another special case of the power-function rule is the *constant-function rule*. Since $x^0 = 1$, then

$$y = f(x) = ax^0 = a$$

Thus,

$$\frac{dy}{dx} = f'(x) = 0(ax^{0-1}) = 0$$

Example

$$y = 5 = 1 \cdot 5^0$$

$$\frac{dy}{dx} = f'(x) = 0(1 \cdot 5^{0-1}) = 0$$

SUMS AND DIFFERENCES RULE

There are a number of economic and business relationships that are derived by combining one or more separate, but related, functions. A firm's profit function, for example, is equal to the firm's total revenue function minus the firm's total cost function. If we define g and h to be functions of the variable x, then

$$u = g(x); v = h(x)$$

$$y = f(x) = u \pm v = g(x) \pm h(x)$$

$$\frac{dy}{dx} = f'(x) = \frac{du}{dx} \pm \frac{dv}{dx} \qquad (2.46)$$

Example

$$u = g(x) = 2x; v = h(x) = x^2$$

$$y = f(x) = g(x) + h(x) = 2x + x^2$$

$$\frac{dy}{dx} = f'(x) = 2 + 2x$$

Example
a. Consider the general case of the linear function

$$y = f(x) = g(x) + h(x) = a + bx$$

$$\frac{dy}{dx} = f'(x) = \frac{du}{dx} + \frac{dv}{dx} = 0 + b = b \qquad (2.5)$$

b. $y = f(x) = 5 - 4$

$$\frac{dy}{dx} = f'(x) = -4$$

c. From Problem 2.1

$$Q_D = 25 - 3P$$

$$Q_S = 10 + 2P$$

$$\frac{dQ_D}{dP} = -3$$

$$\frac{dQ_S}{dP} = 2$$

Example

$$y = 0.04x^3 - 0.9x^2 + 10x + 5$$

$$\frac{dy}{dx} = f'(x) = 0.12x^2 - 1.8x + 10$$

PRODUCT RULE

Similarly, there are many relationships in business and economics that are defined as the product of two or more separate, but related, functions. The total revenue function of a monopolist, for example, is the product of price, which is a function of output, and output, which is a function of itself. Again, if we define g and h to be functions of the variable x, then

$$u = g(x); v = h(x)$$

Further, let

$$y = f(x) = uv = g(x) \cdot h(x)$$

Although intuition would suggest that the derivative of a product is the product of the derivatives, this is not the case. The derivative of a product is defined as

$$\frac{dy}{dx} = f'(x) = u\left(\frac{dv}{dx}\right) + v\left(\frac{du}{dx}\right) = uh'(x) + vg'(x) \qquad (2.47)$$

Example

$$y = 2x^2(3 - 2x)$$

$$u = g(x) = 2x^2$$

$$\frac{du}{dx} = g'(x) = 4x$$

$$v = (3 - 2x)$$

$$\frac{dv}{dx} = h'(x) = -2$$

Substituting into Equation (2.47)

$$\frac{dy}{dx} = f'(x) = 2x^2(-2) + (3 - 2x)(4x) = -12x^2 + 12x$$

QUOTIENT RULE

Even less intuitive than the product rule is the quotient rule. Again, defining g and h as functions of x, we write

$$u = g(x); v = h(x)$$

Further, let

$$y = f(x) = \frac{u}{v} = \frac{g(x)}{h(x)}$$

then

$$\frac{dy}{dx} = f'(x) = \frac{v(du/dx) - u(dv/dx)}{v^2}$$
$$= \frac{h(x)[dg(x)/dx] - g(x)[dh(x)/dx]}{h(x)^2} \qquad (2.48)$$
$$= \frac{h(x) \cdot g'(x) - g(x) \cdot h'(x)}{h(x)^2}$$

Example

$$y = f(x) = (3 - 2x)/2x^2$$
$$u = g(x) = 3 - 2x$$
$$\frac{du}{dx} = g'(x) = -2$$
$$v = h(x) = 2x^2$$
$$\frac{dv}{dx} = h'(x) = 4x$$

Substituting into Equation (2.48), we have

$$\frac{dy}{dx} = f'(x) = \frac{2x^2(-2) - (3-2x)4x}{(2x^2)^2} = \frac{4x^2 - 12x}{4x^4} = \frac{x-3}{x^3}$$

Interestingly, in some instances it is convenient, and easier, to apply the product rule to such problems. This becomes apparent when we remember that

$$y = \frac{u}{v} = uv^{-1}$$

Example

$$y = f(x) = \frac{g(x)}{h(x)} = \frac{2x^2}{3x} = 2x^2(3x)^{-1} = 2x^2[(1/3)x^{-1}]$$

$$\frac{dy}{dx} = f'(x) = 2x^2[(-1/3)x^{-2}] + (1/3)x^{-1}(4x) = -2/3 + 4/3 = 2/3$$

It is left to the student to demonstrate that the same result is derived by applying the quotient rule.

CHAIN RULE

Often in business and economics a variable that is a dependent variable in one function is an independent variable in another function. Output Q, for example, is the dependent variable in a perfectly competitive firm's short-run production function

$$Q = f(L, K_0) = 4L^{0.5}$$

where L represents the variable labor, and K_0 represents a constant amount of capital labor utilizes in the short run. On the other hand, output is the independent variable in the firm's total revenue function

$$TR = g(Q) = PQ = 10Q$$

where P is the (constant) selling price.

In the example just given, we might be interested in determining how total revenue can be expected to change given a change in the firm's labor usage. For this we require a technique for taking the derivative of one function whose independent variable is the dependent variable of another function. Here we might be interested in finding the derivative dTR/dL. To find this derivative value, we avail ourselves of the chain rule. Let $y = f(u)$ and $u = g(x)$. Substituting, we are able to write the composite function

$$y = f[g(x)]$$

The chain rule asserts that

$$\frac{dy}{dx} = \left(\frac{dy}{du}\right)\left(\frac{du}{dx}\right)$$
$$= \left[\frac{df(u)}{du}\right]\left[\frac{dg(x)}{dx}\right] \qquad (2.49)$$
$$= f'(u) \cdot g'(x)$$

Applying the chain rule, we get

$$\frac{dTR}{dL} = \left(\frac{dTR}{dQ}\right)\left(\frac{dQ}{dL}\right) = 10(2L^{-0.5}) = 20L^{-0.5} = 20/\sqrt{L}$$

Example

$$y = (2x^2)^3 + 10$$
$$y = f(u) = u^3 + 10$$

$$\frac{dy}{du} = f'(u) = 3u^2 = 3(2x^2)^2 = 12x^4$$

$$u = g(x) = 2x^2$$

$$\frac{du}{dx} = g'(x) = 4x$$

$$\frac{dy}{dx} = f'(x) = (3u^2)4x = 3(2x^2)^2 \cdot 2(4x) = 12x^4 \cdot 4x = 48x^5$$

EXPONENTIAL AND LOGARITHMIC FUNCTIONS

Now we consider the derivative of two important functions–the exponential function and the logarithmic function. The number e is the base of the natural exponential function, $y = e^x$. The natural logarithmic function is $y = \log_e x = \ln x$. The number e is itself generated as the limit to the series

$$e = \lim_{h \to \infty}\left(1 + \frac{1}{h}\right)^h = 2.71829\ldots \tag{2.50}$$

To illustrate the practical importance of the number e, suppose, for example, that you were to invest \$1 in a savings account that paid an interest rate of i percent. If interest was compounded continuously (see Chapter 12), the value of the deposit at the year end would be

$$\lim_{h \to \infty}\left(1 + \frac{i}{h}\right)^h = e^i \tag{2.51}$$

Now, suppose that a deposit of D dollars was compounded continuously for n years. At the end of n years the deposit would be worth

$$\lim_{h \to \infty}\left[D\left(1 + \frac{1}{h}\right)^h\right]^{in} = \left[D \lim_{h \to \infty}\left(1 + \frac{1}{h}\right)^n\right]^t = De^{in}$$

The derivative of the exponential function $y = e^x$ is

$$\frac{dy}{dx} = \frac{d(e^x)}{dx} = e^x \tag{2.52}$$

That is, the derivative of the exponential function is the exponential function itself.

The derivative of the natural logarithm of a variable with respect to that variable, on the other hand, is the reciprocal of that variable. That is, if

$$y = \log_e x$$

then

$$\frac{dy}{dx} = \frac{d(\log_e x)}{dx} = \frac{1}{x} \tag{2.53}$$

When more complicated functions are involved, we can apply the chain rule. Suppose, for example, that $y = \ln x^2$. Letting $u = x^2$ this becomes $y = \ln u$. The derivative of y with respect to x then becomes

$$\frac{dy}{dx} = \left(\frac{dy}{du}\right)\left(\frac{du}{dx}\right) = (1/u)(2x) = \left(\frac{1}{x^2}\right)(2x) = \frac{2}{x}$$

It may also be demonstrated that the result for the derivative of an exponential function follows directly from a special relationship that exists between the exponential function and the logarithmic function. Given the function $x = e^y$, then $y = \ln x$. Moreover, if $x = \ln y$, then $y = e^x$. These functions are said to be reciprocal functions. When two functions are related in this way, the derivatives are also related; that is, $dy/dx = 1/(dx/dy)$. Using this rule, we can prove the exponential function rule:

$$\frac{d(e^x)}{dx} = \frac{dy}{dx} = \frac{1}{d(\ln y)/dy} = \frac{1}{1/y} = y = e^x$$

Returning to the earlier discussion of continuous compounding, suppose that the value of an asset is given by

$$D(t) = De^{rt}$$

where r is the rate of interest, t time, and D the initial value of the asset. The rate of change of the value of the asset over time is

$$\frac{d(De^{rt})}{dt} = D\left(\frac{de^{rt}}{dt}\right) + e^{rt}\left(\frac{dD}{dt}\right)$$

$$= D\left(\frac{de^u}{du}\right)\left(\frac{du}{dt}\right) + e^{rt}\left(\frac{dD}{dt}\right)$$

$$= De^u r + e^{rt}(0) = rDe^{rt}$$

That is, the rate of change in the value of the asset is the rate of interest times the value of the asset at time t.

INVERSE-FUNCTION RULE

Earlier in this chapter we discussed the existence of inverse functions. It will be recalled that if the function $y = f(x)$ is a one-to-one correspondence, then not only will a given value of x correspond to a unique value of y, but a given value of y will correspond to a unique value of x. In this case, the function f has the inverse function $g(y) = f^{-1}(y) = x$, which is also a one-to-one correspondence. Given an inverse function, its derivative is

$$g'(y) = \frac{dx}{dy} = \frac{1}{dy/dx} = \frac{1}{f'(x)} \tag{2.54}$$

Equation (2.54) asserts that the derivative of an inverse function is the reciprocal of the derivative of the original function.

It will also be recalled that functions with a one-to-one correspondence are said to be *monotonically increasing* if $x_2 > x_1 \Rightarrow f(x_2) > f(x_1)$. Functions in which a one-to-one correspondence exist are said to be *monotonically decreasing* if $x_2 > x_1 \Rightarrow f(x_2) < f(x_1)$. In general, for an inverse function to exist, the original function must be monotonic. In other words, it is not possible to write $x = g(y) = f^{-1}(y)$ until we have determined whether the function $y = f(x)$ is monotonic.

It is possible to determine whether a function is monotonic by examining its first derivative. If the first derivative of the function is positive for all values of x, then the function $y = f(x)$ is monotonically increasing. If the first derivative of the function is negative for all values of x, then the function $y = f(x)$ is monotonically decreasing.

Problem 2.5. Consider the function

$$y = f(x) = 4x + 0.2x^5 + x^7$$

a. Is this function monotonic?
b. If the function is monotonic, use the inverse-function rule to find dx/dy.

Solution
a. The derivative of this function is

$$\frac{dy}{dx} = f'(x) = 4 + x^4 + 7x^6$$

which is positive for all values of x. Thus, the function $f(x)$ is a monotonically increasing function.
b. Because $f(x)$ is a monotonically increasing function, the inverse function $g(y) = f^{-1}(y)$ exists. Thus, it is possible to use the inverse-function rule to determine the derivative of the inverse function, that is,

$$\frac{dx}{dy} = \frac{1}{dy/dx} = \frac{1}{4 + x^4 + 7x^6}$$

It should be noted that the inverse-function rule may also be applied to nonmonotonic functions, provided the domain of the function is restricted. For example, $y = f(x) = x^2$ is nonmonotonic because its derivative does not have the same sign for all values of x. On the other hand, if the domain of this function is restricted to positive values for x, then $dy/dx > 0$.

Problem 2.6. Consider the function

$$y = f(x) = -3x - x^4$$

a. Is this function monotonic?
b. If the function is monotonic, use the inverse-function rule to find dx/dy.

Solution
a. The derivative of this function is

$$\frac{dy}{dx} = f'(x) = -3 - 4x^3 = -(3 + 4x^3)$$

This function is not monotonic, since the sign of dy/dx depends on whether x is positive or negative. On the other hand, the derivative is negative for all positive values for x.
b. Because the derivative of $f(x)$ is positive for all $x > 0$, then it is possible to use the inverse-function rule to determine the derivative of the inverse function, that is,

$$g'(y) = \frac{dx}{dy} = \frac{1}{dy/dx} = 1/f'(y) = \frac{1}{-(3 + 4x^3)}$$

for all $x > 0$.

IMPLICIT DIFFERENTIATION

The functions we have been discussing are referred to as explicit functions. Explicit functions are those in which the dependent variable is on the left-hand side of the equation and the independent variables are on the right-hand side. In many cases in business and economics, however, we may also be interested in what are called implicit functions.

Implicit functions are those in which the dependent variable is also functionally related to one or more of the right-hand-side variables. Such functions often arise in economics as a result of some equilibrium condition that is imposed on a model. A common example of an implicit function in macroeconomic theory is in the definition of the equilibrium level of national income Y, which is given as the sum of consumption spending C, which is itself assumed to be a function of national income, net investment spending I, government expenditures G, and net exports $X - M$. This equilibrium condition is written

$$Y = C + I + G + (X - M) \tag{2.55}$$

Clearly, any change in the value of Y must come about because of changes in any and all changes in the components of aggregate demand. The total derivative of this relationship may be written

$$dY = dC + dI + dG + d(X - M) \qquad (2.56)$$

Equation (2.56) is a differential equation. We may express the relationship between consumption expenditures and national income as $C = C(Y)$. Suppose that the consumption function is well defined and the derivative $dC/dY = C'(Y)$ exists, which may be rewritten as

$$dC = C'(Y)dY = \left(\frac{dC}{dY}\right)dY \qquad (2.57)$$

Equation (2.57) may be rewritten as

$$dY = \left(\frac{dC}{dY}\right)dY + dI + dG + d(X - M) \qquad (2.58)$$

Suppose that we were specifically interested in the derivative dY/dI. It is possible to find the derivative dY/dI by implicit differentiation. Assuming that a change in I has no effect on G and none on $X - M$; that is, $dG = d(X - M) = 0$, but does change Y. Equation (2.59) reduces to

$$dY = \left(\frac{dC}{dY}\right)dY + dI \qquad (2.59)$$

Collecting the dY terms on the left-hand side and dividing, we obtain

$$dY - \left(\frac{dC}{dY}\right)dY = dI$$

$$\left(1 - \frac{dC}{dY}\right)dY = dI \qquad (2.60)$$

$$\frac{dY}{dI} = \frac{1}{1 - dC/dY}$$

This well-known result in macroeconomic theory is the simplified investment multiplier.

To implicitly differentiate a function, we treat changes in the two variables, dY and dI, as unknowns and solve for the ratio of the change in the dependent variable to the change in the independent variable, which is the derivative in explicit form.

TOTAL, AVERAGE, AND MARGINAL RELATIONSHIPS

Now that we have discussed the concept of the derivative, we are in a position to discuss an important class of functional relationships. There are several "total" concepts in business and economics that are of interest to the managerial decision maker: total profit, total cost, total revenue, and so on. Related to each of these total concepts are the analytically important average and marginal concepts, such as average (per-unit) profit and marginal profit; average total cost and marginal cost, average variable cost and marginal cost, and average total revenue and marginal revenue. An understanding of the nature of the relation between total, average, and marginal relationships is essential in optimization analysis.

To make the discussion more concrete, consider the total cost function $TC = f(Q)$, where Q represents the output of a firm's good or service and $dTC/dQ > 0$. As we will see in Chapter 6, related to this are two other important functional relationships. Average total, or per-unit, cost of production (ATC) is defined as $ATC = TC/Q$. Marginal cost of production (MC), which is given by the relationship $MC = dTC/dQ$, measures the incremental change in total cost arising from an incremental change in total output. Clearly, ATC and MC are not the same. Nevertheless, these two cost concepts are systematically related. Indeed, the nature of this relationship is fundamentally the same for all average and marginal relationships. Before presenting a formal statement of the nature of this relationship, consider the following noneconomic example.

Suppose you are enrolled in an economics course, and your final grade is based on the average of 10 quizzes that you are required to take during the semester. Assume that the highest grade you can earn on any individual quiz is 100 points. Thus, if you earn the maximum number of points during the semester, your average quiz grade will be $1,000/10 = 100$. Now, suppose that you have taken 6 quizzes and have earned a total of 480 points. Clearly, your average quiz grade is $480/6 = 80$. How will your average be affected by the grade you receive on the seventh quiz? Since the number of points you earn on the seventh quiz will increase the total number of points earned, we will call the number of additional points earned your marginal grade. How will this marginal grade affect your average? Clearly, if the grade that you receive on the seventh quiz is greater than your average for the first six quizzes, your average will rise. For example, if you receive a grade of 90, your average will increase from 80 to $570/7 = 81.4$. On the other hand, if the grade you receive is less than the average, the average will fall. For example, if you receive a grade of 70, your average will decline to $550/7 = 78.6$. Finally, if the grade you receive on the next quiz is the same as your average, the average will remain unchanged (i.e., $560/7 = 80$).

In general, it can be easily demonstrated that when any marginal value M is greater than its corresponding average A value (i.e., $M > A$), then A will rise. Analogously, when $M < A$, then A will fall. Finally, when $M = A$, then A will neither rise nor fall. In many economic models, when $M = A$ the value of A will be at a local maximum or local minimum. These relationships will be formalized in the following paragraphs.

Consider again the functional relationship in Equation (2.1).

$$y = f(x) \qquad (2.1)$$

Define the average and marginal functions of Equation (2.1) as

$$A = \frac{y}{x} = \frac{f(x)}{x} \qquad (2.61)$$

$$M = \frac{dy}{dx} = f'(x) \qquad (2.62)$$

Fundamentally, we are asking how a marginal change in the value of y with respect to a change in x will affect the average value of y. To understand what is going on, we begin by taking the first derivative of Equation (2.61). Using the quotient rule, we obtain

$$\frac{dA}{dx} = \frac{xf'(x) - f(x)}{x^2} \qquad (2.63)$$

Since the value of the denominator in Equation (2.63) is positive, the sign of dA/dx will depend on the sign of the expression $xf'(x) - f(x)$. That is, for the average to be increasing ($dA/dx > 0$), then $[xf'(x) - f(x)] > 0$. This, of course, implies that $f'(x) > f(x)/x$, or $M > A$. For the average to fall ($dA/dx < 0$), then $[xf'(x) - f(x)] < 0$, or $f'(x) < f(x)/x$. That is, the marginal must be less than the average ($M < A$). Finally, for no change in the average ($dA/dx = 0$), then $[xf'(x) - f(x)] = 0$, or $f'(x) = f(x)/x$. That is, for no change in the average, the marginal is equal to the average. For the functional relationship in Equation (2.1), these relationships are summarized as follows:

$$\frac{dA}{dx} > 0 \Rightarrow f'(x) > \frac{f(x)}{x}, \text{ or } M > A \qquad (2.64a)$$

$$\frac{dA}{dx} < 0 \Rightarrow f'(x) > \frac{f(x)}{x}, \text{ or } M < A \qquad (2.64b)$$

$$\frac{dA}{dx} = 0 \Rightarrow f'(x) = \frac{f(x)}{x}, \text{ or } M = A \qquad (2.64c)$$

Let us return to the example of the total cost function $TC = f(Q)$ introduced earlier. Consider the hypothetical total cost function in Figure 2.13, and the corresponding average total cost and marginal cost curves in Figure 2.14.

In Figure 2.13, the numerical value of ATC is the same as a slope of a ray from the origin to a point on the TC curve corresponding to a given level of output. The equation of a ray from the origin is $TC = bQ$, where b is the slope of the ray from the origin to a point on the TC curve, which is given as

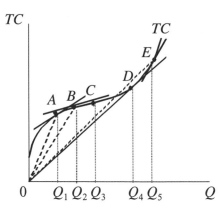

FIGURE 2.13 The total cost curve
and its relationship to marginal and average
total cost.

$$b = \frac{\Delta TC}{\Delta Q} = \frac{TC_2 - TC_1}{Q_2 - Q_1} \tag{2.65}$$

where the values where Q_1 represents the initial value of output and Q_2 represents the changed level of output. Since the ray passes through the origin, then the initial values (Q_1, TC_1) are $(0,0)$. Setting $TC_2 = TC$ and $Q_2 = Q$, Equation (2.66) reduces to

$$b = ATC = \frac{TC}{Q} \tag{2.66}$$

Of course, the value of b will change as we move along the total cost curve. This is illustrated in Figure 2.13. MC, of course, is the value of the slope of the TC curve and may be illustrated diagrammatically in Figure 2.13 as the slope a line that is tangent to TC at some level of output. By comparing the value of the slope of the tangent with the slope of the ray from the origin, we are able to illustrate the relationship between MC and ATC in Figure 2.14.

Note that output at point A in Figure 2.13, the slope of the tangent (MC), is less than the slope of the ray from the origin (ATC). Thus, at output level Q_1, MC is less than ATC. This is illustrated in Figure 2.14. Now let us move to point B. Note that at Q_2 the slopes of the tangent and the ray are less than they were at point A. Thus, in Figure 2.14 MC and ATC at Q_2 are less than at Q_1. Although both MC and ATC have fallen, the slope of the tangent (MC) at Q_2 is still less than the slope of the ray (ATC). Thus, since $MC < ATC$ at Q_2, then ATC has declined. By analogous reasoning, as we move from Q_2 to Q_3, since $MC < ATC$, then ATC will fall. The reader will note that point C in the Figure 2.13 is an inflection point. Beyond output level Q_3, the slope of the TC curve (MC) begins to increase. Thus, at output level Q_3, marginal cost is minimized. Nevertheless, as illustrated in Figure 2.14, as long as $MC < ATC$, then ATC will continue to fall.

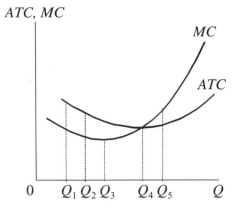

ATC, MC

FIGURE 2.14 The relationship between average total cost and marginal cost.

At output level Q_4 the slopes of the ray and tangent are identical ($ATC = MC$). Thus, at Q_4 ATC is neither rising nor falling (i.e., $dATC/dQ = 0$). After Q_4 the slope of the tangent not only becomes greater than the slope of the ray, but the slope of the ray changes direction and starts to increase. Thus, we see that at output level Q_5, $MC > ATC$ and ATC are rising. These relationships are illustrated in Figure 2.14.

The situation depicted in Figure 2.14 illustrates a U-shaped average total cost curve in which the MC intersects ATC from below. The reader should visually verify that when $MC < ATC$, even when MC is rising, ATC is falling. Moreover, when $MC > ATC$, then ATC is rising. Finally, when $MC = ATC$, then ATC is neither rising nor falling (i.e., ATC is minimized). In some cases, the average curve is shaped not like U but like a hill: that is, the marginal curve intersects the average curve from above at its maximum point. An example of this would be the relationship between the average and marginal physical products of labor, which will be discussed in detail in Chapter 5.

PROFIT MAXIMIZATION: THE FIRST-ORDER CONDITION

We are now in a position to use the rules for taking first derivatives to find the level of output Q that maximizes π, as illustrated in Table 2.3. Consider again the total revenue and total cost functions introduced earlier:

$$TR(Q) = PQ; P = \$18$$
$$TC(Q) = 6 + 33Q - 9Q^2 + Q^3$$
$$\pi = TR - TC = 18Q - (6 + 33Q - 9Q^2 + Q^3)$$
$$\pi = -6 - 15Q + 9Q^2 - Q^3$$

(2.67)

It should be noted in Table 2.3 and Figure 2.11 that profit is maximized ($\pi = 19$) at $Q = 5$. What is more, it should be immediately apparent that if a smooth curve is fitted to Figure 2.11, the value of the slope at $Q = 5$ is zero: that is, the profit function is neither upward sloping nor downward sloping. Alternatively, at $Q = 5$, then $d\pi/dQ = 0$. These observations imply that the value of a function will be optimized (maximized or minimized) where the slope of the function is equal to zero. In the present context, the first-order condition for profit maximization is $d\pi/dQ = 0$, thus

$$\frac{d\pi}{dQ} = -3Q^2 + 18Q - 15 = 0 \tag{2.68}$$

This equation is of the general form:

$$ax^2 + bx + c = 0 \tag{2.69}$$

where $a = -8$, $b = 10$ and $c = -15$. Quadratic equations generally admit to two solutions, which may be determined using the quadratic formula. The quadratic formula is given by the expression:

$$x_{1,2} = \frac{-b \pm \sqrt{b^2 - 4ac}}{2a} \tag{2.70}$$

After substituting the values of Equation (2.68) into Equation (2.70) we get

$$Q_1 = \frac{-18 + \sqrt{(18^2) - 4(-3)(-15)}}{2(-3)}$$

$$= \frac{-18 + \sqrt{324 - 180}}{-4} = \frac{-18 - 12}{-6} = \frac{-30}{-6} = 5$$

$$Q_2 = \frac{-18 + 12}{-6} = \frac{-6}{-6} = 1$$

Referring again to Figure 2.11, we see that the value of π reaches a minimum and a maximum at output levels of $Q = 1$ and $Q = 5$, respectively. Substituting these values back into the Equation (2.67) yields values of $\pi = -13$ (at $Q = 1$) and $\pi = 19$ (at $Q = 5$). In this example, therefore, the entrepreneur of the firm would maximize his profits at $Q = 5$. As this example illustrates, simply setting the first derivative of the function equal to zero is not sufficient to ensure that we will achieve a maximum, since a zero slope is also required for a minimum value as well. Thus, we need to specify the second-order conditions for a maximum or a minimum value to be achieved.

PROFIT MAXIMIZATION: THE SECOND-ORDER CONDITION

MAXIMA AND MINIMA

For functions of one independent variable, $y = f(x)$, a second-order condition for $f(x)$ to have a maximum at some value $x = x_0$ is that together with $dy/dx = f'(x) = 0$, the second derivative (the derivative of the derivative) be negative, that is,

$$\frac{d(dy/dx)}{dx} = \frac{d^2 y}{dx^2} = f''(x) < 0 \tag{2.71}$$

where $f''(x)$ is an alternative way to denote the second derivative.

This condition expresses the notion that in the case of a maximum, the slope of the total function is first positive, zero, and then negative as we "walk" over the top of the "hill." Functions that are locally maximum are said to be "concave downward" in the neighborhood of the maximum value of the dependent variable. Similarly, the second-order condition for $f(x)$ to have a minimum at some value $x = x_0$, then is

$$\frac{d(dy/dx)}{dx} = d^2 y/dx^2 = f''(x) > 0 \tag{2.72}$$

The first-order and second-order conditions for a function with a maximum or minimum are summarized in Table 2.4.

Consider again the π maximization example, which is also illustrated in Figure 2.11. Taking the second derivative of the π function yields

$$\frac{d^2 \pi}{dQ^2} = -6Q + 18$$

At $Q_1 = 5$,

$$\frac{d^2 \pi}{dQ^2} = -6(5) + 18 = -30 + 18 = -12 < 0$$

which is, as we have already seen, a π maximum. At $Q_2 = 1$,

TABLE 2.4   First-order and second-order conditions for functions of one independent variable.

	Maximum	Minimum
First-order condition	$\dfrac{dy}{dx} = 0$	$\dfrac{dy}{dx} = 0$
Second-order condition	$\dfrac{d^2 y}{dx^2} < 0$	$\dfrac{d^2 y}{dx^2} > 0$

$$\frac{d^2\pi}{dQ^2} = -6(1) + 18 = -6 + 18 = 12 > 0$$

which is a π minimum.

Problem 2.7. A monopolist's total revenue and total cost functions are

$$TR(Q) = PQ = 20Q - 3Q^2$$

$$TC(Q) = 2Q^2$$

a. Determine the output level (Hint: $\pi(Q) = TR(Q) - TC(Q)$) that will maximize profit π.
b. Determine maximum π.
c. Determine the price per unit at which the π-maximizing output is sold.

Solution
a. $\pi = TR - TC$
$\quad = 20Q - 3Q^2 - 2Q^2 = 20Q - 5Q^2$
$\dfrac{d\pi}{dQ} = 20 - 10Q = 0$ (i.e., the first-order condition for a profit maximum).
$Q = 2$ units
$\dfrac{d^2\pi}{dQ^2} = -10 < 0$ (i.e., the second-order condition for a profit maximum).
b. $\pi = 20(2) - 5(2)^2 = 40 - 20 = \$20$
c. $TR = PQ = 20Q - 3Q^2 = (20 - 3Q)Q$
$\quad P = 20 - 3Q = 20 - 3(2) = 20 - 6 = \$14$

Problem 2.8. Another monopolist has the following TR and TC functions:

$$TR(Q) = 45Q - 0.5Q^2$$

$$TC(Q) = 2 + 57Q - 8Q^2 + Q^3$$

Find the π-maximizing output level.

Solution

$\pi = TR - TC$
$\quad = (45Q - 0.5Q^2) - (2 + 57Q - 8Q^2 + Q^3) = -2 - 12Q + 7.5Q^2 - Q^3$

$\dfrac{d\pi}{dQ} = -12 + 15Q - 3Q^2 = 0$ (i.e., the first-order condition for a local maximum)

Utilizing the quadratic formula:

$$Q_{1,2} = \frac{-15 \pm \sqrt{15^2 - 4(-3)(-12)}}{2(-3)}$$

$$= \frac{-15 \pm \sqrt{81}}{-6} = \frac{-15 \pm 9}{-6}$$

$$Q_1 = \frac{-15 - 9}{-6} = \frac{-24}{-6} = 4$$

$$Q_2 = \frac{-15 + 9}{-6} = \frac{-6}{-6} = 1$$

To determine whether these values constitute a minimum or a maximum, we can substitute the values into the profit function and determine the minimum and maximum values directly, or we can examine the values of the second derivatives:

$$\frac{d^2\pi}{dQ^2} = -6Q + 15$$

For $Q_1 = 4$,

$$\frac{d^2\pi}{dQ^2} = -6(4) + 15 = -24 + 15 = -9 < 0$$

(i.e., the second-order condition for a local maximum)

For $Q_2 = 1$,

$$\frac{d^2\pi}{dQ^2} = -6(1) + 15 = -6 + 15 = 9 > 0$$

(i.e., the second-order condition for a local minimum)

Substituting $Q_1 = 4$ into the π function yields a maximum profit of

$$\pi^* = -2 - 12(4) + 7.5(4)^2 - Q^3 = -2 - 48 + 120 - 64 = 6$$

INFLECTION POINTS

What if *both* the first and second derivatives are equal to zero? That is, what if $f'(x) = f''(x) = 0$? In this case, we have a stationary point, which is neither a maximum nor a minimum. That is, stationary values for which $f'(x) = 0$ need not be a relative extremum (maximum or minimum). Stationary values at x_0 that are neither relative maxima nor minima are illustrated in Figures 2.15 and 2.16.

To determine whether the stationary value at x_0 is the situation depicted in Figure 2.15 or Figure 2.16, it is necessary to examine the third derivative: $d(d^2y/dx^2)/dx = d^3y/dx^3 = f'''(x)$. The value of the third derivative for the

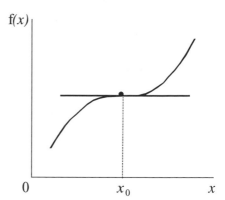

FIGURE 2.15 Inflection point: a stationary value at x_0 that is neither a maximum nor a minimum.

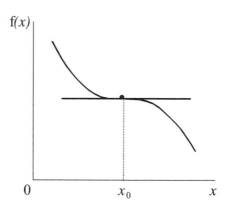

FIGURE 2.16 Inflection point: a stationary value at x_0 that is neither a maximum nor a minimum.

situation depicted in Figure 2.15 is $d^3y/dx^3 = f'''(x) > 0$. The value of the third derivative for the situation depicted in Figure 2.16 is $d^3y/dx^3 = f'''(x) < 0$.

PARTIAL DERIVATIVES AND MULTIVARIATE OPTIMIZATION: THE FIRST-ORDER CONDITION

Most economic relations involve more than one independent (explanatory) variable. For example, consider the following sales (Q) function of a firm that depends on the price of the product (P) and levels of advertising expenditures (A):

$$Q = f(P, A) \tag{2.73}$$

To determine the marginal effect of each independent variable, we take the first derivative of the function with respect to each variable separately, treating the remaining variables as constants. This process, known as taking partial derivatives, is denoted by replacing d with ∂.

Example

Consider the following explicit relationship:

$$Q = f(P, A) = 80P - 2P^2 - PA - 3A^2 + 100A \tag{2.74}$$

(where A is in thousands of dollars). Taking first partial derivatives with respect to P and A yields

$$\frac{\partial Q}{\partial P} = 80 - 4P - A \tag{2.75}$$

$$\frac{\partial Q}{\partial A} = -P - 6A + 100 \tag{2.76}$$

To determine the values of the independent variables that maximize the objective function, we simply set the first partial derivatives equal to zero and solve the resulting equations simultaneously.

Example

To determine the values of P and A that maximize the firm's total sales, Q, set the first partial derivatives in Equations (2.69) and (2.70) equal to zero.

$$80 - 4P - A = 0 \tag{2.77}$$

$$-P - 6A + 100 = 0 \tag{2.78}$$

Equations (2.77) and (2.78) are the first-order conditions for a maximum. Solving these two linear equations simultaneously in two unknowns yields (in thousands of dollars).

$$P = \$16.52$$

$$A = \$13.92$$

Substituting these results back into Equation (2.74) yields the optimal value of Q.

$$Q^* = 80(16.52) - 2(16.52)^2 - (16.52)(13.92) - 3(13.92)^2 + 100(13.92)$$
$$= \$1,356.52$$

PARTIAL DERIVATIVES AND MULTIVARIATE OPTIMIZATION: THE SECOND-ORDER CONDITION[8]

Unfortunately, a general discussion of the second-order conditions for multivariate optimization is beyond the scope of this book. It will be sufficient within the present context, however, to examine the second-order conditions for a maximum and a minimum in the case of two independent variables. Consider the following function:

---

[8] For a more complete discussion of the second-order conditions for the multivariate case, see Silberberg (1990), Chapter 4.

$$y = f(x_1, x_2) \qquad (2.79)$$

As discussed earlier, the first-order conditions for a maximum or a minimum are given by

$$\frac{\partial y}{\partial x_1} = f_1 = 0 \qquad (2.80a)$$

$$\frac{\partial y}{\partial x_2} = f_2 = 0 \qquad (2.80b)$$

The second-order conditions for a maximum are given by

$$\frac{\partial^2 y}{\partial x_1^2} = f_{11} < 0 \qquad (2.81a)$$

$$\frac{\partial^2 y}{\partial x_2^2} = f_{12} < 0 \qquad (2.81b)$$

$$\left(\frac{\partial^2 y}{\partial x_1^2} \right)\left(\frac{\partial^2 y}{\partial x_2^2} \right) - \left(\frac{\partial^2 y}{\partial x_1 \partial x_2} \right)^2 = f_{11}f_{22} - f_{12}^2 > 0 \qquad (2.81c)$$

The second-order conditions for a minimum are given by:

$$\frac{\partial^2 y}{\partial x_1^2} = f_{11} > 0 \qquad (2.82a)$$

$$\frac{\partial^2 y}{\partial x_2^2} = f_{22} > 0 \qquad (2.82b)$$

$$\left(\frac{\partial^2 y}{\partial x_1^2} \right)\left(\frac{\partial^2 y}{\partial x_2^2} \right) - \left(\frac{\partial^2 y}{\partial x_1 \partial x_2} \right)^2 = f_{11}f_{22} - f_{12}^2 > 0 \qquad (2.82c)$$

Example
Consider once again our sales maximization problem. The appropriate second-order conditions are given by:

$$f_{PP} = -4 < 0 \qquad (2.83a)$$

$$f_{AA} = -6 < 0 \qquad (2.83b)$$

$$f_{PP}f_{AA} - f_{PA}^2 = (-4)(-6) - (-1)^2 = 24 + 1 > 0 \qquad (2.83c)$$

The second-order conditions for sales maximization are satisfied.[9] The first- and second-order conditions for sales maximization are illustrated in Figure 2.17.

[9] By Young's theorem

$$f_{xy} = f_{yx}$$

That is, the same "cross partial" derivative results regardless of the order in which the variables are differentiated. For a more complete discussion of Young's theorem, see Silberberg (1990), Chapter 3. According to Silberberg, the reference is to W. H. Young who published a

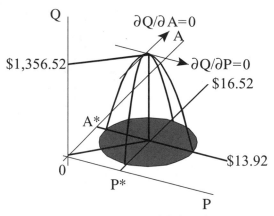

FIGURE 2.17 A global maximum.

CONSTRAINED OPTIMIZATION

Unfortunately, most decision problems managers faced are not of the unconstrained variety just discussed. The manager often is required to maximize some objective function subject to one or more side constraints. A production manager, for example, may be required to maximize the total output of a given commodity subject to a given budget constraint and fixed prices of factors of production. Alternatively, the manager might be required to minimize the total costs of producing some specified level of output. The cost minimization problem might be written as:

$$\text{Maximize (or minimize): } y = f(x_1, x_2) \tag{2.84a}$$

$$\text{Subject to: } k = g(x_1, x_2) \tag{2.84b}$$

Example

The total cost function of a firm that produces its product on two assembly lines is given as

$$TC(x, y) = 3x^2 + 6y^2 - xy$$

The problem facing the firm is to determine the least-cost combination of output on assembly lines x and y subject to the side condition that total output equal 20 units. This problem may be formally written as

$$\text{Minimize: } TC(x, y) = 3x^2 + 6y^2 - xy$$

$$\text{Subject to: } x + y = 20$$

formal proof of this theorem in 1909 using the concept of the limit (see, e.g., Cambridge Tract No. 11, *The Fundamental Theorems of the Differential Calculus*, Cambridge University Press, reprinted in 1971 by Hafner Press). According to Silberberg, the result was first published by Euler in 1734 ("De infinitis curvis eiusdem generis...," Commentatio 44 Indicis Enestroemiani).

SOLUTION METHODS TO CONSTRAINED OPTIMIZATION PROBLEMS

There are generally two methods of solving constrained optimization problems:

1. The substitution method
2. The Lagrange multiplier method

SUBSTITUTION METHOD

The substitution method involves first solving the constraint, say for x, and substituting the result into the original objective function. Consider, again, the foregoing example.

$$x = g(y) = 20 - y \qquad (2.85)$$

Substituting into the objective function yields

$$TC = f[g(y)] = F(y) = 30(20 - y)^2 + 6y^2 - (20 - y)y$$
$$= 3(400 - 40y + y^2) + 6y^2 - (20y - y^2) \qquad (2.86)$$

$$TC = 1200 - 140y + 10y^2 \qquad (2.87)$$

In other words, this problem reduces to one of solving for one decision variable, y, and inserting the solution into the objective function. Taking the first derivative of the objective function with respect to y and setting the result equal to zero, we get

$$\frac{dTC}{dy} = -140 + 20y = 0 \qquad (2.88)$$

$$20y = 140$$

$$y = 7$$

Note also that the second-order condition for total cost minimization is also satisfied:

$$\frac{d^2TC}{dy^2} = 20 > 0 \qquad (2.89)$$

Substituting $y = 7$ into the constraint yields

$$x + 7 = 20$$

$$x = 13$$

Finally, substituting the values of x and y into the original TC function yields:

$$TC = 3(13)^2 + 6(7)^2 - (13)(7) = 507 + 294 - 91 = 710$$

LAGRANGE MULTIPLIER METHOD

Sometimes the substitution method may not be feasible because of more than one side constraint, or because the objective function or side constraints are too complex for efficient solution. Here, the *Lagrange multiplier method* can be used, which directly combines the objective function with the side constraint(s).

The first step in applying the Lagrange multiplier technique is to first bring all terms to the right side of the equation.[10]

$$20 - x - y = 0$$

With this, we can now form a new objective function called the Lagrange function, which will be used in subsequent chapters to find solution values to constrained optimization:

$$\begin{aligned}
\mathscr{L}(x,y) &= f(x,y) + \lambda g(x,y) \\
&= 3x^2 + 6y^2 - xy + \lambda(20 - x - y)
\end{aligned} \tag{2.90}$$

Note that this expression is equal to the original objective function, since all we have done is add zero to it. That is, $\mathscr{L}$ always equals f for values of x and y that satisfy g. To solve for optimal values of x and y, we now take the first partials of this more complicated expression with respect to three unknowns—x, y, and λ. The first-order conditions therefore become:

$$\frac{\partial \mathscr{L}}{\partial x} = \mathscr{L}_x = 6x - y - \lambda = 0 \tag{2.91a}$$

$$\frac{\partial \mathscr{L}}{\partial y} = \mathscr{L}_y = 12y - x - \lambda = 0 \tag{2.91b}$$

$$\frac{\partial \mathscr{L}}{\partial \lambda} = \mathscr{L}_\lambda = 12 - x - y = 0 \tag{2.91c}$$

Note that Equation (2.91c) is, conveniently, our original constraint. Since the first-order conditions given constitute three linear equations in three unknowns, this system of equations may be solved simultaneously. The solution values are

$$x = 13; y = 17; \lambda = -71$$

---

[10] Actually, it does not really matter whether the terms are brought to the right- or to the left-hand side of the equation, although it will affect the interpretation of the value of the Lagrange multiplier, λ. In other words, it is of no consequence whether one writes $\mathscr{L} = f + \lambda g$ or $\mathscr{L} = f - \lambda g$, since one's choice merely changes the sign of the Lagrangian multiplier.

Note that the values for x and y are the same as those obtained using the substitution method. The Lagrange multiplier technique is more powerful, however, because we are also able to solve for the Lagrange multiplier, λ. What is the interpretation of λ? From Equations (2.91) it can be demonstrated that the Lagrange multiplier is defined as

$$\lambda^*(k) = \frac{\partial \mathcal{L}}{\partial k} \tag{2.92}$$

That is, the Lagrange multiplier is the marginal change in the maximum value of the objective function with respect to parametric changes in the value of the constraint.[11] In the context of the present example, $\lambda = -71$ says that if we relax our production constraint by, say, one unit of output (i.e., if we reduce output from 20 units to 19 units), our total cost of production will decline by \$71. It is important to note that because marginal cost is a nonlinear function, the value of λ may be interpreted only in the neighborhood of $Q = 20$. In other words, the value of λ will vary at different output levels.

Problem 2.9. A profit-maximizing firm faces the following constrained maximization problem:

$$\text{Maximize: } \pi(x, y) = 80x - 2x^2 - xy - 3y^2 + 100y$$

$$\text{Subject to: } x + y = 12$$

Determine profit-maximizing output levels of commodities x and y subject to the condition that total output equals 12 units.

Solution. Form the Lagrange expression

$$\mathcal{L}(x, y) = 80x - 2x^2 - xy - 3y^2 + 100y + \lambda(12 - x - y)$$

The first-order conditions are:

$$\frac{\partial \mathcal{L}}{\partial x} = \mathcal{L}_x = 80 - 4x - y - \lambda = 0$$

$$\frac{\partial \mathcal{L}}{\partial y} = \mathcal{L}_y = -x - 6y + 100 - \lambda = 0$$

$$\frac{\partial \mathcal{L}}{\partial \lambda} = \mathcal{L}_\lambda = 12 - x - y = 0$$

This system of three linear equations in three unknowns can be solved for the following values:

[11] Silberberg (1990). Chapter 7.

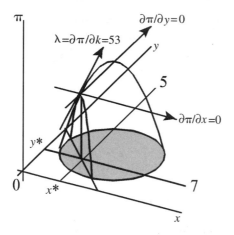

FIGURE 2.18 Constrained maximization.

$$x = 5; y = 7; \lambda = 53$$

Substituting the values of x and y back into our original objective function yields the maximum value for profits:

$$\pi^* = \$868$$

The interpretation of λ is that if our constraint is relaxed by one unit, say increased from an output level of 12 units to 13 units, the firm's profits will increase by $53. Similarly, if output is reduced from say 12 units to 11 units, profits will be decreased by $53. This result is illustrated in Figure 2.18, which shows that the value of $\lambda = \partial \pi / \partial k$ approaches zero as the output constraint becomes non binding, that is, as we approach the top of the profit "hill."

INTEGRATION

INDEFINITE INTEGRALS

The discussion thus far has been concerned with *differential* calculus. In differential calculus we began with the function $y = f(x)$ and then used it to derive another function $dy/dx = f'(x) = g(x)$, which represented slope values along the function $f(x)$ at different values of x. This information was valuable because it allowed us to examine relative maxima and minima.

Suppose, on the other hand, that we are given the function $dy/dx = f'(x) = g(x)$ and wish to recover the function $y = f(x)$. In other words, what function $y = f(x)$ has as its derivative $dy/dx = f'(x) = g(x)$?

Suppose, for example, that we are given the expression

$$\frac{dy}{dx} = 3x^2 \qquad (2.93)$$

From what function was this expression derived? We know from experience that Equation (2.93) could have been derived from each of the expressions

$$y = x^3; y = 100 + x^3; y = -10,000 + x^3$$

By examination we see that Equation (2.93) may be derived from the general class of equations

$$y = c + x^3 \qquad (2.94)$$

where c is an arbitrary constant. The general procedure for finding Equation (2.94) is called *differentiation*. The process of recovering Equation (2.94) from Equation (2.93) is called *integration*.

In general, suppose that $y = f(x)$, and that

$$\frac{df(x)}{dx} = f'(x) = g(x)$$

where $y = f(x)$ is referred to as the *integral* of $g(x)$. If we are given $g(x)$ and wish to recover $f(x)$, the general solution is

$$y = f(x) + c \qquad (2.95)$$

The term c is referred to as an arbitrary *constant of integration*, which may be unknown. Since $dy/dx = g(x)$, then

$$dy = g(x)dx \qquad (2.96)$$

Integrating both sides of Equation (2.96), we obtain

$$\int dy = \int g(x)dx \qquad (2.97)$$

By definition $\int dy = y$. The integral of $g(x)dx$ is $f(x) + c$. Thus, Equation (2.97) may be rewritten as

$$y = \int g(x)dx + c = f(x) + c$$

The term $\int g(x)dx + c$ is called an *indefinite* integral because c is unknown from the integration procedure.

The process of integration is sometimes fairly straightforward. For example, the expression

$$\int x^m dx = \left(\frac{x^{m+1}}{m+1}\right) + c \qquad (2.98)$$

is readily apparent upon careful examination because the derivative of the right is clearly x^m.[12] On the other hand, the integral

---

[12] In fact, Equation (2.98) is a rule that may be applied to many integration problems.

$$\int x^2 e^x \, dx = x^2 e^x - 2xe^x + c$$

may take a while to figure out.

Examples
a. $\int (2x + 100)dx = x^2 + 100x + c$
b. $\int (4x^2 + 3x + 50)dx = (\frac{4}{3})x^3 + (\frac{3}{2})x^2 + 50x + c$

THE INTEGRAL AS THE AREA UNDER A CURVE

The importance of integration stems from its interpretation as the area under a curve. Consider, for example, the marginal cost function $MC(Q)$ illustrated in Figure 2.19.

Marginal cost represents the addition to total cost from producing additional units of a commodity, Q. The process of adding up (or integrating) the cost of each additional unit of Q will result in the total cost of producing Q units of the commodity less any other costs not directly related to the production process, such as insurance payments and fixed rental payments. Such "indirect" (to the actual production of Q) costs are collectively referred to as total fixed cost TFC. Costs that vary directly with output of Q are referred to as total variable cost TVC. Total cost is defined as

$$TC(Q) = TFC + TVC(Q) \tag{2.99}$$

Note that in Equation (2.99) TFC is not functionally related to the level of output, Q.

The marginal cost function illustrated in Figure 2.19 is simply the first derivative of Equation (2.99), or

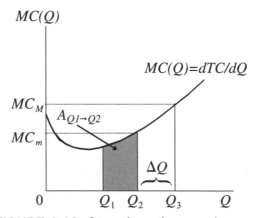

FIGURE 2.19　Integration as the area under a curve.

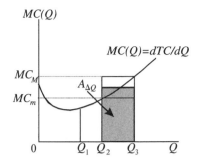

FIGURE 2.20 Approximating the increase in the area under a curve.

$$\frac{dTC(Q)}{dQ} = MC(Q) \tag{2.100}$$

From the foregoing discussion, we realize that integrating Equation (2.100) will yield

$$\int MC(Q)dQ = TVC(Q) + c \tag{2.101}$$

That is, by integrating the marginal cost function, we will recover the total variable cost function, with the constant of integration c representing *TFC*. This process is illustrated in Figure 2.19.

Consider the area beneath $MC(Q)$ in Figure 2.19 between Q_1 and Q_2. Let us denote the value of this area as $A_{Q1 \to Q2}$. Suppose that we wish to consider the effect of an increase in the value of the area under the curve resulting from an increase in output from Q_2 to Q_3, where $Q_3 = Q_2 + \Delta Q$. The value of the area under the curve will increase by ΔA, where

$$\Delta A = A_{Q1 \to Q3} - A_{Q1 \to Q2} = A_{Q2 \to Q3} = A_{\Delta Q}$$

In the interval Q_2 to Q_3 there is a minimum and maximum value of $MC(Q)$, which we will denote as MC_m, and MC_M, respectively. It must be the case that

$$MC_m \Delta Q \le \Delta A \le MC_M \Delta Q$$

This is illustrated in Figure 2.20 as the shaded rectangle. Thus, estimating the value of ΔA by using discrete changes in the value of Q results in an approximation of the increase in the value of the area under the curve.

How can we improve upon this estimate of ΔA? One way is to divide ΔQ into smaller intervals. This is illustrated in Figure 2.21.

Taking the limit as $\Delta Q \to 0$ "squeezes" the difference between MC_m and MC_M to its limiting value $MC(Q)$. Thus,

$$\frac{\lim_{\Delta Q \to 0} \Delta A}{\Delta Q} = \frac{dA}{dQ} = MC(Q)$$

MC(Q)

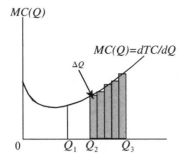

$MC(Q)=dTC/dQ$

ΔQ

0   Q_1 Q_2 Q_3

FIGURE 2.21 Improving on the estimate of the value of the area under a curve by "squeezing" ΔQ.

As noted, A and $TC(Q)$ can differ only by the value of some arbitrary constant c, which in this case is TFC.

Consider, now, the area under the marginal cost curve from Q_1 to Q_3. The total cost of production over that interval is

$$TC = \int_{Q1}^{Q3} MC(Q)dQ = TVC(Q)+TFC \qquad (2.102)$$

Problem 2.10. Suppose that a firm's the marginal cost function is $MC(x)$ = 50x + 600.
a. Find the total cost function if total fixed cost is $4,000.
b. What is the firm's total cost of producing 5 units of output?
c. What is the firm's total cost of producing from 2 to 5 units of output?

Solution
a. $\int MC(x)dx = \int(50x + 600)dx$

$$= TVC(Q)+TFC$$
$$= 25x^2 + 600x + 4,000 = TC(x)$$

b. $TC(x) = 25(5)^2 + 600(5) + 4{,}000 = 625 + 3{,}000 + 4{,}000 = \$7{,}624$
c. $TC_2^5 = \int_2^5 (50x + 600)dx$

$$= \int_2^5 \left[25(5)^2 + 600(5) + 4{,}000\right]$$
$$= \left[25(5)^2 + 600(5) + 4{,}000\right] - \left[25(2)^2 + 600(2) + 4{,}000\right]$$
$$= (625 + 3{,}000 + 4{,}000) - (100 + 1{,}200 + 4{,}000)$$
$$= \$7{,}625 - \$5{,}300 + \$2{,}325$$

CHAPTER REVIEW

Economic and business relationships may be represented in a variety of ways, including tables, charts, graphs, and algebraic expressions. These relationships are very often expressed as functions. In mathematics, a functional relationships of the form $y = f(x)$ is read "y is a function of x." This relationship indicates that the value of y depends in a systematic way on the value of x. The expression says that there is a unique value for y for each value of x. The y variable is referred to as the *dependent variable*. The x variable is referred to as the *independent variable*.

Functional relationships may be linear and nonlinear. The distinguishing characteristic of a *linear function* is its constant slope; that is, the ratio of the change in the value of the dependent variable given a change in the value of the independent variable is constant. The graphs of linear functions are straight lines. With *nonlinear functions* the slope is variable. The graphs of nonlinear functions are "curved." *Polynomial functions* constitute a class of functions that contain an independent variable that is raised to some nonnegative power greater than unity.

Two of the most common polynomial functions encountered in economics and business are the *quadratic function* and the *cubic function*.

Many economic and business models use a special set of functional relations called total, average, and marginal functions. These relations are especially useful in the theories of consumption, production, cost, and market structure. In general, whenever a function's marginal value is greater than its corresponding average value, the average value will be rising. Whenever the function's marginal value is less than its corresponding average value, the average value will be falling. Whenever the marginal value is equal to the average value, the average value is neither rising nor falling.

Many problems in economics involve the determination of "optimal" solutions. For example, a decision maker might wish to determine the level of output that would result in maximum profit. In essence, economic optimization involves maximizing or minimizing some objective function, which may or may not be subject to one or more constraints. Finding optimal solutions to these problems involves *differentiating* an objective function, setting the result equal to zero, and solving for the values of the decision variables. For a function to be differentiable, it must be well defined; that is, it must be continuous or "smooth." Evaluating optimal solutions requires an evaluation of the appropriate first- and second-order conditions. There are generally two methods of solving constrained optimization problems: the *substitution* and *Lagrange multiplier methods*.

Integration is the reverse of differentiation. Integration involves recovering an original function, such as a total cost equation, from its first derivative, such as a marginal cost equation. The resulting function is called an indefinite integral because the value of the constant term in the original equation, such as total fixed cost, cannot be found by integrating the first derivative. Thus, the integral of the marginal cost equation is the equation for total variable cost. Integration is particularly useful in economics when trying to determine the area beneath a curve.

CHAPTER QUESTIONS

2.1 Economic optimization involves maximizing an objective function, which may or may not be subject to side constraints. Do you agree with this statement? If not, why not?

2.2 For an inverse function to exist, the original function must be monotonic. Do you agree? Explain.

2.3 What does it mean for a function to be well defined?

2.4 The inverse-function rule may be applied only to monotonic functions. Do you agree with this statement? If not, why not?

2.5 Suppose that a firm's total profit is a function of output [i.e., $\pi = f(Q)$]. To maximize total profits, the firm must produce at an output level at which $M\pi = d\pi/dQ = 0$. Do you agree? Explain.

2.6 Suppose that a firm's total profit is a function of output [i.e., $\pi = f(Q)$]. Marginal and average profit are defined as $M\pi = d\pi/dQ$ and $A\pi = \pi/Q$. Describe the mathematical relationship between total, marginal, and average profit.

2.7 Maximizing per-unit profit is equivalent to maximizing total profit. Do you agree? Explain.

2.8 Describe briefly the difference between the substitution and Lagrange multiplier methods for finding optimal solutions to constrained optimization problems.

2.9 The Lagrange multiplier is an artificial variable that is of no importance when one is finding optimal solutions to constrained optimization problems. Do you agree with this statement? Explain.

CHAPTER EXERCISES

2.1 Solve each of the following systems of equations and check your answers.

a. $2x + y = 100$
$-4x + 2y = 40$

b. $x - y = 20$
$(\frac{1}{3})x - y = 0$

c. $x^2 - y = 20$
$x^2 + y = 10$

d. $2x + y^2 = 4$
$-x + y^2 = 16$

2.2 Solve the following system of equations:

$$x + y + z = 1$$

$$-x - \left(\frac{1}{2}\right)y - \left(\frac{2}{3}\right)z = 4$$

$$2x + 2y - z = 5$$

2.3 Find the first derivatives and the indicated values of the derivatives.
a. $y = f(x) = 9 + 6x$. Find $f'(0), f'(2), f'(12)$.
b. $y = f(x) = (2 + x)(3 - x)$. Find $f'(-2), f'(3), f'(6)$.
c. $y = f(x) = (x - 2)/(x^2 + 4)$. Find $f'(-4), f'(0), f'(2)$.
d. $y = f(x) = [(x - 1)/(x + 4)]^3$. Find $f'(-2), f'(0), f'(2)$.
e. $y = f(x) = 2x^2 - 4/x + \sqrt{(4x)} - 3\sqrt{(x)}$. Find $f'(1), f'(5), f'(10)$.
f. $y = f(x) = 3\log_e x - (\frac{3}{4})\log_e x$. Find $f'(0), f'(1), f'(100)$.
g. $y = f(x) = 6e^x$. Find $f'(-1), f'(0), f'(1), f'(2)$.
h. $y = f(x) = x^4 - 2x^3 + 3x^2 - 5x + x^{-1} - x^{-2} + 24$. Find $f'(-3), f'(0), f'(3)$.
2.4 Find the second derivatives.
a. $y = f(x) = 8x + 3x^2 - 13$
b. $y = f(x) = e^x + x^2 - (2x - 4)^2$
c. $y = f(x) = x/3 + 4\sqrt{(x)} - (x - 3)^2(x^2 + 2)$
d. $y = f(x) = 2\log_e(x^2 + 4x) - [(x - 2)/(x + 3)]^2$
2.5 The total cost function of a firm is given by:

$$TC = 800 + 12Q + 0.018Q^2$$

where TC denotes total cost and Q denotes the quantity produced per unit of time.
a. Graph the total cost function from $Q = 0$ to $Q = 100$.
b. Find the marginal cost function.
c. Find the marginal cost of production from $Q = 0$ to $Q = 100$.
2.6 The total cost of production of a firm is given as

$$TC = 2{,}000 + 10Q - 0.02Q^2 + 0.001Q^3$$

where TC denotes total cost and Q denotes the quantity produced per unit of time.
a. Graph the total cost function from $Q = 0$ to $Q = 200$.
b. Find the marginal cost function.
c. Find the average cost function.
d. Graph in the same diagram average and marginal costs of production from $Q = 0$ to $Q = 200$.
2.7 Here are three total cost functions:

$$TC = 500 + 100Q - 10Q^2 + 2Q^3$$

$$TC = 500 + 100Q - 10Q^2$$

$$TC = 500 + 100Q$$

a. Determine for each equation the average variable cost, average cost, and marginal cost equations.
b. Plot each equation on a graph.
c. Use calculus to determine the minimum total cost for each equation.

2.8 The market demand function for a commodity x is given as

$$Q = 300 - 30\sqrt{(P)}$$

where Q denotes the quantity demanded and P its price.
a. Find the average revenue function (i.e., price as a function of quantity).
b. Find the marginal revenue function for a monopolist who produces Q.
c. Graph the average revenue curve and the marginal revenue curve from $Q = 1$ to $Q = 100$.

2.9 A firm has the following total revenue and total cost functions:

$$TR = 21Q - Q^2$$

$$TC = \frac{Q^3}{3} - 3Q^2 + 9Q + 6$$

a. At what level of output does the firm maximize total revenue?
b. Define the firm's total profit as $\pi = TR - TC$. At what level of output does the firm maximize total profit?
c. How much is the firm's total profit at its maximum?

2.10 Assume that the firm's operation is subject to the following production function and price data:

$$Q = 3X + 5Y - XY$$

$$P_x = \$3; P_y = \$6$$

where X and Y are two variable input factors employed in the production of Q.
a. In the unconstrained case, what levels of X and Y will maximize Q?
b. It is possible to express the cost function associated with the use of X and Y in the production of Q as $TC = 3X + 6Y$. Assume that the firm has an operating budget of $250. Use the Lagrange multiplier technique to determine the optimal levels of X and Y. What is the firm's total output at these levels of input usage?
c. What will happen to the firm's output from a marginal increase in the operating budget?

2.11 Evaluate the following integrals:
a. $\int (8x^2 + 600)dx$
b. $\int (5x + 3)dx$
c. $\int (10x^2 + 5x - 25)dx$

2.12 Suppose that the marginal cost function of a firm is

$$MC(Q) = Q^2 - 4Q + 5$$

The firm's total fixed cost is 10.

a. Determine the firm's total cost function.
b. What is the firm's total cost of production at $Q = 3$?

SELECTED READINGS

Allen, R. G. D. Mathematical Analysis for Economists. New York: Macmillan, 1938.
————. Mathematical Economics, 2nd ed. New York: Macmillan, 1976.
Brennan, M. J., and T. M. Carroll. Preface to Quantitative Economics & Econometrics, 4th ed. Cincinnati, OH: South-Western Publishing, 1987.
Chiang, A. Fundamental Methods of Mathematical Economics, 3rd ed. New York: McGraw-Hill, 1984.
Draper, J. E., and J. S. Klingman. Mathematical Analysis: Business and Economic Applications, 2nd ed. New York: Harper & Row, 1972.
Fine, H. B. College Algebra. New York: Dover, 1961.
Glass, J. C. An Introduction to Mathematical Methods in Economics. New York: McGraw-Hill, 1980.
Henderson, J. M., and R. E. Quandt. Microeconomic Theory: A Mathematical Approach, 3rd ed. New York: McGraw-Hill, 1980.
Marshall, A. Principles of Economics, 8th ed. London: Macmillan, 1920.
Purcell, E. J. Calculus with Analytic Geometry, 2nd ed. New York: Meredith, 1972.
Rosenlicht, M. Introduction to Analysis. Glenview, Ill: Scott, Foresman, 1968.
Silberberg, Eugene. The Structure of Economics: A Mathematical Analysis, 2nd ed. New York: McGraw-Hill, 1990.
Youse, B. K. Introduction to Real Analysis. Boston: Allyn & Bacon, 1972.

3

THE ESSENTIALS OF
DEMAND AND SUPPLY

Managerial economics is the synthesis of microeconomic theory and quantitative methods to find optimal solutions to managerial decision-making problems. In Chapters 1 and 2 we reviewed the basic elements of two of the quantitative methods most frequently used in managerial economics: mathematical economics and econometrics. In this chapter, we will demonstrate how presumably quantifiable economic functional relationships involving one dependent variable and one or more explanatory variables may be used to predict market-clearing prices in idealized, perfectly competitive markets.

Students who have made it this far in their economic studies have already been exposed to the market paradigm of demand and supply. While the principles of demand and supply presented in this chapter may be familiar, the manner in which this material is presented may not be. The discussion that follows establishes the procedural framework for much of what is to come.

The basic market paradigm presented in this chapter is a stylized version of what occurs in the real world. The model is predicated on a number of assumptions that are rarely, if ever, satisfied in practice, including *perfect and symmetric information*, market transactions that are restricted to *private goods and services*, and that no market participants having *market power*.

When there is "perfect and symmetric information," all that is knowable about the goods and services being transacted is known in equal measure by all market participants. For markets to operate efficiently, both the buyer and the seller must have complete and accurate information about the quantity, quality, and price of the good or service being exchanged. Asymmetric information exists when some market participants have more and better information about the goods and services being exchanged. Fraud can arise in the presence of asymmetric information. In extreme cases, the knowledge that some market participants have access to privileged information may result in a complete breakdown of the market, such as might occur if it became widely believed that stock market transactions were dominated by insider trading.

Goods and services are said to be "private" when all the production costs and consumption benefits are borne exclusively by the market participants. That is, there are no indirect, third-party effects. Such third-party effects, called *externalities*, may affect either consumers or producers. The most common example of a *negative externality* in production is pollution. Finally, "market power" refers to the ability to influence the market price of a good or service by shifting the demand or supply curve.

A violation of any of the three assumptions just given could lead to failure of the market to provide socially optimal levels of particular goods or services. When this occurs, direct or indirect government intervention in the market may be deemed to be in the public's best interest. Market failure and government intervention will be discussed at some length in Chapter 15.

For many readers, most of what is presented in this chapter will constitute a review of material learned in a course in the fundamentals of economics. Students who are familiar with the application of elementary algebraic methods to the concepts of demand, supply, and the market process may proceed to Chapter 4 without any loss of continuity.

THE LAW OF DEMAND

The assumption of profit-maximizing behavior assumes that owners and managers know the demand for the firm's good or service. The demand function asserts that there is a measurable relationship between the price that a company charges for its product and the number of units that buyers are willing and able to purchase during a specified time period. Economists refer to this behavioral relationship as the *law of demand*, which is sometimes called the *first fundamental law of economics*.

Definition: The law of demand states that the quantity demanded of a good or service is inversely related to the selling price, *ceteris paribus* (all other determinants remaining unchanged).

The term "law of demand" is actually a misnomer. As discussed in Chapter 1, laws are facts. Laws are assertions of fact. Laws predict events with certainty. By contrast, theories are probabilistic statements of cause

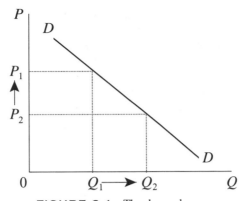

FIGURE 3.1 The demand curve.

and effect. The law of demand is a theory, as is invariably the case when human nature is involved.

Symbolically, the law of demand may be summarized as

$$Q_D = f(P) \qquad (3.1a)$$

and

$$\frac{dQ_D}{dP} < 0 \qquad (3.1b)$$

Equation (3.1a) states that Q_D, the quantity demanded of a good or service, is functionally related to the selling price P. Inequality (3.1b) asserts that quantity demanded and price are inversely related. This relationship is illustrated in Figure 3.1. The downward-sloping *demand curve* illustrates the inverse relationship between the quantity demanded of a good or service and its selling price.

The validity of the law of demand may be argued on the basis of common sense and simple observation. At a more sophisticated level, the validity of the law of demand may be argued on the basis of diminishing marginal utility and income and substitution effects.[1]

INCOME EFFECT

For most goods, the *income effect* asserts that as a product's price declines (increases), an individual's real income (purchasing power) increases (decreases). The increase in real purchasing power resulting from a fall in prices enables the individual to consume greater quantities of a commodity, while the opposite is true for an increase in prices. In other words, an

---

[1] A formal derivation of the demand curve is presented in Appendix 3A.

increase in real purchasing power generally (although not always) leads to increase in quantity demanded. The goods of the types for which this phenomenon holds are referred to as *normal goods*. Unfortunately, the income effect does not always have the expected positive effect on the quantity demanded of a good. In some cases, as an individual's purchasing power increases, the quantity demand for that good falls. Goods of these types are called *inferior goods*. Examples of such goods may be potatoes, bus tickets, soup bones, and bologna. We will return to this issue shortly when considering separately the effect of changes in money income on the demand for goods and services.

SUBSTITUTION EFFECT

The more powerful *substitution effect* entails no such ambiguitys. The substitution effect reflects changes in consumers' opportunity costs. The substitution effect states that as a product's price declines, consumers will substitute the now less expensive product for similar goods that are more expensive.[2]

In the majority of cases, the income effect and the substitution effect complement and reinforce each other. That is, a decline in the price of a good will not only have a positive substitution effect, but will have a positive income effect as well. As a result, the ordinary demand curve will be downward sloping. Even in the case of inferior goods, where the income effect is negative, the ordinary demand curve will exhibit a downward slope because the substitution effect, which is always positive with a drop in price, outweighs the negative income effect.[3]

THE MARKET DEMAND CURVE

The law of demand is a theoretical explanation of the expected behavior of individual economic units when confronted with a change in the price of a commodity. Yet our concern, at the present, is less with the behavior

[2] The interaction of the income and substitution effects are summarized in the Slutsky equation, the proof of which may be found in Silberberg (1990), Chapter 10.

[3] If, on the other hand, the negative income effect, which is associated with inferior goods, outweighs the always positive substitution effect, the ordinary demand curve will be upward sloping! This is precisely what happened in 1845 when famine in Ireland greatly increased the price of potatoes, which in turn caused real incomes to fall sharply. Irish families ended up consuming more rather than less of the high-priced potatoes. Why? Being forced to pay so high a price for a basic necessity made it impossible for the average family to purchase any meat at all, and hence most were forced to become even more dependent on potatoes. The explanation of this curious phenomenon was first attributed to the Victorian economist Sir Robert Giffen. As a result, such goods have been dubbed Giffen goods. See Samuelson and Nordhaus (1985), p. 416.

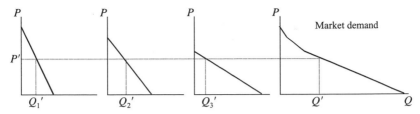

FIGURE 3.2 The market demand curve is the horizontal summation of the individual demand curves.

of individual economic agents than with the market demand for the product of an industry. We must, therefore, extend our analysis to justify what we would hope to be a downward-sloping market demand curve. To derive the hypothetical market demand function for a particular industry's product, let us first consider three hypothetical individual demand functions for the product in question

$$Q_{D,1} = a_1 + b_1 P \qquad (3.2a)$$

$$Q_{D,2} = a_2 + b_2 P \qquad (3.2b)$$

$$Q_{D,3} = a_3 + b_3 P \qquad (3.2c)$$

where the $Q_{D,i}$ terms represent the individual's demand for the commodity, the a_i terms are positive constants, and the b_i terms the unit change in quantity demanded given a change in the selling price.

Definition: The market demand curve is the horizontal summation of the individual demand curves.

For any given price, the market demand curve is the sum of the horizontal distances from the vertical axis to each individual demand curve. Summing together Equations (3.2) we get

$$Q_{D,1} + Q_{D,2} + Q_{D,3} = (a_1 + a_2 + a_3) + (b_1 + b_2 + b_3)P \qquad (3.3)$$

or

$$Q_D = a + bP \qquad (3.4)$$

where $a = a_1 + a_2 + a_3$ and $b = b_1 + b_2 + b_3$. In general, for the n-consumer case

$$Q_{D,M} = \sum_{i=1 \to n} Q_{D,i} = \sum_{i=1 \to n} a_i + \sum_{i=1 \to n} b_i P \qquad (3.5)$$

where $Q_{D,M}$ is market demand. Equation (3.5) is illustrated in Figure 3.2.

Problem 3.1. Suppose that the total market demand for a product comprises the demand of three individuals with identical demand equations.

$$Q_{D,1} = Q_{D,2} = Q_{D,3} = 50 - 25P$$

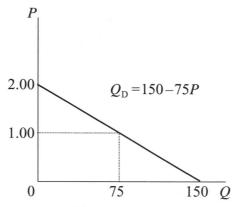

FIGURE 3.3   Diagrammatic solution to problem 3.1.

What is the market demand equation for this product?

Solution. The market demand curve is the horizontal summation of the individual demand curves. The market demand equation is

$$Q_D = Q_{D,1} + Q_{D,2} + Q_{D,3}$$
$$= (50 - 25P) + (50 - 25P) + (50 - 25P) = 150 - 75P$$

This result is illustrated in Figure 3.3.

Problem 3.2. Suppose that the total market demand for a product consists of the demands of individual 1 and individual 2. The demand equations of the two individuals are given by the following equations:

$$Q_{D,1} = 20 - 2P$$

$$Q_{D,2} = 40 - 5P$$

What is the market demand equation for this product?

Solution. Solving the individuals' demand curves for price we obtain

$$P = 10 - 0.5Q_{D,1}$$

$$P = 8 - 0.2Q_{D,2}$$

These demand equations are illustrated in Figure 3.4.

It should be apparent from Figure 3.4 that for $P > \$8$, only individual 1 will purchase units of commodity Q. Thus, the market demand curve is $Q_{D,1} = 20 - 2P$. For prices $P \leq \$8$, both individuals 1 and 2 will purchase units of the commodity Q. Thus, the market demand curve is $Q = Q_{D,1} + Q_{D,2} =$

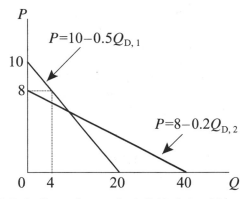

FIGURE 3.4 Demand curves for individuals 1 and 2 in problem 3.2.

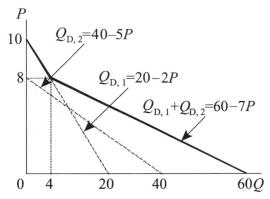

FIGURE 3.5 The market demand curve as the sum of the demand curves for individuals 1 and 2 in problem 3.2.

$(20 - 2P) + (40 - 5P) = 60 - 7P$. The market demand curve for commodity Q is illustrated by the heavy line in Figure 3.5.

The reader will note that the demand curve for commodity Q is discontinuous at $P = \$8$. Figure 3.5 is often referred to as a "kinked" demand curve. Compare this with the smooth and continuous curve in Problem 3.1 (Figure 3.3), in which both individuals enter the market at the same time (i.e., for $P < \$2$).

The market demand curve establishes a relationship between the product's price and the quantity demanded; all other determinants of market demand are held constant. The relationship between changes in price and changes in quantity demanded are illustrated as movements along the demand curve. When economists refer to a change in the quantity demanded (in response to a change in price), they are referring to a movement along the demand curve. As we will see, this is to be distinguished from a change in demand (illustrated as a shift in the entire demand curve), which results when a determinant of demand, other than its selling price, is changed. This semantic distinction is made necessary because two-dimensional representations of a demand function can accommodate a relationship between two variables only—in this case price and quantity, the independent and dependent variables, respectively.[4] What are some of these other determinants of demand?

OTHER DETERMINANTS OF MARKET DEMAND

We know, of course, that price is not the only factor that influences an economic agent's decision to purchase quantities of a given good or service. Other demand determinants include income, consumer preferences, the prices of related goods, price expectations, and population.

INCOME (I)

Typically, an increase in a consumer's money income will result in increased purchases of goods and services, other things remaining equal (including the selling price). More precisely, a *ceteris paribus* increase in an individual's money income will usually lead to an increase in the demand for a good or service. Conceptually, this is not the same thing as an increase in quantity demanded of a good or service due to an increase in an individual's real income that has resulted from a fall in price. Similarly, a *ceteris paribus* decline in an individual's money income will result in a decrease in demand. As before, such goods are called normal goods. Most goods and services fall into this category. An increase in demand for a normal good resulting from an increase in income may be illustrated in Figure 3.6.

In the case of so-called interior goods, however, the demand for a good or a service actually declines with an increase in money income. The result would be a leftward shift in the demand curve. Inferior goods are largely a matter of individual preferences. As their income rises, some individuals prefer to substitute train or plane travel for slower, and presumably less expensive, long-distance bus rides. On the other hand, other people really like riding buses. For this group, long-distance bus travel is a normal good.

---

[4] Although it is possible to represent a three-dimensional object on a two-dimensional surface, such as in a photograph, in practice, drawing such diagrams is quite difficult. More-over, beyond three dimensions, graphically illustrating a relationships that includes, say, four variables is impossible, although depicting its three-dimensional shadow on a two-dimensional surface is not! After all, we live in three-dimensional space, so what does a fourth-dimensional object look like?

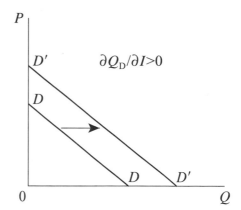

FIGURE 3.6 An increase in demand resulting from an increase in money income.

TASTES OR PREFERENCES (T)

Another determinant of market demand is individuals' tastes, or preferences, for a particular product. After seeing a McDonald's television commercial, for example, one person might be compelled to purchase an increased quantity of hamburgers, even though the price of hamburgers had not fallen or his income had remained the same. This increased demand for hamburgers would be represented as a rightward shift in the demand curve. Similarly, if after reading an article in the *New York Times* about the health dangers associated with diets high in animal fat and salt, the same person might decide to cut down on his intake of hamburgers, which would be shown as a left-shift in his demand curve for hamburgers. The effect of an increase in taste is similar to that depicted for an increase in income in Figure 3.6.

PRICES OF RELATED GOODS: SUBSTITUTES (P_s) AND COMPLEMENTS (P_c)

The prices of related goods can also affect the demand for a particular good or service. Related goods are generally classified as either substitute goods or complementary goods.

Substitutes are goods that consumers consider to be closely related. As the price of good X rises, the quantity demanded of that good will fall according to the law of demand. If good Y is a substitute for good X, the demand for good Y will rise as the consumer substitutes into it. The willingness of the consumer to substitute one good for another varies from good to good and is rarely an either/or proposition. For example, although not perfect substitutes for most consumers, Coca-Cola and Pepsi-Cola might be classified as "close" substitutes. Other examples of goods that may

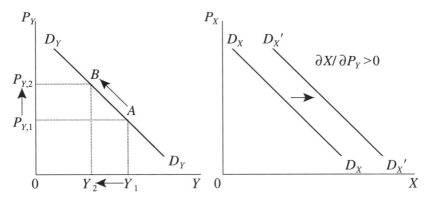

FIGURE 3.7   An increase in demand resulting from a decrease in the price of a substitute good.

be classified as substitutes are oleomargarine and butter, coffee and tea, and beer and ale.

If goods X and Y are substitutes, then we would expect that as the price of Y rises the quantity demanded of Y falls, and the demand for X, other things remaining constant (including the price of X, income, etc.) increase. This interrelationship is illustrated in Figure 3.7.

Note that in Figure 3.7 as the price of good Y rises from $P_{Y,1}$ to $P_{Y,2}$ the quantity demanded of good Y falls from Y_1 to Y_2 (a movement along the $D_Y D_Y$ curve from point A to point B), resulting in an increase in the demand for good X. This is illustrated by a right-shift in the demand function for X from $D_X D_X$ to $D_X' D_X'$. Analogously, a fall in the price of product Y, say from $P_{Y,2}$ to $P_{Y,1}$, would result in an increase in the quantity demanded of good Y, or a movement along the demand curve from point B to point A, would result in a left-shift of the demand curve for good X (not shown in Figure 3.7).

Complements are products that are normally consumed together. Examples of such product pairs include corned beef and cabbage, tea and lemon, coffee and cream, peanut butter and jelly, tennis rackets and tennis balls, ski boots and skis, and kites and kite string.

If goods X and Y are complements, we would expect that as the price of good Y falls and the quantity demanded of good Y increases, we will also witness an increase in the demand for good X. In Figure 3.8 as the price of Y falls from $P_{Y,1}$ to $P_{Y,2}$ the quantity demanded of good Y increases from Y_1 to Y_2 (a movement along the $D_Y D_Y$ curve from point A to point B). The lower price of good Y, say for kites, not only results in an increase in the quantity demanded of kites, but also results in an increase in the demand for good X, kite string. This increase in the demand for good X is shown as a right-shift in the entire demand function for good X. Similarly, an increase

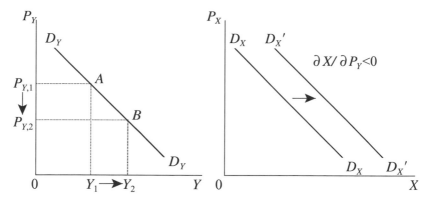

FIGURE 3.8   An increase in demand resulting from a decrease in the price of a complementary good.

in the price of good Y not only would result in a decline in the quantity demanded of good Y, but also would result in a fall in the demand for good X, which is illustrated as left-shift in the demand function for good X.

PRICE EXPECTATIONS (P_e)

If we expect that the price of a good or service will be lower in the future, the demand for that product will be lower today, resulting in a left-shift of today's demand function. Conversely, if we expect the price to be higher tomorrow, the demand will be greater today, resulting in a right-shift in the demand function.

POPULATION (N)

As we discussed earlier, the market demand curve for a good or a service is the horizontal summation of demand curves of individuals that make up the market. Changes in the number of consumers in the market, perhaps because of an increase in the general population, will result in changes in demand. An increase in population, perhaps because of immigration, increased birthrates, or demographic changes, likely will cause an increase in the demand for a product, which will be illustrated diagrammatically as a right-shift in the demand curve. Similarly, a decrease in population will likely cause a decrease in the demand for a product, which will be illustrated diagrammatically as a left-shift in the demand curve.

The relationship between the demand for a good and service and the set of determinants just discussed may be expressed as

$$Q_D = f(P, I, T, P_s, P_c, P_e, N) \qquad (3.6)$$

TABLE 3.1   Impacts on Demand Arising from Changes
in Demand Determinants

Determinant	Change	Demand shift
Income		
Normal good, I	$\Delta\uparrow$	$\rightarrow$
	$\Delta\downarrow$	$\leftarrow$
Inferior good, I	$\Delta\uparrow$	$\leftarrow$
	$\Delta\downarrow$	$\rightarrow$
Tastes or preferences, T	$\Delta\uparrow$	$\rightarrow$
	$\Delta\downarrow$	$\leftarrow$
Price of substitutes, P_s	$\Delta\uparrow$	$\rightarrow$
	$\Delta\downarrow$	$\leftarrow$
Price of complements, P_c	$\Delta\uparrow$	$\leftarrow$
	$\Delta\downarrow$	$\rightarrow$
Price expectations, P_e	$\Delta\uparrow$	$\rightarrow$
	$\Delta\downarrow$	$\leftarrow$
Population, N	$\Delta\uparrow$	$\rightarrow$
	$\Delta\downarrow$	$\leftarrow$

where $\partial Q_D/\partial P < 0, \partial Q_D/\partial I > 0, \partial Q_D/\partial T > 0, \partial Q_D/\partial P_s > 0, \partial Q_D/\partial P_c < 0, \partial Q_D/\partial P_e > 0$, and $\partial Q_D/\partial N > 0$. The diagrammatic effects of changes in determinants on the demand curve are summarized in Table 3.1.

OTHER DEMAND DETERMINANTS

We have mentioned only a very few of the possible factors that will influence the demand for a product. Other demand determinants might include income expectations, changes in interest rates, changes in foreign exchange rates, and the impact of wealth effects. In actual demand analysis, an in-depth familiarity with specific market conditions will usually help one to identify the relevant demand determinants that need to be considered in analyzing market behavior.

THE MARKET DEMAND EQUATION

The functional relationship summarized in Equation (3.6) suggests only that a relationship exists between Q_D and a collection of hypothesized explanatory variables. While such an expression of causality is useful, it says nothing about the specific functional relationship, nor does it say anything about the magnitude of the interrelationships. To quantify the hypothesized relationship in Equation (3.6), it is necessary to specify a functional form. Using the techniques discussed in Green (1997), Gujarati (1995), and

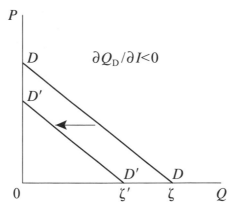

FIGURE 3.9   A decline in consumer income that results in a lower value for the horizontal intercept of a linear demand equation.

Ramanathan (1998), we may proceed to estimate the values of the coefficients. As indicated earlier, the most commonly used functional form is the linear equation. We might, therefore, express Equation (3.6) as

$$Q_D = b_0 + b_1 P + b_2 I + b_3 P_s + b_4 P_c + b_5 P_e + b_6 N \qquad (3.7)$$

where

$$b_1 < 0, b_2 > 0, b_3 > 0, b_4 < 0, b_5 > 0, b_6 > 0$$

The coefficients b_i are the first partial derivatives of the demand function. They indicate how Q_D will change from a one unit change in the value of the independent variables. For many purposes, it is useful to concentrate only on the relationship between quantity demanded and the price of the commodity under consideration while holding the other variables constant. Equation (3.7) may be rewritten as

$$Q_D = \zeta + b_1 P \qquad (3.8)$$

where

$$\zeta = b_0 + b_2 I_0 + b_3 P_{s,0} + b_4 P_{c,0} + b_5 P_{e,0} + b_6 N_0$$

It should be clear from Equation (3.8) and the discussion thus far that a change in P will result in a change in the quantity demanded and, thus, a movement along the curve labeled DD. On the other hand, a change in any of the demand determinants will result in a change in the value of the horizontal intercept (ζ) resulting in a change in demand and a shift in the entire demand curve. For example, a decline in consumers income will result in a decline in the value of ζ to ζ', resulting in a left-shift of the demand function from DD to $D'D'$. Consider Figure 3.9.

Problem 3.3. The demand equation for a popular brand of fruit drink is given by the equation

$$Q_x = 10 - 5P_x + 0.001I + 10P_y$$

where Q_x = monthly consumption per family in gallons
P_x = price per gallon of the fruit drink = \$2.00
I = median annual family income = \$20,000
P_y = price per gallon of a competing brand of fruit drink = \$2.50
a. Interpret the parameter estimates.
b. At the stated values of the explanatory variables, calculate the monthly consumption (in gallons) of the fruit drink.
c. Rewrite the demand equation in a form similar to Equation (3.8).
d. Suppose that median annual family income increased to \$30,000. How does this change your answer to part b?

Solution
a. According to our demand equation in Q_x, a \$1 increase in the price of the fruit drink will result in a 5-gallon decline in monthly consumption of fruit drink per family. A \$1,000 increase in median annual family income will result in a 1-gallon increase in monthly consumption of fruit drink per family. Finally, a \$1 increase in the price of the competing brand of fruit drink will result in a 10-gallon increase in monthly consumption of the fruit drink per family. In other words, the two brands of fruit drink are substitutes.
b. Substituting the stated values into the demand equation yields

$$Q_x = 10 - 5(2.00) + 0.001(20,000) + 10(2.50) = 45 \text{ gallons}$$

c. $Q_x = 55 - 5P_x$
d. $Q_x = 10 - 5(2.00) + 0.001(30,000) + 10(2.50) = 55$ gallons

MARKET DEMAND VERSUS FIRM DEMAND

While the discussion thus far has focused on the market demand curve, it is, in fact, the demand curve facing the individual firm that is of most interest to the manager who is formulating price and output decisions. In the case of a monopolist, when firm output constitutes the output of the industry, the market demand curve is identical to the demand curve faced by the firm. Consequently, the firm will bear the entire impact of changes in such demand determinants as incomes, tastes, and the prices of related goods. Similarly, the pricing policies of the monopolist will directly affect the consumer's decisions to purchase the firm's output.

In most cases, however, the firm supplies only a small portion of the total output of the industry. Thus, the firm's demand curve is not identical to that of the market as a whole. One major difference between firm and market demand may be the existence of additional demand determinants, such as pricing decisions made by the firm's competitors. Another important difference is that the quantitative impact of changes in such determinants as taste, income, and prices of related goods will be smaller because of the firm's smaller share of the total market supply. It is the demand function faced by the individual firm that is of primary concern in managerial economics.

THE LAW OF SUPPLY

While we have discussed some of the conditions under which consumers are willing, and able, to purchase quantities of a particular good or service, we have yet to say anything about the willingness of producers to produce those very same goods and services. Once we have addressed this matter, we will be in a position to give form and substance to the elusive concept of "the market."

Definition: The law of supply asserts that quantity supplied of a good or service is directly (positively) related to the selling price, *ceteris paribus*.

As we will see in later chapters on production and cost, under certain conditions, including short-run production, the hypothesis of a profit maximization, and perfect competition in resource markets, the law of supply is based on the law of diminishing marginal returns (sometimes called the law of diminishing marginal product). In fact, as we will see later, the supply curve of an individual firm is simply a portion of the firm's marginal cost curve, which at some point rises in response to the law of diminishing returns.

The law of diminishing returns is not an economic relationship but a technological relationship that is empirically consistent. In fact, the law of diminishing marginal returns may be the only true law in economics. The law of diminishing marginal returns in fact makes the law of supply a stronger relationship than the "law" of demand. With that, consider the following hypothetical market supply function.

Symbolically, the law of supply may be summarized as follows:

$$Q_s = g(P) \tag{3.9a}$$

and

$$\frac{dQ_s}{dP} > 0 \tag{3.9b}$$

Equation (3.9a) states that the quantity supplied Q_s of a good or service is functionally related to the selling price P. Inequality (3.9b) asserts that

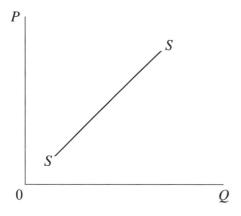

FIGURE 3.10   The supply curve.

quantity supplied of a product and its price are directly related. This relationship is illustrated in Figure 3.10. The upward-sloping *supply curve* illustrates the positive relationship between the quantity demanded of a good
or service and its selling price. The market supply curve shows the various
amounts of a good or service that profit-maximizing firms are willing to
supply at each price. As with the market demand curve, the market supply
curve is also the horizontal summation of the individual firms' supply
curves. Unlike the earlier discussion of the market demand schedule as the
horizontal summation of the individual consumer demand schedules, an
investigation of the supply schedule for an individual firm will be deferred.

The market supply curve establishes a relationship between price and
quantity supplied. Changes in the price and the quantity supplied of a good
or service are represented diagrammatically as a movement along the
supply curve. Changes in supply determinants are illustrated as a shift in
the entire supply curve.

DETERMINANTS OF MARKET SUPPLY

Of course, the market price of a good or service is not the only factor
that influences a firm's decision to alter the quantity supplied of a particular good or service. To get a "feel" for whether a firm will increase or
decrease the quantity supplied of a particular good or service (assuming the
product's price is given) in response to a particular supply-side stimulus, let
us assume that the firms that make up the supply side of the market are
"profit maximizers." Total profit is defined as

$$\pi(Q) = TR(Q) - TC(Q) \tag{3.10}$$

where π is total profit, TR is total revenue, and TC is the total cost, which
are defined as functions of total output Q. Moreover, total revenue may be

DETERMINANTS OF MARKET SUPPLY

expressed as the product of the selling price of the product times the quantity sold.

$$TR = PQ \tag{3.11}$$

Total cost, on the other hand, is assumed to be an increasing function of a firm's output level, which is a function of the productive resources used in its production. Equation (3.12) expresses total cost as a function of labor and capital inputs.

$$TC = h(Q) = h[k(L,K)] = l(L,K) \tag{3.12}$$

If the firm purchases productive resources in a perfectly competitive factors market, the total cost function might be expressed as

$$\begin{aligned} TC &= TFC + TVC \\ &= TFC + P_L L + P_K K \end{aligned} \tag{3.13}$$

where TFC represents total fixed cost (a constant), P_L is the price of labor, which is determined exogenously, L the units of labor employed, P_K is the rental price of capital, also determined exogenously, and K the units of capital employed. Fixed costs represent the cost of factors of production that cannot be easily varied in the short run. Rental payments for office space as specified for the term of a lease represent a fixed cost.

Equation (3.13) indicates that as a firm's output level expands, the costs associated with higher output levels increase. In general, let us say that the change in any factor that causes a firm's profit to increase will result in a decision to increase the quantity the firm supplies to the market, other things remaining the same. Conversely, any change that causes a decline in profits will result in a decline in quantity supplied, other things remaining the same. We have already seen that an increase in product price, which increases total revenue, will result in an increase in the quantity supplied, or a movement to the right and along the supply function. Now let's consider other supply side determinants.

PRICES OF PRODUCTIVE INPUTS (P_L)

By the logic just set forth, a drop in the price of a resource used to produce a product will reduce the total cost of production. If the selling price of the product is parametric, the decrease in the price of resources will result in an increase in the firm's profits, resulting in a right-shift of the supply function. Conversely, a rise in input prices, which increases total cost and reduces profit, at a given price, will result in a left-shift in the supply function. The relationship between supply and a decline in the price of a resource is illustrated in Figure 3.11.

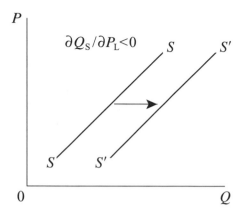

FIGURE 3.11   An increase in supply resulting from a decrease in factor prices.

TECHNOLOGY (*E*)

Advances in methods of management or production imply increases in productive efficiency. Increased efficiency means that either more output can be obtained from some given level of inputs, or some given level of output can be obtained using fewer inputs. In either case, improvements in the managerial or technological arts imply lower total costs of production, other things remaining the same, which implies increased profits, and, therefore, a right-shift in the entire supply schedule.

TAXES AND SUBSIDIES (*R*)

An increase in taxes levied on a firm's operations translates to an increase in the total cost of production, which implies a reduction in profits, other things remaining the same. The result would be a reduction in supply, or a left-shift in the supply curve. Conversely, a reduction in taxes, which is analytically equivalent to, say, a government subsidy, improves the firm's profits, thereby resulting in a right-shift in the supply schedule (an increase in supply).

PRICES OF RELATED GOODS: SUBSTITUTES (*P*$_s$) AND COMPLEMENTS (*P*$_c$)

The prices of related goods can also affect the supply of a particular good or service. As in the case of demand, these related goods are generally classified as either substitute goods or complementary goods.

Substitutes are goods that may be produced using the same (fixed) production facilities. Suppose, for example, that land can be used to grow wheat or corn. An increase in the price of corn would cause farmers to devote more land to the production of corn and less to the production of wheat. Thus, even though the price of wheat may have initially remained unchanged, the increase in the price of corn causes a reduction in the supply of wheat.

Complements are goods that are produced together. Beef and cowhide leather, for example, are complements in production. An increase in the price of beef will cause an increase in the quantity supplied of beef, which may also result in an increase in the supply of cowhide leather, even though the price of cowhide leather initially remained unchanged.

PRICE EXPECTATIONS (P_e)

If firm owners expect an increase in the product's selling price, they can be expected to withhold some output from the market, thereby building up inventories, for later sale at the anticipated higher price. Notice that this would probably result in a reduction in total revenues, and profits, today in favor of expected higher profits tomorrow. This would result in a reduction in supply, or a left-shift in the supply curve. Conversely, firm owners who anticipate a decline in selling prices can be expected to draw down inventories below what are considered optimal levels for sale today, thereby causing the supply curve to shift to the right.

NUMBER OF FIRMS IN THE INDUSTRY (F)

Other things being equal, including the selling price of a given product, an influx of firms into an industry will result in an increase in total supply. The result would be a right-shift in the supply function. Conversely, if firms exit the industry, the supply curve would be expected to shift to the left.

The relationship between the supply of a good and service and the set of supply determinants discussed thus far may be expressed as

$$Q_S = f(P, P_L, E, R, P_s, P_c, P_e, F) \tag{3.14}$$

where $\partial Q_S/\partial P > 0, \partial Q_S/\partial P_L < 0, \partial Q_S/\partial E > 0, \partial Q_S/\partial R < 0, \partial Q_S/\partial P_s < 0, \partial Q_S/\partial P_c > 0, \partial Q_S/\partial P_e < 0$, and $\partial Q_S/\partial F > 0$. The effects of changes in these supply determinants on the curve are summarized in Table 3.2.

Remember that a change in the quantity supplied of a good or service refers to the relationship between changes in the price of the good or service in question and changes in the quantity supplied. This is illustrated diagrammatically as a movement along the supply curve. A change in supply, on the other hand, refers to the relationship between changes in any other supply determinant, such as factor prices and production technology, which is shown diagrammatically shift in the entire supply curve.

TABLE 3.2   Impacts on Supply Arising from Changes in Supply Determinants

Determinant	Change	Supply shift
Resource prices, P_L	$\Delta\uparrow$	$\leftarrow$
	$\Delta\downarrow$	$\rightarrow$
Technology, E	$\Delta\uparrow$	$\rightarrow$
	$\Delta\downarrow$	$\leftarrow$
Taxes and subsidies, R	$\Delta\uparrow$	$\leftarrow$
	$\Delta\downarrow$	$\rightarrow$
Price of substitutes, P_s	$\Delta\uparrow$	$\leftarrow$
	$\Delta\downarrow$	$\rightarrow$
Price of complements, P_c	$\Delta\uparrow$	$\rightarrow$
	$\Delta\downarrow$	$\leftarrow$
Price expectations, P_e	$\Delta\uparrow$	$\leftarrow$
	$\Delta\downarrow$	$\rightarrow$
Number of firms, F	$\Delta\uparrow$	$\rightarrow$
	$\Delta\downarrow$	$\leftarrow$

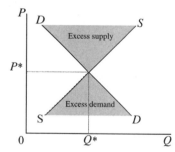

FIGURE 3.12 Market equilibrium.

THE MARKET MECHANISM: THE INTERACTION OF DEMAND AND SUPPLY

We can now use the concepts of demand and supply to explain the functioning of the market mechanism. Consider Figure 3.12, which brings together the market demand and supply curves. In our hypothetical market, the market equilibrium price is P^*. At that price, the quantity of a good or service that buyers are able and willing to buy is precisely equal to Q^*, the amount that firms are willing to supply. At a price below P^*, the quantity demanded exceeds the quantity supplied. In this situation, consumers will bid among themselves for the available supply of Q, which will drive up the selling price. Buyers who are unable or unwilling to pay the higher price will drop out of the bidding process. At the higher price, profit-maximizing producers will increase the quantity supplied. As long as the selling price is below P^*, excess demand for the product will persist and the bidding process will continue. The bidding process will come to an end when, at the equilibrium price, excess demand is eliminated. In other words, at the equilibrium price, the quantity demanded by buyers is equal to the quantity supplied.

It is important to note that in the presence of excess demand, the adjustment toward equilibrium in the market emanates from the demand side. That is, prices are bid up by consumers eager to obtain a product that is in relatively short supply. Suppliers, on the other hand, are, in a sense, passive participants, taking their cue to increase production as prices rise.

On the other side of the market equilibrium price is the situation of excess supply. At a price above P^*, producers are supplying amounts of Q in excess of what consumers are willing to purchase. In this case, producers' inventories will rise above optimal levels as unwanted products go unsold. Since holding inventories is costly, producers will lower price in an effort to move their product. At the lower price, the number of consumers who are willing and able to purchase, say, hamburgers increases. Producers, on the other hand, will adjust their production schedules downward to reflect the reduced consumer demand.

In this case, where the quantity supplied exceeds the quantity demanded, producers become active players in the market adjustment process. That is, in the presence of excess supply, producers provide the impetus for lower product prices in an effort to avoid unwanted inventory accumulation. Consumers, on the other hand, are passive participants, taking their cue to increase consumption in response to lower prices initiated by the actions of producers but having no direct responsibility for the lower prices.

Problem 3.4. The market demand and supply equations for a product are

$$Q_D = 25 - 3P$$

$$Q_S = 10 + 2P$$

where Q is quantity and P is price. What are the equilibrium price and quantity for this product?

Solution. Equilibrium is characterized by the condition $Q_D = Q_S$. Substituting the demand and supply equations into the equilibrium condition, we obtain

$$25 - 3P = 10 + 2P$$

$$P^* = 3$$

$$Q^* = 25 - 3(3) = 10 + 2(3) = 16$$

Problem 3.5. Adam has an extensive collection of *Flash* and *Green Lantern* comic books. Adam is planning to attend a local community college in the fall and wishes to sell his collection to raise money for textbooks. Three local comic book collectors have expressed an interest in buying Adam's collection. The individual demand equation for each of these three individuals is

$$Q_{D,1} = Q_{D,2} = Q_{D,3} = 550 - 2.5P$$

where P is measured in dollars per comic book.
a. What is the market demand equation for Adam's comic books?
b. How many more comic books can Adam sell for each dollar reduction in price?
c. If Adam has 900 comic books in all, what price should he charge to sell his entire collection?

Solution

a. The market demand for Adam's comic books is equal to the sum of the individual demands, that is,

$$Q_{D,M} = Q_{D,1} + Q_{D,2} + Q_{D,3} = (55 - 2.5P) + (55 - 2.5P) + (55 - 2.5P)$$
$$= 165 - 7.5P$$

b. Since price is measured in dollars, each one-dollar reduction in the price of comic books will result in an increase in quantity demanded of 7.5 comic books.
c. Since Adam is offering his entire comic book collection for sale, the total quantity supplied of comic books is 90, that is,

$$Q_S = 90$$

To determine the price Adam must charge to sell his entire collection, equate market demand to market supply and solve:

$$Q_D = Q_S$$
$$165 - 7.5P = 90$$
$$P^* = 75/7.5 = \$10$$

That is, in order for Adam to sell his entire collection, he should sell his comic books for $10 each. Consider Figure 3.13.

Problem 3.6. Consider, again, the market demand curve in Figure 3.5.
a. Suppose that the total market supply is given by the equation

$$Q_S = -16 + 2P$$

What are the market equilibrium price and quantity?
b. Suppose that because of a decline in labor costs, market supply increases to

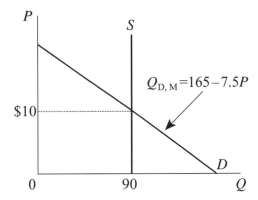

FIGURE 3.13   Diagrammatic solution to problem 3.5.

$$Q'_S = 6 + 2P$$

What are the new equilibrium price and quantity?

c. Diagram your answers to parts a and b.

Solution

a. Equilibrium is characterized by the condition $Q_D = Q_S$. Recall from Problem 3.2 that the market demand curve for $Q \leq 6$ is $Q_{D,1} = 20 - 2P$ and $Q_{D,M} = Q_{D,1} + Q_{D,2} = 60 - 7P$ for $Q \geq 4$. The equilibrium price and quantity are

$$-16 + 2P = 20 - 2P$$

$$P^* = 9$$

$$Q^* = 20 - 2(9) = -16 + 2(9) = 2$$

b. The new equilibrium price and quantity are

$$6 + 2P = 60 - 7P$$

$$P^* = 6$$

$$Q^* = 60 - 7(6) = 6 + 2(6) = 18$$

c. Figure 3.14 shows the old and new market equilibrium price and quantity.

Problem 3.7. Universal Exports has estimated the following monthly demand equation for its new brand of gourmet French pizza, Andrew's Appetizer:

$$Q_D = 500 - 100P + 50I + 20P_r + 30A$$

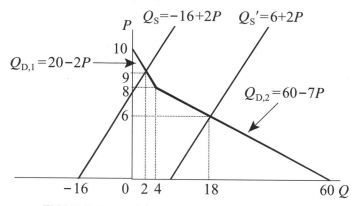

FIGURE 3.14   Diagrammatic solution to problem 3.6.

where Q_D = quantity demanded per month
         P = price per unit
         I = per-capita income (thousands of dollars)
         P_r = price of another gourmet product, François's Frog Legs
         A = monthly advertising expenditures (thousands of dollars) of
             U niversal Exports

The supply equation for Andrew's Appetizer is

$$Q_S = 1,350 + 450P$$

a. What is the relationship between Andrew's Appetizer and François's Frog Legs?
b. Suppose that $I = 200$, $P_r = 80$, and $A = 100$. What are the equilibrium price and quantity for this product?
c. Suppose that per-capita income increases by 55 (i.e., $I = 255$). What are the new equilibrium price and quantity for this product?

Solution
a. By the law of demand, an increase in the price of a product will result in a decrease in the quantity demanded of that product, other things being equal. In this case, an increase in the price of François's Frog Legs would result in a decrease in the quantity demanded of frogs legs, other things equal. Since this results in an increase in the demand for Andrew's Appetizer, we would conclude that Andrew's Appetizer and François's Frog Legs are substitutes.
b. Substituting the information from the problem statement into the demand equation yields

$$Q_D = 500 - 100P + 50(200) + 20(80) + 30(100)$$
$$= 500 - 100P + 10,000 + 1,600 + 3,000 = 15,100 - 100P$$

Market equilibrium is defined as $Q_D = Q_S$. Substituting the supply and demand to equations into the equilibrium condition, we obtain

$$15,100 - 100P = 1,350 + 450P$$

$$P* = \$25$$

$$Q* = 15,100 - 100(25) = 12,600$$

c. Substituting the new information into the demand equation yields

$$Q_D = 500 - 100P + 50(255) + 20(80) + 30(100)$$
$$= 500 - 100P + 12,750 + 1,600 + 3,000 = 17,850 - 100P$$

Substituting this into the equilibrium condition, we write

$$17,850 - 100P = 1,350 + 450P$$

$$P* = \$30$$

$$Q* = 17,850 - 100(30) = 14,850$$

It is interesting to note that the increase in per-capita income is represented diagrammatically as an increase in the intercept Q from 15,100 to 17,850, with no change in the slope of the demand curve. The student should verify diagrammatically that an increase in the Q intercept will result in right-shift of the demand curve, which is exactly what we would expect for a normal good given an increase in per capita income.

CHANGES IN SUPPLY AND DEMAND: THE ANALYSIS OF PRICE DETERMINATION

Now let us use the analytical tools of supply and demand to analyze the effects of a change in demand and/or a change in supply on the equilibrium price and quantity. Consider first the case of a change in demand.

DEMAND SHIFTS

Suppose, for example, that medical research finds that hamburgers have highly desirable health characteristics, triggering an increase in the public's preference for hamburgers. Other things remaining constant, this would result in a right-shift in the demand curve for hamburgers. This results in an increase in the equilibrium price and quantity demanded for hamburgers. Consider Figure 3.15.

If medical research, on the other hand had discovered that hamburgers exhibited highly undesirable health properties, one could have predicted a reduction in the demand for hamburgers, or a left-shift in the demand curve,

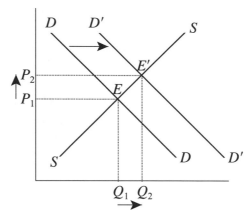

FIGURE 3.15 A rise in the equilibrium price and quantity resulting from an increase in demand.

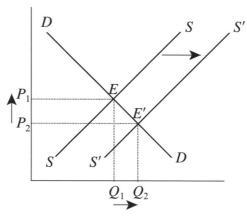

FIGURE 3.16 A fall in the equilibrium price and a rise in the equilibrium quantity resulting from an increase in supply.

resulting, in turn, in a decline in both equilibrium price and quantity demanded.

SUPPLY SHIFTS

Suppose there is a sharp decline in the price of cattle feed. The result will be an increase in the supply of hamburgers at every price, other things remaining the same. This, of course, would result in a right-shift of the supply function. The result, which is illustrated in Figure 3.16, is a decline in the equilibrium price and an increase in quantity supplied. Conversely, a

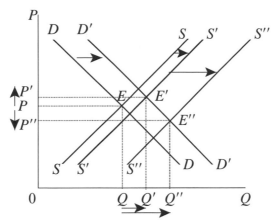

FIGURE 3.17 An increase in demand and supply may result in an unambiguous rise in the equilibrium quantity and an ambiguous change in the equilibrium price.

left-shift in the supply curve would have raised the equilibrium price and lowered the equilibrium quantity. In either the case of a demand shift or a supply shift, the effect on the equilibrium price and quantity is unambiguous. Can as much be said if both the demand curve and the supply curve shift simultaneously?

DEMAND AND SUPPLY SHIFTS

As illustrated in Figure 3.16, a shift in the demand curve or a shift in the supply curve resulted in unambiguous changes in equilibrium price and quantity demanded. When changes in both demand and supply occur simultaneously, however, it is more difficult to predict the effect on price and quantity demanded. This can be illustrated by considering four possible cases.

Case 1: An Increase in Demand and an Increase in Supply

As illustrated in Figure 3.17, a right-shift in both the demand and supply curves yields an unambiguous increase in quantity demanded. The effect on the equilibrium price, however, is indeterminate.

As shown earlier, if the increase in supply is relatively less than the increase in demand, the result will be a net increase in price. This is seen in Figure 3.17 by comparing the market clearing price at E with E'. On the other hand, if there occurs a large increase in supply, relative to the increase in demand, the result will be a net decrease in the equilibrium price. This is seen by comparing the market clearing price at E with E'' in Figure 3.17.

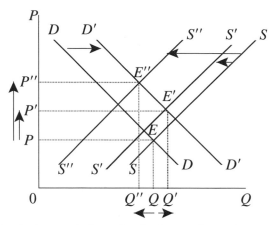

FIGURE 3.18   An increase in demand and a decrease in supply may result in an unambiguous rise in the equilibrium price and an ambiguous change in the equilibrium quantity.

Case 2: An Increase in Demand and a Decrease in Supply

As illustrated in Figure 3.18, a right-shift in the demand curve and a left-shift in The supply curve result in an unambiguous increase in the equilibrium price, although the effect on the equilibrium quantity is indeterminate.

If the decrease in supply is relatively less than the increase in demand, the result will be an increase in equilibrium price and quantity. This is seen in Figure 3.18 by comparing the equilibrium price and quantity at E with E'. If, however, the decrease in supply is relatively more than the increase in demand, the result will be an increase in the equilibrium price but a decrease in the equilibrium quantity. This can be seen by comparing the equilibrium price and quantity at E with E'' in Figure 3.18.

Case 3: A Decrease in Demand and a Decrease in Supply

As can be seen in Figure 3.19, a left-shift in both the demand and supply curves will result in an unambiguous decline in the equilibrium quantity and an indeterminate change in the equilibrium price.

If the decrease in supply is relatively less than the decrease in demand, the result will be a decrease in the equilibrium price and quantity. This is seen by comparing equilibrium price and quantity at E with E' in Figure 3.19. If, however, the decrease in supply is relatively greater than the decrease in demand, the result will be a decrease in the equilibrium quantity, but an increase in the equilibrium price. This can be seen by comparing the equilibrium price and quantity at E with E'' in Figure 3.19.

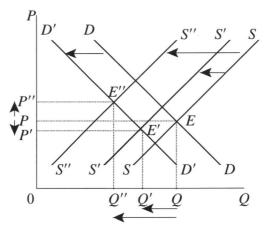

FIGURE 3.19 A decrease in both demand and supply may result in an unambiguous fall in the equilibrium quantity but an ambiguous change in the equilibrium price.

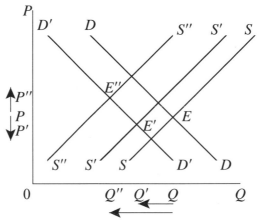

FIGURE 3.20 A decrease in demand and an increase in supply may result in an unambiguous fall in the equilibrium quantity and an ambiguous change in the equilibrium price.

Case 4: A Decrease in Demand and an Increase in Supply

In our final case, a left-shift in the demand curve and a right-shift in the supply curve will result in an unambiguous decline in the equilibrium price, but an indeterminate change in the equilibrium quantity. This situation is depicted in Figure 3.20.

If the increase in supply is relatively less than the decrease in demand, the result will be a decrease in the equilibrium price and quantity. This is seen by comparing the equilibrium price and quantity at E with E' in

Figure 3.20. If, however, the increase in supply is relatively greater than the decrease in demand, the result will be an increase in the equilibrium quantity and a decrease in the equilibrium price. This can be seen by comparing the equilibrium price and quantity at E with E'' in Figure 3.20.

Problem 3.8. The market supply and demand equations for a given product are given by the expressions

$$Q_D = 200 - 50P$$

$$Q_S = -40 + 30P$$

a. Determine the equilibrium price and quantity.
b. Suppose that there is an increase in demand to

$$Q_D = 300 - 50P$$

Suppose further that there is an increase in supply to

$$Q_S = -20 + 30P$$

What are the new equilibrium price and quantity?
c. Suppose that the increase in supply had been

$$Q_S = 140 + 30P$$

Given the demand curve in part b, what are the equilibrium price and quantity?
d. Diagram your results.

Solution
a. Equilibrium is characterized by the condition $Q_D = Q_S$. Substituting, we have

$$200 - 50P = -40 + 30P$$

$$P^* = 3$$

$$Q^* = 200 - 50(3) = -40 + 30(3) = 50$$

b. Substituting the new demand and supply equations into the equilibrium equations yields

$$300 - 50P = -20 + 30P$$

$$P^* = 4$$

$$Q^* = 300 - 50(4) = -20 + 30(4) = 100$$

c. $$300 - 50P = 140 + 30P$$

$$P^* = 2$$

$$Q^* = 300 - 50(2) = 140 + 30(2) = 200$$

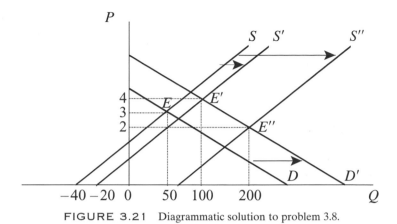

FIGURE 3.21 Diagrammatic solution to problem 3.8.

d. Figure 3.21 diagrams the foregoing results.

THE RATIONING FUNCTION OF PRICES

How realistic is the assumption of market equilibrium? In a dynamic economy it is unrealistic to presume that markets adjust instantaneously to demand and supply disturbances. Although temporary shortages and surpluses are inevitable, it is important to realize that unfettered markets are stable in the sense that the prices tend to converge toward equilibrium following an exogenous shock. The converse would be to assume that markets are inherently unstable and that prices diverge or spiral away from equilibrium, which would be a recipe for market disintegration on a regular basis. The fact that we do not observe this kind of chaos should reinforce our faith in the underlying logic and stability of the free market process.

The system of markets and prices performs two closely related, and very important, functions. In Figure 3.12 we observed that when the market price of a good or service is above or below the equilibrium price, surpluses or shortages arise. The question confronting any economy when the quantity demanded exceeds the quantity supplied is how to allocate available supplies among competing consumers. In free-market economies, this task is typically accomplished by an increase in prices. The process by which shortages are eliminated by allocating available goods and services to consumers willing and able to pay higher prices calls on control the *rationing function* of prices. Price rationing means that whenever there is a need to distribution of a good or service that is in limited supply, the price will rise until the quantity demanded equals the quantity supplied and equilibrium in the market is restored.

Definition: The rationing function of prices refers to the increase or a decrease in the market price to eliminate a surplus or a shortage of a good or service. The rationing function is considered to be a short-run phenomenon because other demand determinants are assumed to be constant.

As we observed earlier, shortages set into motion a process whereby consumers effectively bid among themselves for available goods and services. As the price is bid up, suppliers make more goods and services available for sale, while some consumers drop out of the bidding process. Fundamental to this bidding process is the notion of willingness and ability to pay. The ideal of "willingness and ability to pay" is fundamental to the allocation of available goods and services. The willingness and ability of a consumer to pay for a good or service is fundamentally a function of consumers' tastes and preferences, and income and wealth. What all this implies, of course, is that in market economies the more well-to-do participants have greater command over goods and services than consumers of more modest means.

While price rationing is a fundamental characteristic of market economies, it is not the only way to allocate goods and services that are in short supply. Alternative rationing mechanisms are necessary when the market is constrained from performing this function. Under what circumstances might the market price fail to increase to eliminate a shortage?

PRICE CEILINGS

At various times, and under a variety of circumstances, state and federal governments have found it necessary to "interfere" in the market. This interference has sometimes involved measures that short-circuit the price-rationing function of markets. Government officials accomplish this by prohibiting price increases to eliminate shortages when they arise. A ban on price increases above a certain level is called a *price ceiling*. The rationale underlying the imposition of a price ceiling typically revolves around the issue of "fairness." Sometimes such interference is justified, but more often than not price ceilings result in unintended negative consequences. To understand what is involved, consider Figure 3.21.

Definition: A price ceiling is a maximum price for a good or service that has been legally imposed on firms in an industry.

Figure 3.21 depicts the situation of excess demand $Q_1' - Q_1''$ at price P_1 arising from a decrease in the supply. Of course, the excess demand might also have arisen from an increase in the demand for a good or service. Figure 3.21 might be used to illustrate the market for consumer goods and services in the United States during World War II. As resources were shifted into the production of military goods and services to prosecute the war effort, fewer commodities were available for domestic consumption. If the

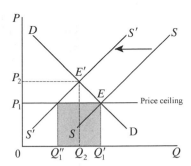

FIGURE 3.22   Market intervention: the effects
of price ceilings in times of shortage.

government had done nothing, prices on a wide range of consumer goods
(gasoline, meat, sugar, butter, automobile tires, etc.) would have risen
sharply from P_1 to P_2. Without price controls, the equilibrium quantity
would have fallen from Q_1' to Q_2. Thus, the rationing function of prices
would have guaranteed that only the well-to-do had access to available,
nonmilitary commodities. In the interest of "fairness," and to maintain
morale on the home front, the government imposed *price ceilings*, such as
P_1 in Figure 3.21, on a wide range of consumer goods.

The imposition of a price ceiling means shortages will not be automatically eliminated by increases in price. With price ceilings, the price-rationing
mechanism is not permitted to operate. Some other mechanism for allocating available supplies of consumer goods is required. When shortages
were created by the imposition of price ceilings during World War II, the
federal government instituted a program of *ration coupons* to distribute
available supplies of consumer goods. Ration coupons are coupons or
tickets that entitle the holder to purchase a given amount of a particular
good or service during a given time period. During World War II, families
were issued ration coupons monthly to purchase a limited quantities of
gasoline, meat, butter, and so on.

Definition: Ration coupons are coupons or tickets that entitle the holder
to purchase a given amount of a particular good or service during a given
time period.

It should be noted that the use of ration coupons to bypass the price-
rationing mechanism of the market will be effective as long as no trading
in ration coupons is all owed. If transactions in trading coupons are not
effectively prohibited, the results will be almost identical to a market-driven
outcome. Illegal transactions are referred to as "black markets." Individuals who are willing and able to pay will simply bid up the price of coupons
and eliminate the price differential between the market and ceiling prices.

In addition to ration coupons, there are a variety of other non–price
rationing mechanisms. Perhaps the most common of all such non–
price rationing mechanisms is *queuing*, or waiting in line. This was the

non–price rationing mechanism that arose in response to the decision by Congress to impose a price ceiling of 57¢ per gallon of unleaded gasoline following the 1973–74 OPEC embargo on shipments of crude oil to the United States.

Definition: Queuing is a non–price rationing mechanism that involves waiting in line.

Analytically, higher crude oil prices resulted in a left-shift in the supply of curve of gasoline (why?). Without the price ceiling, the result would have been a sharp increase of gasoline prices at the pump, which the Congress deemed to be "unfair." As a result, shortages of gasoline developed. Since the price rationing mechanism was not permitted to operate, there were very long lines at gas stations. Under the circumstances, gasoline still went to drivers willing and able to pay the price, which in this case, in addition to the pump price, included the opportunity cost of waiting in line for hours on end.

Another version of queuing is the *waiting list*. Waiting lists are prevalent in metropolitan areas with rent control laws. Rent control is a price ceiling on residential apartments. When controlled rents are below market clearing rents, a shortage of rent-controlled apartments is created. Prospective tenants are placed on a waiting list to obtain apartments as housing units become available. Rent controls were initially imposed during World War II. With the end of the war and the return of the GIs, and the subsequent baby boom, the demand curve for rental housing units soared. Elected politicians, sensing the pulse of their constituency, decided to continue with rent controls in some form, no doubt intoning the "fairness" mantra."

The initial result was a serious housing shortage in urban centers. Applicants were placed on waiting lists, but the next available rental units were slow to materialize. Other non–price rationing mechanisms included so-called *key money* (bribes paid by applicants to landlords to move up on the waiting list), the requirement that prospective tenants purchase worthless furniture at inflated prices, exorbitant, non refundable *security deposits*, and, of course, so-called *favored customers* or individuals who receive special treatment. One of the more despicable incarnations of the favored customer relates to racial, religious, and other forms of group discrimination.

Definition: A favored customer is an individual who receives special treatment.

Rent controls tend to create housing shortages that become more severe over time. Population growth shifts the demand for rental units to the right, which tends to exacerbate shortages in the rental housing market. What is more, if permitted rent increases do not keep pace with rising maintenance costs, fuel bills, and taxes, the supply of rental units may actually decline as landlords abandoned unprofitable buildings. This was particularly notable in New York City in the 1960s and 1970s, when apartment buildings abandoned by landlords in the face of rising operating costs transformed the

South Bronx into an area reminiscent of war-ravaged Berlin in 1945. Rent stabilization in the cities encouraged the development of suburban communities, which ultimately led to "urban sprawl."

Another tactic for dealing with the economic problems associated with rent controls was the genesis, at least in New York City, of the cooperative. "Co-ops," which are not subject to rent controls, are former rental units in apartment buildings. Ownership of shares in the corporation convey the right to occupy an apartment. The prices of these shares are market determined. Unfortunately, the transformation of rental units into co-ops and office space further exacerbated New York City's housing shortage.

Just why rent controls in New York City have persisted for so long is understandable. To begin with, landlords are a particularly unlikable lot. Second, there are many more tenants than landlords, and each tenant has a vote. Pleasing this population is a lure not easily overlooked by politicians, whose planning horizon tends to extend only as far as the next election.

But there is some good news. Having recognized the fundamental flaws associated with interfering in the housing market, newer generations of politicians, obliged to deal with the problems of inner-city blight in part created by rent controls have undertaken to revitalize urban centers. Among these measures has been the elimination or dramatic reduction in the number of rental units subject to price ceilings. The result has been a resurgence in new rental housing construction, which has put downward pressure on rents (why?).

Problem 3.9. The market demand and supply equations for a product are

$$Q_D = 300 - 3P$$
$$Q_S = 100 + 5P$$

where Q is quantity and P is price.
a. What are the equilibrium price and quantity for this product?
b. Suppose that an increase in consumer income resulted in the new demand equation

$$Q_D = 420 - 3P$$

What are the new equilibrium price and quantity for this product?
c. Suppose the government enacts legislation that imposes a price ceiling equivalent to the original equilibrium price. What is the result of this legislation?

Solution
a. Equilibrium is characterized by the condition $Q_D = Q_S$ Substituting, we have

$$300 - 3 = 100 + 5P$$

$$P^* = \$25$$

$$Q^* = 300 - 3(25) = 100 + 5(25) = 225$$

b. Substituting the new demand and supply equations into the equilibrium equations yields

$$420 - 3P = 100 + 5P$$

$$P^* = 40$$

$$Q^* = 420 - 3(40) = 100 + 5(40) = 300$$

c. At the price ceiling of $P = \$25$ the quantity demand is

$$Q_D = 420 - 3P = 420 - 3(25) = 345$$

At the price ceiling the quantity supplied is

$$Q_S = 100 + 5P = 100 + 5(25) = 225$$

Based on these results, there is a shortage in this market of

$$Q_D - Q_S = 345 - 225 = 120$$

PRICE FLOORS

The counterpart to price ceilings is the price floor. Whereas price ceilings are designed to keep prices from rising above some legal maximum, price floors are designed to keep prices from falling below some legal minimum. Perhaps the most notable examples of prices floors are agricultural price supports and minimum wages. This situation is depicted in Figure 3.22.

The situation depicted in Figure 3.22 is that of an excess supply (surplus) for a commodity, say tobacco, resulting from an increase in supply. Of course, the excess supply might also have arisen from a decrease in the demand. Here, the government is committed to maintaining a minimum tobacco price at P_1, perhaps for the purpose of assuring tobacco farmers a minimum level of income. The result of a price floor is to create an excess supply of tobacco of $Q_1'' - Q_1'$. In the absence of a price floor, the equilibrium price of tobacco would have fallen from P_1 to P_2 and the equilibrium quantity would have increased from Q_1' to Q_2. In the labor market, price floors in the form of minimum wage legislation are ostensibly designed to provide unskilled workers with a "living wage," although the result is usually an increase in the unemployment rate of unskilled labor.

Definition: A price floor is a legally imposed minimum price that may be charged for a good or service.

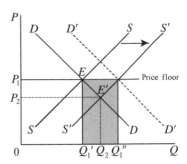

FIGURE 3.23 Market intervention: the effects of price floors in times of surplus.

The problem with price floors is that they create surpluses, which ultimately have to be dealt with. In the case of agricultural price supports, to maintain the price of the product at P_1 in Figure 3.22 the government has two policy options: either pay certain farmers not to plant, thereby keeping the supply curve from shifting from SS to $S'S'$, or enter the market and effectively buy up the surplus produce, which is analytically equivalent to shifting the demand curve from DD to $D'D'$. In either case, the taxpayer picks up the bill for subsidizing the income of the farmers for whose benefit the price floor has been imposed.

Actually, the tobacco farmer case illustrates the often schizophrenic nature of government policies. On the one hand, the federal government goes to great lengths to extol the evils of smoking, while at the same time subsidizing tobacco production.

Minimum wage legislation also impacts the taxpayer. Suppose, for example, that there is an increase in unskilled labor in a particular industry because of immigration. This results in a shift to the right of the labor supply curve, which could drive the wage rate below the mandated minimum. A surplus of unskilled labor leads to unemployment. This is a serious result, since not only would many unskilled workers be willing to accept a wage below the minimum (as opposed to no wage at all), but these workers now are hard put to obtain on-the-job experience needed to enable them to earn higher wages and income in the future. The taxpayer picks up the bill for many of these unemployed workers, who show up on state welfare rolls.

Problem 3.10. Consider the following demand and supply equations for the product of a perfectly competitive industry:

$$Q_D = 25 - 3P$$

$$Q_S = 10 + 2P$$

a. Determine the market equilibrium price and quantity algebraically.

b. Suppose that government regulatory authorities imposed a "price floor" on this product of $P = \$4$. What would be the quantity supplied and quantity demanded of this product? How would you characterize the situation in this market?

Solution

a. Equilibrium in this market occurs when, at some price, quantity supplied equals quantity demanded. Algebraically, this condition is given as $Q_D = Q_S$. Substituting into the equilibrium condition we get

$$25 - 3P = 10 + 2P$$

$$P* = \frac{15}{5} = 3$$

The equilibrium quantity is determined by substituting the equilibrium price into either the demand or the supply equation.

$$Q_D^* = 25 - 3(3) = 25 - 9 = 16$$

$$Q_S^* = 10 + 2(3) = 10 + 6 = 16$$

b. At a mandated price of $P = \$4$, the quantity demanded and quantity supplied can be determined by substituting this price into the demand and supply equations and solving:

$$Q_D = 25 - 3(4) = 25 - 12 = 13$$

$$Q_S = 10 + 2(4) = 10 + 8 = 18$$

Since $Q_S > Q_D$, these equations describe a situation of excess supply (surplus) of 5 units of output.

THE ALLOCATING FUNCTION OF PRICES

While the price rationing mechanism of the market may be viewed as a short-run phenomenon, the allocating function of price tends to be a long-run phenomenon. In the long run, all price and nonprice demand and supply determinants are assumed to be variable. In the long run, price changes signal consumers and producers to devote more or less of their resources to the consumption and production of goods and services. In other words, free markets determine not only final distribution of final goods and services, but also what goods and services are produced and how productive resources will be allocated for their production.

Definition: The allocating function of prices refers to the process by which productive resources are reallocated between and among production processes in response to changes in the prices of goods and services.

To see this, consider the increase in the demand for restaurant meals in the United States that developed during the 1970s. This increase in demand for restaurant meals resulted in an increase in the price of eating out, which increased the profits of restauranteurs. The increase in profits attracted investment capital into the industry. As the output of restaurant meals increased, the increased demand for restaurant workers resulted in higher wages and benefits. This attracted workers into the restaurant industry and away from other industries, where the diminished demand for labor resulted in lower wages and benefits.

CHAPTER REVIEW

The interaction of supply and demand is the primary mechanism for the allocations of goods, services, and productive resources in market economies. A *market system* comprises markets for productive resources and markets for final goods and services.

The *law of demand* states that a *change in quantity demanded* of a good or service is inversely related to a change in the selling price, other factors (*demand determinants*) remaining unchanged. Other demand determinants include income, tastes and preferences, prices of related goods and services, number of buyers, and price expectations.

The law of demand is illustrated graphically with a *demand curve*, which slopes downward from left to right, with price on the vertical axis and quantity on the horizontal axis. A change in the quantity demanded of a good, service, or productive resource resulting from a change in the selling price is depicted as a *movement along the demand curve*. A *change in demand* for a good or service results from a change in a nonprice demand determinant, other factors held constant, including the price of the good or service under consideration. An increase in per-capita income, for example, results in an increase in the demand for most goods and services and is illustrated as a *shift of the demand curve* to the right.

The *law of supply* states that a *change in quantity supplied* of a good or service is directly related to the selling price, other factors (supply determinants) held constant. Other *supply determinants* include factor costs, technology, prices of other goods the producers can supply, number of firms producing the good or service, price expectations, and weather conditions.

The law of supply is illustrated graphically with a *supply curve*, which slopes upward from left to right with price on the vertical axis and quantity on the horizontal axis. A change in the quantity supplied of a good or service resulting from a change in the selling price is depicted as a *movement along the supply curve*. A *change in supply* of a good or service results from a change in some other supply demand determinant, other factors held constant, including the price of the good or service under consideration. An increase in the number of firms producing the good, for example, will result in a *shift of the supply curve* to the right.

Market equilibrium exists when the quantity supplied is equal to quantity demanded. The price that equates quantity supplied with quantity demanded is called the *equilibrium price*. If the price rises above the equilibrium price, the quantity supplied will exceed the quantity demanded, resulting in a *surplus* (excess supply). If the price falls below the equilibrium price, quantity demanded will exceed the quantity supplied, resulting in a *shortage* (excess demand).

An increase or a decrease in price to clear the market of a surplus or a shortage is referred to as the *rationing function* of prices. The rationing function is considered to be a short-run phenomenon. In the short run, one or more explanatory variables are assumed to be constant. A *price ceiling* is a government-imposed maximum price for a good or service produced by a given industry. Price ceilings create market shortages that require a non–price rationing mechanism to allocate available supplies of goods and services. There are a number of non-price rationing mechanisms, including *ration coupons*, *queuing*, *favored customers*, and *black markets*.

The *allocating* function of price, on the other hand, is assumed to be a long-run phenomenon. In the long run, all explanatory variables are assumed to be variable. In the long run, price changes signal consumers and producers to devote more or less of their resources to the consumption and production of goods and services. In other words, the allocating function of price allows for changes in all demand and supply determinants.

KEY TERMS AND CONCEPTS

Allocating function of price   The process by which productive resources are reallocated between and among production processes in response to changes in the prices of goods and services.

Change in demand   Results from a change in one or more demand determinants (income, tastes, prices of complements, prices of substitutes, price expectations, income expectations, number of consumers, etc.) that causes an increase in purchases of a good or service at all prices. An increase in demand is illustrated diagrammatically as a right-shift in the entire demand curve. A decrease in demand is illustrated diagrammatically as a left-shift in the entire demand curve.

Change in supply   Results from a change in one or more supply determinants (prices of productive inputs, technology, price expectations, taxes and subsidies, number of firms in the industry, etc.) that causes an increase in the supply of a good or service at all prices. An increase in supply is illustrated diagrammatically as a right-shift in the entire supply curve. A decrease in supply curve is illustrated diagrammatically as a left-shift in the entire supply curve.

Change in quantity demanded Results from a change in the price of a good or service. As the price of a good or service rises (falls), the quantity demanded decreases (increases). An increase in the quantity demanded of a good or service is illustrated diagrammatically as a movement from the left to the right along a downward-sloping demand curve. A decrease in the quantity demanded of a good or service is illustrated diagrammatically as a movement from the right to the left along a downward-sloping demand curve.

Change in quantity supplied Results from a change in the price of a good or service. As the price of a good or service rises (falls), the quantity supplied increases (decreases). An increase in the quantity supplied of a good or service is illustrated diagrammatically as a movement from the left to the right to left along an upward-sloping demand curve. A decrease in the quantity supplied of a good or service is illustrated diagrammatically as a movement from the right to the left along an upward-sloping supply curve.

Demand curve A diagrammatic illustration of the quantities of a good or service that consumers are willing and able to purchase at various prices, assuming that the influence of other demand determinants remaining unchanged.

Demand determinants Nonprice factors that influence consumers' decisions to purchase a good or service. Demand determinants include, income, tastes, prices of complements, prices of substitutes, price expectations, income expectations, and number of consumers.

Equilibrium price The price at which the quantity demanded equals the quantity supplied of that good or service.

Favored customer Describing a non–price rationing mechanism in which certain individuals receive special treatment. In the extreme, the favored customer as a form of non–price rationing may take the form of racial, religious, and other forms of group discrimination.

Law of demand The change in the quantity demanded of a good or a service is inversely related to its selling price, all other influences affecting demand remaining unchanged (ceteris paribus).

Law of supply The change in the quantity supplied of a good or a service is positively related to its selling price, all other influences affecting supply remaining unchanged (*ceteris paribus*).

Market equilibrium Conditions under which the quantity supplied of a good or a service is equal to quantity demanded of that same good or service. Market equilibrium occurs at the equilibrium price.

Market power Refers to the ability to influence the market price of a good by shifting the demand curve or the supply curve of a good or a service. In perfectly competitive markets, individual consumers and individual suppliers do not have market power.

Movement along the demand curve The result of a change in the quantity demanded of a good or a service.

Movement along the supply curve   The result of a change in the quantity supplied of a good or service.

Price ceiling   The maximum price that firms in an industry can charge for a good or service. Typically imposed by governments to achieve an objective perceived as socially desirable, price ceilings often result in inefficient economic, and social, outcomes.

Price floor   A legally imposed minimum price that may be charged for a good or service.

Queuing   A non–price rationing mechanism that involves waiting in line.

Ration coupons   Coupons or tickets that entitle the holder to purchase a given amount of a particular good or service during a given time period. Ration coupons are sometimes used when the price rationing mechanism of the market is not permitted to operate, as when, say, the government has imposed a price ceiling.

Rationing function of price   The increase or a decrease in the market price to eliminate a surplus or a shortage of a good or service. The rationing function is considered to operate in the short run because other demand determinants are assumed to be constant.

Shift of the demand curve   The result of a change in the demand for a good or a service.

Shift of the supply curve   The result of a change in the supply of a good or a service.

Shortage   The result that occurs when the quantity demanded of a good or a service exceeds the quantity supplied of that same good or service. Shortages exist when the market price is below the equilibrium (market clearing) price.

Supply curve   A diagrammatic illustration of the quantities of a good or service firms are willing and able to supply at various prices, assuming that the influence of other supply determinants remains unchanged.

Surplus   The result that occurs the quantity supplied of a good or a service exceeds the quantity demanded of that same good or service. Surpluses exist when the market price is above the equilibrium (market clearing) price.

Waiting list   A version of queuing.

CHAPTER QUESTIONS

3.1 Define and give an example of each of the following demand terms and concepts. Illustrate diagrammatically a change in each.
   a. Quantity demanded
   b. Demand
   c. Market demand curve

d. Normal good

e. Inferior good

f. Substitute good

g. Complementary good

h. Price expectation

i. Income expectation

j. Advertising

k. Population

3.2 Define and give an example of each of the following supply terms and concepts. Illustrate diagrammatically a change in each.

a. Quantity supplied

b. Supply

c. Market supply curve

d. Factor price

e. Technology

f. Price expectation

g. Advertising

h. Substitute good

i. Complementary good

j. Taxes

k. Subsidies

l. Number of firms

3.3 Does the following statement violate the law of demand? The quantity demanded of diamonds declines as the price of diamonds declines because the prestige associated with owning diamonds also declines.

3.4 In recent years there has been a sharp increase in commercial and recreational fishing in the waters around Long Island. Illustrate the effect of "overfishing" on inflation-adjusted seafood prices at restaurants in the Long Island area.

3.5 New York City is a global financial center. In the late 1990s the financial and residential real estate markets reached record high price levels. Are these markets related? Explain.

3.6 Large labor unions always support higher minimum wage legislation even though no union member earns just the minimum wage. Explain.

3.7 Discuss the effect of a frost in Florida, which damaged a significant portion of the orange crop, on each of the following

a. The price of Florida oranges

b. The price of California oranges

c. The price of tangerines

d. The price of orange juice

e. The price of apple juice

3.8 Discuss the effect of an imposition of a wine import tariff on the price of California wine.

3.9 Explain and illustrate diagrammatically how the rent controls that were imposed during World War II exacerbated the New York City housing shortage during the 1960s and 1970s.

3.10 Explain what is meant by the rationing function of prices.

3.11 Discuss the possible effect of a price ceiling.

3.12 The use of ration coupons to eliminate a shortage can be effective only if trading ration coupons is effectively prohibited. Explain.

3.13 Scalping tickets to concerts and sporting events is illegal in many states. Yet, it may be argued that both the buyer and seller of "scalped" tickets benefit from the transaction. Why, then, is scalping illegal? Who is really being "scalped"? Explain.

3.14 The U.S. Department of Agriculture (USDA) is committed to a system of agricultural price supports. To maintain the market price of certain agricultural products at a specified level, the USDA has two policy options. What are they? Illustrate diagrammatically the market effects of both policies.

3.15 Minimum wage legislation represents what kind of market interference? What is the government's justification for minimum wage legislation? Do you agree? Who gains from minimum wage legislation? Who loses?

3.16 Explain the allocating function of prices. How does this differ from the rationing function of prices?

CHAPTER EXERCISES

3.1 Yell-O Yew-Boats, Ltd. produces a popular brand of pointy birds called Blue Meanies. Consider the demand and supply equations for Blue Meanies:

$$Q_{D,x} = 150 - 2P_x + 0.001I + 1.5P_y$$

$$Q_{S,x} = 60 + 4P_x - 2.5W$$

where Q_x = monthly per-family consumption of Blue Meanies
$\quad P_x$ = price per unit of Blue Meanies
$\quad I$ = median annual per-family income = $25,000
$\quad P_y$ = price per unit of Apple Bonkers = $5.00
$\quad W$ = hourly per-worker wage rate = $8.60

a. What type of good is an Apple Bonker?
b. What are the equilibrium price and quantity of Blue Meanies?
c. Suppose that median per-family income increases by $6,000. What are the new equilibrium price and quantity of Blue Meanies?
d. Suppose that in addition to the increase in median per-family ncome, collective bargaining by Blue Meanie Local #666 resulted in

a $2.40 hourly increase in the wage rate. What are the new equilib
rium price and quantity?

e. In a single diagram, illustrate your answers to parts b, c, and d.

3.2 Consider the following demand and supply equations for sugar:

$$Q_D = 1,000 - 1,000P$$

$$Q_S = 800 + 1,000P$$

where P is the price of sugar per pound and Q is thousands of pounds of
sugar.

a. What are the equilibrium price and quantity for sugar?

b. Suppose that the government wishes to subsidize sugar production by
placing a floor on sugar prices of $0.20 per pound. What would be the
relationship between the quantity supplied and quantity demand for
sugar?

3.3 Occidental Pacific University is a large private university in
California that is known for its strong athletics program, especially in
football. At the request of the dean of the College of Arts & Sciences, a
professor from the economics department estimated a demand equation
for student enrollment at the university

$$Q_x = 5,000 - 0.5P_x + 0.1I + 0.25P_y$$

where Q_x is the number of full-time students, P_x is the tuition charged
per full-time student per semester, I is real gross domestic product (GDP)
($ billions) and P_y is the tuition charged per full-time student per semester
by Oriental Atlantic University in Maryland, Occidental Pacific's closest
competitor on the grid iron.

a. Suppose that full-time enrollment at Occidental is 4,000 students. If
$I = $7,500$ and $P_y = $6,000$, how much tuition is Occidental charging
its full-time students per semester?

b. The administration is considering a $750,000 promotional campaign
to bolster admissions and tuition revenues. The economics professor
believes that the promotional campaign will change the demand
equation to

$$Q_x = 5,100 - 0.45P_x + 0.1I + 0.25P_y$$

If the professor is correct, what will Occidental's full-time enrollment
be?

c. Assuming no change in real GDP and no change in full-time tuition
charged by Oriental, will the promotional campaign be effective?
(*Hint*: Compare Occidental's tuition revenues before and after the
promotional campaign.)

d. The director of Occidental's athletic department claims that the increase in enrollment resulted from the football team's NCAA Division I national championship. Is this claim reasonable? How would it show up in the new demand equation?

3.4 The market demand and supply equations for a commodity are

$$Q_D = 50 - 10P$$

$$Q_S = 20 + 2.5P$$

a. What is the equilibrium price and equilibrium quantity?
b. Suppose the government imposes a price ceiling on the commodity of $3.00 and demand increases to $Q_D = 75 - 10P$. What is the impact on the market of the government's action?
c. In a single diagram, illustrate your answers to parts a and b.

3.5 The market demand for brand X has been estimated as

$$Q_x = 1,500 - 3P_x - 0.05I - 2.5P_y + 7.5P_z$$

where P_x is the price of brand X, I is per-capita income, P_y is the price of brand Y, and P_z is the price of brand Z. Assume that $P_x = \$2$, $I = \$20,000$, $P_y = \$4$, and $P_z = \$4$.

a. With respect to changes in per-capita income, what kind of good is brand X?
b. How are brands X and Y related?
c. How are brands X and Z related?
d. How are brands Z and Y related?
e. What is the market demand for brand X?

SELECTED READINGS

Baumol, W. J., and A. S. Blinder. Microeconomics: Principles and Policy, 8th ed. New York: Dryden, 1999.

Boulding, K. E. Economic Analysis, Vol. 1, Microeconomics. New York: Harper & Row, 1966.

Case, K. E., and R. C. Fair. Principles of Macroeconomics, 5th ed. Upper Saddle River, NJ: Prentice Hall, 1999.

Green, W. H. Econometric Analysis, 3rd ed. Upper Saddle River, NJ: Prentice-Hall, 1997.

Gujarati, D. Basic Econometrics, 3rd ed. New York: McGraw-Hill, 1995.

Marshall, A. Principles of Economics, 8th ed. London: Macmillan, 1920.

Ramanathan, R. Introductory Econometrics with Applications, 4th ed. New York: Dryden Press, 1998.

Samuelson, P. A., and W. D. Nordhans. Economics, 12th ed. New York: McGraw-Hill, 1985.

Silberberg, E. The Structure of Economics: A Mathematical Analysis, 2nd ed. New York: McGraw-Hill, 1990.

APPENDIX 3A

FORMAL DERIVATION OF THE DEMAND CURVE

The objective of the consumer is to maximize utility subject to a budget constraint. The constrained utility maximization model may be formally written as

$$\text{Maximize: } U = U(Q_1, Q_2) \tag{3A.1a}$$

$$\text{Subject to: } M = P_1 Q_1 + P_2 Q_2 \tag{3A.1b}$$

where P_1 and P_2 are the prices of goods Q_1 and Q_2, respectively, and M is money income. The Lagrangian equation (see Chapter 2) for this problem is

$$\mathcal{L} = U(Q_1, Q_2) + \lambda(M - P_1 Q_1 - P_2 Q_2) \tag{3A.2}$$

The first-order conditions for utility maximization are

$$\mathcal{L}_1 = U_1 - \lambda P_1 = 0 \tag{3A.3a}$$

$$\mathcal{L}_2 = U_2 - \lambda P_2 = 0 \tag{3A.3b}$$

$$\mathcal{L}_\lambda = M - P_1 Q_1 - P_2 Q_2 = 0 \tag{3A.3c}$$

where $\mathcal{L}_i = \partial\mathcal{L}/\partial Q_i$ and $U_i = \partial U/\partial Q_i$. Assuming that the second-order conditions for constrained utility maximization are satisfied,[5] the solutions to the system of Equations (3A.3) may be written as

$$Q_1 = Q_{M,1}(P_1, P_2, M) \tag{3A.4a}$$

$$Q_2 = Q_{M,2}(P_1, P_2, M) \tag{3A.4b}$$

$$\lambda = \lambda_M(P_1, P_2, M) \tag{3A.4c}$$

Note that the parameters in Equations (3A.4) are prices and money income. Equations (3A.4a) and (3A.4b) indicate the consumption levels for any given set of prices and money income. Thus, these equations are commonly referred to as the *money-held-constant demand curves*.

Dividing Equation (3A.4a) by (3A.4b) yields

$$\frac{U_1}{U_2} = \frac{P_1}{P_2} \tag{3A.5}$$

or

$$\frac{U_1}{P_1} = \frac{U_2}{P_2} \tag{3A.6}$$

[5] For an excellent discussion of the mathematics of utility maximization see Eugene Silberberg (1990), Chapter 10.

Equation (3A.6) asserts that to maximize consumption, the consumer must allocate budget expenditures such that the marginal utility obtained from the last dollar spent on good Q_1 is the same as the marginal utility obtained from the last dollar spent on Q_2. For the n-good case, Equation (3A.6) may be generalized as

$$\frac{U_1}{P_1} = \frac{U_2}{P_2} = \ldots = \frac{U_n}{P_n} \tag{3A.7}$$

Problem 3A.1. Suppose that a consumer's utility function is $U = Q_1^2 Q_2^2$.
a. If $P_1 = 5$, $P_2 = 10$, and the consumer's money income is $M = 1,000$, what are the optimal values of Q_1 and Q_2?
b. Derive the consumer's demand equations for goods Q_1 and Q_2. Verify that the demand curves are downward sloping and convex with respect to the origin.

Solution
a. The consumer's budget constraint is

$$1,000 = 5Q_1 + 10Q_2$$

The Lagrangian equation for this problem is

$$\mathcal{L} = Q_1^2 Q_2^2 + \lambda(1,000 - 5Q_1 - 10Q_2)$$

The first-order conditions are
1. $\mathcal{L}_1 = 2Q_1 Q_2^2 - 5\lambda = 0$
2. $\mathcal{L}_2 = 2Q_1^2 Q_2 - 10\lambda = 0$
3. $\mathcal{L}_\lambda = 1,000 - 5Q_1 - 10Q_2 = 0$
Dividing the first equation by the second yields

$$\frac{2Q_1 Q_2^2}{2Q_1^2 Q_2} = \frac{5}{10}$$

$$\frac{Q_2}{Q_1} = \frac{1}{2}$$

$$Q_1 = 2Q_2$$

Substituting this result into the budget constraint yields

$$1,000 = 5(2Q_2) + 10Q_2 = 20Q_2$$

$$Q_2^* = 50$$

Substituting this result into the budget constraint yields

$$1,000 = 5Q_1 + 10(50) = 5Q_1 + 500$$

$$5Q_1 = 500$$

$$Q_1^* = 100$$

b. From the optimality condition [Equation (3A.5)]:

$$\frac{U_1}{U_2} = \frac{P_1}{P_2}$$

From the consumer's utility function this becomes

$$\frac{Q_2}{Q_1} = \frac{P_1}{P_2}$$

$$Q_2 = \left(\frac{P_1}{P_2}\right)Q_1$$

Substituting this result into the budget constraint yields

$$M = P_1Q_1 + P_2\left(\frac{P_1}{P_2}\right)Q_1$$

$$= P_1Q_1 + P_1Q_1 = 2P_1Q_1$$

$$Q_1 = \frac{M}{2P_1}$$

For $M = 1,000$, the consumer's demand equation for Q_1 is

$$Q_1 = \frac{500}{P_1}$$

Similarly, the consumer's demand equation for Q_2 is

$$Q_2 = \frac{500}{P_2}$$

For a demand curve to be downward sloping, the first derivative with respect to price must be negative. For a demand curve to be convex with respect to the origin, the second derivative with respect to price must be positive. The first and second derivatives of Q_1 with respect to P_1 are

$$\frac{dQ_1}{dP_1} = -\frac{500}{P_1^2} < 0$$

$$\frac{d^2Q_1}{dP_1^2} = \frac{2(500)}{P_1^3} = \frac{1,000}{P_1^3} > 0$$

Similarly for Q_2

$$\frac{dQ_2}{dP_2} = -\frac{500}{P_2^2} < 0$$

$$\frac{d^2Q_2}{dP_2^2} = \frac{2(500)}{P_2^3} = \frac{1,000}{P_2^3} > 0$$

4

ADDITIONAL TOPICS IN DEMAND THEORY

Although the law of demand tells us that consumers will respond to a price decline (increase) by purchasing more (less) of a given good or service, it is important for a manager to know how sensitive is the demand for the firm's product, given changes in the price of the product and other demand determinants. The decision maker must be aware of the degree to which consumers respond to, say, a change in the product's price, or to a change in some other explanatory variable. Is it possible to derive a numerical measurement that will summarize this kind of sensitivity, and if so, how can the manager make use of such information to improve the performance of the firm? It is to this question that we now turn our attention.

PRICE ELASTICITY OF DEMAND

In this section we consider the sensitivity of a change in the quantity demanded of a good or service given a change in the price of the product. Recall from Chapter 3 the simple linear, market demand function

$$Q_D = b_0 + b_1 P \qquad (4.1)$$

where, by the law of demand, it is assumed that $b_1 < 0$. One possible candidate for a measure of sensitivity of quantity demanded to changes in the price of the product is, of course, the slope of the demand function, which in this case is b_1, where

$$b_1 = \frac{\Delta Q_D}{\Delta P}$$

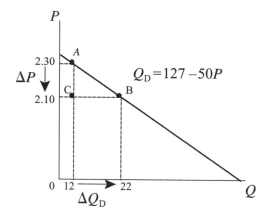

FIGURE 4.1   The linear demand curve.

Consider, for example, the linear demand equation

$$Q_D = 127 - 50P \qquad (4.2)$$

Equation (4.2) is illustrated in Figure 4.1. The slope of this demand curve is calculated quite easily as we move along the curve from point A to point B. The slope of Equation (4.2) between these two points is calculated as

$$
\begin{aligned}
b_1 &= \frac{\Delta Q_D}{\Delta P} = \frac{Q_2 - Q_1}{P_2 - P_1} \\
&= \frac{22 - 12}{2.10 - 2.30} = \frac{10}{-0.20} = -50
\end{aligned}
\qquad (4.3)
$$

That is, for every $1 decrease (increase) in the price, the quantity demanded increases (decreases) by 50 units.

Although the slope might appear to be an appropriate measure of the degree of consumer responsiveness given a change in the price of the commodity, it suffers from at least two significant weaknesses. First, the slope of a linear demand curve is invariant with respect to price; that is, its value is the same regardless of whether the firm charges a high price or a low price for its product. Since its value never changes, the slope is incapable of providing insights into the possible repercussions of changes in the firm's pricing policy. Suppose, for example, that an automobile dealership is offering a $1,000 rebate on the purchase of a particular model. The dealership has estimated a linear demand function, which suggests that the rebate will result in a monthly increase in sales of 10 automobiles. But, a $1,000 rebate on the purchase of a $10,000 automobile, or 10%, is a rather significant price decline, while a $1,000 rebate on the same model priced at $100,000, or 1%, is relatively insignificant. In the first instance, potential buyers are likely to view the lower price as a genuine bargain. In the second instance, buyers may view the rebate as a mere marketing ploy.

Suppose, on the other hand, that instead of offering a $1,000 rebate on new automobile purchases, management offers a 10% rebate regardless of sticker price. How will this rebate affect unit sales? What impact will this rebate have on the dealership's total sales revenue? By itself, the constant value of the slope, which in this case is $\Delta Q_D/\Delta P = 10/{-}1,000 = -0.01$ provides no clue to whether it will be in management's best interest to offer the rebate.

The second weakness of the slope as a measure of responsiveness is that its value is dependent on the units of measurement. Consider, again, the situation depicted in Figure 4.1, where the value of the slope is $b_1 = \Delta Q_D/\Delta P = (22 - 12)/(2.10 - 2.30) = 10/{-}0.2 = -50$. Suppose, on the other hand, that prices had been measured in hundredths (cents) rather than in dollars. In that case the value of the slope would have been calculated as $b_1 = \Delta Q_D/\Delta P = (22 - 12)/(210 - 230) = 10/{-}20 = -0.50$. Although we are dealing with identically the same problem, by changing the units of measurement we derive two different numerical measures of consumer sensitivity to a price change. To overcome the problem associated with the arbitrary selection of units of measurement, economists use the concept of the price elasticity of demand.

Definition: The price elasticity of demand is the percentage change in the quantity demanded of a good or a service given a percentage change in its price.

As we will soon see, the price elasticity of demand overcomes both weaknesses associated with the slope as a measure of consumer responsiveness to a price change. Symbolically, the price elasticity of demand is given as

$$E_p = \frac{\%\Delta Q_D}{\%\Delta P} \tag{4.4}$$

Before discussing the advantages of using the price elasticity of demand in preference to slope as a measure of sales responsiveness to a change in price, we will consider how the percentage in Equation (4.4) should be calculated. It is conventional to divide the change in the value of a variable by its starting value. We might, for example, define a percentage change in price as

$$\%\Delta P = \frac{P_2 - P_1}{P_1}$$

There is nothing particularly sacrosanct about this approach. We could easily have defined the percentage change in price as

$$\%\Delta P = \frac{P_2 - P_1}{P_2}$$

Clearly, the selection of the denominator to be used for calculating the percentage change depends on whether we are talking about a price increase or a price decrease. In terms of Figure 4.1, do we calculate percentage changes by starting at point A and moving to point B, or vice versa? The law of demand asserts only that changes in price and quantity demanded are inversely related; it does not specify direction. But, how we define a percentage change will affect the calculated value of the price elasticity of demand. For example, if we choose to move from point A to point B, the value of the price elasticity of demand is

$$E_p = \frac{(22-12)/12}{(2.10-2.30)/2.30}$$

$$= \frac{10/12}{-0.20/2.30} = \frac{0.833}{-0.087} = -9.57$$

On the other hand, if we calculate the price elasticity of demand in moving from point B to point A then

$$E_p = \frac{(12-22)/22}{(2.30-2.10)/2.10}$$

$$= \frac{-10/12}{0.20/2.10} = \frac{0.455}{-0.095} = -4.79$$

Problem 4.1. Suppose that the price elasticity of demand for a product is -2. If the price of this product fell by 5%, by what percentage would the quantity demanded for a product change?

Solution. The price elasticity of demand is given as

$$E_p = \frac{\%\Delta Q_D}{\%\Delta P}$$

Substituting, we write

$$-2 = \frac{\%\Delta Q_D}{-5}$$

$$\%\Delta Q_D = 10$$

PRICE ELASTICITY OF DEMAND: THE MIDPOINT FORMULA

It should be clear from Problem 4.1 that the choice of A or B as the starting point can have a significant impact on the calculated value of E_p. One way of overcoming this dilemma is to use the average value of Q_D and P as the point of reference in calculating the averages. The resulting expression for the price elasticity of demand is referred to as the midpoint formula. The derivation of the midpoint formula is

$$E_p = \frac{(Q_2 - Q_1)/[(Q_1 + Q_2)/2]}{(P_2 - P_1)/[(P_1 + P_2)/2]}$$

$$= \left(\frac{Q_2 - Q_1}{Q_1 + Q_2}\right)\left(\frac{P_2 - P_1}{P_1 + P_2}\right)$$

$$= \left(\frac{Q_2 - Q_1}{P_2 - P_1}\right)\left(\frac{P_1 + P_2}{Q_1 + Q_2}\right) \qquad (4.5)$$

$$= \left(\frac{\Delta Q}{\Delta P}\right)\left(\frac{P_1 + P_2}{Q_1 + Q_2}\right)$$

$$= b_1\left(\frac{P_1 + P_2}{Q_1 + Q_2}\right)$$

Using the data from the foregoing illustration, we find that the price elasticity of demand as we move from point A to point B is

$$E_p = \left(\frac{Q_2 - Q_1}{P_2 - P_1}\right)\left(\frac{P_1 + P_2}{Q_1 + Q_2}\right)$$

$$= \left(\frac{22 - 12}{2.10 - 2.30}\right)\left(\frac{2.30 + 2.10}{12 + 22}\right)$$

$$= \left(\frac{10}{-0.20}\right)\left(\frac{4.40}{34}\right) = -50 \times 0.129 = -6.45$$

On the other hand, moving from point B to point A yields identically the same result.

$$E_p = \left(\frac{Q_2 - Q_1}{P_2 - P_1}\right)\left(\frac{P_1 + P_2}{Q_1 + Q_2}\right)$$

$$= \left(\frac{12 - 22}{2.30 - 2.10}\right)\left(\frac{2.10 + 2.30}{22 + 12}\right)$$

$$= \left(\frac{-10}{0.20}\right)\left(\frac{4.40}{34}\right) = -6.45$$

The price elasticity of demand is always negative by the law of demand. When referring to the price elasticity of demand, however, it is conventional to refer to its absolute value. The reason is largely semantic. When an economist identifies one good as relatively more or less elastic than another good, reference is made to the absolute percentage change in the quantity demanded of the good or service, given some absolute percentage change in its price without reference to the nature of the relationship. Suppose, for example, that E_p of good X is calculated as –4, and that the value of E_p for good Y is calculated as –2, good X is "more elastic" than good Y because the consumer's response to a change in price is greater. Numerically, however, −4 is less than −2. To avoid this confusion arising from this inconsistency, the price elasticity of demand is typically indicted in terms of absolute values.

As a measure of consumer sensitivity, the price elasticity of demand overcomes the measurement problem that is inherent in the use of the slope. Elasticity measures are dimensionless in the sense that they are independent of the units of measurement. When prices are measured in dollars, the price elasticity of demand is calculated as

$$
E_p = \left(\frac{Q_2 - Q_1}{P_2 - P_1} \right) \left(\frac{P_1 + P_2}{Q_1 + Q_2} \right)
$$

$$
= \left(\frac{22 - 12}{2.10 - 2.30} \right) \left(\frac{2.30 + 2.10}{12 + 22} \right) = -6.45
$$

When measured in hundredths of dollars (cents), the price elasticity of demand is

$$
E_p = \left(\frac{Q_2 - Q_1}{P_2 - P_1} \right) \left(\frac{P_1 + P_2}{Q_1 + Q_2} \right)
$$

$$
= \left(\frac{22 - 12}{210 - 230} \right) \left(\frac{230 + 210}{12 + 22} \right)
$$

$$
= \left(\frac{10}{-20} \right) \left(\frac{440}{34} \right) = -0.50 \times 12.94 = -6.47
$$

Except for rounding, the answers are identical.

Problem 4.2. Suppose that the price and quantity demanded for a good are \$5 and 20 units, respectively. Suppose further that the price of the product increases to \$20 and the quantity demanded falls to 5 units. Calculate the price elasticity of demand.

Solution. Since we are given two price–quantity combinations, the price elasticity of demand may be calculated using the midpoint formula.

$$
E_p = \left(\frac{Q_2 - Q_1}{P_2 - P_1} \right) \left(\frac{P_1 + P_2}{Q_1 + Q_2} \right)
$$

$$
= \left(\frac{5 - 20}{20 - 5} \right) \left(\frac{5 + 20}{20 + 5} \right)
$$

$$
= \left(\frac{-15}{15} \right) \left(\frac{25}{25} \right) = -1.00
$$

Problem 4.3. At a price of \$25, the quantity demanded of good X is 500 units. Suppose that the price elasticity of demand is −1.85. If the price of the good increases to \$26, what will be the new quantity demanded of this good?

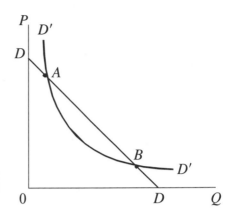

FIGURE 4.2 The midpoint formula obscures the shape of the underlying demand curve.

Solution. The midpoint formula for the price elasticity of demand is

$$E_p = \left(\frac{Q_2 - Q_1}{P_2 - P_1}\right)\left(\frac{P_1 + P_2}{Q_1 + Q_2}\right)$$

Substituting and solving for Q_2 yields

$$-1.85 = \left(\frac{Q_2 - 500}{26 - 25}\right)\left(\frac{25 + 26}{500 + Q_2}\right)$$

$$= \left(\frac{Q_2 - 500}{1}\right)\left(\frac{51}{500 + Q_2}\right) = \frac{51Q_2 - 25,500}{500 + Q_2}$$

$$-925 - 1.85Q_2 = 51Q_2 - 25,500$$

$$52.85Q_2 = 24,575$$

$$Q_2 = 465$$

PRICE ELASTICITY OF DEMAND: WEAKNESS OF THE MIDPOINT FORMULA

In spite of its advantages over the slope as a measure of sensitivity, the midpoint formula also suffers from a significant weakness. By taking averages, we obscure the underlying nature of the demand function. Using the midpoint formula to calculate the price elasticity of demand requires knowledge of only two price–quantity combinations along an unknown demand curve. To see this, consider Figure 4.2.

In Figure 4.2, both demand curves DD and $D'D'$ pass through points A and B. In both cases, the price elasticity of demand calculated by means of the midpoint formula is the same. In fact, the price elasticity of demand is an average elasticity along the cord AB. For this reason, the value of E_p calculated by means of the midpoint formula is sometimes referred to as the

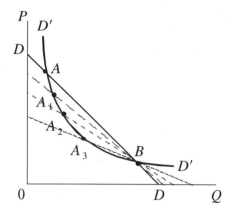

FIGURE 4.3 Estimates of the arc-price elasticity of demand are improved as the points along the demand curve are moved closer togther.

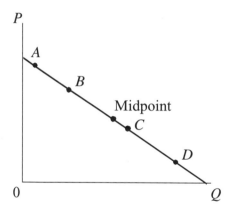

FIGURE 4.4 Demand is price elastic when it is calculated by using the midpoint formula for points above the midpoint, and price inelastic when it is calculated below the midpoint.

arc-price elasticity of demand. Note, however, that as point A is arbitrarily moved closer to point B along the true demand curve $D'D'$, the approximated value of the price elasticity of demand found by using the midpoint formula will approach its true value, which occurs when the two points converge at point B. This is illustrated in Figure 4.3.

The ability to calculate the price elasticity of demand on the basis of only two price–quantity combinations clearly is a source of strength of the midpoint formula. On the other hand, the arbitrary selection of these two points obscures the shape of the underlying demand function and will affect the calculated value of the price elasticity of demand. One solution to this problem is to calculate the price elasticity of demand at a single point. This measure is called the *point-price elasticity of demand.*

Another problem with the midpoint formula is that it often obscures the nature of the relationship between price and quantity demanded. Consider Figure 4.4. Suppose that the price elasticity of demand is calculated between any two points below the midpoint, such as between points C and D, on a linear demand curve. As we will see later, for all points below the midpoint, the price elasticity of demand is less than unity in absolute value. In such cases, demand is said to be inelastic. For all points above the midpoint, the price elasticity of demand is greater than unity in absolute value, such as between points A and B. In these cases, demand is said to be elastic. Finally, at the midpoint the value of the price elasticity of demand is equal to unity. In this unique case, demand is said to be unit elastic.

Since the use of the midpoint formula assumes that only two price–quantity vectors are known, it is important that the two points chosen be "close" in the sense that they do not span the midpoint. If we were to choose, say, points B and C to calculate the price elasticity of demand, it would be difficult to determine the nature of the relationship between changes in the price of the commodity and the quantity demanded of that commodity. For this and other reasons, an alternative measure of the price elasticity of demand is preferred. It is to this issue that we now turn our attention.

REFINEMENT OF THE PRICE ELASTICITY OF DEMAND FORMULA: POINT-PRICE ELASTICITY OF DEMAND

The point-price elasticity of demand overcomes the second major weakness of using the slope of a linear demand equation as a measure of consumer responsiveness to a price change. Unlike the slope, which is the same for every price–quantity combination, there is a unique value for the price elasticity of demand at each and every point along the linear demand curve. The point-price elasticity of demand is defined as

$$\varepsilon_p = \left(\frac{dQ_D}{dP} \right)\left(\frac{P}{Q_D} \right) \tag{4.6}$$

where dQ_D/dP is the slope of the demand function at a single point. It is, in fact, the first derivative of the demand function. Diagrammatically, Equation (4.6) is illustrated in Figure 4.3 as the price elasticity of demand evaluated at point B, where dQ_D/dP is the slope of the tangent along $D'D'$. Consider again the hypothetical demand curve from Equation (4.2) and illustrated in Figure 4.5. We can use the midpoint formula, to calculate the values of the price elasticity of demand as we move from point A to point B as follows:

$$E_p(AB) = -50(0.129) = -6.45$$

$$E_p(A'B) = -50(0.116) = -5.80$$

$$E_p(A''B) = -50(0.099) = -5.12$$

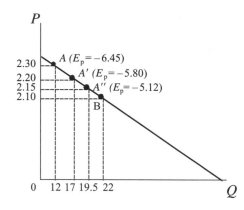

FIGURE 4.5 Alternative calculations of the arc–price elasticity from the demand equation $Q_D = 127 - 50P$.

Note that the value of the slope of the linear demand curve, $b_1 = \Delta Q_D / \Delta P$, is constant at -50. But, as we move along the demand curve from point A to point B, the value of E_p not only changes but will converge to some limiting value. At a price of $2.125, for example, $E_p = -5.12$. Additional calculations are left to the student as an exercise.

What, then, is this limiting value? We can calculate this convergent value by setting the difference between P_1 and P_2, and Q_1 and Q_2 at zero:

$$E_p = -50\left(\frac{P_1 + P_2}{Q_1 + Q_2}\right)$$

$$= -50\left(\frac{2.10 + 2.10}{22 + 22}\right) = -50\left(\frac{4.20}{44}\right) = -4.77$$

Now, calculating the point-price elasticity of demand at point B we find

$$\varepsilon_p(B) = \left(\frac{dQ_D}{dP}\right)\left(\frac{P}{Q_D}\right) = -50\left(\frac{2.10}{22}\right) = -4.77$$

When we calculate ε_p at point A we find that

$$\varepsilon_p(A) = \left(\frac{dQ_D}{dP}\right)\left(\frac{P}{Q_D}\right) = -50\left(\frac{2.30}{12}\right) = -9.58$$

Unlike the value of the slope, the point-price elasticity of demand has a different value at each of the infinite number of points along a linear demand curve. In fact, for a downward-sloping, linear demand curve, the absolute value of the point-price elasticity of demand at the "P intercept" is ∞ and steadily declines to zero as we move downward along the demand curve to the "Q intercept." This variation in the calculated price elasticity of demand is significant because it can be used to predict changes in the firm's total revenues resulting from changes in the selling price of the product. In fact, assuming that the firm has the ability to influence the market price of its product, the price elasticity of demand may be used as a management tool to determine an "optimal" price for its product.

Point-price elasticities may also be computed directly from the estimated demand equation. Consider, again, Equation (4.2). The point-price elasticity of demand may be calculated as

$$\varepsilon_p = \left(\frac{dQ_D}{dP}\right)\left(\frac{P}{Q_D}\right) = -50\left(\frac{P}{127-50P}\right) = \frac{-50P}{127-50P}$$

Suppose, as in the foregoing example, that $P = 2.10$. The point-price elasticity of demand is

$$\varepsilon_p = \frac{-50(2.10)}{127-50(2.10)} = -4.77$$

Problem 4.4. The demand equation for a product is $Q_D = 50 - 2.25P$. Calculate the point-price elasticity of demand if $P = 2$.

Solution

$$\varepsilon_p = \left(\frac{dQ_D}{dP}\right)\left(\frac{P}{Q_D}\right)$$

$$= -2.25\left(\frac{P}{50-2.25P}\right) = \frac{-2.25P}{50-2.25P}$$

$$= \frac{-2.25(2)}{50-2.25(2)} = \frac{-4.5}{45.5} = -0.099$$

Problem 4.5. Suppose that the demand equation for a product is $Q_D = 100 - 5P$. If the price elasticity of demand is -1, what are the corresponding price and quantity demanded?

Solution

$$\varepsilon_p = \left(\frac{dQ_D}{dP}\right)\left(\frac{P}{Q_D}\right)$$

$$= -5\left(\frac{P}{100-5P}\right)$$

$$-1 = \frac{-5P}{100-5P}$$

$$5P - 100 = -5P$$

$$10P = 100$$

$$P = 10$$

$$Q_D = 100 - 5(10) = 50$$

RELATIONSHIP BETWEEN ARC-PRICE AND
POINT-PRICE ELASTICITIES OF DEMAND

Consider, again, Figure 4.5. What is the relationship between the arc-price elasticity of demand as calculated between points A and B, and the point-price elasticity of demand? We saw that when the midpoint formula was used, $E_p = -6.45$. Intuitively, it might be thought that the arc-price elasticity of demand is the simple average of the corresponding point-price elasticities. If we calculate the point-price elasticity of demand at points A and B from Equation (4.2) we find that

$$\varepsilon_p(A) = \left(\frac{dQ_D}{dP}\right)\left(\frac{P}{Q_D}\right) = -50\left(\frac{2.30}{12}\right) = \frac{-115}{12} = -9.58$$

$$\varepsilon_p(B) = \left(\frac{dQ_D}{dP}\right)\left(\frac{P}{Q_D}\right) = -50\left(\frac{2.10}{22}\right) = \frac{-105}{22} = -4.77$$

Taking a simple average of these two values we find

$$\frac{\varepsilon_p(A) + \varepsilon_p(B)}{2} = \frac{-9.58 + -4.77}{2} = \frac{-14.35}{2} = -7.18$$

which is clearly not equal to the arc-price elasticity of demand. It can be easily proven, however, that the calculated arc-price elasticity of demand over any interval along a linear demand curve will be equal to the point-price elasticity of demand calculated at the midpoint along that interval. For example, calculating the point-price elasticity of demand at point A' yields

$$\varepsilon_p(A') = \left(\frac{dQ_D}{dP}\right)\left(\frac{P}{Q_D}\right) = \frac{-50(2.20)}{17} = \frac{-110}{17} = -6.47$$

which is the same as the arc-price elasticity of demand adjusted for rounding errors. It is important to remember that this relationship only holds for linear demand functions.

PRICE ELASTICITY OF DEMAND: SOME
DEFINITIONS

Now that we are able to calculate the price elasticity of demand at any point along a demand curve, it is useful to introduce some definitions. As indicated earlier, in general we will consider only absolute values of ε_p, denoted symbolically as $|\varepsilon_p|$. Since ε_p may assume any value between zero and negative infinity, then $|\varepsilon_p|$ will lie between zero and infinity.

ELASTIC DEMAND

Demand is said to be *price elastic* if $|\varepsilon_p| > 1$ ($-\infty < \varepsilon_p < 1$), that is, $|\%dQ^d|$ > $|\%dP|$. Suppose, for example, that a 2% increase in price leads to a 4% decline in quantity demanded. By definition, $|\varepsilon_p| = 4/2 = 2 > 1$. In this case, the demand for the commodity is said to be price elastic.

INELASTIC DEMAND

Demand is said to be *price inelastic* if $|\varepsilon_p| < 1$ ($-1 < \varepsilon_p < 0$), that is, $|\%dQ_D|$ < $|\%dP|$. Suppose, for example, that a 2% increase in price leads to a 1% decline in quantity demanded. By definition, $|\varepsilon_p| = 1/2 = 0.5 < 1$. In this case, the demand for the commodity is said to be price inelastic.

UNIT ELASTIC DEMAND

Demand is said to be *unit elastic* if $|\varepsilon_p| = 1$ ($\varepsilon_p = -1$), that is, $|\%dQ_D| =$ $|\%dP|$. Suppose, for example, that a 2% increase in price leads to a 2% decline in quantity demanded. By definition, $|\varepsilon_p| = 2/2 = 1$. In this case, the demand for the commodity is said to be unit elastic.

EXTREME CASES

Demand is said to be *perfectly elastic* when $|\varepsilon_p| = \infty$ ($\varepsilon_p = -\infty$). There are two circumstances in which this situation might, occur, assuming a linear demand function. Consider, again, Equation (4.6). The absolute value of the price elasticity of demand will equal infinity when $dQ_D/dP = -\infty$, when P/Q_D equals infinity, or both. Note that P/Q_D will equal infinity when $Q_D = 0$. Consider Figure 4.6, which illustrates two hypothetical demand curves, DD and $D'D'$. In Figure 4.6 the demand curve DD will be perfectly elastic at point

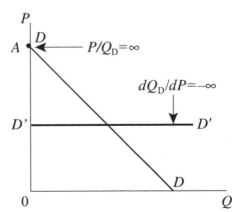

FIGURE 4.6 Perfectly elastic demand.

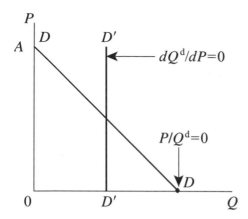

FIGURE 4.7 Perfectly inelastic demand.

A regardless of the value of the slope, since at that point $Q = 0$. In the case of demand curve $D'D'$ the slope of the function is infinity even though the function appears to have a zero slope. This is because by economic convention the dependent variable Q is on the horizontal axis instead of the vertical axis.

Demand is said to be *perfectly inelastic* when $|\varepsilon_p| = 0$ ($\varepsilon_p = -0$). There are three circumstances in which this situation might occur, assuming a linear-demand function. When $dQ_D/dP = 0$, when $P/Q_D = 0$, or both. Note that P/Q_D will equal zero when $P = 0$. Consider Figure 4.7, which illustrates two hypothetical demand curves, DD and $D'D'$.

POINT-PRICE ELASTICITY VERSUS ARC-PRICE ELASTICITY

We have thus far introduced two dimensionless measures of consumer responsiveness to changes in the price of a good or service: the arc-price and point-price elasticities of demand. The arc-price elasticity of demand may be derived quite easily on the basis of only two price–quantity vectors. The arc-price elasticity of demand, however, suffers from significant weaknesses. On the other hand, if the demand is known or can be estimated, then we are able to calculate the point-price elasticity of demand for every feasible price–quantity vector.

We also learned that along any linear demand curve the absolute value of the price elasticity of demand ranges between zero and infinity. Finally, it was demonstrated that where the demand function intersects the price axis, the price elasticity of demand will be perfectly elastic ($|\varepsilon_p| = \infty$) and where it intersects the quantity axis the price elasticity of demand will be perfectly inelastic ($|\varepsilon_p| = 0$). This, of course, suggests, that along any linear

TABLE 4.1 Solution to problem 4.6.

P	Q	dQ/dP	P/Q	ε_p
0	80	−10	0	0
1	70	−10	0.014	−0.14
2	60	−10	0.033	−0.33
3	50	−10	0.060	−0.60
4	40	−10	0.100	−1.00
5	30	−10	0.167	−1.67
6	20	−10	0.300	−3.00
7	10	−10	0.700	−7.00
8	0	−10	∞	$-\infty$

demand curve the values of ε_p will become increasingly larger as we move leftward along the demand curve.

Problem 4.6. Consider the demand equation $Q = 80 - 10P$. Calculate the point-price elasticity of demand for $P = 0$ to $P = 8$.

Solution. By definition

$$\varepsilon_p = \left(\frac{dQ}{dP} \right)\left(\frac{P}{Q} \right)$$

$$= \frac{-10P}{80 - 10P}$$

The solution values are summarized in Table 4.1.

As illustrated in Problem 4.6, the value of ε_p ranges between 0 and $-\infty$. This is true of all linear demand curves. Moreover, demand is unit elastic at the midpoint of a linear demand curve, as illustrated at point B in Figure 4.8. In fact, this is true of all linear demand curves.

By using the proof of similar triangles, we can also define $|\varepsilon_p|$ as the ratio of the line segments BC/BA. For points above the midpoint, where $AB < BC$, then $|\varepsilon_p| > 1$; that is, demand is elastic. For points below the midpoint, where $AB > BC$, then $|\varepsilon_p| < 1$; that is, demand is inelastic. Where $AB = BC$, then $|\varepsilon_p| = 1$; that is, demand is unit elastic.

The choice between the point-price and arc-price elasticity of demand depends primarily on the information set that is available to the decision maker, as well as its intended application. The arc-price elasticity of demand is appropriate when one is analyzing discrete changes in price; it is most appropriate for small firms that lack the resources to estimate the demand equation for their products. Because of its precision, the point-price elasticity of demand is preferable to the arc-price elasticity. Calculation of the point-price elasticity requires knowledge of a specific demand

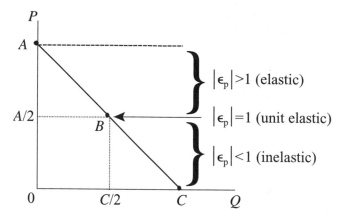

FIGURE 4.8 Elastic, inelastic, and unit-elastic demand along a linear demand curve.

equation. The expense and expertise associated with estimating the demand equation for a firm's product, however, typically are available only to the largest of business enterprises. In addition to its business applications, the point-price elasticity of demand is more useful in theoretical economic analysis.

INDIVIDUAL AND MARKET PRICE ELASTICITIES OF DEMAND

In Chapter 3 it was demonstrated that the market demand curve is the horizontal summation of the individual demand curves. What is the relationship between the individual and market price elasticity of demand? It is easily demonstrated that the market price elasticity of demand is the weighted sum of the individual price elasticities. The weights are equal to each individual's share of the total quantity demanded at each price. To see this, suppose that the market quantity demanded is the sum of three individual demand curves

$$Q_M(P) = Q_1(P) + Q_2(P) + Q_3(P) \tag{4.7}$$

where Q_M is the market quantity demanded and Q_1, Q_2 and Q_3 are the individual quantities demanded, which are each a function of a common selling price, P. Taking the derivative of both sides of Equation (4.7) with respect to P, we obtain

$$\frac{dQ_M}{dP} = \frac{dQ_1}{P} = \frac{dQ_2}{P} + \frac{dQ_3}{dP} \tag{4.8}$$

Multiplying both sides of Equation (4.8) by P/Q_M yields

$$\frac{dQ_M}{dP(P/Q_M)} = \frac{dQ_1}{P(P/Q_M)} = \frac{dQ_2}{P(P/Q_M)} + \frac{dQ_3}{dP(P/Q_M)} \qquad (4.9)$$

Multiplying each term on the right-hand side of Equation (4.9) by Q_i/Q_i, $i = 1, 2, 3$, we get

$$\frac{dQ_M}{dP(P/Q_M)} = \frac{dQ_1}{P(P/Q_M)}\left(\frac{Q_1}{Q_1}\right) + \frac{dQ_2}{P(P/Q_M)}\left(\frac{Q_2}{Q_2}\right)$$
$$+ \frac{dQ_3}{dP(P/Q_M)}\left(\frac{Q_3}{Q_3}\right) \qquad (4.10)$$

Rearranging Equation (4.10) yields

$$\frac{dQ_M}{dP(P/Q_M)} = \frac{dQ_1}{P(P/Q_1)}\left(\frac{Q_1}{Q_M}\right) = \frac{dQ_2}{P(P/Q_2)}\left(\frac{Q_2}{Q_M}\right)$$
$$+ \frac{dQ_3}{dP(P/Q_3)}\left(\frac{Q_3}{Q_M}\right) \qquad (4.11)$$

Equation (4.11) may be rewritten as

$$\varepsilon_M = \omega_1\varepsilon_1 + \omega_2\varepsilon_2 + \omega_3\varepsilon_3 \qquad (4.12)$$

where ε_M is the market price elasticity of demand, $\omega_i = Q_i/Q_M$ ($i = 1, 2, 3$) the proportion of total market demand that is accounted for by each individual, and ε_i ($i = 1, 2, 3$) the individual price elasticities of demand.

DETERMINANTS OF THE PRICE ELASTICITY OF DEMAND

There are a number of factors that bear upon the price elasticity of demand. These determinants include the number of substitutes available for the commodity, the proportion of the consumer's income devoted to the consumption of the commodity, the time available to the consumer to make adjustments to price changes, and the nature of the commodity itself.

SUBSTITUTABILITY

An important factor determining the price elasticity of demand for a particular good or service is the number of substitutes available to the consumer. The larger the number of close substitutes available, the greater will be the price elasticity of demand at any given price. The number of substitutes available will depend, of course, upon how narrowly we choose to define the good in question. The logic behind this explanation is fairly straightforward. Consumers and reluctant to reduce their purchases of goods and service following a price increase when no close substitutes exist.

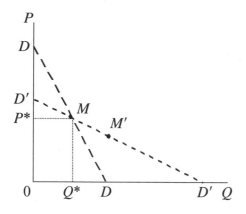

FIGURE 4.9   All linear demand curves have elastic and inelastic regions.

Thus, a percentage increase in the price of the good in question is not likely to be matched by as large a percentage decline in the demand for that good as might have occurred had there been one, or more, close substitutes available.

If the demand curve is linear, then the availability of a large number of substitutes will be shown diagrammatically as a curve with a small slope. The greater the number of substitutes, the flatter will be the market demand curve for the good. In the extreme case of an infinite number of close substitutes, the demand curve will be horizontal, where $|\varepsilon_p| = \infty$ at every point on the curve. At the other extreme, where no other close substitutes exist, the demand function will be vertical; that is, $|\varepsilon_p| = 0$ at every point.

Care should be taken, however, not to interpret a steep linear demand curve as an indication that the demand for a good is relatively price inelastic. As we saw earlier, the slope of the demand curve is not an adequate measure of a consumer's response to price changes. Moreover, all linear demand curves have elastic and inelastic regions. The slope will offer no clue to the price elasticity of demand for a commodity unless that demand is evaluated at a given price. Consider Figure 4.9.

Figure 4.9 compares two demand curves, DD and $D'D'$. Clearly $D'D'$ is flatter than DD. Point M represents the midpoint on curve DD. Thus, at the price P^*, $|\varepsilon_p| = 1$. Point M', on the other hand, represents the midpoint on the curve $D'D'$. Since M lies above M' on the $D'D'$ curve, then at P^* on $D'D'$ the price elasticity of demand for this commodity is clearly price elastic, that is, $|\varepsilon_p| > 1$. Note that although the slope of $D'D'$ is less than that of DD, this is not what makes the demand for the good price elastic, since at some point on $D'D'$ below M' the demand for the good would be price inelastic, that is, $|\varepsilon_p| < 1$. In short, it is not the steepness of the demand curve for a particular commodity that characterizes the good as either demand elastic or inelastic, but rather whether the prevailing price of that commodity lies above, below, or at the midpoint of a linear demand curve.

PROPORTION OF INCOME

Another factor that has a bearing on the price elasticity of demand is the proportion of income devoted to the purchase of a particular good or service. It is generally argued that the larger the proportion of an individual's income that is devoted to the purchase of a particular commodity, the greater will be the elasticity of demand for that good at a given price. This argument is based on the idea that if the purchase of a good constitutes a large proportion of a person's total expenditures, then a drop in the price will entail a relatively large increase in real income. Thus, if the good is normal (i.e., demand varies directly with income), the increase in real income will lead to an increase in the purchase of that good, and other normal goods as well. For example, suppose that a person's weekly income is $2,000. Suppose also that a person's weekly consumption of chewing gum consists of five 10-stick packages, at a price of $0.50 apiece, or a total weekly expenditure of $2.50. The total percentage of the person's weekly income devoted to chewing gum is, therefore, 0.125%. Under such circumstances, a given percentage increase in the price of chewing gum is not likely to significantly alter the amount of chewing gum consumed.

Unfortunately, this line of reasoning is not entirely compelling. To begin with, demand elasticity measures deal with relative changes in consumption. To say that an absolute increase in the purchases of a good or service results from an increase in real income tell us nothing about relative changes in consumption. If the absolute consumption of a good or service is already large, then there is no *a priori* reason to believe that there will be a relative increase in expenditures. There is, however, an alternative argument to explain why goods and services that constitute a small percentage of total expenditures are expected to have a low price elasticity of demand. This explanation introduces the added consideration of search costs. These search costs may simply be "too high" to justify the time and effort involved in finding a substitute for a good whose price has increased. In short, the consumer will engage in a cost–benefit analysis. If the marginal cost of looking for a close substitute, which includes such considerations as the marginal value of the consumer's time, is greater than the dollar value of the anticipated marginal benefits, including, of course, any psychic satisfaction that the consumer may derive in the search process, the search cost will be deemed to be "too high."

ADJUSTMENT TIME

It takes time for consumers to adjust to changed circumstances. In general, the longer it takes them to adjust to a change in the price of a commodity, the less price elastic will be the demand for a good or service. The reason for this is that it takes time for consumers to search for substitutes.

The more time consumers have to adjust to a price change, the more price elastic the commodity becomes. To see this, suppose that members of OPEC, upset over the Middle East policies of the U.S. government, embargo shipments of crude oil to the United States and its allies. Suppose that the average retail price of regular gasoline, which is produced from crude oil, soars from $1.50 per gallon to $10 per gallon. In the short run, consumers and producers will pay the higher price because they have no alternative. Over time, however, drivers of, say, sports utility vehicles (SUVs) will substitute out of these "gas guzzlers" into more fuel-efficient models, while firms will adopt more energy-efficient production technologies. Of course, such retaliatory policies could be self-defeating, since the higher price of crude oil will encourage the development of alternative energy sources and more energy-efficient technologies. This would dramatically reduce OPEC's ability to influence the market price of this most important commodity.

COMMODITY TYPE

The value of $|\varepsilon_p|$ also depends on whether the commodity in question is considered to be an essential item in the consumer's budget. Although the characterization of a good as a luxury or a necessity is based on the related concept of the income elasticity of demand, it nonetheless seems reasonable to conclude that if a product is an essential element in a consumer's budget, the demand for that product will be relatively less sensitive to price changes than a more discretionary budget item would be. Table 4.2 summarizes estimated price and income elasticities (to be discussed shortly) for a selected variety of goods and services.

PRICE ELASTICITY OF DEMAND, TOTAL REVENUE, AND MARGINAL REVENUE

Calculating price elasticities of demand would be a rather sterile exercise if it did not have some practical application to the real world. As we have already seen, the price elasticity of demand is defined by the price of a commodity, the quantity demanded of that commodity, and knowledge of the underlying demand function. Moreover, somewhat trivially, there is also a very close relationship between the price a firm charges for its product and the firm's total revenue. Intuitively, therefore, there must also be a very close relationship between the price elasticity of demand for a commodity and the total revenue earned by the firm that offers that commodity for sale.

Another method for gauging whether the demand for a commodity is elastic, inelastic, or unit elastic is to consider the effect of a price change on

TABLE 4.2   Selected Price and Income Elasticities of Demand

Commodity	Price elasticity	Income elasticity
Food	−0.21	0.28
Medical services	−0.22	0.22
Housing		
Rental	−0.18	1.00
Owner occupied	−1.20	1.20
Electricity	−1.14	0.61
Automobiles	−1.20	3.00
Beer	−0.26	0.38
Wine	−0.88	0.97
Marijuana	−1.50	0.00
Cigarettes	−0.35	0.50
Abortions	−0.81	0.79
Transatlantic air travel	−1.30	1.40
Imports	−0.58	2.73
Money	−0.40	1.00

Source: Nicholson (1995), p. 219.

the total expenditures of the consumer, or alternatively, the effect of a price change on the total revenues from the sale of the commodity. By the definition of ε_p, a percentage change in the price of a good will result in some percentage change in the quantity purchased (sold) of that good.

Suppose that we are talking about a decline in the selling price of, say, 10%. With no change in the quantity demanded, this will result in a 10% decline in expenditures, or a 10% decline in revenues earned by the firm selling the good. By the law of demand, however, we know that the quantity demanded will not remain the same but will, in fact, result in an increase in purchases. Intuitively, if the resulting percentage increase in Q is greater than the percentage decline in price, an increase in total expenditures (revenues) will result. If, on the other hand, the percentage increase in Q is less than the percentage decline in price, we would expect a decline in total expenditures (revenues). Finally, if the percentage increase in Q is equal to the percentage decline in price, we would expect total expenditures to remain unchanged.

Problem 4.7. Consider the demand equation $Q = 80 − 10P$. Calculate the point-price elasticity of demand (ε_p) and total revenue (TR) for $P = 0$ to $P = 8$.

Solution. By definition $\varepsilon_p = (dQ/dP)(P/Q)$ and $TR = P \times Q$. The solution values are summarized in Table 4.3.

When the price of the commodity is $6, the quantity demanded is 20 units. Total revenue is $120. The price elasticity of demand at the price–quantity

TABLE 4.3   Solution to problem 4.7.

P	Q	dQ/dP	P/Q	ε_p	TR
0	80	−10	0	0	0
1	70	−10	0.014	−0.14	70
2	60	−10	0.033	−0.33	120
3	50	−10	0.060	−0.60	150
4	40	−10	0.100	−1.00	160
5	30	−10	0.167	−1.67	150
6	20	−10	0.300	−3.00	120
7	10	−10	0.700	−7.00	70
8	0	−10	∞	−∞	0

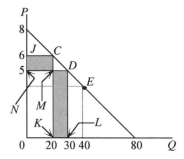

FIGURE 4.10   Price-elastic demand: a decrease (increase) in price and an increase (decrease) in total revenue.

combination is –3.00; that is, a 1% decline in price instantaneously will result in 3% increase in the quantity demanded. When the price is lowered to $5, the quantity demanded increases to 30 units. The price elasticity of demand at that price–quantity combination is –1.67. Intuitively, since the quantity demanded for this product is price elastic within this range of values, we would expect an increase in total expenditures (revenues) for this product as the price declines from $6 to $5, and that is exactly what happens. As the price declines from $6 to $5, total revenues earned by the firm rises from $120 to $150. This phenomenon is illustrated in Figure 4.10.

The fact that total revenues increased following a decrease in price in the elastic region of the demand curve (above the midpoint E in Figure 4.10) can be seen by comparing the rectangles $0JCK$ and $0NMK$ in Figure 4.10, which represent total revenue ($TR = P \times Q$) at $P = \$6$ and $P = \$5$, respectively. Note that both rectangles share the area of the rectangle $0NMK$ in common. When the price declines from $6 to $5, total expenditures decline by the area of the rectangle $NJCM = -\$1(20) = -\$20$. This is not the end of the story, however. As a result of the price decline, the quantity demanded increases by 10 units, or an offsetting increase in revenue equal to the area of the rectangle $KMDL = \$5(10) = \$50$, or a net increase in total revenue of $KMDL + NJCM = \$50 - \$20 = \$30$.

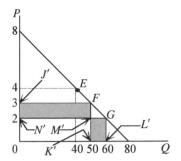

FIGURE 4.11   Price-inelastic demand: a decrease (increase) in price and a decrease (increase) in total revenue.

Suppose, on the other hand, that the price declined in the inelastic region of the demand curve. At $P = \$3$ the quantity demanded is 50 units, for total expenditures of $150. This is shown in Figure 4.11 as the area of the rectangle $0J'FK'$. We saw in Table 4.3 that at $P = \$3$, $Q = 50$, $|\varepsilon_p| = 0.60$, and $TR = \$150$. When price falls to $2, the quantity demanded increased to 60 units, $|\varepsilon_p| = 0.33$, and $TR = \$120$. In other words, when the price is lowered in the inelastic region of a demand curve then total revenue falls.

The fact that total revenues (expenditures) fall as the price declines in the inelastic region of the demand curve can also be illustrated diagrammatically. In Figure 4.11, as the price declines from $3 to $2 total revenues decline by the area of the rectangle $N'J'FM' = -\$1(50) = -\$50$. As a result of this price decline, however, the quantity demanded increases by 10 units, or an offsetting increase in total revenue equal to the area of the rectangle $K'M'GL' = \$2(10) = \$20$, or a net decrease in total revenue of $K'M'GL' - N'J'FM' = \$20 - \$50 = -\$30$. Since the gain in revenues to the firm as a result of increased sales is lower than the loss in revenues due to the lower price, there was a net reduction in total revenues. Again, as price was lowered in the inelastic region, total revenues (expenditures) declined.

The relationship between total revenues and the price elasticity of demand is illustrated in Figure 4.12. As the selling price of the commodity is lowered in the elastic region of the demand curve, the quantity demanded increases and total revenue rises. As the selling price is lowered in the inelastic region of the demand curve, the quantity demanded increases, although total revenue falls. Similarly, as the selling price of the product is increased in the inelastic region of the demand curve, the quantity demanded falls and total revenue increases. As the selling price is increased in the elastic region of the demand curve, quantity demanded falls, as does total revenue.

Finally, total revenues are maximized where $|\varepsilon_p| = 1$. This is illustrated for a linear demand curve in Figure 4.12a at an output level of $b_0/2$, at a price of $a_0/2$, and maximum total revenue of $b_0a_0/4$. Diagrammatically, maximum total revenue is shown as the largest rectangle that can be inscribed below

a

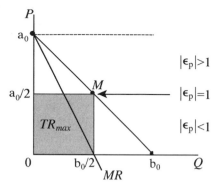

b

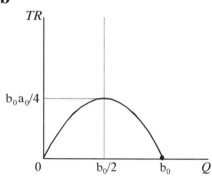

FIGURE 4.12 Price elasticity of demand and total revenue.

TABLE 4.4 The Relationship between Price Changes and Changes in Total Revenue

$|\varepsilon_p|$	ΔP	ΔQ	ΔTR
>1	−	+	+
>1	+	−	−
<1	−	+	−
<1	+	−	+

the demand curve, and the top of the total revenue function in the Figure 4.12b.

The relationship between changes in the selling price of the product, changes in quantity demanded, and changes in total revenues for different price elasticities of demand are summarized in Table 4.4. Note that these relationships are confined to price changes within elastic or inelastic regions of the demand curve. Without additional information, it is not possible to generalize the effect on total revenue of a price change that results in a movement along the demand curve from the elastic region to the inelastic region, or vice versa.

Note that in Figure 4.12 marginal revenue is zero at the output level $\beta_0/2$, which is where total revenue is maximized. The derivation of the marginal revenue equation from a linear demand curve is straightforward. Consider, again, the simple linear demand equation

$$Q = b_0 - b_1 P \tag{4.1}$$

Rewriting the equation as a function of Q yields

$$P = a_0 - a_1 Q \tag{4.13}$$

where $a_0 = b_0/b_1$ and $a_1 = 1/b_1 < 0$. The total revenue equation in terms of Q is

$$TR = PQ = (a_0 - a_1 Q)Q = a_0 Q - a_1 Q^2$$

Marginal revenue, which is the slope of the total revenue function, is simply the first derivative of the total revenue equation, which is given as

$$\frac{dTR}{dQ} = MR = a_0 - 2a_1 Q \tag{4.14}$$

Equation (4.14) has the same intercept as Equation (4.13), but twice the slope. To find the output level that maximizes total revenue set the right-hand side of Equation (4.14) to zero and solve:

$$MR = a_0 - 2a_1 Q = 0$$

$$Q = \frac{a_0}{2a_1} = \frac{b_0/b_1}{2(1/b_1)} = \frac{b_0}{2}$$

The corresponding revenue maximizing price is

$$\frac{b_0}{2} = b_0 - b_1 P$$

$$P = \frac{b_0}{2b_1} = \frac{a_0}{2}$$

Since the total revenue-maximizing price and quantity are $a_0/2$ and $b_0/2$, respectively, then the right triangles $a_0(a_0/2)M$ and $M(b_0/2)b_0$ in Figure 4.12 must be congruent. Thus, point M must be the midpoint of the linear demand equation, Equation (4.1). In other words, total revenue is maximized at the price–quantity combination that corresponds to the midpoint of a linear demand curve. At this price–quantity combination, demand is unit elastic.

FORMAL RELATIONSHIP BETWEEN THE PRICE ELASTICITY OF DEMAND AND TOTAL REVENUE

The relationship between the price elasticity of demand (ε_p) and total revenue (TR) may be demonstrated by using elementary differential calculus. To begin with, consider again the general form of the demand function

$$Q = f(P)$$

where

$$\frac{dQ}{dP} < 0$$

In other words, the quantity demanded of a product is negatively related to the selling price. Total revenue is defined as price P times quantity Q, or

$$TR = PQ$$

Differentiating TR with respect to Q, and utilizing the inverse-function rule,[1] it is possible to write the inverse of the demand function

$$P = g(Q)$$

where $dP/dQ < 0$. We use the product rule to find the appropriate first-order condition for total revenue maximization:

$$\frac{dTR}{dQ} = MR = P\left(\frac{dQ}{dQ}\right) + Q\left(\frac{dP}{dQ}\right)$$

$$= P(1) + Q\left(\frac{dP}{dQ}\right) = P\left[1 + \left(\frac{Q}{P}\right)\left(\frac{dP}{dQ}\right)\right]$$

Since $(dP/dQ)(Q/P) = 1/\varepsilon_p$, then

$$MR = P\left(1 + \frac{1}{\varepsilon_p}\right) \tag{4.15}$$

where $\varepsilon_p < 0$, since $(dQ/dP) < 0$. Thus, MR is a function of ε_p. For example, when $\varepsilon_p = -1$, then

$$MR = P\left(1 + \frac{1}{-1}\right) = 0$$

---

[1] The *inverse-function rule* asserts that there exists for the function $y = f(x)$ an inverse function $g(y) = f^{-1}(y) = x$ if for each value of x there is a unique value of y, and for each value of y there exists a unique value of x. The inverse-function rule allows us to rewrite the demand function $Q = f(P)$ as $P = g(Q)$. For more details, see Chapter 2.

TABLE 4.5   Solution to problem 4.8.

P	Q	ε_p	Demand is	TR
0	50	0	Perfectly inelastic	0
5	37.5	−0.33	Inelastic	187.5
10	25	−1.00	Unit elastic	250
15	12.5	−3.00	Elastic	187.5
20	0	−∞	Perfectly elastic	0

Since $P > 0$, $MR = 0$ requires that $1 + 1/\varepsilon_p = 0$. This implies, given the appropriate second-order conditions, that total revenue is maximized. When $\varepsilon_p < -1$ ($|\varepsilon_p| > 1$), then $MR > 0$, which implies that TR may be increased by lowering price, thereby increasing the quantity demanded. Finally, when $-1 < \varepsilon_p < 0$ ($|\varepsilon_p| < 1$), then $MR < 0$, which implies that TR may be increased by increasing price.

Problem 4.8. Consider the demand equation $Q = 50 - 2.5P$, where Q is the quantity demanded and P is the selling price. Calculate the point-price elasticity of demand and corresponding total revenue for $P = 0$, $P = 5$, $P = 10$, $P = 15$, and $P = 20$. What, if anything, can you conclude about the relationship between the price elasticity of demand and total revenue?

Solution. The point-price elasticity of demand is defined as

$$\varepsilon_p = \left(\frac{dQ}{dP}\right)\left(\frac{P}{Q}\right)$$

Total revenue is defined as

$$TR = PQ$$

Applying the preceding definition to the demand equation yields

$$\varepsilon_p < 0 = (-2.5)\left(\frac{P}{50 - 2.5P}\right)$$

$$TR = P(50 - 2.5P)$$

Consider Table 4.5, which summarizes the values of the price elasticity of demand and total revenue at the values indicated.

Problem 4.9. Consider the demand equation $Q = 25 - 3P$, where Q represents quantity demanded and P the selling price.
a. Calculate the arc-price elasticity of demand when $P_1 = \$4$ and $P_2 = \$3$.
b. Calculate the point-price elasticity of demand at these prices. Is the demand for this good elastic or inelastic at these prices?

c. What, if anything, can you say about the relationship between the price elasticity of demand and total revenue at these prices?

d. What is the price elasticity of demand at the price that maximizes total revenue?

Solution

a. The arc-price elasticity of demand is given by the expression

$$E_p = \frac{(Q_2 - Q_1)/(Q_1 + Q_2)/2}{(P_2 - P_1)/(P_1 + P_2)/2}$$

$$= \frac{(Q_2 - Q_1)/(Q_1 + Q_2)}{(P_2 - P_1)/(P_1 + P_2)}$$

Solving for Q_1 and Q_2 yields

$$Q_1 = 25 - 3(4) = 25 - 12 = 13$$

$$Q_2 = 25 - 3(3) = 25 - 9 = 16$$

Substituting these results into the expression for arc-price elasticity of demand yields

$$E_p = \frac{(16 - 13)/(13 + 16)}{(3 - 4)/(4 + 3)}$$

$$= \frac{(3/29)}{(-1/7)} = \left(\frac{3}{29}\right)\left(\frac{7}{-1}\right) = -0.724$$

b. The point-price elasticity of demand is given by the expression:

$$\varepsilon_p = \left(\frac{dQ}{dP}\right)\left(\frac{P}{Q}\right)$$

The point-price-elasticities of demand at $P = \$4$ and $P = \$3$ are

$$\varepsilon_p(P = \$4) = -3\left(\frac{4}{13}\right) = \frac{-12}{13} = -0.923$$

$$\varepsilon_p(P = \$3) = -3\left(\frac{3}{16}\right) = \frac{-9}{16} = -0.563$$

At both prices, demand is price inelastic, since $-1 < \varepsilon_p < 0$.

c. Total revenue is given by the expression:

$$TR = PQ = P(25 - 3P) = 25P - 3P^2$$

$$TR(P = \$4) = 4(13) = \$52$$

$$TR(P = \$3) = 3(16) = \$48$$

These solutions illustrate that total revenue will decline as the price falls in the inelastic region of the linear demand function.

d. Maximizing the expression for total revenue yields:

$$\frac{dTR}{dP} = 25 - 6P = 0$$

Solving for P, we write

$$P = \frac{25}{6} = 4.167$$

$$TR = 25(4.167) - 3(4.167)^2 = 104.175 - 52.092 = \$52.083$$

Solving for the point-price elasticity of demand,

$$\varepsilon_p = \frac{-3(4.167)}{25 - 3(4.167)} = \frac{-12.5}{12.5} = -1$$

This solution illustrates that total revenue is maximized where marginal revenue is equal to zero where the point-price elasticity of demand is equal to negative unity.

Problem 4.10. It is not possible for a demand curve to have a constant price elasticity throughout its entire length. Comment.

Solution. The statement is false. Consider the demand equation $Q = \alpha P^{-\beta}$, where Q is quantity demanded (units), P is price, and α and β are positive constants. The point-price elasticity of demand (ε_p) is

$$\varepsilon_p = \left(\frac{dQ}{dP}\right)\left(\frac{P}{Q}\right) = (-\beta\alpha P^{-\beta-1})\left(\frac{P}{\alpha P^{-\beta}}\right) = \frac{-\beta\alpha P^{-\beta}}{\alpha P^{-\beta}} = -\beta$$

which is a constant. In other words, regardless of the values of Q and P, $\varepsilon_p = -\beta$. Consider, for example, the following demand equation:

$$Q = 25P^{-2.5}$$

The point-price elasticity of demand (ε_p) is

$$\varepsilon_p = \left(\frac{dQ}{dP}\right)\left(\frac{P}{Q}\right) = (-2.5(25)P^{-3.5})\left(\frac{P}{25P^{-2.5}}\right) = \frac{-2.5(25)P^{-2.5}}{25P^{-2.5}} = -2.5$$

Problem 4.11. Determine the price elasticity of demand for each of the following demand equations when $P = 4$:
a. $Q_D = 98 - P^2/2$
b. $Q_D = 14P^{-5}$

Solution

a. $\varepsilon_p = \left(\frac{dQ_D}{dP}\right)\left(\frac{P}{Q_D}\right)$

$$= -P\left(\frac{P}{Q_D}\right) = \frac{-P^2}{(98 - P^2/2)} = \frac{-4^2}{(98 - 4^2/2)} = \frac{-16}{90} = -0.18$$

TABLE 4.6   Solution to problem 4.12.

P	Q	ε_p	Demand is	TR
0	∞	−2.5	Elastic	∞
0.5	56.57	−2.5	Elastic	28.29
1	10.00	−2.5	Elastic	10.00
5	0.18	−2.5	Elastic	0.90
10	0.03	−2.5	Elastic	0.30
15	0.01	−2.5	Elastic	0.15
20	0.006	−2.5	Elastic	0.12

b. $\varepsilon_p = \left(\dfrac{dQ_D}{dP}\right)\left(\dfrac{P}{Q_D}\right) = -70P^{-6}\left(\dfrac{P}{14P^{-5}}\right) = \dfrac{-70P^{-5}}{14P^{-5}} = \dfrac{-70}{14} = -5$

Problem 4.12. Consider the demand equation $Q = 10P^{-2.5}$, where Q is quantity demanded and P is the selling price. Calculate the point-price elasticity of demand and corresponding total revenue for $P = 0$, $P = 0.5$, $P = 1$, $P = 10$, $P = 15$, and $P = 20$. What, if anything, can you conclude about the relationship between the price elasticity of demand and total revenue?

Solution. The point-price elasticity of demand is defined as

$$\varepsilon_p = \left(\frac{dQ}{dP}\right)\left(\frac{P}{Q}\right)$$

Total revenue is defined as $TR = PQ$. Applying the definition of ε_p to the demand equation yields

$$\varepsilon_p = (-25P^{-3.5})\left[\frac{P}{(10P^{-2.5})}\right] = \frac{-25P^{-2.5}}{10P^{-2.5}} = \frac{-25}{10} = -2.5$$

$$TR = P(50P^{-0.5})$$

Consider Table 4.6, which summarizes the values of the price elasticity of demand and total revenue at the values indicated.

The first thing to note is that the demand equation is nonlinear (multiplicative). Diagrammatically, the demand curve is a generalized rectangular hyperbola. Contrary to the general class of linear demand curves, the slope of this demand curve is different at every price–quantity combination. On the other hand, the price elasticity of demand is the same at every price–quantity combination. In fact, the price elasticity of demand is the same as the value of the exponent of P (i.e., −2.5). In other words, the forego nonlinear demand equation is elastic throughout.

These results also illustrate the general proposition that as price is raised (lowered) when demand is elastic ($\varepsilon_p < -1$), then total revenue decreases (increases). Since the price elasticity of demand is a constant, as price is lowered, total revenue, in the limit, is infinity. Conversely, as price is raised, total revenue, in the limit, is zero. This result is consistent with the fact that the demand curve is a generalized equilateral hyperbola.

Problem 4.13. Consider the general form of the demand function $Q = f(P)$, where $dQ/dP < 0$; that is, quantity demanded of a product is negatively related to the selling price.

a. Demonstrate that average revenue is equal to the selling price of the product.
b. Demonstrate the general proposition that at the output level of which total revenue TR is maximized, the price elasticity of demand is unity (i.e., $\varepsilon_p = -1$).
c. In general, what is the relationship between marginal revenue MR and the price elasticity of demand?

Solution
a. Total revenue is defined as price P times quantity Q, or $TR = PQ$. Average revenue is defined as $AR = TR/Q = PQ/Q = P$.
b. Solving for price and applying the inverse-function rule, we may write the inverse demand function as $P = g(Q)$, where $dP/dQ < 0$. By using the product rule, we find the appropriate first-order condition for total revenue maximization

$$\frac{dTR}{dQ} = MR = P\left(\frac{dQ}{dQ}\right) + Q\left(\frac{dP}{dQ}\right) = P(1) + Q\left(\frac{dP}{dQ}\right)$$

$$= P\left[1 + \left(\frac{Q}{P}\right)\left(\frac{dP}{dQ}\right)\right] = P\left(1 + \frac{1}{\varepsilon_p}\right) = 0$$

where $\varepsilon_p = (dQ/dP)(P/Q)$. Since $P > 0$, $MR = 0$ requires that $1 + 1/\varepsilon_p = 0$. Solving for ε_p, we have

$$1 + \frac{1}{\varepsilon_p} = 0$$

$$\frac{1}{\varepsilon_p} = -1$$

$$\varepsilon_p = -1$$

In summary, at the output level that maximizes TR ($MR = 0$), $\varepsilon_p = -1$.
b. From the foregoing considerations, the relationship

$$MR = P\left(1 + \frac{1}{\varepsilon_p}\right)$$

illustrates the general result that when demand is elastic (i.e., when $\varepsilon_p < -1$, $MR > 0$), total revenue rises (falls) when quantity demanded increases (decreases) following a price decline (increase). Alternatively,

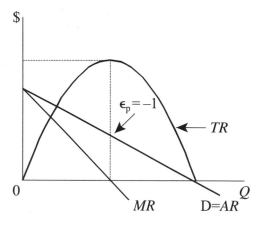

FIGURE 4.13 Diagrammatic solution to problem 4.13.

when demand is inelastic (i.e., when $-1 < \varepsilon_p < 0$, $MR < 0$), total revenue falls (rises) when quantity demanded increases (decreases) following a price decline (increase). These results are summarized in Figure 4.13.

Problem 4.14. PDQ Company specializes in rapid parcel delivery. Cross-sectional data from PDQ's regional "hubs" were used to estimate the demand equation for the company's services. Holding income and prices of other goods constant, the demand equation is estimated to be

$$P = 66Q^{-1/3}$$

where P is the price per pound and Q is pounds delivered. The marginal cost of delivery is constant and equal to $2 per pound.
a. What is the point-price elasticity of demand?
b. What are the profit-maximizing price and quantity?
c. What are the total revenue maximizing price and quantity?

Solution
a. The point-price elasticity of demand is

$$\varepsilon_p = \left(\frac{dQ}{dP}\right)\left(\frac{P}{Q}\right)$$

$$\frac{dP}{dQ} = \left(\frac{-1}{3}\right)(66)Q^{-4/3} = -22Q^{-4/3}$$

Since $dQ/dP = 1/(dP/dQ)$, we write

$$\frac{dQ}{dP} = \frac{1}{-22Q^{-4/3}}$$

$$\varepsilon_p = \left(\frac{1}{-22Q^{-4/3}}\right)\left(\frac{66Q^{-1/3}}{Q}\right) = \left(\frac{1}{-22Q^{-4/3}}\right)(66Q^{-4/3}) = \frac{-66}{22} = -3$$

for all values of Q. Demand is price elastic.

b. The profit-maximizing condition is $MR = MC$.

$$TR = PQ = (66Q^{-1/3})Q = 66Q^{2/3}$$

$$MR = \frac{dTR}{dQ} = \left(\frac{2}{3}\right)(66Q^{-1/3}) = 44Q^{-1/3}$$

$$MR = MC$$

$$44Q^{-1/3} = 2$$

$$Q^{1/3} = 22$$

$$Q = (22)^3 = 10,648$$

$$P = 66Q^{-1/3}$$

$$Q^{1/3} = 22$$

$$Q^{-1/3} = \frac{1}{22}$$

$$P = 66Q^{-1/3} = \frac{66}{22} = 3$$

c. $\dfrac{dTR}{dQ} = \left(\dfrac{2}{3}\right)(66Q^{-1/3})$

This result suggests that there are no TR maximizing P and Q. The demand function is a generalized equilateral hyperbola. As $Q \to \infty$ and $P \to 0$, $TR \to \infty$. This result follows because the price elasticity of demand is constant (-3). In general, when demand is elastic, a price decline (increase in quantity demanded) will result in an increase in total revenue. Since demand is always elastic, total revenue will continue to rise as price is lowered.

USING ELASTICITIES IN MANAGERIAL DECISION MAKING

Suppose that a linear demand equation for the following functional relationship has been estimated

$$Q_D = f(P, A, I, P_s) \tag{4.16}$$

where P is the price of the commodity, A is the level of advertising expenditures, I is per-capita income, and P_s is the price of a competitor's product. With knowledge of a specific demand equation, the manager can easily estimate all relevant demand elasticities. In addition to the price elasticity of demand, the manager can estimate elasticity measures for each of the other explanatory variables.

INCOME ELASTICITY OF DEMAND

Perhaps the second most frequently estimated measure of elasticity, after the price elasticity of demand, is the income elasticity of demand, which is defined as

$$\varepsilon_I = \left(\frac{\partial Q_D}{\partial I}\right)\left(\frac{I}{Q_D}\right) \tag{4.17}$$

where I represents some measure of aggregate consumer income. The income elasticity of demand measures the percentage change in the demand for a good or service given a percentage change in income. From the managerial decision-making perspective, the income elasticity of demand is used to evaluate the sales sensitivity of a good or service to economic fluctuations. Selected income elasticities of demand were summarized in Table 4.6.

Commodities for which $\varepsilon_I > 0$ are referred to as *normal goods*. Sales of normal goods rise with increases in income, and vice versa. Normal goods may be further classified as either *necessities* or *luxuries*. A commodity is classified as a necessity if $0 < \varepsilon_I < 1$. The sales of such goods (electricity, rent, food, etc.) are relatively insensitive to economic fluctuations. A commodity is classified as a luxury if $\varepsilon_I \geq 1$. Such commodities (jewelry, luxury automobiles, yachts, furs, restaurant meals, etc.) are very sensitive to economic fluctuations.

Commodities in which $\varepsilon_I < 0$ are referred to as *inferior goods*. Sales of inferior good fall with increases in income, and vice versa. While it is difficult to identify inferior goods at the market level, it is easy to hypothesize the existence of inferior goods for individuals. For some individuals, such goods might include bus rides from New York City to Washington, D.C. An increase in that individual's income might result in fewer bus trips and more train, plane, or automobile trips.

It is easy to show that while an individual's consumption bundle might consist of only normal goods, or a combination of normal goods and inferior goods, it is not possible for the individual's consumption bundle to comprise only inferior goods. To see this, consider an individual with money income M who consumes two goods, Q_1 and Q_2. Although the following discussion is restricted to the two-good case, it is easily generalized to n goods. The reader is cautioned not to confuse the individual's money income with aggregate consumer income, I. The demand functions for the two goods are assumed to be functionally related to the prices of the two goods and the consumers money income, that is, $Q_1 = Q_1(P_1, P_2, M)$ and $Q_2 = Q_2(P_1, P_2, M)$. From Appendix 3A the consumer's budget constraint may be written as

$$M = P_1 Q_1 + P_2 Q_2 \tag{3A, 1t}$$

Differentiating Equation (3A, 1t) with respect to money income yields

$$P_1\left(\frac{\partial Q_1}{\partial M}\right) + P_2\left(\frac{\partial Q_2}{\partial M}\right) = 1 \qquad (4.18)$$

Multiplying each term of the left-hand side of Equation (4.18) by unity yields

$$P_1\left(\frac{Q_1}{M}\right)\left(\frac{M}{Q_1}\right)\left(\frac{\partial Q_1}{\partial M}\right) + P_2\left(\frac{Q_2}{M}\right)\left(\frac{M}{Q_2}\right)\left(\frac{\partial Q_2}{\partial M}\right) = 1 \qquad (4.19)$$

where $(Q_1/M)\ (M/Q_1) = (Q_2/M)\ (M/Q_2) = 1$. Rearranging, Equation (4.19) becomes

$$\omega_1 \varepsilon_{1,M} + \omega_2 \varepsilon_{2,M} = 1 \qquad (4.20)$$

where $\omega_1 = P_1(Q_1/M)$ and $\omega_2 = P_2(Q_2/M)$ is the proportion of money income spent on Q_1 and Q_2, respectively. The respective income elasticities for the two goods are $\varepsilon_{1,M}$ and $\varepsilon_{2,M}$.

Equation (4.20) asserts that the weighted sum of the income elasticities of demand for both goods must equal unity. Since ω_1 and ω_2 are both positive, it cannot be true that both $\varepsilon_{1,M}$ and $\varepsilon_{2,M}$ can be inferior goods. The value of at least one of the income elasticities must be positive (i.e., a normal good).

Equation (4.20) also says something else. If the consumer's money income increases by, say, 20%, then total purchases must increase by 20%.[2] Moreover, Equation (4.20) shows that for each good in the consumption bundle with an income elasticity of demand with a value less than unity, there must also exist a good or goods with an income elasticity of demand with a value greater than unity. Finally, assuming that the income elasticity of demand for all goods in the consumption bundle is not equal to unity, an individual who consumes only normal goods must consume both necessities ($0 < \varepsilon_M < 1$) and luxuries ($\varepsilon_M \geq 1$).

Problem 4.15. Suppose that an individual consumes three goods, Q_1, Q_2, and Q_3. Suppose further that the respective proportions of total income devoted to the consumption of these three goods are 80, 20 and 20%. The income elasticities for Q_1 and Q_2 are $\varepsilon_{1,M} = 0.5$ and $\varepsilon_{2,M} = 1.5$. How would you classify the three goods?

Solution. Since $0 < \varepsilon_{1,M} < 1$, then Q_1 is a necessity. Since $\varepsilon_{2,M} \geq 1$, then Q_2 is a luxury good. Finally, substituting the information provided into Equation (4.20) yields

---

[2] Some readers may be concerned about the possibility that the individual does not spend all of his or her income on goods and services (i.e., the consumer saves). This dilemma is easily resolved if saving is viewed, correctly, as just another normal good.

TABLE 4.7 Selected Cross-Price Elasticities of Demand

Demand for	Effect of price on	ε_y
Butter	Margarine	1.53
Electricity	Natural gas	0.50
Coffee	Tea	0.15

Source: Nicholson, (1995), p. 220.

$$\omega_1\varepsilon_{1,M} + \omega_2\varepsilon_{2,M} + \omega_3\varepsilon_{3,M} = 1$$

$$(0.8)(0.5) + (0.2)(1.5) + (0.2)\varepsilon_{3,M} = 1$$

$$0.7 + (0.2)\varepsilon_{3,M} = 1$$

$$\varepsilon_{3,M} = 1.5$$

Since $\varepsilon_{3,M} \geq 1$, then Q_2 is a luxury good as well.

CROSS-PRICE ELASTICITY OF DEMAND

Another frequently used elasticity measure is the cross-price elasticity of demand, which is defined as

$$\varepsilon_y = \left(\frac{\partial Q_x^d}{d\partial P_y}\right)\left(\frac{P_y}{Q_x^d}\right) \tag{4.21}$$

The cross-price elasticity of demand measures the percentage change in the demand for good X given a percentage change in the price of good Y. The cross-price elasticity of demand is used to evaluate the sales sensitivity of a good or service to changes in the price of a related good or service.

An interpretation of the cross-price elasticity of demand follows from the sign of the first derivative, since the second term on the right-hand side of Equation (4.21) is always positive. When $\varepsilon_y > 0$, this indicates that the good in question is a *substitute*, and when the $\varepsilon_y < 0$, the good in question is a complement. Selected cross-price elasticities of demand are summarized in Table 4.7.

OTHER ELASTICITIES OF DEMAND

Elasticity is a perfectly general concept. Whenever a functional relationship exists, then an elasticity measure in principle exists. That is, for any function $y = f(x_1, \ldots, x_n)$, there exists an elasticity measure such that $\varepsilon = (dy/dx_i)(x_i/y)$, for all $i = 1, \ldots, n$. In Equation (4.16), the explanatory variable A is the level of advertising expenditures. The advertising elasticity of demand is, therefore,

$$\varepsilon_A = \left(\frac{\partial Q_D}{\partial A}\right)\left(\frac{A}{Q_D}\right) \qquad (4.22)$$

Equation (4.22) measures the percentage change in the demand for the commodity given a percentage change in advertising expenditures.

Problem 4.16. Suppose that the demand equation for good X is

$$Q_x = 100 - 10P_x - 2P_y + 0.1I + 0.2A$$

where Q_x represents sales of good X in units of output, P_x is the price of good X, P_y is the price of related good Y, I is per-capita income ($$\bullet\bullet$s), and A is the level of advertising expenditures ($$\bullet\bullet$s). Suppose that $P_x = \$2$, $P_y = \$3$, $I = 10$, and $A = 20$. Calculate the price elasticity of demand.

Solution. Substituting the values for the explanatory variables into the demand equation yields

$$
\begin{aligned}
Q_x &= 100 - 10P_x - 2P_y + 0.1I + 0.2A \\
&= 100 - 10P_x - 2(3) + 0.1(10) + 0.2(20) \\
&= 100 - 10P_x - 6 + 1 + 4 = 99 - 10P_x
\end{aligned}
$$

Using this result and calculating the price elasticity of demand yields

$$\varepsilon_p\left(\frac{\partial Q_D}{\partial P_x}\right)\left(\frac{P_x}{Q_D}\right) = -10\frac{P_x}{(99 - 10P_x)} = \frac{-10P_x}{99 - 10P_x}$$

$$= \frac{-10(2)}{99 - 10(2)} = \frac{-20}{79} = -0.253$$

Problem 4.17. Rubicon & Styx has estimated the following demand function for its world-famous hot sauce, Sergeant Garcia's Revenge,

$$Q = 62 - 2P + 0.2I + 25A$$

where Q is the quantity demanded per month ($\bullet\bullet$'s), P is the price per 6-oz. bottle, I is an index of consumer income, and A is the company's advertising expenditures per month ($$\bullet\bullet$'s). Assume that $P = 4$, $I = 150$, and $A = \$4$.

a. Calculate the number of bottles of Sergeant Garcia's Revenge demanded.
b. Calculate the price elasticity of demand. According to your calculations, is the demand for this product elastic, inelastic, or unit elastic? What, if anything, can you say about the demand for this product?
c. Calculate the income elasticity of demand. Is Sergeant Garcia's Revenge a normal good or an inferior good? Is it a luxury or a necessity?
d. Calculate the advertising elasticity of demand. Explain your result.

Solution

a. Substituting the given information into the demand function yields

$$Q = 62 - 2P + 0.2I + 25A$$
$$= 62 - 2(4) + 0.2(150) + 25(4) = 62 - 8 + 30 + 100 = 184$$

b. The price elasticity of demand is given by the expression

$$\varepsilon_p = \left(\frac{\partial Q}{\partial P}\right)\left(\frac{P}{Q}\right) = -2\left(\frac{4}{184}\right) = \frac{-8}{184} = -0.04$$

This result indicates that a 1% reduction in the price of Sergeant Garcia's Revenge results in a 0.04% increase in quantity demanded. Since $|\varepsilon_p| < 1$, the demand for this product is price inelastic. It suggests, perhaps, that Sergeant Garcia's Revenge has no close substitutes.

c. The income elasticity of demand is given as

$$\varepsilon_I = \left(\frac{\partial Q}{\partial I}\right)\left(\frac{I}{Q}\right) = 0.2\left(\frac{150}{184}\right) = \frac{30}{184} = 0.16$$

This result suggests that a 1% increase in consumer income results in a 0.16% increase in the demand for this product. Since $\varepsilon_I > 0$, this good is characterized as a "normal" good. Moreover, since $0 < \varepsilon_I < 1$, this product is also characterized as a "necessity." This suggests that people just cannot get along without Sergeant Garcia's Revenge hot sauce.

d. The advertising elasticity of demand is given as

$$\varepsilon_A = \left(\frac{\partial Q}{\partial A}\right)\left(\frac{A}{Q}\right) = 25\left(\frac{4}{184}\right) = \frac{100}{184} = 0.54$$

This result suggests that a 1% increase in Rubicon & Styx's advertising budget would result in a 0.54% increase in sales.

CHAPTER REVIEW

Elasticity is a general concept that relates the sensitivity of a dependent variable to changes in the value of some explanatory (independent) variable. Suppose, for example, that the value of variable *y* depends in some systematic way on the value of variable *x*. This relationship can be read "*y* is a function of *x*." Elasticity measures the percentage change in the value of *y* given a percentage change in the value of *x*. There are several elasticity concepts associated with the demand curve including *price elasticity of demand*, *income elasticity*, *cross* (or *cross-price*) *elasticity*, *advertising elasticity*, and *interest elasticity*.

There are two measures of elasticity: the *arc-price* and the *point-price elasticities of demand*. The elasticity measure calculated will depend on the purpose of the analysis and the type of information available. The point-price elasticity of demand requires a rudimentary knowledge of differential calculus.

The price elasticity of demand measures the percentage increase (decrease) in the quantity demanded of a good or service given a percentage decrease (increase) in its price. By the law of demand, the price elasticity of demand is always negative. If the price elasticity of demand is between zero and negative unity (<1 in absolute terms), then demand is said to be *price inelastic*. If the price elasticity of demand is equal to negative unity, then demand is said to be *unit elastic*. If the price elasticity of demand is less than negative unity (greater than unity in absolute terms), then demand is said to be *price elastic*.

If the demand curve is linear, all price–quantity combinations above the midpoint of the curve are price elastic. All price–quantity combinations below the midpoint are price inelastic. At the midpoint of the demand curve, demand is unit elastic.

There is also an important relationship between the price elasticity of demand and total revenue. If demand is price elastic, a decrease (increase) in price will result in an increase (decrease) in total revenue. If demand is price inelastic, then a decrease (increase) in price will result in a decrease (increase) in total revenue. Finally, total revenue is maximized at the price–quantity combination at which demand is unit elastic. Since marginal revenue is zero when total revenue is maximized, it must also be true that the price elasticity of demand is equal to negative unity when marginal revenue is zero. This further implies that for linear demand curves, total revenue is maximized at the price–quantity combination that corresponds to the midpoint of a linear demand curve.

The income elasticity of demand measures the percentage change in the demand for a good or service given a percentage change in consumers' income. The income elasticity of demand is used to classify goods and services as *normal goods* and *inferior goods*. Normal goods are further classified as *luxury (superior) goods* and *necessities*. A good or service is a luxury if the income elasticity of demand is greater than unity. A good or service is a necessity if the income elasticity of demand is less than unity. Finally, a good or service is inferior if the income elasticity of demand is negative.

The cross-price elasticity of demand measures the percentage change in the demand for a good or service given a percentage change in the price of a *related good or service*. Related goods and services may be either *substitutes* or *complements*. If two products are substitutes, the cross-elasticity of demand is positive. If two products are complements, the cross-elasticity of demand is negative.

KEY TERMS AND CONCEPTS

Advertising elasticity of demand A measure of the sensitivity of consumer demand for a good or a service in response to a change in the advertising expenditures of a firm or an industry. The advertising elasticity of demand is computed as the percentage change in the demand for a good or a service divided by the percentage change in advertising expenditures. In practice, advertising expenditures are often used as a proxy for tastes and preferences in the demand function.

Arc-price elasticity of demand The price elasticity of demand that is calculated over a price–quantity interval by using the simple average as the base. A knowledge of only two price–quantity combinations is required to calculate an arc-price elasticity of demand.

Complement In the case of a complement, the change in the demand for a good or service is inversely related to a change in the price of a related good or service, and the cross-price elasticity of demand is negative.

Cross-price elasticity of demand A measure of the sensitivity of consumer demand for a good or a service in response to a change in the price of a related good or service. The cross-price elasticity of demand is computed as the percentage change in the demand for a good or a service divided by the percentage change in the price of a related good or service.

Elastic demand Demand is elastic when the percentage increase (decrease) in the quantity demanded of a good or a service is greater than the percentage decrease (increase) in its price. When the demand for a good or a service is price elastic, an increase (decrease) in the price of that good or service will result in a decrease (increase) in the total revenue earned by the firm or industry selling that good or service.

Elasticity Whenever there is a functional relationship between a dependent variable and an independent (explanatory) variable, it is theoretically possible to calculate a measure of elasticity. Elasticity is a measure of the sensitivity of a dependent variable to changes in an independent (explanatory) variable. Elasticities are computed as the percentage change in the value of the dependent variable divided by the percentage change in the value of the independent (explanatory) variable.

Income elasticity of demand A measure of the sensitivity of consumer demand for a good or a service in response to a change in income. The income elasticity of demand is computed as the percentage change in the demand for a good or a service divided by the percentage change in income.

Inelastic demand Demand is inelastic when the percentage increase (decrease) in the price of a good or a service is less than the percentage decrease (increase) in its price. When the demand for a good or a service is price inelastic, an increase (decrease) in the price of that good or a service will result in an increase (decrease) in the total revenue earned by the firm or industry selling that good or service.

Inferior good A good or service is inferior when changes in the demand for it are inversely related to changes in income. In the case of an inferior good, the value of the income elasticity of demand is negative.

Luxury In the case of a luxury, the percentage increase (decrease) in the demand for a good or service is greater than the percentage increase (decrease) in income, and the value of the income elasticity of demand is greater than unity.

Marginal revenue The change in the total revenue earned by a firm in response to a change in output sold. When marginal revenue is positive then total revenue is increasing. When marginal revenue is negative then total revenue is decreasing. If marginal revenue is positive at lower output levels and negative at higher levels, total revenue is maximized when marginal revenue is zero.

Necessity In the case of a necessity, the percentage increase (decrease) in the demand for a good or service is less than the percentage increase (decrease) in income, and the value of the income elasticity of demand is positive and less than unity (i.e., a positive fraction).

Normal good or service In the case of a normal good or service, changes in the demand are positively related to changes in income, and the value of the income elasticity of demand is positive. Normal goods and services may be further classified as luxuries and necessities.

Point-price elasticity of demand The price elasticity of demand that is calculated at a specific price–quantity combination. A knowledge of the demand equation for a good or a service is required to calculate a point-price elasticity of demand

Price elasticity of demand A measure of the sensitivity of the quantity demanded of a good or a service in response to a change in the price of that good or service. The price elasticity of demand is computed as the percentage increase (decrease) in the quantity demanded of a good or a service divided by the decrease (increase) in the price of that good or service.

Price elasticity of supply A measure of the sensitivity of the quantity supplied of a good or a service in response to a change in the price of that good or service. The price elasticity of supply is computed as the percentage increase (decrease) in quantity supplied of a good or service given a percentage increase (decrease) in the price of that good or service.

Related good or service Changes in the demand for a good or a service are sometimes related to changes in the price of some other good or service. Related goods and services may be further classified as complements and substitutes.

Substitute   In the case of a substitute, the change in the demand for a good or service is positively related to a change in the price of a related good or service, and the cross-price elasticity of demand is positive.

Total revenue   The price of a product multiplied by the quantity sold (i.e., $TR = PQ$).

Unit elastic demand   In the case of unit elastic demand the percentage increase (decrease) in the price of a good or a service is equal to the percentage decrease (increase) in its price, and the value of the price elasticity of demand is negative unity. Total revenue is maximized at the price–quantity combination for which the price elasticity of demand is equal to negative unity.

CHAPTER QUESTIONS

4.1 Suppose that the demand equations for heart surgery and cosmetic surgery are both linear. The demand for heart surgery is more price inelastic than the demand for cosmetic surgery. Do you agree? Explain.

4.2 The price elasticity of demand of gasoline is more elastic in the long run than it is in the short run. Do you agree? Explain.

4.3 Suppose that you are a portfolio manager for a large, diversified mutual fund. The fund's chief economist is forecasting a slowdown in aggregate economic activity (i.e., a recession). How would you use your knowledge of estimated income elasticities of demand to alter the composition of the portfolio?

4.4 What is the advertising elasticity of demand? What, if anything, can you say about the effect of advertising expenditures on company profits?

4.5 Consider two linear demand curves drawn on the same diagram. The first demand curve has a larger intercept but a numerically smaller (steeper) slope than the second demand curve. What, if anything, can you say about the price elasticity of demand for both goods at the point where the two demand curves intersect?

4.6 What, if anything, can you say about the relationship between the price elasticity of demand for a good and the percentage of an individual's income spent on that good?

4.7 The price elasticity of demand of a good at a given price is more elastic for wealthy individuals than for individuals who are less affluent. Do you agree? Explain.

4.8 Demonstrate that the market price elasticity of demand is equal to the weighted sum of the individual price elasticities.

4.9 A severe frost significantly damages the Florida orange crop. As a result, revenues earned by Florida orange growers decline dramatically. Do you agree? Explain.

4.10 The demand for canal transportation was more inelastic after the development of regional railroads than before. Do you agree? Explain.

4.11 Suppose that the market for illegal drugs is perfectly competitive. Suppose further that domestic crime rates are positively related to the value of illegal drug sales and that the demand for drugs is price inelastic. The government's primary weapon in the war on drugs is to interdict then flow into the country from outside its borders. What is the likely effect of interdiction on domestic crime rates? Do you support such a policy? What alternative approach to the war on drugs would you recommend?

4.12 A monopolist would never produce a good along the inelastic portion of a linear demand curve. Do you agree? Explain.

4.13 A consortium is formed of the world's leading oil producers form a cartel to control crude oil supplies and international oil prices. The objective of the cartel is to reduce output, raise prices, and increase cartel revenues. Under what circumstances will the cartel's efforts be successful? Do you believe that this is a realistic scenario?

4.14 The world's leading coffee bean producers form a cartel to control coffee bean supplies and international coffee prices. The objective of the cartel is to increase output, lower prices, and increase cartel revenues. Under what circumstances will the cartel's efforts be successful? Do you believe that this is a realistic scenario?

4.15 Suppose that the demand equation for a firm's product has been estimated as $Q_x = 100P^{-3.5}I^{0.25}$, where P and I are price and income, respectively.
   a. What, if anything, can you say about the price elasticity of demand for good X?
   b. What, if anything, can you say about the income elasticity of demand for good X?
   c. What, if anything, can you say about the relationship between the slope of the demand curve and the price elasticity of demand?
   d. What, if anything, can you say about the effect of a price decrease on firm revenues?
   e. How would your answer to part c be different if the demand equation had been linear?

CHAPTER EXERCISES

4.1 The Sylvan Corporation has estimated the price elasticity of demand for synthetic wood sorrel to be −0.25.
   a. If the price of Sylvan wood sorrel increases by 10%, what will happen to the quantity demanded of wood hewers?
   b. What will happen to Sylvan's revenues as a result of the price increase?

4.2 Suppose that the cross-price elasticity of demand for good X is 2.5. The price of good Y increases by 25%.

a. What is the relationship between good X and good Y?

b. How will the increase in the price of good Y affect sales of good X?

4.3 Suppose that the cross-price elasticity of demand for good M is -1.75 and the price of good N falls by 10%.

a. What is the relationship between good M and good N?

b. How will the fall in the price of good N affect sales of good M?

4.4 Suppose that the income elasticity of demand for a good is 3.5.

a. What type of good is this?

b. What increase in income will be necessary for the demand for the good to increase by 21%?

4.5 Silkwood Enterprises specializes in gardening supplies. The demand for its new brand of fertilizer, Meadow Muffins, is given by the equation $Q = 120 - 4P$.

a. Silkwood is currently charging $10 for a pound of Meadow Muffins. At this price, what is the price elasticity of demand for Meadow Muffins?

b. At a price of $10, what is Silkwood's marginal revenue?

c. What price should Silkwood charge if it wishes to maximize its total revenue?

d. At the total revenue maximizing price, what is the price elasticity of demand for Meadow Muffins?

e. Diagram your answers to parts a through d.

4.6 Just-the-Fax, Max, Inc. has determined that the demand for its fax machines is $Q = 3,000 - 1.5P$.

a. Calculate the point-price elasticity of demand when $P = \$600$.

b. At $P = \$600$, what is the firm's marginal revenue?

c. Find the total revenue maximizing price and quantity for the firm.

4.7 The market research department of Paradox Enterprises has determined that the demand for fingolds is $Q = 1,000 - 5P + 0.05I - 50P_z$, where P is the price of glibdibs, I is income, and P_z is the price of ballzacks. Suppose that $P = \$5$, $I = \$20,000$, and $P_z = \$15$.

a. Compute the price elasticity of demand for fingolds.

b. Is the firm maximizing its total revenue at $P = \$5$. If not, what price should it charge?

c. At $P = \$5$, compute the income elasticity of demand for fingolds.

d. At $P = \$5$, compute the cross-price elasticity of demand for fingolds.

4.8 The demand equation for a firm's product has been estimated as log $Q_x = 1,500 - 2 \log P_x + 0.5 \log I + 0.25 \log P_y - 1.5 \log P_z$, where Q_x represents unit sales of brand X, P_x is the price of brand X, I is per-capita income, P_y is the price of brand Y, and P_z is the price of brand Z.

a. What is the price elasticity of demand for brand X?

b. What is the income elasticity of demand for brand X? What type of good is brand X?

c. What is the cross-price elasticity of demand for brand X in relation to the price of brand Y? What is the relationship between brand X and brand Y?

d. What is the cross-price elasticity of demand for brand X in relation to the price of brand Z? What is the relationship between brand X and brand Z?

e. What effect will an increase in the price of brand X have on the firm's total revenues?

4.9 The demand curve for widgets is $Q_D = 10,000 - 25P$.

a. How many widgets could be sold for $100?

b. At what price would widget sales fall to zero?

c. What is the total revenue (TR) equation for widgets in terms of output, Q? What is the marginal revenue equation in terms of Q?

d. What is the point-price elasticity of demand when $P = \$200$? What is total revenue at this price? What is marginal revenue at this price? Explain your result.

e. Suppose that the price of widgets fell to $P = \$150$. What would be the new point-price elasticity of demand? What is total revenue at this price? What is marginal revenue at this price? Explain your result.

f. Suppose that the price of widgets rose to $P = \$250$. What would be the new point-price elasticity of demand? What is total revenue at this price? What is marginal revenue at this price? Explain your result.

g. Suppose that the supply of widgets is given by the equation $Q_S = -5,000 + 50P$. What is the relationship between quantity supplied and quantity demanded at a price of $300?

h. In this market, what is the equilibrium price and what is the quantity?

4.10 The demand for high-top bell-knots is given by the equation $Q = 50 - 2P$.

a. What is the point-price elasticity of demand at $P = \$20$?

b. If the price were to fall to $15, what would happen to total expenditures on this product and what would this imply about the price elasticity of demand?

c. Verify your answer to part b by computing the arc-price elasticity over this interval.

d. What, if anything, can you say about the relationship between the point-price elasticities of demand calculated in parts a and b and the arc-price elasticity of demand calculated in part c?

4.11 The demand equation for product X is given by $Q_x = (2IP_y)/(5P_x)$, where I is income, P_x the price of product X, and P_y the price of product Y. Also, $I = \$1,000$, $P_x = \$20$, and $P_y = \$5$.

a. Write the demand equation in linear form.
b. Write an equation for the point-price elasticity. For what values of I, P_x, and P_y is demand unitary elastic? Explain.
c. Write an equation for the point-income elasticity. For what values of I, P_x, and P_y is demand unitary elastic? Explain.
d. Write an equation for the point–cross-price elasticity. For what values of I, P_x, and P_y is demand unitary elastic? Explain.

4.12 An individual consumes three goods, Q_1, Q_2, and Q_3. The proportions of total income devoted to the consumption of Q_1 and Q_2 are 75 and 15%, respectively. The income elasticities for Q_1 and Q_2 are $\varepsilon_{1,M} = 0.75$ and $\varepsilon_{2,M} = -1.5$, respectively. How would you classify the three goods?

SELECTED READINGS

George, P. S., and G. A. King. *Consumer Demand for Food Commodities in the United States with Projections for 1980*. Berkeley: University of California, 1971.

Glass, J. C. *An Introduction to Mathematical Methods in Economics*. New York: McGraw-Hill, 1980.

Hicks, J. R. *Value and Capital*, 2nd ed. London: Oxford University Press, 1946.

Hope, S. *Applied Microeconomics*. New York: John Wiley & Sons, 1999.

Houthakker, H. S., and L. D. Taylor. *Consumer Demand in the United States: Analysis and Projections*, 2nd ed. Cambridge, MA: Harvard University Press, 1970.

Mansfield, E. *Microeconomics: Theory and Applications*. New York: W. W. Norton, 1985.

McCloskey, D. N. *The Applied Theory of Price*. New York: Macmillan, 1982.

McConnell, C. R., and S. L. Brue. *Economics: Principles, Problems, and Policies*. New York: McGraw-Hill, 1982.

Miller, R. L. *Intermediate Microeconomics: Theory, Issues, Applications*, 2nd ed. New York: McGraw-Hill, 1982.

Nicholson, W. *Microeconomic Theory: Basic Principles and Extensions*, 6th ed. New York: Dryden Press, 1995.

Palm, T., and A. Qayum. *Private and Public Investment Analysis* Cincinnati, OH: South-Western Publishing, 1985.

Silberberg, E. *The Structure of Economics: A Mathematical Analysis*, 2nd ed. New York: McGraw-Hill, 1990.

Slutsky, E., "Sulla Teoria del Bilancio del Consumatore." *Giornale degli Economisti*, 51 (1915), pp. 19–23. Translated as "On the Theory of the Budget of the Consumer," in G. Stigler and K. Boulding, eds., *Readings in Price Theory*. Homewood, IL: Richard D. Irwin, 1952.

Stigler, G. *The Theory of Price*. 4th ed. New York: Macmillan, 1987.

5

PRODUCTION

The discussion thus far has focused primarily on the demand side of the market. We have seen, for example, that a firm's total revenue will depend, in part, on the selling price of the product, which is determined by the interaction of consumer and producer behavior in the market. We have also investigated the conditions under which a firm might increase its revenues by changing the selling price of its product.

In spite of all that has thus far been accomplished, we have yet to examine the conditions under which firms produce the goods and services that are demanded by consumers, and perhaps more importantly from the perspective of senior management, the associated costs of production. If we are to investigate more closely the first-order and second-order conditions for a firm to maximize its profits, we must understand not only the revenue component of the profit equation, but the cost component as well. In this chapter we will examine the general problem of transforming productive resources in goods and services for sale in the market.

THE ROLE OF THE FIRM

The firm is an organizational activity that transforms factors of production, or productive inputs, into outputs of goods and services. Economics itself is the study of how society chooses to satisfy virtually unlimited human wants subject to scarce productive resources. In fact, this economic problem can be viewed as a constrained optimization problem in which the objective is to maximize some index of human happiness, which is assumed to be a function of the consumption of limited, or scarce, amounts of goods and services.

Let us examine this fundamental economic paradigm a bit more closely. For theoretical purposes, it is useful to assume that human material wants and desires are insatiable. While this might not be so for any individual commodity, by and large the vast majority of individuals are never completely satisfied with what they have. Consumers will, in general, always want more of something. Unfortunately, consumers cannot have everything they want for the simple reason that the productive inputs necessary to produce these goods and services are finite. In other words, outputs of goods and services (Q) are limited because the productive resources necessary to produce them are limited.

Productive resources, or *inputs*, or *factors of production* are used by firms to produce goods and services. These productive resources may conceptually be divided into two broad categories—human and nonhuman resources. Nonhuman resources may be further classified as *land*, *raw materials*, and *capital*. While these classifications are arbitrary, they are conceptually convenient.

Land (e.g., arable land for farming, or the land under buildings and roads) may be described as a "gift of nature." Raw materials include such natural resources as coal, oil, copper, sand, and trees. Finally, capital represents manufactured inputs that are used in the production of final goods and services. Capital goods include tools, machinery, equipment, office buildings, and storage facilities.

In an economic sense, "capital" does not refer to such financial assets as money, corporate equities, savings accounts, and U.S. Treasury securities. There is a loose conceptual connection between the economic and financial definitions of the term in that firms that wish to acquire capital equipment will do so only if the additional return from an investment in capital goods is sufficient to cover the opportunity cost of the interest that might have been earned by investing in a financial asset.

Human resources, on the other hand, might be classified as *labor* and *entrepreneurial ability*. Labor consists of the physical and mental talents of individuals engaged in the production process. Labor services are similar to services derived from nonhuman resources in that the rental value of labor services (wages, salaries, health benefits, etc.) is determined by the interaction of supply and demand conditions in the market for factors of production. Labor is unique among the other factors of production, however, in that in a free society, labor decides for itself how intensively its services will be made available in the production process.

Entrepreneurial ability is a special subset of human resources because without the entrepreneur, all other factors of production cannot be combined. In other words, the services of land, labor, and capital are "rented" to the highest bidder through the interaction of supply and demand. The bidders are entrepreneurs. An individual may, of course, be both a laborer and entrepreneur in the same production process. Nevertheless, the entrepreneur is unique in that it is through his or her initiative and enterprise that the other factors of production are organized in the first place.

The entrepreneur is distinguished from the "hired hand" in a number of other ways. The entrepreneur, for example, makes the nonroutine decisions for the firm. The entrepreneur determines the firm's organizational objectives. The entrepreneur is an innovator, constantly on the alert for the best (least expensive) production techniques. The entrepreneur also endeavors to ascertain the wants and needs of the public to be able to introduce new and better products, and to discontinue production of goods and services that are no longer in demand. The entrepreneur is a risk taker in the expectation of earning a profit.

It should be pointed out once again that it is assumed that the expectation of earning profit is the motivating incentive for all commercial activities in a free economy. Without the profit motive, it is assumed that entrepreneurs would not incur risk the financial risks associated with combining productive resources to produce final goods and services for sale in the market. In the absence of the profit motive, the production of goods and services in quantities that are most in demand by society would not occur. Moreover, whenever the profit incentive is diluted—say, through a tax on profits—fewer goods and services will be produced by the private sector in exchange for an increase in goods and services produced by the public sector. Whether society is better off or worse off will ultimately depend on which sector is most responsive to society's needs and preferences and which sector is most efficient in the utilization of productive resources in the delivery of those goods and services. The disappointing economic experiences of centrally planned economies in the communist countries of eastern Europe and Asia in the latter half of the twentieth century, compared with that of the essentially free market economies of western Europe, North America, and Japan often convincing testimony to the power of the profit motive in promoting the general economic well-being of society at large. To quote from Adam Smith: "By pursuing his own interest he (the entrepreneur) frequently promotes that of society more effectively than when he really intends to promote it."[1]

THE PRODUCTION FUNCTION

The technological relationship that describes the process whereby factors of production are efficiently transformed into goods and services is

---

[1] Adam Smith, *The Wealth of Nations*. (New York: Modern Library, 1937) p. 423. (Originally published in 1776.)

called the *production function*. Mathematically, a production function utilizing capital, labor, and land inputs may be written as

$$Q = f(K, L, M) \tag{5.1}$$

where K is capital, L is labor, and M is land.

The production function defines the maximum rate of output per unit of time obtainable from a given set of productive inputs. Obviously, some firms organize inputs inefficiently, thereby producing less than the maximum possible level of goods and services. In a competitive market environment, however, firms that do not adopt the most efficient (cost-effective) production technology will not prosper and may, if fact, be forced to curtail operations as their market position is undermined by more aggressive competitors. In free-market economies there is a tendency for more efficient operations to drive less efficient firms out of an industry.

For the sake of pedagogical, theoretical, and graphical convenience, let us assume that all productive inputs may be classified as either labor (L) or capital goods (K). Equation (5.1) may therefore be rewritten as

$$Q = f(K, L) \tag{5.2}$$

In most cases, labor and capital may be substituted, albeit in varying degrees. As we will see, the precise manner in which these inputs are combined will depend on the relative rental price and marginal productivity of the factor of production. A firm that operates efficiently will choose that combination of productive inputs that minimizes the total cost of producing a given level of output. Equivalently, a firm that operates efficiently will choose that combination of productive inputs that will maximize production subject to a given operating budget.

It should be noted that the production function signifies the technological relationship between inputs and outputs. It is an engineering concept, devoid of any economic content. The production function defines the maximum output obtainable from a particular combination of inputs. Input prices must be combined with the production function to determine which of the many possible combinations of inputs is the most desirable given the firm's objectives, such as profit maximization.

THE COBB–DOUGLAS PRODUCTION FUNCTION

Production functions take many forms. In fact, there is a unique production function associated with each and every production process. In practice, it may not be possible to precisely define the mathematical relationship between the output of a good or service and a set of productive inputs. In spite of this, it is possible to approximate a firm's production function. Perhaps the most widely used functional form of the production process for empirical and instructional purposes is the *Cobb–Douglas pro-*

duction function. The appeal of the Cobb–Douglas production function stems from certain desirable mathematical properties. The general form of the Cobb–Douglas production function for the two-input case may be written

$$Q = AK^{\alpha}L^{\beta} \tag{5.3}$$

where A, α and β are known parameters and K and L represent the explanatory variables capital and labor, respecitvely. It is further assumed that $0 \leq (\alpha, \beta) \leq 1$.

Consider, for example, the following empirical Cobb–Douglas production function:

$$Q = 25K^{0.5}L^{0.5} \tag{5.4}$$

Table 5.1, which summarizes the different output levels associated with alternative combinations of labor and capital usage, illustrates three important relationships that highlight the desirable mathematical properties of the Cobb–Douglas production function. These are the relationships of *substitutability* of inputs and *returns to scale*, and the *law of diminishing marginal product*. Although these properties of production functions are discussed at greater length later, a brief discussion of their significance in terms of the example illustrated in Table 5.1 is useful here.

Substitutability

When a given level of output is generated, factors of production may or may not be substitutable for each other. Table 5.1 illustrates the substitutability of labor and capital for the production function summarized in Equation (5.4). It can be seen, for example, that to produce 122 units of output, labor and capital may be combined in (row, column) combinations of (3, 8), (4, 6), (6, 4), and (8, 3).

TABLE 5.1   Substitutability

Capital	Labor							
	1	2	3	4	5	6	7	8
1	25	35	43	50	56	61	66	71
2	35	50	61	71	79	87	94	100
3	43	61	75	87	97	106	115	**122**
4	50	71	87	100	112	**122**	132	141
5	56	79	97	112	125	137	148	158
6	61	87	106	**122**	137	150	162	173
7	66	94	115	132	148	162	175	187
8	71	100	**122**	141	158	173	187	200

The Cobb–Douglas production function also illustrates the fundamental economic problem of constrained optimization. Although there are theoretically an infinite number of output levels possible, the firm is typically subject to a predetermined operating budget that limits the amount of productive resources that can be acquired by the firm. Because of this restriction, an increase in the use of one factor of production requires that less of some other factor be employed. The degree of substitutability of inputs is important because it suggests that managers are able to alter the input mix required to produce a given level of output in response to changes in input prices.

Returns to Scale

Suppose that output is described as a function of capital and labor. Suppose that capital and labor are multiplied by some scalar. If output increases by that same scalar, the term *constant returns to scale* (*CRTS*) opplies. In Table 5.1 we observe that when labor and capital inputs are raised by a factor of 2, as when labor and capital are doubled from 2 units to 4 units, then output is raised by the same scalar (i.e., output increases from 50 to 100 units). If capital and labor are multiplied by a scalar and output increases by a multiple greater than the scalar, the condition is referred to as *increasing returns to scale* (IRTS). Finally, if capital and labor are multiplied by a scalar and output increases by a multiple less than the scalar, the condition is referred to as *decreasing returns to scale* (DRTS).

Law of Diminishing Marginal Product

Finally, the Cobb–Douglas production function exhibits a very important technological relationship—*the law of diminishing marginal product* (also referred to as the *law of diminishing returns*). This law, sometimes referred to as the *second fundamental law of economics*, states that when at least one productive input is held fixed while at least one other productive resource is increased, output will also increase but by successively smaller increments. The law of diminishing marginal product is a short-run production concept. As will be discussed in the next section, the "short run" in production refers to that period of time during which at least one factor of production is held fixed in amount. Mathematically, the law of diminishing marginal product requires that the first partial derivative of the production function with respect to a variable input be positive and the second partial derivative negative. In Table 5.1, for example, when capital is held constant at $K = 1$, and labor is successively increased from $L = 1$ to $L = 6$, output increases from 25 to 61 units, but successive marginal increments are 10, 8, 7, 6, and 5.

It was noted earlier that the production function is characterized as efficient (i.e., the most output obtainable from a given level of input usage). Efficient utilization of productive inputs is characterized by production pos-

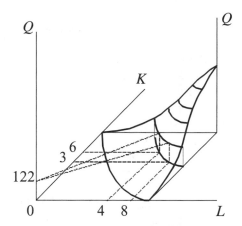

FIGURE 5.1 The production surface.

sibilities defined on the production surface in Figure 5.1. Any point above the production surface is unobtainable given the level of inputs available to the firm and the prevailing state of production technology. Any point below the production surface characterizes inefficiency.

SHORT-RUN PRODUCTION FUNCTION

In the production process, economists distinguish between the *short run* and the *long run*. The short run in production refers to that period of time during which at least one factor of production is held constant. The law of diminishing marginal product is a short-run phenomenon. The long run in production occurs when all factors of production are variable. Denoting K_0 as a fixed amount of capital, the short-run production function may be written

$$Q_L = f(K_0, L) = TP_L \qquad (5.5)$$

Equation (5.5) is sometimes referred to as to *total product of labor*, or more simply as TP_L.

The decision maker must determine the optimal amount of the variable input (L) given its price (P_L) and the price of the resulting output (P). It is assumed that the state of technology is captured in the specification of the production function and that production is efficient. Note that the subscript L in Equation (5.5) denotes the level of output dependent on the level of labor usage. Equivalently, if labor is assumed to be the fixed input, the short-run production function would be written

$$Q_K = f(K, L_0) = TP_K \qquad (5.6)$$

KEY RELATIONSHIPS: TOTAL, AVERAGE, AND MARGINAL PRODUCTS

There is a crucial relationship between any total concept and its related average and marginal concepts. Since the present discussion deals with production, we will explore the relationship between the total product of labor and the related *average product of labor* (AP_L) and *marginal product of labor* (MP_L). The reader is advised, however, that the fundamental relationships established here are perfectly general and may be applied to any functional relationship.

TOTAL PRODUCT OF LABOR

If we assume that the level of capital usage is fixed, the total product of labor is described by Equation (5.5). This short-run production function defines the maximum amount of output attainable from any given level of labor usage given some fixed level of capital usage.

AVERAGE PRODUCT OF LABOR

The average product of labor AP_L is simply the total product per unit of labor usage and is determined by dividing the total product of labor by the total amount of labor usage. This relationship is defined in Equation (5.7).

$$AP_L = \frac{TP_L}{L} = \frac{Q_L}{L} = \frac{f(K_0, L)}{L} \tag{5.7}$$

MARGINAL PRODUCT OF LABOR

The *marginal product of labor* MP_L is defined as the incremental change in output associated with an incremental change in the amount of labor usage. Mathematically, since the amount of capital is constant, this is equivalent to the first partial derivative of the production function with respect to labor:

$$MP_L = \frac{\partial TP_L}{\partial L} = \frac{\partial Q_L}{\partial L} = \frac{\partial f(K_0, L)}{\partial L} \tag{5.8}$$

Similarly, the marginal product of capital is defined as

$$MP_K = \frac{\partial TP_K}{\partial K} = \frac{\partial Q_K}{\partial K} = \frac{\partial f(K, L_0)}{\partial K} \tag{5.9}$$

Consider, for example, the Cobb–Douglas production function

$$Q = AK^{\alpha}L^{\beta} \tag{5.3}$$

The respective marginal products are

$$MP_L = \frac{\partial Q_L}{\partial L} = \beta A K^\alpha L^{\beta-1} \tag{5.10}$$

$$MP_K = \frac{\partial Q_K}{\partial K} = \alpha A K^{\alpha-1} L^\beta \tag{5.11}$$

Problem 5.1. Suppose that you are given the following production function:

$$Q = 100 K^{0.6} L^{0.4}$$

Determine the marginal product of capital and the marginal product of labor when $K = 25$ and $L = 100$.

Solution. The marginal product of capital is given as

$$MP_K = \frac{\partial Q_K}{\partial K} = 0.6(100) K^{0.6-1} L^{0.4} = 60\ K^{-0.4} L^{0.4} = \frac{60 L^{0.4}}{K^{0.4}}$$

$$= 60\left(\frac{L}{K}\right)^{0.4} = 60\left(\frac{100}{25}\right)^{0.4} = 60(4)^{0.4} = 63.4$$

The marginal product of labor is given as

$$MP_L = \frac{\partial Q_L}{\partial L} = 0.4(100) K^{0.6} L^{0.4-1} = 40\ K^{0.6} L^{-0.6} = \frac{40 K^{0.6}}{L^{0.6}}$$

$$= 40\left(\frac{K}{L}\right)^{0.6} = 40\left(\frac{25}{100}\right)^{0.6} = 40(0.25)^{0.6} = 17.4$$

MATHEMATICAL RELATIONSHIP BETWEEN AP_L AND MP_L

The mathematical relationship between the average product of labor (or any average concept) and the marginal product of labor (or any related marginal concept) may be illustrated by the use of optimization analysis. Consider again the definition of the average product of labor

$$AP_L = \frac{TP_L}{L} = \frac{Q_L}{L} = \frac{f(K_0, L)}{L} \tag{5.7}$$

Taking the first derivative of Equation (5.7) with respect to labor and setting the results equal to zero yields

$$\frac{\partial AP_L}{\partial L} = \frac{L(\partial Q_L / \partial L) - Q_L(\partial L / \partial L)}{L^2} = 0$$

which implies

$$MP_L - \frac{Q_L}{L} = 0 \qquad (5.12)$$

or

$$MP_L = AP_L$$

since $1/L^2$ is positive. That is, when the average product of labor is maximized, the marginal product of labor is equal to the average product of labor.

Equation (5.12) may also be used to highlight another important relationship between the average product of labor and the marginal product of labor. When $MP_L > AP_L$, then $\partial AP_L/\partial L > 0$, which implies that the average product of labor is rising. When $MP_L < AP_L$, then $\partial AP_L/\partial L < 0$, which says that the average product of labor is falling. Only when $MP_L = AP_L$ and $\partial AP_L/\partial L = 0$ will the average product of labor be stationary (either a maximum or a minimum). The second-order condition for minimum average product of labor is $\partial^2 AP_L/\partial L^2 < 0$.

In general, for any total function it can be easily demonstrated that when the marginal value is greater than the average value (i.e., $M > A$), then A will be rising. When $M < A$, A will be falling. Finally, when $M = A$, A will neither be falling nor rising but at a local optimum (maximum or minimum). To illustrate this relationship, consider the simple example of a student who takes a course in which the final grade is based on the average of 10 quizzes. A maximum of 100 points may be earned on each quiz. Thus, a maximum of 1,000 points may be earned during the semester, or a maximum average for the course of $1,000/10 = 100$. Suppose that the student has taken six quizzes and has earned a total of 480 points, for an average grade of $480/6 = 80$. If the student receives a grade of 90 on the seventh quiz, then the student's average will rise from 80 to $570/7 = 81.4$. That is, since the marginal grade is greater than the average grade to that point, the student's average will rise. On the other hand, if the student received a grade of 70 on the seventh quiz, the student's average will fall to $550/7 = 78.6$. Finally, if the student receives a grade of 80 on the seventh quiz then, clearly, there will be no change in the student's average (i.e., $560/7 = 80$).

Problem 5.2. Consider again the Cobb–Douglas production function:

$$Q = 25K^{0.5}L^{0.5}$$

Verify that when the average product of labor is maximized, it is identical to the marginal product of labor.

Solution. The average product of labor is

$$AP_L = \frac{Q}{L} = \frac{(25K^{0.5}L^{0.5})}{L}$$

Maximizing this expression with respect to labor yields

$$\frac{\partial AP_L}{\partial L} = \frac{0.5(25K^{0.5}L^{-0.5})L - 25K^{0.5}L^{.5}}{L^2}$$

Since $L > 0$, this implies that

$$0.5(25K^{0.5}L^{-0.5})L - 25K^{0.5}L^{0.5} = 0$$

$$0.5(25K^{0.5}L^{-0.5}) = \frac{25K^{0.5}L^{0.5}}{L}$$

As demonstrated earlier, the term on the left-hand side of the expression is the marginal product of labor, while the term on the right is the average product of labor. Thus, this expression may be rewritten as

$$MP_L = AP_L$$

THE LAW OF DIMINISHING MARGINAL PRODUCT

It was noted earlier that the Cobb–Douglas production function exhibits a number of useful mathematical properties. One of these properties is the important technological relationship known as the *law of diminishing marginal product* (*law of diminishing returns*). This concept can be described with the use of a simple illustration.

Consider a tomato farmer who has a 10-acre farm and as much fertilizer, capital equipment, water, labor, and other productive resources as is necessary to grow tomatoes. The only input that is fixed in supply is farm acreage. The farmer decides that to maximize output, additional workers will have to be hired. With the exception of farm acreage, each worker has as many productive resources to work with as necessary.

Initially, as one might expect, output expands rapidly. At least in the early stages of production, as more workers are assigned to the cultivation of tomatoes, the additional output per worker might be expected to increase. This is because in the beginning land is relatively abundant and labor is relatively scarce. While each worker has as much land and other resources to work with as is necessary for efficient production, at least some land initially stands fallow. Labor can be said to be fully utilized while land can be said to be underutilized. As more laborers are added to the production process, total output rises; beyond some level of labor usage, however, incremental additions to output from the addition of more workers, while positive, will begin to decline. That is, while each additional worker contributes positively to total output, beyond some point the amount of land allocated to each worker will decline. No matter how much water, fertilizer, and other inputs are made available to each worker, the amount of output per worker will begin to fall. At this point, land has become over utilized while labor has become fully utilized.

The law of diminishing marginal product sets in at the point at which the contribution to total output from an additional worker begins to fall. In fact, if successively more workers are added to the production process, the amount of land allocated to each worker becomes so small that we might even expect zero marginal product; that is, total output has been maximized. It is even conceivable that beyond the point of maximum production, as more workers are added to the production process, output will actually decline. This is because workers may interfere with each other or will perhaps trample on some of the tomatoes. In the extreme, we cannot rule out the possibility of negative marginal product of a variable input.

Definition: The law of diminishing marginal product states that as increasing amounts of a variable input are combined with one or more fixed inputs, at some point the marginal product of the variable input will begin to decline.

Numerous empirical studies have attested to the veracity of the law of diminishing marginal product. As noted earlier, this phenomenon is exhibited mathematically in the Cobb–Douglas production function. A necessary condition for the law of diminishing returns is that the first partial derivative of the production function be positive, indicating that as more of the variable input is added to the production process, output will increase. A sufficient condition, however, is that the second partial derivative be negative, indicating that the additions to total output from additions of the variable input will become smaller. Consider again Equation (5.10).

$$MP_L = \frac{\partial Q_L}{\partial L} = \beta A K^\alpha L^{\beta-1} > 0 \qquad (5.10)$$

Since A, α, and β are assumed to be positive constant, and $|\alpha|$, $|\beta| < 1$, then Equation (5.10) is clearly positive, since $L^{\beta-1} > 0$. A positive marginal product of labor is expected, since we would expect output to increase as incremental units of a variable input are added to the production process. Our concern is with the change in marginal product, given incremental increases in the amount of labor used. To determine this we must take the second partial derivative of the total product of labor function or, which is the same thing, the first partial derivative of Equation (5.10).

$$\frac{\partial MP_L}{\partial L} = \frac{\partial^2 Q_L}{\partial L^2} = \beta(\beta - 1)AK^\alpha L^{\beta-2} < 0$$

since $\beta - 1 < 0$ and $L^{\beta-2} > 0$.

Problem 5.3. Consider the following Cobb–Douglas production function:

$$Q = 25K^{0.5}L^{0.5}$$

Verify that this expression exhibits the law of diminishing marginal product with respect to capital.

Solution. The marginal product of capital is given as

$$MP_K = \frac{\partial Q_K}{\partial K} = 0.5(25)K^{0.5-1}L^{0.5} = 12.5K^{-0.5}L^{0.5} > 0$$

since L and K are positive. The second partial derivative of the production function is

$$\frac{\partial MP_K}{\partial K} = \frac{\partial^2 Q_K}{\partial K^2} = -0.5(12.5)K^{-1.5}L^{0.5} < 0$$

which is clearly negative, since $K^{-1.5} = 1/K^{1.5} > 0$.

THE OUTPUT ELASTICITY OF A VARIABLE INPUT

Another useful relationship in production theory is the *coefficient of output elasticity of a variable input*, which illustrates an interesting relationship between the marginal product and the average product of a productive input. By definition, the *output elasticity of labor* is

$$\varepsilon_L = \frac{\%\Delta Q}{\%\Delta L} = \left(\frac{\partial Q_L}{\partial L}\right)\left(\frac{L}{Q_L}\right)$$
$$= MP_L\left(\frac{1}{AP_L}\right) = \frac{MP_L}{AP_L} \tag{5.13}$$

The output elasticity of labor is simply the ratio of the marginal product of labor and the average product of labor. As we will see later, this relationship has some interesting implications for production theory.

Problem 5.4. The *Cobb–Douglas production function* is widely used in economic and empirical analysis because it possesses several useful mathematical properties. The general form of the *Cobb–Douglas production function* is given as

$$Q = AK^\alpha L^\beta$$

where A is a positive constant and $0 < \alpha < 1, 0 < \beta < 1$.

a. The *law of diminishing marginal product* states that as units of a variable input are added to a fixed input, output will increase at a decreasing rate. Suppose that capital (K) is the fixed input and that labor (L) is the variable input. Demonstrate the *law of diminishing marginal product* using the *Cobb–Douglas production function*.

b. Assuming that capital is the constant factor of production, what is the proportional change in output resulting from a proportional change in labor input?

Solution

a. With capital the constant factor of production, the mathematical conditions for the law of diminishing returns are

$$MP_L = \frac{\partial Q}{\partial L} > 0$$

$$\frac{\partial MP_L}{\partial L} = \frac{\partial^2 Q}{\partial L^2} < 0$$

Taking the partial derivative of the Cobb–Douglas production function with respect to labor yields

$$\frac{\partial Q}{\partial L} = \beta A K^\alpha L^{\beta-1} = \beta(A K^\alpha L^\beta) L^{-1} = \frac{\beta Q}{L} > 0 \qquad \text{for} \quad K, L > 0$$

This result demonstrates that as more labor is added to fixed capital, output will rise. Taking the second partial derivative of Q with respect to L, we obtain

$$\frac{\partial^2 Q}{\partial L^2} = (\beta-1)\beta A K^\alpha L^{\beta-2} = (\beta-1)\beta(A K^\alpha L^\beta) L^{-2}$$

$$= \frac{(\beta-1)\beta Q}{L} < 0 \qquad \text{for} \quad K, L > 0$$

This result demonstrates that output increases at a decreasing rate.

b. The output elasticity with respect to L is given as

$$\varepsilon_L = \left(\frac{\partial Q}{\partial L}\right)\left(\frac{L}{Q}\right) = \frac{MP_L}{AP_L} = \left(\frac{\beta Q}{L}\right)\left(\frac{L}{Q}\right) = \beta$$

That is, the proportional change in output resulting from proportional changes in labor input (the *output elasticity of labor*) is equal to β, a constant. It can be easily demonstrated that the output elasticity of capital (ε_K) is equal to α.

RELATIONSHIPS AMONG THE PRODUCT FUNCTIONS

MARGINAL PRODUCT

In Figure 5.2, illustrates the short-run relationships among the total, average, and marginal product functions, which the marginal product of

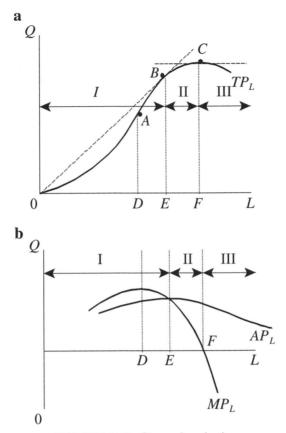

FIGURE 5.2 Stages of production.

labor, which is the first partial derivative of the total product of labor function, is the value of the slope of a tangent at a particular point on the TP_L curve. We can see from Figure 5.2a that as we move from point 0 on the TP_L curve, the slope of the tangent steadily increases in value until we reach inflection point A. From point A to point C the marginal product of labor is still positive, but its value steadily decreases to zero, which is at the top of the TP_L "hill." Beyond point C the slope of the value of the tangent (MP_L) becomes negative. These relationships are illustrated in Figure 5.2b, where the MP_L function reaches its maximum at the labor usage level $0D$, which is at the inflection point, thereafter declining steadily until $MP_L = 0$ at $0F$. For labor usage beyond point $0F$, then MP_L becomes negative, resulting in the decline in TP_L.

In Figure 5.2a the distance $0A$ along TP_L represents *increasing marginal product of labor*. This range of labor usage is represented by the distance

0*D* and is characterized by increasing incremental contributions to total output arising from incremental applications of labor input. This phenomenon, if it occurs at all, is likely to take place at lower output levels. This is because at low output levels the fixed input is likely to be underutilized, making it likely that additional applications of the variable input will result in increased efficiency arising from specialization, management, communications, and so on.

Once efficiency gains from specialization have been exhausted, however, the production process will be characterized by the law of diminishing marginal product. This phenomenon sets in at the labor usage *DF*, which corresponds to the distance *AC* along the TP_L curve. The law of diminishing marginal product sets in at the inflection point *A* and continues until MP_L = 0 at point *C*. To reiterate, the law of diminishing marginal product says that as more and more of the variable input is added to the production process with the amount utilized of at least one factor of production remaining constant, beyond some point, incremental additions to output will become smaller and smaller.

Finally, movement along the TP_L curve beyond point *C* is characterized by *negative marginal product of labor*. Beyond the level of labor usage 0*F* in Figure 5.2a, incremental increases in labor usage will actually result in a fall in total output. In Figure 5.2b this phenomenon is illustrated by $MP_L <$ 0; that is, the MP_L curve falls below the horizontal axis for output levels in excess of 0*F*.

AVERAGE PRODUCT

The average product of labor may be illustrated diagrammatically as the value of the slope of a ray through the origin to a given point on the total product curve. To see this, consider the definition of the marginal product of labor for discrete changes in output.

$$MP_L = \frac{\Delta Q}{\Delta L} = \frac{Q_2 - Q_1}{L_2 - L_1} \qquad (5.14)$$

Suppose that we arbitrarily select as our initial price quantity combination the origin (i.e., $Q_1 = L_1 = 0$). Substituting these values into Equation (5.14) we get

$$MP_L = \frac{Q_2 - 0}{L_2 - 0} = \frac{Q_2}{L_2} = AP_L \qquad (5.15)$$

This is the same result as in Equation (5.12).

Referring to Figure 5.2a, we see that as we move up along the TP_L curve from the origin, AP_L reaches a maximum at point *B*, steadily declining thereafter. Note also that at point *B* the average product of labor is precisely the value of the marginal product of labor because at that point the ray from the origin and the tangent at that point are identical. This is seen in Figure 5.2b at the labor usage $0E$, where the AP_L curve intersects the MP_L curve. Finally, unlike the marginal product of labor (or any other productive input), the average product of labor cannot be negative because labor and output can never be negative.

THE THREE STAGES OF PRODUCTION

Figure 5.2 can also be used to define the three stages of production. *Stage I of production* is defined as the range of output from $L = 0$ to, but not including, the level of labor usage at which $AP_L = MP_L$. Alternatively, stage I of production is defined up to the level of labor usage at which the average product of labor is maximized. In this range, labor is over utilized, whereas capital is underutilized. This can be seen by the fact that $MP_L > AP_L$ thus "pulling up" output per unit of labor. If we assume that the wage rate per worker and the price per unit of output are constant, then increasing output per worker suggests that average revenue generated per worker is rising, which suggests that average profit per worker is also rising. It stands to reason, therefore, that no firm would ever actually operate within this region of labor usage (0 to $MP_L = AP_L$), since additions to the labor force will increase average worker productivity and, under the appropriate assumptions, average profit generated per worker as well.

Stage II of production is defined in Figure 5.2 as the labor usage levels $0E$ to $0F$. In this region, the marginal product of labor is positive but is less than the average product of labor, thus "pulling down" output per worker, which implies that average revenue generated per worker is also falling. In this region, labor becomes increasingly less productive on average.

Finally, *stage III of production* is defined along the TP_L function for labor input usage in excess of $0F$, where $MP_L < 0$. As it is apparent that production will not take place in stage I of production because an incremental increase in labor usage will result in an increase in output per worker and, under the appropriate assumptions, an increase in profit per worker, so it is also obvious that production will not take place in stage III. This is because an increase in labor usage will result in a decline in total output accompanied by an increase in total cost of production, implying a decline in profit.

Stage III is also the counterpart to stage I of production. Whereas in stage I labor is overutilized and capital is underutilized, in stage III the reverse is true; that is, labor is underutilized and capital is overutilized. In other words, because of the symmetry of production, labor that is overutilized implies that capital is underutilized, and *vice versa*. Since stages I and III of production for labor have been ruled out as illogical from a profit maximization perspective, it also follows that stages III and I of production for capital have been ruled out for the same reasons.

We may infer that stage II of production for labor, and also for capital, is the only region in which production will take place. The precise level of labor and capital usage in stage II in which production will occur cannot be ascertained at this time. For a profit-maximizing firm, the efficient capital–labor combination will depend on the prevailing rental prices of labor (P_L) and capital (P_K), and the selling price of a unit of the resulting output (P). More precisely, as we will see, the optimal level of labor and capital usage subject to the firm's operating budget will depend on resource and output prices, and the marginal productivity of productive resources. A discussion of the optimal input combinations will be discussed in the next chapter.

ISOQUANTS

Figure 5.3 illustrates once again the production surface for Equation (5.4). From our earlier discussion we noted that because of the substitutability of productive inputs, for many productive processes it may be possible to utilize labor and capital in an infinite number of combinations (assuming that productive resources are infinitely divisible) to produce, say, 122 units of output. Using the data from Table 5.1, Figure 5.3 illustrates four such input combinations to produce 122 units of output. It should be noted once again that efficient production is defined as any input combination on the production surface. The locus of points *II* in Figure 5.3 is called an *isoquant*.

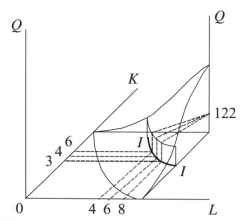

FIGURE 5.3 The production surface and an isoquant at $Q = 122$.

Definition: An isoquant defines the combinations of capital and labor (or any other input combination in n-dimensional space) necessary to produce a given level of output.

If fractional amounts of labor and capital are assumed, then an infinite number of such combinations is possible. While Figure 5.3 explicitly shows only one such isoquant at $Q = 122$ for Equation (5.4), it is easy to imagine that as we move along the production surface, an infinite number of such isoquants are possible corresponding to an infinite number of theoretical output levels. Projecting downward into capital and labor space, Figure 5.4 illustrates seven such isoquants corresponding to the data presented in Table 5.1.

Figure 5.4 is referred to as an *isoquant map*. For any given production function there are an infinite number of isoquants in an isoquant map. In general, the function for an isoquant map may be written

$$Q_0 = f(K, L) \tag{5.16}$$

where Q_0 denotes a fixed level of output. Solving Equation (5.16) for K yields

$$K = g(L, Q_0) \tag{5.17}$$

The slope of an isoquant is given by the expression

$$\frac{dK}{dL} = g_K(L, Q_0) = MRTS_{KL} < 0 \tag{5.18}$$

It measures the rate at which capital and labor can be substituted for each other to yield a constant rate of output. Equation (5.18) is also referred

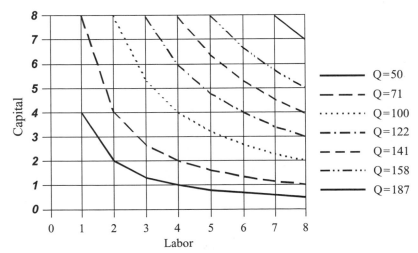

FIGURE 5.4   Selected isoquants for the production function $Q = 25K^{0.5}L^{0.5}$.

to as the *marginal rate of technical substitution* of capital for labor ($MRTS_{KL}$). The marginal rate of technical substitution summarizes the concept of substitutability discussed earlier. $MRTS_{KL}$ says that to maintain a fixed output level, an increase (decrease) in the use of capital must be accompanied by a decrease (increase) in the use of labor. It may also be demonstrated that

$$MRTS_{KL} = -\frac{MP_L}{MP_K} \tag{5.19}$$

Equation (5.19) says that the marginal rate of technical substitution of capital for labor is the ratio of the marginal product of labor (MP_L) to the marginal product of capital (MP_K).

Definition: If we assume two factors of production, capital and labor, the marginal rate of technical substitution ($MRTS_{KL}$) is the amount of a factor of production that must be added (subtracted) to compensate for a reduction (increase) in the amount of a factor of production to maintain a given level of output. The marginal rate of technical substitution, which is the slope of the isoquant, is the ratio of the marginal product of labor to the marginal product of capital (MP_L/MP_K).

To see this, consider Figure 5.5, which illustrates a hypothetical isoquant. By definition, when we move from point A to point B on the isoquant, output remains unchanged. We can conceptually break this movement down into two steps. In going from point A to point C, the reduction in output is equal to the loss in capital times the contribution of that incremental change in capital to total output (i.e., $MP_K \Delta K < 0$). In moving from point C to point B, the contribution to total output is equal to the incremental increase in labor time marginal product of that incremental increase

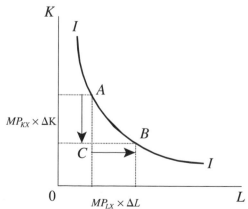

FIGURE 5.5 Slope of an isoquant: marginal rate of technical substitution.

(i.e., $MP_L \Delta L > 0$). Since to remain on the isoquant there must be no change in total output, it must be the case that

$$-MP_K \times \Delta K = MP_L \times \Delta L \tag{5.20}$$

Rearranging Equation (5.20) yields

$$\frac{\Delta K}{\Delta L} = -\frac{MP_L}{MP_K}$$

For instantaneous rates of change, Equation (5.20) becomes

$$\frac{dK}{dL} = -\frac{MP_L}{MP_K} = MRTS_{KL} < 0 \tag{5.21}$$

Equation (5.21) may also be derived by applying the implicit function theorem to Equation (5.2). Taking the total derivative of Equation (5.2) and setting the results equal to zero yields

$$dQ = \left(\frac{\partial Q}{\partial L}\right) dL + \left(\frac{\partial Q}{\partial K}\right) dK = 0 \tag{5.22}$$

Equation (5.22) is set equal to zero because output remains unchanged in moving from point A to point B in Figure 5.5. Rearranging Equation (5.22) yields

$$\frac{\partial Q/\partial L}{\partial Q/\partial K} = \frac{dK}{dL}$$

or

$$\frac{dK}{dL} = -\frac{MP_L}{MP_K}$$

Another characteristic of isoquants is that for most production processes they are convex with respect to the origin. That is, as we move from point A to point B in Figure 5.5, increasing amounts of labor are required to substitute for decreased equal increments of capital. Mathematically, convex isoquants are characterized by the conditions $dK/dL < 0$ and $d^2K/dL^2 > 0$. That is, as MP_L declines as more labor is added by the law of diminishing marginal product, MP_K increases as less capital is used. This relationship illustrates that inputs are not perfectly substitutable and that the rate of substitution declines as one input is substituted for another. Thus, with MP_L declining and MP_K increasing, the isoquant becomes convex to the origin.

The degree of convexity of the isoquant depends on the degree of substitutability of the productive inputs. If capital and labor are perfect substitutes, for example, then labor and capital may be substituted for each other at a fixed rate. The result is a linear isoquant, which is illustrated in Figure 5.6. Mathematically, linear isoquants are characterized by the

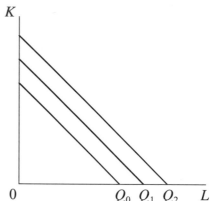

FIGURE 5.6 Perfect input substitutability.

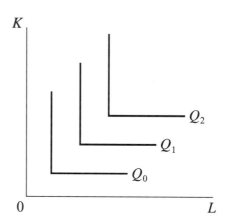

FIGURE 5.7 Fixed input combinations.

conditions $dK/dL < 0$ and $d^2K/dL^2 = 0$. Examples of production processes in which the factors of production are perfect substitutes might include oil versus natural gas for some heating furnaces, energy versus time for some drying processes, and fish meal versus soybeans for protein in feed mix.

Some production processes, on the other hand, are characterized by fixed input combinations, that is, $MRTS_{K/L} = KL$. This situation is illustrated in Figure 5.7. Note that the isoquants in this case are "L shaped." These isoquants are discontinuous functions in which efficient input combinations take place at the corners, where the smallest quantity of resources is used to produce a given level of output. Mathematically, discontinuous functions do not have first and second derivatives. Examples of such fixed-input production processes include certain chemical processes that require that basic elements be used in fixed proportions, engines and body parts for automobiles, and two wheels and a frame for a bicycle.

Problem 5.5. The general form of the Cobb–Douglas production function may be written as:

$$Q = AK^\alpha L^\beta$$

where A is a positive constant and $0 < \alpha < 1, 0 < \beta < 1$.
a. Derive an equation for an isoquant with K in terms of L.
b. Demonstrate that this isoquant is convex (bowed in) with respect to the origin.

Solution
a. An isoquant shows the various combinations of two inputs (say, labor and capital) that the firm can use to produce a specific level of output. Denoting an arbitrarily fixed level of output as Q_0, the *Cobb–Douglas production function* may be written

$$Q_0 = AK^\alpha L^\beta$$

Solving this equation for K in terms of L yields

$$K^\alpha = Q_0 A^{-1} L^{-\beta}$$

$$K = Q_0^{1/\alpha} A^{-1/\alpha} L^{-\beta/\alpha}$$

b. The necessary and sufficient conditions necessary for the isoquant to be convex (bowed in) to the origin are

$$\frac{\partial K}{\partial L} < 0$$

$$\frac{\partial^2 K}{\partial L^2} > 0$$

The first condition says that the isoquant is downward sloping. The second condition guarantees that the isoquant is convex with respect to the origin. Taking the respective derivatives yields

$$\frac{\partial K}{\partial L} = \left(-\frac{\beta}{\alpha} \right) Q_0^{1/\alpha} A^{-1/\alpha} L^{-\beta/\alpha-1} < 0$$

since $(-\beta/\alpha) < 0$ and $(Q_0^{1/\alpha} A^{-1/\alpha} L^{-\beta/\alpha-1}) > 0$. Taking the second derivative of this expression, we obtain

$$\frac{\partial^2 K}{\partial L^2} = \left[-\left(\frac{\beta}{\alpha} \right) - 1 \right] \left(-\frac{\beta}{\alpha} \right) \left(Q_0^{1/\alpha} A^{-1/\alpha} L^{-\beta/\alpha-2} \right) > 0$$

since $[-(\beta/\alpha) - 1](-\beta/\alpha) > 0$ and $(Q_0^{1/\alpha} A^{-1/\alpha} L^{-\beta/\alpha-2}) > 0$.

Problem 5.6. The Spacely Company has estimated the following production function for sprockets:

$$Q = 25K^{0.5}L^{0.5}$$

a. Suppose that $Q = 100$. What is the equation of the corresponding isoquant in terms of L?
b. Demonstrate that this isoquant is convex (bowed in) with respect to the origin.

Solution

a. The equation for the isoquant with $Q = 100$ is written as

$$100 = 25K^{0.5}L^{0.5}$$

Solving this equation for K in terms of L yields

$$K^{0.5} = 100(25L^{0.5})^{-1} = 100(25^{-1}L^{-0.5}) = 4L^{-0.5}$$

$$K = (4L^{-0.5})^2 = \frac{16}{L}$$

b. Taking the first and second derivatives of this expression yields

$$\frac{dK}{dL} = 16L^{-2} < 0$$

$$\frac{d^2K}{dL^2} = -2(-16)L^{-3} = \frac{2(16)}{L^3} = \frac{32}{L^3} > 0$$

That the first derivative is negative and the second derivative is positive are necessary and sufficient conditions for a convex isoquant.

LONG-RUN PRODUCTION FUNCTION

RETURNS TO SCALE

It was noted earlier that the long run in production describes the situation in which all factors of production are variable. A firm that increases its employment of all factors of production may be said to have increased its scale of operations. Returns to scale refer to the proportional increase in output given some equal proportional increase in all productive inputs. As discussed earlier, constant returns to scale (*CRTS*) refers to the condition where output increases in the same proportion as the equal proportional increase in all inputs. Increasing returns to scale (*IRTS*) occur when the increase in output is more than proportional to the equal proportional increase in all inputs. Decreasing returns to scale (*DRTS*) occur when the proportional increase in output is less than proportional increase in all inputs. To illustrate these relationships mathematically, consider the production function

TABLE 5.2   Production functions
homogenous of degree r.

r	Returns to scale
=1	Constant
>1	Increasing
<1	Decreasing

$$Q = f(x_1, x_2, \ldots, x_n) \tag{5.23}$$

where output is assumed to be a function of n productive inputs. A function is said to be homogeneous of degree r if, and only if,

$$f(tx_1, tx_2, \ldots, tx_n) \equiv t^r f(x_1, x_2, \ldots, x_n)$$

or

$$t^r Q \equiv f(tx_1, tx_2, \ldots, tx_n) \tag{5.24}$$

where $t > 0$ is some factor of proportionality. Note the identity sign in expression (5.24). This is not an equation that holds for only a few points but for all $t, x_1, x_2, \ldots, x_n$. This relationship expresses the notion that if all productive inputs are increased by some factor t, then output will increase by some factor t^r, where $r > 0$. Expression (5.24) is said to be a function that is homogeneous of degree r.

Returns to scale are described as constant, increasing, or decreasing depending on whether the value of r is greater than, less than, or equal to unity. Table 5.2 summarizes these relationships. Constant returns to scale is the special case of a production function that is homogeneous of degree one, which is often referred to as *linear homogeneity*.

Problem 5.7. Consider again the general form of the Cobb–Douglas production function

$$Q_0 = AK^\alpha L^\beta$$

where A is a positive constant and $0 < \alpha < 1, 0 < \beta < 1$. Specify the conditions under which this production function exhibits constant, increasing, and decreasing returns to scale.

Solution. Suppose that capital and labor are increased by a factor of t. Then,

$$f(tK, tL) \equiv A(tK)^\alpha (tL)^\beta \equiv At^\alpha K^\alpha t^\beta L^\beta \equiv t^{\alpha+\beta} AK^\alpha L^\beta \equiv t^{\alpha+\beta} Q$$

The production function exhibits constant, increasing, and decreasing returns to scale as $\alpha + \beta$ is equal to, greater than, and less than unity, respectively. For example, suppose that $\alpha = 0.3$ *and* $\beta = 0.7$ and that capital and labor are doubled ($t = 2$). The production function becomes

$$A(2K)^{0.3}(2L)^{0.7} \equiv A2^{0.3}K^{0.3}2^{0.7}L^{0.7} \equiv 2^{0.3+0.7}AK^{0.3}L^{0.7} \equiv 2Q$$

Since doubling all inputs results in a doubling of output, the production function exhibits constant returns to scale. This is easily seen by the fact that $\alpha + \beta = 1$.

Consider again Equation (5.4).

$$Q = 25K^{0.5}L^{0.5} \tag{5.4}$$

This Cobb–Douglas production function clearly exhibits constant returns to scale, since $\alpha + \beta = 1$. When $K = L = 1$, then $Q = 25$. When inputs are doubled to $K = L = 2$, then output doubles to $Q = 50$. This result is illustrated in Figure 5.8.

It should be noted that adding exponents to determine whether a production function exhibits constant, increasing, or decreasing returns to scale is applicable only to production functions that are in multiplicative (Cobb–Douglas) form. For all other functional forms, a different approach is required, as is highlighted in Problem 5.8.

Problem 5.8. For each of the following production functions, determine whether returns to scale are decreasing, constant, or increasing when capital and labor inputs are increased from $K = L = 1$ to $K = L = 2$.
a. $Q = 25K^{0.5}L^{0.5}$
b. $Q = 2K + 3L + 4KL$
c. $Q = 100 + 3K + 2L$
d. $Q = 5K^{\alpha}L^{\beta}$, where $\alpha + \beta = 1$

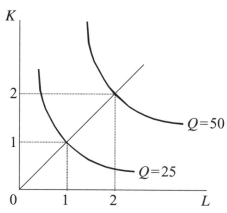

FIGURE 5.8 Constant returns to scale.

e. $Q = 20K^{0.6}L^{0.5}$
f. $Q = K/L$
g. $Q = 200 + K + 2L + 5KL$

Solution
a. For $K = L = 1$,

$$Q = 25(1)^{0.5}(1)^{0.5} = 25$$

For $K = L = 2$ (i.e., inputs are doubled),

$$Q = 25(2)^{0.5}(2)^{0.5} = 25(2)^{1} = 50$$

Since output doubles as inputs are doubled, this production function exhibits constant returns to scale. It should also be noted that for Cobb–Douglas production functions, of which this is one, returns to scale may be determined by adding the values of the exponents. In this case, $0.5 + 0.5 = 1$ indicates that this production function exhibits constant returns to scale.

b. For $K = L = 1$,

$$Q = 2(1) + 3(1) + 4(1)(1) = 2 + 3 + 4 = 9$$

For $K = L = 2$,

$$Q = 2(2) + 3(2) + 4(2)(2) = 4 + 6 + 16 = 26$$

Since output more than doubles as inputs are doubled, this production function exhibits increasing returns to scale for the input levels indicated.

c. For $K = L = 1$,

$$Q = 100 + 3(1) + 2(1) = 100 + 3 + 2 = 105$$

For $K = L = 2$,

$$Q = 100 + 3(2) + 2(2) = 100 + 6 + 4 = 110$$

Since output less than doubles as inputs are doubled, this production function exhibits decreasing returns to scale for the input levels indicated.

d. As noted earlier, returns to scale for Cobb–Douglas production functions may be determined by adding the values of the exponents. This production function clearly exhibits constant returns to scale.

e. For $K = L = 1$,

$$Q = 20(1)^{0.6}(1)^{0.5} = 20(1)(1) = 20$$

For $K = L = 2$,

$$Q = 20(2)^{0.6}(2)^{0.5} = 20(1.516)(1.414) = 42.872$$

Since output more than doubles as inputs are doubled, this production function exhibits increasing returns to scale. Since this is a Cobb–Douglas production function, this result is verified by adding the values of the exponents (i.e., $0.6 + 0.5 = 1.1$). Since this result is greater than unity, we may conclude that this production function exhibits increasing returns to scale.

f. For $K = L = 1$,

$$Q = \frac{1}{1} = 1$$

For $K = L = 2$,

$$Q = \frac{2}{2} = 1$$

Since output does not double (it remains unchanged) as inputs are doubled, this production function exhibits decreasing returns to scale.

g. For $K = L = 1$,

$$Q = 200 + 1 + 2(1) + 5(1)(1) = 208$$

For $K = L = 2$

$$Q = 200 + 2 + 2(2) + 5(2)(2) = 226$$

Since output does not double as inputs are doubled, this production function exhibits decreasing returns to scale for the input levels indicated. The reader should verify that when $K = L = 100$, then $Q = 50,500$. When input levels are doubled to $K = L = 200$, then $Q = 200,800$. In this case, a doubling of input usage resulted in an almost fourfold increase in output (i.e., increasing returns to scale). The important thing to note is that some production functions may exhibit different returns to scale depending on the level of input usage. Fortunately, Cobb–Douglas production functions exhibit the same returns-to-scale characteristics regardless of the level of input usage.

ESTIMATING PRODUCTION FUNCTIONS

The Cobb–Douglas production function is also the most commonly used production function in empirical estimation. Consider again Equation (5.3).

$$Q = AK^{\alpha}L^{\beta} \tag{5.3}$$

Cobb–Douglas production functions may be estimated using ordinary-least-squares regression methodology.[2] Ordinary least squares regression

---

[2] See, for example, W. H. Green, *Econometric Analysis*, 3rd ed. (Upper Saddle River: Prentice-Hall, 1997), D. Gujarati, *Basic Econometrics*, 3rd ed. (New York: McGraw-Hill, 1995), and R. Ramanathan, *Introductory Econometrics with Applications*, 4th ed. (New York: Dryden, 1998).

analysis is the most frequently used statistical technique for estimating business and economic relationships. In the case of Equation (5.3), ordinary least squares may be used to derive estimates of the parameters A, α and β on the basis observed values of the dependent variable Q and the independent variables K and L. To apply the ordinary-least-squares methodology, however, the equation to be estimated must be linear in parameters, which Equation (5.3) clearly is not. This minor obstacle is easily overcome. Taking logarithms of Equation (5.3) we obtain

$$\log Q = \log A + \alpha \log K + \beta \log L \tag{5.25}$$

The estimated parameter values α and β are no longer slope coefficients but elasticity values. To begin, recall that $y = \log x$, then

$$\frac{dy}{dx} = \frac{1}{x}$$

or

$$dy = \frac{dx}{x}$$

Now, taking the first partial derivatives of Equation (5.25) with respect to K and L, we obtain

$$\frac{\partial \log Q}{\partial \log K} = \alpha$$

and

$$\frac{\partial \log Q}{\partial \log L} = \beta$$

But $\partial \log Q = \partial Q/Q$, $\partial \log K = \partial K/K$, and $\partial \log L = \partial L/L$. Therefore

$$\frac{\partial \log Q}{\partial \log K} = \frac{\partial Q/Q}{\partial K/K} = \left(\frac{\partial Q}{\partial K}\right)\left(\frac{K}{Q}\right) = \alpha = \varepsilon_K \tag{5.26}$$

Similarly,

$$\frac{\partial \log Q}{\partial \log L} = \frac{\partial Q/Q}{\partial L/L} = \left(\frac{\partial Q}{\partial L}\right)\left(\frac{L}{Q}\right) = \beta = \varepsilon_L \tag{5.27}$$

These parameter values represent output elasticities of capital and labor, while the sum of these parameters is the coefficient of output elasticity (returns to scale), that is,

$$\varepsilon_Q = \varepsilon_K + \varepsilon_L \tag{5.28}$$

Problem 5.9. Consider the following Cobb–Douglas production function

$$Q = 56K^{0.38}L^{0.72}$$

a. Demonstrate that the elasticity of production with respect to labor is 0.72.
b. Demonstrate that the elasticity of production with respect to capital is 0.38.
c. Demonstrate that this production function exhibits increasing returns to scale.

Solution

a. The elasticity of production with respect to labor is

$$\varepsilon_L = \left(\frac{\partial Q}{\partial L}\right)\left(\frac{L}{Q}\right) = [(0.72)56K^{0.38}L^{0.72-1}]\left(\frac{L}{56K^{0.38}L^{0.72}}\right)$$

$$= \frac{0.72(56^{0.38}L^{-0.28})L}{56K^{0.38}L^{0.72}} = \frac{0.72Q}{Q} = 0.72$$

b. The elasticity of production with respect to capital is

$$\varepsilon_K = \left(\frac{\partial Q}{\partial K}\right)\left(\frac{K}{Q}\right) = [(0.38)56K^{0.38-1}L^{0.72}]\left(\frac{K}{56K^{0.38}L^{0.72}}\right)$$

$$= \frac{0.38(56^{-0.62}L^{0.72})K}{56K^{0.38}L^{0.72}} = \frac{0.38Q}{Q} = 0.38$$

c. The Cobb–Douglas production function is

$$Q = 56K^{0.38}L^{0.72}$$

Returns to scale refer to the additional output resulting from an equal proportional increase in all inputs. If output increases in the same proportion as the increase in all inputs, then the production function exhibits constant returns to scale. If output increases by a greater proportion than the equal proportional increase in all inputs, then the production function exhibits increasing returns to scale. Finally, if output increases by a lesser proportion than the equal proportional increase in all inputs, the production function exhibits decreasing returns to scale. To determine the returns to scale of the foregoing production function, multiply all factors by some scalar ($t > 1$), that is,

$$56(tK)^{0.38}(tL)^{0.72} = 56t^{0.38}K^{0.38}t^{0.72}L^{0.72} = t^{(0.38+0.72)}56K^{0.38}L^{0.72}$$

$$= t^{1.1}56K^{0.38}L^{0.72} = t^{1.1}Q$$

From this result, it is clear that if inputs are, say, doubled ($t = 2$), then output will increase by 2.14 times. From this we conclude that the production function exhibits increasing returns to scale. In fact, for Cobb–Douglas production functions, returns to scale are determined by the sum of the exponents. From the general form of the Cobb–Douglas production function

TABLE 5.3 Cobb-Douglas production function and returns to scale.

$\alpha + \beta$	Returns to scale
<1	Decreasing
=1	Constant
>1	Increasing

$$Q = AK^{\alpha}L^{\beta}$$

we can derive Table 5.3

CHAPTER REVIEW

A production function is the technological relationship between the maximum amount of output a firm can produce with a given combination of inputs (factors of production). The *short run in production* is defined as that period of time during which at least one factor of production is held fixed. The *long run in production* is defined as that period of time during which all factors of production are variable. In the short run, the firm is subject to the *law of diminishing returns* (sometimes referred to as the law of diminishing marginal product), which states that as additional units of a variable input are combined with one or more fixed inputs, at some point the additional output (marginal product) will start to diminish.

The short-run production function is characterized by three stages of production. Assuming that output is a function of labor and a fixed amount of capital, *stage I of production* is the range of labor usage in which the *average product of labor* (AP_L) is increasing. Over this range of output, the *marginal product of labor* (MP_L) is greater than the average product of labor. Stage I ends and stage II begins where the average product of labor is maximized (i.e., $AP_L = MP_L$).

Stage II of production is the range of output in which the average product of labor is declining and the marginal product of labor is positive. In other words, stage II of production begins where AP_L is maximized and ends with $MP_L = 0$.

Stage III of production is the range of product in which the marginal product of labor is negative. In stage II and stage III of production, $AP_L > MP_L$. According to economic theory, production in the short run for a "rational" firm takes place in stage II.

If we assume two factors of production, the marginal rate of technical substitution ($MRTS_{KL}$) is the amount of a factor of production that must be added (subtracted) to compensate for a reduction (increase) in the amount of another input to maintain a given level of output. If capital and labor are substitutable, the marginal rate of technical substitution is defined as the ratio of the marginal product of labor to the *marginal product of capital*, that is, MP_L/MP_K.

Returns to scale refers to the proportional increase in output given an equal proportional increase in all inputs. Since all inputs are variable, "returns to scale" is a long-run production phenomenon. *Increasing returns to scale (IRTS)* occur when a proportional increase in all inputs results in a more than proportional increase in output. *Constant returns to scale (CRTS)* occur when a proportional increase in all inputs results in the same proportional increase in output. *Decreasing returns to scale (DRTS)* occur when a proportional increase in all inputs results in a less than proportional increase in output.

Another way to measure returns to scale is the coefficient of output elasticity (ε_Q), which is defined as the percentage increase (decrease) in output with respect to a percentage increase (decrease) in all inputs. The coefficient of output elasticity is equal to the sum of the output elasticity of labor (ε_L) and the output elasticity of capital (ε_K), that is, $\varepsilon_Q = \varepsilon_L + \varepsilon_K$. *IRTS* occurs when $\varepsilon_Q > 1$. *CRTS* occurs when $\varepsilon_Q = 1$. *DRTS* occurs when $\varepsilon_Q < 1$.

The *Cobb–Douglas production function* is the most popular specification in empirical research. Its appeal is largely the desirable mathematical properties it exhibits, including substitutability between and among inputs, conformity to the law of diminishing returns to a variable input, and returns to scale. The Cobb–Douglas production function has several shortcomings, however, including an inability to show marginal product in stages I and III.

Most empirical studies of cost functions use time series accounting data, which present a number of problems. Accounting data, for example, tend to ignore opportunity costs, the effects of changes in inflation, tax rates, social security contributions, labor insurance costs, accounting practices, and so on. There are also other problems associated with the use of accounting data including output heterogeneity and asynchronous timing of costs.

Economic theory suggests that short-run total cost as a function of output first increases at an increasing rate, then increases at a decreasing rate. Cubic cost functions exhibit this theoretical relationship, as well as the expected "*U*-shaped" average total, average variable, and marginal cost curves.

KEY TERMS AND CONCEPTS

Average product of capital (AP_K)   The total product per unit of capital usage. It is the total product of capital divided by the total amount of capital employed by the firm.

Average product of labor (AP_L)   The total product per unit of labor usage. It is the total product of labor divided by the total amount of labor employed by the firm.

Cobb–Douglas production function   It may not in practice be possible precisely to define the mathematical relationship between the output of a good or service and a set of productive inputs employed by the firm to produce that good or service. In spite of this, because of certain desirable mathematical properties, perhaps the most widely used functional form to approximate the relationship between the production of a good or service and a set of productive inputs is the Cobb–Douglas production function. For the two-input case (capital and labor), the Cobb–Douglas production function is given by the expression $Q = AK^{\alpha}L^{\beta}$.

Coefficient of output elasticity   The percentage change in the output of a good or service given a percentage change in all productive inputs. Since all inputs are variable, the coefficient of output elasticity is a long-run production concept.

Constant returns to scale ($CRTS$)   The case in which the output of a good or a service increases in the same proportion as the proportional increase in all factors of production. Since all inputs are variable, $CRTS$ is a long-run production concept. In the case of $CRTS$ the coefficient of output elasticity is equal to unity.

Decreasing returns to scale ($DRTS$)   The case in which the output of a good or a service increases less than proportionally to a proportional increase in all factors of production used to produce that good or service. Since all inputs are variable, $DRTS$ is a long-run production concept. In the case of $DRTS$ the coefficient of output elasticity is less than unity.

Factor of production   Inputs used in the production of a good or service. Factors of production are typically classified as land, labor, capital, and entrepreneurial ability.

Increasing returns to scale ($IRTS$)   The case in which the output of a good or a service increases more than proportionally to a proportional increase in all factors of production used to produce that good or service. Since all inputs are variable, $IRTS$ is a long-run production concept. In the case of $IRTS$ the coefficient of output elasticity is greater than unity.

Isoquant   A curve that defines the different combinations of capital and labor (or any other input combination in n-dimensional space) necessary to produce a given level of output.

Law of diminishing marginal product   As increasing amounts of a variable input are combined with one or more fixed inputs, at some point the marginal product of the variable input will begin to decline. Because at least one factor of production is held fixed, the law of diminishing returns is a short-run concept.

Long run in production In the long run, all factors of production are variable.

Marginal product of capital (MP_k) The incremental change in output associated with an incremental change in the amount of capital usage. If the production function is given as $Q = f(K, L)$, then the marginal product of capital is the first partial derivative of the production function with respect to capital ($\partial Q/\partial K$), which is assumed to be positive.

Marginal product of labor (MP_L) The incremental change in output associated with an incremental change in the amount of labor usage. If the production function is given as $Q = f(K, L)$, then the marginal product of labor is the first partial derivative of the production function with respect to labor ($\partial Q/\partial L$), which is assumed to be positive.

Marginal rate of technical substitution ($MRTS_{KL}$) Suppose that output is a function of variable labor and capital input, $Q = f(K, L)$. The marginal rate of technical substitution is the rate at which capital (labor) must be substituted for labor (capital) to maintain a given level of output. The marginal rate of technical substitution, which is the slope of the isoquant, is the ratio of the marginal product of labor to the marginal product of capital (MP_L/MP_K).

Production function A mathematical expression that relates the maximum amount of a good or service that can be produced with a set of factors of production.

$Q = AK^{\alpha}L^{\beta}$ The Cobb–Douglas production function, which asserts that the output of a good or a service as a multiplicative function of capital (K) and labor (L).

Short run in production That period of time during which at least one factor of production is constant.

Stage I of production Assuming that output is a function of variable labor and fixed capital, this is the range of labor usage in which the average product of labor is increasing. Over this range of output, the marginal product of labor is greater than the average product of labor. Stage I ends, and stage II begins, where the average product of labor is maximized (i.e., $AP_L = MP_L$). According to economic theory, production in the short run for a "rational" firm takes place in stage II of production.

Stage II of production Assuming that output is a function of variable labor and fixed capital, this is the range of output in which the average product of labor is declining and the marginal product of labor is positive. Stage II of production begins where AP_L is maximized, and ends with $MP_L = 0$.

Stage III of production Assuming that output is a function of variable labor and fixed capital, this is the range of production in which the marginal product of labor is negative.

Total product of capital Assuming that output is a function of variable capital and fixed labor, this is the total output of a firm for a given level of labor input.

Total product of labor Assuming that output is a function of variable labor and fixed capital, this is the total output of a firm for a given level of labor input.

CHAPTER QUESTIONS

5.1 What is the difference between a production function and a total product function?

5.2 What is meant by the short run in production?

5.3 What is meant by the long run in production?

5.4 What is the total product of labor? What is the total product of capital? Are these short-run or long-run concepts?

5.5 Suppose that output is a function of labor and capital. Assume that labor is the variable input and capital is the fixed input. Explain the law of diminishing marginal product. How is the law of diminishing marginal product reflected in the total product of labor curve?

5.6 Assume that a production function exhibits the law of diminishing marginal product. What are the signs of the first and second partial derivatives of output with respect to variable labor input?

5.7 Suppose that the total product of labor curve exhibits increasing, diminishing and negative marginal product. Describe in detail the shapes of the marginal product and average product curves.

5.8 Suppose that the total product of labor curve exhibits only diminishing marginal product. Describe in detail the shapes of the marginal product and average product curves.

5.9 Explain the difference between the law of diminishing marginal product and decreasing returns to scale.

5.10 Suppose that output is a function of labor and capital. Define the output elasticity of variable labor input. Define the output elasticity of variable capital input. What is the sum of the output elasticity of variable labor and variable capital input?

5.11 Suppose that a firm's production function is $Q = 75K^{0.4}L^{0.7}$. What is the value of the output elasticity of labor? What is the value of the output elasticity of capital? Does this firm's production function exhibit constant, increasing, or decreasing returns to scale?

5.12 Define "marginal rate of technical substitution."

5.13 Suppose that output is a function of labor and capital. Diagrammatically, what is the marginal rate of technical substitution?

5.14 Explain the difference between perfect and imperfect substitutability of factors of production.

5.15 What does an "L-shaped" isoquant illustrate? Can you give an example of a production process that would exhibit an "L-shaped" isoquant?

5.16 What does a linear isoquant illustrate?

5.17 Isoquants cannot intersect. Do you agree? Explain.

5.18 The degree of convexity of an isoquant determines the degree of substitutability of factors of production. Do you agree? Explain.

5.19 Suppose that output is a function of capital and labor input. Assume that the production function exhibits imperfect substitutability between the factors of production. What, if anything, can you say about the values of the first and second derivatives of the isoquant?

5.20 Suppose that a firm's production function is $Q = KL^{-1}$. Does this production function exhibit increasing, decreasing, or constant returns to scale? Explain.

5.21 Define each of the following:
a. Stage I of production
b. Stage II of production
c. Stage III of production

5.22 When the average product of labor is equal to the marginal product of labor, the marginal product of labor is maximized. Do you agree? Explain.

5.23 Suppose that output is a function of labor and capital input. The slope of an isoquant is equal to the ratio of the marginal products of capital and labor. Do you agree? Explain.

5.24 Suppose that output is a function of labor and capital input. If a firm decides to reduce the amount of capital employed, how much labor should be hired to maintain a given level of output?

5.25 What is the ratio of the marginal product of labor to the average product of labor?

5.26 Isoquants may be concave with respect to the origin. Do you agree? Explain.

5.27 Firms operate in the short run and plan in the long run. Do you agree? Explain.

5.28 Describe at least three desirable properties of Cobb–Douglas production functions.

5.29 What is the relationship between the average product of labor and the marginal product of labor?

5.30 What is the coefficient of output elasticity?

5.31 Suppose that output is a function of labor and capital input. Suppose further that the corresponding isoquant is linear. These conditions indicate that labor and capital are not substitutable for each other. Do you agree? Explain.

5.32 Suppose that output is a function of labor and capital input. Suppose further that capital and labor must be combined in fixed proportions. These conditions indicate that returns to scale are constant. Do you agree? Explain.

5.33 An increase in the size of a company's labor force resulted in an increase in the average product of labor. For this to happen, the firm's total output must have increased. Do you agree? Explain.

5.34 An increase in the size of a company's labor force will result in a shift of the average product of labor curve up and to the right. This indicates that the company is experiencing increasing returns to scale. Do you agree? Explain.

5.35 Suppose that output is a function of labor and capital input and exhibits constant returns to scale. If a firm doubles its use of both labor and capital, the total product of labor curve will become steeper. Do you agree? Explain.

CHAPTER EXERCISES

5.1 Suppose that the production function of a firm is given by the equation

$$Q = 2K^{.5}L^{.5}$$

where Q represents units of output, K units of capital, and L units of labor. What is the marginal product of labor and the marginal product of capital at $K = 40$ and $L = 10$?

5.2 A firm's production function is given by the equation

$$Q = 100K^{0.3}L^{0.8}$$

where Q represents units of output, K units of capital, and L units of labor.

    a. Does this production function exhibit increasing, decreasing, or constant returns to scale?

    b. Suppose that $Q = 1,000$. What is the equation of the corresponding isoquant in terms of labor?

    c. Demonstrate that this isoquant is convex with respect to the origin.

5.3 Determine whether each of the following production functions exhibits increasing, decreasing, or constant returns to scale for $K = L = 1$ and $K = L = 2$.

    a. $Q = 10 + 2L^2 + K^3$

    b. $Q = 5 + 10K + 20L + KL$

    c. $Q = 500K^{0.7}L^{0.1}$

    d. $Q = K + L + 5LK$

5.4 Suppose that a firm's production function has been estimated as

$$Q = 5K^{0.5}L^{0.5}$$

where Q is units of output, K is machine hours, and L is labor hours. Suppose that the amount of K available to the firm is fixed at 100 machine hours.

   a. What is the firm's total product of labor equation? Graph the total product of labor equation for values $L = 0$ to $L = 200$.

   b. What is the firm's marginal product of labor equation? Graph the marginal product of labor equation for values $L = 0$ to $L = 200$.

   c. What is the firm's average product of labor equation? Graph the average product of labor equation for values $L = 0$ to $L = 200$.

5.5 Suppose that a firm's short-run production function has been estimated as

$$Q = 2L + 0.4L^2 - 0.002L^3$$

where Q is units of output and L is labor hours.

   a. Graph the production function for values $L = 0$ to $L = 200$.

   b. What is the firm's marginal product of labor equation? Graph the marginal product of labor equation for values $L = 0$ to $L = 200$.

   c. What is the firm's average product of labor equation? Graph the average product of labor equation for values $L = 0$ to $L = 200$.

5.6 Lothian Company has estimated the following production function for its product lembas

$$Q = 10K^{0.3}L^{0.7}$$

where Q represents units of output, K units of capital, and L units of labor. What is the coefficient of output elasticity? What are the returns to scale?

5.7 The average product of labor is given by the equation

$$AP_L = 600 + 200L - L^2$$

   a. What is the equation for the total product of labor (TP_L)?

   b. What is the equation for the marginal product of labor (MP_L)?

   c. At what level of labor usage is $AP_L = MP_L$?

SELECTED READINGS

Brennan, M. J., and T. M. Carrol. *Preface to Quantitative Economics & Econometrics*, 4th ed. Cincinnati, OH: South-Western Publishing, 1987.

Cobb, C. W., and P. H. Douglas. "A Theory of Production." *American Economic Review* March (1928), pp. 139–165.

Douglas, P. H. "Are There Laws of Production?" *American Economic Review*, March (1948), pp. 1–41.

———. "The Cobb–Douglas Production Function Once Again: Its History, Its Testing, and Some New Empirical Values." *Journal of Political Economy*, October (1984), pp. 903–915.

Glass, J. C. *An Introduction to Mathematical Methods in Economics.* New York: McGraw-Hill, 1980.

Henderson, J. M., and R. E. Quandt. *Microeconomic Theory: A Mathematical Approach*, 3rd ed. New York: McGraw-Hill, 1980.

Maxwell, W. D. Production Theory and Cost Curves. *Applied Economics*, 1, August (1969), pp. 211–224.

Silberberg, E. *The Structure of Economics: A Mathematical Approach*, 2nd ed. New York: McGraw-Hill, 1990.

Walters, A. A. Production and Cost Functions: An Econometric Survey. *Econometrica*, January (1963), pp. 1–66.

6

COST

In Chapter 5 we reviewed the theoretical implications of the technological process whereby factors of production are efficiently transformed into goods and services for sale in the market. The production function defines the maximum rate of output per unit of time obtainable from a given set of productive inputs. The production function, however, was presented as a purely technological relationship devoid of any behavioral assertions underlying motives of management. The optimal combination of inputs used in the production process will differ depending on the firm's organizational objectives. The objective of profit maximization, for example, may require that the firm use one set of productive resources, while maximization of revenue or market share may require a completely different set. The substitutability of inputs in the production process indicates that any given level of output may be produced with multiple factor combinations. Deciding which of these combinations is optimal not only depends on a well-defined organizational objective but also requires that management attempt to achieve this objective while constrained by a limited operating budget and constellation of factor prices. Changes in the budget constraints or factor prices will alter the optimal combination of inputs. The purpose of this chapter is to bridge the gap between production as a purely technological relationship and the cost of producing a level of output to achieve a well-defined organizational objective.

THE RELATIONSHIP BETWEEN PRODUCTION AND COST

The cost function of a profit-maximizing firm shows the minimum cost of producing various output levels given market-determined factor prices and the firm's budget constraint. Although largely the domain of accountants, the concept of cost to an economist carries a somewhat different connotation. As already discussed in Chapter 1, economists generally are concerned with any and all costs that are relevant to the production process. These costs are referred to as *total economic costs*. *Relevant costs* are all costs that pertain to the decision by management to produce a particular good or service.

Total economic costs include the *explicit costs* associated with the day-to-day operations of a firm, but also *implicit* (*indirect*) costs. All costs, both explicit and implicit, are opportunity costs. They are the value of the next best alternative use of a resource. What distinguishes explicit costs from implicit costs is their "visibility" to the manager. Explicit costs are sometimes referred to as "out-of-pocket" costs. Explicit costs are visible expenditures associated with the procurement of the services of a factor of production. Wages paid to workers are an example of an explicit cost.

By contrast, implicit costs are, in a sense, invisible: the manager will not receive an invoice for resources supplied or for services rendered. To understand the distinction, consider the situation of a programmer who is weighing the potential monetary gains from leaving a job at a computer software company to start a consulting business. The programmer must consider not only the potential revenues and out-of-pocket expenses (explicit costs) but also the salary forgone by leaving the computer company. The programmer will receive no bill for the services he or she brings to the consulting company, but the forgone salary is just as real a cost of running a consulting business as the rent paid for office space. As with any opportunity cost, implicit costs represent the value of the factor's next best alternative use and must therefore be taken into account. As a practical matter, implicit costs are easily made explicit. In the scenario just outlines, the programmer can make the forgone salary explicit by putting himself or herself "on the books" as a salaried employee of the consulting firm.

SHORT-RUN COST

The theory of cost is closely related to the underlying production technology. We will begin by assuming that the firm's short-run total cost (TC) of production is given by the expression

$$TC = f(Q) \tag{6.1}$$

As we discussed in Chapter 5, the short run in production is defined as that period of time during which at least one factor of production is held at some fixed level. Assuming only two factors of production, capital (K) and labor (L), and assuming that capital is the fixed factor (K_0), then Equation (6.1) may be written

$$TC = f[g(K_0, L)] \qquad (6.2)$$

Equation (6.2) simply says that the short-run total cost of production is a function of output, which is itself a function of the level of capital and labor usage. In other words, total cost is a function of output, which is a function of the production technology and factors of production, and factors of production cost money.

Equation (6.2) is a general statement that relates the total cost of production to the usage of the factors of production, fixed capital and variable labor. Equation (6.2) also makes clear that total cost is intimately related to the characteristics of the underlying production technology. As we will see, concepts such as total cost (TC), average total cost (ATC), average variable cost (AVC), and marginal cost (MC) are defined by their production counterparts, total physical product, average physical product, and marginal physical product of both labor and capital.

To begin with, let us assume that the prices of labor and capital are determined in perfectly competitive factor markets. The short-run total economic cost of production is given as

$$TC = P_K K_0 + P_L L \qquad (6.3)$$

where P_K is the rental price of capital, P_L is the rental price of labor, K_0 is a fixed amount of capital, and L is variable labor input. The most common example of the rental price of labor is the wage rate. An example of the rental price of capital might be what a construction company must pay to lease heavy equipment, such as a bulldozer or a backhoe. If the construction company already owns the heavy equipment, the rental price of capital may be viewed as the forgone income that could have been earned by leasing its own equipment to someone else. In either case, both P_K and P_L are assumed to be market determined and are thus parametric to the output decisions of the firm's management. Thus, Equation (6.3) may be written

$$TC(Q) = TFC + TVC(Q) \qquad (6.4)$$

where TFC and TVC represent total fixed cost and total variable cost, respectively.

Total fixed cost is a short-run production concept. Fixed costs of production are associated with acquiring and maintaining fixed factors of production. Fixed costs are incurred by the firm regardless of the level of production. Fixed costs are incurred by the firm even if no production takes place at all. Examples often include continuing expenses incurred under a binding contract, such as rental payments on office space, certain insurance payments, and some legal retainers.

Total variable costs of production are associated with acquiring and maintaining variable factors of production. In stages I and II of production, total variable cost is an increasing function of the level of output. *Total cost* is the sum of total fixed and total variable cost.

KEY RELATIONSHIPS: AVERAGE TOTAL COST, AVERAGE FIXED COST, AVERAGE VARIABLE COST, AND MARGINAL COST

The definitions of average fixed cost, average variable cost, average total cost, and marginal cost are, appropriately, as follows:

$$\text{Average fixed cost: } AFC = \frac{TFC}{Q} \tag{6.5}$$

$$\text{Average variable cost: } AVC = \frac{TVC}{Q} \tag{6.6}$$

$$\text{Average total cost: } ATC = \frac{TC}{Q} = \frac{TFC + TVC}{Q} = AFC + AVC \tag{6.7}$$

$$\text{Marginal cost: } MC = \frac{dTC}{dQ} = \frac{dTVC}{dQ} \tag{6.8}$$

Average total cost is the total cost of production per unit. It is the total cost of production divided by total output. Average total cost is a short-run production concept if total cost includes fixed cost. It is a long-run production concept if all costs are variable costs. *Average fixed cost*, which is a short-run production concept, is total fixed cost per unit of output. It is total fixed cost divided by total output. *Average variable cost* is total variable cost of production per unit of output. Average variable cost is total variable cost divided by total output.

Marginal cost is the change in the total cost associated with a change in total output.[1] Contrary to conventional belief, this is not the same thing as the cost of producing the "last" unit of output. Since it is total cost that is changing, the cost of producing the last unit of output is the same as the

---

[1] Strictly speaking, it is incorrect to assert that marginal cost is the rate of change in total cost with respect to a change in output unless total cost has been properly specified. The total cost equation $TC = P_K K + P_L L$ is a function of inputs K and L, and factor prices P_K and P_L. Mathematically, it is incorrect to differentiate total cost with respect to the nonexistent argument, Q. As we saw from our discussion of isoquants in Chapter 5, it is possible to produce a given level of output with numerous combinations of inputs. For the profit-maximizing firm, however, only the cost-minimizing combination of inputs is of interest. Marginal cost is not, therefore, an arbitrary increase in total cost given an increase in output. Rather, marginal cost is the *minimum* increase in total cost with respect to an increase in output. The appropriate total cost equation is

$$TC = P_K K^*(P_K, P_L, Q) + P_L L^*(P_K, P_L, Q) = TC^*(P_K, P_L, Q)$$

where L^* and K^* represent the optimal input levels for a cost-minimizing firm. Once the total cost function has been properly defined, marginal cost is $MC = \partial TC^*(P_K, P_L, Q)/\partial Q$. For a more detailed discussion, see Silberberg (1990, Chapter 10, pp. 226–227).

per-unit cost of producing any other level of output. More specifically, the marginal cost of production for a profit-maximizing firm is equal to average total cost plus the per-unit change in total cost, multiplied by total output.[2] Equation (6.8) shows that marginal cost is the same as marginal variable cost, since total fixed cost is a constant.

Related to marginal cost is the more general concept of *incremental cost*. While marginal cost is the change in total cost given a change in output, incremental cost is the change in the firm's total costs that result from the implementation of decisions made by management, such as the introduction of a new product or a change in the firm's advertising campaign. By contrast, *sunk costs* are invariant with respect to changes in management decisions. Since sunk costs are not recoverable once incurred, they should not be considered when one is determining, say, an optimal level of output or product mix. Suppose, for example, that a textile manufacture purchases a loom for $1 million. If the firm is able to dispose of the loom in the resale market for only $750,000, the firm, in effect, has permanently lost $250,000. In other words, the firm has incurred a sunk cost of $250,000.

Related to the concept of sunk cost is the analytically more important concept of total fixed cost. Total fixed cost, which represents the cost of a firm's fixed inputs, is invariant with respect to the profit-maximizing level of output. This is demonstrated in Equation (6.8). Changes in total cost with respect to changes in output are the same as changes in total variable cost with respect to changes in output. In other words, marginal variable cost is identical to marginal cost.

The distinction between sunk and fixed cost is subtle. Suppose that when the firm operated the loom to produce cotton fabrics, the rental price of the loom was $100,000 per year. This rental price is invariant to the firm's level of production. In other words, the firm would rent the loom for $100,000 per year regardless of whether it produced 5,000 or 100,000 yards of cloth during that period. A sunk cost is essentially the difference between the purchase price of the loom and its salvage value.

---

[2] As discussed in footnote 1, the appropriate total cost equation for a profit-maximizing firm is $TC = P_K K^*(P_K, P_L, Q) + P_L L^*(P_K, P_L, Q) = TC^*(P_K, P_L, Q)$. Thus, appropriate average total cost function is

$$ATC^*(P_K, P_L, Q) = \frac{TC^*(P_K, P_L, Q)}{Q}$$

Differentiating this expression with respect to output yields

$$\frac{\partial ATC^*}{\partial Q} = \frac{Q(\partial TC^*/\partial Q) - TC^*}{Q^2}$$

Rearranging, and noting that $MC^* = \partial TC^*/\partial Q$, yields

$$MC^* = ATC^* + \left(\frac{\partial ATC^*}{Q}\right)Q$$

For a more detailed exposition and discussion, see Silberberg (1990, Chapter 10, pp. 229–230).

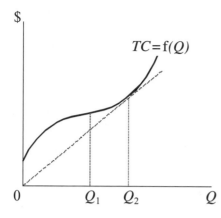

FIGURE 6.1   Total cost curve exhibiting increasing then diminishing marginal product.

Additional insights into the relationship between total cost and production may be seen by examining Equation (6.8). Recalling that $Q = f(K, L)$ and applying the chain rule we obtain

$$MC = \frac{dTC}{dQ} = \left(\frac{dTC}{dL}\right)\left(\frac{dL}{dQ}\right)$$

Recalling from Equation (6.3) that $TC = P_K K_0 + P_L L$, then marginal cost may be written as

$$MC = P_L\left(\frac{dL}{dQ}\right) = \frac{P_L}{MP_L} \tag{6.9}$$

where P_L is the rental price of homogeneous labor input and MP_L is the marginal product of labor. Equation (6.9) establishes a direct link between marginal cost and the marginal product of labor, which was discussed in Chapter 5. Since P_L is a constant, it is easily seen that MC varies inversely with MP_L. Recalling Figure 5.2 in the preceding chapter, the shapes of the $TC, ATC, AVC,$ and MC curves may easily be explained. When MP_L is rising (falling), for example, MC will be falling (rising). These relationships are illustrated in Figures 6.1 and 6.2.

Equation (6.9) indicates clearly the relation between the theory of production and the theory of cost. The cost curves are shaped as they are because the production function exhibits the properties it does, especially the law of diminishing marginal product. In other words, underlying the short-run cost functions are the short-run production functions.

Problem 6.1. For most of his professional career, David Ricardo was a computer programmer for International Megabyte Corporation (IMC). During his last year at IMC, David earned an annual salary of $120,000. Last year, David founded his own consulting firm, Computer Compatriots, Inc. His monthly fixed costs, including rent, property and casualty insurance,

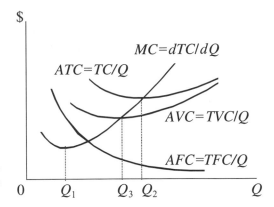

FIGURE 6.2 Marginal, average total, average variable, and average fixed cost curves.

and group health insurance, amounted to $5,000. David's monthly variable costs, including wages and salaries, telecommunications services (telephone, fax, e-mail, conference calling, etc.), personal computer rentals and maintenance, mainframe computer time sharing, and office supplies, amounted to $20,000.

a. Assuming that David does not pay himself a salary, what are the total monthly explicit costs of Computer Compatriots?
b. What are the firm's total monthly economic costs?

Solution

a. Total explicit cost refers to all "out-of-pocket" expenses. The total monthly explicit costs of Computer Compatriots are

$$TC_{explicit} = TFC + TVC_{explicit} = \$5,000 + \$20,000 = \$25,000$$

b. "Total economic cost" is the sum of total explicit costs and total implicit costs. In this case, the total monthly implicit (opportunity) cost to David Ricardo of founding Computer Compatriots is $10,000, which was the monthly salary earned by him while working for IMC. The new firm's total monthly economic costs are

$$TC_{economic} = TFC + TVC_{explicit} + TVC_{implicit}$$
$$= \$5,000 + \$20,000 + \frac{\$120,000}{12} = \$35,000$$

THE FUNCTIONAL FORM OF THE TOTAL COST FUNCTION

Figure 6.1 illustrated a short-run total cost function exhibiting both increasing and diminishing marginal product. In the diagram, increasing marginal product occurs over the range of output from 0 to Q_1, while diminishing marginal product characterizes output levels greater than Q_1. The inflection point, which occurs at output level Q_1, corresponds to minimum marginal cost. The short-run total cost function in Figure 6.1 may be characterized by a cubic function of the form

$$TC(Q) = b_0 + b_1 Q + b_2 Q^2 + b_3 Q^3 \qquad (6.10)$$

For Equation (6.10) to make sense, the values of the coefficients (b_i s) must make economic sense. The value of the constant term, for example, must be restricted to some positive value, $b_0 > 0$, since total fixed cost must be positive.

To determine the restrictions that should be placed on the remaining coefficient values, consider again Figure 6.1. Note that as illustrated in Figure 6.2, in which marginal cost is always positive, total cost is an increasing function of output. Since the minimum value of MC is positive, it is necessary to restrict the remaining coefficients so that the absolute minimum value of the marginal cost function is also positive. These restrictions are[3]

[3] To see this, consider output level at which MC is minimized. Taking the first derivative of the total cost function to derive the marginal cost function, we find that

$$\frac{dTC}{dQ} = MC(Q) = b_1 + 2b_2 Q + 3b_3 Q^2$$

Taking the first derivative of the marginal cost function (the second derivative of the total cost function) and setting the results equal to zero, we get

$$\frac{dMC}{dQ} = \frac{d^2 TC}{dQ^2} = 2b_2 + 6b_3 Q = 0$$

which reduces to

$$Q = \frac{-b_2}{3b_3}$$

The second-order condition for a minimum is

$$\frac{d^2 MC}{dQ^2} = 6b_3 > 0$$

That is, the value of b_3 must be positive. Since we expect the optimal value of Q (Q^*) to be positive, then by implication b_2 must be negative. Upon substituting Q^* into the marginal cost function, the minimum value of MC becomes

$$MC_{\min} = b_1 + 2b_2 \left(\frac{-b_2}{3b_3} \right) + 3b_3 \left(\frac{-b_2}{3b_3} \right)^2$$

$$= -\frac{b_2^2}{3b_3} + b_1 = \frac{3b_3 b_1 - b_2^2}{3b_3}$$

The equation for $MC_{\min}$ indicates that the restrictions $b_3 > 0$ and $b_2 < 0$ are not sufficient to guarantee that the absolute minimum of marginal cost will be positive. This requires the additional condition that $(3b_3 b_1 - b_2^2) > 0$. The last restriction implies that $b_1 > 0$ and that $3b_3 b_1 > b_2^2 > 0$.

$$b_0 > 0; b_1 > 0; b_2 < 0; b_3 > 0; 3b_3b_1 > b_2^2 > 0$$

Equation (6.10) is the most general form of the total cost function because it reflects both increasing marginal product and diminishing marginal product. But, as we saw in Chapter 5, while the production function *may* exhibit increasing marginal product at low levels of output, this is not guaranteed. The only thing of which we may be certain is that in the short run, at some level of output (and this may occur as soon as the firm commences operations), total cost will begin to increase at an increasing rate. For firms that experience only diminishing marginal product, the total cost equation may be written as

$$TC(Q) = b_0 + b_1Q^2 \qquad (6.11)$$

As before, positive total fixed cost guarantees that $b_0 > 0$. Increasing marginal cost requires that $dMC/dQ = d^2TC/dQ^2 > 0$. From Equation (6.11), the reader will verify that $MC = 2b_1Q$ and $dMC/dQ = 2b_1$. Increasing marginal cost also requires, therefore, that $b_1 > 0$.

Problem 6.2. A firm's total cost function is

$$TC = 12 + 60Q - 15Q^2 + Q^3$$

Suppose that the firm produces 10 units of output. Calculate total fixed cost (*TFC*), total variable cost (*TVC*), average total cost (*ATC*), average fixed cost (*AFC*), average variable cost (*AVC*), and marginal cost (*MC*).

Solution

$$TFC = 12$$

$$TVC = 60Q - 15Q^2 + Q^3 = 60(10) - 15(10)^2 + (10)^3 = 100$$

$$ATC = 12Q^{-1} + 60 - 15Q + Q^2 = \frac{12}{10} + 60 - 15(10) + (10)^2 = 11.2$$

$$AFC = 12Q^{-1} = \frac{12}{10} = 1.2$$

$$AVC = 60 - 15Q + Q^2 = 60 - 15(10) + (10)^2 = 10$$

$$MC = \frac{dTC}{dQ} = 60 - 30Q + 3Q^2 = 60 - 30(10) + 3(10)^2 = 60$$

MATHEMATICAL RELATIONSHIP BETWEEN ATC AND MC

An examination of Figure 6.2 indicates that the marginal cost (*MC*) curve intersects the average total cost (*ATC*) curve and average variable cost (AVC) curve from below at their minimum points. The relation between total, marginal, and average functions were discussed in Chapters 2 and 5. This section will extend that discussion to the specific relation between MC and ATC. The approach is to minimize the average total cost function and determine if the condition observed in Figure 6.2 is satisfied. Consider, again, the definition of average total cost

$$ATC = \frac{TC}{Q} \tag{6.7}$$

Minimizing Equation (6.7) by taking the first derivative with respect to output and setting the results equal to zero yields

$$\frac{dATC}{dQ} = \frac{Q(dTC/dQ) - TC}{Q^2} = 0 \tag{6.12}$$

Since $Q^2 > 0$, then, from Equation (6.12),

$$\frac{dTC}{dQ} = \frac{TC}{Q}$$

That is, the first-order condition for a minimum ATC is

$$MC = ATC \tag{6.13}$$

The second-order condition for minimum is that the second derivative of Equation (6.7) is positive. Taking the derivative of Equation (6.12) yields

$$\frac{d^2 ATC}{dQ^2}$$
$$= \frac{Q^2[Q(d^2 TC/dQ^2 + dTC/dQ - dTC/dQ)] - [Q(dTC/dQ) - TC](2Q)}{Q^4}$$
$$= \frac{(d^2 TC/dQ^2)}{Q} - \frac{(2dTC/dQ)}{Q^2} + \frac{2TC}{Q^3}$$

Substituting the first-order condition $Q(dTC/dQ) - TC$ yields

$$\frac{d^2 ATC}{dQ^2} = \frac{(d^2 TC/dQ^2)}{Q} - \frac{(2dTC/dQ)}{Q^2} + \frac{2Q(dTC/dQ)}{Q^3}$$
$$= \frac{(d^2 TC/dQ^2)}{Q} = \frac{(dMC/dQ)}{Q} > 0 \tag{6.14}$$

for a minimum ATC. Since $Q > 0$, at a minimum ATC the second-order condition requires that marginal cost is increasing. As indicated in Figure 6.2, at the point at which ATC is minimized, $ATC = MC$, and the MC curve intersects the ATC curve from below.

It is also easy to demonstrate that the marginal cost curve also intersects the minimum point on the average variable cost (AVC) curve from below. From Equation (6.4)

$$TC(Q) = TFC + TVC(Q) \tag{6.4}$$

Dividing both sides of Equation (6.4) by output, and rearranging, we obtain

$$AVC(Q) = ATC(Q) - AFC \tag{6.15}$$

Taking the derivative of Equation (6.15) with respect to output yields

$$\frac{dAVC(Q)}{dQ} = \frac{dATC(Q)}{dQ} \tag{6.16}$$

since AFC is a constant. Thus, minimizing average variable cost with respect to output is equivalent to minimizing average total cost with respect to output, and generates identical conclusions.

It should be pointed out that although the MC curve intersects both the ATC and AVC curve at their minimum points that minimum AVC occurs at a lower output level than minimum ATC. To see why this is the case, refer again to Equation (6.15). For any output level, including the output level that minimizes ATC and AVC, ATC exceeds AVC by the amount of AFC. In Figure 6.2, since the marginal cost curve is upward sloping, the MC curve cannot intersect both the AVC and ATC curves at their minimum points unless it does so at different output levels as long as $AFC > 0$ (otherwise $ATC = AVC$). Since $ATC > AVC$, the output level corresponding to the minimum point on the ATC curve must be above and to the right of the output level that corresponds to the minimum point on the AVC curve. Finally, referring again to Figure 6.2, from Equation (6.15), AFC must equal the vertical distance between the ATC and the AVC curves at any output level. Since AFC falls as Q increases, the ATC and AVC curves must be asymptotic vertically.

Problem 6.3. Suppose that the total cost function of a firm is given as

$$TC = 1,000 + 10Q^2$$

a. Determine the output level that minimizes average total cost (ATC). At this output level, what is TC? ATC? MC? Verify that at this output level $MC = ATC$, and that ATC intersects MC from below.
b. Determine the output level that minimizes average variable cost (AVC). At this output level, what is TC? AVC? MC?
c. Diagram your answers to parts a and b.

Solution
a. ATC is calculated as

$$ATC = \frac{TC}{Q} = \frac{1,000 + 10Q^2}{Q} = 1,000Q^{-1} + 10Q$$

To determine the output level that minimizes this expression, take the first derivative of the ATC equation, set the resulting expression equal to zero, and solve.

$$\frac{dATC}{dQ} = -1,000Q^{-2} + 10 = 0$$

$$Q^* = 10$$

At $Q^* = 10$, total cost is

$$TC = 1,000 + 10(10)^2 = 2,000$$

It should also be noted that since $TC = ATC \times Q$, then

$$TC = 200(10) = 2,000$$

The first-order condition for average total cost minimization is satisfied at an output level of 10 units. To verify that ATC is minimized at this output level, the second-order condition requires that the second derivative be positive, that is,

$$\frac{d^2ATC}{dQ^2} = 2(1,000Q^{-3}) = \frac{2,000}{Q^3} > 0$$

At $Q = 10$, average total cost is

$$ATC_{min} = \frac{1,000 + 10(10)^2}{10} = \frac{1,000 + 1,000}{10} = 200$$

The marginal cost equation is

$$\frac{dTC}{dQ} = MC = 20Q$$

Marginal cost at $Q^* = 10$ is

$$MC = 20(10) = 200$$

Not surprisingly, $MC = ATC$ at the output level that minimizes ATC. For MC to intersect ATC from below, it must be the case that at $Q^* = 10$, $dMC/dQ > 0$. The reader will verify that is condition is satisfied.

b. AVC is calculated as follows:

$$AVC = \frac{TVC}{Q} = \frac{10Q^2}{Q} = 10Q$$

Note that AVC is linear in output. This follows directly becomes the total cost is specified as a quadratic equation. Although linear equations do not have a minimum or a maximum value, since total cost is restricted to nonnegative values of Q, the foregoing suggests that AVC is

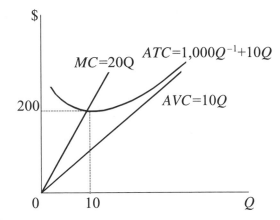

FIGURE 6.3

minimized where $Q = 0$. Substituting this into the AVC equation, we obtain

$$AVC = 10(0) = 0$$

In other words, at zero output the firm incurs only fixed cost, that is,

$$TC = 1,000 + 10(0)^2 = TFC$$

Again, the marginal cost equation is

$$MC = 20Q$$

Marginal cost at $Q* = 0$ is

$$MC = 20(0) = 0$$

Again, not surprisingly, $MC = AVC$ at the output level that minimizes AVC.

c. Figure 6.3 diagrams the answers to parts a and b.

LEARNING CURVE EFFECT

The discussion in Chapter 5 noted that the profit-maximizing firm will operate in *stage II* of production. It will be recalled that in *stage II* the marginal product of a factor, say labor, is positive, but declining at an increasing rate. The phenomenon is a direct consequence of the law of diminishing marginal product. At constant factor prices this relationship implies that as output is expanded, the marginal cost of a variable factor increases at an increasing rate.

An important assumption implicit in the law of diminishing marginal product is that the quality of the variable input used remains unchanged.

TABLE 6.1   Learning Curve Effects: Unit Labor Costs

Output	$m = 0.9$	$m = 0.8$	$m = 0.7$
1	$10,000.00	$10,000.00	$10,000.00
2	9,000.00	8,000.00	7,000.00
4	8,100.00	6,400.00	4,900.00
8	7,290.00	5,120.00	3,430.00
16	6,561.00	4,096.00	2,401.00
32	5,904.90	3,276.80	1,680.70
64	5,314.41	2,621.44	1,176.49
128	4,782.97	2,097.15	823.54
256	4,340.67	1,677.72	576.48

In the case of labor, for example, the "productivity" of labor is assumed to remain unchanged regardless of the level of production. In fact, this restriction is an oversimplification: it is reasonable to expect that as output expands over time, the typical laborer "gets better" at his or her job. In other words, it is reasonable to assume that workers become more productive as they gain experience. This would suggest that over some range of production, per-unit labor input might, in fact, fall. At constant labor prices, this implies that per-unit labor costs may in fact fall.

We are not, of course, talking about *stage I* of production, where per-unit costs fall because of increased specialization as additional units of, say, labor are added to underutilized amounts of capital. On-the-job training and experience will make workers more productive, which has important implications for the cost structure of the firm. It is precisely the expectation of greater productivity that compels many firms to underwrite on-site employee training and off-site continuing education programs. The relationship between increased per-worker productivity and reduced per-worker cost at fixed labor prices associated with an increase in output and experience is called the *learning curve effect*.

Definition: The learning curve effect measures the relation between an increase in per-worker productivity (a decrease in per-unit labor cost at fixed labor prices) associated with an improvement in labor skills from on-the-job experience.

One measure of the learning curve effect is

$$\Gamma = \text{Per-unit labor cost} = \varphi Q^\beta \qquad (6.17)$$

where φ is the per-unit cost of producing the first unit of output, Q is the level of output, $\beta = (\ln m)/(\ln \lambda)$, m is the learning factor, and λ is a factor of output proportionality. In fact, β is a measure of the learning curve effect. It determines the rate at which per-unit labor requirements fall given the rate at which workers "learn" (m) following a scalar (proportional) increase in production (λ). The value of m varies from zero to unity ($0 \leq m \leq 1$). As the value of m approaches zero, the learning curve effect on lowering per-unit labor costs becomes more powerful.

Table 6.1 presents data for 90% ($m = 0.9$), 80% ($m = 0.8$), and 70% ($m = 0.7$) learning curves for a factor of output proportionality (λ) of 2. That is, each time output is doubled, the per-unit labor cost drops to become 90, 80, or 70% of its previous level. It is assumed that it takes 1,000 labor units (say, labor hours) to produce the first unit of output, and that the wage rate is constant at $10 per hour. Thus, the per-unit labor cost of producing the first unit of output is $10,000. If the learning factor is $m = 0.9$ (i.e., the learning process is relatively slow), the per-unit labor cost when $Q = 2$ is $9,000. When $Q = 4$, per unit labor cost is $8,100, and so on.

The reader will note that the lower the learning factor (i.e., the quicker the learning process), the more rapidly per-unit labor costs fall as output expands. Since the wage rate in this example is constant at $10 per hour, the learning curve effect implies that fewer labor units per unit of output are required as output increases. The extreme cases are $m = 1$ and $m = 0$. When $m = 1$, no learning whatsoever takes place, and $\beta = (\ln 1/\ln \lambda) = 0$. In this case, there are no learning curve effects, and the per-unit labor cost remains unchanged. On the other hand, when $m = 0$, then $\beta = -\infty$. In this case, learning is so complete and production so efficient that the per-unit labor cost reduces to zero, which implies that at a constant wage rate no labor is required at all. In the two-input case, this suggests that all production technology is embodied in the amount of capital employed.

Learning curve effects are usually thought to result from the development of labor skills, especially for tasks of a repetitive nature, over time. More broadly, however, incremental reductions in per-unit labor costs may result from a variety of factors, such as the adoption of new production, organizational, and managerial techniques, the replacement of higher cost with lower cost materials, an new product design. Consideration of these additional factors has given rise to the broader term *experience curve effects*.

Definition: The experience curve effect is a measure of the relationship between an increase in per-worker productivity (a decrease in per-worker cost at fixed labor prices) associated with an improvement in labor skills from on-the-job experience, the adoption of new production, organizational and managerial techniques, the replacement of higher cost with lower cost materials, new product design, and so on.

Problem 6.4. Suppose that the labor cost to a firm of producing a single unit of output is $5,000.

a. If the learning factor is 0.74 and the factor of proportionality is 2.5, estimate the per-unit labor cost of producing 120 units of output.
b. If the wage rate is constant at $15 per hour, how many labor hours are required to produce the first unit of output? How many labor hours are required per unit of output when 120 units are produced?

Solution

a. From Equation (6.17),

$$\text{Per-unit labor cost} = \varphi Q^{\beta} = 5,000(120)^{\ln 0.74 / \ln 2.5} = \$1,037 \text{ per unit}$$

b. The first unit will require \$5,000/\$15 = 333.33 labor hours. When 120 units are produced, the per-unit labor requirement is \$1,037/\$15 = 69.13 labor hours.

LONG-RUN COST

In the long run all factors of production are assumed to be variable. Since there are no fixed inputs, there are no fixed costs. All costs are variable. Unlike the short-run production function, however, there is little that can be said about production in the long run. There is no long-run equivalent of the law of diminishing marginal product.

As in the case of the firm's short-run cost functions, long-run cost functions are intimately related to the long-run production function. In particular, the firm's long-run cost functions are related to the concept of returns to scale, which was discussed in Chapter 5. In general, economists have theorized that an increase in the firm's scale of operations (i.e., a proportional increase in all inputs), is likely to be accompanied by increasing, constant, and decreasing returns to scale. The relation between total output and all inputs, the *long-run total product curve* (*LRTP*) is illustrated in Figure 6.4.

It will be recalled from Chapter 5 that the coefficient of output elasticity for increasing returns to scale, constant returns to scale, and decreasing returns to scale, which is the sum of the output elasticities of each input, is greater than unity, equal to unity, and less than unity, respectively. Although the shapes of the long-run and short-run total product curves are similar, the reasons are quite different. The short-run total product curve derives

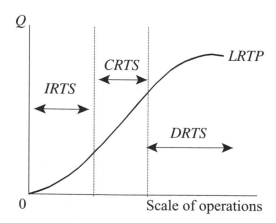

FIGURE 6.4 Long-run total product curve: the increase in total output from a proportional increase in all inputs.

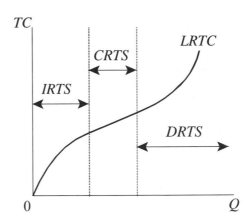

FIGURE 6.5 Long-run total cost curve.

its shape from the law of diminishing marginal product. The long-run total product curve derives its shape from quite different considerations. To begin with, firms might experience increasing returns to scale during the early stages of production because of the opportunity for increased specialization of both human and nonhuman factors, which would lead to gains in efficiency. Only large firms, for example, can rationalize the use of in-house lawyers, accountants, economists, and so on. Another reason is that equipment of larger capacity may be more efficient than mochinery of smaller capacity.

Eventually, as the firm gets larger, the efficiencies from increased size may be exhausted. As a firm grows larger, so too do the demands on management. Increased administrative layers may become necessary, resulting in a loss of efficiency as internal coordination of production processes become more difficult. At some large level of output, factors of production may become overworked and diminishing returns to management may set in. Problems of interdepartmental and interdivisional coordination may become endemic. The result would be decreasing returns to scale.

Since there are no fixed costs in the long run, the firm's corresponding *long-run total cost curve* (*LRTC*), which is similar in appearance to the short-run total cost curve, intersects *TC* at the origin. This is illustrated in Figure 6.5.

ECONOMIES OF SCALE

Scale refers to size. What is the effect on the firm's per-unit cost of production following an increase in all factors of production? In other words, does the size of a firm's operations affect its per-unit cost of production? The answer to the second questions is that it may. Regardless of what we have learned about the short-run production function and the law of diminishing marginal product, it is difficult to make generalizations about the effect of size on per-unit cost of production, although we may speculate about the most likely possibilities.

Economies of scale are intimately related to the concept of increasing returns to scale. If per-unit costs of production decline as the scale of a firm's operations increase, the firm is said to experience economies of scale. The reason is simple. If we assume constant factor prices, while the firm's total cost of production rises proportionately with an increase in total factor usage, per-unit cost of production falls because output has increased more than proportionately. In other words, an increase in the firm's scale of operations results in a decline in *long-run average total cost (LRATC)*.

Conversely, *diseconomies of scale* are intimately related to the concept of decreasing returns to scale. Once again, the explanation is straightforward. Assuming constant factor prices, the firm's total cost of production rises proportionately with an increase in total factor usage, but the per-unit cost of production increases because output increases less than proportionately. In other words, an increase in the firm's scale of operations results in an increase in the firm's long-run average total cost.

Finally, in the case of *constant returns to scale*, per-unit cost of production remains constant as production increases or decreases proportionately with an increase or decrease in factor usage. In other words, an increase or decrease in the firm's size will have no effect on the firm's long-run average total cost.

Definition: Assuming constant factor prices, economies of scale occur when per-unit costs of production decline following a proportional increase in all factors of production.

Definition: Assuming constant factor prices, diseconomies of scale occur when per-unit costs of production increase following a proportional increase in all factors of production.

Assume that $Q = f(L, K)$, where Q is output, L is variable labor, and K is fixed capital. Figure 6.6 illustrates several possible *short-run average total cost curves (SRATC)*, each corresponding to a different level of capital usage. Here, $SRATC_2$ represents the short-run average total cost curve of the firm utilizing a higher level of fixed capital input than $SRATC_1$, $SRATC_3$ represents the short-run average total cost curve of the firm utilizing a higher level of fixed capital input than $SRATC_2$, and so on. We can see that the firm may produce a given level of output with one or more short-run production functions: for example, the firm may produce output level Q_1 along $SRATC_1$ (point A) or $SRATC_2$ (point B).

If the firm believes that the demand for its product in the foreseeable future is Q_1, it will choose to employ a level of capital consistent with $SRATC_2$ to realize lower per-unit cost of production. As the demand for the firm's output increases, the firm will choose that production technology such that its per-unit costs are minimized. All such points are illustrated by the

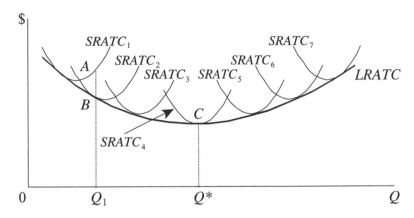

FIGURE 6.6 Long-run average total cost curve as the "envelope" of the short-run average total cost curves.

"envelope" of the short-run average total cost curves. This curve is called the *long-run average total cost curve*, which is labeled *LRATC* in Figure 6.6.

Unlike the short-run average total cost curves, which derive their shape from the law of diminishing returns, the long-run average total cost curve derives its shape from the returns to scale characteristics of the underlying production function. In Figure 6.6, the range of output levels 0 to Q^* corresponds to the underlying production characteristic of increasing returns to scale. Over this range of output, *LRATC* is downward sloping (i.e., $dLRATC/dQ < 0$). Output levels greater than Q^* reflect decreasing returns to scale. Over this range of output *LRATC* is upward sloping (i.e., $dLRATC/dQ > 0$). Where the long-run average total cost curve is neither rising nor falling, $dLRATC/dQ = 0$, the underlying production function exhibits constant returns to scale.

The output level that corresponds to minimum long-run ATC is commonly referred to as the *minimum efficient scale (MES)*. Minimum efficient scale is the level of output that corresponds to the lowest per-unit cost of production in the long run.

The shape of the long-run average total cost curve will vary from industry to industry. There is, in fact, no *a priori reason* for the *LRATC* curve to be U shaped. Figures 6.7 through 6.9 illustrate three other possible shapes of the long-run average total cost curve.

Problem 6.5. A firm's long-run total cost (*LRTC*) equation is given by the expression

$$LRTC = 2,000Q - 5Q^2 + 0.005Q^3$$

a. What is the firm's long-run average cost equation?
b. What is the firm's minimum efficient scale (*MES*) of production?

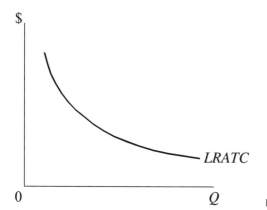

FIGURE 6.7   Economies of scale.

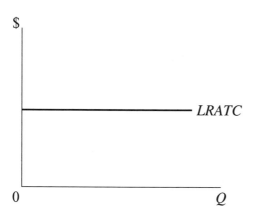

FIGURE 6.8   Constant return to scale.

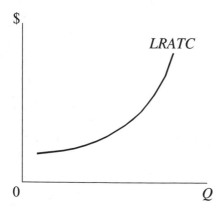

FIGURE 6.9   Diseconomies of scale.

Solution

a. The long-run average total cost equation of the firm is given as

$$LRATC = \frac{LRTC}{Q} = \frac{2,000Q - 5Q^2 + 0.005Q^3}{Q} = 2,000 - 5Q + 0.005Q^2$$

b. To find the minimum efficient scale of production, take the first derivative of the $LRATC$ function, set the results equal to zero (the first-order condition), and solve for Q.

$$\frac{dLRATC}{dQ} = -5 + 0.01Q = 0$$

$$Q = 500$$

The minimum efficient scale of production is 500 units.

The second-order condition for minimizing the $LRATC$ function is $d^2LRATC/dQ^2 > 0$. Taking the second derivative of the $LRATC$ function we obtain

$$\frac{d^2LRATC}{dQ^2} = 0.01 > 0$$

$LRATC$, therefore, is minimized at $Q^* = 500$ (i.e., the minimum efficient scale of production).

REASONS FOR ECONOMIES AND DISECONOMIES OF SCALE

As firms grow larger, economies of scale may be realized as a result of specialization in production, sales, marketing, research and development, and other areas. Specialization may increase the firm's productivity in greater proportion than the increase in operating cost associated with greater size. Some types of machinery, for example, are more efficient for large production runs. Examples include large electrical-power generators and large blast furnaces that generate greater output than smaller ones. Large companies may be able to extract more favorable financing terms from creditors than small companies.

Large size, however, does not guarantee that improvement in efficiency and lower per-unit costs. Large size is often accompanied by a dis proportionately great increase in specialized management. Coordination and communication between and among departments becomes more complicated, difficult, and time-consuming. As a result, time that would be better spent in the actual process of production declines and overhead expenses increase dis proportionately. The result is that diminishing returns to scale set in, and per-unit costs rise. In other words, growth usually is accompanied by diseconomies of scale.

MULTIPRODUCT COST FUNCTIONS

We have thus far discussed manufacturing processes involving the production of a single output. Yet, many firms use the same production facilities to produce multiple products. Automobile companies, such as Ford Motor Company, produce both cars and trucks at the same production facilities. Chemical and pharmaceutical companies, such as Dow Chemical and Merck, use the same basic production facilities to produce multiple different products. Computer companies, such as IBM, produce monitors, printers, scanners, modems and, of course, computers. Consumer product companies, such as General Electric, produce a wide range of household durables, such refrigerators, ovens, and light-bulbs. In each of these examples it is reasonable to suppose that total cost of production is a function of more than a single output. In the case of a firm producing two products, the *multiproduct cost function* may be written as

$$TC = TC(Q_1, Q_2) \tag{6.18}$$

where Q_1 and Q_2 represent the number of units produced of goods 1 and 2, respectively.

Definition: A multiproduct cost function summarizes the cost of efficiently using the same production facilities to produce two or more products.

The multiproduct cost function summarized in Equation (6.18) has the same basic interpretation as a single product cost function, although the specific relationship depends on the manner in which these goods are produced. Two examples of multiproduct cost relationships are *economies of scope* and *cost complementarities*.

ECONOMIES OF SCOPE

Economies of scope exist when the total cost of using the same production facilities to produce two or more goods is less than that of producing these goods at separate production facilities. In the case of a firm that produces two goods, economies of scope exist when

$$TC(Q_1, 0) + TC(0, Q_2) > TC(Q_1, Q_2) \tag{6.19}$$

It may be less expensive, for example, for Ford Motor Company to produce cars and trucks by more intensively utilizing a single assembly plant than to produce these products at two separate, less intensively utilized, manufacturing facilities. It is less expensive for the restaurants in the Olive Garden chain to use the same ovens, tables, refrigerators, and so on to produce both pasta and parmigiana meals than to duplicate the factors of production.

Definition: Economies of scope in production exist when the total cost of producing two or more goods is lower when the same production facilities are used than when separate production facilities are used to produce the goods.

COST COMPLEMENTARITIES

Cost complementarities exist when the marginal cost of producing Q_1 is reduced by increasing the production of Q_2. From Equation (6.18), the marginal cost of producing Q_1 may be written as

$$MC_1(Q_1, Q_2) = \frac{\partial TC}{\partial Q_1}$$

The multiproduct cost function exhibits cost complementarities if the cross-second partial derivative of the multiproduct cost function is negative, that is,

$$\frac{\partial MC_1(Q_1, Q_2)}{\partial Q_2} = \frac{\partial^2 TC}{\partial Q_1 \partial Q_2} < 0 \qquad (6.20a)$$

$$\frac{\partial MC_2(Q_1, Q_2)}{\partial Q_1} = \frac{\partial^2 TC}{\partial Q_2 \partial Q_1} < 0 \qquad (6.20b)$$

Equations (6.20) says that an increase in the production of Q_2 reduces the marginal cost of producing Q_1.[4]

Definition: Cost complementarities exist when the marginal cost of producing one good is reduced by increasing the production of another good.

Examples of cost complementarities include the simultaneous production of beef and leather, and doughnuts and doughnut "holes." Slaughtering cattle for beef without considering the potential usefulness of leather by-products, and vice versa, is not only poor business but wasteful. Producing doughnuts and doughnut holes is certainly more cost efficient when these snacks are produced together than when they are produced separately.

---

[4] Parenthetically, it may be demonstrated using Young's theorem that $\partial^2 TC / \partial Q$, $\partial Q_2 = \partial^2 TC / \partial Q_2 \partial Q_1$. For a discussion of young's theorem, see Eugene Silberberg, the structure of Economics: A Mathematical Analysis, 2nd edition, McGraw-Hill, 1990, chapter 3, pp. 70–76.

Problem 6.6. Suppose that a firm's total cost function is

$$TC = 100 - Q_1 Q_2 + Q_1^2 + Q_2^2$$

where Q_1 and Q_2 represent the number of units of goods 1 and 2, respectively.

a. If the firm produces 2 units of good 1 and 4 units of good 2, do cost complementarities exist?

b. Do economies of scope exist for this firm?

c. How will the firm's total cost of production be affected if it decides to discontinue the production of good 2?

Solution

a. For costs complementarities to exist then, from Equations (6.20)

$$\frac{\partial MC_1(Q_1, Q_2)}{\partial Q_2} = \frac{\partial^2 TC}{\partial Q_1 \partial Q_2} < 0$$

$$\frac{\partial MC_2(Q_1, Q_2)}{\partial Q_1} = \frac{\partial^2 TC}{\partial Q_2 \partial Q_1} < 0$$

$$\frac{\partial TC}{\partial Q_1} = -Q_2 + 2Q_1$$

$$\frac{\partial^2 TC}{\partial Q_1 \partial Q_2} = -1 < 0$$

Similarly,

$$\frac{\partial TC}{\partial Q_2} = -Q_1 + 2Q_2$$

$$\frac{\partial^2 TC}{\partial Q_2 \partial Q_1} = -1 < 0$$

Thus, cost complementarities exist.

b. For economies of scope to exist then

$$TC(Q_1, 0) + TC(0, Q_2) > TC(Q_1, Q_2)$$

$$TC(Q_1, 0) = 100 - Q_1(0) + Q_1^2 + (0)^2 = 100 + Q_1^2 = 100 + 2^2 = 104$$

$$TC(0, Q_2) = 100 - (0)Q_2 + (0)^2 + Q_2^2 = 100 + Q_2^2 = 100 + 4^2 = 116$$

$$TC(Q_1, Q_2) = 100 - (2)(4) + 2^2 + 4^2 = 100 - 8 + 4 + 16 = 112$$

Since $104 + 116 = 220 > 112$, economies of scope exist.

c. Clearly the firm's cost will fall by $112 - $104 = $8 if the firm discontinues production of good 2.

Problem 6.6 illustrates two aspects of corporate of mergers and divestitures that involve multiproduct cost functions. In the presence of economies of scope, a merger of two firms could result in significant cost reductions. Moreover, a firm that divests itself of an unprofitable subsidiary might enjoy only modest cost reductions. Economies of scope make it difficult for firms to spread production costs across product lines.

CHAPTER REVIEW

The cost function of a profit-maximizing firm shows the minimum cost of producing various output levels given market-determined factor prices, and the firm's budget constraint. Although cost is largely the domain of accountants, to an economist the concept carries a somewhat different connotation. Economists are concerned with any and all costs that are relevant to the managerial decision-making process. *Relevant costs* include not only *direct*, *explicit*, or *out-of-pocket costs* associated with the day-to-day operations of a firm, but also *implicit* (*indirect*) *costs*.

The relevant cost concept is *economic cost*, which includes all *opportunity costs*, including explicit and implicit costs. Opportunity cost is the value of a forgone opportunity (e.g., the salary sacrificed by a computer programmer who leaves Microsoft to start a consulting business). Implicit costs may be made explicit, as occurs when the computer programmer pays himself or herself a salary equivalent to the forgone salary. In this case, implicit opportunity costs have been made explicit.

An analysis of the firm's *short-run cost function* follows directly from an analysis of the firm's short-run production function. Assuming constant factor prices, increasing *marginal cost* is a direct consequence of the law of diminishing returns, which in turn affects the pattern of behavior of the firm's *average total cost* and *average variable cost*. Short-run production functions assume that at least one factor of production is held fixed. The cost associated with these fixed inputs is called *total fixed cost*.

Long-run production functions assume that all inputs are variable, which implies that there are no fixed costs. Moreover, the law of diminishing returns is no longer operable. The long-run cost concept of *economies of scale* follows directly from the long-run production concept of increasing returns to scale. Economies of scale occur when long-run average total costs fall as the firm increases its capacity, and the concept itself is related to the production concept of increasing returns to scale.

Diseconomies of scale occur when long-run average total cost increases, as when the firm increases its capacity; the long-run production concept of decreasing returns to scale is related to the notion of diseconomies of scale. It can be argued that the firm's optimal scale of operation occurs when long-run average total cost is minimized (i.e., when the firm experiences constant returns to scale).

Other important cost concepts are the *learning curve* effect, *cost complementarities*, and *economies of scope*. The learning curve effect is the reduction in per-unit cost resulting from increased worker productivity due to increased worker experience. "Economies of scope" refers to the reduction in per-unit cost resulting from the joint production of two or more goods or services, such as the production of automobiles and trucks, or beef and leather, by the same producer. Cost complementarities exist when the marginal cost of producing one good is reduced by increasing the production of another good.

KEY TERMS AND CONCEPTS

Average fixed cost (AFC)   Total fixed cost of production per unit of output. AFC is total fixed cost divided by total output (i.e., $AFC = TFC/Q$). Average fixed cost is a short-run production concept. It is the average cost associated with the firm's fixed factor of production.

Average total cost (ATC)   The total cost of production per unit of output: ATC is total cost divided by total output (i.e., $ATC = TC/Q$). Average total cost is a short-run production concept if total costs include total fixed costs. It is a long-run production concept if all costs are variable costs.

Average variable cost (AVC)   Total variable cost of production per unit of output: AVC is total variable cost divided by total output (i.e., $AVC = TVC/Q$).

Constant returns to scale   Output rises proportionately with the increase in all productive inputs, and per-unit costs remain constant.

Cost complementarities   When the marginal cost of producing one good is reduced by increasing the production of another good, there are cost complementarities.

Direct cost   Same as explicit cost.

Diseconomies of scale   An increase in long-run average total cost. It is conceptually related to the long-run production concept of decreasing returns to scale.

Economies of scale   A decrease in long-run average total cost. It is conceptually related to the long-run production concept of increasing returns to scale.

Economies of scope   Realized when the total cost of using a single production facility to produce two or more goods or services is lower than the cost of using separate production facilities.

Experience curve effect   A measure of the relation between an increase in per-worker productivity (a decrease in per-unit labor cost at fixed labor prices) associated with an improvement in labor skills from on-the-job experience, the adoption of new production, organizational, and managerial techniques, the replacement of higher cost with lower cost materials, new product design, and so on.

Explicit cost Sometimes referred to as out-of-pocket expenses, explicit costs are "visible" in the sense that they are direct payments for factors of production. Wages paid to workers and rental payments are examples of explicit costs.

Implicit cost The value of the next best alternative use of a resource. Implicit costs are "invisible" in the sense that no direct monetary payments are involved. They are the value of any forgone opportunities. Implicit costs, however, may be made explicit.

Incremental cost Related to the concept of marginal cost, incremental cost is the change in total cost associated with an innovation in management policy, such as introducing a new product line or changing in firm's marketing strategy.

Learning curve effect A measure of the relationship between an increase in per-worker productivity (a decrease in per-unit labor cost at fixed labor prices) associated with an improvement in labor skills resulting from on-the-job experience.

Long-run average-total cost (*LRATC*) The least-cost combination of resources in the long run (i.e., when all productive inputs are variable).

Marginal cost (*MC*) The change in total cost of production associated with an incremental change in output.

Minimum efficient scale (*MES*) The output level that corresponds to minimum long-run average total costs.

Multiproduct cost function The total cost function that summarizes the cost of using the same production facilities to efficiently produce two or more products.

Opportunity cost The highest valued forgone alternative associated with a decision.

Sunk cost A cost that is invariant to innovations in management decisions, such as the introduction of a new product line or a change in marketing strategy. Sunk costs are not recoverable in the sense that once incurred, they are forever lost.

Total cost (*TC*) The sum of total fixed cost and total variable cost. It is the total cost of production.

Total economic cost All costs incurred during the production of a good or service. Total economic cost is the sum of explicit and implicit costs.

Total fixed cost (*TFC*) A short-run production concept. Total fixed costs of production are associated with acquiring and maintaining fixed factors of production. Fixed costs are incurred by the firm regardless of the level of output. They are incurred by the firm even if no production takes place at all.

Total variable cost (*TVC*) The cost associated with acquiring and maintaining variable factors of production. In stages I and II of production, total variable cost is an increasing function of the level of production.

CHAPTER QUESTIONS

6.1 Explain the difference between marginal cost and incremental cost.

6.2 Marginal cost is the cost of producing the "last" unit of output. Do you agree? If not, then why not.

6.3 Consider the production function $Q = f(K, L)$, where Q represent units of output, and K and L represent units of capital and labor inputs, respectively. In the short run, demonstrate that for fixed input prices, the shape of the total variable cost curve is identical to the shape of the total product of labor curve.

6.4 All costs are opportunity costs. Do you agree? Explain.

6.5 Only implicit costs are opportunity costs. Do you agree with this statement? If not, then why not?

6.6 Since the prices of productive inputs must always be positive, and since the cost of hiring another unit of, say labor, is the wage rate, it must also be true that marginal cost of producing one more unit of output must also be positive. Do you agree? Explain.

6.7 Demonstrate that $MC = ATC$ when ATC is minimized.

6.8 Demonstrate that $MC = AVC$ when AVC is minimized.

6.9 Explain the difference between total fixed cost and sunk cost. Give examples of each.

6.10 For the production function $Q = f(K, L)$, demonstrate that in the short run marginal cost is equal to the wage rate divided by the marginal product of labor.

6.11 For the total cost function $TC = b_0 + b_1 Q + b_2 Q_2 + b_3 Q^3$, demonstrate that $(3b_3 b_1 - b_2^2) > 0$ is required for minimum marginal cost to be positive.

6.12 Explain the difference between the learning curve effect and the experience curve effect.

6.13 The learning curve effect is summarized by the equation $\Gamma = \varphi Q^\beta$, where φ is the cost of producing the first unit of output, $\beta = (\log m)/(\log \lambda)$, m is the learning factor, and λ is a scalar increase in production. How would you go about estimating the values of φ and β?

6.14 Suppose that learning factor is zero. What does this imply about the amount of labor that should be used in the production process?

6.15 Large firms tend to be more management "top heavy." That is, a larger proportion of their personnel are management than is true of small firms. Do you agree with this statement? Why?

6.16 Large companies are more likely to experience diseconomies of scale than small companies. Do you agree? If not, then why not?

6.17 Explain some of the reasons a firm might experience economies of scale. What is the relation between economies of scale and increasing returns to scale? Be specific.

6.18 Economies of scale and economies of scope are the same thing. Do you agree with this statement? If not, then why not?

6.19 Economies of scope imply that cost complementarities exist, but cost complementarities do not imply the existence of economies of scope. Do you agree with this statement? If not, then why not?

6.20 Explain the difference between economies of scope and cost complementarities.

6.21 Provide examples of economies of scope and cost complementarities other than those given in the text.

CHAPTER EXERCISES

6.1 The total cost equation of a firm is given by the equation

$$TC = 5,000 + 2,000Q - 10Q^2 + 0.25Q^3$$

where TC is total cost and Q is the level of output.
   a. What is the firm's total fixed cost?
   b. What is the equation for the firm's total variable cost (TVC)?
   c. What is the equation for the firm's average total cost (ATC)?
   d. What is the equation for the firm's marginal cost (MC)?

6.2 Suppose that a firm's total cost equation is

$$TC = 10,000 + 100Q + 0.25Q^2$$

where TC is total cost and Q is the level of output.
   a. What output level will minimize the firm's average total cost?
   b. Calculate the average and marginal cost at the average cost minimizing output level.

6.3 Suppose that a firm's total cost equation is

$$TC = 125,000 + 100Q + 0.5Q^2$$

   a. Determine the output level that minimizes average total cost.

   b. Calculate average total cost and marginal cost at the level of output that will minimize average total cost.

6.4 The long-run average total cost equation for a perfectly competitive firm is

$$LRATC = 620 - 5Q + 0.025Q^2$$

   a. Determine the minimum efficient scale of production.
   b. Calculate total cost at the minimum efficient scale of production.
   c. If the total level of output in the industry is 50,000 units, how many firms can profitably operate in this industry?

6.5 The total cost equation for a firm producing two products is

$$TC(Q_1, Q_2) = 25 + Q_1^2 + 4Q_2^2 + 5Q_1Q_2$$

a. Do cost complementarities exist for this firm?
b. Under what circumstances do economies of scope exist for this firm?
c. Suppose that $Q_1 = Q_2 = 2$. Do cost complementarities exist?
d. Suppose that $Q_1 = Q_2 = 3$. Do cost complementarities exist?
e. Suppose that the firm is currently producing 5 units of Q_1 and 10 units of Q_2. What is the firm's total cost of production?
f. Suppose that the firm divests itself of the division selling Q_1 to a competitor. How much will it cost the firm to continue producing 10 units of Q_2? What is the total cost of producing both Q_1 and Q_2 if the firm producing Q_1 produces 5 units?

6.6 Suppose that per-unit labor cost of producing a single unit of output is $25,000.

a. If the learning factor is 0.87 and the factor of proportionality is 2.2, estimate the per-unit labor cost of producing 151 units of output.
b. If the hourly wage is constant at $25, how many labor hours are required to produce the first unit of output? How many labor hours are required per unit of output when 151 units are produced?

SELECTED READINGS

Brennan, M. J., and T. M. Carroll. *Preface to Quantitative Economics & Econometrics*, 4th ed. Cincinnati, OH: South-Western Publishing, 1987.

Glass, J. C. *An Introduction to Mathematical Methods in Economics*. New York: McGraw-Hill, 1980.

Gold, B. "Changing Perspectives on Size, Scale, and Returns: An Interpretative Survey." *Journal of Economic Literature*, 19 (March 1981), pp. 5–33.

Henderson, J. M., and R. E. Quandt. *Microeconomic Theory: A Mathematical Approach*, 3rd ed. New York: McGraw-Hill, 1980.

Hope, S. *Applied Microeconomics*. New York: John Wiley & Sons, 1999.

Maxwell, W. D. "Production Theory and Cost Curves." *Applied Economics*, 1 (August 1969), pp. 211–224.

McCloskey, D. N. *The Applied Theory of Price*. New York: Macmillan, 1982.

Mills, D. "Capacity Expansion and the Size of Plants." *Rand Journal of Economics*, 21 (Winter 1990), pp. 555–566.

Nicholson, W. *Microeconomic Theory: Basic Principles and Extensions*, 6th ed. New York: Dryden Press, 1995.

Silberberg, E. *The Structure of Economics: A Mathematical Analysis*, 2nd ed. New York: McGraw-Hill, 1990.

Stigler, G. J. "The Economies of Scale." *Journal of Law and Economics*, April (1958), pp. 251–274.

Walters, A. A. "Production and Cost Functions: An Econometric Survey." *Econometrica* (January 1963), pp. 1–66.

7

PROFIT AND REVENUE
MAXIMIZATION

Firms transform factors of production into goods and services for sale in the market. In Chapter 5, we discussed several important production relationships at length. We saw, for example, that firms produce in the short run, but plan in the long run. The short run in production was defined at that period of time during which at least one factor of production is held constant. In the short run, firms are subject to the law of diminishing marginal product with respect to the variable inputs. We also saw that in is generally possible to produce a given level of output with several different input combinations. In other words, generally, but not always, factors of production are substitutable. The substitutability of the factors of production was illustrated diagrammatically with the use of an isoquant map, with each isoquant corresponding to a different level of output. By contrast, the long run in production was defined as the period of time in which all factors of production are variable. When all factors of production are variable, the optimal scale of the firm's future operations becomes an important managerial decision-making consideration.

Chapter 5 left a number of important short-run production questions unanswered. For one thing, what is the firm's "optimal" level of output? Not surprisingly, the optimal level of output is defined by the firm's organizational objective. The output level that maximizes the firm's profits, for example, will generally be different from the output level that maximizes the firm's sales revenues or market share. Once the firm's organizational objective has been defined, management must determine the least-cost combination of inputs necessary to achieve that target output level. Clearly, this will depend not only on the firm's operating budget, but also on the market prices of the factors of production. As we saw in Chapter 6, many of the most important cost relationships confronting managers are reflections of the firm's underlying production technology.

In this chapter we develop a general framework for finding optimal solutions to managerial decision-making problems. This framework will be expanded in subsequent chapters to take into consideration alternative market structures and operating environments. This chapter will consider the decision-making process with respect to two organizational objectives: profit maximization and total revenue maximization. We begin by considering profit maximization from two perspectives. At a more practical level, management will attempt to maximize profits by employing just the right amount of each factor of production subject to a predefined budget constraint. At a much more general level, profit maximization may be viewed as an unconstrained or constrained optimization problem in which the decision variable is the firm's level of output.

PROFIT MAXIMIZATION

Although discussion of the production function developed in Chapter 5 has intuitive appeal in its own right, its usefulness to the business manager is in its application to profit maximization. It was demonstrated, for example, that with precise specification of the production function and a given output level, infinite input combinations are at least theoretically possible. The specific combination of inputs used to produce that output level, however, will be that which can be produced at least cost. Alternatively, given the firm's operating budget and the prices of productive resources, the perfectly competitive firm will choose that combination of resources that generates the greatest output level.[1]

OPTIMAL INPUT COMBINATION

ISOCOST LINE

Given the prices of productive resources and the firm's operating budget, and assuming only two factors of production, labor and capital, the various combinations of inputs that a firm can employ in the production process may be summarized as

$$TC_0 = P_L L + P_K K \tag{7.1}$$

[1] As we shall see later, for a perfectly competitive firm in output and factor markets, output price and the prices of productive resources are given exogenously. In other words, the firm's output level will have no effect on the selling price of the particular good or service, nor will the level of the firm's demand for a productive factor affect the input prices.

where TC_0 is the firm's operating budget, or total cost, P_L is the rental price of labor (or the wage rate), and P_K is the rental price of capital (or the interest rate). Equation (7.1) is known as the *isocost equation*. This expression is also known as the firm's cost constraint in the two-variable input case. Suppose, for example, that the firm's weekly operating budget is $1,000, the weekly per worker wage rate is $100, and the weekly rental price of capital is $150. Expression (7.1), therefore, becomes

$$1,000 = 100L + 150K \qquad (7.2)$$

Equation (7.2) may be solved for K to yield the firm's isocost line,

$$K = 6.67 - 0.67L \qquad (7.3)$$

The negative slope coefficient indicates that more capital may be hired only at the expense of fewer units of labor. In this example, when zero labor is employed, at a rental price of capital of $150, the total amount of labor that can be hired is 6.67 units (per operating period). Similarly, if no units of capital are employed, then 10 units of labor may be hired. In general, from Equation (7.1) the isocost line may be written as

$$K = \frac{TC_0}{P_K} - \left(\frac{P_L}{P_K}\right)L \qquad (7.4)$$

Equation (7.4) indicates that the rate at which a unit of labor may be substituted for a unit of capital is given by the ratio of the input prices. In summary, the isocost line denotes the various combinations of inputs that a firm may hire at a given cost.

From Equation (7.3), Table 7.1 illustrates the various combination of labor and capital that may be used given the firm's fixed operating budget of $1,000.

TABLE 7.1   Alternative combinations of labor and capital hired with a fixed operating budget of $1,000.

Labor, L	Capital, K
0	6.7
1	6.0
2	5.3
3	4.7
4	4.0
5	3.3
6	2.7
7	2.0
8	1.3
9	0.7
10	0.0

Equation (7.4) is illustrated diagrammatically in Figure 7.1, where the isocost line (given an operating budget of TC_0 and labor and capital prices of P_L and P_K, respectively) is denoted by the line RAS. Consider, for example, point A on the RAS isocost line. At a total operating budget of TC_0, $0K$ units of capital and $0L$ units of labor may be hired.

Now suppose that there is a change in the operating budget from TC_0 to TC_0', where $TC_0 > TC_0'$ and with unchanged resource prices. In Figure 7.1 this is illustrated by a parallel shift from RAS to TBU, where the vertical intercept has declined from TC_0/P_K to TC_0'/P_K. Since input prices are unchanged, the slope of the isocost line is unaffected. If the firm chooses to hire the same amount of labor as before ($0L_0$), then the new combination of capital and labor hired given the new, lower budget is illustrated by the movement from point A to point B. Here, the number of units of capital hired will fall from $0K_0$ to $0K_1$ because there is less money in the budget. Of course, any combination of labor and capital is possible along the TBU isocost line.

Suppose, on the other hand, that the operating budget remains the same but there is a change in the price of one of the productive factors. Suppose, for example, that the price of labor increases to P_L' (i.e., $P_L' > P_L$). The result of this change is illustrated in Figure 7.2.

Note that in Figure 7.2, line RAS is the isocost line before the change in the wage rate. An increase in the wage rate from P_L to P_L', however, results in a change in the slope of the isocost line from $-P_L/P_K$ to $-P_L'/P_K$; that is, the RBU line is steeper than the RAS line because $|P_L'/P_K| > |P_L/P_K|$. The result of this change is that the isocost line "rotates" clockwise. Assuming, as before, that the level of labor input usage remains unchanged at $0L_0$, the amount of capital that may now be hired falls from $0K_0$ to $0K_1$. This is because labor has become more expensive and there is less money in the budget to hire capital. Note also that since the wage rate does not appear

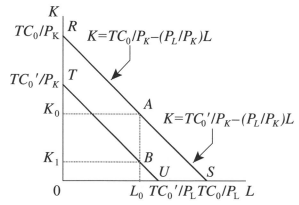

FIGURE 7.1   Isocost line and a budget increase.

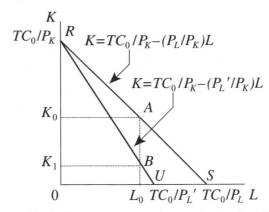

FIGURE 7.2   Isocost line and an increase in the price of labor.

in the vertical intercept term, the maximum amount of capital that may be hired remains TC_0/P_K, although the maximum amount of labor that may be hired falls from TC_0/P_L to TC_0/P_L'.

Problem 7.1. Suppose that the wage rate (P_L) is \$25 and the rental price of capital (P_K) is \$40. In addition, suppose that the firm's operating budget is \$2,500.

a. What is the isocost equation for the firm?
b. If capital is graphed on the vertical axis, what happens to the isocost line if the wage rate increases?
c. If capital is graphed on the vertical axis, what happens to the isocost line if the rental price of capital falls?
d. If the wage rate and the rental price of capital remain unchanged, what happens to the isocost line if the firm's operating budget falls?
e. If the firm's operating budget remains unchanged, what happens to the isocost line if the wage rate and the rental price of capital fall by the same percentage?

Solution

a. The firm's isocost line is given by the expression

$$TC_0 = P_L L + P_K K$$

Substituting into this expression we obtain

$$2,500 = 25L + 40K$$

b. Solving the isocost line for K yields

$$K = \frac{TC_0}{P_K} - \left(\frac{P_L}{P_K}\right)L$$

From this expression, if the wage rate increases, the isocost line will rotate clockwise. In other words, the K intercept will remain unchanged while the L intercept will move to the left.

c. If the rental price of capital falls, the solution of the isocost line for K shows that the isocost line will rotate clockwise. In other words, the L intercept will remain unchanged while the K intercept will move up.

d. If the operating budget falls, the isocost line will experience a parallel shift to the left. In other words, the K intercept will move down, the L intercept will move to the left, and the slope of the isocost line will remain unchanged.

e. If the wage rate and the rental price of capital fall by the same percentage, the isocost line will experience a parallel shift to the right. In other words, the K intercept will move up, the L intercept will move to the right, and the slope of the isocost line will remain unchanged.

FINDING THE OPTIMAL INPUT COMBINATION

We are, at last, in a position to answer the fundamental question facing the firm. That is, given fixed input prices and a known production function, what is the optimal combination of labor and capital. The term "optimal" in this context can be considered from two perspectives. We may consider it to mean maximizing output subject to a fixed operating budget. Somewhat equivalently, we may interpret it is the minimizing of total cost subject to a predetermined level of output. Either approach represents the kind of constrained optimization problem discussed in Chapter 2. As we will see, both approaches represent the first-order conditions for profit maximization.

The optimal combination of labor and capital is illustrated diagrammatically in Figure 7.3, which combines the isocost line, illustrated in Figure 7.1 with the isoquant map introduced in Chapter 5.

Three of the infinite number of possible isoquants are illustrated in Figure 7.3. The isoquant furthest from the origin represents the combinations of labor and capital that generate the highest constant output level. Also illustrated in Figure 7.3 is an isocost line representing the different combinations of labor and capital that may be hired at the fixed input prices P_L and P_K, and the fixed operating budget TC_0. Graphically, it is not difficult to understand why this particular firm will operate at point B on isoquant labeled Q_1. Clearly, as we move from left to right from the horizontal axis along the isocost line, we move to successively higher and higher isoquants. At point C, for example, we are only able to produce an output of Q_0 with an operating budget of TC_0. On the other hand, as we move closer to point B, substituting labor for capital, total output rises. Beyond point B, however, output levels steadily decline as we move to lower isoquants. To understand why this is so, consider what is happening algebraically.

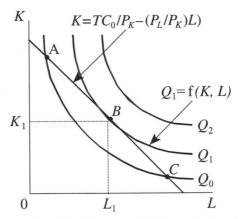

FIGURE 7.3   Optimal input combination: output maximization.

From Chapter 5 recall that the slope of the isoquant is given by the marginal rate of technical substitution, or

$$\frac{dK}{dL} = -\frac{MP_L}{MP_K} = MRTS_{KL} < 0 \tag{5.21}$$

Likewise, the slope of the isocost line is given by the expression

$$\frac{dK}{dL} = \frac{P_L}{P_K} < 0 \tag{7.5}$$

At point C on the diagram we note that the absolute value of the slope of the isoquant is less than of the isocost line. That is

$$\frac{MP_L}{MP_K} < \frac{P_L}{P_K}$$

Rearranging, this expression becomes

$$\frac{MP_L}{P_L} < \frac{MP_K}{P_K} \tag{7.6}$$

Equation (7.6) says that at point C, the marginal product of labor per dollar spent on labor is less than the marginal product of capital per dollar spent on capital. It should be clear, therefore, that by reallocating a dollar from the fixed operating budget from labor into capital, we should generate a net increase in output. Similarly, at point A in the diagram we have

$$\frac{MP_L}{MP_K} > \frac{P_L}{P_K}$$

Rearranging, this expression becomes

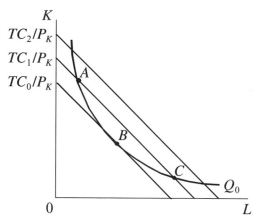

FIGURE 7.4   Optimal input combination: cost minimization.

$$\frac{MP_L}{P_L} > \frac{MP_K}{P_K} \tag{7.7}$$

Equation (7.7) says that reallocating a dollar from capital to labor should generate an increase in output. The only point at which no gain in output will result by reallocating the firm's fixed operating budget dollars is point B, where

$$\frac{MP_L}{MP_K} = \frac{P_L}{P_K} \tag{7.8}$$

In other words, only where the isocost line is just tangent to the isoquant will the firm be hiring the proper combination of labor and capital to generate the most output possible from its fixed operating budget.[2] Of course, rearranging this expression yields

$$\frac{MP_L}{P_L} = \frac{MP_K}{P_K} \tag{7.9}$$

The same optimization conditions apply to the slightly different problem of minimizing the firm's total cost of production subject to a fixed level of production. This situation is illustrated in Figure 7.4.

In Figure 7.4 we have one isoquant and three isocost lines representing the different operating budgets TC_0, TC_1, and TC_2, where $TC_0 < TC_1 < TC_2$. Clearly, by the reasoning just outlined, total production costs will be minimized at point B in the diagram where, as before, $MP_L/P_L = MP_K/P_K$.

---

[2] A formal derivation of this optimality condition is presented in Appendix 7A.

In general, to minimize total production costs subject to a fixed level of output, or to maximize total output subject to a fixed operating budget, the marginal product per last dollar spent on each input must be the same for all inputs. That is, efficient production requires that the isoquant be tangent to the isocost line.

Problem 7.2. Suppose that a firm produces at an output level where the marginal product of labor (MP_L) is 50 units and the wage rate (P_L) is \$25. Suppose, further, that the marginal product of capital (MP_K) is 100 units and the rental price of capital (P_K) is \$40.
a. Is this firm producing efficiently?
b. If the firm is not producing efficiently, how might it do so?

Solution
a. The optimal input combination is given by the expression

$$\frac{MP_L}{P_L} = \frac{MP_K}{P_K}$$

Substituting into this expression we get

$$\frac{50}{25} = \frac{2}{1} < \frac{2.5}{1} = \frac{100}{40}$$

That is, the firm is not operating efficiently.
b. According to these results, the marginal product of labor is 2 units of output for every dollar spent on labor. The marginal product of capital is 2.5 units of output for every dollar spent on capital. To produce more efficiently, therefore, this firm should reallocate its budget dollars away from labor and toward capital.

Problem 7.3. Lotzaluk Tire, Inc., a small producer of motorcycle tires, has the following production function:

$$Q = 100K^{0.5}L^{0.5}$$

During the last production period, the firm operated efficiently and used input rates of 100 and 25 for capital and labor, respectively.
a. What is the marginal product of capital and the marginal product of labor based on the input rates specified?
b. If the rental price of capital was \$20 per unit, what was the wage rate?
c. Suppose that the rental price of capital is expected to increase to \$25 while the wage rate and the labor input will remain unchanged under the terms of a labor contract. If the firm maintains efficient production, what input rate of capital will be used?

Solution

a. $MP_K = \dfrac{\partial Q}{\partial K} = 0.5(100)K^{-0.5}L^{0.5} = \dfrac{50(25)^{0.5}}{(100)^{0.5}} = \dfrac{50(5)}{10} = \dfrac{250}{10} = 25$

$MP_L = \dfrac{\partial Q}{\partial L} = 0.5(100)K^{0.5}L^{-0.5} = \dfrac{50(100)^{0.5}}{(25)^{0.5}} = \dfrac{50(10)}{5} = \dfrac{500}{5} = 100$

b. Efficiency in production requires that

$$\frac{MP_L}{P_L} = \frac{MP_K}{P_K}$$

where P_L is the wage rate and P_K is the rental price of capital. Substituting into the efficiency condition we obtain

$$\frac{100}{P_L} = \frac{25}{20}$$
$$P_L = \$80$$

c. $\dfrac{MP_L}{P_L} = \dfrac{MP_K}{P_K}$

$$\frac{50K^{.5}L^{-0.5}}{P_L} = \frac{50K^{-0.5}L^{0.5}}{P_K}$$

Substituting into the efficiency condition and solving for K yields

$$\frac{50K^{0.5}(25)^{-0.5}}{80} = \frac{50K^{-0.5}(25)^{0.5}}{25}$$
$$\frac{K^{0.5}(25)^{-0.5}}{80} = \frac{K^{-0.5}(25)^{0.5}}{25}$$
$$\frac{K^{0.5}}{400} = \frac{5K^{-0.5}}{25}$$
$$K = 80$$

As a result of the increase in the rental price of capital, the amount of capital used in the production process falls from 100 units to 80 units.

EXPANSION PATH

Note that Equations (7.8) and (7.9) are perfectly general in the sense that they represent the optimal combinations of productive resources independent of the budget or output constraint. In fact, Equations (7.8) and (7.9) are sometimes referred to as the *expansion path* of the firm because they represent the locus of all efficient input combinations. Figure 7.5 might be taken to represent one such expansion path.

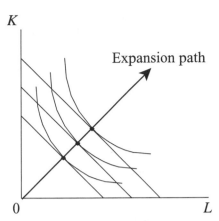

K

Expansion path

FIGURE 7.5 Expansion path.
0
L

Definition: The expansion path is the locus of points for which the isocost and isoquant curves are tangent. It represents the cost-minimizing (profit-maximizing) combinations of capital and labor for different operating budgets.

The expansion path, which represents the optimal combination of capital and labor used in the production process for different operating budgets, is characterized by Equations (7.8) and (7.9). In particular, Equation (7.9) says that a profit-maximizing firm will allocate its budget in such a way that the last dollar spent on labor will yield the same additional output as the last dollar spent on capital.

Problem 7.4. Suppose you are given the production function

$$Q = 30K^{0.7}L^{0.5}$$

where input prices are $P_L = 20$ and $P_K = 30$. Determine the expansion path.

Solution. The expansion path is determined by the expression

$$\frac{MP_L}{P_L} = \frac{MP_K}{P_K}$$

where

$$MP_L = \frac{\partial Q}{\partial L} \quad \text{and} \quad MP_K = \frac{\partial Q}{\partial K}$$

$$\frac{0.5(30)K^{0.7}L^{-0.5}}{20} = \frac{0.7(30)K^{-0.3}L^{0.5}}{30}$$

$$K \approx 0.9L$$

In this case, the expansion path is linear with a slope of about 0.9 and a zero intercept. In fact, the expansion path of all *Cobb–Douglas production functions* is linear with a zero intercept.

Problem 7.5. Muck Rakers is a cable television industry construction contractor that specializes in laying fiberoptic cable. Muck Rakers lays fiberoptic cables according to the following short-run production function:

$$Q = K(5L - 1.25L^2)$$

where Q the length of fiberoptic laid in meters per week, L is labor hours, and K is hours of excavating equipment, which is fixed at 200 hours. The rental price is the same for both labor (P_L) and capital (P_K): $25 per hour. Muck Rakers has received an offer from Telecablevision, Inc. to install 1,000 meters for a price of $10,000.
a. Should Muck Rakers accept the offer?
b. Does this production function exhibit constant, increasing, or decreasing returns to scale?

Solution
a. Substituting the weekly amount of capital available to Muck Rakers into the production function yields

$$Q = 200(5L - 1.25L^2) = 1,000L - 250L^2$$

The amount of labor required to install 1,000 meters of fiberoptic cable is

$$1,000 = 1,000L - 250L^2 - 250L^2 + 1,000L - 1,000 = 0$$

The amount of labor employed can be determined by solving this equation for L. This equation is of the general form

$$aL^2 + bL + c = 0$$

The solution values may be determined by factoring this equation, or by application of the quadratic formula, which is

$$L_{1,2} = \frac{-b \pm \sqrt{b^2 - 4ac}}{2a}$$

$$= \frac{-1,000 \pm \sqrt{\left[(1,000)^2 - 4(-250)(1,000)\right]}}{2(-250)}$$

$$= \frac{-1,000 \pm \sqrt{(0)}}{-500} = -\frac{1,000}{-500} = 2$$

The total cost to Muck Rakers to lay 1,000 meters of fiberoptic cable is, therefore,

$$TC = P_L L + P_K K = 25(2) + 25(200) = 50 + 5,000 = \$5,050$$

Since TR ($10,000) is greater than TC ($5,050), then Muck Rakers should accept the contract.

b. To determine the returns to scale of Muck Rakers production, set $K = L = 1$ and solve:

$$Q = (1)\left[5(1) - 1.25(1)^2\right] = 5 - 1.25 = 3.75$$

Now, set $K = L = 2$ and solve:

$$Q = (2)\left[5(2) - 1.25(2)^2\right] = (2)(10 - 5) = 10$$

Since output more than doubles as inputs are doubled, Muck Rakers production function exhibits increasing returns to scale.

Problem 7.6. Suppose that you are given the following production function:

$$Q = 250(L + 4K)$$

Suppose further that the price of labor (w) is $25 per hour and the rental price of capital (r) is $100 per hour.
a. What is the optimal capital/labor ratio?
b. Suppose that the price of capital were lowered to $25 per hour? What is the new optimal ratio of capital to labor?

Solution
a. In general, the optimal capital/labor ratio is determined along the expansion path

$$\frac{MP_L}{w} = \frac{MP_K}{r}$$

where $MP_L = \partial Q/\partial L$ and $MP_K = \partial Q/\partial K$. The term MP_L/w measures the marginal contribution to output from the last dollar spent on labor, and MP_K/r measures the marginal contribution to output from the last dollar spent on capital. Production is efficient (output maximized) at the point at which the last dollar spent on capital yields the same additional output as the last dollar spent on labor.

Taking the first partial derivative of the production function and substituting the results into the efficiency condition yields

$$\frac{250}{25} = \frac{1,000}{100}$$
$$10 = 10$$

Since the values of MP_L and MP_K are constants, any combination of K and L is an optimal combination. Diagrammatically, both the isocost and isoquant curves are linear in K and L, and have the same slope. To see

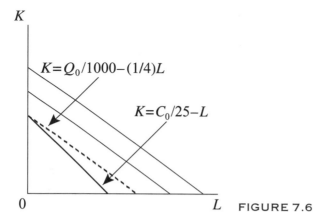

K

$K=Q_0/1000-(1/4)L$

$K=C_0/25-L$

0 L FIGURE 7.6

this, solve the production function for K in terms of L at some arbitrary output level $Q = Q_0$ to obtain the equation of the isoquant at that output level.

$$Q_0 = 250L + 1,000K$$

$$1,000K = Q_0 - 250L$$

$$K = \frac{Q_0}{1,000} - \left(\frac{1}{4}\right)L$$

where the slope of the isoquant is $-1/4$.

The budget constraint for this firm may be written as

$$C_0 = 100K + 25L$$

where C_0 is the total dollar amount of the budget to be allocated between capital and labor. Solving this equation for K in terms of L yields

$$100K = C_0 - 25L$$

$$K = \frac{C_0}{100} - \left(\frac{1}{4}\right)L$$

where the slope of the isocost line is also $-1/4$. Consider the Figure 7.6.
b. Substituting into the efficiency condition yields

$$\frac{250}{25} < \frac{1,000}{25}$$

$$10 < 40$$

This result says that since 40 additional units of output are obtained per dollar spent on capital compared with only 10 additional units of output per dollar spent on labor, then output will be maximized by using all

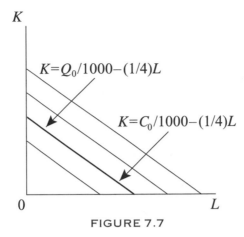

FIGURE 7.7

capital and no labor. Diagrammatically, this is a "corner" solution. Consider Figure 7.7.

UNCONSTRAINED OPTIMIZATION: THE PROFIT FUNCTION

The objective of profit maximization facing the decision maker may, of course, be dealt with more directly. The optimality conditions just discussed are all by-products of this more direct approach. The problem confronting the decision maker is to choose an output level that will maximize profit. We will begin by defining profit as the difference between total revenue and total cost.

$$\pi(Q) = TR(Q) - TC(Q) \tag{7.10}$$

where $TR(Q)$ represents total revenue and $TC(Q)$ represents total cost, both of which are assumed to be functions of output. As we discussed in Chapter 2, Equation (7.10) is an unconstrained objective function in which the object is to maximize total profit, which in this case is a function of the output level.

As was discussed in Chapter 2, to meet the first-order and second-order conditions for a maximum, the first derivative must be equal to zero and the second derivative must be negative. In this case, the first- and second-order conditions, respectively, are $d\pi/dQ = 0$ and $d^2\pi/dQ^2 < 0$. Applying these conditions to Equation (7.10), we obtain

$$\frac{d\pi}{dQ} = \frac{dTR}{dQ} - \frac{dTC}{dQ} = 0 \tag{7.11}$$

or

$$MR = MC \qquad (7.12)$$

Equation (7.12) simply says that the first-order condition for the firm to maximize profits is to select an output level such that marginal revenue ($MR = dTR/dQ$) equals marginal cost ($MC = dTC/dQ$). Alternatively, a first-order condition for the firm to maximize profits is to select an output level for which marginal profit ($M\pi = d\pi/dQ$) is zero.

To ensure that the solution value for Equation (7.10) maximizes profit, the second-order condition must also be satisfied. Differentiating Equation (7.10) with respect to Q, we obtain

$$\frac{d^2\pi}{dQ^2} = \frac{d^2TR}{dQ^2} - \frac{d^2TC}{dQ^2} < 0 \qquad (7.13)$$

or

$$\frac{d^2TR}{dQ^2} < \frac{d^2TC}{dQ^2} \qquad (7.14)$$

In economic terms, Equation (7.14) simply says that to ensure that profit is maximized given that the first-order condition is satisfied, the rate of change in marginal revenue must be less than the rate of change in marginal cost. Diagrammatically, at the profit-maximizing level of output, where marginal revenue equals marginal cost, the marginal cost curve would intersect the marginal revenue curve from below. Alternatively, from Equation (7.13) the second-order condition for profit maximization requires that at the profit-maximizing level of output Q^*, not only must marginal profit be zero but the slope of the profit function must be falling. Diagrammatically this would be illustrated as a profit "hill," where profit is maximized at an output level (Q^*) that corresponds to the top of the profit "hill."

In two common illustrations of the foregoing concepts, which will be discussed at greater length in subsequent chapters, the selling price Q is taken to be parametric ($P = P_0$) or is assumed to be a function of output [$P = f(Q)$]. The first instance is typical of the market structure known as *perfect competition*. The second instance is typical of the market structure known as *monopoly*.

Problem 7.7. The Squashed Apple Company manufactures a variety of bottled fruit juices under the trade name Squapple. The company faces the following total profit function

$$\pi = -2,000 + 450Q - 50Q^2$$

a. At what output level is profit maximized?

b. What is Squapple's marginal profit function?
c. What is Squapple's marginal profit at the profit maximizing output level? At $Q = 3$?
d. At what output level is marginal profit optimized (maximized or minimized)? Which is it?
e. What is Squapple's average profit function?
f. At what output level is average profit optimized (maximized or minimized)? Which is it?
g. What, if anything, do you observe about the relationship between marginal profit and average profit? [*Hint*: Take the first derivative of $A\pi = \pi/Q$, where $\pi = f(Q)$. Examine different values of $M\pi$ and $A\pi$ in the neighborhood of your answer to part f.]

Solution

a. Take the first derivative of the profit function, set the results equal to zero, and solve.

$$\frac{d\pi}{dQ} = 450 - 100Q = 0$$

$$Q* = 4.5$$

To verify that profit corresponding to this output level is maximized, take the second derivative.

$$\frac{d^2\pi}{dQ^2} = -100 < 0$$

A negative second derivative verifies that π is maximized at $Q = 4.5$.

b. $M\pi = \dfrac{d\pi}{dQ} = 450 - 100Q$

c. $M\pi = 450 - 100(3) = 450 - 300 = 150$

d. The marginal profit function is linear. Mathematically, linear functions have neither a maximum nor a minimum. The student is cautioned, however, that mathematics is a means, not an end, to understanding the principles of economics. In our example, since output levels are limited to nonnegative values, while the marginal profit function does not have a maximum value, it is minimized at $Q = 0$.

e. The average profit function is given as

$$A\pi = \frac{\pi}{Q} = -2,000Q^{-1} + 450 - 50Q$$

f. Taking the first derivative, setting the results equal to zero, and solving, we obtain

$$\frac{dA\pi}{dQ} = 2,000Q^{-2} - 50 = 0$$

$$Q^2 = 40$$

$$Q* = (Q^2)^{0.5} = (40)^{0.5} = 6.325$$

$$\frac{d^2 A\pi}{dQ^2} = -4,000Q^{-3} = \frac{-4,000}{252.988} = -15.811 < 0$$

Average profit is maximized at $Q = 6.325$, which is verified by a negative second derivative.

g. $A\pi = \pi Q^{-1}$

$$\frac{dA\pi}{dQ} = -\pi Q^{-2} + Q^{-1}\left(\frac{d\pi}{dQ}\right) = \frac{1}{Q(d\pi/dQ - \pi/Q)} = \frac{1}{Q(M\pi - A\pi)}$$

Since $Q^{-1} > 0$, when $M\pi = A\pi$, then $dA\pi/dQ = 0$ and $A\pi$ is maximized. When $M\pi > A\pi$, $dA\pi/dQ > 0$ and $A\pi$ is rising. When $M\pi < A\pi$, $dA\pi/dQ < 0$, and $A\pi$ is falling. Note that in the answer to part f, $A\pi$ is maximized at $Q = 6.325$. Substituting this result into the $A\pi$ and $M\pi$ equations yields

$$A\pi = \frac{-2,000}{6.325} + 450 - 50(6.325)$$

$$= -316.206 + 450 - 316.25 = -182.456$$

$$M\pi = 450 - 100(6.325) = 450 - 632.50 = -182.50$$

Notwithstanding errors in rounding, these equations verify that when $A\pi$ is maximized, $A\pi = M\pi$. Now, choose $Q = 6 < 6.325$.

$$dA\pi/dQ = \frac{2,000}{(6)^2} - 50 = \frac{2,000}{36} - 50 = 5.556 > 0$$

$$A\pi = \frac{-2,000}{6} + 450 - 50(6) = -333.333 + 450 - 300 = -183.333$$

$$M\pi = 450 - 100(6) = 450 - 600 = -150$$

That is, when $A\pi$ is rising, $M\pi > A\pi$.

Finally, choose $Q = 6.5 > 6.325$.

$$dA\pi/dQ = \frac{2,000}{(6.5)^2} - 50 = \frac{2,000}{42.25} - 50 = 47.337 - 50 = -2.663 < 0$$

$$A\pi = \frac{-2,000}{6.5} + 450 - 50(6.5) = -307.692 + 450 - 325 = -182.692$$

$$M\pi = 450 - 100(6.5) = 450 - 650 = -200$$

That is, when $A\pi$ is falling, $M\pi < A\pi$.

PERFECT COMPETITION

As before, assume that total cost is an increasing function of output [i.e., $TC = TC(Q)$]. If we assume that the selling price per unit of Q is given, the total revenue function becomes

$$TR = P_0 Q \tag{7.15}$$

Substituting Equation (7.15) into Equation (7.10) yields

$$\pi(Q) = P_0 Q - TC(Q) \tag{7.16}$$

The first- and second-order conditions for Equation (7.16) are, respectively,

$$\frac{d\pi}{dQ} = P_0 - \frac{dTC}{dQ} = 0 \tag{7.17}$$

or

$$P_0 = MC \tag{7.18}$$

and

$$d^2\pi / dQ^2 = -\frac{d^2TC}{dQ^2} < 0 \tag{7.19}$$

or

$$\frac{d^2TC}{dQ^2} = \frac{dMC}{dQ} > 0 \tag{7.20}$$

Equation (7.18) says that at the profit-maximizing level of output, the fixed selling price is equal to marginal cost, while Equation (7.20) says that at the profit-maximizing level of output, total cost is increasing at an increasing rate (i.e., marginal cost is rising). Equation (7.19) says that at the profit-maximizing output level, marginal profit is zero and falling. These concepts are illustrated in Figure 7.8.

The shape of the total cost curve (TC) Figure 7.8a was discussed in Chapter 6 and justified largely on the basis of the law of diminishing marginal product, which was introduced in Chapter 5. The total revenue curve in Figure 7.8a is a straight line through the origin. The slope of the total revenue curve is equal to the fixed price of the product, P_0. In Figure 7.8a total profit (π) is illustrated by the vertical distance between the TR and TC curves. Total profit is also illustrated separately in Figure 7.8b.

Total profit is maximized at output levels Q_1 and Q^*, where $d\pi/dQ = 0$. This is the first-order condition for profit maximization. At both Q_1 and Q^* the first-order conditions for profit maximization are satisfied, however only at Q^* is the second-order condition for profit maximization satisfied. In the neighborhood around point B in Figure 7.6b, the slope of the profit

a

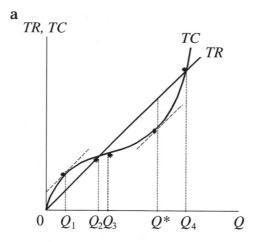

b

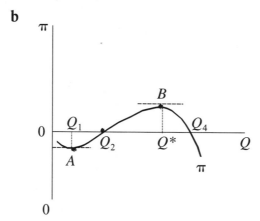

c

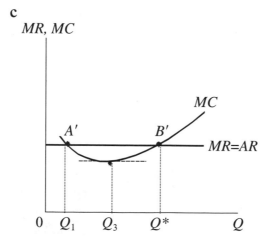

FIGURE 7.8   Profit maximization: perfect competition.

function is falling (i.e., $d^2\pi/dQ^2 < 0$. At point A, $d^2\pi/dQ^2 > 0$, which is a second-order condition for a local minimum. In other words, it is evident from the Figure 7.6a and b that total profit reaches a minimum at point A and a maximum at point B. Finally, note that at B' the profit-maximizing condition $MC = MR$, with MC intersecting the MR curve from below, is satisfied. At A', $MC = MR$ but MC intersects MR from above, indicating that this point corresponds to a minimum profit level.

Note that the marginal cost curve in Figure 7.8c reaches its minimum value at output level Q_3, which corresponds to the inflection point on the total cost function in Figure 7.6a. Also note in Figure 7.6c that because price is constant, marginal revenue is equal to average revenue.

Problem 7.8. The XYZ Company is a perfectly competitive firm that can sell its entire output for $18 per unit. XYZ's total cost equation is

$$TC = 6 + 33Q - 9Q^2 + Q^3$$

where Q represents units of output.
a. What is the firm's total revenue function?
b. What are the marginal revenue, marginal cost, and average total cost equations?
c. Diagram the marginal and average total cost equations for values $Q = 0$ to $Q = 10$.
d. What is the total profit equation?
e. What is the marginal profit equation?
f. Use optimization techniques to find the profit-maximizing output level.

Solution
a. Total revenue is defined as

$$TR = P_0 Q = 18Q$$

b. $MR = \dfrac{dTR}{dQ} = 18$

$MC = \dfrac{dTC}{dQ} = 33 - 18Q + 3Q^2$

$AC = \dfrac{TC}{Q} = 33 - 9Q + Q^2 + \dfrac{6}{Q}$

c. $\pi = TR - TC = 18Q - (6 + 33Q - 9Q^2 + Q^3) = -6 - 15Q + 9Q^2 - Q^3$
d. $M\pi = d\pi/dQ = -15 + 18Q - 3Q^2$
e. To find the profit-maximizing output level, take the first derivative of the total profit function, set the results equal to zero (the first-order condition), and solve for Q.

$$\frac{d\pi}{dQ} = -15 + 18Q - 3Q^2 = 0$$

This equation, which has two solution values, is of the general form

$$aQ^2 + bQ + c = 0$$

The solution values may be determined by factoring this equation, or by application of the quadratic formula, which is

$$Q_{1,2} = \frac{\left[-b \pm \sqrt{b^2 - 4ac}\right]}{2a}$$

$$= \frac{-18 \pm \sqrt{\left[(18)^2 - 4(-3)(-15)\right]}}{2(-3)}$$

$$= \frac{-18 \pm \sqrt{(324 - 180)}}{-6}$$

$$= \frac{-18 \pm \sqrt{144}}{-6} = \frac{-18 \pm 12}{-6}$$

$$Q_1 = \frac{-18 - 12}{-6} = \frac{-30}{-6} = 5$$

$$Q_2 = \frac{-18 + 12}{-6} = \frac{-6}{-6} = 1$$

The second-order condition for profit maximization is $d^2\pi/dQ^2 < 0$. Taking the second derivative of the profit function, we obtain

$$\frac{d^2\pi}{dQ^2} = -6Q + 18$$

Substitute the solution values into this condition.

$$\frac{d^2\pi}{dQ^2} = -6(1) + 18$$

$$= -6 + 18 = 12 > 0, \text{ for a local minimum}$$

$$\frac{d^2\pi}{dQ^2} = -6(5) + 18$$

$$= -30 + 18 = -12 < 0, \text{ for a local minimum}$$

Total profit, therefore, is maximized at $Q^* = 5$.

Another, and perhaps more revealing, way of looking at the profit maximization problem is to substitute Equations (5.2) from Chapter 5 and Equation (7.1) into Equation (7.16) to yield

$$\pi(Q) = P_0 f(K, L) - P_L L - P_K K \tag{7.21}$$

Equation (7.21) expresses profit not directly as a function of output, but as a function of the inputs employed in the production process, in this case capital and labor. Equation (7.21) allows us to examine the profit-maximizing conditions from the perspective of input usage rather than output levels. Taking partial derivatives of Equation (7.21) with respect to capital and labor, the first-order conditions for profit maximization are

$$\frac{\partial \pi}{\partial K} = P_0 \left(\frac{\partial Q}{\partial K} \right) - P_K = 0 \tag{7.22a}$$

$$\frac{\partial \pi}{\partial L} = P_0 \left(\frac{\partial Q}{\partial L} \right) - P_L = 0 \tag{7.22b}$$

The second-order condition for a profit maximum is

$$\frac{\partial^2 \pi}{\partial K^2} < 0; \ \frac{\partial^2 \pi}{\partial^2 L} < 0; \left(\frac{\partial^2 \pi}{\partial K^2} \right)\left(\frac{\partial^2 \pi}{\partial^2 L} \right) - \left(\frac{\partial^2 \pi}{\partial K \partial K} \right) > 0 \tag{7.23}$$

Equations (7.22) may be rewritten as

$$P_0 \times MP_K = P_K \tag{7.24a}$$

$$P_0 \times MP_L = P_L \tag{7.24b}$$

The term on the left-hand side of Equations (7.24) is called the *marginal revenue product of the input* while the term on the right, which is the rental price of the input, is called the marginal resource cost of the input. Equations (7.24) may be expressed as

$$MRP_K = MRC_K \tag{7.25a}$$

$$MRP_L = MRC_L \tag{7.25b}$$

Equations (7.24) are easily interpreted. Equation (7.24a), for example, says that a firm will hire additional incremental units of capital to the point at which the additional revenues brought into the firm are precisely equal to the cost of hiring an incremental unit of capital. Since the marginal product of capital (and labor) falls as additional units of capital are hired because of the law of diminishing marginal product, and since $MRP_K < MRC_K$, hiring one more unit of capital will result in the firm losing money on the last unit of capital hired. Hiring one unit less than the amount of capital required to satisfy Equation (7.24a) means that the firm is for going profit that could have been earned by hiring additional units of capital, since $MRP_K > MRC_K$.

Problem 7.9. The production function facing a firm is

$$Q = K^5 L^5$$

The firm can sell all of its output for \$4. The price of labor and capital are \$5 and \$10, respectively.

a. Determine the optimal levels of capital and labor usage if the firm's operating budget is \$1,000.

b. At the optimal levels of capital and labor usage, calculate the firm's total profit.

Solution

a. The optimal input combination is given by the expression

$$\frac{MP_L}{P_L} = \frac{MP_K}{P_K}$$

Substituting into this expression we get

$$\frac{(0.5K^{0.5}L^{-0.5})}{5} = \frac{(0.5K^{-0.5}L^{0.5})}{10}$$

$$K = 0.5L$$

Substituting this value into the budget constraint we get

$$1,000 = 5L + 10K$$

$$1,000 = 5L + 10(0.5L)$$

$$L^* = 80$$

$$1,000 = 5(80) + 10K$$

$$K^* = 40$$

b. $\pi = TR - TC = P(K^{0.5}L^{0.5}) - TC = 4[(40)^{0.6}(80)^{0.4}] - 1,000 = -\$821.11$

MONOPOLY

We continue to assume that total cost is an increasing function of output [i.e., $TC = TC(Q)$]. Now, however, we assume that the selling price is a function of Q, that is,

$$P = P(Q) \qquad (7.26)$$

where $dP/dQ < 0$. This is simply the demand function after applying the inverse-function rule (see Chapter 2). Substituting Equation (7.26) into Equation (7.10) yields

$$\pi(Q) = P(Q)Q - TC(Q) \qquad (7.27)$$

For a profit maximum, the first- and second-order conditions for Equation (7.16) are, respectively,

$$d\pi/dQ = P + Q\left(\frac{dP}{dQ}\right) - \frac{dTC}{dQ} = 0 \qquad (7.28)$$

or

$$P + Q\left(\frac{dP}{dQ}\right) = MC \qquad (7.29)$$

The term on the left-hand side of Equation (7.29) is the expression for marginal revenue. The second-order condition for a profit maximum is

$$\frac{d^2\pi}{dQ^2} = Q\left(\frac{d^2P}{dQ^2}\right) + 2\frac{dP}{dQ} - \frac{d^2TC}{dQ^2} < 0 \qquad (7.30)$$

If we assume that the demand equation is linear, then Equation (7.26) may be written as

$$P = a + bQ \qquad (7.31)$$

where $b < 0$. Substituting Equation (7.31) into (7.27) yields

$$\pi(Q) = (a + bQ)Q - TC(Q) = aQ + bQ^2 - TC(Q) \qquad (7.32)$$

The first- and second-order conditions become

$$\frac{d\pi}{dQ} = a + 2bQ - \frac{dTC}{dQ} = 0$$

where

$$a + 2bQ = MR \qquad (7.33)$$

Note that the marginal revenue equation is similar to the demand equation in that it has the same vertical intercept but twice the (negative) slope. Note also that, by definition, Equation (7.31) is the average revenue equation, that is,

$$AR = \frac{TR}{Q} = \frac{aQ + bQ^2}{Q} = a + bQ = P$$

The second-order condition for a profit maximum is

$$\frac{d^2\pi}{dQ^2} = 2b - \frac{d^2TC}{dQ^2} < 0 \qquad (7.34)$$

The conditions for profit maximization assuming a linear demand curve are shown in Figure 7.9. The cost functions displayed in Figure 7.9a are essentially the same as those depicted in Figure 7.9. All of the cost functions represent the short run in production in which 7.8, the prices of the factors of production are assumed to be fixed. The fundamental difference between the two sets of figures is that in the case of perfect competition the firm is assumed to be a "price taker," in the sense that the firm owner can sell as much product as required to maximize profit without affecting the market price of the product. The conditions under which this occurs will be

a

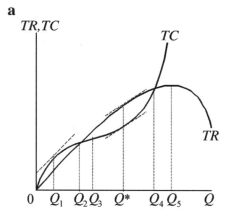

b

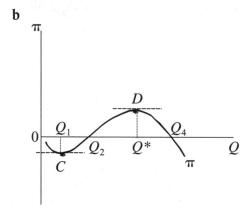

c

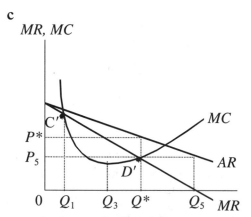

FIGURE 7.9   Profit maximization: monopoly.

discussed in Chapter 8. In the case of monopoly, on the other hand, the firm is a "price maker," since increasing or decreasing output will raise or lower the market price. The simple explanation of this is that because the monopolist is the only firm in the industry, increasing or decreasing output will result in a right- or a left-shift in the market supply curve.

As always, the firm maximizes profit by producing at an output level where $MR = MC$, which in Figure 7.9 occurs at an output level of Q^*. As before, total profit is optimized at output levels Q_1 and Q^*, where $d\pi/dQ = 0$. At both Q_1 and Q^* the first-order conditions for profit maximization are satisfied, however only at Q^* is the second-order condition for profit maximization satisfied. In the neighborhood around point D in Figure 7.9b, while the slope of the profit function is positive, it is falling (i.e., $d^2\pi/dQ^2 < 0$). At point C $d^2\pi/dQ^2 > 0$, which is the second-order condition for a local minimum. Again, note that at D' the profit-maximizing condition $MC = MR$, with MC intersecting the MR curve from below, is satisfied. At C', $MC = MR$ but, MC intersects MR from above, indicating that this point corresponds to a minimum profit level.

Note that the marginal cost curve in Figure 7.9c reaches its minimum value at output level Q_3, which corresponds to the inflection point on the total cost function in Figure 7.9a. Unlike the case of perfect competition, however, while the selling price is by definition equal to average revenue, in the case of monopoly the price is greater than marginal revenue. Once output has been determined by the firm, the selling price of the product will be defined along the demand curve. In fact, any market structure in which the firm faces a downward-sloping demand curve for its product will exhibit this characteristic. Only in the case of perfect competition, where the demand curve for the product is perfectly elastic, will the condition $P = MR$ be satisfied for a profit-maximizing firm.

Problem 7.10. The demand and total cost equations for the output of a monopolist are

$$Q = 90 - 2P$$

$$TC = Q^3 - 8Q^2 + 57Q + 2$$

a. Find the firm's profit-maximizing output level.
b. What is the profit at this output level?
c. Determine the price per unit output at which the profit-maximizing output is sold.

Solution
a. Define total profit as

$$\pi = TR - TC$$

Using the inverse-function rule to solve the demand equation for P yields

$$P = 45 - 0.5Q$$

The expression for total revenue is, therefore,

$$TR = 45Q - 0.5Q^2$$

Substituting the expressions for TR and TC into the profit equation yields

$$\pi = (45Q - 0.5Q^2) - (Q^3 - 8Q^2 + 57Q + 2)$$
$$= 45Q - 0.5Q^2 - Q^3 + 8Q^2 - 57Q - 2 = -Q^3 + 7.5Q^2 - 12Q - 2$$

$$\frac{d\pi}{dQ} = -3Q^2 + 15Q - 12 = 0$$

This equation, which has two solution values, is of the general form

$$aQ^2 + bQ + c = 0$$

The solution values may be determined by factoring this equation, or by application of the quadratic formula, which is

$$Q_{1,2} = \frac{-b \pm \sqrt{(b^2 - 4ac)}}{2a}$$

$$= \frac{-15 \pm \sqrt{[(15)^2 - 4(-3)(-12)]}}{2(-3)}$$

$$= \frac{-15 \pm \sqrt{(225 - 144)}}{-6}$$

$$= \frac{-15 \pm \sqrt{81}}{-6} = \frac{-15 \pm 9}{-6}$$

$$Q_1 = \frac{-15 + 9}{-6} = \frac{-6}{-6} = 1$$

$$Q_2 = \frac{-15 - 9}{-6} = \frac{-24}{-6} = 4$$

The second-order condition for profit maximization is $d^2\pi/dQ^2 < 0$. Taking the second derivative of the profit function, we obtain

$$\frac{d^2\pi}{dQ^2} = -6Q + 15$$

Substitute the solution values into this condition.

$$\frac{d^2\pi}{dQ^2} = -6(1) + 15 = -6 + 15 = 9 > 0, \text{ for a local minimum}$$

$$\frac{d^2\pi}{dQ^2} = -6(4) + 15 = -24 + 15 = -9 < 0, \text{ for a local minimum}$$

Total profit, therefore, is maximized at $Q = 4$.

b. $\pi = -Q^3 + 7.5Q^2 - 12Q - 2 = -(4)^3 + 7.5(4)^2 - 12(4) - 2$
$= -64 + 120 - 48 - 2 = \$6$

c. Total revenue is defined as

$$TR = PQ = 45Q - 0.5Q^2 = (45 - 0.5Q)Q$$

Thus,

$$P = 45 - 0.5Q = 45 - 0.5(4) = 45 - 2 = \$43$$

Problem 7.11. Suppose that the demand function for a product produced by a monopolist is given by the equation

$$Q = \frac{20}{3} - \left(\frac{1}{3}\right)P$$

Suppose further that the monopolist's total cost of production function is given by the equation

$$TC = 2Q^2$$

a. Find the output level that will maximize profit (π).
b. Determine the monopolist's profit at the profit-maximizing output level.
c. What is the monopolist's average revenue (AR) function?
d. Determine the price per unit at the profit-maximizing output level.
e. Suppose that the monopolist was a sales (total revenue) maximizer. Compare the sales maximizing output level with the profit-maximizing output level.
f. Compare total revenue at the sales-maximizing and profit-maximizing output levels.

Solution

a. Total profit is defined as the difference between total revenue TR and total cost, that is,

$$\pi = TR - TC$$

where TR is defined as

$$TR = PQ$$

Solving the demand function for price yields

$$P = 20 - 3Q$$

Substituting this result into the definition of total revenue yields

$$TR = (20 - 3Q)Q = 20Q - 3Q^2$$

Combining this expression with the monopolist's total cost function yields the monopolist's total profit function, that is,

$$\pi = TR - TC = (20Q - 3Q^2) - (2Q^2) = 20Q - 3Q^2 - 2Q^2 = 20Q - 5Q^2$$

Differentiating this expression with respect to Q and setting the result equal to zero (the first-order condition for maximization) yields

$$\frac{d\pi}{dQ} = 20 - 10Q = 0$$

Solving this expression for Q yields

$$10Q = 20$$
$$Q^* = 2$$

The second-order condition for a maximum requires that

$$\frac{d^2\pi}{dQ^2} = -10 < 0$$

b. At $Q = 2$, the monopolist's maximum profit is

$$\pi = 20(2) - 5(2)^2 = 40 - 20 = 20$$

c. Average revenue is defined as

$$AR = \frac{TR}{Q} = \frac{20Q - 3Q^2}{Q} = 20 - 3Q = P$$

Note that the average revenue function is simply the market demand function.

d. Substituting the profit-maximizing output level into the market demand function yields the monopolist's selling price.

$$P = 20 - 3(2) = 20 - 6 = 14$$

e. Total revenue is defined as

$$TR = PQ = 20Q - 3Q^2$$
$$\frac{dTR}{dQ} = 20 - 6Q = 0$$
$$6Q = 20$$
$$Q^* = 3.333$$

The output level that maximizes total revenue is greater than the output level that maximizes total profit ($Q = 2$). This result demonstrates that, in general, revenue maximization is not equivalent to profit maximization.

f. At the sales-maximizing output level, total revenue is

$$TR = (20 - 3Q)Q = [20 - 3(3.333)]3.333 = (20 - 10)3.333 = \$33.333$$

At the profit-maximizing output level, total revenue is

$$TR = [(20 - 3(2)]2 = (20 - 6)2 = 14(2) = \$28$$

Not surprisingly, total revenue at the sales-maximizing output level is greater than total revenue at the profit-maximizing output level.

CONSTRAINED OPTIMIZATION: THE PROFIT FUNCTION

The preceding discussion provides valuable insights into the operations of a profit-maximizing firm. Unfortunately, that analysis suffers from a serious drawback. Implicit in that discussion was the assumption that the profit-maximizing firm possesses unlimited resources. No limits were placed on the amount the firm could spend on factors of production to achieve a profit-maximizing level of output. A similar solution arises when the firm's limited budget is nonbinding in the sense that the profit-maximizing level of output may be achieved before the firm's operating budget is exhausted. Such situations are usually referred to as unconstrained optimization problems.

By contrast, the operating budget available to management may be depleted long before the firm is able to achieve a profit-maximizing level of output. When this happens, the firm tries to earn as much profit as possible given the limited resources available to it. Such cases are referred to as constrained optimization problems. The methodology underlying the solution to constrained optimization problems was discussed briefly in Chapter 2. It is to this topic that the current discussion returns.

Consider, for example, a profit-maximizing firm that faces the following demand equation for its product

$$Q = \frac{20}{3} - \left(\frac{1}{3}\right)P + \left(\frac{10}{3}\right)A \qquad (7.35)$$

where Q represents units of output, P is the selling price, and A is the number of units of advertising purchased by the firm.

The total cost of production equation for the firm is given as

$$TC = 100 + 2Q^2 + 500A \qquad (7.36)$$

Equation (7.36) indicates that the cost per unit of advertising is $500 per unit.

If there are no constraints placed on the operations of the firm, this becomes an unconstrained optimization problem. Solving Equation

(7.35) for P and multiplying through by Q yields the total revenue equation

$$TR = 20Q + 10AQ - 3Q^2 \tag{7.37}$$

The total profit equation is

$$\pi = TR - TC = (20Q + 10AQ - 3Q^2) - (100 + 2Q^2 + 500A)$$
$$\pi = -100 + 20Q - 5Q^2 + 10AQ - 500A \tag{7.38}$$

The first-order conditions for profit maximization are

$$\frac{\partial \pi}{\partial Q} = 20 - 10Q + 10A = 0 \tag{7.39a}$$

$$\frac{\partial \pi}{\partial A} = 10Q - 500 = 0 \tag{7.39b}$$

Solving simultaneously Equations (7.39a) and (7.39b), and assuming that the second-order conditions for a maximum are satisfied, yields the profit-maximizing solutions

$$P^* = \$350; Q^* = 50; A^* = 48$$

In this example, profit-maximizing advertising expenditures are $500(48) = \$24,000$. In other words, to achieve a profit-maximizing level of sales, the firm must spend $24,000 in advertising expenditures. Suppose, however, that the budget for advertising expenditures is limited to $5,000. What, then, is the profit-maximizing level of output. A formal statement of this problem is

Maximize: $\pi(Q, A) = -100 + 20Q - 5Q^2 + 10AQ - 500A$

Subject to: $500A = 5,000$

SUBSTITUTION METHOD

One approach to this constrained profit maximization problem is the substitution method. Solving the constraint for A and substituting into Equation (7.38) yields

$$\pi = -100 + 20Q - 5Q^2 + 10(10)Q - 500(10)$$
$$= -5,100 + 120Q - 5Q^2 \tag{7.40}$$

Maximizing Equation (7.40) with respect to Q and solving we obtain.

$$\frac{d\pi}{dQ} = 120 - 10Q = 0$$

$$Q^* = 12$$

The second derivative of the profit function is

$$\frac{d^2\pi}{dQ^2} = -10 < 0$$

The negative value of the second derivative of Equation (7.40) guarantees that the second-order condition for a maximum is satisfied.

LAGRANGE MULTIPLIER METHOD

A more elegant solution to the constrained optimization is the Lagrange multiplier method, also discussed in Chapter 2. The elegance of this method can be found in the interpretation of the new variable, the Lagrange multiplier, which is usually designated as λ.

The first step in the Lagrange multiplier method is to bring all terms to right side of the constraint.

$$500A - 5,000 = 0 \tag{7.41}$$

Actually, it does not matter whether the terms are brought to the right or left side, although it will affect the interpretation of the value of λ. With Equation (7.41) we now form a new objective function called the Lagrange function, which is written as

$$\mathcal{L}(Q, A, \lambda) = -100 + 20Q - 5Q^2 + 10AQ - 500A + \lambda(500A - 5,000) \tag{7.42}$$

It is important to note that the Lagrange function is equivalent to the original profit function, since the expression in the parentheses on the right is equal to zero. The first-order conditions for a maximum are

$$\frac{\partial \mathcal{L}}{\partial Q} = 20 + 10A - 10Q = 0 \tag{7.43a}$$

$$\frac{\partial \mathcal{L}}{\partial A} = 10Q - 500 - \lambda = 0 \tag{7.43b}$$

$$\frac{\partial \mathcal{L}}{\partial \lambda} = 500A - 5,000 = 0 \tag{7.43c}$$

Note that, conveniently, Equation (7.43c) is the constraint. Equations (7.43) represent a system of three linear equations in three unknowns. Assuming that the second-order conditions for a maximum are satisfied, the simultaneous solution to Equations (7.43) yield

$$P^* = \$84; \, Q^* = 12; \, A^* = 10; \, \lambda^* = 380$$

Note that these solution values are identical to the solution values in the unconstrained case. The Lagrange multiplier technique is a more powerful approach to the solution of constrained optimization problems because it allows us to solve for the Lagrange multiplier, λ. It can be demonstrated that the Lagrange multiplier is the marginal change in the maximum value of the objective function with respect to parametric changes in the value of the constraint (see, e.g., Silberberg, 1990, p. 7). In the present example, the constraint is the firm's advertising budget. Defining the advertising budget as B_A, the value of the Lagrange multiplier is

$$\lambda^* = \frac{\partial \mathcal{L}}{\partial B_A} = \frac{\partial \pi^*}{\partial B_A} = 380 \qquad (7.44)$$

In the present example, the value of the Lagrange multiplier says that, in the limit, an increase in the firm's advertising budget by \$1 will result in a \$380 increase in the firm's maximum profit. Note that, by construction, the optimization procedure guarantees that the firm's profit will always be maximized subject to the constraint. Changing the constraint simply changes the maximum value of π.

Problem 7.12. The total profit equation of a firm is

$$\pi(x, y) = -1,000 - 100x - 50x^2 - 2xy - 12y^2 + 50y$$

where x and y represent the output levels for the two product lines.
a. Use the substitution method to determine the profit-maximizing output levels of goods x and y subject to the side condition that the sum of the two product lines equal 50 units.
b. Use the Lagrange multiplier method to verify your answer to part a.
c. What is the interpretation of the Lagrange multiplier?

Solution
a. The formal statement of this problem is

$$\text{Maximize: } \pi(x, y) = -1000 - 100x - 50x^2 - 2xy - 12y^2 + 50y$$

$$\text{Subject to: } x + y = 50$$

Solving the side constraint for y and substituting this result into the objective function yields

$$\pi(x) = -1,000 - 100x - 50x^2 - 2x(50 - x) - 12(50 - x)^2 + 50(50 - x)$$

$$= -28,500 + 950x + 60x^2$$

The first-order condition for a profit maximization is

$$\frac{d\pi}{dx} = 950 - 120x = 0$$

$$x^* = 7.92 \text{ units of output}$$

The optimal output level of y is determined by substituting this result into the constraint, that is,

$$y^* = 50 - 7.92 = 42.08$$

The second derivative of the profit equation is

$$\frac{d^2\pi}{dx^2} = -120 < 0$$

which verifies that the second-order condition for profit maximization is satisfied.

b. Forming the Lagrangian expression

$$\mathcal{L}(x, y) = -1,000 - 100x - 50x^2 - 2xy - 12y^2 + 50y + \lambda(50 - x - y)$$

The first-order conditions are

$$\frac{\partial \mathcal{L}}{\partial x} = -100 - 100x - 2y - \lambda = 0$$

$$\frac{\partial \mathcal{L}}{\partial y} = -2x - 24y + 50 - \lambda = 0$$

$$\frac{\partial \mathcal{L}}{\partial \lambda} = 50 - x - y = 0$$

This is a system of three linear equations in three unknowns. Solving this system simultaneously yields the optimal solution values

$$x^* = 7.92;\ y^* = 42.08;\ \lambda^* = -975$$

c. Denoting total combined output capacity of the firm as k, which in this case is $k = x + y = 50$, the value of the Lagrangian multiplier is given as

$$\lambda^* = \frac{\partial \mathcal{L}}{\partial k} = \frac{\partial \pi^*}{\partial k} = -\$975$$

The Lagrange multiplier says that, in the limit, a decrease in the firm's combined output level by 1 unit will result in a \$975 increase in the firm's maximum profit level.

TOTAL REVENUE MAXIMIZATION

Although profit maximization is the most commonly assumed organizational objective, it is by no means the only goal of the firm. Firms that are not owner operated and firms that operate in an imperfectly competitive environment often adopt an organizational strategy that focuses on maximizing market share. Unit sales are one way of defining market share. Total revenue generated is another. In this section we will assume that the objective of the firm is to maximize total revenue. The first- and second-order conditions are, respectively,

$$\frac{dTR}{dQ} = 0 \tag{7.45}$$

and

$$\frac{d^2TR}{dQ^2} < 0 \tag{7.46}$$

In Figure 7.9a, c the profit-maximizing and revenue-maximizing levels of output are Q^* and Q_5, respectively. If we assume that firms are price takers in resource markets (the price of labor and capital are fixed) because price and output are always positive, it can be easily demonstrated that the output level that maximizes total revenue will always be greater than the output level that maximizes total profit. This is because of the law of diminishing marginal product guarantees that the rate of increase in marginal cost is greater than the rate of increase in marginal revenue.

Note that in Figure 7.9 total revenue is maximized where $MR = 0$, which occurs at an output level of Q_5. As before, in the case of a monopolist facing a downward-sloping demand curve, once output has been determined, the selling price of the product is determined along the demand curve. In Figure 7.9, the revenue-maximizing price is P_5. Of course, revenue maximization is not possible in the perfectly competitive case, since the selling price of the product is fixed and parametric. The total revenue function is linear and revenue maximization, therefore, is not possible.

Problem 7.13. Thadeus J. Wren and Joshua K. Skimpy have written a new managerial economics textbook: *Managerial Economics: Decision Making for the Chronically Confused.* The publisher, Nock, Downe & Owt (NDO), Inc., has offered Wren and Skimpy the following contract options: royalty payments amounting to 10% of total revenues 15% of total profits. NDO's total revenue and total cost functions associated with publishing the text-book are given as

$$TR = 10,000Q - 5Q^2$$

$$TC = 10,000 - 20Q + 5Q^2$$

a. If we assume that NDO is a profit maximizer, which contract should Wren and Skimpy choose?
b. Would your answer to part a have been different if NDO were a sales (total revenue) maximizer?

Solution
a. Total profit is defined as

$$\pi = TR - TC = 10,000Q - 5Q^2 - 10,000 + 20Q - 5Q^2$$
$$= -10,000 + 10,020Q - 10Q^2$$

Take the first derivative of the total profit function, set the result equal to zero, and solve.

$$\frac{d\pi}{dQ} = 10,020 - 20Q = 0$$

$$Q* = 501$$

To verify that this is a local maximum, the second derivative should be negative.

$$\frac{d^2\pi}{dQ^2} = -20 < 0$$

If Wren and Skimpy select the first contract, their royalties will be

$$TR* = 10,000(501) - 5(501)^2$$

$$TR* = 5,010,000 - 1,255,005 = \$3,754,995$$

$$\text{Royalty} = 0.1(3,754,995) = \$375,499.50$$

If Wren and Skimpy choose the second contract, their royalties will be

$$\pi* = -10,000 + 10,020(501) - 10(501)^2$$

$$= -10,000 + 5,020,020 - 2,510,010 = \$2,500,010$$

$$\text{Royalty} = 0.15(2,500,010) = \$375,001.50$$

According to these results, Wren and Skimpy will marginally favor the first contract.

b. Take the first derivative of the total revenue function, set the result equal to zero, and solve.

$$\frac{dTR}{dQ} = 10,000 - 10Q = 0$$

$$10Q = 10,000$$

$$Q* = 1,000$$

To verify that this is a local maximum, the second derivative should be negative.

$$\frac{d^2\pi}{dQ^2} = -20 < 0$$

If Wren and Skimpy choose the first contract, their royalties will be

$$TR* = 10,000(1,000) - 5(1,000)^2 = \$5,000,000$$

$$\text{Royalty} = 0.1(5,000,000) = \$5000,000$$

If Wren and Skimpy choose the second contract, their royalties will be

$$\pi^* = -10,000 + 10,020(1,000) - 10(1,000)^2 = \$10,000$$

$$\text{Royalty} = 0.15(10,000) = \$1,500$$

Clearly, when NDO is a sales maximizer, Wren and Skimpy will choose the first contract.

CHAPTER REVIEW

The *marginal product of labor* (MP_L) is the change in total output given a unit change in the amount of labor used. The *marginal revenue product of labor* (MRP_L) is the change in the firm's total revenue resulting from a unit change in the amount of labor used. The marginal revenue product is the marginal product of labor times the selling price of the product (i.e., $MRP_L = P \times MP_L$).

Total labor cost is the total cost of labor. The total cost of labor is the wage rate times the total amount of labor employed. The *marginal resource cost of labor* (MRC_L) is the change in total labor cost resulting from a unit change in the number of units of labor used. If the wage rate (P_L) is constant, then the wage rate is equal to the marginal cost of labor.

A profit-maximizing firm that operates in perfectly competitive output and input markets will employ additional units of labor up to the point at which the marginal revenue product of labor is equal to the marginal labor cost (i.e., $P \times MP_L = P_L$). In general, for any variable input i, the optimal level of variable input usage is defined by the condition $P \times MP_i = P_i$.

The *optimal combination of multiple inputs* is defined at the point of tangency between the *isoquant* and *isocost curves*. The isoquant curve represents the different combinations of capital and labor that produce the same level of output. The slope of the isoquant is the marginal rate of technical substitution. The isocost curve represents the different combinations of capital and labor the firm can purchase with a fixed operating budget and fixed factor prices. The slope of the isocost curve is the ratio of the input prices.

The optimal combination of capital and labor usage is defined by the condition $MP_L/MP_K = P_L/P_K$. This condition may be rewritten as $MP_L/P_L = MP_K/P_K$, which says that a profit-maximizing firm will allocate its budget in such a way that the last dollar spent on labor yields the same amount of additional output as the last dollar spent on capital. This condition defines the firm's *expansion path*.

The objective of *profit maximization* facing the decision maker may be dealt with more directly. The problem confronting the decision maker is to choose an output level that will maximize profit. Define profit as the difference between total revenue and total cost, both of which are functions of output [i.e., $\pi(Q) = TR(Q) - TC(Q)$]. The objective is to maximize this unconstrained objective function with respect to output. The first- and second-order conditions for a maximum are $d\pi/dQ = 0$ and $d^2\pi/dQ^2 < 0$, respectively. The profit-maximizing condition is to produce at an output level at which $MR = MC$.

Although profit maximization is the most commonly assumed organizational objective, firms that are not owner operated and firms that operate in an imperfectly competitive environment often adopt an organizational strategy of *total revenue maximization*. The first- and second-order conditions are $dTR/dQ = 0$ and $d^2TR/dQ^2 < 0$, respectively. Assuming that firms are price takers in resource markets (the price of labor and capital are fixed), because price and output are always positive, it can be easily demonstrated that the output level that maximizes total revenue will always be greater than the output level that maximizes total profit. This is because the law of diminishing marginal product guarantees that the rate of increase in marginal cost will be greater than the rate of increase in marginal revenue.

KEY TERMS AND CONCEPTS

Expansion path The expansion path is given by the expression $MP_L/P_L = MP_K/P_K$. The expansion path is the locus of points for which the isocost and isoquant curves are tangent to each other. It represents the cost-minimizing (profit-maximizing) combinations of capital and labor for different operating budgets.

First-order condition for total profit maximization Define total economic profit as the difference between total revenue and total cost, $\pi(Q) = TR(Q) - TC(Q)$, where $TR(Q)$ represents total revenue and $TC(Q)$ represents total cost, both of which are assumed to be functions of output. The first-order condition for profit maximization is $d\pi/dQ = 0$; that is, the first derivative of the profit function with respect to output is zero. This yields $dTR/dQ - dTC/dQ = 0$, which may be solved to yield $MR = MC$.

First-order condition for total revenue maximization Define total revenue as the product of total output (Q) times the selling price of the product (P), $TR(Q) = PQ$. The first-order condition for profit maximization is $dTR/dQ = MR = 0$; that is, the first derivative of the total revenue function with respect to output is zero.

Isocost curve A diagrammatic representation of the isocost equation. Solving the isocost equation for capital yields $K = C/P_K \times (P_L/P_K)L$. If we assume a given operating budget and fixed factor prices, the isocost curve is a straight line with a vertical intercept equal to C/P_K and slope of P_L/P_K.

Isocost equation The firm's isocost equation is $C = P_L L + P_K K$, where C represents the firm's operating budget (total cost), L represents physical units of labor input, K represents physical units of capital input, is P_L is the rental price of labor (wage rate), and P_K is the rental price of capital (or the interest rate). The isocost equation defines all the possible combinations of labor and capital input that firm can purchase with a given operating budget and fixed factor prices.

Marginal resource cost of capital   The increase in the firm's total cost arising from an incremental increase in capital input. Sometimes referred to as the rental price of capital, the marginal resource cost of capital is the return to the owner of capital services used in the production process. The marginal resource cost of capital is sometimes referred to as the interest rate.

Marginal resource cost of labor   The increase in the firm's total cost arising from an incremental increase in labor input. Sometimes referred to as the rental price of labor, in a perfectly competitive labor market, the marginal resource cost of capital is the return to the owner of labor services used in the production process. The marginal resource cost of labor is sometimes referred to as the wage rate.

Marginal revenue product of capital   The product of the selling price of a good or service and the marginal product of capital. The marginal revenue product of capital is given by the expression $P \times MP_K$, where P is the selling price of the product and MP_K is the marginal product of capital. It is the incremental increase in a firm's total revenues arising from the incremental increase in capital input, which results in an incremental increase in total output (the amount of labor input is constant).

Marginal revenue product of labor   The product of the selling price of a good or service and the marginal product of labor. The marginal revenue product of labor is given by the expression $P \times MP_L$, where P is the selling price of the product and MP_L is the marginal product of labor. It is the incremental increase in a firm's total revenues arising from the incremental increase in labor input, which results in an incremental increase in total output (the amount of capital input is constant).

$MP_L/P_L = MP_K/P_K$ The expansion path. This expression represents the cost-minimizing (profit-maximizing) combinations of capital and labor for different operating budgets.

$MR = MC$ The first-order condition for profit maximization. Profit is maximized at the output level at which marginal revenue is equal to rising marginal cost.

$P \times MP_L = P_L$ To maximize profit, a firm will hire resources up to the point at which the marginal revenue product of the labor ($P \times MP_L$) is equal to the marginal resource cost of labor (P_L). In other words, a firm will hire additional incremental units of labor until the additional revenue generated from the sale of the extra output resulting from the application of an incremental unit of labor to the production process is precisely equal to the cost of hiring an incremental unit of labor.

$P \times MP_K = P_K$ To maximize profit, a firm will hire resources up to the point at which the marginal revenue product of the capital ($P \times MP_K$) is equal to the marginal resource cost of capital (P_K). In other words, a firm will hire additional incremental units of capital until the additional revenue generated from the sale of the extra output resulting from the application of an incremental unit of capital to the production process is precisely equal to the cost of hiring an incremental unit of capital.

Second-order condition for total profit maximization   Define profit as the difference between total revenue and total cost [i.e., $\pi(Q) = TR(Q) - TC(Q)$], where $TR(Q)$ represents total revenue and $TC(Q)$ represents total cost, both of which are assumed to be functions of output. The second-order condition for profit maximization is that the second derivative of the profit function with respect to output is negative (i.e., $d^2\pi/dQ^2 < 0$).

Second-order condition for total revenue maximization   Define total revenue as the product of total output times the selling price of the product, $TR(Q) = PQ$. The second-order condition for total revenue maximization is that the second derivative of the profit function with respect to output is negative (i.e., $d^2TR/dQ^2 = dMR/dQ < 0$).

CHAPTER QUESTIONS

7.1 Suppose that a unit of labor is more productive than a unit of capital. It must be true that a profit-maximizing firm will produce as long as $MP_L/P_L > MP_K/P_K$. Do you agree? If not, then why not?

7.2 What is a firm's expansion path?

7.3 Suppose that a firm's production function exhibits increasing returns to scale. It must also be true that the firm's expansion path increases at an increasing rate. Do you agree with this statement? Explain.

7.4 The nominal purpose of minimum wage legislation is to increase the earnings of relatively unskilled workers. Explain how an increase in the minimum wage affects the employment of unskilled labor.

7.5 A smart manager will always employ a more productive worker over a less productive worker. Do you agree? If not, then why not?

CHAPTER EXERCISES

7.1 WordBoss, Inc. uses 4 word processors and 2 typewriters to produce reports. The marginal product of a typewriter is 50 pages per day and the marginal product of a word processor is 500 pages per day. The rental price of a typewriter is $1 per day, whereas the rental price of a word processor is $50 per day. Is WordBoss utilizing typewriters and word processors efficiently?

7.2 Numeric Calculators produces a line of abacuses for use by professional accountants. Numeric's production function is

$$Q = 2L^{0.6}K^{0.4}$$

Numeric has a weekly budget of $400,000 and has estimated unit capital to be cost $5.

   a. Numeric produces efficiently. If the cost of labor is $10 per hour, what is the Numeric's output level?

   b. The labor union is presently demanding a wage increase that will raise the cost of labor to $12.50 per hour. If the budget and capital cost remain constant, what will be the level of labor usage at the new cost of labor if Numeric is to continue operating efficiently?

   c. At the new cost of labor, what is Numeric's new output level?

7.3 A firm has an output level at which the marginal products of labor and capital are both 25 units. Suppose that the rental price of labor and capital are $12.50 and $25, respectively.

   a. Is this firm producing efficiently?

   b. If the firm is not producing efficiently, how might it do so?

7.4 Magnabox installs MP3 players in automobiles. Magnabox production function is:

$$Q = 2KL - 1.5KL^2$$

where Q represents the number of MP3 players installed, L the number of labor hours, and K the number of hours of installation equipment, which is fixed at 250 hours. The rental price of labor and the rental price of capital are $10 and $50 per hour, respectively. Magnabox has received an offer from Cheap Rides to install 1,500 MP3 players in its fleet of rental cars for $15,000. Should Magnabox accept this offer?

7.5 If a production function does not have constant returns to scale, the cost-minimizing expansion path could not be one in which the ratio of inputs remains constant. Comment.

7.6 Suppose that the objective of a firm's owner is not to maximize profits *per se* but rather to maximize the utility that the owner derives from these profits [i.e., $U = U(\pi)$, where $dU/d\pi > 0$]. We assume that $U(\pi)$ is an ordinal measure of the firm owner's satisfaction that is not directly observable or measurable. If the firm owner is required to pay a per-unit tax of tQ, demonstrate that an increase in the tax rate t will result in a decline in output.

7.7 The demand for the output of a firm is given by the equation $0.01Q^2 = (50/P) - 1$. What unit sales will maximize the firm's total revenues?

7.8 A firm confronts the following total cost equation for its product:

$$TC = 100 + 5Q^2$$

a. Suppose that the firm can sell its product for $100 per unit of output. What is the firm's profit-maximizing output? At the profit-maximizing level of output, what is the firm's total profit.

b. Suppose that the firm is a monopolist. Suppose, further, that the demand equation for the monopolist's product is $P = 200 - 5Q$. Calculate the monopolist's profit-maximizing level of output. What is the monopolist's profit-maximizing price? At the profit-maximizing level of output, calculate the monopolist's total profit.

c. What is the monopolist's total revenue maximizing level of output? At the total revenue maximizing level of output, calculate the monopolist's total profit.

7.9 The total revenue and total cost equations of a firm are

$$TR = 50Q$$
$$TC = 100 + 25Q + 0.5Q^2$$

a. What is the total profit function?

b. Use optimization analysis to find the profit-maximizing level of output.

7.10 The total revenue and total cost equations of a firm are

$$TR = 25Q$$
$$TC = 100 + 20Q + 0.025Q^2$$

a. Graph the total revenue and total cost equations for values $Q = 0$ to $Q = 200$.

b. What is the total profit function?

c. Use optimization analysis to find the output level at which total profit is maximized?

d. Graph the total profit equation for values $Q = 0$ to $Q = 200$. Use your graph to verify your answer to part c.

7.11 Suppose that total revenue and total cost are functions of the firm's output [i.e., $TR = TR(Q)$ and $TC = TC(Q)$]. In addition, suppose that the firm pays a per-unit tax of tQ. Demonstrate that an increase in the tax rate t will cause a profit-maximizing firm to decrease output.

7.12 The W. V. Whipple Corporation specializes in the production of whirly-gigs. W. V. Whipple, the company's president and chief executive officer, has decided to replace 50% of his workforce of 100 workers with industrial robots. Whipple's current capital requirements are 30 units. Whipple's current production function is given by the equation

$$Q = 25L^{0.3}K^{0.7}$$

After automation, Whipple's production function will be

$$Q = 100L^{0.2}K^{0.8}$$

Under the terms of Whipple's current collective bargaining agreement with United Whirly-Gig Workers Local 666, the cost of labor is $12 per worker. The cost of capital is $93.33 per unit.

a. Before automation, is Whipple producing efficiently? (*Hint*: Round all calculations and answers to the nearest hundredth.)
b. After automation, how much capital should Whipple employ?
c. By how much will Whipple's total cost of production change as a result of automation?
d. What was Whipple's total output before automation? After automation?
e. Assuming that the market price of whirly-gigs is $4, what will happen to Whipple's profits as a result of automation?

7.13 Suppose that a firm has the following production function:

$$Q = 100K^{0.5}L^{0.5}$$

Determine the firm's expansion path if the rental price of labor is $25 and the rental price of capital is $50.

7.14 The Omega Company manufactures computer hard drives. The company faces the total profit function

$$\pi = -3,000 + 650Q - 100Q^2$$

a. What is the marginal profit function?
b. What is Omega's marginal profit at $Q = 3$?
c. At what output level is marginal profit maximized or minimized? Which is it?
d. At what level of output is total profit maximized?
e. What is the average total profit function?
f. At what level of output is average total profit maximized or minimized? Which is it?
g. What, if anything, do you observe about the relationship between marginal profit and average total profit? (*Hint*: Take the first derivative of $A\pi = \pi/Q$ and examine the different values of $M\pi$ and $A\pi$ in the neighborhood of your answer to part f.)

7.15 The total profit equation for a firm is

$$\pi = -500 - 25x - 10x^2 - 4xy - 5y^2 + 15y$$

where x and y represent the output levels of the two product lines.

a. Use the substitution method to determine the profit-maximizing output levels for goods x and y subject to the side condition that the sum of the two product lines equal 100 units.

b. Use the Lagrange multiplier method to verify your answer to part a.

c. What is the interpretation of the Lagrange multiplier?

SELECTED READINGS

Allen, R. G. D. *Mathematical Analysis for Economists*. New York: St. Martin's Press, 1938.

Brennan, M. J., and T. M. Carroll. *Preface to Quantitative Economics & Econometrics*, 4th ed. Cincinnati, OH: South-Western Publishing, 1987.

Chiang, A. *Fundamental Methods of Mathematical Economics*, 3rd ed. New York: McGraw-Hill, 1984.

Glass, J. C. *An Introduction to Mathematical Methods in Economics*. New York: McGraw-Hill, 1980.

Henderson, J. M., and R. E. Quandt. *Microeconomic Theory: A Mathematical Approach*, 3rd ed. New York: McGraw-Hill, 1980.

Layard, P. R. G., and A. A. Walters. *Microeconomic Theory*. New York: McGraw-Hill, 1978.

Nicholson, W. *Microeconomic Theory: Basic Principles and Extensions*, 6th ed. New York: Dryden Press, 1995.

Silberberg, E. *The Structure of Economics: A Mathematical Analysis*, 2nd ed. New York: McGraw-Hill, 1990.

APPENDIX 7A

FORMAL DERIVATION OF EQUATION (7.8)

Consider the following constrained optimization problem:

$$\text{Maximize } Q = f(L, K) \tag{7A.1a}$$

$$\text{Subject to } TC_0 = P_L L + P_K K \tag{7A.1b}$$

where Equation (7A.1a) is the firm's production function and Equation (7A.1b) is the budget constraint (isocost line). The objective of the firm is to maximize output subject to a fixed budget TC_0 and constant prices for labor and capital, P_L and P_K, respectively. From Chapter 2, we form the Lagrange expression as a function of labor and capital input:

$$\mathcal{L}(L, K) = f(L, K) + \lambda(TC_0 - P_L L - P_K K) \tag{7A.2}$$

The first-order conditions for output maximization are:

$$\frac{\partial \mathcal{L}}{\partial L} = \mathcal{L}_L = \frac{\partial Q}{\partial L} - \lambda P_L = 0 \tag{7A.3a}$$

$$\frac{\partial \mathcal{L}}{\partial y} = \mathcal{L}_K = \frac{\partial Q}{\partial K} - \lambda P_K = 0 \tag{7A.3b}$$

$$\frac{\partial \mathcal{L}}{\partial \lambda} = \mathcal{L}_\lambda = TC_0 - P_L L - P_K K = 0 \tag{7A.3c}$$

We will assume that the second-order conditions for output maximization are satisfied. Dividing Equation (7A.3a) by Equation (7A.3b), and noting that $MP_L = \partial Q/\partial L$ and $MP_K = \partial Q/\partial K$, factoring out λ, and rearranging yields Equation (7.8).

Problem 7A.1. Suppose that a firm has the following production function:

$$Q = 10K^{0.6}L^{0.4}$$

Suppose, further that the firms operating budget is $TC_0 = \$500$ and the rental price of labor and capital are \$5 and \$7.5, respectively.
a. If the firm's objective is to maximize output, determine the optimal level of labor and capital usage.
b. At the optimal input levels, what is the total output of the firm?

Solution
a. Formally this problem is

$$\text{Maximize: } Q = 10L^{0.6}K^{0.4}$$

$$\text{Subject to: } 500 = 5L + 7.5K$$

Forming the Lagrangian expression, we write

$$\mathcal{L}(L, K) = 10K^{0.6}L^{0.4} + \lambda(500 - 5L - 7.5K)$$

The first-order conditions for output maximization are

$$\frac{\partial \mathcal{L}}{\partial L} = \mathcal{L}_L = 6L^{-0.4}K^{0.4} - \lambda 5 = 0$$

$$\frac{\partial \mathcal{L}}{\partial y} = \mathcal{L}_K = 4L^{0.6}K^{-0.6} - \lambda 7.5 = 0$$

$$\frac{\partial \mathcal{L}}{\partial \lambda} = \mathcal{L}_\lambda = 500 - 5L - 7.5K = 0$$

Dividing the first equation by the second yields

$$\frac{6L^{-0.4}K^{0.4} - \lambda 5}{4L^{0.6}K^{-0.6}} = \frac{5}{7.5}$$

which may be solved for K as

$$\frac{K}{L} = \frac{4}{9}$$

This results says that output maximization requires 4 units of capital be employed for every 9 units of labor. Substituting this into the budget constraint yields

$$500 = 5L + 7.5(4/9)L$$
$$500 = 35L$$
$$L^* = 14.29$$
$$K^* = (4/9)(14.29) = 6.35$$

b. $Q = 10(14.29)^{0.6}(6.35)^{0.4} = 103.31$

8

MARKET STRUCTURE: PERFECT COMPETITION AND MONOPOLY

One of the most important decisions made by a manager is how to price the firm's product. If the firm is a profit maximizer, the price charged must be consistent with the realities of the market and economic environment within which the firm operates. Remember, price is determined through the interaction of supply and demand. A firm's ability to influence the selling price of its product stems from its ability to influence the market supply and, to a lesser extent, on its ability to influence consumer demand, as, say, through advertising.

One important element in the firm's ability to influence the economic environment within which it operates is the nature and degree of competition. A firm operating in an industry with many competitors may have little control over the selling price of its product because its ability to influence overall industry output is limited. In this case, the manager will attempt to maximize the firm's profit by minimizing the cost of production by employing the most efficient mix of productive resources. On the other hand, if the firm has the ability to significantly influence overall industry output, or if the firm faces a downward-sloping demand curve for its product, the manager will attempt to maximize profit by employing an efficient input mix and by selecting an optimal selling price.

Definition: Market structure refers to the environment within which buyers and sellers interact.

CHARACTERISTICS OF MARKET STRUCTURE

There are, perhaps, as many ways to classify a firm's competitive environment, or market structure, as there are industries. Consequently, no single economic theory is capable of providing a simple system of rules for optimal output pricing. It is possible, however, to categorize markets in terms of certain basic characteristics that can be useful as benchmarks for a more detailed analysis of optimal pricing behavior. These characteristics of market structure include the number and size distribution of sellers, the number and size distribution of buyers, product differentiation, and the conditions of entry into and exit from the industry.

NUMBER AND SIZE DISTRIBUTION OF SELLERS

The ability of a firm to set its output price will largely depend on the number of firms in the same industry producing and selling that particular product. If there are a large number of equivalently sized firms, the ability of any single firm to independently set the selling price of its product will be severely limited. If the firm sets the price of its product higher than the rest of the industry, total sales volume probably will drop to zero. If, on the other hand, the manager of the firm sets the price too low, then while the firm will be able to sell all that it produces, it will not maximize profits. If, on the other hand, the firm is the only producer in the industry (monopoly) or one of a few large producers (oligopoly) satisfying the demand of the entire market, the manager's flexibility in pricing could be quite considerable.

NUMBER AND SIZE DISTRIBUTION OF BUYERS

Markets may also be categorized by the number and size distribution of buyers. When there are many small buyers of a particular good or service, each buyer will likely pay the same price. On the other hand, a buyer of a significant proportion of an industry's output will likely be in a position to extract price concessions from producers. Such situations refer to monopsonies (a single buyer) and oligopsonies (a few large buyers).

PRODUCT DIFFERENTIATION

Product differentiation is the degree that the output of one firm differs from that of other firms in the industry. When products are undifferentiated, consumers will decide which product to buy based primarily on price. In these markets, producers that price their product above the market price will be unable to sell their output. If there is no difference in price, consumers will not care which seller buy from. A given grade of wheat is an example of an undifferentiated good. At the other extreme, firms that produce goods having unique characteristics may be in a position to exert considerable control over the price of their product. In the automotive industry, for example, product differentiation is the rule.

CONDITIONS OF ENTRY AND EXIT

The ease with which firms are able to enter and exit a particular industry is also crucial in determining the nature of a market. When it is difficult for firms to enter into an industry, existing firms will have much greater influence in their output and pricing decisions than they would if they had to worry about increased competition from new comers, attracted to the industry by high profits. In other words, managers can make pricing decisions without worrying about losing market share to new entrants. Thus if a firm owns a patent for the production of a good, this effectively prohibits other firms from entering the market. Such patent protection is a common feature of the pharmaceutical industry.

Exit conditions from the industry also affect managerial decisions. Suppose that a firm had been earning below-normal economic profit on the production and sale of a particular product. If the resources used in the production of that product are easily transferred to the production of some other good or service, some of those resources will be shifted to another industry. If, however, resources are highly specialized, they may have little value in another industry.

In this and the next two chapters we will examine four basic market structures: perfect competition, monopoly, oligopoly, and monopolistic competition. For purposes of our analysis we will assume that the firms in each of these market structures are price takers in resource markets and that they are producing in the short run. The result of these assumptions is that the cost curves of each firm in these industries will have the same general shape as those presented in Chapter 6.

Firms differ in the proportion of total market demand that is satisfied by the production of each. This is illustrated in Figure 8.1. At one extreme is perfect competition, in which the typical firm produces only a very small percentage of total industry output. At the other extreme is monopoly, where the firm is responsible for producing the entire output of the industry. The percentage of total industry output produced is critical in the analysis of profit maximization because it defines the shape of the demand curve facing the output of each individual firm. The market structures that will be examined in this and the next chapter can be viewed as lying along a spectrum, with the position of each firm defined by the percentage of the market

FIGURE 8.1   Market structure is defined in terms of the proportion of total market demand that is satisfied by the output of each firm in the industry.

satisfied by the typical firm in each industry—from perfect competition at one extreme to monopoly at the other.

PERFECT COMPETITION

The expression "perfect competition" is somewhat misleading because overt competition among firms in perfectly competitive industries is nonexistent. The reason for this is that managers of perfectly competitive firms do not take into consideration the actions of other firms in the industry when setting pricing policy. The reason for this is that changes in the output of each firm are too small relative to the total output of the industry to significantly affect the selling price. Thus, the selling price is parametric to the decision-making process.

The characteristics of a perfectly competitive market may be identified by using the criteria previously enumerated. Perfectly competitive industries are characterized by a large number of more or less equally sized firms. Because the contribution of each firm to the total output of the industry is small, the output decisions of any individual firm are unlikely to result in a noticeable shift in the supply curve. Thus, the output decisions of any individual firm will not significantly affect the market price. Thus, firms in perfectly competitive markets may be described as *price takers*. The inability to influence the market price through output changes means that the firm lacks *market power*.

Definition: Market power refers to the ability of a firm to influence the market price of its product by altering its level of output. A firm that produces a significant proportion of total industry output is said to have market power.

Definition: A firm is described as a price maker if it has market power. A price maker faces a downward-sloping demand curve for its product, which implies that the firm is able to alter the market price of its product by changing its output level.

Definition: Perfect competition refers to the market structure in which there are many utility-maximizing buyers and profit-maximizing sellers of a homogeneous good or service in which there is perfect mobility of factors of production and buyers, sellers have perfect information about market conditions, and entry into and exit from the industry is very easy.

Definition: A perfectly competitive firm is called a price taker because of its inability to influence the market price of its product by altering its level of output. This condition implies that a perfectly competitive firm should be able to sell as much of its good or service at the prevailing market price.

A second requirement of a perfectly competitive market is that there also be a large number of buyers. Since no buyer purchases a significant proportion of the total output of the industry, the actions of any single buyer will not result in a noticeable shift in the demand schedule and, therefore, will not significantly affect the equilibrium price of the product.

A third important characteristic of perfectly competitive markets is that the output of one firm cannot be distinguished from that of another firm in the same industry. The purchasing decisions of buyers, therefore, are based entirely on the selling price. In such a situation, individual firms are unable to raise their prices above the market-determined price for fear of being unable to attract buyers. Conversely, price cutting is counterproductive because firms can sell all their output at the higher, market-determined, price. Remember, the market clearing price of a product implies that there is neither a surplus nor a shortage of the commodity.

A final characteristic of perfectly competitive markets is that firms may easily enter or exit the industry. This characteristic allows firms to easily reallocate productive resources to be able to exploit the existence of economic profits. Similarly, if profits in a given industry are below normal, firms may easily shift productive resources out of the production of that particular good into the production of some other good for which profits are higher.

THE EQUILIBRIUM PRICE

As we have already discussed, the market-determined price of a good or service is accepted by the firm in a perfectly competitive industry as datum. Moreover, the equilibrium price and quantity of that good or service are determined through the interaction of supply and demand. The relation between the market-determined price and the output decision of a firm is illustrated in Figure 8.2.

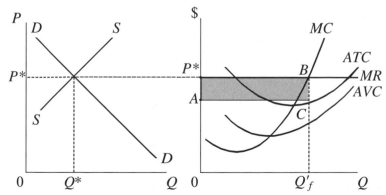

FIGURE 8.2   Short-run competitive equilibrium with positive (above-normal) economic profit.

The market demand for a good or service is the horizontal summation of the demands of individual consumers, while the market supply curve is the sum of individual firms' marginal cost (above-average variable cost) curves. As discussed earlier, if the prevailing price is above the equilibrium price ($P*$), a condition of excess supply forces producers to lower the selling price to rid themselves of excess inventories. As the price falls, the quantity of the product demanded rises, while the quantity supplied from current production falls (Q_F). Alternatively, if the selling price is below $P*$ a situation of excess demand arises. This causes consumers to bid up the price of the product, thereby reducing the quantity available to meet consumer demands, while compelling producers to increase production. This adjustment dynamic will continue until both excess demand and excess supply have been eliminated at $P*$.

Problem 8.1. Suppose that a perfectly competitive industry comprises 1,000 identical firms. Suppose, further, that the market demand (Q_D) and supply (Q_S) functions are

$$Q_D = 170,000,000 - 10,000,000P$$

$$Q_S = 70,000,000 + 15,000,000P$$

a. Calculate the equilibrium market price and quantity?
b. Given your answer to part a, how much output will be produced by each firm in the industry?
c. Suppose that one of the firms in the industry goes out of business. What will be the effect on the equilibrium market price and quantity?

Solution
a. Equating supply and demand yields

$$170,000,000 - 10,000,000P = 70,000,000 + 15,000,000P$$

$$P* = \$4.00$$

Substituting the equilibrium price into either the market supply or demand equation yields

$$Q* = 170,000,000 - 10,000,000(4)$$
$$= 70,000,000 + 15,000,000(4) = 130,000,000$$

b. Since there are 1,000 identical firms in the industry, the output of any individual firm Q_i is

$$Q_i = \frac{Q*}{1,000} = \frac{130,000,000}{1,000} = 130,000$$

c. The supply equation of any individual firm in the industry is

$$Q_i = \frac{Q*}{1,000} = 70,000 + 15,000P$$

Subtracting the supply of the individual firm from market supply yields

$$Q^* - Q_i = (70,000,000 + 15,000,000P) - (70,000 + 15,000P)$$
$$= 69,930,000 + 14,985,000P$$

Equating the new market demand and supply equations yields

$$170,000,000 - 10,000,000P = 69,930,000 + 14,985,000P$$

$$P^* = \$4.0052$$

$$Q^* = 170,000,000 - 10,000,000(4.0052)$$
$$= 69,930,000 + 14,985,000(4.0052) = 129,948,000$$

This problem illustrates the virtual inability of an individual firm in a perfectly competitive industry, which is characterized by a large number of firms, to significantly influence the market equilibrium price of a good or service by changing its level of output. For this reason, it is generally assumed that the market price for a perfectly competitive firm is parametric.

SHORT-RUN PROFIT MAXIMIZATION PRICE AND OUTPUT

If we assume that the perfectly competitive firm is a profit maximizer, the pricing conditions under which this objective is achieved are straightforward. First, define the firm's profit function as:

$$\pi(Q) = TR(Q) - TC(Q) \tag{8.1}$$

To determine the optimal output level that is consistent with the profit-maximizing objective of this firm, the first-order condition dictates that we differentiate this expression with respect to Q and equate the resulting expression to zero. This procedure yields the following results

$$\frac{d\pi(Q)}{dQ} = \frac{dTR(Q)}{dQ} - \frac{dTC(Q)}{dQ} = 0 \tag{8.2}$$

or

$$MR - MC = 0 \tag{8.3}$$

That is, the profit-maximizing condition for this firm is to equate marginal revenue with marginal cost, $MR = MC$.

To carry this analysis a bit further, recall that the definition of total revenue is $TR = PQ$. The preceding analysis of a perfectly competitive market reminds us that the selling price is determined in the market and is unaffected by the output decisions of any individual firm. Therefore,

$$\frac{dTR(Q)}{dQ} = MR = P_0 \tag{8.4}$$

where the selling price is determined in the market and parametric to the firm's output decisions. Thus, the profit-maximizing condition for the perfectly competitive firm becomes

$$P_0 = MC \tag{8.5}$$

To maximize its short-run (and long-run) profits, the perfectly competitive firm must equate the market-determined selling price of its product with the marginal cost of producing that product. This condition was illustrated in Figure 8.2 (right).

Assuming that the firm has U-shaped average total and marginal cost curves, Figure 8.2 illustrates that the perfectly competitive firm maximizes profits by producing $0Q_f$ units of output, that is, the output level at which $P^* = MC$. The economic profit earned is illustrated by the shaded area AP*BC in the figure. This can be seen when we remember that

$$\pi = TR - TC = P^*Q_f - ATC(Q_f) \tag{8.6}$$

This is illustrated in Figure 8.2 as

$$\text{Area}\{AP^*BC\} = \text{Area}\{0P^*BQ_f\} - \text{Area}\{0ACQ_f\} \tag{8.7}$$

It should be remembered that the cost curves of Figure 8.2 include a normal rate of profit. As a consequence, any time the firm has an average revenue greater than average cost, it is earning an economic profit.

Definition: A firm earns economic (above-normal) profit when total revenue is greater than total economic cost.

Problem: 8.2. Consider the firm with the following total monthly cost function, which includes a normal profit.

$$TC = 1,000 + 2Q + 0.01Q^2$$

The firm operates in a perfectly competitive industry and sells its product at the market-determined price of $10. To maximize total profits, what should be the firm's monthly output level, and how much economic profit will the firm earn each month?

Solution. First, determine the firm's marginal cost function by taking the first derivative of the total cost function with respect to Q.

$$\frac{dTC}{dQ} = MC = 2 + 0.02Q$$

As discussed earlier, profit is maximized by setting $MC = P^*$, thus

$$10 = 2 + 0.02Q$$

$$Q = 400$$

Economic profit is given by the expression

$$\pi = TR - TC = P*Q - 1,000 - 2Q - 0.01Q^2$$
$$= \$10(400) - 1,000 - 2(400) - 0.01(4002) = \$600$$

Problem 8.3. A perfectly competitive industry consists of 300 firms with identical cost structures. The respective market demand (Q_D) and market supply (Q_S) equations for the good produced by this industry are

$$Q_D = 3,000 - 60P$$
$$Q_s = 500 + 40P$$

a. What are the profit-maximizing price and output for each individual firm?
b. Assume that each firm is in long-run competitive equilibrium. Determine each firm's total revenue, total economic cost, and total economic profit.

Solution
a. Firms in a perfectly competitive industry are characterized as "price takers." The profit-maximizing condition for firms in a perfectly competitive industry is $P = MC$, where the price is determined in the market. The market equilibrium price and quantity are determined by the condition

$$Q_D = Q_S$$
$$3,000 - 60P = 500 + 40P$$
$$P^* = \$25$$
$$Q^* = 500 + 40(25) = 500 + 1,000 = 1,500$$

The market equilibrium price, which is the price for each individual firm, is P^* = $25. The market equilibrium output is Q = 1,500. Since there are 300 firms in the industry, each firm supplies Q_i = 1,500/300 = 5 units.
b. The total revenue of each firm in the industry is

$$TR = P*Q_i = 25(5) = \$125$$

In long-run competitive equilibrium, each firm earns zero economic profit. Since economic profit is defined as the difference between total revenue and total economic cost, then the total economic cost of each firm is

$$TC_{\text{economic}} = \$125$$

Problem 8.4. The market-determined price in a perfectly competitive industry is P = $10. Suppose that the total cost equation of an individual firm in the industry is given by the expression

$$TC = 100 + 5Q + 0.02Q^2$$

a. What is the firm's profit-maximizing output level?
b. Given your answer to part a, what is the firm's total profit?
c. Diagram your answers to parts a and b.

Solution

a. The profit-maximizing condition for a firm in a perfectly competitive industry is

$$P_0 = MC$$

The firm's marginal cost equation is

$$MC = \frac{dTC}{dQ} = 5 + 0.04Q$$

Substituting these results into the profit-maximizing condition yields

$$10 = 5 + 0.04Q$$

$$0.04Q = 5$$

$$Q^* = 125$$

b. The perfectly competitive firm's profit at $P^* = \$10$ and $Q^* = 125$ is

$$\pi^* = TR - TC$$
$$= P^* Q^* - (100 + 5Q^* + 0.02Q^{*2})$$
$$= 10(125) - \left[100 + 5(125) + 0.02(125)^2\right]$$
$$= 1{,}250 - 1{,}037.50 = \$212.50$$

c. Figure 8.3 diagrams the answers to parts a and b.

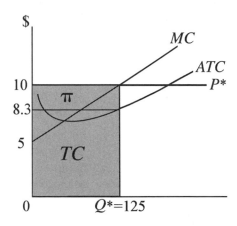

FIGURE 8.3   Diagrammatic solution to problem 8.4.

LONG-RUN PROFIT MAXIMIZATION PRICE
AND OUTPUT

The shaded area in Figure 8.2 represents the firm's total economic profit, that is, the excess of total revenue over total cost of production after a normal rate of return (normal profit) has been taken into consideration. In a perfectly competitive industry, however, this situation will not long persist.

We have already mentioned that a key characteristic of a perfectly competitive industry is ease of entry and exit by potentially competing firms. The existence of economic profits in an industry will attract productive resources into the production of that particular good or service. This transfer of resources will not, however, be instantaneous. It takes time for new firms to build production facilities and for existing firms to increase output. Nevertheless, in the long run all inputs are variable, and the increased output by new and existing firms will result in a right-shift of the market supply curve. Consider Figure 8.4.

In Figure 8.4, a right-shift of the industry supply function has resulted in a fall of the equilibrium price from P^* to P' and an increase in the equilibrium output from Q^* to Q'. But note what has happened to the typical firm in this perfectly competitive industry. The decline in the market equilibrium price has reduced the economic profit to the firm to the shaded area $A'P'B'C'$. In fact, because of the upward sloping marginal cost function, not only has the selling price of the firm's product fallen but the output of the typical firm has dropped as well.

It should, of course, be noted that this result holds only for the "typical" firm. In fact, there is no *a priori* reason to suppose that all firms in a perfectly competitive industry are of equal size. Some existing firms after all

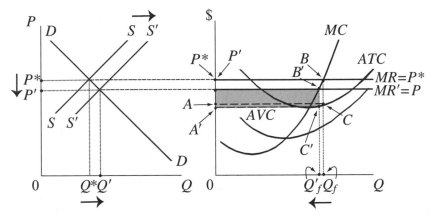

FIGURE 8.4 A price decline, short-run competitive equilibrium, and a reduction in economic (above-normal) profit.

will have increased their output by expanding operations in response to the existence of economic profits. The firm depicted in Figures 8.2 and 8.4 is not such a firm. If we assume that all firms in this industry are approximately the same size, then the output of each firm will decline, although industry output will increase because there are a larger number of firms.

The situation depicted in Figure 8.4 is not, however, stable in the long run, since the area $A'P'B'C'$ still represents a situation in which the firm is earning economic profits. The continued existence of economic profits will continue to attract resources to the production of the particular good or service in question. The situation of long-run competitive equilibrium is illustrated in Figure 8.5.

Figure 8.5 represents a break-even situation for the firm. Since normal profit is included in total cost, at the point where $MR'' = P'' = P = MC$, total revenues equal total costs. In Figure 8.5, P and Q represent the break-even price and output level for the individual firm, respectively. In this situation, the firm described in Figure 8.4 is no longer earning an economic profit, and thus there is no further incentive for firms outside the industry to transfer productive resources into this industry to earn above-normal profits. In a sense, economic profits have been "competed" away. Since there is no further incentive for firms to enter, or for that matter exit, this industry, it may be said that the firm is in a position of long-run competitive equilibrium.

Definition: The break-even price is the price at which total revenue is equal to total economic cost.

Definition: Economic cost is the sum of the firm's total explicit and implicit costs.

Unfortunately, the process of adjustment to long-run competitive equilibrium may not be as smooth as described in connection with Figure 8.5. If uncertainty and incomplete information lead managers to miscalculate,

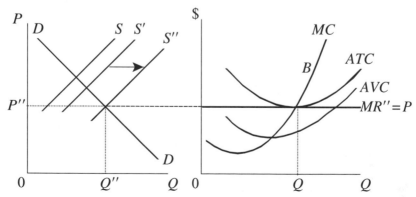

FIGURE 8.5 Long-run competitive equilibrium: zero economic (normal) profit.

too many firms will enter the industry. This situation is depicted in Figure 8.6: this firm is earning an economic loss (below-normal profit), illustrated by the area $P^\dagger A^\dagger B^\dagger C^\dagger$. This can be seen when we remember that

$$\pi = TR - TC = P^\dagger Q_f^\dagger - ATC \times Q_f^\dagger \qquad (8.8)$$

This is illustrated in Figure 8.6 as

$$\text{Area}\{P^\dagger A^\dagger B^\dagger C^\dagger\} = \text{Area}\{0A^\dagger B^\dagger Q_f^\dagger\} - \text{Area}\{0P^\dagger C^\dagger Q_f^\dagger\} < 0 \qquad (8.9)$$

In this situation, firms in this industry are earning below-normal profits. Under such circumstances, productive resources are transferred out of the production of this particular good or service, and output declines, resulting in a left-shift in the market supply function. Eventually, the selling price will rise and long-term competitive equilibrium will be reestablished.

Definition: A firm earns an economic loss when total revenue is less than total economic cost.

ECONOMIC LOSSES AND SHUTDOWN

For firms earning economic profits, the only meaningful decision facing management is the appropriate level of output. When firms are posting economic losses, however, the manager must decide whether it is in the long-run interests of the shareholders to continue producing that particular product. The course of action to be adopted by the manager will be based on a number of alternatives. The manager may decide, for example, to continue producing at the least unprofitable rate of output in the hope that prices will rebound, or the manager might decide to shut down operations completely. In the short run, the consequences of shutting down are illustrated in Figure 8.7.

Recall from Chapter 6 that total cost is the sum of total variable and total fixed cost, that is,

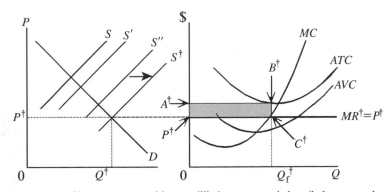

FIGURE 8.6   Short-run competitive equilibrium: economic loss (below-normal profit).

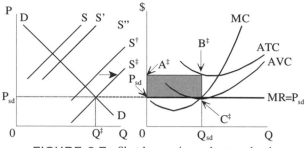

FIGURE 8.7 Shutdown price and output level.

$$TC = TFC + TVC$$

Definition: Total fixed cost refers to the firm's expenditures on fixed factors of production.

Definition: Total variable cost refers to the firm's expenditures on variable factors of production.

Dividing total cost by the level of output, we get

$$ATC = AFC + AVC$$

or

$$AFC = ATC - AVC$$

Diagrammatically, average fixed cost is measured by the vertical distance between the average total cost and average variable cost curves. It follows, therefore, that if the firm in Figure 8.6 produces at $Q^{\dagger}_{f}$ it will recover all of its variable costs and at least some of its fixed costs.

The essential element in the manager's decision is the discrepancy between the selling price of the product and average variable cost. As long as price is greater than average variable cost, the firm minimizes its loss by continuing to produce. Otherwise, the firm will suffer larger short-run losses, since it is still responsible for its fixed costs. On the other hand, when the price falls below average fixed cost, it will be in the firm's best interest to shut down operations, since to continue to produce would result in losses greater than its fixed cost obligations. This concept is illustrated in Figure 8.7.

In Figure 8.7, P_{sd} and Q_{sd} represent the firm's shutdown price and output level, respectively. A profit-maximizing firm that produces at all will produce Q_{sd}, where $MR = P_{sd} = MC$. In fact, the firm is indifferent to producing Q_{sd}, since the firm's economic loss, which is given by the area of the rectangle $P_{sd}A^{\ddagger}B^{\ddagger}C^{\ddagger}$ is equivalent to the firm's total fixed costs (i.e., the firm's economic loss if it shuts down). Below the price P_{sd}, however, the optimal decision by the firm's manager is to cease production, since the firm's total economic loss is greater than its total fixed cost.

Diagrammatically, it is often argued that the portion of the marginal cost curve that lies the average variable cost curve represents the firm's supply curve. The reason for this is that a profit-maximizing firm will produce at an output level at which $P = MC$. Since the marginal cost curve is upward sloping, then an increase in price essentially traces out the firm's supply curve.[1]

In Chapter 3 it was asserted that the market supply curve is the horizontal summation of the individual firms' supply curves. This assertion, however, is correct only as long as input prices remain unchanged. It is entirely possible that a simultaneous increase in the demand for inputs resulting from an increase in industry output will cause input prices to rise. When this occurs, the industry supply curve will be less price elastic than if input prices remained constant.

Definition: Shutdown price is equal to the minimum average variable cost of producing a good or service. Below this price the firm will shut down because the firm's loss, which will equal the total fixed cost, will be less than if the firm continues to stay in business.

We have mentioned that the optimal rule for the manager of the firm in the short run is to shut down when the selling price of the product falls below P_{sd}. This decision rule is subject to two qualifications. First, the firm will not shut down every time $P < AVC$. In many cases, the firm will incur substantial costs when a production process is shut down or restarted, as in the case of a blast furnace for manufacturing steel, which may require several days to bring up to operating temperature. Similarly, a firm that shuts down and then reopens may find that its customers are buying from other suppliers. The decision to shut down operations, therefore, is made only if in the opinion of the manager the price will stay below average variable cost for an extended period of time.

The second qualification involves the distinction between the short run and the long run. The decision to shut down depends on whether the firm can make a contribution to its fixed cost by continuing to produce. In the long run, however, there are no fixed costs. Buildings are sold, equipment is auctioned off, contracts expire, and so on. Thus, in the long run, as long as price is expected to remain below average variable cost, the firm will shut down. This decision rule applies in both the short and the long run.

Problem 8.5. A perfectly-competitive firm faces the following total variable cost function

---

[1] Strictly speaking, the assertion that the portion of the marginal cost curve that lies above the minimum average variable cost is the firm's supply curve is incorrect. The supply function is $Q_S = Q(P)$, where $dQ_S/dP > 0$; that is, output is a function of price. By contrast, the firm's total cost function is $TC = TC(Q)$, where $MC = MC(Q) = dTC/dQ > 0$; that is, marginal cost function is a function of output. Thus, the supply curve is really the inverse of the MC function. A formal derivation of the firm's supply curve is presented in Appendix 8A.

$$TVC = 150Q - 20Q^2 + Q^3$$

where Q is quantity. Below what price should the firm shut down its operations?

Solution. Find the output level that corresponds to the minimum average variable cost. First, calculate average variable cost

$$AVC = \frac{TVC}{Q} = 150 - 20Q + Q^2$$

Next, take the first derivative, equate the result to zero, and solve.

$$\frac{dAVC}{dQ} = -20 + 2Q = 0$$

$$Q = 10$$

Since the firm operates at the point where $P = MC$, substitute this result into the marginal cost function to yield

$$P = MC = \frac{dTVC}{dQ} = 150 - 40Q + 3Q^2 = 150 - 40(10) + 3(102) = \$50$$

Thus, if the price falls below $50 per unit, then the firm should shut down.

Problem 8.6. Hale and Hearty Limited (HH) is a small distributor of B&Q Foodstores, Inc., in the highly competitive health care products industry. The market-determined price of a 100-tablet vial of HH's most successful product, papaya extract, is $10. HH's total cost ($TC$) function is given as

$$TC = 100 + 2Q + 0.01Q^2$$

a. What is the firm's profit-maximizing level of output? What is the firm's profit at the profit-maximizing output level? Is HH in short-run or long-run competitive equilibrium? Explain.
b. At $P = \$10$, what is HH's break-even output level?
c. What is HH's long-run break-even price and output level?
d. What is HH's shutdown price and output level? Does this price–output combination constitute a short-run or a long-run competitive equilibrium? Explain.

Solution
a. Total profit is defined as the difference between total revenue (TR) and total cost, that is,

$$\pi = TR - TC = PQ - TC = 10Q - (100 + 2Q + 0.01Q^2)$$
$$= -100 + 8Q - 0.01Q^2$$

Differentiating this expression with respect to Q and setting the result equal to zero (the first-order condition for a local maximization) yields

$$\frac{d\pi}{dQ} = 8 - 0.02Q = 0$$

$$Q^* = 400$$

To verify that this output constitutes a maximum, differentiate the marginal profit function (take the second derivative of the total profit function). A negative value for the resulting expression constitutes a second-order condition for a local maximum.

$$\frac{d^2\pi}{dQ^2} = -0.02 < 0$$

Total profit at the profit-maximizing output level is

$$\pi^* = -100 + 8(400) - 0.01(400)^2 = -100 + 3,200 - 1,600 = \$1,500$$

HH is in short-run competitive equilibrium. In perfectly competitive markets, individual firms earn no economic profit in the long run. HH, however, is earning an economic profit of $1,500, which will attract new firms into the industry, which will increase supply and drive down the selling price of papaya extract (assuming that the demand for the product remains unchanged).

b. The break-even condition is defined as

$$TR = TC$$

Substituting into this definition gives

$$10Q = 100 + 2Q + 0.01Q^2$$

$$100 - 8Q + 0.01Q^2 = 0$$

This equation, which has two solution values, is of the general form

$$aQ^2 + bQ + c = 0$$

The solution values may be determined by factoring this equation, or by applying the quadratic formula, which is given as

$$Q_{1,2} = \frac{-b \pm \sqrt{(b^2 - 4ac)}}{2a}$$

$$= \frac{-(-8) \pm \sqrt{[(-8)^2 - 4(0.01)(100)]}}{2(0.01)}$$

$$= \frac{8 \pm \sqrt{(64 - 4)}}{0.02} = \frac{8 \pm 7.746}{0.02}$$

$$Q_1 = \frac{8 + 7.746}{0.02} = 787.3$$

$$Q_2 = \frac{8 - 7.746}{0.02} = 12.7$$

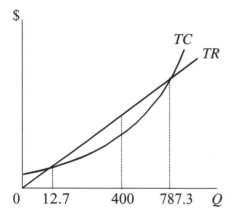

FIGURE 8.8   Diagrammatic solution to problem 8.6, part b.

These results indicate that there are two break-even output levels at $P = \$10$. Consider Figure 8.8.

c. In long-run competitive equilibrium, no firm in the industry earns an economic profit. It is an equilibrium in that while each firm earns a "normal" profit, there is no incentive for new firms to enter the industry, nor is there an incentive for existing firms to leave. The break-even price is defined in terms of the output level of which price is equal to minimum average total cost (ATC), that is,

$$P_{be} = ATC_{min}$$

ATC is given by the expression

$$ATC = \frac{TC}{Q} = \frac{100 + 2Q + 0.01Q^2}{Q} = 100Q^{-1} + 2 + 0.01Q$$

Minimizing this expression yields

$$\frac{dATC}{dQ} = -100Q^{-2} + 0.01 = 0$$

which is a first-order condition for a local minimum.

$$0.01Q^2 = 100$$

$$Q^2 = 10,000$$

$$Q_{be} = 100$$

$$\frac{d^2ATC}{dQ^2} = 200Q^{-3} = \frac{200}{(100)^3} > 0$$

which is a second-order condition for a local minimum. Substituting this result into the preceding condition yields

$$P_{be} = ATC_{min} = 100Q^{-1} + 2 + 0.01Q = \frac{100}{100} + 2 + 0.01(100) = 4$$

d. The firm's shutdown price is defined in terms of the output level of which price is equal to minimum average variable cost (AVC), that is,

$$P_{sd} = AVC_{min}$$

AVC is given by the expression

$$AVC = \frac{TVC}{Q} = \frac{2Q + 0.01Q^2}{Q} = 2 + 0.01Q$$

Since this expression is linear, AVC is minimized where $Q_{sd} = 0$. Substituting this result into the preceding condition we get

$$P_{sd} = AVC_{min} = 2 + 0.01Q = 2 + 0.01(0) = \$2$$

This result is a short-run competitive equilibrium. At a price below \$2, the firm's loss will exceed its fixed costs. Under these circumstances, it will pay the firm to go out of business, in which case its short-run loss will be limited to its fixed costs. Because the firm is earning an economic loss for $P < ATC$, there will be an incentive for firms to exit the industry, which will reduce supply. If the demand for papaya extract is constant, the result will be an increase in price. Firms will continue to exit the industry until economic losses have been eliminated, as illustrated in Figure 8.9.

MONOPOLY

We now turn out attention to the other market extreme, monopoly. Monopolies may be described in terms of the same characteristics used to discuss perfect competition.

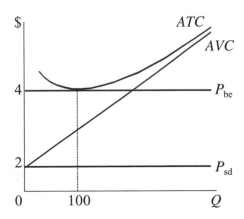

FIGURE 8.9   Diagrammatic solution to problem 8.6, part d.

In the case of a monopoly, the industry is dominated by a single producer. The most obvious implication of this is that the demand curve faced by the monopolist is the same downward-sloping market demand curve. Unlike the perfectly competitive firm, which produces too small a proportion of total industry output to significantly affect the market price, the output of the monopolist, is total industry output. Thus, for the monopolist, market prices are no longer parametric. An increase or decrease in the output will lower or raise the market price of the monopolist's product. For this reason, monopolists may be characterized as price makers.

Definition: The term "monopoly" is used to describe the market structure in which there is only one producer of a good or service for which there are no close substitutes and entry into and exit from the industry is impossible.

In the case of a monopoly, the number and size distribution of buyers is largely irrelevant, since the buyers of the firm's output have no bargaining power with which to influence prices. Such bargaining power is usually manifested through the explicit or implicit threat to obtain the desired product from a competing firm, which is nonexistent in a market sewed by a monopoly.

Goods and services produced by monopolies are unique. That is, the output of a monopolist has no close substitutes. In one respect, monopolies are diametrically opposed to perfectly competitive firm in that they do not have to compete with other firms in the industry. The output level of individual firms in perfectly competitive industries is so small relative to total industry output that each firm may effectively ignore the output decisions of other firms. A monopolist, on the other hand, is the only seller in an industry and, therefore, has no competitors.

For the firm to continue as a monopolist in the long run, there must exist barriers that prevent the entry of other firms into the industry. Such restrictions may be the result of the monopolist's control over scarce productive resources, patent rights, access to unique managerial talent, economies of scale, location, and so on. Another significant barrier to entry is found when a firm has a government franchise to be the sole provider of a good or service.

CONTROLLING SCARCE PRODUCTIVE RESOURCES

Until the 1940s, the Aluminum Company of America owned or controlled nearly 100% of the world's bauxite deposits. Since bauxite is needed to manufacture aluminum, that company, now known as Alcoa, was the sole producer and distributor of aluminum. Clearly, a firm that controls the entire supply of a vital factor of production will control production for the entire industry.

PATENT RIGHTS

A legal barrier to the entry of new firms into an industry is the *patent*. A patent, which is granted by a national government, is the exclusive right to a product or process by its inventor.[2] In the United States, patent protection is granted by Congress for a period of 20 years. Of course, during that period, the owner of the patent has the sole authority to produce for sale in the market the commodity protected by the patent.

Definition: A patent is the exclusive right granted to an inventor by government to a product or a process.

The rationale behind the granting of patents is that they provide an incentive for product research, development, invention, and innovation. Without such protection, investors are less likely to incur the often substantial development costs and risks associated with bringing a new product to market. On the other hand, the existence of patents discourages competition, which promotes product innovation, the development of more efficient, less costly production techniques, and lower prices. It is for these reasons that patents are not granted in perpetuity.

Arguments for and against patents have recently taken center stage in the United States in the debate over the escalating cost of health care. A frequently cited culprit has been the high price of prescription drugs. Pharmaceutical companies have been granted thousands of patents for a wide range of new prescription medicines, for which they have been able to charge monopoly prices. While recognizing that the high price of prescription medicines places a financial burden on some consumers, particularly the elderly, these companies nonetheless argue that the high prices are necessary as compensation for the millions of dollars in research and development costs. The companies also argue that these profits are necessary as compensation for the risks incurred in developing new products that are never brought to market or do not receive approval by the U.S. Food and Drug Administration.

GOVERNMENT FRANCHISE

Perhaps the most common example of a monopoly in the United States is the *government franchise*. Many firms are monopolies because the government has granted them the sole authority to supply a particular product within a given region. Public utilities are the most recognizable of government franchises. Government-franchised monopolies are usually justified on the grounds that it is more efficient for a single firm to produce, say,

---

[2] In the United States, patents are granted under Article I, Section 8, of the Constitution, which gives Congress the authority to "promote the progress of science and the useful arts, by securing for limited times to authors and inventors the exclusive right to their respective writings and discoveries."

electricity because of the large economies of scale involved and the desire to eliminate competing power grids. In exchange for this franchise, public utilities have agreed to be regulated. In principle, public utility commissions regulate the rates charged to ensure that the firm does not abuse its monopoly power.

Definition: A government franchise is a publicly authorized monopoly.

Fairness is another reason frequently cited in defense of government regulation. In many states, local telephone service is subject to regulation to ensure that consumers have access to affordable service. In fact, the profits earned by telephone companies from business users subsidize private household use, which is billed to individual consumers at below cost.

LAWSUITS

Monopolists can attempt to protect exclusive market positions by filing lawsuits against potential competitors claiming patent or copyright infringement. Start-up companies typically need to get their products to market as quickly as possible to generate cash flow. Regardless of the merits of lawsuits that may be brought against them, such cash-poor companies are financially unprepared to weather these legal challenges. In the end, the companies may be forced out of business, or may even be acquired by the monopolist.

SHORT-RUN PROFIT-MAXIMIZING PRICE AND OUTPUT

The case of the monopolist is illustrated in Figure 8.10. In the diagram we note that the monopolist faces the downward-sloping market demand curve, and the usual U-shaped marginal and average total cost curves. As

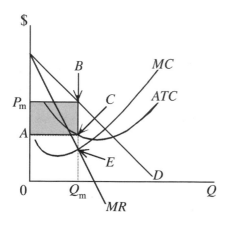

FIGURE 8.10 Monopoly: short-run and long-run profit-maximizing price and output.

in the case of a perfectly competitive firm, the profit-maximizing mono-polist will adjust its output level up to the point at which the marginal cost of producing an addition unit of the good is just equal to the marginal revenue from its sale. This condition is satisfied at point E in Figure 8.7, at output level Q_m.

The selling price of the monopolist output is determined along the market demand function at P_m. At this price–quantity combination, the economic profit earned by the firm is illustrated by the shaded area AP_mBC.

If entry into this industry were relatively easy, the existence of such eco-nomic profits would attract scarce productive resources into the production of the monopolist's product. As new firms entered the industry, the demand function facing the monopolist at any given price would become more elastic (flatter), with economic profit being dissipated as a result of increase competition. Eventually, the industry might even approach the perfectly competitive market structure.

If, on the other hand, the monopolist's position in the industry is secure, economic profits could persist indefinitely. Thus, Figure 8.10 may depict both short-run and long-run profit-maximizing price and output.

Problem 8.7. Suppose that the total cost (TC) and demand equations for a monopolist is given by the following expressions:

$$TC = 500 + 20Q^2$$

$$P = 400 - 20Q$$

What are the profit-maximizing price and quantity?

Solution. The total revenue function for the firm is

$$TR = PQ = 400Q - 20Q^2$$

Define total profit as

$$\pi = TR - TC = 400Q - 20Q^2 - 500 - 20Q^2$$

Taking the first derivative, and setting the resulting expression equal to zero, yields the profit-maximizing output level.

$$\frac{d\pi}{dQ} = 400 - 80Q = 0$$

$$Q^* = 5$$

Substituting this result into the demand equation yields the selling price of the product

$$P^* = 400 - 20(5) = \$300$$

LONG-RUN PROFIT-MAXIMIZING PRICE
AND OUTPUT

The long-run profit-maximizing price and output for a monopolist in the long run are the same as the short-run profit-maximizing price and output. The reason for this is that in the absence of changes in demand, profits to the monopolist will continue because restrictions to entry into the industry guarantee that these profits will not be competed away.

Problem 8.8. Suppose that an industry is dominated by a single producer and that the demand for its product is

$$Q_D = 3,000 - 60P$$

Suppose further that the total cost function of the firm is

$$TC = 100 + 5Q + \frac{1}{480}Q^2$$

a. What is the monopolist's profit-maximizing price and output?
b. Given your answer to part a, what is the firm's economic profit?

Solution
a. The profit-maximizing condition for a monopolist is

$$MR = MC$$

The monopolist's total revenue equation is

$$TR = PQ$$

Solving the demand equation for P yields

$$P = 50 - \frac{1}{60}Q$$

Substituting this result into the total revenue equation yields

$$TR = \left[50 - \left(\frac{1}{60}\right)Q\right]Q = 50Q - \left(\frac{1}{60}\right)Q^2$$

The monopolist's marginal revenue equation is

$$MR = \frac{dTR}{dQ} = 50 - \left(\frac{1}{30}\right)Q$$

The monopolist's marginal cost equation is

$$MC = \frac{dTC}{dQ} = 5 + \left(\frac{1}{240}\right)Q$$

Substituting these results into the profit-maximizing condition yields the profit-maximizing output level

$$50 - \left(\frac{1}{30}\right)Q = 5 + \left(\frac{1}{240}\right)Q$$

$$Q^* = 1,200$$

To determine the profit-maximizing price, substitute this result into the demand equation:

$$P^* = 50 - \left(\frac{1}{60}\right)1,200 = 50 - 20 = \$30$$

b. The monopolists profit at $P^* = \$30$ and $Q^* = 1,200$ is

$$\pi^* = TR - TC = P^*Q^* - \left(100 + 5Q^* + \left(\frac{1}{480}\right)Q^{*2}\right)$$

$$= 30(1,200) - \left[100 + 5(1,200) + \left(\frac{1}{480}\right)(1,200)^2\right] = \$26,900$$

Problem 8.9. Explain why a profit-maximizing monopolist would never produce at an output level (and charge a price) that corresponded to the inelastic portion of a linear market demand curve.

Solution. In the case of a linear market demand curve, when demand is elastic ($\varepsilon_p < -1$), marginal revenue is positive ($MR > 0$) and total revenue is increasing. When the price elasticity of demand is unitary ($\varepsilon_p = -1$), marginal revenue is zero ($MR = 0$) and total revenue is maximized. Finally, when the price elasticity of demand is inelastic ($-1 < \varepsilon_p < 0$), marginal revenue is negative ($MR < 0$) and total revenue is decreasing. Thus, if the monopolist were to produce at an output level corresponding to the inelastic portion of the demand curve, the corresponding marginal revenue would be negative. Since profit is maximized where $MR = MC$, this would imply that $MC < 0$, which is false by assumption. In other words, since total cost is assumed to be an increasing function of total output, then marginal cost cannot be negative, and a profit-maximizing monopolist would not produce where $MC = MR$.

MONOPOLY AND THE PRICE ELASTICITY OF DEMAND

Consider the relationship between the price charged by a profit-maximizing monopolist and the price elasticity of demand. From Equation (8.2)

$$\frac{d\pi(Q)}{dQ} = \frac{dTR(Q)}{dQ} - \frac{dTC(Q)}{dQ} = 0 \tag{8.2}$$

Recall that because the monopolist faces a downward-sloping demand curve, price is functionally related to output. Thus, Equation (8.2) may be rewritten as

$$\frac{d\pi(Q)}{dQ} = P + Q\left(\frac{dP}{dQ}\right) - MC = 0 \qquad (8.10)$$

Rearranging the right-hand side of Equation (8.10) we obtain

$$-Q\left(\frac{dP}{dQ}\right) = P - MC \qquad (8.11)$$

Dividing both sides of Equation (8.11) by P, we write

$$\left(-\frac{Q}{P}\right)\left(\frac{dP}{dQ}\right) = \frac{P - MC}{P}$$

$$\frac{-1}{\varepsilon_P} = \frac{P - MC}{P} \qquad (8.12)$$

The profit-maximizing monopolist produces where $MR = MC$. Since marginal cost is normally positive, the left-hand side of Equation (8.12) implies that $-1 \le \varepsilon_p < -\infty$; that is, demand is price elastic. Thus, a monopolist will produce, and price, along the elastic portion of the demand curve.

LERNER INDEX

Equation (8.12) is referred to as the *Lerner index*. The Lerner index, which is simply the negative of the inverse of the price elasticity of demand, is a measure of monopoly power and takes on values between 0 and 1. The greater the difference between price and marginal cost (marginal revenue) for a profit-maximizing firm, the greater the value of the Lerner index, and thus the greater the monopoly power of the firm. This result also suggests that the more elastic (flatter) the demand curve, the smaller will be the firm's proportional markup over marginal cost. A special case of the Lerner index is the case of a profit-maximizing, perfectly competitive firm where $P = MC$. The reader will verify that in this case the value of the Lerner index is 0 (i.e., no monopoly power).

Definition: The Lerner index is a measure of the monopoly power of a firm.

Problem 8.10. The market-determined price in a perfectly competitive industry is $P = \$10$. The total cost equation of an individual firm in this industry is

$$TC = 100 + 6Q + Q^2$$

Calculate the value of the Lerner index for this firm.

Solution. The profit equation for this firm is

$$\pi = TR - TC = 10Q - (100 + 6Q + Q^2) = -100 + 4Q - Q^2$$

Assuming that the second-order condition is satisfied, the profit-maximizing output level is found by taking the first derivative of the total profit function, setting the results equal to zero, and solving for Q.

$$\frac{d\pi}{dQ} = 4 - 2Q = 0$$

$$Q^* = 2$$

Marginal cost of this firm at $Q^* = 2$ is

$$MC = \frac{dTC}{dQ} = 6 + 2Q = 6 + 2(2) = 10$$

Thus, the value of the Lerner index is

$$\frac{-1}{\varepsilon_P} = \frac{P - MC}{P} = \frac{10 - 10}{10} = \frac{0}{10} = 0$$

Thus, this perfectly competitive firm has no monopoly power. The firm's proportional markup over marginal cost is zero; that is, the firm is earning zero economic profit.

Problem 8.11. The demand equation for a product sold by a monopolist is

$$P = 10 - Q$$

The total cost equation of the firm is

$$TC = 100 + 6Q + Q^2$$

Calculate the value of the Lerner index for this firm.

Solution. The profit equation for this firm is

$$\pi = TR - TC = PQ - TC = (10 - Q)Q - (100 + 6Q + Q^2) = -100 + 4Q - 2Q^2$$

Assuming that the second-order condition is satisfied, the profit-maximizing output level is found by taking the first derivative of the total profit function, setting the results equal to zero, and solving for Q.

$$\frac{d\pi}{dQ} = 4 - 4Q = 0$$

$$Q^* = 1$$

Substituting this into the demand equation gives the profit-maximizing price

$$P^* = 10 - Q = 10 - 1 = 9$$

Marginal cost of this firm at $Q^* = 1$ is

$$MC = \frac{dTC}{dQ} = 6 + 2Q = 6 + 2(1) = 8$$

Thus, the value of the Lerner index is

$$\frac{-1}{\varepsilon_P} = \frac{P - MC}{P} = \frac{9 - 8}{8} = \frac{1}{8} = 0.125$$

Thus, this firm enjoys monopoly power. The firm's proportional markup over marginal cost is 11.1%; that is, the firm is earning positive economic profit.

EVALUATING PERFECT COMPETITION AND MONOPOLY

In closing this chapter a few words are in order about the societal implications of a market structure that is characterized as perfectly competitive versus one that is dominated by a monopolist. In the case of a perfectly competitive output market, the equilibrium price and quantity are determined through the interaction of supply and demand forces. In Figure 8.11, the equilibrium price and quantity are determined at point E. At that point the equilibrium price and quantity in a perfectly competitive market are P_{pc} and Q_{pc}, respectively. In the case of a market dominated by a single producer, however, the equilibrium price and quantity are determined where $MC = MR$. In Figure 8.11 the equilibrium price and quantity are P_m and Q_m, respectively. From society's perspective, perfect competition is clearly preferable to monopoly because it results, even in the short run, in greater output and lower prices. This is not, however, the end of the story.

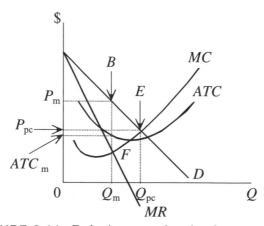

FIGURE 8.11   Evaluating monopoly and perfect competition.

In Figure 8.11 both the monopolist and the perfectly competitive firm are making economic profits. Unlike the case of an industry comprising a single producer, however, this situation will set into motion competitive forces that will eventually drive down prices and increase output further in markets that are characterized as perfectly competitive. Consider Figure 8.12.

As the lure of economic profit attracts new firms into the perfectly competitive industry, the market supply curve shifts to the right. As discussed earlier, long-run competitive equilibrium will be established where demand equals supply at point E'. At this point the typical firm in a perfectly competitive industry is making only normal profits. Since firms will no longer be attracted into the industry or compelled to leave it, the long-run competitive equilibrium price and quantity are P_{pc}' and Q_{pc}', respectively. For the monopolist, however, since new firms may neither enter nor exit the industry, equilibrium continues to be determined at point F and the long-run (and short-run) price and quantity remain P_m and Q_m, respectively. Clearly in this idealized case, society is better off when output is generated by perfectly competitive industries.

Monopolists are also less efficient than perfectly competitive firms, as an examination of Figure 8.12 illustrates. In long-run competitive equilibrium, the selling price of the product is equal to minimum cost per unit (i.e., $P_{pc}' = ATC_{min}$). In the case of an industry dominated by a monopolist, however, this is clearly not the case. At the profit-maximizing output level Q_m, the cost per unit of output is ATC_m. This solution is clearly inefficient and represents a misallocation of society's productive resources in the sense that not enough of the product is being produced. These results have profound implications for government-franchised monopolies, such as public utilities. At what price should the output of these firms be regulated? This

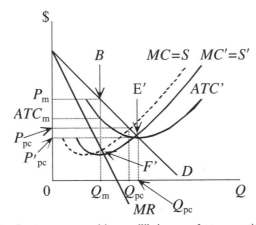

FIGURE 8.12   Long-run competitive equilibrium: perfect competition and monopoly.

question will be taken up in a later chapter. However, considerations of public welfare and efficiency should be central to regulators' concerns.

WELFARE EFFECTS OF MONOPOLY

Another approach to evaluating the relative merits of firms in perfectly competitive industries against those of a monopoly is by employing the concepts of consumer surplus and producer surplus.

CONSUMER SURPLUS

Consider Figure 8.13, which depicts the case of the perfectly competitive market. The area of the shaded region in the diagram $0AEQ^*$ represented the total benefits derived by consumers in competitive equilibrium. Total expenditures on Q^* units, however, is given by the area $0P^*EQ^*$. The difference between the total net benefits received from the consumption of Q^* units of output and total expenditures on Q^* units of output is given by the shaded area $0AEQ^* - 0P^*EQ^* = P^*AE$. *Consumer surplus* is given by the shaded area P^*AE. Consumer surplus is the difference between what consumers would be prepared to pay for a given quantity of a good or service and the amount they actually pay. The idea of consumer surplus is a derivation of the law of diminishing marginal utility. The law of diminishing marginal utility says that individuals receive incrementally less satisfaction from the consumption of additional units of a good or service and thus pay less for those additional units. Thus, in Figure 8.10, consumers are willing to pay more than P^* for the first unit of Q, but are prepared to pay just P^* for the Q^*th unit.

Definition: Consumer surplus is the difference between what consumers are willing to pay for a given quantity of a good or service and the amount

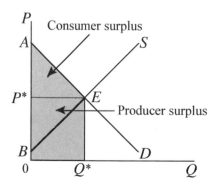

FIGURE 8.13 Consumer and producer surplus.

that they actually pay. Diagrammatically, consumer surplus is illustrated as the area below a downward-sloping demand curve but above the selling price.

PRODUCER SURPLUS

Consider, again, Figure 8.13. Recalling that the firm's supply curve is the marginal cost curve above minimum average variable cost, the total cost of producing Q^* units of output is given by the area $0BEQ^*$. Total revenues (consumer expenditures) earned from the sale of Q^* units of output is given by the area $0P^*EQ^*$. The difference between the total revenues from the sale of Q^* and the total cost of producing Q^* (total economic profit) is given by the shaded area $0BEQ^* - 0P^*EQ^* = BP^*E$. The shaded area BP^*E is referred to as *producer surplus*. Producer surplus is the difference between the total revenues earned from the production and sale of a given quantity of output and what the firm would have been willing to accept for the production and sale of that quantity of output.

Definition: Producer surplus is the difference between the total revenues earned from the production and sale of a given quantity of output and what the firm would have been willing to accept for the production and sale of that quantity of output.

PERFECT COMPETITION

It is often suggested in the economic literature that perfect competition is the "ideal" market structure because it guarantees that the "right" amount of a good or service is being produced. This is because the profit-maximizing firm will increase production up to the point at which marginal revenue (price) equals marginal cost. In this context, the demand curve for a good or service is society's marginal benefit curve. In a perfectly competitive market, output will expand until the marginal benefit derived by consumers, as evaluated along the demand function, is just equal to the marginal opportunity cost to society of producing the last unit of output. This is illustrated at point E in Figure 8.13. A voluntary exchange between consumer and producer will continue only as long as both parties benefit from the transaction. In the long run, perfectly competitive product markets guarantee that productive resources have been efficiently allocated and that production occurs at minimum cost.

Another way to evaluate a perfectly competitive market structure is to examine the relative welfare effects. Point E in Figure 8.13 also corresponds to the point at which the sum of consumer and producer surplus is maximized. The reader will note that no attempt is made to moralize about the relative virtues of consumers and producers. Perfect competition is considered to be a superior market structure precisely because perfect competition maximizes total societal benefits.

MONOPOLY

If it is, indeed, true that perfect competition is the "ideal" market structure because it results in the "right" amount of the product being produced, how are we to assess alternative market structures? It is, of course, tempting to condemn monopolies as avaricious, self-serving, or immoral, but are these characterizations justified? After all, profit-maximizing, perfectly competitive firms follow precisely the same decision criterion as the monopolist: that is, $MR = MC$. Viewed in this way, it is difficult to sustain the argument that the evils of monopolies reside in the hearts of monopolists.

To evaluate the relative societal merits of perfect competition versus monopoly, a more objective standard must be employed. We may infer, for example, that a monopolist earning economic profit benefited at the expense of consumers. We have already noted that consumers are made worse off because monopolists charge a higher price and produce a lower level of output than would be the case with perfect competition. We have also noted that monopolies are inherently inefficient because monopolists do not produce at minimum per unit cost. The real issue is whether the gain by monopolists in the form of higher profits is greater than, less than, or equal to the loss to consumers paying a higher price from a lower level of output. If the gain by monopolists is equal to the loss by consumers, it will be difficult to objectively argue that society is worse off because of the existence of monopolies. After all, monopolists are people too.

There are a number of reasoned economic arguments favoring perfect competition over monopoly. One such argument involves the application of the concepts of consumer and producer surplus. Consider Figure 8.14, which illustrates the situation of a profit-maximizing monopolist. For ease of exposition, the marginal cost curve is assumed to be linear.

In the case of perfect competition, equilibrium price and quantity are determined by the intersection of the supply (marginal cost) and demand (marginal benefit) curves. In Figure 8.14 this occurs at point E. The equilibrium price and quantity are P^* and Q^*, respectively. As in Figure 8.13, consumer surplus is given by the area P^*AE and producer surplus is given by the area BP^*E. The sum of consumer and producer surplus is given by the area BAE.

Suppose that the industry depicted in Figure 8.14 is transformed into a monopoly. A monopolist will maximize profits by producing at the output level at which $MR = MC$. The monopolist in Figure 8.14 will produce Q_m units of output and charge a price of P_m. The reader will verify that under monopoly the consumer is paying a higher price for less output. The reader will also verify that consumer surplus has been reduced from P^*AE to

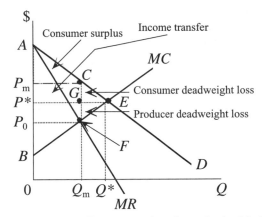

FIGURE 8.14   Consumer and producer deadweight loss.

P_mAC. Clearly, the consumer has been made worse off as a result of the monopolization of this industry by the area P^*P_mCE. To what extent has the monopolist benefited at the expense of the consumer?

An examination of Figure 8.14 clearly indicates that producer surplus has changed from the area BP^*E to BP_mCF. The net change in producer surplus is $P^*P_mCG - FGE$. The portion of lost consumer surplus P^*P_mCE captured by the monopolist (P^*P_mCE) represents an income transfer from the consumer to the producer. If the net change in producer surplus is positive, then the producer has been made better off as a result of the monopolization of the industry. Certainly, in terms of Figure 8.14, this appears to be the case, but is society better off or worse off? To see this we must compare the sums of consumer and producer surpluses before and after monopolization of the industry.

Before the monopolization of the industry, net benefits to society are given by the sum of consumer and producer surplus, $P^*AE + BP^*E = BAE$. After monopolization of the industry the net benefits to society are given by the sum of consumer and producer surplus $P_mAC + BP_mCF = BACF$. Since $BACF < BAE$, society has been made worse off as a result of monopolization of the industry.

DEADWEIGHT LOSS

The reader should note that in Figure 8.14 the portion of lost consumer and producer surplus is given by the area $GCE + FGE = FCE$. The area FCE is referred to as *total deadweight loss*. The area GCE is referred to as *consumer deadweight loss*. Consumer deadweight loss represents the reduction in consumer surplus that is not captured as an income transfer to a monopolist. The area FGE is referred to as *producer deadweight loss*. Producer deadweight loss arises when society's resources are inefficiently employed because the monopolist does not produce at minimum per-unit cost. No assumptions about the relative merits of consumers or producers or the distribution of income are required to assess this outcome. Clearly, the loss of consumer and producer surplus represents a net loss to society.

Definition: Consumer deadweight loss represents the reduction in consumer surplus that is not captured as an income transfer to a monopolist.

Definition: Producer deadweight loss arises when society's resources are inefficiently employed because the monopolist does not produce at minimum per-unit cost.

Definition: Total deadweight loss is the loss of consumption and production efficiency arising from monopolistic market structures. Total deadweight loss is the sum of the losses of consumer and producer surplus for which there are no offsetting gains.

The importance of the foregoing analysis of the welfare effects of monopoly for public policy cannot be underestimated. Demands by public interest groups for remedies against the "abuses" of monopolies are seldom framed in terms of total deadweight loss, and indeed focus on the unfairness of the transfer, with monopoly pricing of income from consumer to producer, (i.e., the net loss of consumer surplus). But as we have seen, part of this loss of consumer surplus is captured by the monopolist in the form of an income transfer. It is important, however, to question the disposition of income transfers before categorically condemning monopolistic pricing and output practices.

Monopolistic market structures that result in increased research and development, such as product invention and innovation, may be considered to be socially preferable to the rough-and-tumble of perfect competition. An example of this is monopolies arising from patent protection that results in the development of lifesaving pharmaceuticals. Another example of a monopoly that is considered to be socially desirable is that of the government franchise, which was also discussed earlier. The static analysis of the welfare effects of monopoly ignores the dynamic implications of monopolistic market structures. The dynamic implications must also be considered when one is evaluating the relative benefits of perfect competition versus monopoly.

Problem 8.12. Consider the monopolist that faces the following market demand and total cost functions:

$$Q = 22 - \frac{P}{5}$$

$$TC = 100 - 10Q + Q^2$$

a. Find the profit-maximizing price (P_m) and output (Q_m) for this firm. At this price–quantity combination, how much is consumer surplus?

b. How much economic profit is this monopoly earning?

c. Given your answer to part a, what, if anything, can you say about the redistribution of income from consumer to producer?

d. Suppose that government regulators required the monopolist to set the selling price at the long-run, perfectly competitive rate. At this price, what is consumer surplus?

e. Relative to the perfectly competitive long-run equilibrium price, what is the deadweight loss to society at P_m?

Solution

a. The total revenue function for the monopolist is

$$TR = PQ = 110Q - 5Q^2$$

The monopolist's total profit function is therefore

$$\pi = -100 + 120Q - 6Q^2$$

Taking the first derivative of this expression yields the profit maximizing output level

$$\frac{d\pi}{dQ} = 120 - 12Q = 0$$

$$Q_m = 10$$

The profit-maximizing price is, therefore

$$P_m = 110 - 5Q_m = 110 - 5(10) = 60$$

Consumer surplus may be determined from the following expression:

$$\text{Consumer surplus} = 0.5(110 - P_m)Q_m$$

where 110 is the price according to the demand function when $Q = 0$. Utilizing this expression yields

$$\text{Consumer surplus} = 0.5(110 - 60)10 = \$250$$

b. The monopolist economic profit is

$$\pi = -100 + 120Q - 6Q^2 = -100 + 120(10) - 6(10^2) = \$500$$

which is the amount of the income transfer from consumer to producer.

c. Unfortunately, economic theory provides no insights about whether this income transfer is an improvement in society's welfare. Such an analysis would require an assumption about the appropriate distribution for the society in question, and this cannot be evaluated by using efficiency criteria.

d. The perfectly competitive long-run equilibrium price is defined as

$$P = MC = ATC$$

Marginal cost is equal to average total cost at the output level where average total cost is minimized. Define average total cost as

$$ATC = 100Q^{-1} - 10 + Q$$

Taking the first derivative and setting the results equal to zero yields

$$\frac{dATC}{dQ} = -100Q^{-2} + 1 = 0$$

$$Q^* = 10$$

Alternatively, setting $MC = ATC$ yields

$$-10 + 2Q = 100Q^{-1} - 10 + Q$$
$$Q^2 = 100$$
$$Q = 10$$

At this output level, the long-run, perfectly competitive price is

$$P_{pc} = -10 + 2Q = -10 + 2(10) = 10$$

with an output level of

$$Q_{pc} = 22 - \frac{P}{5} = 22 - \frac{10}{5} = 20$$

In this case, consumer surplus may be determined from the following expression:

Consumer surplus $= 0.5(110 - P_{pc})Q_{pc} = 0.5(110 - 10)20 = \$1,000$

e. Finally, the deadweight loss to society is

$$\text{Deadweight loss} = 0.5[(P_m - P_{pc})(Q_{pc} - Q_m)]$$
$$= 0.5[(60 - 10)(20 - 10)] = \$250$$

This solution is illustrated in Figure 8.15.

NATURAL MONOPOLY

At the beginning of the discussion about the existence of monopolies, the focus was on such barriers to entry as control over scarce productive resources, patent rights, and government franchises. In each instance, monopoly power was based on exclusive access or special privilege. It is conceivable, however, that a firm may come to dominate a market based on the underlying production technology. In particular, if a single firm is able to realize sufficiently large economies of scale such that alone it can satisfy total market demand at a per-unit cost that is less than an industry

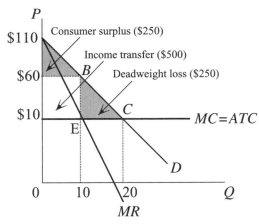

FIGURE 8.15   Diagrammatic solution to problem 8.2, part e.

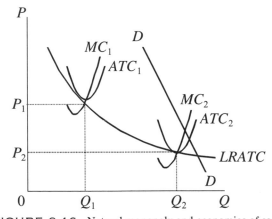

FIGURE 8.16   Natural monopoly and economies of scale.

consisting of two or more firms, then that firm is referred to as *natural monopoly*.

Definition: A natural monopoly is a firm that is able to satisfy total market demand at a per-unit cost of production that is less than an industry comprising two or more firms.

The case of a natural monopoly is illustrated in Figure 8.16, where the MC_1 and ATC_1 curves designate a small-scale plant and MC_2 and ATC_2 a large-scale plant. Suppose that Q_2 represents an output level of 250,000 units and Q_1 represents an output level of 50,000 units. Clearly, it would be more efficient, less costly, and in the public interest for one firm to operate a single large-scale plant than for five firms to operate several small-scale plants. This is, in fact, one rationale underlying the granting of government franchises of public utilities.

COLLUSION

Suppose that an industry initially comprised several firms, which decided to coordinate their pricing and output decisions to limit competition and maximize profits for the group. Such an arrangement is referred to as *collusion*. Analytically, the impact on the consumer would be the same as in the case of a monopoly. In the United States, collusive arrangements are illegal. Collusive pricing and output behavior by firms will be more closely examined in Chapter 10 (Market Structure: Duopoly and Oligopoly) and Chapter 13 (Introduction to Game Theory).

Definition: Collusion refers to a formal agreement among producers in an industry to coordinate pricing and output decisions to limit competition and maximize collective profits.

CHAPTER REVIEW

Market structure refers to the competitive environment within which a firm operates. Economists divide market structure into four basic types: *perfect competition, monopolistic competition, oligopoly*, and *monopoly*. Perfect competition and monopoly represent opposite ends of the competitive spectrum.

The characteristics of a perfectly competitive industry are a large number of sellers and buyers, a standardized product, complete information about market prices, and complete freedom of entry into and exit from the industry. A perfectly competitive firm produces a minuscule proportion of the total industry output. Thus, although the market demand curve is downward sloping, the demand curve from the perspective of the individual firm is perfectly elastic (horizontal). A perfectly competitive firm can sell as much as it wants at an unchanged price. A perfectly competitive firm has no *market power*, and is said to be a *price taker*.

Total revenue is defined as price (P) times output. *Marginal revenue* (MR) is defined as the increase (decrease) in total revenue given an increase (decrease) in output. For a perfectly competitive firm, marginal revenue is identically equal to the selling price. Since, $MR = P$, then $MR = ATR$ (average total revenue).

All profit-maximizing firms produce at an output level at which marginal revenue equals marginal cost (MC), that is, $MR = MC$. Since $MR = P_0$, the profit-maximizing condition for a perfectly competitive firm is $P_0 = MC$. If price is greater than average total cost ($P_0 > ATC$), then a perfectly competitive firm earns positive economic profits, which will attract new firms into the industry, shifting the market supply curve to the right and driving down the selling price. If $P_0 < ATC$, the firm generates economic losses, which cause firms to exit the industry, shifting the market supply curve to the left and driving up the selling price. When $P_0 = ATC$, a perfectly competitive firm breaks even (i.e., earns zero economic profits). At this *break-even price*, the industry is in long-run competitive equilibrium, which implies that $P_0 = MC = ATC$. Finally, since $MC = ATC$, per-unit costs are minimized; that is, perfectly competitive firms produce efficiently in the long run.

In the short run, a perfectly competitive firm earning an economic loss will remain in business as long as price is greater than average variable cost (AVC). This is because the firm's revenues cover all its fixed cost and part of its variable cost. When $P_0 < AVC$, the firm will shut down because revenues cover only part of its variable cost and none of its fixed cost. When $P_0 = AVC$, the firm is indifferent between shutting down and remaining in business. This is because in either case the firm's economic loss is equivalent to its total fixed cost. This price is called the *shutdown price*.

The characteristics of a monopolistic industry are a single firm, a unique product, absolute control over supply within a price range, and highly restrictive entry into or exit from the industry. Unlike the perfectly competitive firm, a monopoly faces the downward-sloping market demand curve, which implies that the selling price is negatively related to the output of the firm. A monopolist has market power and is said to be a *price maker*.

A profit-maximizing monopolist will produce at an output level at which $MR = MC$. Unlike a perfectly competitive firm, selling price is always greater than the marginal revenue (i.e., $P > MR$). Like a perfectly competitive firm, the monopolist earns an economic profit when $P > ATC$. Unlike a perfectly competitive firm, this condition is both a short-run and a long-run competitive equilibrium, since new firms are unable to enter the industry to increase supply, lower selling price, and compete away the monopolist's economic profits. Finally, since $MC < ATC$, per-unit costs are not minimized; that is, monopolists produce inefficiently in the long run.

A *natural monopoly* is a firm that is able to satisfy total market demand at a per-unit cost of production that is less than an industry comprising two or more firms. *Collusion* refers to a formal agreement among producers in an industry to coordinate pricing and output decisions to limit competition and maximize collective profits. Collusive arrangements are illegal in the United States.

KEY TERMS AND CONCEPTS

Break-even price   The price at which total revenue is equal to total economic cost.

Collusion   A formal agreement among producers in an industry to coordinate pricing and output decisions to limit competition and maximize collective profits.

Consumer deadweight loss   The reduction in consumer surplus that is not captured as an income transfer to a monopolist.

Consumer surplus   The difference between what consumers are willing to pay for a given quantity of a good or service and the amount that they actually pay. Diagrammatically, consumer surplus is illustrated as the area below a downward-sloping demand curve but above the selling price.

Economic cost   The sum of total explicit and implicit costs.

Economic loss   Total revenue that is less than total economic cost.

Economic profit   Total revenue that is greater than total economic cost.

Government franchise   A publicly authorized monopoly.

Lerner index   A measure of the monopoly power of a firm.

Market power   The ability of a firm to influence the market price of its product by altering its level of output. Market power is displayed when a firm produces a significant proportion of total industry output.

Market structure   The environment within which buyers and sellers interact.

Monopoly   The market structure in which there is only one producer of a good or service for which there are no close substitutes and entry into and exit from the industry is impossible.

$MR = MC$ Marginal revenue equals marginal cost is the first-order condition for profit maximization by firms in imperfectly competitive markets.

$MR = P_0$ Marginal revenue equals price for firms in perfectly competitive industries.

Natural monopoly   A firm that is able to satisfy total market demand at a per-unit cost of production that is less than an industry comprising two or more firms.

$P_0 = MC$ Price equals marginal cost is the first-order condition for profit maximization by perfectly competitive firms.

$P_0 = MC = ATC$ Price equals marginal cost equals minimum average total cost is the first-order, long-run profit-maximizing condition for perfectly competitive firms.

$P > MR = MC$ The selling price is greater than marginal revenue, which is equal to marginal cost, is the first-order profit maximizing condition for a firm facing downward-sloping demand curve for its good or service.

Patent   The exclusive right granted to an inventor by government to a product or a process.

Perfect competition   The market structure in which there are many buyers and sellers of a homogeneous good or service; in addition, there is perfect mobility of factors of production and buyers, sellers have perfect information about market conditions, and entry into and exit from the industry is very easy.

Price maker   A firm that faces a downward-sloping demand curve for its product. This condition implies that the firm is able to alter the market price of its product by changes its output level.

Price taker   A perfectly competitive firm that prices its good or service at the prevailing market price. A perfectly competitive firm is called a price taker because it is unable to influence the market price of its product by altering its level of output. This condition implies that a perfectly-competitive firm should be able to sell as much of its good or service at the prevailing market price as any other comparable firm.

Producer deadweight loss   Arises when society's resources are inefficiently employed because a monopolist does not produce at minimum per-unit cost.

Producer surplus   The difference between the total revenues earned from the production and sale of a given quantity of output and what the firm would have been willing to accept for the production and sale of that quantity of output.

Shutdown price   The price that is equal to the minimum average variable cost of producing a good or service. Below this price the firm will shut down because the firm's loss, which will equal the firm's total fixed cost, will be less than if the firm continues to stay in business.

Total deadweight loss   The loss of consumption and production efficiency arising from monopolistic market structures. Total deadweight loss is the sum of the losses of consumer and producer surpluses for which there are no offsetting gains.

Total fixed cost   The firm's expenditures on fixed factors of production.

Total variable cost   The firm's expenditures on variable factors of production.

CHAPTER QUESTIONS

8.1 Price competition is characteristic of firms in perfectly competitive industries. Do you agree with this statement? If not, then why not?

8.2 Firms in perfectly competitive industries may be described as price takers. What are the implications of this observation for the price and output decisions of profit-maximizing firms?

8.3 For industries characterized as perfectly competitive, equilibrium price and quantity can never be determined along the inelastic portion of the market demand curve. Do you agree? Explain.

8.4 A perfectly competitive firm earning an economic loss at the profit-maximizing level of output should shut down. Do you agree with this statement? Explain.

8.5 A profit-maximizing firm is producing at an output level at which the price of its product is less than the average total cost of producing that product. Under what conditions will this firm continue to operate? Explain.

8.6 A profit-maximizing firm is producing at an output level at which the price of its product is less than the average total cost of producing that product. Under what conditions will this firm shut down? Explain.

8.7 A perfectly competitive firm in short-run competitive equilibrium must also be in long-run competitive equilibrium. Do you agree? Explain.

8.8 A perfectly competitive firm in long-run competitive equilibrium must also be in short-run competitive equilibrium. Do you agree? Explain.

8.9 A perfectly competitive firm in long-run competitive equilibrium earns a zero rate of return on investment. Do you agree? If not, then why not?

8.10 No firm in a perfectly competitive industry would ever operate at a point on the demand curve at which the price elasticity of demand is equal to or less than one in absolute value. Comment.

8.11 No competitive industry would ever operate at a point on the industry demand curve at which the price elasticity of demand is equal to or less than one in absolute value. Comment.

8.12 A perfectly competitive firm in long-run competitive equilibrium produces at minimum per-unit cost. Do you agree? Explain.

8.13 A perfectly competitive firm maximizes profits by producing at an output level at which marginal revenue equals declining marginal cost. Do you agree? If not, then why not?

8.14 A perfectly competitive firm will continue to operate in the short run as long as total revenues cover all the firm's total variable costs and some the firm's total fixed costs. Explain.

8.15 The marginal cost curve is a perfectly competitive firm's supply curve. Do you agree with this statement? If not, then why not?

8.16 In a perfectly competitive industry, the market supply curve is the summation of the individual firm's marginal cost curves. Do you agree? Explain.

8.17 When price is greater than average variable cost for a typical firm in a perfectly competitive industry, we can be quite certain that the price will fall. Explain.

8.18 A profit-maximizing monopolist will never produce along the inelastic portion of the market demand curve. Do you agree? Explain.

8.19 To maximize total revenue, the monopolist must charge the highest price possible. Do you agree? Explain.

8.20 Suppose that an unregulated electric utility is a government-franchised, profit-maximizing monopoly. At the prevailing price of electricity, an empirical study indicates that the price elasticity of demand for electricity is −0.8. Something is wrong. What? Explain.

8.21 A monopolist does not have a supply curve. Explain.

8.22 For a profit-maximizing firm subject to the law of diminishing marginal product, maximizing total revenue is equivalent to maximizing total profit. Do you agree? Explain.

8.23 Under what circumstances will maximizing the firm's total revenues result in maximum total profits.

8.24 Indicate whether the following statements are true, false, or uncertain. Explain.

    a. A profit-maximizing monopoly charges the highest price possible for its product.

    b. Profit-maximizing monopolies are similar to profit-maximizing perfectly competitive firms in that $P_0 = MR$.

    c. It is possible to describe the market demand for the output of a perfectly competitive industry as price inelastic.

    d. It is possible to describe the market demand for the output of a profit-maximizing monopolist as price inelastic.

    e. Suppose that a monopolist employs only one factor of production and that marginal and average total cost are constant. A 10% increase in the price of that input will cause the monopolist to increase product price by 10%.

    f. Suppose that a profit-maximizing monopolist can shift the linear demand curve for the firm's product to the right by advertising. The monopolist's total cost equation is $TC = \theta Q$, where θ is a positive constant. An increase in the price of advertising will result in an increase in the price of the monopolist's output.

8.25 The Lerner index is a measure of a firm's monopoly power. It is also a measure of the firm's per-unit proportional markup over marginal cost. Explain.

8.26 Describe the social welfare effects of monopolies versus those of perfect competition.

8.27 Compared with perfect competition, for consumers monopolies are always and inferior market structure. Do you agree? If not, then why not?

8.28 Why do governments grant patents and copyrights?

CHAPTER EXERCISES

8.1 A firm faces the following total cost equation for its product

$$TC = 500 + 5Q + 0.025Q^2$$

The firm can sell its product for $10 per-unit of output.

    a. What is the profit-maximizing output level?

    b. Verify that the firm's profit corresponding to this level of output represents a maximum.

8.2 The total cost (TC) and demand equations for a monopolist is

$$TC = 100 + 5Q^2$$

$$P = 200 - 5Q$$

  a. What is the profit-maximizing quantity?
  b. What is the profit-maximizing price?

8.3 Bucolic Farms, Inc., is a dairy farm that supplies milk to B&Q Food-stores, Inc. Bucolic has estimated the following total cost function

$$TC = 100 + 12Q + 0.06Q^2$$

where Q is 100 gallons of milk.

  a. Determine the following functions:
    i. Average total cost (ATC)
    ii. Average variable cost (AVC)
    iii. Marginal cost (MC)
    iv. Total fixed cost (TFC)
  b. What are Bucolic's shutdown and break-even price and output levels?
  c. Suppose that there are 5,000 nearly identical milk producers in this industry. What is the market supply curve?
  d. Suppose that the market demand function is

$$Q_D = 660,000 - 16,333,33P$$

  What are the market equilibrium price and quantity?

  e. Determine Bucolic's profit.
  f. Assuming no change in demand or costs, how many milk producers will remain in the industry in the long run?

8.4 A monopoly faces the following demand and total cost equations for its product.

$$Q = 30 - \frac{P}{3}$$

$$TC = 100 - 5Q + Q^2$$

  a. What are the firm's short-run profit-maximizing price and output level?
  b. What is the firm's economic profit?

8.5 The demand equation for a product sold by a monopolist is

$$Q = 25 - 0.5P$$

The total cost equation of the firm is

$$TC = 225 + 5Q + 0.25Q^2$$

  a. Calculate the profit-maximizing price and quantity.
  b. What is the firm's profit?

8.6 The market equation for a product sold by a monopolist is

$$Q = 100 - 4P$$

The total cost equation of the firm is

$$TC = 500 + 10Q + 0.5Q^2$$

a. What are the profit-maximizing price and quantity?
b. What is the firm's maximum profit?

8.7 A firm faces the following total cost equation for its product

$$TC = 6 + 33Q - 9Q^2 + Q^3$$

The firm can sell its product for $18 per-unit of output.

a. What is the profit-maximizing output level?
b. What is the firm's profit?

8.8 Suppose initially that the blodget industry in Ancient Elam is in long-run competitive equilibrium, with each firm in the industry just earning normal profits. This situation is illustrated in Figure E8.8.

a. Find the equilibrium price and the industry output level.
b. Suppose that venture capitalists organize a syndicate to acquire all the firms in the blue blodget industry. The resulting company, Kablooy, is a profit-maximizing monopolist. Find the equilibrium price and output level. What is the monopolist's economic profit?
c. Suppose that the Antitrust Division of the U.S. Department of Justice is concerned about the economic impact of consolidation in the blue blodget industry but is generally of the opinion that it is not in the national interest to "break up" Kablooy. Instead, Justice Department lawyers recommend that the blue blodget industry be regulated. In your opinion, what are the economic concerns of Justice Department? In your answer, explain whether consumers were made better off or worse off as a result of consolidation in the blue blodget industry?

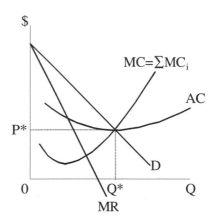

FIGURE E8.8 Chapter exercise 8.8.

Also, be sure to compare prices, output levels, production efficiency, and consumer surplus before and after consolidation.

d. If you believe that consumers have been made worse off, what regulatory measures would you suggest be recommended by the Justice Department?

e. Do you foresee any potential long-run economic problems arising from the decision to allow the blue blodget industry from continuing as a monopoly (*Hint*: What are the implications for product innovation, development, and adoption of efficient production technology)?

SELECTED READINGS

Brennan, M. J., and T. M. Carroll. *Preface to Quantitative Economics & Econometrics*, 4th ed. Cincinnati, OH: South-Western Publishing, 1987.

Case, K. E., and R. C. Fair. *Principles of Microeconomics*, 5th ed. Upper Saddle River, NJ: Prentice-Hall, 1999.

Friedman, L. S. *Microeconomic Analysis*. New York: McGraw-Hill, 1984.

Glass, J. C. *An Introduction to Mathematical Methods in Economics*. New York: McGraw-Hill, 1980.

Henderson, J. M., and R. E. Quandt. *Microeconomic Theory: A Mathematical Approach*, 3rd ed. New York: McGraw-Hill, 1980.

Nicholson, W. *Microeconomic Theory: Basic Principles and Extensions*, 6th ed. New York: Dryden Press, 1995.

Silberberg, E. *The Structure of Economics: A Mathematical Analysis*, 2nd ed. New York: McGraw-Hill, 1990.

APPENDIX 8A

FORMAL DERIVATION OF THE FIRM'S SUPPLY CURVE

Suppose that the objective of the firm is to maximize the profit function

$$\pi(Q) = PQ - TC(Q) \tag{8A.1}$$

where Q represents the firm's output and the parameter P the market determined price of the product. The first-order condition for profit maximization is

$$P - MC(Q) = 0 \tag{8A.2}$$

where $MC = dTC/dQ$, the firm's marginal cost. Equation (8A.2) asserts that the firm will maximize profit by producing at an output level at which price equals marginal cost. The second-order condition for profit maximization is

$$\frac{d^2\pi}{dQ^2} = \frac{-d^2TC}{dQ^2} = \frac{-dMC}{dQ} < 0 \tag{8A.3}$$

Equation (8A.3) merely asserts that the marginal cost curve of the firm is upward sloping. An upward sloping marginal cost curve with the product price constant is a reflection of the law of diminishing marginal product.

In principle, Equation (8A.2) may be solved for Q in terms of P, that is,

$$Q = Q^*(P) \tag{8A.4}$$

Equation (8A.4) is the firm's supply function. The question, of course, is how the firm's output will change when as price varies. To see this, substitute Equation (8A.4) into Equation (8A.2) to yield

$$P - MC[Q^*(P)] \equiv 0 \tag{8A.5}$$

Note that Equation (8A.5) is an identity, since the left-hand side is always zero because the profit-maximizing firm will always set price equal marginal cost for any P. Differentiating Equation (8A.5) with respect to price, and using the chain rule (see Chapter 2), we obtain

$$\frac{dP}{dP} - \frac{dMC(Q)}{dQ}\frac{dQ^*}{dP} \equiv 0 \tag{8A.6}$$

which yields

$$\frac{dQ^*}{dP} \equiv \frac{1}{dMC(Q)/dQ} > 0 \tag{8A.7}$$

Since $(dMC(Q)/dQ) > 0$ by the second-order condition for profit maximization, this ends our proof.

9

MARKET STRUCTURE: MONOPOLISTIC COMPETITION

Although the conditions necessary for the existence of perfect competition and monopoly, which were discussed in Chapter 8, are unlikely to be found in the real world, an analysis of these market structures is important because it provides insights into more commonly encountered industry types. These insights provide guidance in the formulation of public policy to promote the general economic welfare. We saw in Chapter 8, for example, that unlike monopolies, perfectly competitive firms produce at minimum per-unit cost. Thus, perfectly competitive market structures efficiently allocate society's scarce productive resources and tend to maximize consumer and producer surplus. For these reasons, economists tend to favor policies that move industries closer to the perfectly competitive paradigm.

Despite the unlikelihood encountering the conditions that define perfect competition in reality, the insights gleaned from an analysis of this market structure yield important insights into real-world phenomena. As Milton Friedman (1981) observed: "I have become increasingly impressed with how wide is the range of problems and industries for which it is appropriate to treat the economy as if it were competitive" (p. 120). What is important is not that the characteristics that define perfect competition are religiously satisfied, but that in large measure the interactions of market participants simulate the competitive model.

Although models of perfect competition and monopoly are useful, it is important analytically to bridge the gap between these two extreme cases. The first significant contributions in this direction were provided by Edward Chamberlin and Joan Robinson. These economists observed that in many intensely competitive markets individual firms were able to set the market price of their product. Since these firms exhibit characteristics of both perfect competition and monopoly, this market structure is referred to as *monopolistic competition.*

The market power of monopolistically competitive firms, such as fast-food restaurants, is derived from product differentiation and market segmentation. Through subtle and not-so-subtle distinctions, each firm in a monopolistically competitive industry is a sort of minimonopolist. But, unlike monopolists, these firms are severely constrained in their ability to set the market price for their product by the existence of many close substitutes. Thus, the demand for the output of monopolistically competitive firms is much more price elastic (flatter) than the demand curve confronting the monopolist. A firm in a perfectly competitive industry faces a perfectly elastic (horizontal) demand curve because its output is a perfect substitute for the output of other firms in the industry. Unlike monopolies and monopolistically competitive firms, which may be described as price makers, perfectly competitive firms are price takers.

CHARACTERISTICS OF MONOPOLISTIC COMPETITION

Monopolistic competition has characteristics in common with both perfect competition and monopoly. The most salient features of monopolistically competitive markets are as follows.

NUMBER AND SIZE DISTRIBUTION OF SELLERS

As in perfect competition, a monopolistically competitive industry is assumed to have a large number of firms, each producing a relatively small percentage of total industry output. As in perfect competition, the actions of any individual firm are unlikely to influence the actions of its competitors.

NUMBER AND SIZE DISTRIBUTION OF BUYERS

Also as in perfect competition, monopolistic competition assumes that there are a large number of buyers for its output and that resources are easily transferred between alternative uses.

PRODUCT DIFFERENTIATION

Unlike perfect competition, while each firm in a monopolistically competitive industry produces essentially the same type of product, each firm produces a product that is considered by consumers to be somewhat different from those of its competitors. The products of each firm in the industry are close, albeit not perfect, substitutes. Monopolistic competition is frequently encountered in the retail and service industries. Examples of product differentiation are most frequently encountered in the same industries and include such products as clothing, soft drinks, beer, cosmetics, gasoline stations, and restaurants.

Product differences may be real or imagined. For example, regular (87 octane) gasoline has a precise chemical composition. Many consumers, however, believe brand-name gasoline stations, such as Exxon and Mobile, sell better gasoline than little-known vendors. Firms often reinforce these perceived differences by introducing real or cosmetic additives into their product. Monopolistically competitive firms commit substantial sums in advertising expenditures to reinforce real and perceived product differences. These efforts are intended not only to attract new buyers but also to create brand-name recognition and solidify customer loyalty. By segmenting the market in this manner, these producers are able to charge higher prices. Within each segment of the market, the individual firm is a monopolist that is able to exercise market power.

CONDITIONS OF ENTRY AND EXIT

Finally, as in perfect competition, it is relatively easy for new firms to enter the industry, or for existing firms to leave it.

Definition: Monopolistic competition is a market structure that is characterized by buyers and sellers of a differentiated good or service and in which it is relatively easy to enter the industry or to leave it.

SHORT-RUN MONOPOLISTICALLY COMPETITIVE EQUILIBRIUM

Clearly, then, the one condition that differentiates the perfectly competitive firm from the monopolistically competitive firm is that the latter faces a downward-sloping demand curve for its product, which implies that, like a monopolist, the firm has some control over the selling price of its product. This market power stems from consumers' belief that each firm in the industry produces a somewhat different product, with different qualities and different customer appeal.

The typical firm's ability to affect the selling price of its product implies that the firm is able, within bounds, to raise the price of its product without completely losing its customer base. This situation is illustrated in Figure 9.1, which assumes the usual U-shaped marginal and average total cost curves.

In Figure 9.1, we observe that a typical monopolistically competitive firm maximizes its short-run profit by producing at the level of output at which

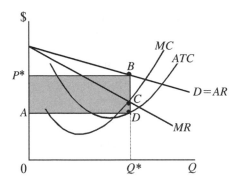

FIGURE 9.1 Short-run monopolistically competitive equilibrium and positive economic (above-normal) profit.

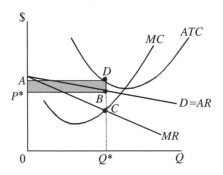

FIGURE 9.2 Short-run monopolistically competitive equilibrium and negative economic (below-normal) profit.

marginal cost equals marginal revenue. This occurs at the output level Q^*. At this output level, the firm charges a price of P^*, which is determined along the demand (average revenue) curve. The firm's total revenue is illustrated by the area of the rectangle $0P^*BQ^*$. The firm's total cost at output level Q^* is illustrated by the area of the rectangle $0ADQ^*$. Since total profit is defined as the difference between total revenue and total cost, the firm's profit at output level Q^* is illustrated by the area of the rectangle AP^*BD.

Of course, in the short run the monopolistically competitive firm might just as easily have generated an economic loss. This is illustrated by the area of the rectangle P^*ADB in Figure 9.2. Note, again, that profit is maximized at Q^*, where marginal cost equals marginal revenue.

LONG-RUN MONOPOLISTICALLY COMPETITIVE EQUILIBRIUM

Each firm in a monopolistically competitive industry produces a somewhat different version of the same product. The objective of product differentiation is market segmentation. By producing a product that is perceived to be different from those produced by every other firm in the industry, firms in monopolistically competitive markets are able to carve out their own market niche. In doing so, each firm faces a downward-sloping demand curve for its product. Within a relatively narrow range of prices, each firm exercises a degree of market power by exploiting brand-name identification and customer loyalty.

There is, however, a limit to the ability of firms in a monopolistically competitive industry to exercise market power by exploiting customer loyalty. Since all firms produce fundamentally the same type of product, the demand for each firm's product is more price elastic because of the existence of many close substitutes. By contrast, there are not close substitutes for the output of a monopolist. Moreover, as more firms enter the market, the number of close substitutes increases, which not only reduces each firm's market share but also increases the price elasticity of demand for each firm's product.

The short-run analysis of the profit-maximizing, monopolistically competitive firm is similar to that of the monopolist, but that is where the similarity ends. Relatively easy entry into and exit from the industry guarantees that in the long run monopolistically competitive firms will earn zero economic profit. To see this, consider, again, the short-run monopolistically competitive equilibrium condition in Figure 9.1.

The opportunity to obtain positive economic profits attracts new firms into the industry. Each firm offers for sale in the market a product that is somewhat different from those of its competitors, which results in increased market segmentation. As a result, the demand curve firm not only shifts to the left (because each firm has a smaller market share), but also becomes more price elastic (because of an increase in the number of close substitutes). Conversely, as firms exit the industry in the face of economic losses, the market share of each firm increases and the demand curve shifts to the right and becomes less price elastic (because fewer substitutes are available to the consumer). As in the case of perfect competition, this process will continue until each firm earns zero economic (normal) profit. This final, long-run monopolistically competitive equilibrium, is illustrated in Figure 9.3.

In the long run, the demand curve of the monopolistically competitive firm is tangent to the average total cost curve at the profit-maximizing output level Q^*. At this output level, total revenue ($P^* \times Q^*$) is just equal to total economic cost ($ATC^* \times Q^*$). This result is similar to the long-run equilibrium solution for the perfectly competitive industry, where $P^* = ATC^*$ at the profit-maximizing output level. Unlike the perfectly competitive firm, where $P^* = MR$, profit-maximizing, monopolistically competitive firms produce at an output level at which $P^* > MR$, which is the same as that for monopolies.

The long-run competitive equilibrium for a monopolistically competitive industry can also be demonstrated as follows. By definition, total profit is defined as

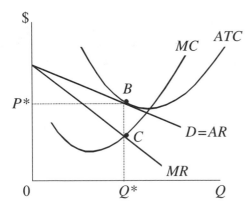

FIGURE 9.3 Long-run monopolistically competitive equilibrium and zero economic (normal) profit.

$$\pi = TR - TC = P^*Q^* - TC$$

Average profit is defined as

$$A\pi = \frac{\pi}{Q^*} = \frac{TR}{Q^*} - \frac{TC}{Q^*} = AR - ATC^*$$

$$= \frac{P^*Q^*}{Q^*} - ATC^*$$

Since $\pi = 0$, then $A\pi = 0$, then

$$P^* = ATC^*$$

This result is identical to the situation that arises in long-run perfectly competitive equilibrium.

The long-run monopolistically competitive equilibrium output level is to the left of the minimum point on its average total cost curve. Price equals average total cost, as in the case of long-run perfectly competitive equilibrium; however, price does not equal marginal revenue or marginal cost. Thus, output is lower and the price is higher than would be the case in a perfectly competitive industry. This result is similar to that found in the case of monopoly.

Problem 9.1. A typical firm in a monopolistically competitive industry faces the following demand and total cost equations for its product.

$$Q = 20 - \frac{P}{3}$$
$$TC = 100 - 5Q + Q^2$$

a. What is the firm's short-run, profit-maximizing price and output level?
b. What is the firm's economic profit?
c. Suppose that the existence of economic profit attracts new firms into the industry such that the new demand curve facing the typical firm in this

industry is $Q = 35/3 - P/3$. Assuming no change in the firm's total cost function, find the new profit-maximizing price and output level.
d. Is the firm earning an economic profit?
e. What, if anything, can you say about the relationship between the firm's demand and average cost curves? Is this result consistent with your answer to part c?

Solution

a. To maximize profit, the monopolistically competitive firm produces at the output level at which marginal cost equals marginal revenue. Price is determined along the demand curve. Solving the demand equation for price yields

$$P = 60 - 3Q$$

Substituting this result into the definition of total revenue yields

$$TR = PQ = (60 - 3Q)Q = 60Q - 3Q^2$$

Substituting this into the definition of total profit yields

$$\pi = TR - TC = 600Q - 3Q^2 - 100 + 5Q - Q^2 = -100 + 65Q - 4Q^2$$

Taking the first derivative of this expression with respect to Q and setting the resulting equation equal to zero yields

$$\frac{d\pi}{dQ} = 65 - 8Q = 0$$

The profit-maximizing output level is

$$Q^* = 8.125$$

Substituting this result into the demand equation results in

$$P^* = 60 - 3(8.125) = 35.625$$

b. The firm's economic profit is

$$\pi = -100 + 65(8.125) - 4(8.125)^2 = \$164.0625$$

These results are illustrated in the Figure 9.4.
c. The firm's new profit equation is

$$\pi = -100 + 40Q - 4Q^2$$

Taking the first derivative of this expression and setting the results equal to zero yields

$$\frac{d\pi}{dQ} = 40 - 8Q = 0$$

$$Q^* = 5$$

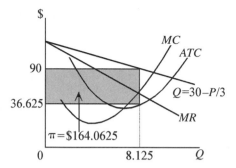

FIGURE 9.4 Diagrammatic solution
to problem 9.1 part b.

Substituting this result into the demand equation yields

$$P* = 35 - 3(35) = 20$$

d. The firm's economic profit is

$$\pi = -100 + 40(5) - 4(5)^2 = -100 + 200 - 100 = 0$$

This result is consistent with the profit-maximizing condition that marginal revenue must equal marginal cost, that is,

$$MR = MC$$

$$35 - 6Q = -5 + 2Q$$

$$Q* = 5$$

e. The firm's average total cost equation is

$$ATC = \frac{TC}{Q} = \frac{100}{Q} - 5 + Q$$

The slope of this function is

$$\frac{dATC}{dQ} = \frac{-100}{Q^2} + 1$$

In long-run monopolistically competitive equilibrium, the slope of the ATC curve and the slope of the demand function are the same, therefore

$$\frac{-100}{Q^2} + 1 = -3$$

$$Q* = 5$$

Moreover, at $Q* = 5$, $ATC = 20 = P*$. These results are consistent with the results in part c and are illustrated in Figure 9.5.

Problem 9.2. The demand equation for a product sold by a monopolistically competitive firm is

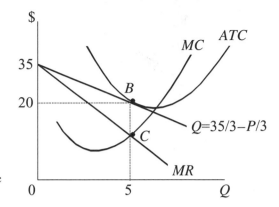

FIGURE 9.5 Diagrammatic solution to problem 9.1 part e.

$$Q_D = 25 - 0.5P$$

The total cost equation of the firm is

$$TC = 225 + 5Q + 0.25Q^2$$

a. Calculate the equilibrium price and quantity.
b. Is this firm in long-run or short-run equilibrium at the equilibrium price and quantity?
c. Diagram your answers to parts a and b.

Solution
a. The profit-maximizing condition is

$$MR = MC$$

The total revenue equation is

$$TR = PQ$$

Solving the demand equation for P yields

$$P = 50 - 2Q$$

Substituting this result into the total revenue equation yields

$$TR = (50 - 2Q)Q = 50Q - 2Q^2$$

The monopolist's marginal revenue equation is

$$MR = \frac{dTR}{dQ} = 50 - 4Q$$

The monopolist's marginal cost is

$$MC = \frac{dTC}{dQ} = 5 + 0.5Q$$

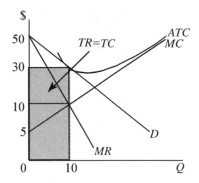

FIGURE 9.6 Diagrammatic solution to problem 9.2.

Substituting these results into the profit-maximizing condition yields the profit-maximizing output level:

$$50 - 4Q = 5 + 0.5Q$$

$$Q^* = 10$$

To determine the profit-maximizing (equilibrium) price, substitute this result into the demand equation:

$$P^* = 50 - 2(10) = \$30$$

b. Long-run competitive equilibrium is defined as the condition under which $\pi = 0$. In the short run, $\pi \neq 0$. The profit for the monopolistically competitive firm at $P^* = \$30$ and $Q^* = 10$ is

$$\pi = TR - TC = P^* Q^* - (225 + 5Q^* + 0.25Q^{*2})$$

$$= 30(10) - \left[225 + 5(10) + 0.25(10)^2\right] = 300 - 300 = \$0$$

We can conclude from this result that the monopolistically competitive firm is in long-run competitive equilibrium.

c. Figure 9.6 shows the answers to parts a and b.

Problem 9.3. The market equation for a product sold by a monopolistically competitive firm is

$$Q_D = 100 - 4P$$

The total cost equation of the firm is

$$TC = 500 + 10Q + 0.5Q^2$$

a. Calculate the equilibrium price and quantity.
b. Is this firm in long-run or short-run equilibrium at the equilibrium price and quantity?

Solution
a. The profit-maximizing condition is

$$MR = MC$$

The total revenue equation is

$$TR = PQ$$

Solving the demand equation for P yields

$$P = 25 - 0.25Q$$

Substituting this result into the total revenue equation yields

$$TR = (25 - 0.25Q)Q = 25Q - 0.25Q^2$$

The monopolist's marginal revenue equation is

$$MR = \frac{dTR}{dQ} = 25 - 0.5Q$$

The monopolist's marginal cost is

$$MC = \frac{dTC}{dQ} = 10 + Q$$

Substituting these results into the profit-maximizing condition yields the profit-maximizing output level:

$$25 - 0.5Q = 10 + Q$$

$$Q^* = 10$$

To determine the profit-maximizing (equilibrium) price, substitute this result into the demand equation:

$$P^* = 25 - 0.25(10) = \$22.5$$

b. Long-run competitive equilibrium is defined as the condition under which $\pi = 0$. In the short run, $\pi \neq 0$. The profit for the monopolistically competitive firm at $P^* = \$40$ and $Q^* = 20$ is

$$\pi = TR - TC = P^*Q^* - [500 + 10Q^* + 0.5Q^{*2}]$$
$$= 22.5(10) - [500 + 10(10) + 0.5(10^2)] = -\$425$$

Since $\pi < 0$, we can conclude from this result that the firm is in short-run monopolistically-competitive equilibrium.

ADVERTISING IN MONOPOLISTICALLY COMPETITIVE INDUSTRIES

The importance of advertising in monopolistic industries is readily apparent. Advertising highlights real or perceived product differences between and among products of firms in the industry. Advertising creates

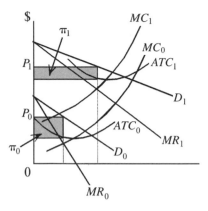

FIGURE 9.7 Successful advertising by a monopolistically competitive firm.

and reinforces customer loyalty, which gives the firm limited market power. The effect of successful advertising by firms in monopolistically competitive firms is illustrated in Figure 9.7.

In Figure 9.7 the demand curve for the firm's product shifts from D_0 to D_1 as a result of the firm's advertising expenditures. The costs of advertising are illustrated by the shifts in the marginal and average total cost curves from MC_0 to MC_1 and ATC_0 to ATC_1, respectively. These changes result in an increased unit sales and prices. In the situation depicted the Figure 9.7, the firm is clearly better off as a result of its presumably successful advertising campaign. This is seen by the increase in profits from π_0 to π_1.

How much advertising is optimal? In principle, the optimal level of advertising expenditure maximizes the firm's profits from having spent that money. As a general rule, the firm will maximize its profits from advertising by producing at an output level at which marginal production cost (including incremental advertising expenditures) equals marginal revenue.

EVALUATING MONOPOLISTIC COMPETITION

Many of the same criticisms of monopolistic market structures compared with perfect competition are applicable when one is evaluating monopolistic competition. As with monopoly, perfect competition may be considered to be a superior market structure because it results in greater output and lower prices than are obtained with monopolistic competition. This is because as with a monopolist, the demand curve confronting the monopolistically competitive firm is downward sloping. On the other hand, the demand curve confronting the monopolistically competitive firm is generally more elastic than that confronting the monopolist because of the existence of many close substitutes. Thus, the disparity between perfectly competitive and monopolistically competitive prices and output levels will generally be less than what is found for the pricing and output decisions of the monopolist.

Another criticism of monopolistic competition in comparison to perfect competition is that production in the long run does not occur at minimum per-unit cost. Thus, monopolistically competitive firms are inherently less efficient than firms in perfectly competitive industries. On the other hand, as with perfect competition, relatively easy entry into and exit from the industry ensures that in the long-run monopolistically competitive firms earn zero economic profits. Moreover, unlike monopolies, entry and exit are relatively easy, which encourage product innovation and development.

Can we say anything good about monopolistic competition? Indeed, we can. Although production is less efficient, the consumer is rewarded with the greater product variety. In fact, it might be argued that the cost to the consumer of increased product variety is somewhat higher per-unit cost of production. This, of course, differs significantly from monopolies from which, in the long run, the consumer receives nothing in return for sluggish product innovation, production inefficiency, and higher per-unit costs.

At a more general level, the model of monopolistic competition has been the subject of numerous criticisms since it was first proposed by Chamberlin and Robinson in the early 1930s. To begin with, the existence of monopolistically competitive industries has been difficult to identify empirically. Product differentiation in industries comprising a large number of firms has been found to be minimal, which implies that the demand curves facing individual firms in the industry are approximately perfectly elastic (horizontal). Thus, the model of perfect competition has been found to provide a reasonably accurate approximation of the behavior of firms in monopolistically competitive industries.

It has also been found that industries characterized by products with strong brand-name recognition typically consist of a few large firms that dominate total industry output. As we will see in Chapter 10, these industries are best classified as oligopolistic. Finally, as with perfect competition, monopolistic competition assumes that the pricing and output decisions of one firm in the industry are unrelated to the pricing and output decisions of its competitors. This assumption has been found to be unrealistic, since a change in product price by one firm, say a local gasoline station, will prompt price changes by neighboring firms. Interdependency of pricing and output decisions of firms is characteristic of oligopolistic market structures.

CHAPTER REVIEW

Monopolistic competition is an example of an imperfect competition. Firms in such industries exercise a degree of market power, albeit less than that exercised by a monopoly. As in the cases of perfect competition and monopoly, profit-maximizing monopolistically competitive and oligopolistic firms will produce at an output level at which $MR = MC$.

The characteristics of a monopolistically competitive industry are a large number of sellers acting independently, differentiated products, partial (and limited) control over product price, and relatively easy entry into and exit from the industry.

Product differentiation refers to real or perceived differences in goods or services produced by different firms in the same industry. Product differentiation permits market segmentation, which enables individual firms to set their own prices within limits. As in the case of a monopoly, each firm in a monopolistically competitive industry faces a downward-sloping demand curve, which implies that $P > MR$.

The short-run profit-maximizing condition for a monopolistically competitive firm is $P > MR = MC$. As in the case of perfect competition, the firm earns economic profit when $P > ATC$, which will attract new firms into the industry. As new firms enter the industry, existing firms lose market share. This is illustrated graphically by a shift to the left of each firm's demand curve. If $P < ATC$, the firm earns an economic loss, which will cause firms to exit the industry, resulting in an increase in market share and a shift to the right of the demand curve.

In the long run, the firm earns no economic profit because $P = ATC$. The demand curve for the firm's product is just tangent to the firm's average total cost curve. The long-run competitive equilibrium in monopolistically competitive industries is $P = ATC > MR = MC$. As in the case of monopoly, since $MC < ATC$, per-unit cost is not minimized; that is, monopolistically competitive firms produce inefficiently in the long run.

Advertising is an important element of monopolistic competition because it reinforces customer loyalty by highlighting real or perceived product differences between and among products of firms in the industry. The optimal level of advertising expenditures maximizes the firm's profits; profit maximization occurs when the firm is produced at an output level at which marginal cost (which includes incremental advertising expenditures) equals marginal revenue.

When compared with the model of perfect competition, in many respects monopolistic competition is considered to be an inferior market structure. As in the case of monopoly, the demand curve confronting a monopolistically competitive firm is downward sloping. Thus, monopolistic competition results in lower output levels and higher prices than are characteristic of perfect competition. Moreover, monopolistically competitive firms do not produce at minimum per-unit cost. On the other hand, although production is not as efficient as in perfect competition, the consumer is rewarded with the greater product variety. As in the case of perfect competition, relatively easy entry and exit encourage product innovation and development. In the long run, monopolistically competitive firms earn only a normal rate of return.

The model of monopolistic competition itself has been subjected to numerous criticisms. First, it has been empirically difficult to identify monopolistically competitive industries. Product differentiation in industries comprising a large number of firms has been found to be minimal. Industries characterized by strong brand-name recognition typically consist of a few large firms. Such industries are best described as oligopolistic. Finally, the assumption that the pricing and output decisions of one firm are unrelated to the pricing and output decisions of its competitors is unrealistic.

KEY TERMS AND CONCEPTS

Monopolistic competition   The market structure in which there are many buyers and sellers of a differentiated good or service and it is relatively easy to enter and leave the industry.

P > MR = MC   The selling price is greater than marginal revenue, which is equal to marginal cost, is the first-order profit-maximizing condition for a firm facing a downward-sloping demand curve for its good or service.

Product differentiation   Exists when goods or services that are in fact somewhat different, or are so perceived by the consumer, nonetheless perform the same basic function.

CHAPTER QUESTIONS

9.1 Describe the similarities and differences between perfectly competitive and monopolistically competitive market structures.

9.2 In monopolistically competitive industries it is not important for each firm to supply products that are, in fact, different from those of competitors. It is important only that the public think that the products are different. Do you agree? Explain.

9.3 Monopolistically competitive firms are similar to monopolies in that they are able to earn economic profits in the long run. Do you agree with this statement? If not, then why not?

9.4 Monopolistically competitive firms are similar to monopolies in that they tend to charge a higher price and supply less product than firms in perfectly competitive industries. Do you agree? Explain.

9.5 In the long run, monopolistically competitive firms are inherently inefficient. Do you agree? Explain.

9.6 Explain the importance of advertising in monopolistically competitive industries. How does this compare with the importance of advertising in perfectly competitive industries?

9.7 In monopolistically competitive industries, what is the optimal level of advertising expenditure? Explain.

9.8 The demand for the product of a typical firm in a monopolistically competitive industry tends to be more price inelastic than the demand for the product of a monopolist. Do you agree? Explain.

9.9 In the long run, the selling price of a monopolistically competitive firm's product is equal to the minimum per-unit cost of production. Do you agree with this statement? If not, then why not?

9.10 If a typical firm in a monopolistically competitive industry earns an economic loss, should the firm shut down? Would your answer be different if the firm were perfectly competitive?

9.11 If some firms exit a monopolistically competitive industry, what will happen to the demand curve for the typical firm remaining in the industry?

9.12 Compared with perfect competition, how is monopolistic competition similar to monopoly? How different?

9.13 What are some of the criticisms of the model of monopolistic competition?

CHAPTER EXERCISES

9.1 Glamdring Enterprises produces a line of fine cutlery. The demand equation for the firm's top-of-the-line cutlery set, Orcrist, is

$$Q = 10 - 0.2P$$

Glamdring's total cost equation is

$$TC = 50 - 4Q + 2Q^2$$

a. Give the firm's short-run profit-maximizing price and output level. Verify that Glamdring is earning a positive economic profit. What is the relationship between price and average total cost?

b. Suppose that the existence of economic profits calculated in part a attracts new firms into the industry. As a result, the demand curve facing Glamdring becomes $Q = 4.38 - 0.095P$. Assuming no change in the firm's total cost function, give the new profit-maximizing price and output level.

c. Is this firm in long-run monopolistically competitive equilibrium?

d. What, if anything, can you say about the relation between the firm's demand and average cost curves? Is this result consistent with your answer to part c?

9.2 Suppose that a firm in a monopolistically competitive industry faces the following demand equation for its product:

$$Q = 9 - 0.1P$$

The firm's total cost equation is

$$TC = 75 - Q + 3Q^2$$

a. Give the firm's short-run profit-maximizing price and output.
b. Verify that the firm is earning a positive economic profit. What is the relationship between price and average total cost?
c. Suppose that the existence of positive economic profits attracts new firms into the industry. As a result, the new demand curve facing the firm is

$$Q = 3.891 - 0.04545P$$

Is this firm in long-run monopolistically competitive equilibrium?
d. What is the relationship between selling price and average total cost? Is this consistent with your answer to part c?

9.3 Suppose that in Exercise 9.2 the demand curve for the firm's product had been

$$Q = 3 - 0.04P$$

As before, the firm's total cost equation is

$$TC = 75 - Q + 3Q^2$$

a. Give the firm's short-run profit-maximizing price and output.
b. Verify that the firm is earning a negative economic profit. What is the relation between price and average total cost?
c. Suppose that the existence of negative economic profits causes some firms to exit the industry. As before, the demand curve facing the firm becomes

$$Q = 3.891 - 0.04545P$$

What is the relation between selling price and average total cost? Is this consistent with your answer to part b?

SELECTED READINGS

Chamberlin, E. *The Theory of Monopolistic Competition*. Cambridge, MA: Harvard University Press, 1933.

Demsetz, H. "The Welfare and Empirical Implications of Monopolistic Competition." *Economic Journal*, September (1964), pp. 623–641.

———. "Do Competition and Monopolistic Competition Differ?" *Journal of Political Economy*, January–February (1968), pp. 146–168.

Friedman, M. *Capitalism and Freedom*. Chicago: University of Chicago Press, 1981.

Galbraith, J. K. *Economics and the Public Purpose*. Boston: Houghton Mifflin, 1973.

Henderson, J. M. and R. E. Quandt. *Microeconomic Theory: A Mathematical Approach*, 3rd ed. New York: McGraw-Hill, 1980.

Hope, S. *Applied Microeconomics*. New York: John Wiley & Sons, 1999.

Robinson, J. *The Economics of Imperfect Competition*. London: Macmillan, 1933.

Silberberg, E. *The Structure of Economics: A Mathematical Analysis*, 2nd ed. New York: McGraw-Hill, 1990.

Stigler, G. J. *The Organization of Industry*. Homewood, IL: Richard D. Irwin, 1968.

Telser, L. G. "Monopolistic Competition: Any Impact Yet?" *Journal of Political Economy*, March–April (1968), pp. 312–315.

10

MARKET STRUCTURE:
DUOPOLY AND OLIGOPOLY

Despite its shortcomings, the analysis of monopolistically competitive industries provides valuable insights into the operations of markets in general. We will next examine the cases of duopoly and oligopoly. An oligopoly is an industry comprising "a few" firms. What constitutes "a few" in this context, however, is somewhat debatable. A duopoly, which is a special case of oligopoly, is an industry comprising two firms.

The distinguishing feature of oligopolistic or duopolistic market structures, especially compared with perfect competition or monopoly, is not simply a matter of the number of firms in the industry. Rather, it is the degree to which the output, pricing, and other decisions of one firm affect, and are affected by, similar decisions made by other firms in the industry. What is important is the interdependence of the managerial decisions among the various firms in the industry.

The interdependence of firm behavior in duopolistic or oligopolistic industries contrasts with market structures encountered in earlier chapters. There was previously no need to consider the strategic behavior of rival firms, either because the output of each firm was very small relative to industry output (perfect competition) or because the firm had no competitors (monopoly) or because of some combination of the two (monopolistic competition). In the United States, where collusion between and among firms is illegal, oligopolistic behavior may be modeled analytically as a noncooperative game in which the actions of one firm to increase market share will, unless countered, result in a reduction of the market share of other firms in the industry. Thus, action will be followed by reaction. This interdependence is the essence of an analysis of duopolistic or oligopolistic market structures.

CHARACTERISTICS OF DUOPOLY AND OLIGOPOLY

There are a number of approaches to the analysis of duopolistic and oligopolistic markets. Each of the models we discuss is developed for the duopolistic market but can easily be generalized to the case of oligopolies. Before examining these analytical approaches, we make some general statements about the basic characteristics of duopolies and oligopolies.

NUMBER AND SIZE DISTRIBUTION OF SELLERS

"Oligopoly" refers to the condition in which industry output is dominated by relatively few large firms. Although there is no precise definition attached to the word "few," two to eight firms controlling 75% or more of a market could be defined as an oligopoly. However an oligopolistic market structures is defined, its distinguishing characteristic is strategic interaction, which refers to the extent to which the pricing, output, and other decisions of one firm affect, and are affected by, the decisions of other firms.

The interdependence of firms in an industry is illustrated in Figure 10.1, which shows the demand curve faced by all firms in the industry, DD, and the demand curve faced by an individual firm, dd. The rationale behind the diagram is as follows. If all firms in the industry decide to lower their price, say from P_1 to P_2, then the quantity demanded by consumers will increase from Q_1 to Q_2.

Suppose, however, that a single firm in the industry decided to reduce price from P_1 to P_2 in the expectation that other firms would not respond in a similar manner. In this case, the firm could anticipate a substantial increase in its sales, say from Q_1 to Q_3. This implies that over this price range, the demand curve facing the individual firm is more price elastic than the

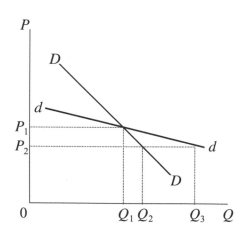

FIGURE 10.1   Oligopolistic industry and individual demand curves.

demand curve faced by the entire industry. The decision by one firm to unilaterally lower its selling price will result in a substantially larger market share, provided this price reduction is not matched by the firm's rivals—a dubious assumption, indeed.

NUMBER AND SIZE DISTRIBUTION OF BUYERS

The number and size distribution of buyers in duopolistic and oligopolistic is usually unspecified, but generally is assumed to involve a large number of buyers.

PRODUCT DIFFERENTIATION

Products sold by duopolies and oligopolies may be either homogeneous or differentiated. If the product is homogeneous, the industry is said to be purely duopolistic or purely oligopolistic. Examples of pure oligopolies are the steel and copper industries. Examples of industries producing differentiated products are the automobile and television industries.

CONDITIONS OF ENTRY AND EXIT

For either duopolies or oligopolies to persist in the long run, there must exist conditions that prevent the entrance of new firms into the industry. There is disagreement among economists over just what these conditions are. Bain (1956) has argued that these conditions should be defined as any advantage that existing firms hold over potential competitors, while Stigler (1968) argues that these barriers to entry comprise any costs that must be paid by potential competitors that are not borne by existing firms in the industry. Many of the barriers to entry erected by oligopolists are the same as those used by monopolists (see Chapter 8). Oligopolist also can control the industry supply of a product and enhance its market power through the control of distribution outlets, such as by persuading retail chains to carry only its product. Persuasion may take the form of selective discounts, long-term supply contracts, or gifts to management. Devices such as product warranties also serve as an effective barrier to entry. New car warranties, for example, typically require the exclusive use of authorized parts and service. Such warranties limit the ability of potential competitors from offering better or less-expensive products.

Definition: A duopoly is an industry comprising two firms producing homogeneous or differentiated products; it is difficult to enter or leave the industry.

Definition: A oligopoly is an industry comprising a few firms producing homogeneous or differentiated products; it is difficult to enter or leave the industry.

MEASURING INDUSTRIAL CONCENTRATION

It was demonstrated in Chapter 8 that perfect competition results in an efficient allocation of resources. Perfect competition results in the production of goods and services that consumers want at least cost. As we move further away from the assumptions underlying the paradigm of perfect competition, with monopoly being the extreme case, firms acquire increasing levels of market power, which usually results in prices that are higher and output levels that are lower than socially optimal levels.

Oligopolies are characterized by a "few" firms dominating the output of an industry. In many respects, an oligopolistic industry is like art—you know it when you see it. But is it possible to measure the extent to which production is attributable to a select number of firms? Is it possible to gauge the degree of industrial concentration? To illustrate the concerns associated with industrial concentration, it is useful to review the historical development of antitrust legislation in the United States, where the federal government has attempted to remedy the socially nonoptimal outcomes of imperfect competition either by enacting regulations to encourage competition and limit market power, or by regulating industries to encourage socially desirable outcomes.

In 1887 Congress created the Interstate Commerce Commission to correct abuses in the railroad industry, and in 1890 it passed the landmark Sherman Antitrust Act, which asserted that monopolies and restraints of trade were illegal. Unfortunately, the Sherman Act was deficient in that its provisions were subject to alternative interpretations. Although the Sherman Act banned monopolies, and certain kinds of monopolistic behavior were illegal, it was unclear what constituted a restraint of trade.

Not surprisingly, actions brought by the U.S. Department of Justice against firms believed to be in violation of the Sherman Act ended up in the courts. Two of the most significant court challenges to prosecution under the Sherman Act involved Standard Oil and American Tobacco. While the U.S. Supreme Court in 1911 found both companies in violation of provisions of the Sherman Act, the Court also made it clear that not every action that seemed to restrain trade was illegal. The Justices ruled that market structure alone was not a sufficient reason for prosecution under the Sherman Act, indicating that only "unreasonable" actions to restrain trade violated the terms of the law. As a result of this "rule of reason," between 1911 and 1920 actions by the Justice Department against Eastman Kodak, International Harvester, United Shoe Machinery, and United States Steel were dismissed. Federal courts ruled that although each of these companies controlled an overwhelming share of its respective market, there was no evidence that these companies engaged in "unreasonable conduct."

In an effort to strengthen the Sherman Act and clarify the *rule of reason*, in 1914 Congress passed the Clayton Act, which made illegal certain specific practices. In general, the Clayton Act limited mergers that lessened competition or tended to create monopolies. In that same year, the Federal Trade Commission was created to investigate "the organization, business conduct, practices, and management of companies" engaged in interstate commerce. Although the Clayton Act clarified many of the provisions of the Sherman Act, the focus remained on the "rule of reason." This changed in 1945, when the Aluminum Corporation of America (Alcoa) was prosecuted for violating the Sherman Act by monopolizing the raw aluminum market.

In a landmark case, *United States* versus *Aluminum Company of America*, the Court ruled that while Alcoa engaged in "normal, prudent, but not predatory business practices" it was the structure of the market *per se* that constituted restraint of trade. On the basis of the *per se rule*, the Court ordered the dissolution of Alcoa. The following year, other court cases resulted in an extension of the Clayton Act that made illegal both tacit and explicit acts of *collusion*. In its extreme form, collusion results in pricing and output results that reflect monopolistic behavior. The implications of collusive behavior by firms in an industry will be discussed at greater length later in this chapter.

In the years to follow, Congress enacted several additional pieces of legislation to deal with the problems associated with monopolistic behavior and restraint of trade. In 1950, for example, the Celler–Kefauver Act, gave the Justice Department the power to monitor and enforce the provisions of the Clayton Act. Nevertheless, there remained considerable uncertainty about what constituted an unacceptable merger. In response, the Justice Department promulgated guidelines for identifying mergers that were deemed to be unacceptable. These guidelines were initially based on the notion of a *concentration ratio*. It was determined, for example, that if the four largest firms in an industry controlled 75% or more of a market, any firm with a 15% market share attempting to acquire another firm in the industry would be challenged under the terms of the Clayton Act.

CONCENTRATION RATIO

The *concentration ratio* compares the dollar value of total shipments in an industry accounted for by a given number of firms in an industry. The U.S. Census Bureau, for example, calculates concentration ratios for the 4, 8, 20, and 50 largest companies, which are grouped according to a standardized industrial classification.[1] (See later: Table 10.1.)

---

[1] In 1997 the U.S. Census Bureau replaced the U.S. Standard Industrial Classification (SIC) system with the North American Industry Classification System (NAICS). NAICS industries are identified with a 6-digit code, which accommodates a larger number of sectors and provides more flexibility in designating subsectors. The new system also provides for greater detail for the three NAICS countries (the United States, Canada, and Mexico). The international NAICS agreement fixes only the first five digits of the code. Thus, the sixth digit in any given item in the U.S. code may differ from that of the Canadian of Mexican code. The SIC system had a 4-digit code.

TABLE 10.1   Concentration Ratios and Herfindahl–Hirschman Indices in Manufacturing, 1997

NAICS	Industry	Number of companies	Value of shipments ($ millions)	Largest 4 companies	Largest 8 companies[a]	HHI for largest 50 companies[a]
312221	Cigarettes	9	29,253	98.9	(D)	(D)
331411	Primary copper	9	6,128	94.5	(D)	2,392.2
327213	Glass containers	11	4,198	91.1	98.0	2,959.9
312120	Breweries	494	18,203	89.7	93.4	(D)
311230	Breakfast cereals	48	6,556	86.7	94.7	2,772.7
336411	Aircraft	172	57,893	84.8	96.0	(D)
336111	Automobiles	173	95,366	79.5	96.3	2,349.7
325611	Soap and detergents	738	17,773	65.6	77.9	1,618.6
325110	Petrochemicals	42	19,468	59.8	83.3	1,187.0
331312	Primary aluminum	13	6,225	59.2	81.7	1,230.6
334413	Semiconductors	993	78,479	52.5	64.0	1,080.1
334111	Electronic computers	531	66,302	45.4	68.5	727.9
337111	Iron and steel	191	56,994	32.7	52.7	445.3
324110	Petroleum refineries	122	158,668	28.5	48.6	422.1
322121	Paper mills	121	42,966	37.6	59.2	541.7
325412	Pharmaceuticals	707	66,735	35.6	50.1	462.4
323117	Book printing	690	5,517	31.9	45.1	363.7
332510	Hardware	906	11,061	17.4	27.7	154.6
321113	Sawmills	4,024	24,632	16.8	23.2	112.3

[a] (D), data omitted because of possible disclosure; data are included in higher level totals.
Source: U.S. Census Bureau, 1997 Economic Census.

Definition: Concentration ratios measure the percentage of the total industry revenue or market share that is accounted for by the largest firms in an industry.

Although the concentration ratios in Table 10.1 will provide useful insights into the degree of industrial concentration, it is important not to read too much into the statistics. To begin with, standard industrial classifications are based on the similarity of production processes but ignore substitutability across products, such as glass versus plastic containers. U.S. Census data describe domestically produced goods and do not include import competing products. Table 10.1 indicates, for example, that the eight largest U.S. makers of motor vehicles and bodies account for 91% of industry output. By omitting data from foreign competitors, especially from Japanese automobile manufacturers, this statistic clearly overstates the actual market share of U.S. automakers.

Another weakness of concentration ratios is that they are not sensitive to differences within categories. The concentration ratio, for example, makes no distinction between industry A, in which the top four companies have 24% of the market, and industry B, in which the largest firm has 90%

of the market, while the next three companies account for an additional 6%. In both industries the concentration ratio for the largest four companies is 96%.

HERFINDAHL–HIRSCHMAN INDEX

In 1982 and 1984, guidelines of the U.S. Department Justice for identifying unacceptable mergers were modified with the development of the *Herfindahl–Hirschman Index* (HHI). The HHI is calculated as

$$\text{HHI} = \sum_{i=1 \to n} S_i^2 \tag{10.1}$$

where n is the number of companies in the industry and S_i is the ith company's market share expressed in percentage points. The Herfindahl–Hirschman Index ranges in value from zero to 10,000. According to the modified guidelines, the Justice Department views any industry with an HHI of 1,000 or less as unconcentrated. Mergers in unconcentrated industries will go unchallenged. If the index is between 1,000 and 1,800, a proposed merger will be challenged by the Justice Department if, as a result of the merger, the index rises by more than 100 points. Finally, if the HHI is greater than 1,800, proposed mergers will be challenged if the index increases by more than 50 points. Table 10.1 summarizes concentration ratios for the largest four and eight companies and the Herfindahl–Hirschman Index for the 19 industries listed.

Definition: The Herfindahl–Hirschman Index is a measure of the size distribution of firms in an industry that considers the market share of all firms and gives a disproportionately large weight to larger firms.

The HHI is superior to the concentration ratio in that it not only uses the market share information of all firms in the industry, but by squaring individual market shares, gives greater weight to larger firms. Thus the HHI for industry A in our earlier example is 2,304, while the HHI for the more concentrated industry B is 8,112. According to the Department of Justice guidelines, both markets are concentrated.

MODELS OF DUOPOLY AND OLIGOPOLY

As mentioned earlier, the distinctive characteristic of duopolies and oligopolies is the interdependence of firms. It is difficult to formulate models of duopoly and oligopoly because of the many ways in which firms deal with this interdependence. Thus, there is no general theory to explain this interdependence. The models presented next are based on specific assumptions regarding the nature of this interaction.

SWEEZY ("KINKED" DEMAND CURVE) MODEL

Although managers of oligopolistic firms are aware of the law of demand, they are also aware that their pricing and output decisions depend on the pricing and output decisions of their competitors. More specifically, such firms know that their pricing and output decisions will provoke pricing and output adjustments by their competitors. Another notable characteristic of oligopolistic industries is the relative infrequency of price changes. Paul Sweezy (1939) attempted to explain this price rigidity by suggesting that oligopolists face a "kinked" demand curve, as illustrated in Figure 10.2.

Definition: Price rigidity is characterized by the tendency of product prices to change infrequently in oligopolistic industries.

Definition: The "kinked" demand curve is a model of firm behavior that seeks to explain price rigidities in oligopolistic industries.

Figure 10.2 depicts the situation of a typical firm operating in an oligopolistic industry. The demand curve for the product of the firm really comprises two demand curves, D_1 and D_2. Unlike a monopoly or monopolistically competitive firm that has a degree of market power along the length of a single demand curve, the oligopolist faces a demand curve characterized by a "kink," illustrated in Figure 10.2 as the heavily darkened portions of demand curves D_1 and D_2.

Suppose initially that the price of the oligopoly's product is P^*. If the firm raises the price of its product above P^* and its competitors do not follow the price increase, it will lose some market share. The firm realizes this and is reluctant to sacrifice its market position to its competitors. On the other hand, if the firm attempts to capture market share by lowering price, the price decrease will be matched by its rivals, who are not willing to cede their market share. The firm whose experience is depicted in Figure

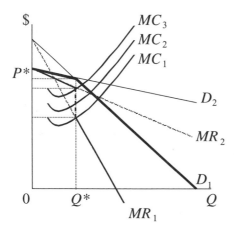

FIGURE 10.2 The "kinked" demand curve (Sweezy) model.

10.2 posts a small increase in sales as the inflation-adjusted purchasing power by consumers increases following an industry-wide decrease in prices, but the increase in sales is considerably less than the loss of sales from a comparable increase in prices. In other words, demand for the oligopolist's product is relatively more elastic for price increases than for price decreases.

Figure 10.2 also illustrates why prices in oligopolistic industries change more infrequently than in market structures characterized by more robust competition. Assume that the few firms in this oligopolistic industry are of comparable size. The marginal revenue curve associated with the "kinked" demand curve is illustrated by the heavy dashed line in Figure 10.2. Because of the "kink" at output level Q^*, the marginal revenue curve is discontinuous.

Figure 10.2 also assumes the usual U-shaped marginal cost curves. As always, the firm maximizes its profit at the output level at which $MR = MC$. This occurs at Q^*. Note, however, that because of the discontinuity of the marginal revenue curve, marginal cost can fluctuate from MC_1 to MC_3 without a corresponding change in the profit-maximizing price or output level. This result differs from cases considered thus for, in which an increase (decrease) in marginal cost will be matched by an increase (decrease) in price and a decrease (increase) in output. The importance of this result is that the adoption of more efficient production technologies, which results in lower marginal costs, may not result in significant reductions in the market price of the product. Conversely, an increase in marginal costs may not be immediately passed along to the consumer.

The "kinked" demand curve analysis has been criticized on two important points. While the analysis offers some explanation for price stability in oligopolistic industries, it offers no insights with respect to how prices are originally determined. Moreover, empirical research generally has failed to verify predictions of the model. Stigler (1947), for example, found that in oligopolistic industries price increases were just as likely to be matched as were price cuts.

Problem 10.1. Lightning Company is a firm in an oligopolistic industry. Lightning faces a "kinked" demand curve for its product, which is characterized by the following equations:

$$Q_1 = 82 - 8P$$

$$Q_2 = 44 - 3P$$

Suppose further that the firm's total cost equation is

$$TC = 8 + Q + 0.05Q^2$$

a. Give the price and output level for Lightning's product.
b. Based on your answer to part a, what is the firm's profit?

c. Determine the range of values within which Lightning's marginal cost may vary without affecting the prevailing price and output level.

d. Based on your answer to part a, what is the firm's marginal cost? Is it consistent with your answer to part c?

e. Suppose that Lightning's total cost equation changed to $TC = 12 + 5Q + 0.1Q^2$. Will the firm continue to operate at the same price and output level? If not, what price will the firm charge and how many units will it produce?

f. Based on your answer to part e, what is the Lightning's profit?

Solution

a. $82 - 8P = 44 - 3P$

$P^* = 7.6$

$Q^* = 82 - 8(7.6) = 21.2$

b. $\pi = TR - TC = 7.6(21.2) - 8 - 21.2 - 0.05(21.1)^2$

$\quad = 161.21 - 8 - 21.2 - 22.47 = 109.45$

c. $P = 10.25 - \dfrac{1}{8}Q_1$

$TR_1 = 10.25Q_1 - \dfrac{1}{8}Q_1^2$

$MR_1 = 10.25 - \dfrac{1}{4}Q_1 = 10.25 - \dfrac{1}{4}(21.2) = 4.95$

$P = 14.67 - \dfrac{1}{3}Q_2$

$TR_2 = 14.67Q_2 - \dfrac{1}{3}Q_2^2$

$MR_2 = 14.67 - \dfrac{2}{3}Q_2 = 14.67 - \dfrac{2}{3}(21.2) = 0.54$

Marginal cost may vary between 0.54 and 4.95 without affecting the prevailing (profit-maximizing) price and output level.

d. $MC = \dfrac{dTC}{dQ} = 1 + 0.1Q = 1 + 0.1(21.2) = 3.12$

This result is consistent with the answer to part c, since it lies between 0.54 and 4.95.

e. The firm will maximize its profit where $MC = MR$. Marginal cost is

$$MC = \frac{dTC}{dQ} = 5 + 0.2Q$$

The relevant portion of the marginal revenue curve is

$$MR_1 = 10.25 - \frac{1}{4}Q_1$$

Equating marginal cost with marginal revenue yields

$$5+0.2Q_1 = 10.25 - 0.25Q_1$$

$$Q^* = 11.67$$

$$P^* = 10.25 - \frac{1}{8}(11.67) = 8.79$$

In other words, Lightning will not continue to produce at the original price and output level. Note that at the new output level Lightning's marginal cost is

$$MC = 5 + 0.2(11.67) = 7.32$$

which falls outside the range of values calculated in part c.

f. $\pi = TR - TC = 8.79(11.67) - 12 - 5(11.67) - 0.1(11.67)^2$
$= 102.58 - 12 - 58.35 - 13.62 = 18.61$

Problem 10.2. Suppose that International Dynamo is a contractor in the oligopolistic aerospace industry. International Dynamo faces a "kinked" demand curve for its product, which is defined by the equations

$$Q_1 = 200 - 2P$$

$$Q_2 = 60 - 0.4P$$

Suppose further that International Dynamo has a constant marginal cost $MC = \$50$.

a. Give the price and output level for International Dynamo's product.
b. Based on your answer to part a, what is International Dynamo's profit?
c. Determine the range of values within which marginal cost may vary without affecting the prevailing market price and output level.
d. Diagram your answers to parts a, b, and c.

Solution

a. We determine the price and output level for International Dynamo's product at the "kink" of the "kinked" demand curve, which occurs at the intersection of the two demand curves. Solving the two demand curves simultaneously yields

$$200 - 2P = 60 - 0.4P$$

$$P^* = \$87.50$$

At $P^* = \$87.50$, International's total output is

$$Q^* = 200 - 2(87.50) = 200 - 175 = 25 \text{ units}$$

b. Since MC is constant, $MC = ATC$. By the definition of ATC

$$ATC = \frac{TC}{Q}$$

$$TC = ATC \times Q = MC \times Q = 50(25) = \$1,250$$

Total revenue is

$$TR = PQ = 87.50(25) = \$2,187.50$$

Total profit is, therefore,

$$\pi = TR - TC = 2,187.50 - 1,250 = \$937.50$$

c. To determine the range of values within which marginal cost may vary without affecting the price and output level, first derive the marginal revenue function for International Dynamo. Solving the demand equations for P yields

$$P = 100 - 0.5Q_1$$
$$P = 150 = 2.5Q_2$$

Total revenue is defined as

$$TR = PQ$$

Applying this definition to the demand functions yields

$$TR_1 = 100Q - 0.5Q^2$$
$$TR_2 = 150Q - 2.5Q^2$$

The corresponding marginal revenue functions are

$$MR_1 = \frac{dTR_1}{dQ} = 100 - Q$$

$$MR_2 = \frac{dTR_2}{dQ} = 150 - 5Q$$

These marginal revenue functions, however, are not relevant for all positive values of Q; MR_1 is relevant only for values $0 \le Q \le 25$; MR_2 is relevant for values $Q \ge 25$. For the firm to maximize profit, MC must equal MR. At $Q = 25$,

$$MR_1 = 100 - 25 = 75$$

$$MR_2 = 150 - 5(25) = 25$$

Thus, marginal cost may vary between 25 and 75 without affecting the prevailing (profit-maximizing) price and output level.
d. Consider Figure 10.3.

COURNOT MODEL

A classic treatment of duopolies (and oligopolies) was first formulated by the French economist Augustin Cournot in the early nineteenth century. (see Cournot, 1897). Cournot began by assuming that duopolies produce a homogeneous product. The critical assumption of the model deals with the firms' output decision-making process. In the Cournot model, each firm

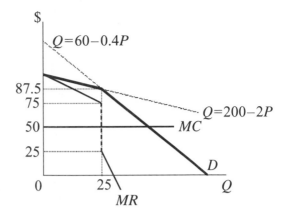

FIGURE 10.3 Diagrammatic solution to problem 10.2.

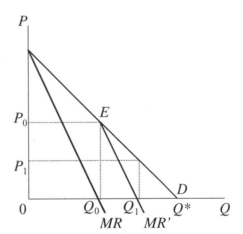

FIGURE 10.4 The Cournot model.

decides how much to produce and assumes that its rival will not alter its level of production in response. Additionally, total output of both firms equals the output for the industry. The process whereby equilibrium is established in the Cournot model may be illustrated by considering Figure 10.4.

Definition: The Cournot model is a theory of strategic interaction in which each firm decides how much to produce by assuming that its rivals will not alter their level of production in response.

To simplify matters, assume that the demand curve for the product is linear and that the marginal cost of production for each firm is zero. Cournot's example was that of a monopolist selling spring water produced at zero cost. Assume that firm A is the first to enter the industry. Thus, to maximize its profits ($MC = MR$), firm A will produce $Q_0 = 1/2Q^*$ units of output and charge a price of P_0. With a linear demand curve and zero marginal cost of production, Q_0 is half the output, where $P = 0$, or Q^*. The latter condition also assumes a perfectly competitive industry, where individual

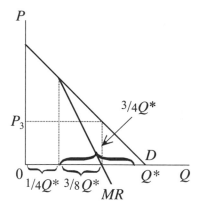

FIGURE 10.5 Determination of market shares in the Cournot model.

firms take the selling price as constant. Since $MC = 0$, maximizing profits is equivalent to maximizing total revenue, since $P = MR = MC = 0$.

Since the barriers to entry into this industry are low, the existence of economic profit attracts firm B into production. firm B also sells spring water that is produced at zero cost. In the Cournot model, firm B takes the output of firm A (Q_0) as given. Thus, from the point of view of firm B the vertical axis has been shifted to Q_0. The demand curve relevant to firm B is the line segment ED. To maximize its profits, firm B will produce such that marginal revenue is equal to zero marginal cost, which occurs at an output level of $Q_1 - Q_0$, which is $\frac{1}{2}Q_0$ or $\frac{1}{4}Q^*$. The combined output of the industry is now $\frac{1}{2}Q^* + \frac{1}{4}Q^* = \frac{3}{4}Q^*$.

This, of course, is not the end of the story. Since total industry output is now Q_1, the market price of the product must fall to P_1. If firm A attempts to maintain a price of P_0, it will lose part of its market share to firm B. In the Cournot model, firm A will assume that firm B will continue to produce $\frac{1}{4}Q^*$. firm A will subsequently adjust its output to maximize its profit based on the remaining $\frac{3}{4}Q^*$ of the market. This situation is depicted in Figure 10.5.

It can be seen in Figure 10.5 that firm A can maximize its profits by producing half of the remaining three-quarters of the market, or $\frac{3}{8}Q^*$. Combined industry output is now $\frac{1}{4}Q^* + \frac{3}{8}Q^* = \frac{5}{8}Q^*$. Firm B will, of course react by taking firm A's output of $\frac{3}{8}Q^*$ units as given and adjusting output to maximize its profit based on the remaining $\frac{5}{8}Q^*$ of the market. Extending the analysis, this means that firm B will increase its output to $\frac{5}{16}Q^*$. This process of action and reaction, which is summarized in Table 10.2, will come to an end when both firms have a market share equal to $\frac{1}{3}Q^*$. When firm A produces $\frac{1}{3}Q^*$, this leaves $\frac{2}{3}Q^*$ remaining for firm B to maximize its profits. Since half of the remaining market is $\frac{1}{3}Q^*$, the process now comes to a halt. The Cournot model can be generalized to include industries comprising of more than two firms. Cournot demonstrated that when the marginal cost of production is zero $(MC = 0)$, then total industry output is given as

TABLE 10.2   Firm and Industry Output

Iteration	Q^A	Q^B	$Q^A + Q^B$
1	$\frac{1}{2} Q*$	0	$\frac{1}{2} Q*$
2	$\frac{1}{2} Q*$	$\frac{1}{4} Q*$	$\frac{3}{4} Q*$
3	$\frac{3}{8} Q*$	$\frac{1}{4} Q*$	$\frac{5}{8} Q*$
4	$\frac{3}{8} Q*$	$\frac{5}{16} Q*$	$\frac{11}{16} Q*$
5	$\frac{11}{32} Q*$	$\frac{5}{16} Q*$	$\frac{21}{32} Q*$
$\vdots$	$\vdots$	$\vdots$	$\vdots$
i	$\frac{1}{3} Q*$	$\frac{1}{3} Q*$	$\frac{2}{3} Q*$

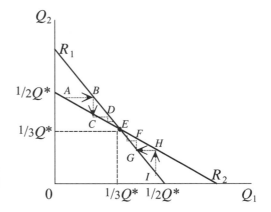

FIGURE 10.6 Reaction functions and the adjustment to a Cournot equilibrium in a duopolistic industry.

$$Q = \frac{nQ*}{n+1} \tag{10.2}$$

where n is the number of firms in the industry.

From Equation (10.2) it is clearly recognized that as $n \to \infty$, then $Q \to Q*$. This is the situation of perfect competition described earlier, where $MC = 0$ and $MR = P$. It may also be seen that the average market share of each firm in the industry is

$$Q_i = \frac{Q}{n} = \frac{Q*}{n+1} \tag{10.3}$$

where i represents the ith firm in the industry, Clearly, as the number of firms in the industry increases, the market share of each individual firm will decrease. Recall that for the two-firm case, the average market share of each was $1/(2 + 1)Q* = \frac{1}{3}Q*$, where $Q*$ is the total output of a perfectly competitive industry.

The adjustment process just described may be illustrated with the use of the reaction functions (to be discussed in greater detail shortly) illustrated in Figure 10.6, where R_1 is the reaction function for firm 1 and R_2 is the reaction function for firm 2. Equilibrium at output levels Q_1^* and Q_2^* will be stable provided the reaction curve of firm 1 is steeper than that of firm 2.

Starting at point I in Figure 10.6, the output of firm 1 is greater than its equilibrium level of output Q_1^* and the output of firm 2 is lower than its equilibrium level of output Q_2^*. Given firm 1's output, firm 2 will increase its output to point H, as was the case, for example, in the move from iteration 3 to iteration 4 in Table 10.2. Firm 1 will react by reducing its output to point G (iteration 5). Continuing in this manner will eventually lead to the equilibrium output level at point E. Analogous reasoning would produce the same result if the process were to begin at point A with firm 2 producing "too much" and firm 1 producing "too little."

The analysis thus far assumes that the demand functions that confront the two firms are identical and that production occurs at zero marginal cost ($MC = 0$). Of course, neither of these assumptions will necessarily be valid. To see this, consider the following, more general, description of the Cournot duopoly model. Since the sum of the output of two firms equals the industry output $Q = Q_1 + Q_2$, the market demand function may be written

$$P = f(Q_1 + Q_2) \tag{10.4}$$

where Q_1 and Q_2 represent the outputs of firm 1 and firm 2, respectively. The total revenue of each duopolist may be written as

$$TR_1 = Q_1 f(Q_1 + Q_2) \tag{10.5a}$$

$$TR_2 = Q_2 f(Q_1 + Q_2) \tag{10.5b}$$

The profits of the firm are

$$\pi_1 = Q_1 f(Q_1 + Q_2) - TC_1(Q_1) \tag{10.6}$$

$$\pi_2 = Q_2 f(Q_1 + Q_2) - TC_2(Q_2) \tag{10.7}$$

The basic behavioral assumption underlying the Cournot model is that each duopolist will maximize its profit without regard to the actions of its rival. In other words, the firm assumes that its rival's output is invariant with respect to its own output decision. Thus, each duopolist maximizes profit holding output of its rival constant. Taking the appropriate first partial derivative, setting the results equal to zero we find

$$\frac{\partial \pi_1}{\partial Q_1} = \frac{\partial TR}{\partial Q_1} - \frac{\partial TC_1}{\partial Q_1} = 0 \tag{10.8}$$

or

$$MR_1 = MC_1 \tag{10.9}$$

Similarly for firm 2,

$$\frac{\partial \pi_2}{\partial Q_2} = \frac{\partial TR}{\partial Q_2} - \frac{\partial TC_2}{\partial Q_2} = 0 \tag{10.10}$$

or

$$MR_2 = MC_2 \qquad (10.11)$$

The marginal revenue of the duopolists is not necessarily equal. Bearing in mind that $Q = Q_1 + Q_2$, then $\partial Q/\partial Q_1 = \partial Q/\partial Q_2 = 1$. The marginal revenues of the duopolists are, therefore

$$\frac{\partial TR_i}{\partial Q} = P + Q_i\left(\frac{dP}{dQ}\right), i = 1,2 \qquad (10.12)$$

Clearly, since $dP/dQ < 0$, the duopolist with the largest output will have the smallest marginal revenue. That is, an increase in the output by either firm will result in a reduction in price, while the marginal revenue of both firms will be affected. The second-order condition for profit maximization is

$$\frac{\partial^2 \pi i}{\partial Q_2^2} = \frac{\partial^2 TR_i}{\partial Q_i^2} - \frac{\partial^2 TC_i}{\partial Q_2^2} < 0, i = 1,2 \qquad (10.13)$$

or

$$\frac{\partial^2 TR_i}{\partial Q_i^2} < \frac{\partial^2 TC_i}{\partial Q_2^2}, i = 1,2 \qquad (10.14)$$

This result simply says that the firm's marginal revenue must be increasing less rapidly than marginal cost.

Thus, the Cournot solution asserts that each duopolist (oligopolist) will be in equilibrium if Q_1 and Q_2 maximize each firm's profits and each firm's output remains unchanged. This process may be described more fully by introducing an additional step before solving for the equilibrium output levels. Reaction functions express the output of each firm as a function of its rival's output. Solving the first-order conditions, these reaction functions may be written as

$$Q_1 = R_1(Q_2) \qquad (10.15)$$

$$Q_2 = R_2(Q_1) \qquad (10.16)$$

In the case of firm 1, the expression states that for any specified value of Q_2 the corresponding value of Q_1 maximizes π_1, and similarly for firm 2. The solution values are illustrated in Figure 10.7.

Problem 10.3. Suppose that an industry comprising two firms produces a homogeneous product. Consider the following demand and individual firm's cost function:

$$P = 200 - 2(Q_1 + Q_2)$$

$$TC_1 = 4Q_1$$

$$TC_2 = 4Q_2$$

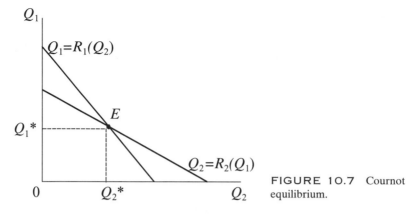

FIGURE 10.7   Cournot equilibrium.

a. Calculate each firm's reaction function.
b. Calculate the equilibrium price, profit-maximizing output levels, and profits for each firm. Assume that each duopolist maximizes its profit and that each firm's output decision is invariant with respect to the output decision of its rival.

Solution

a. The total revenue function for firm 1 is

$$TR_1 = 200Q_1 - 2Q_1^2 - 2Q_1Q_2$$

therefore, the total profit function for firm 1 is

$$\pi_1 = 200Q_1 - 2Q_1^2 - 2Q_1Q_2 - 4Q_1 = 196Q_1 - 2Q_1^2 - 2Q_1Q_2$$

For firm 1, taking the first partial derivative with respect to Q_1, setting equal to zero and solving yields

$$\frac{\partial \pi}{\partial Q_1} = 196 - 4Q_1 - 2Q_2 = 0$$

For firm 2,

$$TR_2 = 200Q_2 - 2Q_1Q_2 + 2Q_2^2$$

$$\pi_2 = 200Q_2 - 2Q_1Q_2 - 2Q_2^2 - 4Q_2 = 196Q_2 - 2Q_1Q_2 - 2Q_2^2$$

Taking the first partial derivative with respect to Q_1, setting equal to zero and solving

$$\frac{\partial \pi_2}{\partial Q_2} = 196 - 2Q_1 - 4Q_2 = 0$$

These first-order conditions yield the reactions functions

$$Q_1 = 49 - 0.5Q_2$$
$$Q_2 = 49 - 0.5Q_1$$

b. These reaction functions may be solved simultaneously to yield the equilibrium output levels

$$Q_1* = Q_2* = 32.67$$

Thus, total industry output is

$$Q_1* = Q_2* = 65.34$$

Substituting these results into the profit functions yields

$$\pi_1* = 196(32.67) - 2(32.67)^2 - 2(32.67)(32.67) = \$2,134$$

$$\pi_2* = 196(32.67) - 2(32.67)^2 - 2(32.67)(32.67) = \$2,134$$

The equilibrium price can be found by using the demand equation

$$P* = 200 - 2(32.67 + 32.67) = \$69.32$$

BERTRAND MODEL

Cournot's constant-output assumption was criticized by the nineteenth-century French mathematician and economist Joseph Bertrand in 1881.[2] Bertrand argued that each firm sets the price of its product to maximize profits and ignores the price charged by its rival. This assumption is analogous to that adopted by Cournot in that both duopolists expect their rival to keep price, rather than output, constant. The demand curve facing each firm in the Bertrand model is

$$Q_1 = f_1(P_1, P_2) \qquad (10.17a)$$
$$Q_2 = f_2(P_1, P_2) \qquad (10.17b)$$

Once again, for simplicity, assume that each firm has constant and equal marginal cost. The total revenue and profit functions for each firm are

$$TR_1 = P_1 f_1(P_1, P_2) \qquad (10.18a)$$
$$TR_2 = P_2 f_2(P_1, P_2) \qquad (10.18b)$$

and

$$\pi_1 = P_1 f_1(P_1, P_2) - TC_1(P_1, P_2) \qquad (10.19a)$$
$$\pi_2 = P_2 f_2(P_1, P_2) - TC_2(P_1, P_2) \qquad (10.19b)$$

In the Bertrand model, the objective of each firm in the industry is to maximize Equations (10.19) with respect to its selling price, and assuming

[2] *Journal des Savants*, September, 1883.

that the price charged by its rival remains unchanged. As Problem 10.4 illustrates, it is easily seen that both firms will charge the same price when $MC_1 = MC_2$.

Definition: The Bertrand model is a theory of strategic interaction in which a firm sets the price of its product to maximize profits and ignores the prices charged by its rivals. The Bertrand model is analogous to Cournot model in that the firms expect their rivals to keep prices, rather than output, constant.

Problem 10.4. Suppose that an industry comprising two firms producing a homogeneous product. Suppose that the demand functions for two profit-maximizing firms in a duopolistic industry are

$$Q_1 = 50 - 0.5P_1 + 0.25P_2$$

$$Q_2 = 50 - 0.5P_2 + 0.25P_1$$

Suppose, further, that the firms' total cost functions are

$$TC_1 = 4Q_1$$

$$TC_2 = 4Q_2$$

where P_1 and P_2 represent the prices charged by each firm producing Q_1 and Q_2 units of output.

a. What is the inverse demand equation for this product?
b. What are the equilibrium price, profit-maximizing output levels, and profits for each firm?

Solution

a. Total industry output is given as

$$Q = Q_1 + Q_2$$
$$= (50 - 0.5P_1 + 0.25P_2) + (50 - 0.5P_2 + 0.25P_1) = 100 - 0.25(P_1 + P_2)$$
$$0.25(P_1 + P_2) = 100 - (Q_1 + Q_2)$$

In equilibrium $P = P_1 = P_2$. Thus

$$0.25(2P) = 100 - (Q_1 + Q_2)$$
$$0.5P = 100 - (Q_1 + Q_2)$$
$$P = 200 - 2(Q_1 + Q_2)$$

which is the demand equation in Problem 10.3.

b. The total revenue function for firm 1 is

$$TR_1 = P_1 Q_1 = P_1(50 - 0.5P_1 + 0.25P_2) = 50P_1 - 0.5P_1^2 + 0.25P_1 P_2$$

Similarly, the total revenue function for firm 2 is

$$TR_2 = P_2 Q_2 = 50P_2 - 0.5P_2^2 + 0.25P_1 P_2$$

The total cost functions for the two firms are

$$TC_1 = 4Q_1 = 4(50 - 0.5P_1 + 0.25P_2) = 200 - 2P_1 + P_2$$
$$TC_2 = 4Q_2 = 200 - 2P_2 + P_1$$

The firms' profit functions are

$$\pi_1 = TR_1 - TC_1 = -200 + 52P_1 - 0.5P_1^2 - P_2 + 0.25P_1P_2$$
$$\pi_2 = TR_2 - TC_2 = -200 + 52P_2 - 0.5P_2^2 - P_1 + 0.25P_1P_2$$

For firm 1, taking the first partial derivative with respect to P_1 and setting the result equal to zero yields

$$\frac{\partial \pi_1}{\partial P_1} = 52 - P_1 + 0.25P_2 = 0$$

For firm 2,

$$\frac{\partial \pi_2}{\partial P_2} = 52 - P_2 + 0.25P_1 = 0$$

These first-order conditions yield the reaction functions

$$P_1 = 52 + 0.25P_2$$
$$P_2 = 52 + 0.25P_1$$

Solving the reaction functions for the equilibrium price yields

$$P_1^* = 52 + 0.25(52 + 0.25P_1) = \$69.33$$
$$P_2^* = 52 + 0.25(69.33) = \$69.33$$

The profit-maximizing output levels are

$$Q_1^* = 50 - 0.5(69.33) + 0.25(69.33) = 32.67$$
$$Q_2^* = 50 - 0.5(69.33) + 0.25(69.33) = 32.67$$

Thus, total industry output is

$$Q_1^* + Q_2^* = 65.34$$

Finally, each firm's profits are

$$\pi_1^* = -200 + 52(69.33) - 0.5(69.33)^2 - 69.33 + 0.25(69.33)(69.33)$$
$$= \$2,134.17$$
$$\pi_2^* = -200 + 52(69.33) - 0.5(69.33)^2 - 69.33 + 0.25(69.33)(69.33)$$
$$= \$2,134.17$$

The reader should note from Problems 10.3 and 10.4 that for identical demand and cost functions, except for rounding the Cournot and Bertrand results, duopoly models are the same. The reader should verify that for firms producing a homogeneous product, the solution to the Bertrand model will be quite different from the solution to the Cournot model if the firms in the industry do not have identical marginal costs. To see this, suppose, initially, that each firm charges a price greater than MC_2. If $MC_1 > MC_2$, then firm 1 will be able to capture the entire market by charging a price that is only slightly below MC_1.

STACKELBERG MODEL

A variation on the Cournot model, the *Stackelberg model* posits two firms. Firm 2, which is referred to as the "Stackelberg leader," believes that firm 1 will behave as in the Cournot model by taking the output of firm 2 as constant. Firm 2 will then attempt to exploit the behavior of firm 1, called the "Stackelberg follower," by incorporating the known reaction of the follower into its production decisions. Depending on the total cost functions of the two firms, different solutions may emerge. But, if the two firms have identical total cost equations, the first mover will capture a larger share of the market and earn greater profits. This is illustrated in Problem 10.5.

Definition: The Stackelberg model is a theory of strategic interaction in which one firm, the "Stackelberg leader," believes that its rival, the "Stackelberg follower," will not alter its level of output. The production decisions of the Stackelberg leader will exploit the anticipated behavior of the Stackelberg follower.

Problem 10.5. Consider once again the situation described in Problems 10.3 and 10.4, where the demand equation for two profit-maximizing firms in a duopolistic industry is

$$P = 200 - 2(Q_1 + Q_2)$$

and the firm's total cost functions are

$$TC_1 = 4Q_1$$
$$TC_2 = 4Q_2$$

where Q_1 and Q_2 represent the output levels of firm 1 and firm 2, respectively. Assume that firm 2 is a Stackelberg leader and firm 1 is a Stackelberg follower. What are the equilibrium price, profit-maximizing output levels, and profits for each firm?

Solution. From the solution to the Cournot duopoly problem, the reaction function of firm 1 is

$$Q_1 = 49 - 0.5Q_2$$

The profit function of firm 2 is

$$\pi_2 = 196Q_2 - 2Q_2^2 - 2Q_1Q_2$$

Substituting firm 1's reaction function into firm 2's profit function yields

$$\pi_2 = 196Q_2 - 2Q_2^2 - 2Q_2(49 - 0.5Q_2) = 98_2 - Q_2^2$$

The first-order condition is

$$\frac{\partial \pi_2}{\partial Q_2} = 98 - 2Q_2 = 0$$

$$Q_2* = 49$$

Substituting into the reaction function, the output of firm 1 is

$$Q_1^* = 49 - 0.5(49) = 24.5$$

Thus, total industry output is

$$Q_1* + Q_2* = 73.5$$

The equilibrium price in this market is

$$P* = 200 - 2(49 + 24.5) = \$53$$

The profits of the two firms are

$$\pi_1* = 98(24.5) - (24.5)^2 = \$1,800.75$$

$$\pi_2* = 98(49) - (49)^2 = \$2,401$$

Compare these answers with the results obtained in Problems 10.3 and 10.4. Note that in the Stackelberg solution total industry output is higher ($73.5 > $65.34) and the product price is lower ($53 < $69.3) than in both the Cournot and Bertrand solutions. Moreover, in both the Cournot and Bertrand solutions both firms' profits were $2,134, which is less than the profit of the Stackelberg follower, but greater than the Stackelberg leader. Finally, in the Stackelberg solution firm 1's profit of $1,800.75 is three-fourths that of firm 2.

The duopoly models discussed have been criticized for the simplicity of their underlying assumptions. As E. H. Chamberlin (1933) noted: "When a move by one seller evidently forces the other to make a countermove, he is very stupidly refusing to look further than his nose if he proceeds on the assumption that it will not" (p. 46). Chamberlin was quick to realize that mutual interdependence would lead oligopolistic firms to explicitly or tacitly agree to charge monopoly prices and divide the profits. Chamberlin's contribution to the analysis of oligopolies was to recognize that the price and output of one firm will affect, and be affected by, the price and output decisions of other firms in the industry.

On the other hand, we can use game theory (discussed briefly in the next section and in more detail in Chapter 13), to illustrate the Cournot and Bertrand models as static games, in which in equilibrium the underlying assumptions are fulfilled. The Stackelberg model can be shown to be a dynamic game and, once again, the equilibrium assumptions are satisfied (see, e.g., Bierman and Fernandez, 1998, Chapters 2 and 6).

Definition: Mutual interdependence in pricing occurs when firms in an oligopolistic industry recognize that their pricing policies depend on the pricing policies of other firms in the industry.

COLLUSION

When duopolists or oligopolists recognize their mutual interdependence, they might agree to coordinate their output decisions to maximize the output of the entire industry. Collusion may take the form of explicit price-fixing agreements, through so-called price leadership, or by means of other practices that lessen competitive pressures. The exact nature of the collusive practices will depend on the particular characteristics of the industry. The implementation of such practices will, however, be constrained by antitrust regulation.

Definition: Collusion represents a formal agreement among firms in an oligopolistic industry to restrict competition to increase industry profits.

Definition: Price fixing is a form of collusion in which firms in an oligopolistic industry conspire to set product prices.

Definition: Price leadership is a form of price collusion in which a firm in an oligopolistic industry initiates a price change that is matched by other firms in the industry.

Perhaps the most well-known manifestation of collusive behavior is the *cartel*. A cartel is a formal agreement among firms in an oligopolistic industry to allocate market share and/or industry profits. The Organization of Petroleum Exporting Countries (OPEC) is probably the most famous of all cartels. In the mid-1970s, OPEC began to restrict the quantity of oil produced, which resulted in a dramatic increase in oil and gasoline prices. Many economists have attributed global recession and inflation to these output restrictions.

Definition: A cartel is an explicit agreement among firms in an oligopolistic industry to allocate market share and/or industry profits.

Many people believe that cartels are organized for the purpose of increasing product prices by restricting output, but in fact the opposite might occur. In the mid-1980s an international coffee cartel attempted to lower prices by increasing output! Why? The answer can be found in the price elasticity of demand, which was discussed in Chapter 4. If the demand for a product is price inelastic, as was the case of petroleum in the 1970s, producers will be able to increase total revenues by lowering output. On the other hand, if demand is price elastic, as was the case of coffee in the 1980s, producers should be able to earn higher revenues by increasing output and lowering prices. Of course, the actions by coffee producers received very little press coverage. After all, consumers rarely complain about lower prices.

When firms in an industry agree to coordinate their output decisions, the profit-maximizing behavior of the cartel is analytically identical to that of a multiplant monopolist in which the profit function is the difference between the total revenue and total costs functions of each firm.

Problem 10.6. Consider, again, the demand and cost equations given in Problem 10.5. Suppose that the two firms in the industry decide to jointly determine output levels for the purpose of maximizing industry profit. Determine the profit-maximizing levels of output, the equilibrium price, and total industry profit.

Solution. The industry profit function is given as

$$\pi = \pi_1 + \pi_2 = 196Q_1 + 196Q_2 - 2Q_1^2 - 2Q_2^2 - 4Q_1Q_2$$

Taking the first partial derivatives, setting the result equal to zero, and solving yields

$$\frac{\partial \pi}{\partial Q_1} = 196 - 4Q_2 - 4Q_1 = 0$$

$$\frac{\partial \pi}{\partial Q_2} = 195 - 4Q_1 - 4Q_2 = 0$$

The firms' reaction functions are

$$Q_1 = 49 - Q_2$$
$$Q_2 = 49 - Q_1$$

This system of linear equations yields the profit maximizing output levels for Q_1 and Q_2 of

$$Q_1^* = Q_2^* = 24.5$$

The product's price is given as

$$P^* = 200 - 2(24.5 + 24.5) = \$102$$

with industry profit given as \$4,802. In the example of the Cournot solution to Problem 10.3, on the other hand, total industry profit was \$4,268 (\$2,134 + \$2,134).

GAME THEORY

Today, *game theory* is perhaps the most important tool in the economist's analytical kit for studying *strategic behavior*. Strategic behavior is concerned with how individuals and groups make decisions when they recognize that their actions affect, and are affected by, the actions of other individuals or groups. In other words, the decision-making process is mutually interdependent.

Definition: Strategic behavior recognizes that decisions of competing individuals and groups are mutually interdependent.

In each of the models thus far discussed, strategic behavior was central to an understanding of how equilibrium prices and quantities were established in oligopolistic industries. We saw in the discussion of the "kinked" demand curve, for example, that the decision by one firm in an oligopolistic industry to lower its product price to capture increased market share is likely to be countered by lower prices from rivals. On the other hand, unless justified by a mutual increase in the marginal cost of production, a price increase by one firm is likely to go unchallenged by other firms in the industry. Similar considerations of move and countermove were also explicit recognized in the form of reaction functions in our discussions of the Cournot, Bertrand, and Stackelberg models.

Game theory represents an improvement over earlier models discussed in this chapter in that it attempts to analyze the strategic interaction of firms in any competitive environment. Although more exhaustive discussion of game theory will be deferred to Chapter 13, a brief introduction is presented here to highlight the potential usefulness of this methodology in the analysis of the interdependency of pricing decisions by firms in oligopolistic industries.

Definition: Game theory is the study of how rivals make decisions in situations involving strategic interaction (i.e., move and countermove) to achieve an optimal outcome.

What is a game? There are a number of elements that are common to all games. To begin with, all games have rules. These rules define the order of play, that is, the sequence of moves by each player. The moves of each player in a game are based on strategies. A *strategy* is a sort of game plan. It is a decision rule that the player will apply when decisions about the next move need to be made. Knowledge of that player's strategy allows us to predict what course of action that player will take when confronted with choices. The collection of strategies for each player is called a *strategy profile*. Strategy profiles are often depicted within curly braces {}. Each strategy profile defines the outcome of the game and the payoffs to each player.

Definition: A strategy is a decision rule that indicates what action a player will take when confronted with a decision.

Definition: A strategy profile represents the collection of strategies adopted by a player.

Definition: A payoff represents the gain or loss to each player in a game.

Each of these basic elements of games is illustrated in what is perhaps the best-known of all game theoretic scenarios—the *Prisoners' Dilemma*. The Prisoners' Dilemma is an example of a two-person, noncooperative, simultaneous-move, one-shot game in which both players have a strictly dominant strategy, that is, one that results in the largest payoff regardless of the strategies adopted by any other player. The Prisoners' Dilemma is an example of a noncooperative game in the sense that the players are unable or unwilling to collude to achieve an outcome that is optimal for both.

In the Prisoners' Dilemma the players are required to move simultaneously. Simultaneous-move games are sometimes referred to as *static games*. An example of a simultaneous-move game would be the children's game rock–paper–scissors. In this game, both players are required to recite in unison the words "rock, paper, scissors." When they say the word "scissors" both are required to simultaneously show a rock (fist), a paper (open hand), or a scissors (index and middle finger separated). The winner of the game depends on what each player shows. If one player shows rock and the other player shows scissors, then rock wins because rock breaks scissors. If one player shows rock and the other player shows paper, then paper wins because paper covers rock. If one player shows scissors and the other player shows paper, then scissors wins because scissors cut paper. Strictly speaking, it is not absolutely necessary that both players actually move at the same time. The important thing is that neither player knows what the other player plans to show until both have moved. It is only necessary that neither player be aware of the decision of the other player until after both have moved.

Finally, the Prisoners' Dilemma is an example of a one-shot game. In a one-shot game, both players have one, and only one, move. In fact, most games, such as chess or checkers, involve multiple moves in which the players "take turns" (i.e., move sequentially). *Sequential-move games* are sometimes referred to as *dynamic games*. Except for the first move, the move of each player will depend on the moves made by the other player.

Definition: In a simultaneous-move game neither player is aware of the decision of the other player until after a pair of moves has been made.

Definition: A strictly dominant strategy results in the largest payoff to a player regardless of the strategy adopted by any other player.

Definition: The Prisoners' Dilemma is a two-person, simultaneous-move, noncooperative, one-shot game in which each player adopts the strategy that yields the largest payoff, regardless of the strategy adopted by the other player.

Suspect *B*

		Do not confess	Confess
	Do not confess	(6 months in jail, 6 months in jail)	(10 years in jail, 0 years in jail)
Suspect *A*			
	Confess	(0 years in jail, 10 years in jail)	(5 years in jail, 5 years in jail)

Payoffs: (Suspect *A*, Suspect *B*)

FIGURE 10.8   Payoff matrix for the Prisoners' Dilemma.

To illustrate the Prisoners' Dilemma, consider the following situation, which is described in Schotter (1985) (see also Luce and Raiffa, 1957, Chapter 5). Two individuals are taken into custody by the police following the robbery of a store, but after of the booty has been disposed of. Although the police believe the suspects to be guilty, they do not have enough evidence to convict them. In an effort to extract a confession, the suspects are taken to separate rooms and interrogated. If neither individual confesses, the most that either one can be convicted of is loitering at the scene of the crime, which carries a penalty of 6 months in jail. On the other hand, if one confesses and turns state's evidence against the other, the person who talks will go free by a grant of immunity, while the other will receive 10 years in prison. Finally, if both suspects confess, both will be convicted, but because of a lack of evidence (the stolen items having been disposed of prior to their arrest) the penalty is 5 years on the lesser charge of breaking and entering. The decision problem and outcomes facing each suspect are illustrated in Figure 10.8.

The entries in the cells of the *payoff matrix* refer to the gain or loss to each player from each combination of strategies. The payoffs are often depicted in parentheses. The first entry in parentheses in each cell refers to the payoff to suspect *A*, while the second entry refers to the payoff to suspect *B*. We will adopt the convention that the first entry refers to the payoff to the player indicated on the left of the payoff matrix, while the second entry refers in each cell refers to the payoff to the player indicated at the top. The situation depicted in Figure 10.8 is sometimes referred to as a *normal-form game*.

Definition: A normal-form game summarizes the players, possible strategies, and payoffs from alternative strategies in a simultaneous-move game.

In the situation depicted in Figure 10.8, the worst outcome is reserved for the suspect who does not confess if the other suspect does confess. To see this, consider the lower left-hand cell of the payoff matrix, which represents the decision by suspect *A* to confess and the decision by suspect *B* not to confess. The result of the strategy profile *{Confess, Do not confess}* is that suspect *A* is set free, while suspect *B* goes to prison for 10 years. Since the payoff matrix is symmetric, the strategy profile *{Do not confess, Confess}* results in the opposite outcome.

It should be remembered that the Prisoners' Dilemma is a noncooperative game. Neither suspect has any idea what the other plans to do before making his or her own move. The key element is strategic uncertainty. Since both suspects are being held incommunicado, they are unable to cooperate. Under the circumstances, if both suspects are rational, the decision of each suspect (i.e., the move that will result in the largest payoff), will be to confess. Why? Consider the problem from suspect *A*'s perspective. If suspect *B* does not confess, the more advantageous response is to confess, since this will result in no prison time as opposed to 6 months by not confessing. On the other hand, if suspect *B* confesses, suspect *A* would be well advised to confess because this would result in 5 years in prison, compared with 10 years by not confessing. In other words, suspect *A*'s best strategy is to confess, regardless of the strategy adopted by suspect *B*. Since the payoff matrix is symmetric, the same thing is true for suspect *B*. In this case, both suspects' strictly dominant strategy is to confess. The strictly dominant strategy equilibrium for this game is *{Confess, Confess}*. In this case, both suspects will receive 5 years in prison.

The foregoing solution is called a *Nash equilibrium*, in honor of John Forbes Nash Jr. who, along with John Harsanyi and Reinhard Selten, received the 1994 Nobel Prize in economic science for pioneering work in game theory. A noncooperative game has a Nash equilibrium when neither player can improve the payoff by unilaterally changing strategies. Nash created quite a stir in the economics profession in 1950, when he first proposed his now famous solution to noncooperative games, which he called a "fixed-point equilibrium." The reason was that his result seemed to contradict Adam Smith's famous metaphor of the invisible hand, which asserts that the welfare of society as a whole is maximized when each individual pursues his or her own private interests. According to the situation depicted in Figure 10.8, it is clearly in the best interest of both suspects to adopt the joint strategy of not confessing. This would result in an optimal solution, at least for the suspects, of only 6 months in prison.

Definition: A Nash equilibrium occurs in a noncooperative game when each player adopts a strategy that is the best response to what is believed to be the strategy adopted by the other players. When a game is in Nash equilibrium, neither player can improve the payoff by unilaterally changing strategies.

The Prisoners' Dilemma provides some very important insights into the strategic behavior of oligopolists. To see this, consider the situation of a duopolistic industry. Suppose that firm *A* and firm *B* are confronted with the decision to charge a "high" price or a "low" price for their product.

In the case of the "kinked" demand curve model discussed earlier, for example, each firm recognizes that a unilateral change in price is likely to precipitate a response from the rival firm. More specifically, if firm A charges a "high" price, but firm B charges a "low" price, then firm B will gain market share at firm A's expense, and *vice versa*. On the other hand, if the two firms were to collude, they could act as a profit-maximizing monopolist and both would benefit. But collusion, at least in the United States, is illegal, so it may be possible to model the strategic behavior of the two firms as a game similar to the Prisoners' Dilemma (i.e., a two-person, noncooperative, simultaneous-move, one-shot game). To see this, suppose that the alternatives facing each firm in the present situation are as summarized in Figure 10.9. The numbers in each cell represent the expected profit that can be earned by each firm given any combination of a high price and a low price strategy.

Does either firm have a strictly dominant strategy in this scenario? To answer this question, consider the problem from the perspective of firm B. If firm A charges a "high" price, it will be in firm B's interest to charge a "low" price. Why? If firm B adopts a *high-price* strategy, it will earn a profit of $1,000,000 compared with a profit of $5,000,000 adopts a low-price strategy. On the other hand, if firm A charges a "low" price, then firm B will earn a profit of $100,000 if it charges a "high" price and $250,000 if it charges a "low" price. In this case, regardless of the strategy adopted by firm A, it will be in firm B's best interest to charge a "low" price. Thus, firm B's dominant strategy is to charge a "low" price. What about firm A? Since the entries in the payoff matrix are symmetric, the outcome will be identical. If firm B charges a "high" price, it will be in firm A's best interest to adopt a *low-price* strategy, since it will earn a profit of $5,000,000, compared with a profit of only $1,000,000 by adopting a high-price strategy. If firm B charges a "low" price, it will again be firm A's best interest to charge a "low" price and earn a profit of $250,000 as opposed to earning a profit of only $100,000 by charging a "high" price. Thus, firm A's dominant strategy is also to charge a "low" price. Thus, in this noncooperative game, where the pricing decision of one firm is independent of the pricing decision of the other firm, it pays for both firms to charge a "low" price, with each firm earning a profit of $250,000. In other words, the strictly dominant strategy equilibrium for this game is *{Low price, Low price}*.

The reader should note that the solution to the game depicted in Figure 10.9 is a Nash equilibrium because neither firm can improve its payoff by unilaterally switching to another strategy. On the other hand, if both firms were to cooperate and charge a "high" price, each firm could earn profits of $1,000,000. Note, however, that a *{High price, High price}* strategy profile is not a Nash equilibrium, since either player could improve its payoff by switching strategies. That is, firm A could earn profits of $5,000,000 by charg-

Firm _B_

	High price	Low price
High price	($1,000,000, $1,000,000)	($100,000, $5,000,000)
Low price	($5,000,000, $100,000)	($250,000, $250,000)

Firm _A_ (label at left of rows)

Payoffs: (Firm _A_, Firm _B_)

FIGURE 10.9   Game theory and interdependent pricing behavior.

ing "low" price, provided firm _B_ continues to charge a "high" price. Of course, if firm _A_ were to charge a "low" price, firm _B_ would respond by lowering its price as well.

Historically, such cartels have proven to be highly unstable. Even if both firms were legally permitted to collude, distrust of the other firm's motives and intentions might compel each to charge a lower price anyway. Whether the collusive arrangement is legal or illegal, the incentive for cartel members to cheat is strong. Economic history is replete with examples of cartels that have collapsed because of the promise of gain at the expense of other members of the cartel. For such cartel arrangements to be maintained, it must be possible to enforce the agreement by effectively penalizing cheaters. The conditions under which this is likely to occur will be discussed in Chapter 13.

Problem 10.7. Why do fast-food restaurants tend to cluster in the same immediate vicinity? Consider the following situation concerning the owners of two hamburger franchises, Burger Queen and Wally's. Route 795 was recently extended from Baconsville to Hashbrowntown. Both franchise owners currently operate profitable restaurants in Hashbrowntown, a small town of about 25,000 residents. The exit off Route 795 is 5 miles from Hashbrowntown. Both franchise owners are considering moving their restaurants from the center of town to a location near the exit ramp. Regardless of location, we will assume that there is only enough business for two fast-food franchises to operate profitably. The franchise owners calculate that by relocating they will continue to receive some in-town business, but will also gain customers who use the exit as a rest stop. The payoff matrix for either strategy in this game is illustrated in Figure 10.10. The first entry in each cell of the payoff matrix refers to the payoff to Wally's and the second entry refers to the payoff to Burger Queen.
a. Does either franchise owner have a strictly dominant strategy?
b. Is the solution to this game a Nash equilibrium?

Burger Queen

		Exit ramp	Hashbrowntown
Wally's	Exit ramp	($150,000, $150,000)	($1,000,000, $100,000)
	Hashbrowntown	($100,000, $1,000,000)	($250,000, $250,000)

Payoffs: (Wally's, Burger Queen)

FIGURE 10.10   Payoff matrix for problem 10.7.

Solution

a. Both franchise owners have a dominant strategy to relocate to the exit ramp. Consider the problem from Burger Queen's perspective. If Wally's relocates near the exit ramp, it will be in Burger Queen's best interest to relocate there as well, since the payoff of $150,000 is greater than the alternative of $100,000 by remaining in Hashbrowntown. If Wally's decides to remain in Hashbrowntown, then, once again, it will be in Burger Queen's best interest to relocate, since the payoff of $1,000,000 is greater than $250,000. Thus, Burger Queen's dominant strategy is to locate near the exit ramp. Since the entries in the payoff matrix are symmetrical, the same must be true for Wally's. Thus, the dominant-strategy equilibrium for this game is *{Exit ramp, Exit ramp}*.

b. Note that the optimal solution for both franchise owners is to agree to remain in Hashbrowntown, since the payoff to both fast-food restaurants will be greater. But, this would require cooperation between Burger Queen and Wally's. If collusive behavior is ruled out, the dominant-strategy equilibrium *{Exit ramp, exit Ramp}* is also a Nash equilibrium, since neither franchise can unilaterally improve its payoff by choosing a different strategy.

CHAPTER REVIEW

The characteristics of oligopoly are relatively few sellers, either standardized or differentiated products, price interdependence, and relatively difficult entry into and exit from the industry. A duopoly is an industry comprising two firms producing homogeneous or differentiated products in which entry and exit into and from the industry is difficult.

Two common measures for determining the degree of industrial concentration are the *concentration ratio* and the *Herfindahl–Hirschman Index*. Concentration ratios measure the percentage of total industry revenue or market share accounted for by the industry's largest firms. The Herfindahl–Hirschman Index is a measure of the size distribution of firms in an industry but assigns greater weight to larger firms.

Mutual interdependence in pricing decisions, which is characteristic of industries with high concentration ratios, makes it difficult to determine the optimal price for a firm's product. *Collusion* occurs when firms coordinate their output and pricing decisions to maximize the output of the entire industry. Collusion may take the form of explicit price-fixing agreements, through so-called price leadership, or by means of other practices that lessen competitive pressures. Perhaps the best-known example of collusive behavior is the *cartel*, which is a formal agreement among producers to allocate market share and/or industry profits.

Four popular models of firm behavior in oligopolistic industries are the *Sweezy ("kinked" demand curve) model*, the *Cournot model*, the *Bertrand model*, and the *Stackelberg model*. The Sweezy model, which provides insights into the pricing dynamics of oligopolistic firms, assumes that firms will follow a price decrease by other firms in the industry but will not follow a price increase. In the Cournot model, each firm decides how much to produce and assumes that its rival will not alter its level of production in response. The Bertrand model argues that each firm sets the price of its product to maximize profits and ignores the price charged by its rival. Finally, the Stackelberg model assumes that one firm will behave as in the Cournot model by taking the output of its rival as constant, but the rival will incorporate this behavior into its production decisions.

Game theory is perhaps the most important tool in the economist's analytical kit for analyzing *strategic behavior*. Strategic behavior is concerned with how individuals make decisions when they recognize that their actions affect, and are affected by, the actions of other individuals or groups. The Prisoners' Dilemma is an example of a two-person, noncooperative, simultaneous-move, one-shot game in which both players have a strictly dominant strategy (i.e., one that results in the largest payoff regardless of the strategy adopted by any other players). A Nash equilibrium occurs in a noncooperative game when each player adopts a strategy that is the best response to what is believed to be the strategy adopted by any other player. When a two-person game is in Nash equilibrium, neither player can improve the payoff by unilaterally changing strategies.

KEY TERMS AND CONCEPTS

Bertrand model   A theory of strategic interaction in which a firm sets the price of its product to maximize profits and ignores the prices charged by its rivals.

Cartel   An agreement among firms in an oligopolistic industry to allocate market share and/or industry profits.

Collusion   A formal agreement among firms in an oligopolistic industry to restrict competition to increase industry profits. Collusion may occur when firms in an oligopolistic industry recognize that their pricing policies are mutually interdependent. Collusion may take the form of explicit price-fixing agreements, so-called price leadership, or other practices that ameliorate competitive pressures.

Concentration ratios   One way to distinguish an oligopoly from other market structures is through the use of *concentration ratios*, which measure the percentage of the total industry revenue or market share that is accounted for by the largest firms in an industry.

Cournot model   The theory of strategic interaction according to which each firm decides how much to produce by assuming that its rivals will not alter their level of production in response.

Duopoly   An industry comprising two firms producing homogeneous or differentiated products; it is very difficult to enter the industry and to leave it.

Game theory   Game theory is the study of how rivals make decisions in situations involving strategic interaction (i.e., move and countermove) to achieve some optimal outcome. The best-known of game theoretic scenarios is the Prisoners' Dilemma, which is a two-person, noncooperative, simultaneous-move, one-shot game.

Herfindahl–Hirschman Index   A measure of the size distribution of firms in an industry that considers the market share of all firms and gives disproportionate weight to larger firms.

"Kinked" demand curve   A model of firm behavior that seeks to explain price rigidities in oligopolistic industries. The model postulates that a firm will not raise its price because the increase will not be matched by its competitors, which would result in a loss of market share. The firm realizes this and is reluctant to sacrifice its market position to its competitors. On the other side, a firm will not lower its price, since the reduction will be matched by its competitors who themselves are not willing to cede market share.

Mutual interdependence in pricing   Exists when firms in an oligopolistic industry recognize that their pricing policies are mutually interdependent. When mutual interdependence in pricing is recognized, firms might agree to coordinate their output decisions to maximize industry profits.

Nash equilibrium   Occurs in a noncooperative game when each player adopts a strategy that is the best response to what is believed to be the strategy adopted by any other player. When a two-person game is in Nash equilibrium, neither player can improve the payoff by unilaterally changing strategies.

Normal-form game   Summarizes the players, possible strategies, and payoffs from alternative strategies in a simultaneous-move game.

Oligopoly   An industry comprising a few firms producing homogeneous or differentiated products, it is very difficult to enter the industry and to leave it.

Payoff   The gain or loss to each player in a game.

Price fixing   A form of collusion in which firms in an oligopolistic industry conspire to set product prices. Price leadership is a form of price fixing.

Price leadership   A form of price collusion in which a firm in an oligopolistic industry initiates a price change that is matched by other firms in the industry.

Price rigidities   The result of the tendency of product prices to change infrequently in oligopolistic industries.

Prisoners' Dilemma   A two-person, simultaneous-move, noncooperative, one-shot game in which each player adopts the strategy that yields the largest payoff, regardless of the strategy adopted by the other player.

Product differentiation   Goods or services that are in fact somewhat different or are perceived to be so by the consumer but nonetheless perform the same basic function are said to exemplify product differentiation.

Reaction function   In the Cournot duopoly model, a firm's reaction function indicates a profit-maximizing firm's output level given the output level of its rival. In The Bertrand duopoly model, a firm's reaction function indicates a profit-maximizing firm's price given the price changed by its rival.

Simultaneous-move game   A game in which neither player is aware of the decision of the other player until after the moves have been made.

Stackelberg model   The theory of strategic interaction in which one firm, the "Stackelberg leader," believes that its rival, the "Stackelberg follower," will not alter its level of output. The production decisions of the Stackelberg leader will exploit the anticipated behavior of the Stackelberg follower.

Strategic behavior   Actions reflecting the recognition that the behavior of an individual or group affects, and is affected by the actions of other individuals or groups.

Strategy   A decision rule that indicates what action a player will take when confronted with the need to make a decision.

Strategy profile   The collection of strategies adopted by a player.

Strictly dominant strategy   A strategy that results in the largest payoff to a player regardless of the strategy adopted by other players.

CHAPTER QUESTIONS

10.1 In contrast to perfect and monopolistic competition, oligopolistic market structures are characterized by interdependence in pricing and output decisions. Explain.

10.2 Oligopolies are characterized by "a few" firms in the industry. What is meant by "a few firms," and when does "a few" become "too many"?

10.3 Product differentiation is an essential characteristic of oligopolistic market structures. Do you agree? Explain.

10.4 What is the concentration ratio? What are the weaknesses of concentration ratios as measures of oligopolistic market structures?

10.5 Explain why the Herfindahl–Hirschman Index is superior to the concentration ratio.

10.6 Bertrand criticized Cournot's duopoly model for its assumption of constant prices. Do you agree with this statement? If not, then why not?

10.7 What is a reaction function?

10.8 How does the Stackelberg duopoly model modify the Cournot duopoly model?

10.9 E. H. Chamberlin criticized the Cournot, Bertrand, and Stackelberg duopoly models for the naivete of their underlying assumptions. To what, specifically, was Chamberlin referring?

10.10 What is a cartel? In what way is an analysis of a cartel similar to an analysis of a monopoly?

10.11 The "kinked" demand curve model suffers from the same weakness as the Cournot, Bertrand, and Stackelberg models in that it fails to consider the interdependence of pricing and output decisions of rival firms in oligopolistic industries. Do you agree? Explain.

10.12 The "kinked" demand curve model has been criticized on two important points. What are these points?

10.13 In what way does the application of game theory as an explanation of interdependent behavior among firms in oligopolistic industries represent an improvement over earlier models?

10.14 What is a Nash equilibrium?

10.15 The Prisoners' Dilemma is an example of a one-shot, two-player, simultaneous-move, noncooperative game. If the players are allowed to cooperate, a Nash equilibrium is no longer possible. Do you agree with this statement? If not, then why not?

CHAPTER EXERCISES

10.1 Suppose that the demand function for an industry's output is $P = 55 - Q$. Suppose, further, that the industry comprises two firms with constant average total and marginal cost, $ATC = MC = 5$. Finally, assume that each firm in the industry believes that its rival will not alter its output when determining how much to produce.

    a. Give the equilibrium price, quantity, and profit of each firm in the industry. (*Hint*: Use the Cournot duopoly model to analyze the situation.)

b. Assuming that this is a perfectly competitive industry, give the price and output level.

c. Suppose that there are 10 firms in this industry. What is output of the industry? What is the output level of each firm?

d. Suppose that the industry is dominated by a single profit-maximizing firm. What is the firm's output? How much will the firm charge for its product? What is the firm's profit?

10.2 Consider the following market demand and cost equations for two firms in a duopolistic industry.

$$P = 100 - 5(Q_1 + Q_2)$$
$$TC_1 = 5Q_1$$
$$TC_2 = 5Q_2$$

a. Determine each firm's reaction function.

b. Give the equilibrium price and profit-maximizing output for each firm, and each firm's maximum profit.

10.3 Suppose that the inverse market demand equation for the homogeneous output of a duopolistic industry is

$$P = A - (Q_1 + Q_2)$$

and that the two firms' cost equations are

$$TC_1 = B$$
$$TC_2 = C$$

where A, B, and C are positive constants. What is the profit-maximizing level of output for each firm?

10.4 Suppose that firm 2 in Exercise 10.2 is a Stackelberg leader and that firm 1 is a Stackelberg follower. What is the profit-maximizing output level for each firm?

10.5 Suppose that the demand functions for the product of two profit-maximizing firms in a duopolistic industry are

$$Q_1 = 50 - 5P_1 + 2.5P_2$$
$$Q_2 = 20 - 2.5P_2 + 5P_1$$

Total cost functions for the two firms are

$$TC_1 = 25Q_1$$
$$TC_2 = 50Q_2$$

a. What are the reaction functions for each firm?

b. Give the equilibrium price, profit-maximizing output, and profits for each firm.

Cord

		750 cars a month	500 cars a month
Auburn	750 cars a month	($5,000,000, $5,000,000)	($3,000,000, $6,000,000)
	500 cars a month	($6,000,000, $3,000,000)	($4,000,000, $4,000,000)

Payoffs: (Auburn, Cord)

FIGURE E10.8   Payoff matrix for chapter exercise 10.8.

10.6 Suppose that an oligopolist is charging a price of $500 and is selling 200 units of output per day. If the oligopolist were to increase price above $500, quantity demanded would decline by 4 units for every $1 increase in price. On the other hand, if the oligopolist were to lower the price below $500, quantity demanded would increase by only 1 unit for every $1 decrease in price. If the marginal cost of producing the output is constant, within what range may marginal cost vary without causing the profit-maximizing oligopolist to change either the price of the product or the level of output?

10.7 Thunder Corporation is an oligopolistic firm that faces a "kinked" demand curve for its product. If Thunder charges more than the prevailing market price, the demand curve for its product may be described by the demand equation

$$Q_1 = 40 - 2P$$

On the other hand, if Thunder charges less than the prevailing market price, it faces the demand curve

$$Q_2 = 12 - 0.4P$$

a. What is the prevailing market price for Thunder's product?
b. At the prevailing market price, what is Thunder's total output?
c. What is Thunder's marginal revenue function?
d. Assuming that Thunder Corporation is a profit maximizer, at the prevailing market price what is the possible range of values for marginal cost?
e. Diagram your answers to parts a, b, and c.

10.8 In the country of Arcadia there are two equal-sized automobile manufacturers that share the domestic market: Auburn Motorcar Company and Cord Automobile Corporation. Each company can produce 500 or 750 midsized automobiles a month. The payoff matrix for either strategy in this game is illustrated in Figure E10.8. The first entry in each cell of the payoff matrix refers to the payoff to Auburn and the second entry refers to the payoff to Cord.

    a. Does either firm have a dominant strategy?

    b. What is the Nash equilibrium for this game?

SELECTED READINGS

Axelrod, R. *The Evolution of Cooperation*. New York: Basic Books, 1984.

Bain, J. S. *Barriers to New Competition*. Cambridge, MA: Harvard University Press, 1956.

Bierman, H. S., and L. Fernandez. *Game Theory with Economic Applications*. New York: Addison-Wesley, 1998.

Case, K. E., and R. C. Fair. *Principles of Microeconomics*, 5th ed. Upper Saddle River, NJ: Prentice Hall, 1999.

Chamberlin, E. H. *The Theory of Monopolistic Competition*. Cambridge, MA: Harvard University Press, 1933.

Cournot, A. *Researches into the Mathematical Principles of the Theory of Wealth*, translated by Nathaniel T. Bacon. New York: Macmillan, 1897. First published in French in 1838.

Henderson, J. M., and R. E. Quandt. *Microeconomic Theory: A Mathematical Approach*, 3rd ed. New York: McGraw-Hill, 1980.

Hope, S. *Applied Microeconomics*. New York: John Wiley & Sons, 1999.

Luce, D. R., and H. Raiffa. *Games and Decisions: Introduction and Critical Survey*. New York: John Wiley & Sons, 1957.

Nash, J. "Equilibrium Points in *n*-Person Games." *Proceedings of the National Academy of Sciences, USA*, 36 (1950), pp. 48–49.

———. "A Simple Three-Person Poker Game" (with Lloyd S. Shapley). *Annals of Mathematics Study*, 24 (1950).

———. "Non-cooperative Games." *Annals of Mathematics*, 51 (1951), pp. 286–295.

———. "Two-Person Cooperative Games." *Econometrica*, 21 (1953), pp. 405–421.

———. "A Comparison of Treatments of a Duopoly Situation" (with J. P. Mayberry and M. Shubik). *Econometrica*, 21 (1953), pp. 141–154.

Nasar, S. *A Beautiful Mind*. New York: Simon & Schuster, 1998.

Schotter, A. *Free Market Economics: A Critical Appraisal*. New York: St. Martin's Press, 1985.

———. *Microeconomics: A Modern Approach*. New York: Addison-Wesley, 1998.

Silberberg, E. *The Structure of Economics: A Mathematical Analysis*, 2nd ed. New York: McGraw-Hill, 1990.

———. "The Kinky Oligopoly Demand Curve and Rigid Prices." *Journal of Political Economy*, October (1947), pp. 432–449.

Stigler, G. J. *The Organization of Industry*. Homewood, IL: Richard D. Irwin, 1968.

Sweezy, P. "Demand Conditions under Oligopoly." *Journal of Political Economy*, August (1939), pp. 568–573.

Tucker, A. W. *Game Theory and Programming*. Stillwater: Department of Mathematics, Oklahoma Agricultural and Mechanical College, 1955.

Von Neumann, J., and O. Morgenstern. *Theory of Games and Economic Behavior*. New York: John Wiley & Sons, 1944.

11

PRICING PRACTICES

We have thus far discussed output and pricing decisions under some very simplistic assumptions. We have assumed, for example, that a firm is a profit maximizer, that it produces and sells a single good or service, that all production takes place in a single location, that the firm operates within a well-defined market structure, and that management has precise knowledge about the firm's production, revenue, and cost functions. In addition, we assumed that the firm sells its output at the same price to all consumers in all markets. These conditions, however, are rarely observed in reality. These in the next two chapters we apply the tools of economic analysis developed earlier to more specific real-world situations, including multiplant and multiproduct operations, differential pricing, and non-profit-maximizing behavior.

PRICE DISCRIMINATION

For firms with market power, price discrimination refers to the practice of tailoring a firm's pricing practices to fit specific situations for the purpose of extracting maximum profit. Price discrimination may involve charging different buyers different prices for the same product or charging the same consumer different prices for different quantities of the same product. Price discrimination may involve pricing practices that limit the consumers' ability to exercise discretion in the amounts or types of goods and services purchased. In whatever guise price discrimination is practiced, it is often viewed by the consumer, when the consumer understands what is going on, as somehow nefarious, or at the very least "unfair."

Definition: Price discrimination occurs when profit-maximizing firms charge different individuals or groups different prices for the same good or service.

The literature generally discusses three degrees of price discrimination. First-degree price discrimination, which involves charging each individual a different price for each unit of a given product, is potentially the most profitable of the three types of price discrimination. First-degree price discrimination is the least often observed because of very difficult informational requirements. Second-degree price discrimination differs from first-degree price discrimination in that the firm attempts to maximize profits by "packaging" its products, rather than selling each good or service one unit at a time. Finally, third-degree price discrimination occurs when firms charge different groups different prices for the same good or service. While not as profitable as first-degree and second-degree price discrimination, third-degree price discrimination is the most commonly observed type of differential pricing. A recurring theme in most, but not all, price discriminatory behavior is the attempt by the firm to extract all or some consumer surplus.

FIRST-DEGREE PRICE DISCRIMINATION

We have noted that price discrimination occurs when different groups are charged different prices for the same product subject to certain conditions. Theoretically, price discrimination could take place at any level of group aggregation. Price discrimination at its most disaggregated level occurs when each "group" consists a single individual. First-degree price discrimination occurs when firms charge each individual a different price for each unit purchased. The price charged for each unit purchased is based on the seller's knowledge of each individual's demand curve. Because it is virtually impossible to satisfy this informational requirement, first-degree price discrimination is extremely rare. Nevertheless, an analysis of first-degree price discrimination is important because it underscores the rationale underlying differential pricing.

Definition: First-degree price discrimination occurs when a seller charges each individual a different price for each unit purchased.

The purpose of first-degree price discrimination is to extract the total amount of *consumer surplus* from each individual customer. The concept of consumer surplus was introduced in Chapter 8. Consumer surplus represents the dollar value of benefits received from purchasing an amount of a good or service in excess of benefits actually paid for. In Figure 11.1, which illustrates an individual's demand (marginal benefit) curve for a particular product, the market price of the product is $3. At that price, the consumer

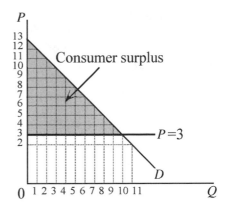

FIGURE 11.1   Consumer surplus.

purchases 10 units of the product. The total expenditure by the consumer, and therefore the total revenues to the firm, is $3 × 10 = $30. It is clear from Figure 11.1, however, that the individual would have been willing to pay much more for the 10 units purchased at $3. In fact, as we will see, only the tenth unit was worth $3 to the consumer. Each preceding unit was worth more than $3.

Suppose that we lived in a world of truth tellers. The consumer whose behavior is represented in Figure 11.1 enters a shop to purchase some amount of a particular product. The consumer is completely knowledgeable of his or her preferences and the value (to the consumer) of each additional unit. The process begins when the shopkeeper inquires how much the consumer is willing to pay for the first unit of the good. The consumer truthfully states a willingness to pay $12. A deal is struck, the sale is made, and the consumer expends $12, which becomes $12 in revenue to the shopkeeper. The process continues. The shopkeeper then inquires how much the consumer is willing to pay for the second unit. By the law of diminishing marginal utility, the consumer truthfully acknowledges a willingness to pay $11. Once again, a deal is struck, the sale is made, and the consumer expends an additional $11, which becomes an additional $11 in revenue to the shopkeeper.

This process continues until the tenth unit is purchased for $3. The consumer will not purchase an eleventh unit, since the amount paid ($3) will exceed the dollar value of the marginal benefits received ($2). By proceeding in this manner, the consumer has paid for each item purchased an amount equivalent to the marginal benefit received, or a total expenditure of $75. This amount is $45 greater than would have been paid in a conventional market transaction. In other words, the shopkeeper was able extract $45 in consumer surplus.

Definition: Consumer surplus is the value of benefits received per unit of output consumed minus the product's selling price.

Of course, this mind experiment is unrealistic in the extreme. Moreover, the amount of consumer surplus we calculated is only a rough approximation. With the price variations made arbitrarily small, the actual value of consumer surplus is the value of the shaded area in Figure 11.1. Our scenario, however, underscores the benefits to the firm being able to engage in first-degree price discrimination.

Alas, we do not live in a world of truth tellers. Even if we were completely cognizant of our individual utility functions, we would more than likely understate the true value of the next additional unit offered for sale. Moreover, even if the firm knew each consumer's demand equation, the realities of actual market transactions make it extremely unlikely that the firm would be able to extract the full amount of consumer surplus. Transactions are seldom, if ever, conducted in such a piecemeal fashion.

More formally, for discrete changes in sales (Q), consumer surplus may be approximated as

$$CS = \sum_{i=1 \to n} (P_i \times \Delta Q) - P_n Q_n \tag{11.1}$$

where Q_n is the quantity demanded by individual i at the market price, P_n. If we assume that the individual's demand function is linear, that is,

$$P_i = b_0 + b_1 Q_i \tag{11.2}$$

then consumer surplus is approximated as

$$CS = \sum_{i=1 \to n} (b_0 + b_1 Q_i) \Delta Q - P_n Q_n \tag{11.3}$$

Examination of Equation (11.3) suggests that the smaller ΔQ, the better the approximation of the shaded area in Figure 11.1. It can be easily demonstrated, and can be seen by inspection, that for a linear demand equation, as $\Delta Q \to 0$ the value of the shaded area in Figure 11.1 may be calculated as

$$CS = 0.5(b_0 - P_n) Q_n \tag{11.4}$$

In Chapter 2 we introduced the concept of the integral as accurately representing the area under a curve. The concept of the integral can be applied in this instance to calculate the value of consumer surplus. Defining the demand curve as $P = f(Q)$, consumer surplus may be defined as

$$CS = \int f(Q) dQ - P^* Q^*$$

where P_n and Q_n are the equilibrium price and quantity, respectively. Substituting Equation (11.2) into the integral equation yields

$$CS = \int_0^n (b_0 + b_1 Q_i) dQ - P_n Q_n$$
$$= [b_0 Q_i + 0.5 b_1 Q_i^2]_0^n - P_n Q_n$$
$$= [b_0 Q_n + 0.5 b_1 Q_n^2] - [b_0(0) + 0.5 b_1(0)^2] - P_n Q_n$$
$$= [b_0 Q_n + 0.5 b_1 Q_n^2] - P_n Q_n$$

If we assume that the demand equation is linear and that the firm is able to extract consumer surplus, how can we find the profit-maximizing price and output level? If the firm is able to extract consumer surplus, total revenue is

$$TR = PQ + 0.5(b_0 - P)Q \tag{11.5}$$

If we assume that total cost as an increasing function of output, then the total profit function is

$$\pi(Q) = TR(Q) - TC(Q) \tag{11.6}$$

Substituting Equations (11.4) and (11.5) into Equation (11.6) yields

$$\pi = (b_0 - b_1 Q)Q + 0.5[b_0 - (b_0 + b_1 Q)Q] - TC$$
$$= b_0 Q + 0.5 b_1 Q^2 - TC \tag{11.7}$$

The first- and second-order conditions for profit maximization are

$$\frac{d\pi}{dQ} = b_0 + b_1 Q - MC = 0 \tag{11.8a}$$

$$\frac{d\pi^2}{dQ^2} = \frac{b_1 - dMC}{dQ} < 0 \tag{11.8b}$$

Solving Equation (11.8a) for output yields

$$Q^* = \frac{MC - b_0}{b_1} \tag{11.9}$$

Substituting Equation (11.9) into Equation (11.2) yields

$$P^* = b_0 + b_1 \left(\frac{MC - b_0}{b_1} \right) = b_0 + (MC - b_0) = MC \tag{11.10}$$

Under the circumstances, the firm attempting to extract consumer surplus does not actually charge a price equal to marginal cost. Instead, the firm will calculate consumer surplus by substituting Equation (11.10) into Equation (11.4). It should be noted that Equation (11.10) looks similar to the one the profit-maximizing firm operating in a perfectly competitive industry. Of course, the crucial difference is that $P > MC$ for a profit-maximizing firm facing a downward-sloping demand curve for its product.

Problem 11.1. Assume that an individual's demand equation is

$$P_i = 20 - 2Q_i$$

Suppose that the market price of the product is $P_n = \$6$.
a. Approximate the value of this individual's consumer surplus for $\Delta Q = 1$.
b. What is value of consumer surplus as $\Delta Q \to 0$?

Solution
a. The equation for approximating the value of consumer surplus for discrete changes in Q when the demand function is linear is

$$CS = \sum_{i=1 \to n} (b_0 + b_1 Q_i) \Delta Q - P_n Q_n$$

For $P_n = \$6$ and $\Delta Q = 1$ this equation becomes

$$CS = \sum_{i=1 \to n} (20 - 2Q_i) - 42$$

For values of Q_i from 0 to 7 this becomes

$$\begin{aligned} CS &= [20 - 2(1)] + [20 - 2(2)] + [20 - 2(3)] + [20 - 2(4)] \\ &\quad + [20 - 2(5)] + [20 - 2(6)] + [20 - 2(7)] - 42 \\ &= 18 + 16 + 14 + 12 + 10 + 8 + 6 - 42 = \$42 \end{aligned}$$

The approximate value of consuming 7 units of this good is approximately \$84 dollars. If the consumer pays \$6 for 7 units of the good, then the individual's total expenditure is \$42. The approximate dollar value of benefits received, but not paid for, is \$42.

b. The value of the individual's consumer surplus as $\Delta Q \to 0$ is given by the expression

$$CS = 0.5(b_0 - P_n)Q_n$$

Substituting into this expression we obtain

$$CS = 0.5(20 - 6)7 = 0.5(14)7 = \$49$$

The actual value of consumer surplus is \$49, compared with the approximated value of \$42 calculated in part a.

SECOND-DEGREE PRICE DISCRIMINATION

Sometimes referred to as *volume discounting*, *second-degree price discrimination* differs from first-degree price discrimination in the manner in which the firm attempts to extract consumer surplus. In the case of second-

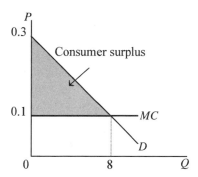

FIGURE 11.2   Block pricing.

degree price discrimination, sellers attempt to maximize profits by selling product in "blocks" or "bundles" rather than one unit at a time. There are two common types of second-degree price discrimination: *block pricing* and *commodity bundling*.

Definition: Second-degree price discrimination occurs when firms sell their product in "blocks" or "bundles" rather than one unit at a time.

Block Pricing

Block pricing, or selling a product in fixed quantities, is similar to first-degree price discrimination in that the seller is trying to maximize profits by extracting all or part of the buyer's consumer surplus. Eight frankfurter rolls in a package and a six-pack of beer are examples of block pricing.

The rationale behind block pricing is to charge a price for the package that approximates, but does not exceed, the total benefits obtained by the consumer. Suppose, for example, that the estimated demand equation of the average consumer for frankfurter rolls is given as $Q = 24 - 80P$. Solving this equation for P yields $P = 0.3 - 0.0125Q$. Suppose, further, that the marginal cost of producing a frankfurter roll is constant at \$0.10. This situation is illustrated in Figure 11.2.

With block pricing the firm will attempt to get the consumer to pay for the full value received for the eight frankfurter rolls by charging a single price for the package. If frankfurter rolls were sold for \$0.10 each, the total expenditure by the typical consumer would be \$0.80. The firm will add the value of consumer surplus to the package of eight frankfurter rolls, as follows:

$$\text{Block price} = TR = PQ + CS = PQ + 0.5(b_0 - P)Q$$
$$= 0.1(8) + 0.5(0.3 - 0.1)8 = \$1.60$$

The profit earned by the firm is

$$\pi = TR - TC = PQ + 0.5(b_0 - P)Q - (MC \times Q) = \$1.60 - \$0.80 = \$0.80$$

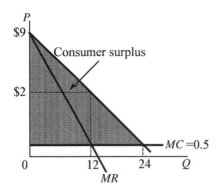

FIGURE 11.3 Amusement park pricing.

If this firm operated in a perfectly competitive industry and frankfurter rolls were sold individually, the selling price would be $0.10 per roll and the firm would break even. In other words, the firm would earn only normal profits, since $TR = TC$.

One interesting variation of block pricing is amusement park pricing. While it is not possible for the management of an amusement park to know the demand equation for each individual entering the park, and therefore first-degree price discrimination is out of the question, suppose that management had estimated the demand equation of the average park visitor. Figure 11.3 illustrates such a demand relationship.

In Figure 11.3 the marginal cost to the amusement park of providing a ride is assumed to be $0.50. If the amusement park is a profit maximizer, it will set the average price of a ride at $2 per ride (i.e., where $MR = MC$). At $2 per ride, the average park visitor will ride 12 times for an average total expenditure of $24 per park visitor. The total profit per visitor is

$$\pi = TR - TC = PQ - (MC \times Q) = 2(12) - 0.5(12) = \$18$$

At the profit-maximizing price, however, the average park visitor will enjoy a consumer surplus on the first 11 rides. The challenge confronting the managers of the amusement park is to extract this consumer surplus.

Rather than charging on a per-ride basis, many amusement parks charge a one-time admission fee, which allows park visitors to ride as often as they like. What admission fee should the amusement park charge? The park will calculate consumer surplus as if the price per ride is equal to the marginal cost to the amusement park of providing a single ride. Substituting Equation (11.22) into Equation (11.16), the amount of consumer surplus is

$$CS = 0.5(9 - 0.5)24 = \$102$$

The one-time admission fee charged by the amusement park should equal the marginal cost of providing a ride multiplied by the number of rides, plus the amount of consumer surplus. On average, the amusement park expects each guest to ride approximately 24 times. Thus, the amusement park should charge a one-time admission of $114 $[(MC \times Q) + CS =$ $0.5(24) + $102]$.

The main difference between the block pricing of frankfurter rolls and admission to an amusement park is that while frankfurter rolls are very much a private good, amusement park rides take on the characteristics of a *public good*. The distinction between private and public goods will be discussed in greater detail in Chapter 15. For now, it is enough to say that the ownership rights of private goods are well defined. The owner of the private property rights to a good or service is able to exclude all other individuals from consuming that particular product. Moreover, once the product has been consumed, as in this case frankfurter rolls, there is no more of the good available for anyone else to consume. In other words, private goods have the properties of *excludability* and *depletability*.

The situation is quite different with public goods. For one thing, use by one person of a public good such as commercial radio programming or television broadcasts does not decrease its availability to others. Another important characteristic of a public good is unlimited access by individuals who have not paid for the good. This is the characteristic of nonexcludability. While cable television broadcasts possess the characteristic of nondepletability, they are not public goods because nonpayers can be excluded from their use.

In the case of public goods, private markets often fail because consumers are unwilling to reveal their true preferences for the good or service, which makes it difficult, if not impossible, to correctly price the good. This phenomenon is often referred to as the *free-rider problem*. In the case of pure public goods, the government is often obliged to step in to provide the good or service. The most commonly cited examples of public goods are national defense and police and fire protection. The provision of public goods is financed through tax levies.

Block pricing by amusement parks is similar to block pricing by cable television companies in that the success of this pricing policy depends crucially on management's ability to deny access to nonpayers. This is usually accomplished by controlling access to the park. It is not unusual for large amusement parks, such as the Six Flags, Busch Gardens, or Disney World theme parks, to be isolated from densely populated areas. Access to the park is typically limited to one or a few points, and the perimeter of the park is characterized by high walls, fences, or *a* natural obstacle, such as a lake, constantly guarded by security personnel. It is much more difficult for older amusement parks, which are usually located in densely populated metropolitan areas, to engage in a one-time admission fee pricing policy because of the difficulty associated with controlling access to park grounds. In such cases, an alternative pricing policy to extract consumer surplus is necessary. One such technique is to sell identifying bracelets that enable park visitors to ride as often as they like for a limited period of time, say, two hours. This approach is often advertised as a POP (pay-one-price) plan. Thus, access to rides is not controlled at the park entrance, but at the entrance to individual rides.

Ironically, whatever technique is used to extract consumer surplus by amusement parks, it is good public relations. Park visitors like the convenience of not having to pay per ride. What is more, most park visitors believe that this pricing practice is a by-product of the management's concern for the comfort and convenience of guests, which is probably true. Finally, and most important, many amusement park visitors believe that they are getting their money's worth by being able to ride as many times as they like, which is, of course, true. But do they get more than their money's worth? This may also be true, but it should not be forgotten that the purpose of this type of pricing is to maximize amusement park profits by extracting as much consumer surplus as possible.

Problem 11.2. Seven Banners High Adventure has estimated the following demand equation for the average summer visitor to its theme park

$$Q = 27 - 3P$$

where Q represents the number or rides by each guest and P the price per ride in U.S. dollars. The total cost of providing a ride is characterized by the equation

$$TC = 1 + Q$$

Seven Banners is a profit maximizer considering two different pricing schemes: charging on a per-ride basis or charging a one-time admission fee and allowing park visitors to ride as often as they like.

a. How much should the park charge on a per-ride basis, and what is the total profit to Seven Banners per customer?
b. Suppose that Seven Banners decides to charge a one-time admission fee to extract the consumer surplus of the average park guest. What is the estimated average profit per park guest? How much should Seven Banners charge as a one-time admission fee? What is the amount of consumer surplus of the average park guest?

Solution
a. Solving the demand equation for P yields

$$P = 9 - \frac{Q}{3}$$

The per-customer total revenue equation is

$$TR = PQ = \left(9 - \frac{Q}{3}\right)Q = 9Q - \frac{Q^2}{3}$$

The per-customer total profit equation is

$$\pi = TR - TC = 9Q - \frac{Q^2}{3} - (1 + Q) = -1 + 8Q - \frac{Q^2}{3}$$

The first- and second-order conditions for profit maximization are $d\pi/dQ = 0$ and $d^2\pi/dQ^2 < 0$, respectively. The profit-maximizing output level is

$$\frac{d\pi}{dQ} = 8 - \frac{2Q}{3} = 0$$

$$Q^* = 12$$

To verify that this is a local maximum, we write the second derivative of the profit function

$$\frac{d^2\pi}{dQ^2} = \frac{-2}{3} < 0$$

which satisfies the second-order condition for a local maximum. The profit-maximizing price per ride is, therefore,

$$P^* = 9 - \frac{12}{3} = 5$$

The estimated average profit per Seven Banners guest with per-ride pricing is

$$\pi = -1 + 8(12) - \frac{(12)^2}{3} = \$47$$

b. If Seven Banners charges a one-time admission fee, it will attempt to extract the total amount of consumer surplus. Since the demand equation is linear, the estimated consumer surplus per average rider is given by the equation

$$CS = 0.5(b_0 - P)Q \qquad \boxed{1}$$

From Equation (11.7) the profit equation for Seven Banners is

$$\pi = TR - TC = (b_0 + b_1 Q)Q + 0.5[b_0 - (b_0 + b_1 Q)]Q - TC$$

$$= \left(9 - \frac{Q}{3}\right)Q + 0.5\left[9 - \left(9 - \frac{Q}{3}\right)\right]Q - (1 + Q)$$

$$= 9Q - \frac{Q^2}{3} + \frac{0.5Q^2}{3} - 1 - Q = 8Q - \frac{Q^2}{6} - 1$$

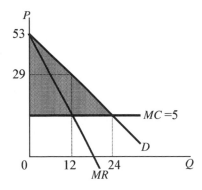

FIGURE 11.4 Two-part pricing.

The first-order condition for profit maximization is

$$\frac{d\pi}{dQ} = 8 - \frac{Q}{3} = 0$$

$$Q^* = 24$$

After substituting this value into the demand equation we get

$$P^* = 9 - \frac{24}{3} = 1 = MC$$

Total profit is, therefore,

$$\pi = 8Q - \frac{Q^2}{6} - 1 = 8(24) - \frac{(24)^2}{6} - 1 = 192 - 96 - 1 = \$95$$

The one-time admission fee should equal the total cost per guest of providing 24 rides plus the total amount of consumer surplus, that is,

$$\text{Admission fee} = TR = (MC \times Q) + CS = (MC \times Q) + 0.5(b_0 - MC)Q$$
$$= 1(24) + 0.5(9 - 1)24 = 24 + 96 = \$120$$

Thus the estimated consumer surplus of the average park guest is $96.

Two-Part Pricing

A variation of block pricing is *two-part pricing*. Two-part pricing is used to enhance a firm's profits by first charging a fixed fee for the right to purchase or use the good or service, then adding a per-unit charge. As in the case of block pricing, two-part pricing is often used by clubs to extract consumer surplus. To see how two-part pricing works, consider Figure 11.4, which illustrates the demand for country club membership.

In Figure 11.4 the per-visit demand to the country club is

$$Q = 26.5 - 0.5P$$

The club's total cost equation is

$$TC = 15 + 5Q$$

If the management of the country club were to charge its members a single price, the profit-maximizing price and output level would be 12 and $29, respectively. The country club's profit would be ($24 × 12) − ($5 × 12) = $288. At this price–quantity combination, each member of the club would receive consumer surplus (value received but not paid for) of 0.5[(53 − 29) × 12] = $144.

If, on the other hand, the country club were to use two-part pricing, it could extract the maximum amount of consumer surplus, which is the shaded area in Figure 11.4. In this case, the club would charge an initiation fee of 0.5[($53 − $5) × $24] = $576 and impose a per-visit charge of $5 to cover the cost of services. It is clear that the initiation fee is pure profit and is a substantial improvement over the profit of $288 earned by charging a single price per visit.

Commodity Bundling

Another form of second-degree price discrimination is *commodity bundling*. Commodity bundling involves combining two or more different products into a single package, which is sold at a single price. Like block pricing, commodity bundling is an attempt to enhance the firm's profits by extracting at least some consumer surplus.

A vacation package offered by a travel agent that includes airfare, hotel accommodations, meals, entertainment, ground transportation, and so on is an example of commodity bundling. Another example of commodity bundling, and one that has elicited considerable attention from the U.S. Department of Justice, is Microsoft's bundling of its Internet Explorer internet web browser with its Windows 98 software package. The federal government's interest stemmed not so much from Microsoft's ability to enhance profits by bundling its products, but from a near monopoly in the market for web browsers. Microsoft was able to ochieve because economies of scale.

To understand how commodity bundling enhances a company's profits, consider the case of a resort hotel that sells weekly vacation packages. Suppose that the package includes room, board, and entertainment. Let us further suppose that the marginal cost to the resort hotel of providing the package is $1,000.

Management has identified two groups of individuals that would be interested in the vacation package. Although the hotel is not able to iden-tify members of either group, it does know that each group values the com-ponents of the package differently. To keep the example simple, assume that

TABLE 11.1   Commodity bundling and vacation packages.

Group	Room and board	Entertainment
1	$2,500	$500
2	$1,800	$750

there are an equal number of members in each group. To further simplify the example, assume that total membership in each group is a single individual. Table 11.1 illustrates the maximum amount that each group will pay for the components of the package.

If the resort hotel could identify the members of each group, it might engage in first-degree price discrimination and charge members of the first group $3,000 and members of the second group $2,550 for the vacation package. Since the marginal cost of providing the service to each group is $1,000, the hotel's profit would be $3,550 per group. Since the hotel is not able to identify members of each group, what price should the hotel charge for the package?

Suppose the hotel decides to price each component of the package separately. If it charges $2,500 for room and board, it would sell only to the first group, and its total revenue would be $2,500. Members of the second group will not be interested because the price is above what the value they attach to room and board. If, on the other hand, the hotel were to charge $1,800 for room and board, it would sell to both groups for a total revenue of $3,600. Clearly, then, the hotel will charge $1,800.

The same scenario holds true for entertainment. If the hotel charges $750, then only members of the second group will purchase entertainment and the hotel will generate revenues of only $750. On the other hand, if the hotel charges $500, both groups will purchase entertainment and generate revenues of $1,000. Thus, whether the hotel charges per item or charges a package price of $1,800 + $500 = $2,300, the profit from each group will be $1,300. Since we have assumed that there is only one individual in each group, the hotel's total profit is $2,600.

Now, although a package price of $2,300 appears to be reasonable from the point of view of the profit-conscious hotel, the story does not end there. As it turns out, the hotel can do even better if it charges a package price of $1,800 + $750 = $2,550. The reason is simple. Management knows that the value of the package to the first group is $2,500 + $500 = $3,000. It also knows that the value to the second group is $1,800 + $750 = $2,550. By bundling room, board, and entertainment and selling the package for $2,550, the hotel will sell both components of the package to members of both groups. At a package price of $2,550, the hotel earns a profit of $1,550, instead of $1,300, from each group. Again, since we have assumed that there is only one person in each group, the hotel's total profit is now $3,100.

TABLE 11.2 Commodity bunding and new car options I.

Group	Power steering	CD stereo system
1	$1,700	$300
2	$1,600	$320
3	$1,500	$340

In the foregoing example, by bundling room, board, and entertainment and charging a single package price, the hotel has enhanced its profits by $250 per group member. The hotel has extracted the entire amount of consumer surplus from members of the second group and some consumer surplus from members of the first group.

Problem 11.3. A car dealership offers power steering and a compact disc stereo system as options in all new models. Suppose that the dealership sells to members of three different groups of new car buyers and that there are five individuals in each group. Table 11.2 illustrates how the members of each group value power steering and a compact disc stereo sound system.

Suppose that the per-unit cost of providing power steering and a CD stereo system is $1,200 and $250, respectively.
a. If the dealership sold each option separately, how much profit would it earn from each group member?
b. If the dealership cannot easily identify the members of each group, how should it price a package consisting of power steering and a CD stereo system? What will be the dealership's profit on each package sold?

Solution
a. If the dealership sells each item separately, it would change $1,500 for power steering, for a profit of $300 per sale. Given that there are five members in each group, the dealership has generated total profits of $4,500. By contrast, if the dealership sells power steering for $1,600, it will earn a profit of $400 per sale. But since only members of the second and third groups will purchase power steering, the dealership's total profit will only be $4,000.

Similarly, the dealership will sell compact disc stereo systems for $300, for a profit of $50 per sale. Again, since there are five members in each group, the dealership's total profit will be $750. By contrast, if the dealership sells the option for $320 it will earn a profit of $70 per sale. Since, however, only members of the first and second group will opt for the CD stereo system at this price, the dealership's total profit will be $700.
b. If the dealership sells power steering and a CD stereo system at a package price of $1,800, as suggested in the answer to part a, the total

TABLE 11.3   Commodity bundling and new car
options II.

Group	Power steering	CD stereo system
1	$2,000	$300
2	$1,800	$350
3	$1,500	$400

profit will be $4,700. However, if the dealership sells the package for
$1,840, it will appeal to members of all three groups. In this way, the
dealership will extract total consumer surplus from members of the third
group, and at least some consumer surplus from the remaining two
groups. The dealership's total profit will be $5,850.

Problem 11.4. Suppose that the members of each group in Problem 11.3
valued power steering and a compact disc stereo sound system as in Table
11.3.

The per-unit cost of providing power steering and a CD stereo system
remains $1,200 and $250, respectively. How much will the dealership now
change for power steering and a CD stereo system as a package? What will
be the dealership's profit on each package sold? What is the dealership's
total profit?

Solution. In Problem 11.3, we saw that the profit-maximizing price for the
package was equivalent to the sum of the prices the third group was willing
to pay for each option separately. If we were to follow that practice in this
case, the profit on each package sold would be $1,900 − $1,450 = $450, for
a total profit of $450 × 15 = $6,750. Suppose, however, that the dealership
charged $2,150 for the package, which is the value placed on the package
by the second group? The profit on each package sold would be $2,150 −
$1,450 = $700, for a total profit of $700 × 10 = $7,000. Finally, if the dealership charged $2,300 for both options, which is the value placed on the
package by the first group, the profit on each package would be $850, for a
total profit of $850 × 5 = $4,250. Clearly, under the conditions specified in
Table 11.3, the dealership will charge a package price of $2,150 and sell only
to the first two groups.

THIRD-DEGREE PRICE DISCRIMINATION

In some cases, it is possible for the firm to charge different groups different prices for its goods or services. It is a common practice, for example,
for theaters, restaurants, and amusement parks to offer senior citizen,
student, and youth discounts. This kind of pricing strategy, which is perceived as altruistic or community spirited, has considerable public relations

appeal. In reality, however, this *third-degree price discrimination* in fact results in increased company profits.

Definition: Third-degree price discrimination occurs when firms segment the market for a particular good or service into easily identifiable groups, then charge each group a different price.

For third-degree price discrimination to be effective, a number of conditions must be satisfied. First, the firm must be able to estimate each group's demand function. As we will see, the degree of price variation will depend of differences in each group's price elasticity of demand. In general, groups with higher price elasticities of demand will be charged a lower price.

A second condition that must be satisfied for a firm to engage in third-degree price discrimination is that members of each group must be easily identifiable by some distinguishable characteristic, such as age; or perhaps groups can be identified in terms of the time of the day in which the good or service, such as movie tickets, is purchased.

Finally, for third-degree price discrimination to be successful, it must not be possible for groups purchasing the good or service at a lower price to be able to resell that good or service to groups changed the higher price. If resales are possible, the firm would not be able to sell anything to the group paying the higher price because they would simply buy the good or service from the group eligible for the lower price.

The rationale behind third-degree price discrimination is straightforward. Different individuals or groups of individuals with different demand functions will have different marginal revenue functions. Since the marginal cost of producing the good is the same, regardless of which group purchases the good, the profit-maximizing condition must be $MC = MR_1 = MR_2 = \cdots = MR_n$, where n is the number of identifiable and separable groups. To see why this must be the case, suppose that $MR_1 > MC$. Clearly, in this case, it would pay for the firm to produce one more unit of the good or service and sell it to group 1, since the addition to total revenues would exceed the addition to total cost from producing the good. As more of the good or service is sold to group 1, marginal revenue will fall until $MR_1 = MC$ is established.

The mathematics of this third-degree price discrimination is fairly straightforward. Assume that a firm sells its product in two easily identifiable markets. The total output of the firm is, therefore,

$$Q = Q_1 + Q_2 \tag{11.11}$$

By the law of demand, the quantity sold in each market will vary inversely with the selling price. If the demand function of each group is known, the total revenue earned by the firm selling its product in each market will be

$$TR(Q) = TR_1(Q_1) + TR_2(Q_2) \tag{11.12}$$

where $TR_1 = P_1Q_1$ and $TR_2 = P_2Q_2$. The total cost of producing the good or service is a function of total output, or,

$$TC(Q) = TC(Q_1 + Q_2) \tag{11.13}$$

Note that the marginal cost of producing the good is the same for both markets. By the chain rule,

$$\frac{\partial TC(Q)}{\partial Q_1} = \left(\frac{dTC}{dQ}\right)\left(\frac{\partial Q}{\partial Q_1}\right) = \frac{\partial TC}{dQ} \tag{11.14}$$

since $\partial Q/\partial Q_1 = 1$. Likewise for Q_2,

$$\frac{\partial TC(Q)}{\partial Q_2} = \left(\frac{dTC}{dQ}\right)\left(\frac{\partial Q}{\partial Q_2}\right) = \frac{\partial TC}{dQ} \tag{11.15}$$

since $\partial Q/\partial Q_2 = 1$. Equations (11.14) and (11.15) simply affirm that the marginal cost of producing the good or service remains the same, regardless of the market in which it is sold.

Upon combining Equations (11.11) to (11.15), the firm's profit function may be written

$$\pi(Q_1, Q_2) = TR_1(Q_1) + TR_2(Q_2) - TC(Q_1 + Q_2) \tag{11.16}$$

Equation (11.16) indicates that profit is a function of both Q_1 and Q_2. The objective of the firm is to maximize profit with respect to both Q_1 and Q_2. Taking the first partial derivatives of the profit function with respect to Q_1 and Q_2, and setting the results equal to zero, we obtain

$$\frac{\partial \pi}{\partial Q_1} = \frac{\partial TR_1}{\partial Q_1} - \left(\frac{dTC}{dQ}\right)\left(\frac{\partial Q}{\partial Q_1}\right) = 0 \tag{11.17a}$$

$$\frac{\partial \pi}{\partial Q_2} = \frac{\partial TR_2}{\partial Q_2} - \left(\frac{dTC}{dQ}\right)\left(\frac{\partial Q}{\partial Q_2}\right) = 0 \tag{11.17b}$$

Solving Equations (11.17) simultaneously with respect to Q_1 and Q_2 yields the profit-maximizing unit sales in the two markets. Assuming that the second-order conditions are satisfied, the first-order conditions for profit maximization may be written as

$$MC = MR_1 = MR_2 \tag{11.18}$$

Finally, since $TR_1 = P_1Q_1$ and $TR_2 = P_2Q_2$, then

$$\begin{aligned} MR_1 &= P_1\left(\frac{dQ_1}{dQ_1}\right) + Q_1\left(\frac{dP_1}{dQ_1}\right) \\ &= P_1\left[1 + \left(\frac{dP_1}{dQ_1}\right)\left(\frac{Q_1}{P_1}\right)\right] = P_1\left(1 + \frac{1}{\varepsilon_1}\right) \end{aligned} \tag{11.19}$$

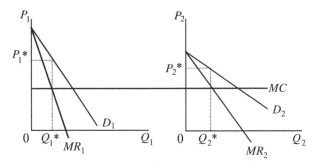

FIGURE 11.5   Third-degree price discrimination.

$$MR_2 = P_2\left(1 + \frac{1}{\varepsilon_2}\right) \tag{11.20}$$

where ε_1 and ε_2 are the price elasticities of demand in the two markets. By the profit-maximizing condition in Equations (11.17), it is easy to see that the firm will charge the same price in the two markets only if $\varepsilon_1 = \varepsilon_2$. When $\varepsilon_1 \neq \varepsilon_2$, the prices in the two markets will not be the same. In fact, when $\varepsilon_1 > \varepsilon_2$, the price charged in the first market will be greater than the price charged in the second market. Figure 11.5 illustrates this solution for linear demand curves in the two markets and constant marginal cost.

Problem 11.5. Red Company sells its product in two separable and identifiable markets. The company's total cost equation is

$$TC = 6 + 10Q$$

The demand equations for its product in the two markets are

$$Q_1 = 10 - (0.2)P_1$$
$$Q_2 = 10 - (0.2)P_2$$

where $Q = Q_1 + Q_2$.
a. Assuming that the second-order conditions are satisfied, calculate the profit-maximizing price and output level in each market.
b. Verify that the demand for Red Company's product is less elastic in the market with the higher price.
c. Give the firm's total profit at the profit-maximizing prices and output levels.

Solution
a. This is an example of price discrimination. Solving the demand equations in both markets for price yields

$$P_1 = 50 - 5Q_1$$

$$P_2 = 30 - 2Q_2$$

The corresponding total revenue equations are

$$TR_1 = 50Q_1 - 5Q_1^2$$

$$TR_2 = 30Q_2 - 2Q_2^2$$

Red Company's total profit equation is

$$\pi = TR_1 + TR_2 - TC = 50Q_1 - 5Q_1^2 + 30Q_2 - 2Q_2^2 - 6 - 10(Q_1 + Q_2)$$

Maximizing this expression with respect to Q_1 and Q_2 yields

$$\frac{\partial \pi}{\partial Q_1} = 50 - 10Q_1 - 10 = 40 - 10Q_1 = 0$$

$$Q_1{}^* = 4$$

$$\frac{\partial \pi}{\partial Q_2} = 30 - 4Q_2 - 10 = 20 - 4Q_2 = 0$$

$$Q_2{}^* = 5$$

$$P_1{}^* = 50 - 5(4) = 50 - 20 = 30$$

$$P_2{}^* = 30 - 2(5) = 30 - 10 = 20$$

b. The relationships between the selling price and the price elasticity of demand in the two markets are

$$MR_1 = P_1\left(1 + \frac{1}{\varepsilon_1}\right)$$

$$MR_2 = P_2\left(1 + \frac{1}{\varepsilon_2}\right)$$

where

$$\varepsilon_1 = \left(\frac{dQ_1}{dP_1}\right)\left(\frac{P_1}{Q_1}\right)$$

$$\varepsilon_2 = \left(\frac{dQ_2}{dP_2}\right)\left(\frac{P_2}{Q_2}\right)$$

From the demand equations, $dQ_1/dP_1 = -0.2$ and $dQ_2/dP_2 = -0.5$. Substituting these results into preceding above relationships, we obtain

$$\varepsilon_1 = (-0.2)\left(\frac{30}{4}\right) = \frac{-6}{4} = -1.5$$

$$\varepsilon_2 = (-0.5)\left(\frac{20}{5}\right) = \frac{-10}{5} = -2$$

This verifies that the higher price is charged in the market where the price elasticity of demand is less elastic.

c. The firm's total profit at the profit-maximizing prices and output levels are

$$\pi^* = 50(4) - 5(4)^2 + 30(5) - 2(5)^2 - 6 - 10(4+5)$$
$$= 200 - 80 + 150 - 50 - 6 - 90 = 124$$

Problem 11.6. Copperline Mountain is a world-famous ski resort in Utah. Copperline Resorts operates the resort's ski-lift and grooming operations. When weather conditions are favorable, Copperline's total operating cost, which depends on the number of skiers who use the facilities each year, is given as

$$TC = 10S + 6$$

where S is the total number of skiers (in hundreds of thousands). The management of Copperline Resorts has determined that the demand for ski-lift tickets can be segmented into adult (S_A) and children 12 years old and under (S_C). The demand curve for each group is given as

$$S_A = 10 - 0.2P_A$$

$$S_C = 15 - 0.5P_C$$

where P_A and P_C are the prices charged for adults and children, respectively.
a. Assuming that Copperline Resorts is a profit maximizer, how many skiers will visit Copperline Mountain?
b. What prices should the company charge for adult and child's ski-lift tickets?
c. Assuming that the second-order conditions for profit maximization are satisfied, what is Copperline's total profit?

Solution
a. Total profit is given by the expression

$$\pi = TR - TC = (TR_A + TR_C) - TC$$
$$= P_A S_A + P_C S_C - TC$$
$$= (50 - 5S_A)S_A + (30 - 2S_C)S_C - [10(S_A + S_C) + 6]$$
$$= -6 + 40S_A + 20S_C - 5S_A^2 - 2S_C^2$$

Taking the first partial derivatives with respect to S_A and S_C, setting the results equal to zero, and solving, we write

$$\frac{\partial \pi}{\partial S_A} = 40 - 10S_A = 0$$

$$S_A = 4$$

$$\frac{\partial \pi}{\partial S_C} = 20 - 4S_C = 0$$

$$S_C = 5$$

The total number of skiers that will visit Copperline Mountain is

$$S = S_A = S_C = 4 + 5 = 9 \, (\times 10^5) \, \text{skiers}$$

b. Substituting these results into the demand functions yields adult and child's, ski-lift ticket prices.

$$4 = 10 - 0.2P_A$$

$$P_A = \$30$$

$$5 = 15 - 0.5P_C$$

$$P_C = \$20$$

c. Substituting the results from part a into the total profit equation yields

$$\pi = -6 + 40(4) + 20(5) - 5(4)^2 - 2(5)^2$$
$$= -6 + 160 + 100 - 80 - 50 = \$124 \, (\times 10^3)$$

Problem 11.7. Suppose that a firm sells its product in two separable markets. The demand equations are

$$Q_1 = 100 - P_1$$

$$Q_2 = 50 - 0.25P_2$$

The firm's total cost equation is

$$TC = 150 + 5Q + 0.5Q^2$$

a. If the firm engages in third-degree price discrimination, how much should it sell, and what price should it charge, in each market?
b. What is the firm's total profit?

Solution
a. Assuming that the firm is a profit maximizer, set $MR = MC$ in each market to determine the output sold and the price charged. Solving the demand equation for P in each market yields

$$P_1 = 100 - Q_1$$

$$P_2 = 200 - 4Q_2$$

The respective total and marginal revenue equations are

$$TR_1 = 100Q_1 - Q_1^2$$

$$TR_2 = 200Q_2 - Q_2^2$$

$$MR_1 = 100 - 2Q_1$$

$$MR_2 = 200 - 8Q_2$$

The firm's marginal cost equation is

$$MC = \frac{dTC}{dQ} = 5 + Q$$

Setting $MR = MC$ for each market yields

$$100 - 2Q_1 = 5 + Q_1$$

$$200 - 8Q_2 = 5 + Q_2$$

$$Q_1^* = 31.67$$

$$Q_2^* = 15$$

$$P_1^* = 100 - 31.67 = \$68.33$$

$$P_2^* = 200 - 4(15) = \$140.00$$

b. The firm's total profit is

$$\pi^* = P_1^* Q_1^* + P_2^* Q_2^* - \left[150 + 5\left(Q_1^* + Q_2^*\right) + 0.5\left(Q_1^* + Q_2^*\right)^2 \right]$$

$$= 68.33(31.67) + 140(15) - (150 + 233.35 + 1,089.04) = \$2,791.62$$

Problem 11.8. Suppose that the firm in Problem 11.7 charges a uniform price in the two markets in which it sells its product.
a. Find the uniform price charged, and the quantity sold, in the two markets.
b. What is the firm's total profit?
c. Compare your answers to those obtained in Problem 11.7.

Solution
a. To determine the uniform price charged in each market, first add the two demand equations:

$$Q = Q_1 + Q_2 = 100 - P_1 + 50 - 0.25P_2 = 150 - 1.25P$$

Next, solve this equation for P:

$$P = 120 - 0.8Q$$

The total and marginal revenue equations are

$$TR = PQ = 120Q - 0.8Q^2$$

$$MR = 120 - 1.6Q$$

The profit-maximizing level of output is

$$MR = MC$$

$$120 - 1.6Q = 5 + Q$$

$$Q^* = 44.23$$

That is, the profit-maximizing output of the firm is 44.23 units. The uniform price is determined by substituting this result into the combined demand equation:

$$P^* = 120 - 0.8(44.23) = 120 - 35.38 = \$84.62$$

The amount of output sold in each market is

$$Q_1^* = 100 - 84.62 = 15.38$$

$$Q_2^* = 50 - 0.25(84.62) = 50 - 21.16 = 28.85$$

Note that the combined output of the two markets is equal to the total output Q^* already derived.

b. The firm's total profit is

$$\pi^* = P^*Q^* - (150 + 5Q^* + 0.5Q^{*2})$$
$$= 84.62(44.23) - \left[150 + 5(44.23) + 0.5(44.23)^2\right]$$
$$= 3,742.74 - (150 + 221.15 + 978.15) = \$2,393.44$$

c. The uniform price charged ($84.62) is between the prices charged in the two markets ($68.33 and $140.00) when the firm engaged in third-degree price discrimination. When the firm engaged in uniform pricing, the amount of output sold is lower in the first market (15.38 units compared with 31.67 units) and higher in the second market (28.85 units compared with 15 units). Finally, the firm's total profit with uniform pricing ($2,393.44) is lower than when the firm engaged in third-degree price discrimination ($2,791.62, from Problem 11.7).

When third-degree price discrimination is practiced in foreign trade it is sometimes referred to as *dumping*. This rather derogatory term is often used by domestic producers claiming unfair foreign competition. Defined by the U.S. Department of Commerce as selling at below fair market value, dumping results when a profit-maximizing exporter sells its product at a different, usually lower, price in the foreign market than it does in its home market. Recall that when resale between two markets is not possible, the monopolist will sell its product at a lower price in the market in which demand is more price elastic. In international trade theory, the difference between the home price and the foreign price is called the *dumping margin*.

NONMARGINAL PRICING

Most of the discussion of pricing practices thus far has assumed that management is attempting to optimize some corporate objective. For the most part, we have assumed that management attempts to maximize the firm's profits, but other optimizing behavior has been discussed, such as revenue maximization. In each case, we assumed that the firm was able to calculate its total cost and total revenue equations, and to systematically use that information to achieve the firm's objectives. If the firm's objective is to maximize profit, for example, then management will produce at an output level and charge a price at which marginal revenue equals marginal cost. This is the classic example of marginal pricing.

In reality, however, firms do not know their total revenue and total cost equations, nor are they ever likely to. In fact, because firms do not have this information, and in spite management's protestations to the contrary, most firms are (unwittingly) not profit maximizers. Moreover, even if this information were available, there are other corporate objectives, such as satisficing behavior, that do not readily lend themselves to marginal pricing strategies. Consequently, most firms engage in nonmarginal pricing. The most popular form of nonmarginal pricing is cost-plus pricing.

Definition: Firms determine the profit-maximizing price and output level by equating marginal revenue with marginal cost. When the firm's total revenue and total cost equations are unknown, however, management will often practice nonmarginal pricing. The most popular form of nonmarginal pricing is cost-plus pricing, also known as markup or full-cost pricing.

COST-PLUS PRICING

As we have seen, profit maximization occurs at the price–quantity combination at which where marginal cost equals marginal revenue. In reality, however, many firms are unable or unwilling to devote the resources necessary to accurately estimate the total revenue and total cost equations, or do not know enough about demand and cost conditions to determine the profit-maximizing price and output levels. Instead, many firms adopt rule-of-thumb methods for pricing their goods and services. Perhaps the most commonly used pricing practice is that of *cost-plus pricing*, also known as *mark up* or *full-cost pricing*. The rationale behind cost-plus pricing is straightforward: approximate the average cost of producing a unit of the good or service and then "mark up" the estimated cost per unit to arrive at a selling price.

Definition: Cost-plus pricing is the most popular form of nonmarginal pricing. It is the practice of adding a predetermined "markup" to a firm's estimated per-unit cost of production at the time of setting the selling price.

The firm begins by estimating the average variable cost (AVC) of producing a good or service. To this, the company adds a per-unit allocation for fixed cost. The result is sometimes referred to as the *fully allocated per-unit cost* of production. With the per-unit allocation for fixed cost denoted AFC and the fully allocated, average total cost ATC, the price a firm will charge for its product with the percentage mark up is

$$P = ATC(1+m) \qquad\qquad (11.21)$$

where m is the percentage markup over the fully allocated per-unit cost of production. Solving Equation (11.21) for m reveals that the mark up may also be expressed as the difference between the selling price and the per-unit cost of production.

$$m = \frac{P - ATC}{ATC} \qquad\qquad (11.22)$$

The numerator of Equation (11.22) can also be written as $P - AVC - AFC$. The expression $P - AVC$ is sometimes referred to as the *contribution margin per unit*. The marked-up selling price, therefore, may be referred to as the profit contribution per unit plus some allocation to defray overhead costs.

Problem 11.9. Suppose that the Nimrod Corporation has estimated the average variable cost of producing a spool of its best-selling brand of industrial wire, Mithril, at $20. The firm's total fixed cost is $20,000.
a. If Nimrod produces 500 spools of Mithril and its standard pricing practice is to add a 25% markup to its estimated per-spool cost of production, what price should Nimrod charge for its product?
b. Verify that the selling price calculated in part a represents a 25% markup over the estimated per-spool cost of production.

Solution
a. At a production level of 500 spools, Nimrod's per-unit fixed cost allocation is

$$AFC = \frac{20,000}{500} = 40$$

The cost-plus pricing equation is given as

$$P = ATC(1+m)$$

where m is the percentage markup and ATC is the sum of the average variable cost of production (AVC) and the per-unit fixed cost allocation (AFC). Substituting, we write

$$P = (20+40)(1+0.25) = 60(1.25) = \$75$$

Nimrod should charge \$75 per spool of Mithril. In other words, Nimrod should charge \$15 over its estimated per-unit cost of production.
b. The percentage markup is given by the equation

$$m = \frac{(P - ATC)}{ATC}$$

Substituting the relevant data into this equation yields

$$m = \frac{75-60}{60} = \frac{15}{60} = 0.25$$

Of course, the advantage of cost-plus pricing is its simplicity. Cost-plus pricing requires less than complete information, and it is easy to use. Care must be exercised, however, when one is using this approach. The usefulness of cost-plus pricing will be significantly reduced unless the appropriate cost concepts are employed. As in the case of break-even analysis, care must be taken to include all relevant costs of production. Cost-plus pricing, which is based only on accounting (explicit) costs, will move the firm further away from an optimal (profit-maximizing) price and output level. Of course, the more appropriate approach would be to calculate total economic costs, which include both explicit and implicit costs of production.

There are two major criticisms of cost-plus pricing. The first criticism involves the assumption of fixed marginal cost, which at fixed input prices is in defiance of the law of diminishing marginal product. It is this assumption that allows us to further assume that marginal cost is approximately equal to the fully allocated per-unit cost of production. If it can be argued, however, that marginal cost is approximately constant over the firm's range of production, this criticism loses much of its sting.

A perhaps more serious criticism of cost-plus pricing is that it is insensitive to demand conditions. It should be noted that, in practice, the size of a firm's markup tends to reflect the price elasticity of demand for of goods of various types. Where the demand for a product is relatively less price elastic, because of, say, the paucity of close substitutes, the markup tends to be higher than when demand is relatively more price elastic. As will be presently demonstrated, to the extent that this observation is correct, the criticism of insensitivity loses some of its bite.

Recall from our discussion of the relationship between the price elasticity of demand and total revenue in Chapter 4, the relationship between marginal revenue, price, and the price elasticity of demand may be expressed as

$$MR = P\left(1 + \frac{1}{\varepsilon_p}\right) \tag{4.15}$$

The first-order condition for profit maximization is $MR = MC$. Replacing MR with MC in Equation (4.15) yields

$$MC = P\left(1 + \frac{1}{\varepsilon_p}\right) \tag{11.23}$$

Solving Equation (11.23) for P yields

$$P = \frac{MC}{1 + 1/\varepsilon_p} \tag{11.24}$$

If we assume that MC is approximately equal to the firm's fully allocated per-unit cost (ATC), Equation (11.24) becomes,

$$P = \frac{ATC}{1 + 1/\varepsilon_p} \tag{11.25}$$

Equating the right-hand side of this result to the right-hand side of Equation (11.21), we obtain

$$\frac{ATC}{1 + 1/\varepsilon_p} = ATC(1 + m)$$

where m is the percentage markup. Solving this expression for the markup yields

$$m = \frac{-1}{\varepsilon_p + 1} \tag{11.26}$$

Equation (11.26) suggests that when demand is price elastic, then the selling price should have a positive markup. Moreover, the greater the price elasticity of demand, the lower will be the markup. Suppose, for example, that $\varepsilon_p = -2.0$. Substituting this value into Equation (11.26), we find that the markup is $m = -1/(-2 + 1) = -1/-1 = 1$, or 100%. On the other hand, if $\varepsilon_p = -5.0$, then $m = -1/(-5 + 1) = -1/-4 = 0.25$, or a 25% markup.

What happens, however, if the demand for the good or service is price inelastic? Suppose, for example, that $\varepsilon_p = -0.8$. Substituting this into Equation (11.26) results in a markup of $m = -1/(-0.8 + 1) = -1/0.2 = -5$. This result suggests that the firm should mark down the price of its product by 500%! Equation (11.26) suggests that if the demand for a product is price inelastic, the firm should sell its output at below the fully allocated per-unit cost of production, a practice that is clearly not observed in the real world. Fortunately, this apparent paradox is easily resolved.

It will be recalled from Chapter 4, and is easily seen from Equation (4.15), that when the demand for a good or service is price inelastic, it marginal revenue must be negative. For the profit-maximizing firm, this suggests that marginal cost is negative, since the first-order condition for profit maximization is $MR = MC$, which is clearly impossible for positive input prices and positive marginal product of factors of production.

Problem 11.10. What is the estimated percentage markup over the fully allocated per-unit cost of production for the following price elasticities of demand?

a. $\varepsilon_p = -11$
b. $\varepsilon_p = -4$
c. $\varepsilon_p = -2.5$
d. $\varepsilon_p = -2.0$
e. $\varepsilon_p = -1.5$

Solution

a. $m = \dfrac{-1}{\varepsilon_p + 1} = \dfrac{-1}{-11 + 1} = 0.10$ or a 10% mark up

b. $m = \dfrac{-1}{\varepsilon_p + 1} = \dfrac{-1}{-4 + 1} = 0.333$ or a 33.3% mark up

c. $m = \dfrac{-1}{\varepsilon_p + 1} = \dfrac{-1}{-2.5 + 1} = 0.667$ or a 66.7% mark up

d. $m = \dfrac{-1}{\varepsilon_p + 1} = \dfrac{-1}{-2.0 + 1} = 1.0$ or a 100% mark up

e. $m = \dfrac{-1}{\varepsilon_p + 1} = \dfrac{-1}{-1.5 + 1} = 2.0$ or a 200% mark up

Problem 11.11. What is the percentage markup on the output of a firm operating in a perfectly competitive industry?

Solution. A firm operating in a perfectly competitive industry faces an infinitely elastic demand for its product. Substituting $\varepsilon_p = -\infty$ into Equation (11.26) yields

$$m = \frac{-1}{\varepsilon_p + 1} = \frac{-1}{-\infty + 1} = 0$$

A firm operating in a perfectly competitive industry cannot mark up the selling price of its product. This is as it should be, since such a firm has no market power; that is, the firm is a price taker. The firm must sell its product at the market-determined price.

Problem 11.12. Suppose that a firm's marginal cost of production is constant at $25. Suppose further that the price elasticity of demand (ε_p) for the firm's product is +5.0.

a. Using cost-plus pricing, what price should the firm charge for its product?

b. Suppose that $\varepsilon_p = -0.5$. What price should the firm charge for its product?

Solution

a. The firm's profit-maximizing condition is

$$MR = MC$$

Recall from Chapter 4 that

$$MR = P\left(1 + \frac{1}{\varepsilon_p}\right)$$

Substituting this result into the profit-maximizing condition yields

$$MC = P\left(1 + \frac{1}{\varepsilon_p}\right)$$

Since MC is constant, then $MC = ATC$. After substituting, and rearranging, we obtain

$$P^* = ATC\frac{\varepsilon_p}{\varepsilon_p + 1} = 25\left(\frac{-5}{-5 + 1}\right) = 25\left(\frac{-5}{-4}\right) = \$31.25$$

b. If $\varepsilon_p = -0.5$, then

$$P^* = 25\left(\frac{-0.5}{-0.5 + 1}\right) = 25\left(\frac{-0.5}{0.5}\right) = -\$25.00$$

This result, however, is infeasible, since a firm would never charge a negative price for its product. Recall that a profit-maximizing firm will never produce along the inelastic portion of the demand curve.

MULTIPRODUCT PRICING

We have thus far considered primarily firms that produce and sell only one good or service at a single price. The only exception to this general statement was our discussion of commodity bundling, in which a firm sells a package of goods at a single price. We will now address the issue of pricing strategies of a single firm selling more than one product under alternative scenarios. These scenarios include the optimal pricing of two or more products with interdependent demands, optimal pricing of two or more products with independent demands that are jointly produced in variable proportions, and optimal pricing of two or more products with independent demands that are jointly produced in fixed proportions.

Definition: Multiproduct pricing involves optimal pricing strategies of firms producing and selling more than one good or service.

OPTIMAL PRICING OF TWO OR MORE PRODUCTS WITH INTERDEPENDENT DEMANDS AND INDEPENDENT PRODUCTION

Often a firm will produce two or more goods that are either complements or substitutes for each other. Dell Computer, for example, sells a number of different models of personal computers. These models are, to a degree, substitutes for each other. Personal computers also come with a variety of accessories (mouses, printers, modems, scanners, etc.). These options not only come in different models, and are, therefore, substitutes for each other, but they are also complements to the personal computers.

Because of the interrelationships inherent in the production of some goods and services, it stands to reason that an increase in the price of, say, a Dell personal computer model will lead to a reduction in the quantity demanded of that model and an increase in the demand for substitute models. Moreover, an increase in the price of the Dell personal computer model will lead to a reduction in the demand for complementary accessories. For this reason, a profit-maximizing firm must ascertain the optimal prices and output levels of each product manufactured jointly, rather than pricing each product independently.

The problem may be formally stated as follows. Consider the demand for two products produced by the same firm. If these two products are related, the demand functions may be expressed as

$$Q_1 = f_1(P_1, Q_2) \tag{11.27a}$$

$$Q_2 = f_2(P_2, Q_1) \tag{11.27b}$$

By the law of demand, $\partial Q_1/\partial P_1$ and $\partial Q_2/\partial P_2$ are negative. The signs of $\partial Q_1/\partial Q_2$ and $\partial Q_2/\partial Q_1$ depend on the relationship between Q_1 and Q_2. If the values of these first partial derivatives are positive, then Q_1 and Q_2 are complements. If the values of these first partials are negative, then Q_1 and Q_2 are substitutes.

Upon solving Equation (11.27a) for P_1 and Equation (11.27b) for P_2, and substituting these results into the total revenue equations, we write

$$TR_1(Q_1, Q_2) = P_1Q_1 = h_1(Q_1, Q_2)Q_1 \qquad (11.28a)$$

$$TR_2(Q_1, Q_2) = P_2Q_2 = h_2(Q_1, Q_2)Q_2 \qquad (11.28b)$$

Since the two goods are independently produced, the total cost functions are

$$TC_1 = TC_1(Q_1) \qquad (11.29a)$$

$$TC_2 = TC_2(Q_2) \qquad (11.29b)$$

The total profit equation for this firm is, therefore,

$$\begin{aligned}
\pi &= TR_1(Q_1, Q_2) + TR_2(Q_1, Q_2) - TC_1(Q_1) - TC_2(Q_2) \\
&= P_1Q_1 + P_2Q_2 + TC_1(Q_1) - TC_2(Q_2) \\
&= h_1(Q_1, Q_2)Q_1 + h_2(Q_1, Q_2)Q_2 - TC_1(Q_1) - TC_2(Q_2)
\end{aligned} \qquad (11.30)$$

The first-order conditions for profit maximization are

$$\frac{\partial \pi}{\partial Q_1} = \frac{\partial TR_1}{\partial Q_1} + \frac{\partial TR_2}{\partial Q_1} - \frac{\partial TC_1}{\partial Q_1} = 0 \qquad (11.31a)$$

$$\frac{\partial \pi}{\partial Q_2} = \frac{\partial TR_2}{\partial Q_2} + \frac{\partial TR_1}{\partial Q_2} - \frac{\partial TC_2}{\partial Q_2} = 0 \qquad (11.31b)$$

which may be expressed as

$$MC_1 = \frac{\partial TR_1}{\partial Q_1} + \frac{\partial TR_2}{\partial Q_1} \qquad (11.32a)$$

$$MC_2 = \frac{\partial TR_2}{\partial Q_2} + \frac{\partial TR_1}{\partial Q_2} \qquad (11.32b)$$

We will assume that the second-order conditions for profit maximization are satisfied.

Equations (11.32) indicate that a firm producing two products with interrelated demands will maximize its profits by producing where marginal cost is equal to the change in total revenue derived from the sale of the product itself, plus the change in total revenue derived from the sale of the related product. If the second term on the right-hand side of Equation (11.31) is positive, then Q_1 and Q_2 are complements. If this term is negative, then Q_1 and Q_2 are substitutes.

Problem 11.13. Gizmo Brothers, Inc., manufactures two types of hi-tech yo-yo: the Exterminator and the Eliminator. Denoting Exterminator output as Q_1 and Eliminator output as Q_2, the company has estimated the following demand equations for its yo-yos:

$$Q_1 = 10 - 0.2P_1 - 0.4Q_2$$

$$Q_2 = 20 - 0.5P_2 - 2Q_1$$

The total cost equations for producing Exterminators and Eliminators are

$$TC_1 = 4 + 2Q_1^2$$

$$TC_2 = 8 + 6Q_2^2$$

a. If Gizmo Brothers is a profit-maximizing firm, how much should it charge for Exterminators and Eliminators? What is the profit-maximizing level of output for Exterminators and Eliminators?
b. What is Gizmo Brothers's profit?

Solution
a. Solving the demand equations for P_1 and P_2, respectively, yields

$$P_1 = 50 - 5Q_1 - 2Q_2$$

$$P_2 = 40 - 2Q_2 - 4Q_1$$

The profit equation is

$$\pi = TR_1(Q_1, Q_2) + TR_2(Q_1, Q_2) - TC_1(Q_1) - TC_2(Q_2)$$
$$= P_1 Q_1 + P_2 Q_2 - TC_1(Q_1) - TC_2(Q_2)$$

Substitution yields

$$\pi = (50 - 5Q_1 - 2Q_2)Q_1 + (40 - 2Q_2 - 4Q_1)Q_2 - (4 + 2Q_1^2) - (8 + 6Q_2^2)$$
$$= 50Q_1 + 40Q_2 - 6Q_1Q_2 - 7Q_1^2 - 8Q_2^2 - 12$$

The first-order conditions for profit maximization are

$$\frac{\partial \pi}{\partial Q_1} = 50 - 14Q_1 - 6Q_2 = 0$$

$$\frac{\partial \pi}{\partial Q_2} = 40 - 6Q_1 - 16Q_2 = 0$$

Recall from Chapter 2 that the second-order conditions for profit maximization are

$$\frac{\partial^2 \pi}{\partial Q_1^2} < 0$$

$$\frac{\partial^2 \pi}{\partial Q_2^2} < 0$$

$$\left(\frac{\partial^2 \pi}{\partial Q_1^2}\right)\left(\frac{\partial^2 \pi}{\partial Q_1^2}\right) - \left(\frac{\partial^2 \pi}{\partial Q_1 \partial Q_2}\right)^2 > 0$$

The appropriate second partial derivatives are

$$\frac{\partial^2 \pi}{\partial Q_1^2} = -14 < 0$$

$$\frac{\partial^2 \pi}{\partial Q_2^2} = -16 < 0$$

$$\frac{\partial^2 \pi}{\partial Q_1 \partial Q_2} = -6$$

$$(-14)(-16) - (6)^2 = 244 - 36 = 208 > 0$$

Thus, the second-order conditions for profit maximization are satisfied. Solving the first-order conditions for Q_1 and Q_2 we obtain

$$14Q_1 + 6Q_2 = 50$$

$$6Q_1 + 16Q_2 = 40$$

which may be solved simultaneously to yield

$$Q_1* = 2.979$$

$$Q_2* = 1.383$$

Upon substituting these results into the price equations, we have

$$P_1* = 50 - 5(2.979) - 2(1.383) = \$32.34$$

$$P_2* = 40 - 2(1.383) - 4(2.979) = \$25.32$$

b. Gizmo Brothers's profit is

$$\pi = 50(2.979) + 40(1.383) - 6(2.979)(1.383) - 7(2.979)^2 - 8(1.383)^2 - 12$$
$$= \$90.17$$

OPTIMAL PRICING OF TWO OR MORE PRODUCTS WITH INDEPENDENT DEMANDS JOINTLY PRODUCED IN VARIABLE PROPORTIONS

Let us now suppose that a firm sells two goods with independent demands that are jointly produced in variable proportions. An example of this might be a consumer electronics company that produces automobile taillight bulbs and flashlight bulbs on the same assembly line. In this case, the demand functions are given by the expressions

$$Q_1 = f_1(P_1) \tag{11.33a}$$

$$Q_2 = f_2(P_2) \tag{11.33b}$$

where $\partial Q_1/\partial P_1$ and $\partial Q_2/\partial P_2$ are negative. The total cost function is given by the expression

$$TC = TC(Q_1, Q_2) \tag{11.34}$$

The firm's total profit function is

$$\pi = TR_1(Q_1) + TR_2(Q_2) - TC(Q_1, Q_2) \tag{11.35}$$

Solving the demand equations for P_1 and P_2 and substituting the results into Equation (11.35) yields

$$\pi = P_1 Q_1 + P_2 Q_2 - TC(Q_1, Q_2)$$
$$= h_1(Q_1)Q_1 + h_2(Q_2)Q_2 - TC(Q_1, Q_2) \tag{11.36}$$

The first-order conditions for profit maximization are

$$\frac{\partial \pi}{\partial Q_1} = \frac{\partial TR_1}{\partial Q_1} - \frac{\partial TC_1}{\partial Q_1} = 0 \tag{11.37a}$$

$$\frac{\partial \pi}{\partial Q_2} = \frac{\partial TR_2}{\partial Q_2} - \frac{\partial TC_2}{\partial Q_2} = 0 \tag{11.37b}$$

which may be written as

$$MR_1 = MC_1 \tag{11.38a}$$

$$MR_2 = MC_2 \tag{11.38b}$$

We will assume that the second-order conditions for profit maximization are satisfied.

Equations (11.38) indicate that a profit-maximizing firm jointly producing two goods with independent demands that are jointly produced in variable proportions will equate the marginal revenue generated from the sale of each good to the marginal cost of producing each product.

Problem 11.14. Suppose Gizmo Brothers also produces Tommy Gunn action figures for boys ages 7 to 12, and Bonzey, a toy bone for pet dogs. Except for the molding phase, both products are made on the same assembly line. Denoting Tommy Gunn as Q_1 and Bonzey as Q_2, the company has estimated the following demand equations:

$$Q_1 = 10 - 0.5P_1$$

$$Q_2 = 20 - 0.2P_2$$

The total cost equation for producing the two products is

$$TC = Q_1^2 + 2Q_1Q_2 + 3Q_2^2 + 10$$

a. As before, Gizmo Brothers is a profit-maximizing firm. Give the profit-maximizing levels of output for Tommy Gunn and for Bonzey. How much should the firm charge for Tommy Gunn and Bonzey?
b. What is Gizmo Brothers's profit?

Solution

a. Solving the demand equations for P_1 and P_2, respectively, yields

$$P_1 = 20 - 2Q_1$$

$$P_2 = 100 - 5Q_2$$

Gizmo Brothers's profit equation is

$$\pi = TR_1(Q_1) + TR_2(Q_2) - TC_1(Q_1, Q_2) = P_1Q_1 + P_2Q_2 - TC_1(Q_1, Q_2)$$

Substituting the demand equations into the profit equation yield

$$\pi = (20 - 2Q_1)Q_1 + (100 - 5Q_2)Q_2 - (Q_1^2 + 2Q_1Q_2 + 3Q_2^2 + 10)$$
$$= -10 + 20Q_1 + 100Q_2 - 3Q_1^2 - 8Q_2^2 - 2Q_1Q_2$$

The first-order conditions for profit maximization are

$$\frac{\partial \pi}{\partial Q_1} = 20 - 6Q_1 - 2Q_2 = 0$$

$$\frac{\partial \pi}{\partial Q_2} = 100 - 16Q_2 - 2Q_1 = 0$$

The second-order conditions for profit maximization are

$$\frac{\partial^2 \pi}{\partial Q_1^2} < 0$$

$$\frac{\partial^2 \pi}{\partial Q_2^2} < 0$$

$$\left(\frac{\partial^2 \pi}{\partial Q_1^2}\right)\left(\frac{\partial^2 \pi}{\partial Q_1^2}\right) - \left(\frac{\partial^2 \pi}{\partial Q_1 \partial Q_2}\right)^2 > 0$$

The appropriate second-partial derivatives are

$$\frac{\partial^2 \pi}{\partial Q_1^2} = -6 < 0$$

$$\frac{\partial^2 \pi}{\partial Q_2^2} = -16 < 0$$

$$\frac{\partial^2 \pi}{\partial Q_1 \partial Q_2} = -2$$

$$(-6)(-16) - (-2)^2 = 96 - 4 = 92 > 0$$

Thus, the second-order conditions for profit maximization are satisfied. Solving the first-order conditions for Q_1 and Q_2 yields

$$6Q_1 + 2Q_2 = 20$$

$$2Q_1 + 16Q_2 = 100$$

which may be solved simultaneously to yield

$$Q_1^* = 1.304$$

$$Q_2^* = 6.087$$

Substituting these results into the price equations yields

$$P_1^* = 20 - 2(1.304) = \$17.39$$

$$P_2^* = 100 - 2(6.087) = \$69.66$$

b. Gizmo Brothers's profit is

$$\pi = 20(1.304) + 100(6.087) - 2(1.304)(6.087) - 3(1.304)^2 - 8(6.087)^2 - 10$$
$$= \$88.17$$

OPTIMAL PRICING OF TWO OR MORE PRODUCTS
WITH INDEPENDENT DEMANDS JOINTLY
PRODUCED IN FIXED PROPORTIONS

Now, let us assume that a firm jointly produces two goods in fixed proportions but with independent demands. In many cases, the second product is a by-product of the first, such as beef and hides. With joint production in fixed proportions, it is conceptually impossible to consider two separate products, since the production of one good automatically determines the quantity produced of the other.

Suppose that the demand functions for two goods produced jointly are given as Equations (11.33). The total cost equation is given as Equation (11.13).

$$TC(Q) = TC(Q_1 + Q_2) \tag{11.13}$$

The analysis differs, however, in that Q_1 and Q_2 are in direct proportion to each other, that is,

$$Q_2 = kQ_1 \tag{11.39}$$

where the constant $k > 0$. Solving Equation (11.33) for P_1 and P_2 yields

$$P_1 = h_1(Q_1) \tag{11.40a}$$

$$P_2 = h_2(Q_2) \tag{11.40b}$$

Substituting Equation (11.39) into Equations (11.13) and (11.40b) yields

$$P_1 = h_1(Q_1)$$

$$P_2 = h_2(Q_1) \tag{11.41}$$

$$TC(Q) = TC(Q_1) \tag{11.42}$$

Substituting Equations (11.39), (11.40a), (11.41), and (11.42) into Equation (11.36) yields the firm's profit equation:

$$\begin{aligned} \pi &= P_1 Q_1 + P_2(kQ_1) - TC(Q_1) \\ &= h_1(Q_1)Q_1 + h_2(Q_1)(kQ_1) - TC(Q_1) \end{aligned} \tag{11.43}$$

Stated another way, the firm's total profit function is

$$\pi(Q_1) = TR_1(Q_1) + TR_2(Q_1) - TC(Q_1) \tag{11.44}$$

Equation (11.44) indicates that total profit is a function of the single decision variable, Q_1. Equation (11.44) may also be written

$$\pi(Q_2) = TR_1(Q_2) + TR_2(Q_2) - TC(Q_2) \tag{11.45}$$

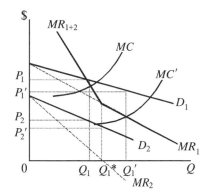

FIGURE 11.6 Optimal pricing of two goods jointly produced in fixed proportions with independent demands.

From Equation (11.44), the first-order condition for profit maximization is

$$\frac{d\pi}{dQ_1} = \frac{dTR_1}{dQ_1} + \frac{dTR_2}{dQ_1} - \frac{dTC_1}{dQ_1} = 0 \qquad (11.46)$$

Equation (11.46) may be rewritten

$$\frac{dTR_1}{dQ_1} + \frac{dTR_2}{dQ_1} = \frac{dTC_1}{dQ_1}$$

$$MR_1(Q_1) + MR_2(Q_1) = MC(Q_1) \qquad (11.47)$$

Equation (11.47) says that a profit-maximizing firm that jointly produces two goods in fixed proportions with independent demands will equate the sum of the marginal revenues of both products expressed in terms of one of the products with the marginal cost of jointly producing both products expressed in terms of the same product. This situation is depicted diagrammatically in Figure 11.6.

In Figure 11.6 the marginal cost curve is labeled MC. According to Equation (11.47) the firm should produce Q_1 units where marginal cost is equal to the sum of MR_1 and MR_2. The amount of Q_2 produced is proportional to Q_1. At that output level the firm charges P_1 for Q_1 and P_2 for Q_2. It should be noted that beyond output level Q_1^* in Figure 11.6, MR_2 becomes negative and MR_{1+2} becomes simply MR_1.

Suppose that marginal cost increases to MC'. In this case, the firm should produce Q_1', but still only sell Q_1^* units. Any output in excess of Q_1^* should be disposed of, since the firm's marginal revenue beyond Q_1^* is negative. The amount of Q_2 produced will be in fixed proportion to Q_1'. The price of Q_1^* is P_2' and the price of Q_2 is P_1'.

Problem 11.15. Suppose that a firm produces two units of Q_2 for each unit of Q_1. Suppose further that the demand equations for these two goods are

$$Q_1 = 10 - 0.5P_1$$

$$Q_2 = 20 - 0.2P_2$$

The total cost of production is

$$TC = 10 + 5Q^2$$

a. What are the profit-maximizing output levels and prices for Q_1 and Q_2?
b. At the profit-maximizing output levels, what is the firm's total profit?

Solution
a. Solving the demand equations for P_1 and P_2 yields

$$P_1 = 20 - 2Q_1$$

$$P_2 = 100 - 5Q_2$$

The firm's total profit equation is

$$\begin{aligned}
\pi &= P_1 Q_1 + P_2 Q_2 - TC(Q_1 + Q_2) \\
&= (20 - 2Q_1)Q_1 + (100 - 5Q_2)Q_2 - (10 + 5Q^2) \\
&= 20Q_1 - 2Q_1^2 + 100Q_2 - 5Q_2^2 - 10 - 5(Q_1 + Q_2)^2
\end{aligned}$$

Since $Q_2 = 2Q_1$, this may be rewritten as

$$\begin{aligned}
\pi &= 20Q_1 - 2Q_1^2 + 100(2Q_1) - 5(2Q_1)^2 - 10 - 5(Q_1 + 2Q_1)^2 \\
&= -10 - 220Q_1 - 67Q_1^2
\end{aligned}$$

The first-order condition for profit maximization is

$$\frac{d\pi}{dQ_1} = 220 - 134Q_1 = 0$$

The second-order condition for profit maximization is

$$\frac{d^2\pi}{dQ_1^2} < 0$$

Since $d^2\pi/dQ_1^2 = -137$ the second-order condition is satisfied. Solving the first-order condition for Q_1 yields

$$Q_1* = 1.64$$

The profit-maximizing level of Q_2 is

$$Q_2* = 2Q_1* = 3.28$$

Substituting these results into the price equations yield

$$P_1* = 20 - 2(1.64) = \$16.72$$

$$P_2* = 100 - 5(3.28) = \$83.60$$

b. The firm's total profit is

$$\pi = 220(1.64) - 67(1.64)^2 - 10 = 360.80 - 180.20 - 10 = \$170.60$$

Problem 11.16. Suppose that a firm jointly produces two goods. Good *B* is a by-product of the production of good *A*. The demand equations for the two goods are

$$Q_A = 200 - 10P_A$$

$$Q_B = 120 - 5P_B$$

The firm's total cost equation is

$$TC = 500 + 15Q + 0.05Q^2$$

a. What is the profit-maximizing price for each product?
b. What is the firm's total profit?

Solution
a. Solving the demand equation for price yields

$$P_A = 20 - 0.1Q_A$$

$$P_B = 24 - 0.2Q_B$$

The respective total and marginal revenue equations are

$$TR_A = 20Q_A - 0.1Q_A^2$$

$$MR_A = 20 - 0.2Q_A$$

$$TR_B = 24Q_B - 0.2Q_B^2$$

$$MR_B = 24 - 0.4Q_B$$

The firm's marginal revenue equation is

$$MR = MR_A + MR_B = 20 - 0.2Q_A + 24 - 0.4Q_B = 44 - 0.6Q$$

The firm's marginal cost equation is

$$MC = \frac{dTC}{dQ} = 15 + 0.1Q$$

The profit-maximizing rate of output is

$$MR = MC$$

$$44 - 0.6Q = 15 + 0.1Q$$

$$Q^* = 41.43$$

The profit-maximizing prices for the two goods are

$$P_A^* = 20 - 0.1(41.43) = 20 - 4.14 = \$15.86$$

$$P_B^* = 20 - 0.2(41.43) = 24 - 8.29 = \$15.71$$

b. The firm's total profit is

$$\pi^* = P_A^*Q^* + P_B^*Q^* - (500 + 15Q^* + 0.05Q^{*2})$$

$$= 15.86(41.43) + 15.71(41.43) - \left[500 - 15(41.43) + 0.05(41.43)^2\right]$$

$$= \$1,343.57$$

PEAK-LOAD PRICING

In many markets the demand for a service is higher at certain times than at others. The demand for electric power, for example, is higher during the day than at night, and during summer and winter than during spring and fall. The demand for theater tickets is greater at night and on the weekends or for midweek matinees. Toll bridges have greater traffic during rush hours than at other times of the day. The demand for airline travel is greater during holiday seasons than at other times. During such "peak" periods it becomes difficult, if not impossible, to satisfy the demands of all customers. Thus the profit-maximizing firm will charge a higher price for the product during "peak" periods and a lower price during "off-peak" periods. This kind of pricing scheme is known as *peak-load pricing*.

Definition: Peak-load pricing is the practice of charging a higher price for a service when demand is high and capacity is fully utilized and a lower price when demand is low and capacity is underutilized.

Figure 11.7 illustrates an example of peak-load pricing for a profit-maximizing firm. Here the marginal cost of providing a service is assumed to be constant until capacity is reached at a peak output level of O_p. At the peak output level the marginal cost curve becomes vertical. This reflects the fact that to satisfy additional demand at O_p, the firm must increase its capacity, by building a new bridge, installing a new hydroelectric generator, or other high-cost measure.

The short-run production function is typically defined in terms of a time interval over which certain factors of production are "fixed." Strictly speaking, this assertion is incorrect. In principle, virtually any factor may be varied if the derived benefits are great enough. It is certainly the case, however, that some factors of production are more easily varied that others. It is clearly easier and less expensive to hire an additional worker at a moment's

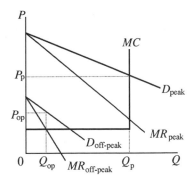

FIGURE 11.7   Peak-load pricing.

notice than to build a new bridge. Thus, it is reasonable to assume that the short-run marginal cost of expanding bridge traffic or increasing hydro-electric capacity is infinite. For that reason, the marginal cost curve at Q_p is assumed to be vertical.

To maximize profits subject to capacity limitations, the firm will charge different prices at different times. Off-peak prices are determined by equating marginal revenue to marginal operating costs. Peak prices, on the other hand, are determined by equating marginal revenue to the marginal cost of increasing capacity. In Figure 11.7, for example, $MR = MC$ for off-peak users at output level Q_{op}. At that output level the firm will charge off-peak users a price of P_{op}. On the other hand, the profit-maximizing level of output for peak users is at the firm's capacity, which in Figure 11.7 occurs at output level Q_p. At that output level the marginal cost curve of producing the service becomes vertical. The profit-maximizing price at that output level is P_p.

Peak-load pricing suggests that users of, say, congested bridges during rush hours, ought to be charged a higher toll than users during non–rush hour periods when there is excess capacity. Since peak-period demand strains capacity, the cost of additional capital investment ought to be borne by peak-period users. This tends to run contrary to the common practice on trains and toll bridges of offering multiple-use discounts to commuters traveling during rush hour, such as lower per-ride prices for, say, monthly tickets on commuter railways.

Problem 11.17. The Gotham Bridge and Tunnel Authority (GBTA) has estimated the following demand equations for peak and off-peak auto-mobile users of the Frog's Neck Bridge:

$$\text{Peak: } T_p = 10 - 0.02 Q_p$$

$$\text{Off-peack: } T_{op} = 5 - 0.05 Q_{op}$$

where T is the toll charged for a one-minute trip (Q) across the bridge. The marginal cost of operating the bridge has been estimated at \$2 per automobile bridge crossing. The peak capacity of the Frog's Neck Bridge has been estimated a 50 automobiles per minute. What toll should the GBTA charge peak and off-peak users of the bridge?

Solution. This is a problem of peak-load pricing. If the GBTA is a profit maximizer, then off-peak drivers should be charged a price consistent with the first-order condition for profit maximization, $MC = MR$. The total revenue equation for off-peak users of the bridge is given as

$$TR_{op} = T_{op}Q_{op} = (5 - 0.05Q_{op})Q_{op} = 5Q - 0.05Q_{op}^2$$

The marginal revenue equation is

$$MR_{op} = \frac{dTR}{dQ_{op}} = 5 - 0.1Q_{op}$$

Equating marginal revenue to marginal cost yields

$$MR_{op} = MC_{op}$$

$$5 - 0.1Q_{op} = 2$$

$$Q_{op} = 30$$

Substituting this result into the off-peak demand equation yields the toll charged to off-peak automobile users of the bridge:

$$T_{op} = 5 - 0.05Q_{op} = 5 - 0.05(30) = \$3.50$$

At a bridge capacity of 50 automobiles per minute, the marginal cost curve is vertical. Substituting bridge capacity into the peak demand equation yields the toll that should be charged to peak automobile users of the bridge:

$$T_p = 10 - 0.02(50) = \$9$$

Peak users of the bridge should be charged \$9 per crossing.

TRANSFER PRICING

In recent years, the growth of large, conglomerate corporations producing a multitude of products has been accompanied by the parallel development of semiautonomous profit centers or subsidiaries. The creation of these "companies within a company" was an attempt to control rising production costs that accompanied the burgeoning managerial and administrative superstructure necessary to coordinate the activities of multiple corporate divisions.

Often the output of a division or subsidiary of a parent company is used as a productive input in the manufacture of the output of another division. A subsidiary of a large, multinational firm, for example, might assemble automobiles, while another subsidiary manufactures automobile bodies. Still another subsidiary might produce air and oil filters, while yet another produces electronic ignition systems, all of which are used in the production of automobiles.

Transfer pricing concerns itself with the correct pricing of intermediate products that are produced and sold between divisions of a parent company. For example, what price should one division of a company that produces, say, ignition systems, charge another division that assembles automobiles. The optimal pricing of intermediary goods is important because the organizational objective of each division is to maximize profit. What is more, the price charged for the output of one division that is used as an input in the production of another division affects not only each division's profits but also profits of the parent company as a whole.

Definition: Transfer pricing involves the optimal pricing of the output of one subsidiary of a parent company that is sold as an intermediate good to another subsidiary of the same parent company.

The literature dealing with transfer pricing typically focuses on three possible scenarios. In the first scenario, there is no external market for the output of the division or subsidiary producing the intermediate good. In other words, the division producing the final product is the sole customer for the output of the division producing the intermediate good. In the second scenario there exists a perfectly competitive external market for the intermediate good. In the third scenario the division or subsidiary operates in an industry that may be characterized as imperfectly competitive.

TRANSFER PRICING WITH NO EXTERNAL MARKET

Assume that a parent company comprises two subsidiary companies. One subsidiary sells its output, Q_1, exclusively to the other subsidiary that is used in the production of Q_2, for final sale in an external market. Assume further that there exists no other demand for Q_1; that is, there is no external market for the intermediate good. Finally assume that one unit of Q_1 is used to produce one unit of Q_2.

Since the parent company comprises only two subsidiaries, the marginal cost of producing Q_2 for final sale must include the marginal cost of producing Q_1. The rationale for this is straightforward. Although the company has been divided into separate profit centers, in the final analysis the company is in the business of producing and selling Q_2 for final sale. The

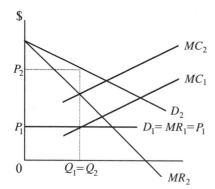

FIGURE 11.8 Transfer pricing with no external market for the intermediate good.

marginal cost of producing Q_2 must, of course, include the marginal cost of producing Q_1. If we assume that the parent company is a profit maximizer, it will produce at the output level where $MR_2 = MC_2$. This situation is illustrated in Figure 11.8.

Since Q_1 and Q_2 are used on a one-to-one basis, the output level that maximizes profit of Q_2 will be the same output level as Q_1. The selling price of Q_2 is P_2. Since the output level of Q_1 has been determined by the output level of Q_2, the profit-maximizing price for Q_1 must be P_1 (i.e., where $MC_1 = MR_1$). Thus, the correct transfer price for the intermediate good Q_1 must be P_1. It should be noted that any increase in the marginal cost of producing Q_1 will result in an increase in the marginal cost of producing Q_2, which will further result in an increase in the selling price of Q_2 and an increase in the transfer price (i.e., the price of the intermediate good that is sold between divisions).

On the other hand, suppose that the marginal cost curve of producing Q_1 remains unchanged, but the marginal cost curve of producing Q_2 shifts upward, perhaps because of an increase in factor or intermediate goods prices purchased in the external market. The result will be an increase in P_2, a decline in the output of Q_2 and Q_1, and, assuming an upward sloping marginal cost curve for Q_1, a fall in the transfer price. When the marginal cost of producing Q_1 is constant, the transfer price remains unaffected by the additional increase in the marginal cost of producing Q_2.

Problem 11.18. Parallax Corporation produces refractive telescopes for amateur astronomers. The demand equation for Parallax telescopes was estimated by the operations research department as

$$Q_T = 2,000 - 20 P_T$$

Parallax's total cost equation was estimated as

$$TC_T = 100 + 2Q_T^2$$

Although the company procures most of its components from outside vendors, each Parallax telescope requires three highly polished lenses that are manufactured on site. Because these components are manufactured to exact specifications, there is no outside market for Parallax lenses. The total cost equation for producing Parallax lenses is

$$TC_L = 200 + 0.025Q_L^2$$

Because of the rapid growth of the company in the 1980s, Parallax management decided to divide the company into two separate profit centers to control costs—the telescope division and the lens division.

a. What is the profit-maximizing price and quantity for Parallax telescopes?
b. What is Parallax's total profit?
c. What transfer price should the lens division charge the telescope division?

Solution
a. Solving the demand equation for P_T yields

$$P_T = 100 - 0.05Q_T$$

The corresponding total revenue equation for Parallax telescopes is

$$TR_T = P_T Q_T = (100 - 0.05Q_T)Q_T = 100Q_T - 0.05Q_T^2$$

The total profit equation for Parallax telescopes is

$$\pi_T = TR_T - TC_T = (100Q_T - 0.05Q_T^2) - (100 + 2Q_T^2)$$
$$= -100 + 100Q_T - 2.05Q_T^2$$

The first-order condition for profit maximization is $d\pi/dQ_T = 0$. Taking the first derivative of the profit equation yields

$$\frac{d\pi}{dQ} = 100 - 4.1Q_T = 0$$

Solving, we have

$$Q_T* = 24.39$$

The second-order condition for profit maximization is $d\pi/dQ_T < 0$. After taking the second derivative of the profit equation, we obtain

$$\frac{d^2\pi}{dQ^2} = -4.1 < 0$$

which guarantees that this output level represents a local maximum.

The profit-maximizing price, therefore, is

$$P_T^* = 100 - 0.05(24.39) = \$98.78$$

b. Parallax's profit at the profit-maximizing price and quantity is

$$\pi = -100 + 100(24.39) - 2.05(24.39)^2 = \$1,119.51$$

c. Since there is no external market for Parallax lenses, the transfer price is equal to the marginal cost of producing the lenses at the profit-maximizing output level. Parallax's marginal cost equation for producing lenses is

$$MC_L = \frac{dTC_1}{dQ_L} = 0.05Q_L$$

Since Parallax needs three lenses for every telescope produced, the total number of lenses required by the telescope division is 73.17 lenses (3×23.39 telescopes). The marginal cost of producing these lenses, therefore, is

$$MC_L = 0.05(70.17) = \$3.51 = P_L$$

The transfer price of the lenses, therefore, is $3.51 per lens.

TRANSFER PRICING WITH A PERFECTLY COMPETITIVE EXTERNAL MARKET

We will now consider the situation in which there exists an external market for the intermediate good. That is, the division or subsidiary producing the final product has the option of purchasing the intermediate good either from a subsidiary of its own parent company or from an outside vendor. If the intermediate good is purchased from within, what will its transfer price be? The answer to this question will depend on whether the external market for the intermediate good is or is not perfectly competitive. We will begin by assuming that there exists a perfectly competitive external market for the intermediate good produced by the subsidiary.

Since both divisions are assumed to be profit maximizers, it stands to reason that the division producing the final good will pay no more for the intermediate good than it would pay in the perfectly competitive external market. Similarly, the division producing the intermediate good will sell its output for nothing less than the perfectly competitive external market price. Thus, the transfer price for the intermediate good is the perfectly competitive price in the external market. This situation is depicted in Figure 11.9, where the price for the intermediate good is the same price depicted in Figure 11.8.

It should be noted that because the price of the intermediate good in Figure 11.9 is assumed to be the same price depicted in Figure 11.8, the mar-

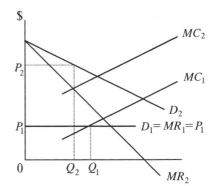

FIGURE 11.9 Transfer pricing with a perfectly competitive external market for intermediate good.

ginal cost of producing the final good remains unchanged. Thus, the profit-maximizing price and the quantity for the final good remain unchanged at P_2 and Q_2. Unlike the situation depicted in Figure 11.8, the amount of output produced by the intermediate good division no longer needs to equal the output of the final good division. Moreover, the transfer price for the intermediate good is the perfectly competitive price in the external market. In the preceding case, with no external market for the intermediate good, the transfer price was determined by the level of output that maximized profits for the final goods division.

In the situation depicted in Figure 11.9, the marginal cost of producing the intermediate good is lower than that depicted in Figure 11.8. The profit-maximizing, intermediate good division will produce at an output level at which $MC_1 = MR_1$. This occurs at an output level that is greater than Q_2. The division producing the intermediate good will sell Q_2 to the division producing the final good and will sell the surplus output of $Q_1 - Q_2$ in the external market at the perfectly competitive price, P_1.

Problem 11.19. Suppose that in the Parallax telescope example of Problem 11.18 the lenses produced by the subsidiary are of a standard variety produced by a perfectly competitive firm. Suppose further that the market-determined price of these lenses is $4.

a. Find the profit-maximizing price and quantity for Parallax telescopes. What is Parallax's total profit?
b. What transfer price should the lens division charge the telescope division?
c. How many lenses will the lens division produce? Will the number of lenses produced be sufficient to satisfy the requirements of the telescope division? If not, what should the telescope division do? If the lens division produces more lenses than the telescope division requires, what should the overproducing division do?

Solution

a. Since there is no change in the demand for Parallax telescopes, there is no change in the firm's total revenue function. However, since lenses are now $0.49 more expensive than before, Parallax must spend $1.47 more to produce each telescope. Parallax's total cost equation for telescopes is now

$$TC_T = 100 - 2Q_T^2 + 1.47Q_T$$

Parallax's total profit equation is

$$\pi = TR - TC_T = (100Q_T - 0.05Q_T^2) - (100 + 2Q_T^2 + 1.47Q_T)$$
$$= -100 + 100Q_T - 2.05Q_T^2 - 1.47Q_T = -100 + 98.53Q_T - 2.05Q_T^2$$

The first-order condition for profit maximization is $d\pi/dQ_T = 0$. Taking the first derivative of the profit equation yields

$$\frac{d\pi}{dQ} = 98.53 - 4.1Q_T = 0$$

Solving, we have

$$Q_T* = 24.03$$

The second-order condition for profit maximization is $d\pi/dQ_T < 0$. Taking the second derivative of the profit equation yields

$$\frac{d^2\pi}{dQ^2} = -4.1 < 0$$

which guarantees that this output level represents a local maximum. The profit-maximizing price, therefore, is

$$P_T* = 100 - 0.05(24.03) = \$98.80$$

Parallax's total profit at the profit-maximizing price and quantity is

$$\pi = -100 + 98.53(24.03) - 2.05(24.03)^2 = \$1,083.93$$

b. The transfer price for lenses is the price set in the perfectly competitive market (i.e., $P_L = \$4$).

c. The lens division will maximize profit by setting the marginal cost of producing lenses equal to the marginal revenue of selling lenses, that is,

$$MC_L = MR_L$$

Since lens production takes place in a perfectly competitive industry, the marginal revenue from selling lenses is $4 per lens. The marginal cost equation of lens production is

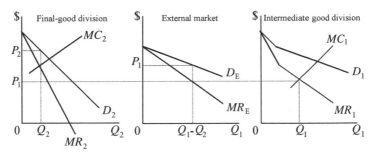

FIGURE 11.10 Transfer pricing with an imperfectly competitive external market for the intermediate good.

$$MC_L = \frac{dTC_L}{dQ_L} = 0.05Q_L$$

Substitution yields

$$4 = 0.05Q_L$$

$$Q_L* = 80$$

The lens division should produce 80 lenses. Since the telescope division needs 72.09 lenses (3×24.03 telescopes), the lens division should sell the remaining 7.91 lenses in the external market.

TRANSFER PRICING WITH AN IMPERFECTLY COMPETITIVE EXTERNAL MARKET

Finally, let us consider an imperfectly competitive external market for the intermediate good. In this case, the price charged by the intermediate good division to the final good division will differ from the price of the intermediate good in the imperfectly competitive external market. The prices charged internally and externally by the intermediate good division become a matter of third-degree price discrimination. Consider Figure 11.10.

In Figure 11.10, the intermediate good division faces a downward-sloping demand curve for its output. The total demand for Q_1 includes the demand for the intermediate good by the final-good division and the demand by the external market. This demand curve is labeled D_1. Once again, the marginal cost of producing the final good Q_2 includes the marginal cost of producing Q_1. The profit-maximizing level of output for the intermediate good division is Q_1. The corresponding $MR_1 = MC_1$ will determine the selling price of the intermediate good to the final good division. This will be the transfer price of the intermediate good.

The amount of Q_1 that will be sold to the final good division will be determined by the profit-maximizing level of output Q_2, since $Q_1 = Q_2$. This leaves $Q_1 - Q_2$ units of Q_1 available for sale in the external market. The intermediate good division will maximize its profits by charging a price in the external market such that $MC_1 = MR_E$. In Figure 11.10, the intermediate good division engages in third-degree price discrimination by charging more in the external market than it charges the final good division.

OTHER PRICING PRACTICES

This chapter has so far focused on the pricing behavior of profit-maximizing firms operating under somewhat unique circumstances. In each case, the firm's pricing practices were predicated on subtle economic concepts. It was also assumed that management had complete information about the realities of the market in which the firm operated. In practice however, a firm's pricing practices are much looser in the sense that they are based less on detailed mathematical analysis than on perception, custom, and intuition. The remainder of this chapter is devoted to a review of five of these alternative pricing practices-*price leadership*, *price skimming*, *penetration pricing*, *prestige pricing*, and *psychological pricing*.

PRICE LEADERSHIP

Price leadership is a phenomenon that is likely to be observed in oligopolistic industries. It was noted in Chapter 10 that oligopolistic industries are characterized by the interdependence of managerial decisions between and among the firms in the industry. Firms in oligopolistic industries are keenly aware that the pricing and output decisions of any individual firm will provoke a reaction by competing firms. A consequence of this interdependence is relatively infrequent price changes.

Definition: Price leadership occurs when a dominant company in an industry establishes the selling price of a product for the rest of the firms in the industry. Two forms of price leadership are barometric price leadership and dominant price leadership.

Barometric Price Leadership

We saw in our discussion of the kinked demand curve that in oligopolistic industries, marginal cost may fluctuate within a fairly narrow range without evoking a price change. The reason for this is the discontinuity in the firm's marginal revenue curve. As a result, prices are relatively stable at the "kink" in the demand curve. What happens, however, when cost conditions for the typical firm in the industry increase significantly because of some exogenous shock? How will the increased cost of production manifest itself in the selling price of the product when, for example, the United Auto Workers negotiate higher wages and benefits for union workers in all firms in the U.S. automobile industry, or OPEC production cutbacks result in higher energy prices?

Definition: Barometric price leadership occurs when a price change by one firm in an oligopolistic industry, usually in response to perceived changes in macroeconomic or market conditions, is quickly followed by price changes by other firms in the industry.

In an oligopolistic industry characterized by firms of roughly the same size, price changes may sometimes be explained by *barometric price leadership*. In this case, a typical firm in the industry initiates, say, a price increase based on management's belief that changes in macroeconomic or market conditions will have a uniform impact on all other firms in the industry. If other firms believe that the firm's interpretations of economic events are correct, they will quickly follow suit. If they disagree, the firm initiating the price increase will be forced to reevaluate its decision and may modify or repeal the price increase. If the price increase is modified, the evaluation process begins again. Ultimately, member firms in the industry will form a consensus and a new, stable, price will be established.

An example of this type of price leadership can be seen in the commercial banking industry. Based on its reading of macroeconomic conditions, a leading money-center commercial bank, such as Citibank, may announce its decision to raise or lower the prime rate (the interest rate on loans to its best customers). If the rest of the industry agrees with Citibank's interpretation of macroeconomic conditions, other money-center commercial banks will quickly follow suit. If not, they will not raise their prime rates and Citibank will quietly lower its prime rate to a level consistent with the sentiments of the industry.

Dominant Price Leadership

Some industries are characterized by a single, dominant firm and many smaller competitors. The dominant firm may be the industry leader because of its leadership in product innovation, or because of economies of scale. If the firm is large enough or efficient enough, it may be able to force smaller competitors out of business by undercutting their prices, or it may simply buy them out. Such behavior, however, often incurs the wrath of the U.S. Department of Justice, which is charged with enforcing federal antitrust legislation.

Definition: Dominant price leadership occurs when one firm in the industry is able to establish the industry price as a result of its profit-maximizing behavior. Once a price has been established by the dominant firm, the remaining firms in the industry become price takers and face a perfectly elastic demand curve for their output.

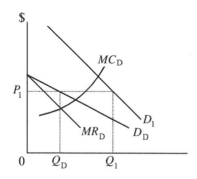

FIGURE 11.11 Dominant price leadership.

Industries dominated by a single large firm are characterized by price stability. The reason for this is that the dominant firm establishes the selling price of the product, and the smaller firms quickly adjust their price and output decisions accordingly. This situation is illustrated in Figure 11.11, which indicates that the dominant firm in the industry will behave like a monopolist by producing at output level Q_D, where its marginal cost is equal to its marginal revenue, $MC_D = MR_D$. The profit-maximizing price P_I will then serve as the industry standard. The amount of output provided by the rest of the industry will be $Q_I - Q_D$.

What is interesting about this analysis is that once the industry price has been established by the dominant firm, the remaining firms take on the appearance of a perfectly competitive industry in which the demand curve for their product is perfectly elastic. The other words, other firms in the industry are price takers. If entry and exit into and from the industry are relatively easy, the existence of above-normal profits will attract new firms into the industry, while below-normal profits will provide an incentive for firms to leave. It is speculative whether the influx or outflow of firms into the industry weakens or strengthens the market power of the dominant firm. In large part, this will depend on the circumstances explaining the firm's rise to industry dominance, and whether those factors are sufficient to maintain the firm's preeminent position.

PRICE SKIMMING

If a firm is first to market with a new product, it may engage in a form of first-degree price discrimination called price skimming. As with first-degree price discrimination, price skimming is an attempt to extract consumer surplus. During the interval between the firm's introduction of a new product and the competition's development of their own versions of the new product, the innovating firm is a virtual monopoly. If the innovating firm wants to extract consumer surplus, however, it must act fast.

Definition: Price skimming is an attempt by a firm that introduces a new product to extract consumer surplus through differential pricing before competitors develop their own versions of the new product.

The firm begins by initially charging a very high price for its product. Consumers willing and able to pay this price will buy first. Before competitors have a chance to sell their versions of the new product, the innovating firm will lower its price just a bit to attract the next, lower tier of consumers. This process is continued until the price charged equals the marginal cost of production. Pricing in this manner will enable the innovating firm to extract consumer surplus to enhance profits. Of course, for this pricing scheme to be successful the firm must have knowledge of the demand curve of the product. Management is unlikely to have such knowledge, however, because of the novel nature of the product. The firm could, of course, conduct consumer surveys, market experiments, and so on, to develop information regarding the demand for the product, but care would have to be taken not to "tip off" the competition.

PENETRATION PRICING

Penetration pricing occurs when a firm entering a new market charges a price that is below the prevailing market price to gain a foothold in the industry. A form of penetration pricing is *dumping*. Dumping is defined by the U.S. Department of Commerce as selling a product at less than fair market value. The most egregious form of this kind of pricing behavior is *predatory dumping*, the attempt by a foreign producer to gain control of the market in another country by selling a product there at less than fair market value with the goal of driving out domestic producers.

Definition: Penetration pricing is the practice of charging a price that is lower than the prevailing market price to gain a foothold in the industry.

PRESTIGE PRICING

Prestige pricing is essentially an attempt by firms to increase sales of certain products by capitalizing on snob appeal. Many consumers derive a degree of personal identity from the ostentatious display of certain brand-name items. For them, an enhanced personal image from the conspicuous consumption of upscale products is as valuable, and sometimes more so, than the usefulness or quality of the product itself. The mere fact that a product sells for a higher price often conveys the impression of higher quality, which may or may not be supported by reality. Prestige pricing is an attempt by some firms to exploit this perception by charging higher prices because of the increased prestige that they believe ownership of their products confers. An often cited example is the luxury automobile market, where higher priced automobiles are perceived to be superior to lower priced automobiles of similar quality.

Definition: Prestige pricing is the practice of charging a higher price for a product to exploit the belief by some consumers that a higher price means better quality, which in turn confers on the owner greater prestige.

PSYCHOLOGICAL PRICING

Finally, psychological pricing is a marketing ploy designed to create the illusion in the mind of the consumer that a product is being sold at a significantly lower price when, in fact, the price differential is inconsequential. Retailer sale of a product for $4.99 instead of $5.00 is psychological pricing. Retailers who engage in psychological pricing are attempting to exploit consumers' initial impressions or their lack of familiarity with the product. The effects of psychological pricing tend to be transitory, however, as initial impressions wear off or the consumer becomes more knowledgeable about the product.

Definition: Psychological pricing is a marketing ploy designed to create the illusion in the mind of the consumer that a product is being sold at a significantly lower price when, in fact, the price differential is inconsequential.

CHAPTER REVIEW

Earlier chapters discussed output and pricing decisions under some very simplistic assumptions. We assumed, for example, that profit-maximizing firms produce a single good or service, that production takes place in a single location, that these firms sell their products in a well-defined market, that managements have perfect information about production, revenue, and cost functions, and that the firms sell their output at a uniform price to all customers. In reality, these assumptions are rarely valid. For that reason, we considered alternative pricing practices, which in some cases are derivatives of the more general cases already encountered.

In *price discrimination*, a firm sells identical products in two or more markets at different prices. Economists have identified three degrees of price discrimination. *First-degree price discrimination* occurs when a firm charges each buyer a different price based on what he or she is willing to pay. In practice, first-degree price discrimination is virtually impossible.

In *second-degree price discrimination*, often referred to as volume discounting, different prices are charged for different blocks of units, or different products are bundled and sold at a package price. An example of second-degree price discrimination is block pricing, in which there are different prices for different blocks of goods and services. Second-degree price discrimination requires that a firm be able to closely monitor the level of services consumed by individual buyers.

In *third-degree price discrimination*, which is by far the most frequently practiced type of price discrimination, firms segment the market for a particular good or service into easily identifiable groups and then charge each group a different price. Such market segregation may be based on such factors as geography, age, product use, or income. For third-degree price discrimination to be successful, firms must be able to prevent resale of the good or service across segregated markets.

Cost-plus pricing, also known as *markup* or *full-cost pricing*, is an example of *nonmarginal pricing*. Firms that engage in nonmarginal pricing are unable or unwilling to devote the resources required to accurately estimate the total revenue and total cost equations, or do not know enough about demand and cost conditions to determine the profit-maximizing price and output levels. In cost-plus pricing, a firm sets the selling price of its product as a markup above its *fully allocated per-unit cost* of production. One criticism of cost-plus pricing is that it is insensitive to demand conditions. In practice, however, the size of a firm's markup tends to be inversely related to the price elasticity of demand for a good or service.

Multi product pricing involves optimal pricing strategies of firms producing and selling more than one good or service. Firms that independently produce two products with interrelated demands will maximize profits by producing at a level at which marginal cost is equal to the change in total revenue derived from the sale of the product itself, plus the change in total revenue derived from the sale of the related product. A profit-maximizing firm selling two goods with independent demands that are jointly produced in variable proportions will equate the marginal revenue generated from the sale of each good to the marginal cost of producing each product. Finally, a profit-maximizing firm that jointly produces two goods in fixed proportions with independent demands will equate the sum of the marginal revenues of both products expressed in terms of one of the products with the marginal cost of jointly producing both products expressed in terms of the same product.

Peak-load pricing occurs when a profit-maximizing firm charges a one price for a service when capacity is fully utilized and a lower price when capacity is underutilized. Off-peak prices are determined by equating marginal revenue to marginal operating costs. Peak prices, on the other hand, are determined by equating marginal revenue to the marginal cost of increasing capacity.

Price leadership appears when an oligopolist establishes a price that is quickly adopted by other firms in the industry. There are two types of price leadership: *barometric price leadership* and *dominant price leadership*.

Barometric price leadership exists when a price change by one firm in an oligopolistic industry, usually in response to perceived changes in macroeconomic or market conditions, is quickly followed by price changes by other firms in the industry.

Dominant price leadership exists when the largest firm in the industry establishes the industry price as a result of its profit-maximizing behavior. Once the industry price has been established, the remaining firms become price takers in the sense that they face a perfectly elastic demand curve for their output.

Other important pricing practices include transfer pricing, price skimming, penetration pricing, prestige pricing, and psychological pricing.

Transfer pricing is a method of correctly pricing a product as it is transferred from one stage of production to another.

Price skimming is the practice of taking advantage of weak or nonexistent competition to change a higher price for a new product than is justified by economic analysis. While competitors are trying to catch up, the firm may have monopoly pricing power.

Penetration pricing is found when a firm entering a new market charges less than its competitors to gain a foothold in the industry.

Prestige pricing is the setting of a high price for a product in the belief that demand will be higher because of the prestige that ownership bestows on the buyer.

Finally, *psychological pricing* is a marketing ploy designed to create the illusion in the mind of the consumer that a product is being sold at a significantly lower price when, in fact, the price differential is inconsequential. A retailer that sells a product for $4.99 instead of $5.00 is engaging in psychological pricing. The effect of psychological pricing tends to be transitory.

KEY TERMS AND CONCEPTS

Barometric price leadership   A price change by one firm in an oligopolistic industry, usually in response to perceived changes in macroeconomic or market conditions, quickly followed by price changes by other firms in the industry.

Block pricing   A form of second-degree price discrimination. It involves charging different prices for different "blocks" of goods and services to enhance profits by extracting at least some consumer surplus.

Commodity bundling   Like block pricing, a form or second-degree price discrimination. Commodity bundling involves the combining of two or more different products into a single package, which is sold at a single price. Like block pricing, commodity bundling is an attempt to enhance profits by extracting at least some consumer surplus.

Consumer surplus   The value of benefits received per unit of output consumed minus the product's selling price.

Cost-plus pricing The most popular form of nonmarginal pricing, cost-plus pricing is the practice of adding a predetermined "markup" to a firm's estimated per-unit cost of production at the time of setting the selling price of its product. Cost-plus pricing is given by the expression $P = ATC(1 + m)$, where m is the percentage markup and ATC is the fully allocated per-unit cost of production. The percentage markup may also be expressed as $m = (P - ATC)/ATC$.

Differential pricing Another term for price discrimination. It involves charging different prices to different groups, for different prices for different blocks of goods or services.

Dominant price leadership Establishment of the industry price by the dominant firm in the industry, as a result of its profit-maximizing behavior. Once the industry price has been established, the remaining firms in the industry become price takers and face a perfectly elastic demand curve for their output.

Dumping Third-degree price discrimination practiced in foreign trade. An exporting company that sells its product at a different, usually lower, price in the foreign market than it does in the home market is practicing dumping.

Dumping margin The difference between the price charged for a product sold by a firm in a foreign market and the price charged in the domestic market.

First-degree price discrimination The changing of a different price for each unit purchased. The price charged for any unit, which is based on the seller's knowledge of the individual buyer's demand curve, reflects the consumer's valuation of each unit purchased. The purpose of first-degree price discrimination is to maximize profits by extracting from each consumer the full amount of consumer surplus.

Full-cost pricing Another term for cost-plus pricing.

Fully allocated per-unit cost The sum of the estimated average variable cost of producing a good or service and a per-unit allocation for fixed cost. It is an approximation of average total cost.

Markup pricing Another term for cost-plus pricing.

Multiproduct pricing Optimal pricing strategies of a firm producing and selling more than one good under a number of alternative scenarios, including pricing of two or more goods with interdependent demands, pricing of two or more goods with independent demands produced in variable proportions, pricing of two or more goods with independent demands jointly produced in fixed proportions, and pricing of two or more goods given capacity limitations.

Nonmarginal pricing The profit maximizing price and output level are determined by equating marginal cost with marginal revenue. Management will often practice nonmarginal pricing, however, when the firm's total cost and total revenue equations are difficult or impossible to estimate. The most popular form of nonmarginal pricing is cost-plus pricing, also known as markup on full-cost pricing.

Peak-load pricing The practice of charging one price for a service when demand is high and capacity is fully utilized and a lower price for the service when demand is low and capacity is underutilized.

Penetration pricing The practice of charging less than the prevailing market price to gain a foothold in the industry; a strategy sometimes selected by firms entering a new market.

Prestige pricing The practice of charging a high price for a product to exploit the belief by some consumers that a high price tag means better quality, which confers upon the owner greater prestige.

Price discrimination The management, by a profit-maximizing firm, to charge different individuals or groups different prices for the same good or service.

Price leadership Seen when a dominant company in an industry establishes the selling price of a product for the rest of the firms in the industry. Two forms of price leadership are barometric price leadership and dominant price leadership.

Price skimming An attempt by a firm that introduces a new product to extract consumer surplus through differential pricing before the firm's competitiors develop their own versions of the new product.

Psychological pricing A marketing ploy designed to create the illusion in the mind of the consumer that a product is being sold at a significantly lower price when, in fact, the price reduction is inconsequential. Retailer sale of a product for $4.99 instead of $5.00 represents psychological pricing.

Relationship between the markup and the price elasticity of demand The size of a firm's markup tends to be inversely related to the price elasticity of demand for a good or service. When the demand for a product is low, the markup tends to be high, and vice versa. This relationship may be expressed as $m = -1/(\varepsilon_p + 1)$.

Second-degree price discrimination Similar in principle to first-degree price discrimination, it involves products in "blocks" or "bundles" rather than one unit at a time.

Third-degree price discrimination Segmenting the market for a particular good or service into easily identifiable groups, with a different price for each group.

Transfer pricing The optimal pricing of the output of one subsidiary of a parent company that is sold as an intermediate good to another subsidiary of the same parent company.

Two-part pricing A variation of second-degree price discrimination, two-part pricing is an attempt to enhance a firm's profits by charging a fixed fee for the right to purchase a good or service, plus a per-unit charge.

The per-unit charge is set equal to the marginal cost of providing the product, while the fixed fee is used to extract maximum consumer surplus, which is pure profit.

Volume discounting   A form of second-degree price discrimination.

CHAPTER QUESTIONS

11.1 Explain each of the following pricing practices.
a. First-degree price discrimination
b. Second-degree price discrimination
c. Third-degree price discrimination

11.2 What is consumer surplus?

11.3 An important objective of firms engaged that practice price discrimination is the extraction of consumer surplus. Do you agree? Explain.

11.4 First-degree price discrimination is a relatively common practice, especially by firms dealing directly with the public, such as restaurants and retail outlets. Do you agree with this statement? If not, then why not?

11.5 What is the difference between block pricing and commodity bundling?

11.6 Sales of frankfurter rolls in packages of eight or beer in six-packs are examples of what pricing practice? What is the objective of the firm?

11.7 Explain the use of block pricing by amusement parks. Why do some amusement parks engage in block pricing while other, usually older, amusement parks do not?

11.8 The pricing of private goods is fundamentally different from the pricing of public goods because of the properties of excludability and depletability. Explain.

11.9 Explain how block pricing by amusement parts is similar to block pricing by cable television companies.

11.10 What is two-part pricing? Provide examples.

11.11 Explain how the practice of commodity bundling may give to a firm an unfair competitive advantage over its rivals.

11.12 Explain cost-plus (markup) pricing. Markup pricing suffers from what theoretical weakness? What are the advantages and disadvantages of markup pricing?

11.13 The more price elastic is the demand for a good or service, the higher will be the price markup over the marginal cost of production. Do you agree with this statement? Explain.

11.14 A firm producing two goods with interrelated demands, such as personal computers and modems, will maximize profits by equating the marginal revenue generated from the sale of each good separately to the marginal cost of producing each good. Do you agree with this statement? Explain.

11.15 A firm producing in variable proportions two goods with independent demands, such as automobile taillight and flashlight bulbs, will maximize profits by equating the marginal cost of producing each good separately to the combined marginal revenue generated from the sale of both goods. Do you agree with this statement? Explain.

11.16 A firm producing two goods with independent demands, which are produced in fixed proportions, will maximize profits by equating the sum of the marginal revenues generated from the sale of both goods, expressed in terms of one of the goods, to the marginal cost of jointly producing both goods. Do you agree? Explain.

11.17 Identify situations in which peak-load pricing may be appropriate. What is the distinguishing characteristic of short-run production functions in these situations?

11.18 Peak-load pricing suggests that users of commuter railroads be charged higher fares during off-peak hours to compensate the company for lost revenues arising from fewer riders. Do you agree with this statement? Explain.

11.19 Suppose a firm that produces a product for sale in the market also produces a vital component of that good for which there is no outside market. How should the firm "price" this component?

11.20 Explain each of the following pricing practices.
a. Barometric price leadership
b. Dominant price leadership
c. Price skimming
d. Penetration pricing
e. Prestige pricing
f. Psychological pricing

CHAPTER EXERCISES

11.1 Assume that an individual's demand for a product is

$$Q = 20 - 0.5P$$

Suppose that the market price of the product $10.
a. Approximate the value of this individual's consumer surplus for $\Delta Q = 1$.
b. What is value of consumer surplus as $\Delta Q \to 0$?

11.2 An amusement park has estimated the following demand equation for the average park guest

$$Q = 16 - 2P$$

where Q represents the number or rides per guest, and P the price per ride. The total cost of providing a ride is characterized by the equation

$$TC = 2 + 0.5Q$$

    a. How much should the park charge on a per-ride basis to maximize its profit? What is the amusement park's total profit per customer?
    b. Suppose that the amusement park decides to charge a one-time admission fee. What admission fee will maximize the park's profit? What is the estimated average profit per park guest?

11.3 A firm sells its product in two separable and identifiable markets. The firm's total cost of production is

$$TC = 5 + 5Q$$

The demand equations for its product in the two markets are

$$Q_1 = 10 - \frac{P_1}{2}$$

$$Q_2 = 20 - \frac{P_2}{5}$$

where $Q = Q_1 + Q_2$.
    a. Calculate the firm's profit-maximizing price and output level in each market.
    b. Verify that the demand for the product is less elastic in the market with the higher price.
    c. Find the firm's total profit at the profit-maximizing prices and output levels.

11.4 Ned Bayward practices third-degree price discrimination when selling barrels of Eastfarthing Leaf in the isolated villages of Toadmorton and Forlorn. The reason for this is that the residents of Toadmorton have a particular preference for Eastfarthing Leaf, while the people in Forlorn can either take it or leave it. Ned's total cost of producing Eastfarthing Leaf is given by the equation

$$TC = 10 + 0.5Q^2$$

The respective demand equations in Forlorn and Toadmorton are

$$Q_1 = 50 - \frac{P_1}{4.5}$$

$$Q_2 = 75 - \frac{P_2}{7.5}$$

where $Q = Q_1 + Q_2$.

   a. Calculate Ned's profit-maximizing price and output level in each market.

   b. Verify that the demand for Eastfarthing Leaf is less elastic in the Toadmorton than in Forlorn. What does your answer imply about Ned's pricing policy?

   c. Find the firm's total profit at the profit-maximizing prices and output levels.

11.5 Suppose a company has estimated the average variable cost of producing its product to be $10. The firms total fixed cost is $100,000.

   a. If the company produces 1,000 units and its standard pricing practice is to add a 35% markup, what price should the company charge?

   b. Verify that the selling price calculated in part a represents a 35% markup over the estimated average cost of production.

11.6 What is the estimated percentage markup over the fully allocated per-unit cost of production for the following price elasticities of demand?

   a. $\varepsilon_p = -10$

   b. $\varepsilon_p = -6$

   c. $\varepsilon_p = -3$

   d. $\varepsilon_p = -2.3$

   e. $\varepsilon_p = -1.8$

11.7 A company produces two products, I and F. The demand equation for F is

$$Q_F = 1,500 - 15P_F$$

The total cost equation is

$$TC_F = 100 + 2Q_F^2$$

The company produces product I exclusively as an intermediate good in the production of product F. The total cost equation for producing good I is

$$TC_1 = 50 - 0.02Q_I^2$$

The company is divided into two semiautonomous profit centers: I division and the F division.

   a. What is the profit-maximizing price and quantity for F division?

   b. What is F division's total profit?

   c. What transfer price should I division charge F division?

SELECTED READINGS

Adams, W. J., and J. I. Yellen. "Commodity Bundling and the Burden of Monopoly." *Quarterly Journal of Economics*, 90 (August 1976), pp. 475–498.

Baye, M. R., and R. O. Beil. *Managerial Economics and Business Strategy*. Burr Ridge, IL: Richard D. Irwin, 1994.

Benson, B. L., M. L. Greenhut, and G. Norman. "On the Basing Point System." *American Economic Review*, 80 (June 1990), pp. 584–588.

Clemens, E. "Price Discrimination and the Multiple Product Firm." *Review of Economic Studies*, 29 (1950–1951), pp. 1–11.

Darden, B. R. "An Operation Approach to Product Pricing." *Journal of Marketing*, April (1968), pp. 29–33.

Hirshleifer, J. "On the Economics of Transfer Pricing." *Journal of Business*, July (1956), pp. 172–184.

———. "Economics of the Divisional Firm." *Journal of Business*, April (1957), pp. 96–108.

Keat, P. G., and P. K. Y. Young. *Managerial Economics: Economic Tools for Today's Decision Makers*, 2nd ed. Upper Saddle River, NJ: Prentice Hall, 1996.

Lanzillotti, R. F. "Pricing Objectives in Large Companies." *American Economic Review*, December (1958), pp. 921–1040.

Littlechild, S. C. "Peak-Load Pricing of Telephone Calls." *The Bell Journal of Economics and Management Science*, Autumn (1970), pp. 191–210.

Oi, W. Y. "A Disneyland Dilemma: Two-Part Tariffs for a Mickey Mouse Monopoly." *Quarterly Journal of Economics*, 85 (February 1971), pp. 77–96.

Robinson, J. *The Economics of Imperfect Competition*. London: Macmillan, 1933.

Salvatore, D. *Managerial Economics*. New York: McGraw-Hill, 1989.

Schneidau, R. E., and R. D. Knutson. "Price Discrimination in the Food Industry: A Competitive Stimulant or Tranquilizer?" *American Journal of Agricultural Economics*, December (1969), pp. 244–246.

Scitovsky, T. "The Benefits of Asymmetric Markets." *Journal of Economic Perspectives*, 4 (Winter 1990), pp. 135–148.

Silberberg, E. S. *The Structure of Economics: A Mathematical Analysis*, 3rd ed. New York: McGraw-Hill, 1990.

Steiner, P. O. Peak Loads and Efficient Pricing. *Quarterly Journal of Economics*, March (1964), pp. 54, 64–76.

Weston, F. J. "Pricing Behavior of Large Firms." *Western Economic Review*, December (1958), pp. 1–18.

Williamson, O. E. "Peak-Load Pricing and Optimal Capacity under Indivisibility Constraints." *American Economic Review*, September (1966), pp. 56, 810–827.

Wirl, F. "Dynamic Demand and Noncompetitive Pricing Strategies." *Journal of Economics*, 54 (1991), pp. 105–121.

Yandle, B., Jr. "Monopoly-Induced Third-Degree Price Discrimination." *Quarterly Review of Economics and Business*, Spring (1971), pp. 71–75.

12

CAPITAL BUDGETING

Much of the preceding discussion was concerned with the manner in which firms organize factors of production during a given period to maximize total economic profits. Clearly this was short-term analysis, with the focus of managerial decision making primarily on day-to-day, operational matters. Whereas short-run profit maximization is certainly important, senior management must also cast an eye to the future well-being of the firm and its shareholders. As a result, senior management must always question whether the current product line is adequate to sustain and enhance the firm's future profitability, or whether current production capacity is sufficient to meet future demand. If production capacity is deemed to be inadequate to meet future needs, the firm must examine its investment options to ascertain its most profitable, risk-adjusted course of action.

This chapter will concentrate on long-term, strategic considerations, focusing primarily on the firm's investment opportunities. The discussions in the preceding chapters have dealt almost entirely with per-period profit maximization. That analysis was fundamentally static. By contrast, investment is fundamentally dynamic, since it involves streams of expenditures and revenues over time. But, $1 received or expended today is worth more than $1 received or expended tomorrow because the $1 may be invested and earn a rate of return. Thus, an essential element of any investment decision is the proper evaluation of alternative investment opportunities involving alternative initial outlays, expected net returns, and time horizons.

In this chapter we evaluate alternative investment opportunities with different characteristics. *Capital budgeting* refers to the process of evaluating the comparative net revenues (expenditures on assets less expected revenues) from alternative investment projects. Since every investment opportunity involves expenditures (cash outflows) and revenues (cash inflows) that are spread out over a number of time periods, capital budgeting is an especially critical element of effective management decision making. Capital budgeting techniques are used to evaluate the potential profitability of possible new product lines, to plan for the replacement of damaged or worn-out (depreciated) plant and equipment, to expand existing production capacity, to engage in research and development, to institute or expand existing worker and management training programs, and evaluate the effectiveness of a major advertising campaign.

Definition: Capital budgeting is the process whereby senior management analyzes the comparative net revenues from alternative investment projects.

CATEGORIES OF CAPITAL BUDGETING PROJECTS

There are several types of capital budgeting decision, including whether to expand facilities, invest in new or improved products, replace worn-out plant and equipment or replace usable equipment with more efficient units; other capital budgeting decisions involve whether to lease or purchase plant and equipment, produce components for a product, or contract components to a vendor. In general, capital budgeting projects may be classified into one of several major categories. We shall discuss *capital expansion*, *replacement*, *new product lines*, *mandated investments*, and *miscellaneous investments*.

CAPITAL EXPANSION

Projected permanent increases in the demand for a firm's output will often lead management to commit significant financial resources to expanding existing production capacity. For companies engaged in the delivery of services (e.g., banking and finance, consulting, the legal profession and other more cerebral activities), capital expansion might take the form of an increase in the number of branch offices, more extensive communications and computing facilities, more intensive and expansive personnel training, and so on.

REPLACEMENT

Over time a firm's plant and equipment may depreciate, be damaged or destroyed, or become obsolete. At a very fundamental level, the replacement of a firm's capital stock is necessary if for no other reason than to maintain existing output levels to meet existing product demand. More subtly, replacement may be necessary to minimize the firm's cash outflows arising from, say, maintenance costs, which is a necessary condition for maximizing the firm's net revenues and shareholder value.

NEW OR IMPROVED PRODUCT LINES

One of the most important roles of management is to keep abreast of changing consumer preferences. Very often, this will require the firm to introduce new or improved goods and services to satisfy often fickle consumer tastes. Once senior management has decided that a change in consumer preferences is likely to continue into the foreseeable future, investment in plant and equipment may be necessary to bring new or improved products to market.

MANDATED INVESTMENTS

The primary obligation of senior management is to satisfy the firm's investors. This obligation often defines the firm's organizational objective, which is usually the maximization of shareholder returns. This concern for the return on shareholders' investment is often tempered, however, by societal or other considerations. These considerations, which often involve quality-of-life issues, such as safety in the workplace or a cleaner environment may entail the construction of access ramps for the disabled or the installation of workplace safety equipment and waste disposal facilities, such as "scrubbers" to treat industrial effluents before they are discharged into the environment.

Mandated capital expenditures often are not undertaken voluntarily because of the obvious negative impact on shareholder returns and company's market share, especially if the firm attempts to pass the increased cost of production along to the customer. In such cases, municipal, state, and federal regulators often step in to mandate such investment expenditures by all firms in an industry, thereby mitigating the competitive disadvantage to any single firm.

MISCELLANEOUS INVESTMENTS

"Miscellaneous investments" is a catchall for capital budgeting projects not easily pigeonholed into any of the foregoing categories. Such capital budgeting projects include the construction of employee parking lots, training and personnel development programs, the purchase of executive jets, or any management decision involving an analysis of cash outflows and inflows that do not easily fall into traditional capital budgeting classifications.

TIME VALUE OF MONEY

At its core, capital budgeting recognizes that $1 received today does not have the same value as $1 received tomorrow. Why not? From a psychological perspective it could be argued that, other things being equal, most people prefer the current consumption and enjoyment of a good or a service to consumption at some future date. There are, however, more practical reasons to conclude that $1 today is worth more than $1 tomorrow. If that $1 were deposited into a savings account paying a certain 5% annual interest rate, the value of that deposit would be worth $1.05 a year later. Thus, receiving $1 today is worth $1.05 a year from now.

Definition: The time value of money reflects the understanding that a dollar received today is worth more than a dollar received tomorrow.

In capital budgeting, future cash inflows and outflows of different capital investment projects are expressed as a single value at a common point in time for purposes of comparison. In most cases, future cash flows are expressed as a single value at the moment of undertaking the project.

CASH FLOWS

FUTURE VALUE WITH DISCRETE (ANNUAL) COMPOUNDING

The *future value* of an investment refers to the final accumulated value of a sum of money at some future time period, usually denoted as $t = n$. The future value of an investment will depend, of course, not only on the rate of return on that investment, i, but also how often that rate of return is calculated. The frequency of calculation of the rate of return is called *compounding*.

Definition: Future value is the final accumulated value of a sum of money at some future time period.

Definition: Compounding refers to the frequency that the rate of return on an investment is calculated.

Suppose, for example, that on May 1, 2000 ($t = 0$) an investor deposits $500 into a certificate of deposit that pays an annually compounded nominal (market) interest rate of 5%. Assume further that the investor plans to make no additional deposits. How much will the certificate of deposit be worth on April 30, 2005 ($t = 5$). It is often useful to visualize such problems with a *cash flow diagram*. Figure 12.1 presents the cash flow diagram for this problem.

Note that in Figure 12.1 the downward-pointing arrow at $t = 0$ represents an outflow of $500 as funds are deposited into the certificate of deposit. When the certificate of deposit matures on April 30, 2005, the future value

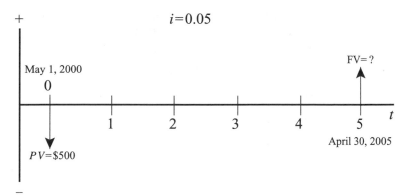

FIGURE 12.1   Future value cash flow diagram.

of the initial investment will be returned in the form of a cash inflow, which is illustrated as the upward-pointing arrow at $t = 5$.

Definition: A cash flow diagram illustrates the cash inflows and cash outflows expected to arise from a given investment.

We define the *present value* as the value of a sum of money at some initial time period, usually denoted as $t = 0$. In Figure 12.1, the present value of the certificate of deposit on May 31, 2000, is $500. What will be the future value of this investment at the end of 5 years if the interest rate earned is 5% ($i = 0.05$) annually. Assume that interest is paid on the last day of each period (April 30) and that interest earnings are reinvested.

Definition: Present value is value of a sum of money at some initial time period.

It is easily seen that the accumulated value of the certificate of deposit at the end of the first year (May 1, 2000, to April 30, 2001) is

$$FV_1 = PV_0 + PV_0 i = PV_0(1+i) = \$500(1.05) = \$525 \qquad (12.1)$$

where PV_0 represents the present value of the investment at the beginning of the first year and FV_1 refers to the future value of the certificate of deposit at the end of the first year.

Suppose further that FV_1 (principal and earned interest) is reinvested in the certificate of deposit for a second year at the same interest rate, $i = 0.05$. The future value of the certificate of deposit at the end of the second year ($t = 2$) is

$$FV_2 = FV_1 + FV_1 i = FV_1(1+i) = \$525(1.05) = \$551.25 \qquad (12.2)$$

Note that Equation (12.1) may be substituted into Equation (12.2) to yield

$$FV_2 = PV_0(1+i)(1+i) = PV_0(1+i)^2 = \$500(1.05)^2 = \$551.25 \qquad (12.3)$$

If we continue to assume that principal and accumulated interest are reinvested at the prevailing rate of interest, then the future value of the certificate of deposit at the end of the third year ($t = 3$) is

$$FV_3 = FV_2 + FV_2 i = FV_2(1+i) = \$551.25(1.05) = \$578.81 \qquad (12.4)$$

Once again, substituting Equation (12.3) into Equation (12.4) we get

$$
\begin{aligned}
FV_3 &= FV_2(1+i) = PV_0(1+i)^2(1+i) \\
&= PV_0(1+i)^3 = 500(1.05)^3 = \$578.81
\end{aligned}
\qquad (12.5)
$$

Repeating this procedure, we find that at the end of 5 years, the value of the certificate of deposit is

$$FV_5 = PV_0(1+i)^5 = \$500(1.05)^5 = \$500(1.2763) = \$638.14 \qquad (12.6)$$

The step-by-step calculation of the future value of $500, compounded annually for 5 years at $i = 0.05$, is illustrated in Figure 12.2, where the downward-pointing arrow at $t = 0$ indicates a cash outflow (−) following the purchase of the certificate of deposit. In $t = 5$ the upward-pointing arrow represents the cash inflow of $638.14 as cash is received when the certificate of deposit matures.

If we generalize the foregoing calculations, the future value of an initial investment for n periods is

$$FV_n = PV_0(1+i)^n \qquad (12.7)$$

Problem 12.1. Adam borrows $10,000 at an interest rate of 6% compounded annually from National Security Bank to buy a new car. If Adam agrees to a lump-sum repayment of the principal and interest, how much must he repay in 3 years?

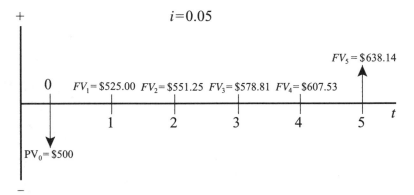

FIGURE 12.2 Future value cash flow diagram.

Solution. Substituting the information provided into Equation (12.7) yields

$$FV_3 = PV_0(1+i)^n = \$10,000(1.06)^3 = \$10,000(1.191) = \$11,910.16$$

This solution is summarized in the cash flow diagram of Figure 12.3.

Note, again, that at $t = 0$ the upward-pointing arrow indicates that the loan of $10,000 represents a cash inflow (+). At $t = 3$ the downward-pointing arrow represents the loan repayment and interest payment, which is a cash outflow (−).

FUTURE VALUE WITH DISCRETE (MORE FREQUENT) COMPOUNDING

The discussion thus far has focused on the future value of a cash amount at some interest rate compounded annually. In most cases, however, interest will be compounded more frequently, say semiannually, quarterly, or monthly. Most bonds, for example, pay interest semiannually; stocks typically pay dividends quarterly, and most mortgages, automobile loans, and student loans require monthly payments.

Consider, again, the example illustrated in Figure 12.1. Suppose that the certificate of deposit pays 5%, which is compounded semiannually. To begin with, the student should note that the number of compounding periods has been doubled from 5 to 10. Since compounding will occur every 6 months instead of every 12 months, the periodic interest rate is now 2.5% semiannually instead of 5% per year. With these adjustments, Equation (12.6) may be rewritten as

$$FV_5 = PV_0\left(1+\frac{i}{2}\right)^{5\times2} = \$500(1.025)^{10} = \$640.04 \qquad (12.8)$$

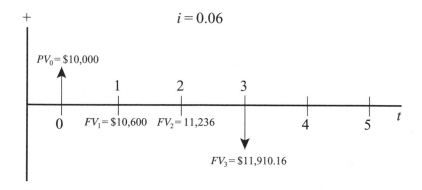

FIGURE 12.3 Diagrammatic solution to problem 12.1.

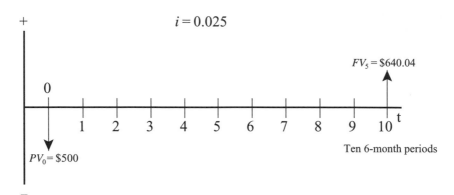

FIGURE 12.4 Future value cash flow diagram with discrete compounding.

This solution is illustrated in Figure 12.4.

The future value calculations just considered are examples of discrete compounding, that is, interest rate compounding that occurs at specific time intervals. In general, for more frequent compounding over n periods Equation (12.7) may be rewritten as

$$FV_n = PV_0 \left(1 + \frac{i}{m}\right)^{mn} \tag{12.9}$$

where i is the nominal (market) interest, n is the number of years, and m is the number of times that compounding takes place per year.

Problem 12.2. Suppose that in Problem 12.1 Adam had borrowed $10,000 from National Security Bank to buy a new car and agreed to repay the loan in 3 years at an annual interest rate of 6% compounded monthly. What is the total amount that Adam must repay?

Solution. Substituting the information provided into Equation (12.7) yields

$$FV_n = PV_0 \left(1 + \frac{i}{m}\right)^{mn}$$

$$FV_3 = \$10,000 \left(1 + \frac{0.06}{12}\right)^{12 \times 3} = \$10,000(1.005)^{36} = \$11,966.81$$

Clearly more frequent compounding results in higher interest payments for Adam of $56.65 than if interest is compounded annually.

Problem 12.3. Suppose that Sergeant Garcia deposits $100,000 in a time deposit that pays 10% interest per year compounded annually. How much will Sergeant Garcia receive when the deposit matures after 5 years? How would your answer have been different for interest compounded quarterly?

Solution. The future value of Sergeant Garcia's deposit of $100,000 that pays an interest rate of 10% compounded annually is

$$FV_n = PV_0(1+i)^n = \$100,000(1.1)^5 = \$100,000(1.61051) = \$161,051$$

The future value of Sergeant Garcia's deposit when compounded quarterly is

$$FV_n = PV_0\left(1+\frac{i}{m}\right)^{mn} = \$100,000\left(1+\frac{0.1}{4}\right)^{5\times4}$$

$$= \$100,000(1.025)^{20} = \$163.861.64$$

FUTURE VALUE WITH CONTINUOUS COMPOUNDING

Referring to Equation (12.9), what happens as the number of compounding periods becomes infinitely large, that is, as $m \to \infty$? This is the case of continuous compounding. To understand the effect of continuous compounding on the future value of a particular sum, recall from Chapter 2 the definition of the natural logarithm of base e:

$$e = \lim_{h\to\infty}\left(1+\frac{1}{h}\right)^h = 2.71829\ldots \tag{2.50}$$

Setting $1/h = i/m$ and substituting into Equation (12.9), we obtain

$$FV_n = PV_0\left(1+\frac{i}{m}\right)^{mn} = PV_0\left(1+\frac{1}{h}\right)^{mn} \tag{12.10}$$

where i is the interest rate and $1/h$ is the interest rate per compounding period. Substituting $m = hi$ into Equation (12.10) yields

$$FV_n = PV_0\left[\left(1+\frac{1}{h}\right)^h\right]^{in} \tag{12.11}$$

From Equation (2.50), the limit of Equation (12.11) as h approaches infinity is

$$FV_n = \lim_{h\to\infty}PV_0\left[\left(1+\frac{1}{h}\right)^h\right]^{i} = PV_0\left[\lim_{h\to\infty}\left(1+\frac{1}{h}\right)^h\right]^{in} = PV_0e^{in} \tag{12.12}$$

Problem 12.4. Suppose that Adam borrows $10,000 from National Security Bank and agrees to repay the loan in 3 years at an interest rate of 6% per year, compounded continuously. How much must Adam repay the bank at the end of 3 years?

Solution. Substituting the information provided into Equation (12.12) yields

$$FV_n = PV_0 e^{in}$$

$$FV_3 = \$10,000 e^{0.06 \times 3} = \$10,000(2.71829\ldots)^{0.18}$$

$$= \$10,000(1.1972) = \$11,972.17$$

This result indicates that Adam will have to pay $5.36 more in interest than if interest is compounded monthly, and $62.01 more than if interest is compounded annually.

FUTURE VALUE OF AN ORDINARY (DEFERRED) ANNUITY (FVOA)

Thus far we have considered the future value of a single cash amount that earns an interest rate of i for n years compounded m times per year. Suppose, however, that an individual wanted to make regular and periodic investment over the life of the investment? Such investments are referred to as annuities. For example, suppose that a person wanted to invest $500 into an interest-bearing account at the end of each of the next 5 years, with an interest rate of 5% per year compounded annually. What is the future value of these investments at the end of the fifth year? This situation, which is illustrated in Figure 12.5, is referred to as an ordinary (deferred) annuity.

In the case of an ordinary annuity, note carefully that the fixed payments are made at the *end* of each period. Thus, the first deposit is made at the end of $t = 0$, which means that no interest will be earned until the start of $t = 1$. Moreover, the final annuity payment is not made until the *end* of $t = 5$. Since the account matures at the end of 5 years, no interest will be earned on the final deposit. At first, the reader may find such an arrangement peculiar. After all, what type of investment requires that the first deposit be made at the end of the first year and the last deposit made at maturity? The confusion quickly disappears, however, when it is recalled that banks often

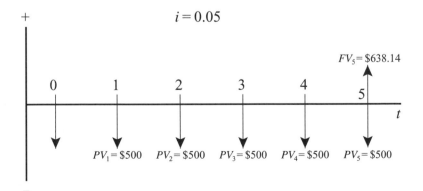

FIGURE 12.5   Future value of an ordinary annuity cash flow diagram.

make loans in which the first repayment is not made until the end of the first month, with the final payment made at maturity. Such an arrangement is called an amortized loan and represents an investment for the bank.

Definition: An annuity is a series of equal payments, which are made at fixed intervals for a specified number of periods.

Definition: An ordinary (deferred) annuity is an annuity in which the fixed payments are made at the end of each period.

Definition: The future value of an ordinary annuity ($FVOA$) is the future value of an annuity in which the fixed payments are made at the end of each period.

For the situation depicted in Figure 12.5, the future value of the ordinary annuity may be determined by calculating the sum of the future value of each of five separate investments, that is,

$$FVOA_5 = PV_1(1+i)^4 + PV_2(1+i)^3 + PV_3(1+i)^2 + PV_4(1+i)^1 + PV_5(1+i)^0$$

Substituting the annuity value and interest rate from Figure 12.5 into the foregoing expression yields

$$FVOA_5 = \$500(1.05)^4 + \$500(1.05)^3 + \$500(1.05)^2 + \$500(1.05)^1 + \$500(1)$$
$$= \$500(1.21551) + \$500(1.15763) + \$500(1.1025)$$
$$+ \$500(1.05) + \$500(1)$$
$$= \$607.76 + \$578.81 + \$551.25 + \$525.00 + \$500 = \$2,762.82$$

In general, if we denote the constant annuity payment as A, the future value of fixed annuity payments for n periods in which the first payment is made at the end of $t = 0$ is

$$FVOA_n = A(1+i)^{n-1} + A(1+i)^{n-2} + \ldots + A(1+i)^0$$
$$= A \sum_{t=1 \to n} (1+i)^{n-1} \tag{12.13}$$

By the algebra of a sum of a geometric progression (see Chapter 2), Equation (12.12) may be rewritten as

$$FVOA_n = \frac{A\left[(1+i)^n - 1\right]}{i} \tag{12.14}$$

Applying Equation (12.14) to the information provided yields the same outcome as before:

$$FVOA_5 = \frac{\$500\left[(1.05)^5 - 1\right]}{0.05} = \frac{\$500(0.2763)}{0.05}$$
$$= \frac{\$138.14}{0.05} = \$2,762.82$$

The value $[(1 + i)^n - 1]/i$ is referred to as the *future value interest factor for an annuity* ($FVIFA_{i,n}$).

FUTURE VALUE OF AN ANNUITY DUE (FVAD)

Suppose that in our example the five payments of \$500 had commenced at the beginning of the first year (i.e., at $t = 0$) rather than at the beginning of the second year ($t = 1$). This is the same thing as saying that an investor has decided to deposit \$500 immediately, and another \$500 each year for the next 4 years. This arrangement is similar to many savings programs. How much will the investor withdraw at the end of the fifth year? This sort of arrangement, which is referred is to as an annuity due, is depicted in Figure 12.6.

Definition: An annuity due is an annuity in which the fixed payments are made at the beginning of each period.

Definition: The future value of an annuity due is the future value of an annuity in which the fixed payments are made at the beginning of each period.

In the case of an annuity due, the fixed payments are made at the *beginning* of each period. Thus, the first deposit is made at the beginning of $t = 0$ and begins to earn interest immediately. Moreover, in the case depicted in Figure 12.6, the final annuity payment is not made until the beginning of $t = 5$. As with an ordinary annuity, the future value of an annuity due may be determined by calculating the sum of the future value of each of five separate investments. The difference, of course, is that the future value of an annuity due is equal to the future value of an ordinary annuity compounded for one additional period.

$$FVAD_n = FVOA_n(1+i) = A\left\{\frac{\left[(1+i)^n - 1\right]}{i}\right\}(1+i) \qquad (12.15)$$

By using the information depicted in Figure 12.6, we find the future value of an annuity due:

$$FVAD_5 = FVOA_5(1.05) = \$2,762.82(1.05) = \$2,900.96$$

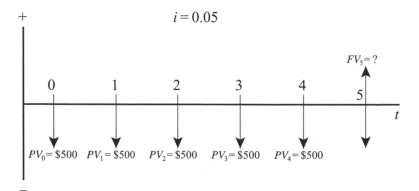

FIGURE 12.6   Future value of an annuity due cash flow diagram.

Compare this amount with the future value of an ordinary annuity of $2,762.82. The difference of $138.14 is attributable to allowing each payment of $500 to compound for one additional period.

Problem 12.5. Andrew's father, Tom, is thinking about putting away a few dollars away to help pay for his son's college tuition. Tom would like to invest $1,000 a year for 10 years into a certificate of deposit. He is reasonably certain of earning an annual interest rate of 5% per annum over the life of the investment. Tom is uncertain, however, whether to open the certificate of deposit immediately, or wait until the end of the year to make his first deposit. Tom realizes that by waiting a year before making his deposit that he will lose a full year of interest compounding. On the other hand, he has the opportunity of earning $100 in interest the first year by lending $1,000 to his Uncle Ned. Assume that Uncle Ned is not a deadbeat and will repays the loan with interest. Suppose that Tom plans to deposit the $100 in interest earned in a regular savings account earning 4% interest annually for 9 years. Should Tom make the loan to Uncle Ned and deposit the initial $1,000 at the end of the year, or should he open the certificate of deposit immediately?

Solution. If Tom decides to deposit $1,000 into a certificate of deposit immediately, the future value of an annuity due is

$$FVAD_n = A\left\{\frac{\left[(1+i)^n - 1\right]}{i}\right\}(1+i) = \$1,000\left\{\frac{\left[(1.05)^{10} - 1\right]}{0.05}\right\}(1.05) = \$13,209$$

On the other hand, if Tom decides to wait a year before making the first deposit, the future value of an ordinary annuity is

$$FVOA_n = \frac{A\left[(1+i)^n - 1\right]}{i} = \frac{\$1,000[(1.05^{10} - 1)]}{0.05} = \$1,000(12.578) = \$12,578$$

To this amount must be added the future value of $100 received from Uncle Ned compounded annually for 9 years at an interest rate of 4%. This amount is given as

$$FV_n = PV_0(1+i)^n = \$100(1.04)^9 = \$100(1.4233) = \$142.33$$

Adding this amount to the future value of an ordinary annuity yields

$$\$12,578 + \$143.33 = \$12,721.33$$

Since he can make $13,209 by opening the certificate of deposit immediately, Tom will not make the loan to Uncle Ned.

FUTURE VALUE OF AN UNEVEN CASH FLOW

The two preceding sections were devoted to calculating the future value of an annuity, which is sometimes referred to as an even cash flow. In this

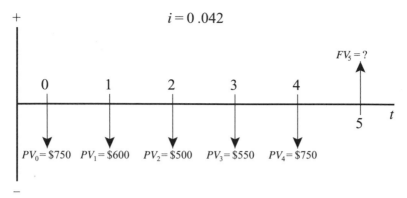

FIGURE 12.7   Uneven cash flow.

section we will discuss the calculation of an uneven cash flow. The future value of an uneven cash flow is determined by compounding each payment and summing the future values. The future value of an uneven cash flow is sometimes referred to as the terminal value. Figure 12.7 illustrates an uneven cash flow diagram.

The future value of the uneven cash flow may be calculated by repeatedly applying Equation (12.7). In particular, the present value of an uneven cash flow is

$$FV_n = PV_0(1+i)^n + PV_1(1+i)^{n-1} + \ldots + PV_{t-1}(1+i)^{n-t}$$
$$= \sum_{t=0\to n} PV_t(1+i)^{n-t} \tag{12.16}$$

The future value of the uneven cash flow depicted in Figure 12.7 at $t = 5$ is

$$FV_5 = 750(1.042)^5 + 600(1.042)^4 + 500(1.042)^3 + 550(1.042)^2 + 750(1.042)^1$$
$$= \$3752.98$$

This solution is illustrated in Figure 12.8.

PRESENT VALUE WITH DISCRETE (ANNUAL) COMPOUNDING

So far we have considered the answer to the question: What will be the value of a payment, or series of payments, at the end of a given period of time? We would now like to turn this around a bit. Suppose that we were interested in determining the value an immediate payment, or series of payments, required to grow to a specified value at some time in the future. Suppose, for example, that Adam wanted to know how much he needed to invest in a certificate of deposit today at 5% interest such that the value of

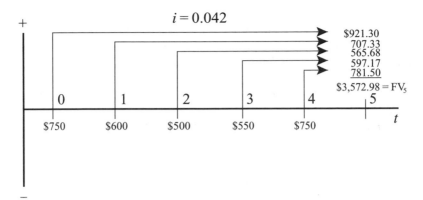

FIGURE 12.8   Future value of an uneven cash flow.

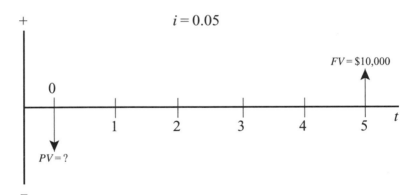

FIGURE 12.9   Present value with discrete (annual) compounding.

the investment in 5 years would be $10,000. This amount is referred to as the *present value* of the investment. The cash flow diagram for this problem is depicted in Figure 12.9.

Definition: Present value is the value today of an investment, or series of investments, that will grow to some future specified amount at a desig-nated rate of interest.

To calculate the present value of a lump-sum investment for n periods at an interest rate of i, consider again Equation (12.7).

$$FV_n = PV_0(1+i)^n \tag{12.7}$$

Solving Equation (12.7) for PV_0 yields

$$PV_0 = \frac{FV_n}{(1+i)^n} \tag{12.17}$$

The present value of an investment, or series of investments, at some designated rate of interest is often referred to as *discounted cash flow*. The rate of interest that is used to discount a cash flow is called the *discount rate*.

Definition: A discounted cash flow is the present value of an investment or series of investments.

Definition: The discount rate is the rate of interest that is used to discount a cash flow.

Substituting the foregoing information into Equation (12.17), we find that the present value of an investment earning 5% interest compounded annually that will be worth $10,000 in 5 years is

$$PV_0 = \frac{\$10,000}{(1.05)^5} = \frac{\$10,000}{1.276} = \$7,835.26$$

That is, if Adam invests $7,835.26 into a certificate of deposit that earns 5% compounded annually, the value of the investment in 5 years will be $10,000.

Problem 12.6. How much should Turin Turambar invest in a certificate of deposit today for that investment to be worth $500 in 7 years if the interest rate is 18% per year, compounded annually?

Solution. Substituting this information into Equation (12.17), we find that the present value of the investment is

$$PV_0 = \frac{FV_n}{(1+i)^n} = \frac{\$500}{(1.18)^7} = \frac{\$500}{3.185} = \$156.96$$

PRESENT VALUE WITH DISCRETE (MORE FREQUENT) AND CONTINUOUS COMPOUNDING

To calculate the present value of a lump-sum investment for n periods at an interest rate of i compounded m times per period, consider again Equation (12.9).

$$FV_n = PV_0 \left(1 + \frac{i}{m}\right)^{mn} \qquad (12.9)$$

Solving Equation (12.9) for PV_0 yields

$$PV_0 = \frac{FV_n}{(1+i/m)^{mn}} \qquad (12.18)$$

To calculate the present value of a lump-sum investment for n periods at an interest rate of i compounded continuously, consider again Equation (12.12).

$$FV_n = PV_0 e^{in} \qquad (12.12)$$

Solving Equation (12.11) for PV_0 yields

$$PV_0 = \frac{FV_n}{e^{in}} \tag{12.19}$$

To continue with our example, suppose that Adam wanted to know how much he needed to invest in a certificate of deposit today at a 5% interest rate compounded quarterly so that the final value of the investment, 5 years from now, would be $10,000. Substituting this information into Equation (12.18), we get

$$PV_0 = \frac{FV_n}{(1+i/m)^{mn}} = \frac{\$10,000}{(1+0.05/4)^{4\times5}} = \$7,800.09$$

How much would the initial investment be if interest were compounded continuously? Substituting this information into Equation (12.19) we obtain

$$PV_0 = \frac{FV_n}{e^{in}} = \frac{\$10,000}{e^{0.05\times5}} = \$7,788.01$$

Compare the present value of $10,000 with annual compounding ($7,835.26) with the present values where interest is compounded quarterly ($7,800.09) and continuously ($7,788.01). Clearly, the more frequent the compounding, the smaller is the required initial investment.

Problem 12.7. If the prevailing interest rate on a time deposit is 8% per year, how much would Sergeant Garcia have to deposit today to receive $200,000 at the end of 5 years if the interest rate were compounded quarterly, monthly, and continuously?

Solution. To receive $200,000 in 5 years on a time deposit that pays 8% compounded quarterly, Sergeant Garcia will have to invest

$$PV_0 = \frac{FV_n}{(1+i/m)^{mn}} = \frac{\$200,000}{(1+0.08/4)^{4\times5}} = \$134,594.27$$

If interest is compounded monthly, Sergeant Garcia will have to invest

$$PV_0 = \frac{FV_n}{(1+i/m)^{mn}} = \frac{\$200,000}{(1+0.08/12)^{12\times5}} = \$134,424.09$$

Finally, if interest is compounded continuously Sergeant Garcia will have to invest

$$PV_0 = \frac{FV_n}{e^{in}} = \frac{\$200,000}{e^{0.08\times5}} = \frac{\$200,000}{e^{0.4}} = \$134,064.01$$

Note, once again, that the more frequent the compounding, the smaller the present value, or the amount to be invested at $t = 0$.

PRESENT VALUE OF AN ORDINARY
ANNUITY (PVOA)

Earlier, we introduced the concept of an annuity as a series of fixed payments made at fixed intervals for a specified period of time. An ordinary (deferred) annuity was defined as a series of payments made at the end of each period. Another way to evaluate ordinary annuities is to calculate their present values. In general, the present value of an ordinary annuity may be calculated by using Equation (12.20):

$$PVOA_n = \frac{A}{(1+i)^1} + \frac{A}{(1+i)^2} + \dots + \frac{A}{(1+i)^n}$$
$$= A \sum_{t=1 \to n} \left(\frac{1}{1+i}\right)^t \qquad (12.20)$$

Consider, again, the situation depicted in Figure 12.5, where an investor deposits $500 at the end of each of the next 5 years and earns 5% per year compounded annually. What is the present value of these investments at the *beginning* of $t = 1$, which is the same thing as the end of $t = 0$? Substituting the information provided into Equation (12.20), the present value of the annuity due is

$$PVOA_5 = \frac{\$500}{(1.05)^1} + \frac{\$500}{(1.05)^2} + \frac{\$500}{(1.05)^3} + \frac{\$500}{(1.05)^4} + \frac{\$500}{(1.05)^5} = \$2,164.73$$

The cash flow diagram for this problem is illustrated in Figure 12.10.

Problem 12.8. Suppose that an individual invests $2,500 at the end of each of the next 6 years and earns an annual interest rate of 8%. Calculate the present value of this series of annuity payments.

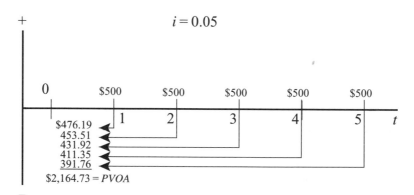

FIGURE 12.10   Present value of an ordinary annuity cash flow diagram.

Solution. Substituting the information provided into Equation (12.20) yields

$$PVOA_n = A \sum_{t=1 \to n} \left(\frac{1}{1+i}\right)^t$$

$$PVOA_6 = \$2,500 \sum_{t=1 \to 6} \left(\frac{1}{1+0.08}\right)^t$$

$$= \frac{\$2,500}{(1.08)^1} + \frac{\$2,500}{(1.08)^2} + \frac{\$2,500}{(1.08)^3} + \frac{\$2,500}{(1.08)^4} + \frac{\$2,500}{(1.02)^5} + \frac{\$2,500}{(1.02)^6}$$

$$= \$11,557.20$$

PRESENT VALUE OF AN ANNUITY DUE (PVAD)

As we saw, an annuity due is an annuity in which the fixed payments are made at the beginning of each period. In general, the present value of an annuity due may be calculated by using Equation (12.21).

$$PVAD_n = \frac{A}{(1+n)^{n-1}} + \frac{A}{(1+n)^{n-2}} + \dots + \frac{A}{(1+n)^0}$$

$$= A \sum_{t=0 \to n} \left(\frac{1}{1+i}\right)^{n-t} \tag{12.21}$$

By substituting the information provided in Figure 12.7 into Equation (12.21), we find that the present value of an annuity due is

$$PVAD_5 = \frac{\$500}{(1.05)^4} + \frac{\$500}{(1.05)^3} + \frac{\$500}{(1.05)^2} + \frac{\$500}{(1.05)^1} + \frac{\$500}{(1.05)^0}$$

$$= \$411.35 + \$431.92 + \$453.51 + \$476.19 + \$500 = \$2,272,97$$

The cash flow diagram for this problem is illustrated in Figure 12.11.

Problem 12.9. Suppose that an individual invests \$2,500 at the beginning of each of the next 6 years and earns an annual interest rate of 8%. Calculate the value of this series of annuity payments. How does this result compare with the solution to Problem 12.8?

Solution. Substituting the information provided into Equation (12.21) yields

$$PVAD_n = A \sum_{t=0 \to n} \left(\frac{1}{1+i}\right)^{n-t}$$

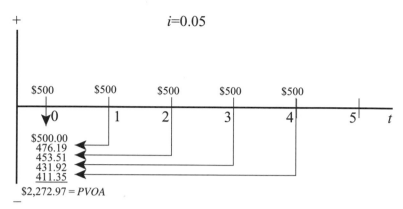

FIGURE 12.11   Present value of an annuity due cash flow diagram.

$$PVAD_6 = \$2,500 \sum_{t=1\to 6}\left(\frac{1}{1.08}\right)^{n-t}$$

$$= \frac{\$2,500}{(1.08)^5} + \frac{\$2,500}{(1.08)^4} + \frac{\$2,500}{(1.08)^3} + \frac{\$2,500}{(1.08)^2} + \frac{\$2,500}{(1.08)^1} + \frac{\$2,500}{(1.08)^0}$$

$$= \$12,481.78$$

The present value of an annuity due in this problem is less than the present value of an ordinary annuity calculated in Problem 12.8 because

$$PVOA_6 - PVAD_6 = \frac{\$2,500}{(1.02)^6} - \frac{\$2,500}{(1.08)^0}$$

where $\$2,500/(1.08)^6 < \$2,500/(1.08)^0$. In other words, since compounding takes place for one less period, $PVOA_6 > PVAD_6$.

AMORTIZED LOANS

Amortized loans represent one of the most useful applications of the future value of an ordinary annuity. These loans are repaid in equal periodic installments. Once again, consider the example in which Adam borrows $10,000 from National Security Bank to buy a new car. Suppose that Adam agrees to repay the loan in 3 years at an interest rate of 6% per year, compounded annually. Adam further agrees to repay the loan in equal annual installments, with the first installment due at the end of the first year. How can he determine the amount of his yearly debt service (principal and interest) payments? This problem is depicted in Figure 12.12.

To determine the amount of Adam's monthly payments, consider again Equation (12.20).

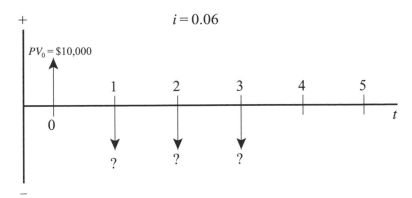

FIGURE 12.12 Amortized loan cash flow diagram.

$$PVOA_n = A \sum_{t=1 \to n} \left(\frac{1}{1+i} \right)^t \qquad (12.20)$$

In this case, we know that $PVOA_3 = \$10,000$ and $i = 0.06$. The task at hand is to determine the amount of Adam's yearly payments, A. Solving Equation (12.20) for A we obtain

$$A = \frac{PVOA_n}{\Sigma_{t=1 \to n}[1/(1+i)]^t} \qquad (12.22)$$

Substituting the information provided in the problem into Equation (12.22) and solving yields

$$A = \frac{PVOA_n}{\Sigma_{t=1 \to n}[1/(1+i)]^t}$$

$$= \frac{\$10,000}{(1/1.06) + (1/1.06)^2 + (1/1.06)^3} = \$3,741.11$$

Thus, Adam must pay National Security Bank $3,741.11 at the end of each of the next three years. Each payment consists of interest due and partial repayment of principal. This series of repayments is referred to as an *amortization schedule*. The reader should verify that the largest interest component of the amortization schedule is paid in at the end of the first year; thereafter, as the amount of the principal outstanding declines, the payments are correspondingly less.

Problem 12.10. Suppose that Andrew borrows $250,000 at 3% to purchase a new home. Andrew agrees to repay the loan in 10 equal annual installments, with the first payment due at the end of the first year.
a. What is the amount of Andrew's mortgage payments?
b. What is the total amount of interest paid?

Solution

a. Substituting the information provided into Equation (12.22) yields

$$A = \frac{PVOA_n}{\Sigma_{t=1 \to n}[1/(1+i)]^t}$$

$$= \frac{\$250,000}{\Sigma_{t=1 \to 10}[1/(1+1.03)]^t} = \frac{\$250,000}{8.5302} = \$29,307.63$$

b. Andrew will make total mortgage payments of 10(29,307.63) = $293,076.27. Thus, the total amount of interest paid will be $293,076.27 − $250,000 = $43,076.27.

METHODS FOR EVALUATING CAPITAL INVESTMENT PROJECTS

Now that the fundamental techniques for assessing the time value of money have been established, we turn our attention to some of the most commonly used methods of assessing the returns on capital investment projects. There are five standard methods for ranking capital investment projects. Each method ranks capital investment projects from the most preferred to the least preferred based on the project's net rate of return (i.e., the rate of return from the investment over and above the total cost of financing the project). The cost to the firm of acquiring funds to finance a capital investment project is commonly referred to as its *cost of capital*.

The five most commonly used methods for ranking capital investment projects are the *payback period*, the *discounted payback period*, the *net present value* (*NPV*) method, the *internal rate of return* (*IRR*), and the *modified rate of return* (*MIRR*). We will, illustrate each method by using the hypothetical cash flows (*CF_t*) for projects *A* and *B* summarized in Table 12.1. To keep the analyses manageable, we will assume that cash flows have been adjusted to reflect inflation, taxes, depreciation, and salvage values.

TABLE 12.1 Net Cash Flows (*CF_t*) for Projects *A* and *B*

Year, t	Project A	Project B
0	−$25,000	−$25,000
1	10,000	3,000
2	8,000	5,000
3	6,000	7,000
4	5,000	9,000
5	4,000	11,000

PAYBACK PERIOD METHOD

The payback period of a capital investment project is the number of periods required to recover the original investment. In general, the shorter the payback period, the more preferred the capital investment project. Using the payback period method to evaluate alternative investment opportunities is perhaps the oldest technique for evaluating capital budgeting projects.

Definition: The payback period is the number of periods required to recover the original investment.

We can see that for project A by the end of year 3 cumulative cash flows are $24,000, or 96% of the original investment has been recovered. By the end of year 4 cumulative cash flows are $29,000, or 116% of the original investment has been recovered. Since only an additional $1,000 cash flow was required in year 4 to fully cover the original $25,000 investment, then the total number of years required to recover the original investment (P_A) was 3 years plus $1,000/$5,000 years, or 3.2 years. The payback period for Project B (P_B) is 4 years plus $1,000/$11,000 years, or 4.09 years In general, the expression for calculating the payback period is

$$P_j = (F-1) + \frac{(-CF_0 - \Sigma_{t=1 \to F-1} CF_t)}{CF_F} \qquad (12.23)$$

where P_k is the payback period of investment j, $(F-1)$ is the year before full recovery of the original investment, CF_0 is the original investment, which is a cash outflow $(-)$, $\Sigma_{t=1 \to F-1} CF_t$ is the sum of all cash flows up to and including the year before full recovery of the original investment, and CF_F is the cash flow in the year of full recovery. Substituting the information in Table 12.1 into Equation (12.23) we obtain

$$P_A = 3 + \frac{-(-\$25,000) - \$24,000}{\$5,000} = 3 + \frac{\$1,000}{\$5,000} = 3.20 \text{ years}$$

$$P_B = 4 + \frac{-(-\$25,000) - \$24,000}{\$11,000} = 4 + \frac{\$1,000}{\$11,000} = 4.09 \text{ years}$$

Assuming that these projects are *mutually exclusive*, investment project A is preferred to project B because project A has a shorter payback period. Projects are said to be mutually exclusive if the acceptance of one project means that all other potential projects are rejected. Projects are said to be *independent* if the cash flows from alternative projects are unrelated to each other.

Definition: Projects are mutually exclusive if acceptance of one project means rejection of all other projects.

Definition: Projects are independent if their cash flows are unrelated.

Problem 12.11. The chief financial analyst of Valaquenta Microprocessors, Inc. has been asked to analyze two proposed capital investment projects, projects A and B. Each project has an initial cost of $10,000. The projects cash flows, which have been adjusted to reflect inflation, taxes, depreciation, and salvage values, are as follows:

Which project should be selected according to the payback period method?

Solution. From the information in Table 12.2, by the end of year 2, the year before full recovery, the cumulative cash flow for project A is $9,500, or 95% of the original investment. By the end of year 3, the year of full recovery, cumulative cash flows are $11,000, or 110 percent of the original investment. The cumulative cash flow for project B by the end of year 2 is $8,000, or 80% of the original investment. By the end of year 3 the cumulative cash flow for Project B is $12,000, or 120% of the original investment. Substituting the rest of the information in the table into Equation (12.23), we see that the payback periods for projects A and B are

$$P_j = (F - 1) + \frac{-CF_0 - \Sigma_{t=1 \to F-1} CF_t}{CF_F}$$

$$P_A = (3 - 1) + \frac{-CF_0 - \Sigma_{t=1 \to 3-1} CF_t}{CF_3}$$

$$= 2 + \frac{-(-10,000) - 7,500 - 2,000}{1,500} = 2 + \frac{500}{1,500} = 2.33 \text{ years}$$

$$P_B = (3 - 1) + \frac{-CF_0 - \Sigma_{t=1 \to 3-1} CF_t}{CF_3}$$

$$= 2 + \frac{-(-10,000) - 4,000 - 4,000}{4,000} = 2 + \frac{2,000}{4,000} = 2.50 \text{ years}$$

Thus, project A is preferred to project B because of its shorter payback period.

TABLE 12.2 Net Cash Flows (CF_t) for Projects A and B

Year, t	Project A	Project B
0	−$10,000	−$10,000
1	7,500	4,000
2	2,000	4,000
3	1,500	4,000
4	1,000	4,000

DISCOUNTED PAYBACK PERIOD METHOD

A variation on the payback period method is the discounted payback period method. The rationale behind the second method is the same as that for the first except that we consider the present value of the projects' cash flows. The projects are discounted to the present using the investor's *cost of capital*. The cost of capital is also referred to as the *discount rate*, the *required rate of return*, the *hurdle rate*, and the *cutoff rate*. The cost of capital is the opportunity cost of finance capital. It is the minimum rate of return required by an investor to justify the commitment of resources to a project.

Definition: The cost of acquiring funds to finance a capital investment project. It is the minimum rate of return that must be earned to justify a capital investment. The cost of capital is the rate of return that an investor must earn on financial assets committed to a project.

Definition: The discounted payback is the number of periods required to recover the original investment where the projects' cash flows are discounted using the cost of capital.

Suppose that the initial cost of a project is $25,000 and that cost of capital (k) is 10%. To determine each project's discounted cash flow (DCF_t), simply divide each period's cash flow by $(1 + k)^t$. The discounted cash flows for projects A and B are summarized in Table 12.3.

Following the procedure already outlined, we see that for project A by the end of year 4 cumulative cash flows are $23,625.44, or 94.5% recovery of the original investment. By the end of year 5 cumulative cash flows are $26, 109.13, or 104.4% recovery of the original investment. Since only an additional $1,374.56 cash flow was required in year 4 to fully cover the original $25,000 investment, the total number of years required to recover the original investment (P_A) was 4 plus $1,374.56/$2,483.69 years, or 4.55 years. Similarly, the payback period for project B (P_B) is 4 plus $6,735.18 years, or 4.99 years. As before, project A is preferred to project B. In general, the expression for calculating the discounted payback period is

TABLE 12.3   Discounted Net Cash Flows (DCF_t) for Projects A and B

Year, t	Project A	Project B
0	−$25,000.00	−$25,000.00
1	9,090.91	2,727.27
2	6,611.57	4,132.23
3	4,507.89	5,259.20
4	3,415.07	6,146.12
5	2,483.69	6,830.13

$$P_j = (F-1) + \frac{-CF_0 - \Sigma_{t=1 \to F-1} DCF_t}{CF_F}$$

$$= (F-1) + \frac{-CF_0 - \Sigma_{t=1 \to F-1}\left[CF_t/(1+k)^t\right]}{CF_F} \qquad (12.24)$$

where $\Sigma_{t=1 \to F-1} DCF_t = \Sigma_{t=1 \to F-1}[CF_t/(1+k)^t]$ is the sum of all discounted cash flows up to and including the year before full recovery of the original investment. Substituting the information in Table 12.3 into Equation (12.24) we obtain

$$P_A = (5-1) + \frac{\begin{array}{c} -(-\$25,000) - \$10,000/(1.10) - \$8,000/(1.10)^2 \\ -\$6,000/(1.10)^3 - \$5,000/(1.10)^4 - \$4,000/(1.10)^5 \end{array}}{\$2,483.69}$$

$$= 4 + \frac{\$1,374.56}{\$2,483.69} = 4.55 \text{ years}$$

$$P_B = (5-1) + \frac{\begin{array}{c} -(-\$25,000) - \$3,000/(1.10) - \$5,000/(1.10)^2 \\ -\$7,000/(1.10)^3 - \$9,000/(1.10)^4 - \$11,000/(1.10)^5 \end{array}}{\$2,483.69}$$

$$= 4 + \frac{\$6,735.18}{\$6,830.13} = 4.99 \text{ years}$$

Since these projects are assumed to be mutually exclusive, then once again project A is preferred to project B because of its shorter discounted payback period. It should be noted that although the payback and discounted payback methods result in the same project rankings here, this is not always the case.

An important drawback of both the payback and discounted payback methods is that they ignore cash flows after the payback period. Suppose, for example that project A generated no additional cash flows after year 5, but project B continued to generate cash flows that increased to, say, $2,000 for each of the next 5 years. Or, suppose project B generates no cash flows for the first 4 years and then generates a cash flow of $100,000 in the fifth year. Because of these deficiencies, other ranking methodologies, such as net present value, internal rate of return, and modified internal rate of return, are more commonly used to rank investment projects. Nevertheless, the payback and discounted period methods are useful because they fell how long funds will be tied up in a project. The shorter the payback period, the greater a project's liquidity.

NET PRESENT VALUE (NPV) METHOD FOR EQUAL-LIVED PROJECTS

The net present value method of evaluating and ranking capital projects was developed in response to the perceived shortcomings of the payback period and discounted payback period approaches. The net present value of a capital project is calculated by subtracting the present value of all cash outflows from the present value of all cash inflows. If the net present value of a project is negative, it is rejected. If the net present value of a project is positive, it is a candidate for further consideration for adoption. Equal-lived projects (i.e., two or more projects that are expected to be in service for the same length of time, with positive net present values) are then ranked from highest to lowest. In general, higher net-present-valued projects are preferred to projects with lower net present values.[1]

Definition: The net present value of a capital project is the difference between the net present value of cash inflows and cash outflows. Projects with higher net present values are preferred to projects with lower net present values.[1]

The net present value of a project is calculated as

$$NPV = CF_0 + \frac{CF_1}{(1+k)^1} + \frac{CF_2}{(1+k)^2} + \ldots + \frac{CF_n}{(1+k)^n}$$
$$= \frac{\Sigma_{t=0 \to n} CF_t}{(1+k)^t} \tag{12.25}$$

where CF_t is the expected net cash flow in period t, k is the cost of capital, and n is the life of the project. Net cash flows are defined as the difference between cash inflows (revenues), R_t, and cash outflows, O_t. Equation (12.25) may thus be rewritten as

$$NPV = \frac{\Sigma_{t=0 \to n} R_t}{(1+k)^t} - \frac{\Sigma_{t=0 \to n} O_t}{(1+k)^t}$$
$$= \frac{\Sigma_{t=0 \to n} (R_t - O_t)}{(1+k)^t} \tag{12.26}$$

[1] The discussion thus far has ignored the possible impact of inflation on the time value of money. In the absence of inflation, the real discount rate and the nominal discount rate, which includes an inflation premium, are one and the same. The same can be said of the relationship between real and nominal expected cash flows. When the expected inflation rate is positive, however, then projected cash flows will increase at the rate of inflation. If the inflation rate is also included in the market cost of capital then inflation-adjusted NPV is identical to the inflation-free NPV, which is calculated using Equation (12.25). On the other hand, if the cost of capital includes an inflation premium, but the cash flows do not, then the calculated NPV will have a downward bias. For more information on the effects of inflation on the capital budgeting process see J.C. VanHorne, "A Note on Biases in Capital Budgeting Introduced by Inflation," *Journal of Financial* and *Quantitative Analysis*, January 1971, pp. 653–658; P.L. Cooley, R.L. Rosenfeldt, and I.K. Chew, "Capital Budgeting Procedures under Inflation, "*Financial Management*, Winter 1975, pp. 18–27; and P.L. Cooley, R.L. Rosenfeldt, and I.K. Chew, "Capital Budgeting Procedures under Inflation: Cooley, Rosenfeldt and Chew vs. Findlay and Frankle," *Financial Management*, Autumn 1974, pp. 83–90.

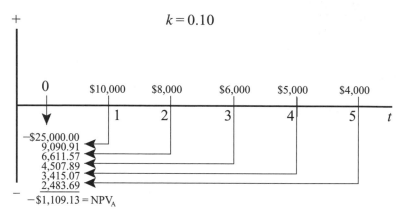

FIGURE 12.13   Net present value calculations for project A.

TABLE 12.4   Net Present Value (*NPV*)
for Projects *A* and *B*

Year, *t*	Project *A*	Project *B*
0	−$25,000.00	−$25,000.00
1	9,090.91	2,727.27
2	6,611.57	4,132.23
3	4,507.89	5,259.20
4	3,415.07	6,146.12
5	2,483.69	6,830.13
Σ	$1,109.13	$94.95

Consider again the cash flows for projects *A* and *B* summarized in Table 12.1. Also assume that the cost of capital (k) is 10%. To determine the net present value of each project, simply divide the cash flow for each period by $(1 + k)^t$. The calculation for the net present value of project *A* (NPV_A) is illustrated in Figure 12.13 as $1,109.13. It can just as easily be illustrated that the net present value of project *B* is $94.95.

Table 12.4 compares the net present values of projects *A* and *B*. If the two are independent, then both investments should be undertaken. On the other hand, if projects *A* and *B* are mutually exclusive, then project *A* will be preferred to project *B* because its net present value is greater.

A positive net present value indicates that the project is generating cash flows in excess of what is required to cover the cost of capital and to provide a positive rate of return to investors. Finally, if the net present value is negative, the present value of cash inflows is not sufficient to cover the present value of cash outflows. A project should not be undertaken if its net present value is negative.

Problem 12.12. Illuvatar International pays the top corporate income tax rate of 38%. The company is planning to build a new processing plant to manufacture silmarils on the outskirts of Valmar, the ancient capital of Valinor. The new plant will require an immediate cash outlay of $3 million but is expected to generate annual profits of $1 million. According to the Valinor Uniform Tax Code, Illuvatar may deduct $500,000 in taxes annually as depreciation. The life of the new plant is 5 years. Assuming that the annual interest rate is 10%, should Illuvatar build the new processing plant? Explain.

Solution. According to the information provided, Illuvatar's taxable return is $R_t = \pi_t - D_t$, where π_t represents profits and D_t is the amount of depreciation that may be deducted in period t for tax purposes. Illuvatar's taxable rate of return is

$$R_t = \$1,000,000 - \$500,000 = \$500,000$$

Illuvatar's annual tax (T_t) is given as $T_t = \tau R_t$, where τ is the tax rate. Illuvatar's annual tax is, therefore,

$$T_t = 0.38(500,000) = \$190,000$$

Illuvatar's after tax income flow (π_t^*) is given as

$$\pi_t^* = \pi_t - T_t = \$1,000,000 - \$190,000 = \$810,000$$

At an interest rate of 10%, the net present value of the after tax income flow is given as

$$NPV = \frac{\Sigma_{t=1 \to 5} \pi_t^*}{(1+i)^5} - \frac{\Sigma_{t=0 \to 0} O_t}{(1+i)^0}$$

where $O_0 = \$3,000,000$, the initial cash outlay. Substituting into this expression, we obtain

$$NPV = \frac{810,000}{(1.10)} + \frac{810,000}{(1.10)^2} + \frac{810,000}{(1.10)^3} + \frac{810,000}{(1.10)^4} + \frac{810,000}{(1.10)^5} - 3,000,000$$

$$= \$70,537.29$$

Because the net present value is positive, Illuvatar should build the new processing plant.

Problem 12.13. Senior management of Bayside Biotechtronics is considering two mutually exclusive investment projects. The projected net cash flows for projects A and B are summarized in Table 12.5. If the discount rate (cost of capital) is expected to be 12%, which project should be undertaken?

TABLE 12.5 Net Cash Flows (CF_t) for Projects A and B

Year, t	Project A	Project B
0	-$25,000	-$19,000
1	7,000	6,000
2	8,000	6,000
3	9,000	6,000
4	9,000	6,000
5	5,000	6,000

Solution

a. The net present value of project A and project B are calculated as

$$NPV_A = \frac{CF_0}{(1+k)^0} + \frac{CF_1}{(1+k)^1} + \frac{CF_2}{(1+k)^2} + \ldots + \frac{CF_n}{(1+k)^5}$$

$$= \frac{-25,000}{(1.12)^0} + \frac{7,000}{(1.12)^1} + \frac{8,000}{(1.12)^2} + \frac{9,000}{(1.12)^3} + \frac{9,000}{(1.12)^4} + \frac{5,000}{(1.12)^5}$$

$$= \$2,590.36$$

$$NPV_B = \frac{-19,000}{(1.12)^0} + \frac{6,000}{(1.12)^1} + \frac{6,000}{(1.12)^2} + \frac{6,000}{(1.12)^3} + \frac{6,000}{(1.12)^4} + \frac{6,000}{(1.12)^5}$$

$$= \$2,628.66$$

Since $NPV_B > NPV_A$, project B should be adopted by Bayside.

Sometimes, mutually exclusive investment projects involve only cash outflows. When this occurs, the investment project with the *lowest* absolute net present value should be selected, as Problem 12.14 illustrates.

Problem 12.14. Finn MacCool, CEO of Quicken Trees Enterprises, is considering two equal-lived psalter dispensers for installation in the employee's recreation room. The projected cash outflows for the two dispensers are summarized in Table 12.6. If the cost of capital is 10% per year and dispense A and B have salvage values after 5 years of $200 and $350, respectively, which dispenser should be installed?

Solution. The net present values of dispenser A and dispenser B are calculated as

$$NPV_A = \frac{CF_0}{(1+k)^0} + \frac{CF_1}{(1+k)^1} + \frac{CF_2}{(1+k)^2} + \ldots + \frac{CF_5}{(1+k)^5}$$

$$= \frac{-2,500}{(1.10)^0} - \frac{900}{(1.10)^1} - \frac{900}{(1.10)^2} - \frac{900}{(1.10)^3} - \frac{900}{(1.10)^4} - \frac{900}{(1.10)^5} + \frac{200}{(1.10)^5}$$

$$= -\$5,787.53$$

TABLE 12.6 Net Cash Flows (CF_t) for Dispensers A and B

Year, t	Dispenser A	Dispenser B
0	-$2,500	-$3,500
1	-900	-700
2	-900	-700
3	-900	-700
4	-900	-700
5	-900	-700

$$NPV_B = \frac{-3,500}{(1.10)^0} - \frac{700}{(1.10)^1} - \frac{700}{(1.10)^2} - \frac{700}{(1.10)^3} - \frac{700}{(1.10)^4} - \frac{700}{(1.10)^5} + \frac{350}{(1.10)^5}$$

$$= -\$5,936.23$$

Since $|NPV_A| < |NPV_B|$, Finn MacCool will install dispenser A.

Problem 12.15. Suppose that an investment opportunity, which requires an initial outlay of $50,000, is expected to yield a return of $150,000 after 20 years.
a. Will the investment be profitable if the cost of capital is 6%?
b. Will the investment be profitable if the cost of capital is 5.5%?
c. At what cost of capital will the investor be indifferent to the investment?

Solution
a. The net present value of the investment with a cost of capital of 6% is given as

$$NPV = \frac{150,000}{(1.06)^{20}} - 50,000 = \frac{150,000}{3.21} - 50,000 = -\$3,229.29$$

Since the net present value is negative, we conclude that the investment opportunity is not profitable.
b. The net present value of the investment with a cost of capital of 5.5% is

$$NPV = \frac{150,000}{(1.055)^{20}} - 50,000 = \frac{150,000}{2.92} - 50,000 = \$1,409.34$$

Since the net present value is positive, we can conclude that the investment opportunity is profitable.
c. The investor will be indifferent to the investment if the net present value is zero. Substituting $NPV = 0$ into the expression and solving for the discount rate yields

$$0 = \frac{150,000}{(1+k)^{20}} - 50,000$$

$$50,000(1+k)^{20} = 150,000$$

$$(1+k)^{20} = 3$$

$$1+k = 1.05646$$

$$k = 0.05647$$

That is, the investor will be indifferent to the investment at a cost of capital of approximately 5.65%.

NET PRESENT VALUE (NPV) METHOD FOR UNEQUAL-LIVED PROJECTS

Whereas comparing alternative investment projects with equal lives is a fairly straightforward affair, how do we compare projects that have different lives? Since net present value comparisons involve future cash flows, an appropriate analysis of alternative capital projects must be compared over the same number of years. Unless capital projects are compared over an equivalent number of years, there will be a bias against shorter lived capital projects involving net cash outflows, and a bias in favor of longer lived capital projects involving net cash inflows. To avoid this time and cash flow bias when one is evaluating projects with different lives, it is necessary to modify the net present value calculations to make the projects comparable.

A fair comparison of alternative capital projects requires that net present values be calculated over equivalent time periods. One way to do this is to compare alternative capital projects over the least common multiple of their lives. To accomplish this, the cash flows of each project must be duplicated up to the least common multiple of lives for each project. By artificially "stretching out" the lives of some or all of the prospective projects until all projects have the same life span, we can reduce the evaluation of capital investment projects with unequal lives to a straightforward application of the net present value approach to evaluating projects discussed in the preceding section. In problem 12.16, for example, project A has a life expectancy of 2 years, while project B has a life expectancy of 3 years. To compare these two projects by means of the net present value approach, project A will be replicated three times and project B will be replicated twice. In this way, both projects will have a 6-year life span.

Problem 12.16. Brian Borumha of Cashel Company, a leading Celtic oil producer, is considering two mutually exclusive projects, each involving drilling operations in the North Sea. The projected net cash flows for each project are summarized in Table 12.7. Determine which project should be adopted if the cost of capital is 8%.

TABLE 12.7 Net Cash Flows (CF_t) for Projects A and B ($ millions)

Year, t	Project A	Project B
0	−$2,000	−$5,000
1	1,000	1,000
2	1,500	2,500
3		3,000

Solution. Since the projects have different lives, they must be compared over the least common multiple of years, which in this case is 6 years.

$$NPV_A = \frac{CF_0}{(1+k)^0} + \frac{CF_1}{(1+k)^1} + \frac{CF_2}{(1+k)^2} + \ldots + \frac{CF_6}{(1+k)^6}$$

$$= \frac{-\$2,000}{(1.08)^0} + \frac{\$1,000}{(1.08)^1} + \frac{\$1,500}{(1.08)^2} - \frac{\$2,000}{(1.08)^2} + \frac{1,000}{(1.08)^3} + \frac{1,500}{(1.08)^4}$$

$$- \frac{2,000}{(1.08)^4} + \frac{1,000}{(1.08)^5} + \frac{1,500}{(1.08)^6}$$

$$= \$549.41$$

$$NPV_B = \frac{-5,000}{(1.08)^0} + \frac{1,000}{(1.08)^1} + \frac{2,500}{(1.08)^2} + \frac{3,000}{(1.08)^3} - \frac{5,000}{(1.08)^3}$$

$$+ \frac{1,000}{(1.08)^4} + \frac{2,500}{(1.08)^5} + \frac{3,000}{(1.08)^6}$$

$$= \$808.61$$

Since $NPV_B > NPV_A$, Brian Borumha will select project B over project A.

INTERNAL RATE OF RETURN (IRR) METHOD AND THE HURDLE RATE

Yet another method of evaluating a capital investment project is by calculating the *internal rate of return (IRR)*. Before discussing the methodology of calculating a project's internal rate of return, it is important to understand the rationale underlying this approach. Consider, for example, the case of an investor who is considering purchasing a 12-year, 10% annual coupon, $1,000 par-value corporate bond for $1,150.70. Before deciding whether the investor should purchase this bond, consider the following definitions.

Coupon bonds are debt obligations of private companies or public agencies in which the issuer of the bond promises to pay the bearer of the bond a series of fixed dollar interest payments at regular intervals for a specified period of time. Upon maturity, the issuer agrees to repay the bearer the par value of the bond. The *par value of a bond* is the face value of the bond, which is the amount originally borrowed by the issuer. Thus, a corporation that issues a $1,000 coupon bond is obligated to pay the bearer of the bond fixed dollar payments at regular intervals. In the present example, the issuer of the bond promises to pay the bearer of the bond $100 per year for the next 12 years plus the face value of the bond at maturity. Parenthetically, the term "coupon bond" comes from the fact that at one time a number of small, dated coupons indicating the amount of interest due to the owner were attached to the bonds. A bond owner would literally clip a coupon from the bond on each payment date and either cash or deposit the coupon at a bank or mail it to the corporation's paying agent, who would then send the owner a check in the amount of the interest.

Definition: Coupon bonds are debt obligations in which the issuer of the bond promises to pay the bearer of the bond fixed dollar interest payments at regular intervals for a specified period of time, with reimbursement of the face value at the end of the period.

Definition: The par value of a bond is the face value of the bond. It is the amount originally borrowed by the issuer.

Why would an investor consider purchasing a bond for an amount in excess of its par value? The reason is simple. In the present example, when the bond was first issued the prevailing rate of interest paid on bonds with equivalent risk and maturity characteristics was 10%. If the bond holder wanted to sell the bond before maturity, the market price would reflect the prevailing rate of interest.

If current market interest rates are higher than the coupon interest rate, the bearer will have to sell the bond at a discount from par value. Otherwise, no one would be willing to buy such a bond. On the other hand, if prevailing interest rates are lower than the coupon interest rate, then the bearer will be able to sell the bond at a premium. The size of the discount or premium reflects the term to maturity and the differential between the prevailing market interest rate and the coupon rate on bonds with similar risk characteristics. Since the market value of the bond in the present example is greater than its par value, prevailing market rates must be lower than the coupon interest rate.

Returning to our example, should the investor purchase this bond? The decision to buy or not to buy this bond will be based upon the rate of return the investor will earn on the bond if held to maturity. This rate of return is called the bond's *yield to maturity* (*YTM*). If the bond's *YTM* is greater than the prevailing market rate of interest, the investor will purchase the bond. If the *YTM* is less than the market rate, the investor will not purchase. If the *YTM* is the same as the market rate, other things being equal, the investor will be indifferent between purchasing this bond and a newly issued bond.

Definition: Yield to maturity is the rate of return earned on a bond that is held to maturity.

Calculating the bond's *YTM* involves finding the rate of interest that equates the bond's offer price, in this case $1,150.70, to the net present value of the bond's cash inflows. Denoting the value price of the bond as V_B, the interest payment as *PMT*, and the face value of the bond as *M*, the yield to maturity can be found by solving Equation (12.27) for *YTM*.

$$
V_B = \frac{PMT}{(1+YTM)^1} + \frac{PMT}{(1+YTM)^2} + \ldots + \frac{PMT}{(1+YTM)^n} + \frac{M}{(1+YTM)^n}
$$
$$
= \frac{\Sigma_{t=1 \to n} PMT}{(1+YTM)^t} + \frac{M}{(1+YTM)^n}
$$

(12.27)

Substituting the information provided into Equation (12.27) yields

$$
\$1,150.72 = \frac{\$100}{(1+YTM)^1} + \frac{\$100}{(1+YTM)^2} + \ldots + \frac{\$100}{(1+YTM)^n} + \frac{\$1,000}{(1+YTM)^n}
$$

Unfortunately, finding the *YTM* that satisfies this expression is easier said than done. Different values of *YTM* could be tried until a solution is found, but this brute force approach is tedious and time-consuming. Fortunately, financial calculators are available that make the process of finding solution values to such problems a trivial procedure. As it turns out, the yield to maturity in this example is $YTM^* = 0.08$, or an 8% yield to maturity. The solution to this problem is illustrated in Figure 12.14.

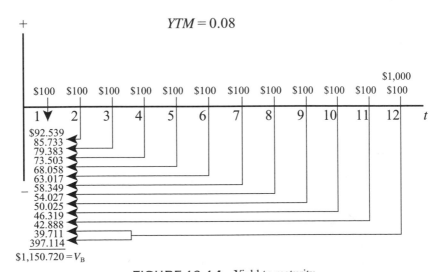

FIGURE 12.14   Yield to maturity.

Thus, the investor will compare the *YTM* to the rate of return on bonds of equivalent risk characteristics before deciding whether to purchase the bond. Parenthetically, the efficient markets hypothesis suggests that the *YTM* on this coupon bond will be the same as the prevailing market interest rate.

We now return to the internal rate of return method for evaluating capital projects, introduced earlier. As we will see shortly, the methodology for determining the yield to maturity on a bond is the same as that used for calculating the internal rate of return. The internal rate of return is the discount rate that equates the present value of a project's expected cash inflows with the project's expected cash outflows. The internal rate of return may be calculated from Equation (12.28).

$$NPV = CF_0 + \frac{CF_1}{(1+IRR)^1} + \frac{CF_2}{(1+IRR)^2} + \ldots + \frac{CF_n}{(1+IRR)^n}$$

$$= \frac{\Sigma_{t=1 \to n} CF_t}{(1+IRR)^t} = 0 \qquad (12.28)$$

Consider, again, the information presented in Table 12.1 for project *A*. This problem is illustrated in Figure 12.15.

To determine the discount rate for which *NPV* is zero, substitute the information provided for project *A* in Table 12.1 into Equation (12.27), which yields

$$NPV = -\$25,000 + \frac{\$10,000}{(1+IRR)^1} + \frac{\$8,000}{(1+IRR)^2} + \frac{\$6,000}{(1+IRR)^3}$$

$$+ \frac{\$5,000}{(1+IRR)^4} + \frac{\$4,000}{(1+IRR)^5} = 0$$

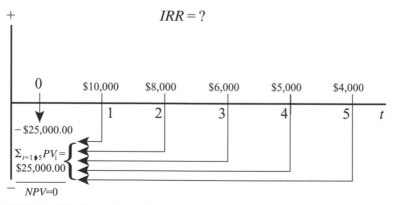

FIGURE 12.15   Internal rate of return is the discount rate for which the net present value of a project is equal to zero.

Of course, finding *IRR* is no easier than solving for *YTM*, as discussed earlier. Once again, a financial calculator comes to the rescue. The internal rate of return for projects *A* and *B* are $IRR_A = 12.05\%$ and $IRR_B = 10.12\%$. Whether these projects are accepted or rejected depends on the cost of capital, which is sometimes referred to as the *hurdle rate, required rate of return,* or *cutoff rate.* The somewhat colorful expression "hurdle rate" is meant to express the notion that a company can increase its shareholder value by investing in projects that earn a rate of return that exceeds (hurdles over) the cost of capital used to finance the project.

Definition: The internal rate of return is the discount rate that equates the present value of a project's expected cash inflows with the project's expected cash outflows.

Definition: The hurdle rate is the cost of capital of a project that must be exceeded by the internal rate of return if the project is to be accepted. Often referred to as the required rate of return or the cutoff rate.

Another way to look at the internal rate of return is that it is the maximum rate of interest that an investor will pay to finance a capital investment project. Alternatively, the internal rate of return is the minimum acceptable rate of return on an investment. Thus, if the internal rate of return is greater than the cost of capital (hurdle rate), a project will be accepted. If the internal rate of return is less than the hurdle rate, a project will be rejected. Finally, if the internal rate of return is equal to the cost of capital, the investor will be indifferent to the project. Of course, the investor would like to earn as much as possible in excess of the internal rate of return.

Suppose that an investor is considering investing in either project *A* or project *B*. If the two projects are independent and the internal rate of return exceeds the hurdle rate, both projects will be accepted. On the other hand, if the projects are mutually exclusive, project *A* will be preferred to project *B* because of its higher internal rate of return. The *NPV* and *IRR* will always result in the same accept and reject decisions for independent projects. This is because, by definition, when *NPV* is positive, then *IRR* will exceed the cost of funds to finance the project. On the other hand, the *NPV* and *IRR* methods can result in conflicting accept/reject decisions for mutually exclusive projects. A comparison of the *NPV* and *IRR* methods of evaluating capital investment projects will be the subject of the next section.

Problem 12.17. Consider, again, Bayside Biotechtronics. The projected net cash flows for projects *A* and *B* are summarized in Table 12.8.
a. Calculate the internal rate of return for both projects.
b. If the cost of capital for financing the projects (hurdle rate) is 17%, which project should be considered?
c. Verify that if the hurdle rate is 1% lower, $NPV_A > 0$
d. Verify that if the hurdle rate is 1% higher, $NPV_B < 0$.

TABLE 12.8 Net Cash Flows CF_t for Projects A and B

Year, t	Project A	Project B
0	-$25,000	-$19,000
1	7,000	6,000
2	8,000	6,000
3	9,000	6,000
4	9,000	6,000
5	5,000	6,000

Solution

a. To determine the internal rate of return for projects A and B, substitute the information provided in the table into the Equation (12.27) and solve for IRR.

$$NPV_A = CF_0 + \frac{CF_1}{(1+IRR_A)^1} + \frac{CF_2}{(1+IRR_A)^2} + \ldots + \frac{CF_5}{(1+IRR_A)^5}$$

$$= -\$25,000 + \frac{\$7,000}{(1+IRR_A)^1} + \frac{\$8,000}{(1+IRR_A)^2} + \frac{\$9,000}{(1+IRR_A)^3}$$

$$+ \frac{\$9,000}{(1+IRR_A)^4} + \frac{\$5,000}{(1+IRR_A)^5} = 0$$

$$NPV_B = -\$19,000 + \frac{\$6,000}{(1+IRR_B)^1} + \frac{\$6,000}{(1+IRR_B)^2} + \frac{\$6,000}{(1+IRR_B)^3}$$

$$+ \frac{\$6,000}{(1+IRR_B)^4} + \frac{\$6,000}{(1+IRR_B)^5} = 0$$

Since calculating IRR_A and IRR_B by trial and error is time-consuming and tedious, the solution values were obtained by using a financial calculator. The internal rates of return for projects A and B are

$$IRR_A = 16.168\%$$

$$IRR_B = 17.448\%$$

b. The internal rate of return is less than the hurdle rate for project A and greater than the hurdle rate for project B. Thus, project A is rejected and project B is accepted.

c. Substituting into Equation (12.28), we write

$$NPV_A = \frac{\Sigma_{t=1 \to n} CF_t}{(1.15168)^t}$$

$$= -\$25,000 + \frac{\$7,000}{(1.15168)^1} + \frac{\$8,000}{(1.15168)^2} + \frac{\$9,000}{(1.15168)^3}$$

$$+ \frac{\$9,000}{(1.15168)^4} + \frac{\$5,000}{(1.15168)^5} = \$584.85$$

d. $NPV_A = \dfrac{\Sigma_{t=1 \to n} CF_t}{(1.17168)^t} = -\$563.64$

COMPARING THE *NPV* AND *IRR* METHODS

Consider, once again, the cash flows for projects A and B presented in Table 12.1. Table 12.9 summarizes the net present values for the cash flows of project A and B for different costs of capital. The data summarized in Table 12.9 are illustrated in Figure 12.16. A diagram that plots the relationship between the net present value of a project and alternative costs of capital is called a *net present value profile*.

Definition: A net present value profile is a diagram that shows the relationship between the net present value of a project and alternative costs of capital.

When the cost of capital is zero, the project's net present value is simply the sum the project's net cash flows. In the present example, the net present values for projects A and B when $k = 0.00\%$ are \$8,000 and \$10,000, respectively. The student will also readily observe from Equation (12.28) that as the cost of capital increases, the net present value of the project declines, which gives rise to the downward-sloping curves in Figure 12.16.

TABLE 12.9 Net Present Value Profiles for Projects A and B

Cost of capital	Project A	Project B
0.00	\$8,000	\$10,000
0.02	6,389	7,621
0.04	4,908	5,465
0.05	4,211	4,462
0.05875	**3,623**	**3,623**
0.06	3,541	3,506
0.08	2,278	1,723
0.10	1,109	96
0.12	24	−1,392
0.14	−985	−2,755

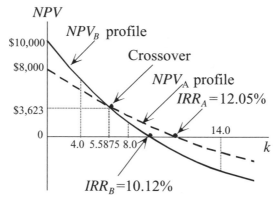

FIGURE 12.16   Internal rates of return and crossover rate.

In one earlier discussion, the internal rate of return was defined as the discount rate at which the *NPV* of a project is zero. For projects *A* and *B*, the internal rates of return (not shown in Table 12.9) are 12.05 and 10.12%, respectively. These values are illustrated in Figure 12.16 at the points at which the net present value profiles for projects *A* and *B* intersect the horizontal axis.

The student will note that when the cost of capital is 5.875%, the net present values of projects *A* and *B* are the same. Additionally, when the cost of capital is less than 5.875% $NPV_A < NPV_B$, and when the cost of capital is greater than 5.875% $NPV_A > NPV_B$. This is illustrated in Figure 12.14 at the point of intersection of the present value profiles of project *A* and *B*. For obvious reasons, the cost of capital at which the *NPV*s of two projects are equal is called the *crossover rate*.

Definition: The crossover rate is the cost of capital at which the net present values of two projects are equal. Diagrammatically, this is the cost of capital at which the net present value profiles of two projects intersect.

An examination of Figure 12.16 also reveals that the marginal change in NPV_B given a change in the cost of capital is greater than that for NPV_A (i.e., $\partial NPV_B/\partial k > \partial NPV_A/\partial k$). In other words, the slope of the net present value profile for project *B* is steeper than the net present value profile for project *A*. The reason for this is that project *B* is more sensitive to changes in the cost of capital than project *A*.

Given the cost of capital, the sensitivity of *NPV* to changes in the cost of capital will depend on the timing of the project's cash flows. To see this, consider once again the cash flows summarized in Table 12.1. Note that these cash flows are received more quickly in the case of project *A* than for project *B*. Referring to Table 12.9, when the cost of capital is doubled from 5.0% to 10.0%, NPV_A falls from $4,211 to $1,109, or a decline of 73.7%. For project *B*, NPV_B falls from $4,462 to $96, or a drop of 97.8%. The reason for the discrepancy is the discounting factor $1/(1 + k)^n$, which will be greater for cash flows received in the distant future than for cash flows received in the near future. Thus, the net present value of projects that receive greater cash flows in the distant future will decline at a faster rate than for projects receiving most of their cash in the early years.

NPV AND *IRR* METHODS FOR INDEPENDENT PROJECTS

It was noted earlier that when the cost of capital is less than *IRR* for both projects, then the *NPV* and *IRR* methods will always result in the same accept and reject decisions. This can be seen in Figure 12.16. If the cost of capital is less than 10.12%, and projects *A* and *B* are independent, both projects will be accepted. If the cost of capital is between 10.12 and 12.05%, project *A* will be accepted and project *B* will be rejected. Finally, If the cost of capital is greater than 12.05%, then both projects will be rejected.

NPV AND *IRR* METHODS FOR MUTUALLY EXCLUSIVE PROJECTS

We noted earlier that if the projects are mutually exclusive (the acceptance of one project means the rejection of the other), the *NPV* and *IRR* methods can result in conflicting accept/reject decisions. To see this, consider again Figure 12.16. If the cost of capital is *greater than the crossover rate*, but less than *IRR* for both projects, in this case 10.12%, then $NPV_A > NPV_B$ and $IRR_A > IRR_B$, in which case both the *IRR* and *NPV* methods indicate that project *A* is preferred to project *B*.

On the other hand, if the cost of capital is *less than the crossover rate*, then although IRR_A is still less than IRR_B, $NPV_B > NPV_A$. Thus, the net present value method indicates that project *B* should be preferred to project *A* and the internal rate of return method ranks project *B* higher than project *A*. In other words, when the cost of capital is less than the crossover rate, a conflict arises between the *NPV* and *IRR* methods. Two questions immediately present themselves:

1. Why do the net present value profiles intersect?
2. When an accept/reject conflict exists because the cost of capital is less than the crossover rate, which method should be used to rank mutually exclusive projects?

The net present value profiles of two projects may intersect for two reasons: differences in project sizes and cash flow timing differences. As noted earlier, the effect of discounting will be greater for cash flows received in the distant future than for cash flows received in the near future. The net present value of projects in which most of the cash flows are received in the distant future will decline at a faster rate than the decline in the net present value for projects in which most of the cash flows are generated in the near future. Thus, if the *NPV* for one project (project *B* in Figure 12.16) is greater than the *NPV* for another project (project *A* in Figure 12.16) when $t = 0$ *and* most of the cash flows for the first project are received in the distant future in comparison to the second project, the net present value profiles of the two projects may intersect.

When the net present value profiles intersect and the cost of capital is less than the crossover rate, which method should be used for selecting a capital investment project? The answer depends on the rate at which the firm reinvests the net cash inflows over the life of the project. The *NPV* method implicitly assumes that net cash inflows are reinvested at the cost of capital. The *IRR* method assumes that net cash inflows are reinvested at the internal rate of return. So, which of these assumptions is more realistic? It may be demonstrated (see Brigham, Gapenski, and Erhardt 1998, Chapter 11) that the best assumption is that a project's net cash inflows are reinvested at the firm's cost of capital. Thus, for ranking mutually exclusive capital investment projects, the *NPV* method is preferred to the *IRR* method.

Problem 12.18. Consider, again, the net cash flows for projects *A* and *B* in Bayside Biotechtronics, summarized in Table 12.10.
a. Illustrate the net present value profiles for projects *A* and *B*.
b. What is the crossover rate for the two projects?
c. Assuming that projects *A* and *B* are mutually exclusive, which project should be selected if the cost of capital is greater than the crossover rate? Which project should be selected if the cost of capital is less than the crossover rate?

Solution
a. A financial calculator was used to find the net present values for projects *A* and *B* for various interest rates are summarized in Table 12.11.

To determine the crossover rate, using Equation (12.25) to equate the net present value of project *A* with the net present value of project *B* and solve for the cost of capital, *k*.

TABLE 12.10 Net Cash Flows (*CF$_t$*) for Projects *A* and *B*

Year, *t*	Project *A*	Project *B*
0	−$25,000	−$19,000
1	7,000	6,000
2	8,000	6,000
3	9,000	6,000
4	9,000	6,000
5	5,000	6,000

TABLE 12.11   Net Present Value
Profiles for Projects A and B

Cost of capital	Project A	Project B
0.00	$13,000	$11,000
0.04	8,931	7,711
0.06	7,145	6,274
0.08	5,503	4,956
0.10	3,989	3,745
0.1172	**2,780**	**2,780**
0.12	2,590	2,629
0.14	1,296	1,598
0.16	97	646
0.18	−1,017	−237

$$NPV_A = NPV_B$$

$$\frac{-\$25,000}{(1+k)^0} + \frac{\$7,000}{(1+k)^1} + \frac{\$8,000}{(1+k)^2} + \frac{\$9,000}{(1+k)^3} + \frac{\$9,000}{(1+k)^4} + \frac{\$9,000}{(1+k)^5} =$$

$$\frac{-\$19,000}{(1+k)^0} + \frac{\$6,000}{(1+k)^1} + \frac{\$6,000}{(1+k)^2} + \frac{\$6,000}{(1+k)^3} + \frac{\$6,000}{(1+k)^4} + \frac{\$6,000}{(1+k)^5}$$

Bringing all the terms in this expression to the left-hand side of the equation, we get

$$\frac{-\$6,000}{(1+k)^0} + \frac{\$1,000}{(1+k)^1} + \frac{\$2,000}{(1+k)^2} + \frac{\$3,000}{(1+k)^3} + \frac{\$3,000}{(1+k)^4} - \frac{\$3,000}{(1+k)^5} = 0$$

The value for k in this expression may be found using the IRR function of a financial calculator. Solving for k yields a crossover rate of 11.72%.

Last, the internal rates of return for projects A and B may be calculated from Equation (12.28).

$$NPV_A = CF_0 + \frac{CF_1}{(1+IRR)^1} + \frac{CF_2}{(1+IRR)^2} + \ldots + \frac{CF_n}{(1+IRR)^5}$$

$$= \frac{-\$25,000}{(1+IRR)^0} + \frac{\$7,000}{(1+IRR)^1} + \frac{\$8,000}{(1+IRR)^2} + \frac{\$9,000}{(1+IRR)^3}$$

$$+ \frac{\$9,000}{(1+IRR)^4} + \frac{\$9,000}{(1+IRR)^5} = 0$$

Solving with a financial calculator yields

$$IRR_A = 16.17\%$$

Similarly for project B,

$$NPV_B = \frac{-\$19,000}{(1+IRR)^0} + \frac{\$6,000}{(1+IRR)^1} + \frac{\$6,000}{(1+IRR)^2} + \frac{\$6,000}{(1+IRR)^3}$$
$$+ \frac{\$6,000}{(1+IRR)^4} + \frac{\$6,000}{(1+IRR)^5} = 0$$

Solving,

$$IRR_B = 17.45\%$$

Finally, using the crossover rate to calculate the net present value of projects A and B yields

$$NPV_A = \frac{-\$25,000}{(1.1172)^0} + \frac{\$7,000}{(1.1172)^1} + \frac{\$8,000}{(1.1172)^2} + \frac{\$9,000}{(1.1172)^3}$$
$$+ \frac{\$9,000}{(1.1172)^4} + \frac{\$9,000}{(1.1172)^5} = \$5,077.91$$

$$NPV_B = \frac{-\$19,000}{(1.1172)^0} + \frac{\$6,000}{(1.1172)^1} + \frac{\$6,000}{(1.1172)^2} + \frac{\$6,000}{(1.1172)^3}$$
$$+ \frac{\$6,000}{(1.1172)^4} + \frac{\$6,000}{(1.1172)^5} = \$2,780$$

With this information, the net present value profiles for projects A and B may be illustrated in Figure 12.17.
b. From Figure 12.17, the crossover rate for the two projects is 11.72%.
c. From Figure 12.17, if the cost of capital is greater than 11.72%, but less than 16.17%, project B is preferred to project A because $NPV_B > NPV_A$. This choice of projects is consistent with the IRR method, since $IRR_B >$

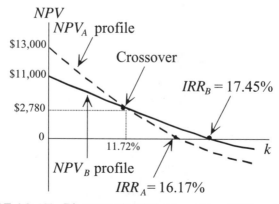

FIGURE 12.17   Diagrammatic solution to problem 12.18, parts b and c.

IRR_A. On the other hand, if the cost of capital is less than 11.72%, project A is preferred to project B, since $NPV_A > NPV_B$. This result conflicts with the choice of projects indicated by the IRR method.

MULTIPLE INTERNAL RATES OF RETURN

In addition to the problems associated with using the IRR method for evaluating capital investment projects, there is yet another potential fly in the ointment: a project may have multiple internal rates of return.

Definition: A project with two or more internal rates of return is said to have multiple internal rates of return.

To illustrate how multiple internal rates of return might occur, consider again Equation (12.28) for calculating the net present value of a project.

$$NPV = CF_0 + \frac{CF_1}{(1+IRR)^1} + \frac{CF_2}{(1+IRR)^2} + \ldots + \frac{CF_n}{(1+IRR)^n}$$

$$= \frac{\Sigma_{t=1 \to n} CF_t}{(1+IRR)^t} = 0$$

(12.28)

The student will immediately recognize that Equation (12.28) is a polynomial of degree n. What this means is that depending on the values of CF_t, Equation (12.28) may have n possible solutions for the internal rate of return! Before discussing the conditions under which multiple internal rates of return are possible, consider Table 12.12, which summarizes the cash flows of a capital investment project.

Substituting the cash flow information from Table 12.12 into Equation (12.28), we obtain

$$NPV = -\$1,000 + \frac{\$6,000}{(1+IRR)^1} - \frac{\$6,000}{(1+IRR)^2} = 0$$

(12.29)

Equation (12.29) is a second-degree polynomial (quadratic) equation, which may have two solution values. To find the solution values, rewrite Equation (12.29) as

$$-\$6,000\left(\frac{1}{1+IRR}\right)^2 + \$6,000\left(\frac{1}{1+IRR}\right) - \$1,000 = 0$$

TABLE 12.12   Net Cash Flows (CF_t) for Project A

Year, t	CF_t
0	-$1,000
1	6,000
2	-6,000

which is of the general form

$$ax^2 + bx + c = 0 \qquad (2.69)$$

The solution values may be found by applying the quadratic equation

$$x_{1,2} = \frac{-b \pm (b^2 - 4ac)^{0.5}}{2a} \qquad (2.70)$$

Substituting the information provided in Equation (12.29) into Equation (2.70) yields

$$\left(\frac{1}{1+IRR}\right)_{1,2} = \frac{-6,000 \pm \left[(6,000)^2 - 4(-6,000)(-1,000)\right]^{0.5}}{2(-6,000)}$$

$$= \frac{-6,000 \pm [36,000,000 - 24,000,000]^{0.5}}{-12,000}$$

$$= \frac{-6,000 \pm (12,000,000)^{0.5}}{-12,000}$$

$$= \frac{-6,000 \pm 3,464.10}{-12,000}$$

The solution values are

$$\left(\frac{1}{1+IRR}\right)_1 = \frac{-6,000 - 3,464.10}{-12,000} = 0.21$$

$$(1+IRR)_1 = 4.76$$

$$IRR_1 = 3.76$$

$$\left(\frac{1}{1+IRR}\right)_2 = \frac{-6,000 + 3,464.10}{-12,000} = 0.79$$

$$(1+IRR)_2 = 1.27$$

$$IRR_2 = 0.27$$

We find that for the cash flows summarized in Table 12.12, this project has internal rates of return of both 27 and 476%. The *NPV* profile for this project is summarized in Table 12.13 and Figure 12.18.

Under what circumstances are multiple internal rates of return possible? Thus, far we have dealt only with *normal cash flows*. A project has normal cash flows when one or more of the cash outflows are followed by a series of cash inflows. The cash flow depicted in Table 12.12 is an example of an *abnormal cash flow*. A large cash outflow during or toward the end of the life of a project is considered to be abnormal. Projects with abnormal cash flows may exhibit multiple internal rates of return.

Definition: A project has a normal cash flow if one or more cash outflows are followed by a series of cash inflows.

TABLE 12.13 Net Present Value Profile
for Project *A*

k	NPV
0.00	−$1,000.00
0.25	−40.00
0.27	**0.00**
0.50	333.33
1.00	500.00
1.50	440.00
2.00	333.33
2.50	224.49
3.00	125.00
3.50	37.04
3.76	**0.00**
4.00	−40.00
4.50	−107.44

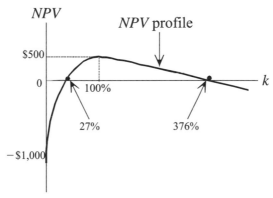

FIGURE 12.18   Multiple internal rates of return.

Definition: A project has an abnormal cash flow when large cash out-flows occur during or toward the end of the project's life.

As before, no difficulties arise when the net present value method is used to evaluate capital investment projects. In our example, if the cost of capital is between 27 and 376% independent projects should be accepted because their net present value is positive. On the other hand, project selection is problematic if the internal rate of return method is employed. It may no longer be automatically presumed that if the internal rate of return is greater than the cost of capital, the project should be accepted. Suppose, for example, that the cost of capital is 10%, which is less than both internal rates of return. Using the *IRR* method, which project should be accepted? In general, the approach will be preferred. Using the *NPV* method, however, the project should be clearly rejected.

TABLE 12.14   Net Cash Flows (CF_t) for
Project X

Year, t	CF_t
0	−$500
1	4,000
2	−5,000

TABLE 12.15   Net Present Value Profile
for Project A

k	NPV
0.00	−$1,500.00
0.10	−995.87
0.25	−500.00
0.50	−55.56
0.56	**0.00**
1.00	250.00
1.50	300.00
2.00	277.78
2.50	234.69
3.00	187.50
3.50	141.98
4.00	100.00
4.50	61.98
5.00	27.78
5.25	**0.00**
5.50	−2.96

Our example illustrates multiple internal rates of return resulting from abnormal cash flows. Abnormal cash flows can also create other problems, such as no internal rate of return at all. Either way, the *NPV* method is a clearly superior method for evaluating capital investment projects.

Problem 12.19. Consider the cash flows for project X, summarized in Table 12.14.
a. Summarize in a table project X's net present value profile for selected costs of capital.
b. Does project X have multiple internal rates of return? What are they?
c. Diagram your answer.

Solution
a. Substituting the cash flows provided and alternative costs of capital into Equation (12.28), we obtain Table 12.15.
b. Substituting the cash flow information into Equation (12.28) yields

$$NPV = -\$500 + \frac{\$4,000}{(1+IRR)^1} - \frac{\$5,000}{(1+IRR)^2} = 0$$

Rearranging, we have

$$-\$5,000\left(\frac{1}{1+IRR}\right)^2 + \$4,000\left(\frac{1}{1+IRR}\right)^1 - \$500 = 0$$

which is of the general form

$$a\left(\frac{1}{1+IRR}\right)^2 + b\left(\frac{1}{1+IRR}\right)^1 + c = 0$$

The solution values to this expression may be found by solving the quadratic equation

$$\left(\frac{1}{1+IRR}\right)_{1,2} = \frac{-b \pm (b^2 - 4ac)^{0.5}}{2a}$$

$$= \frac{-4,000 \pm \left[(4,000)^2 - 4(-5,000)(-500)\right]^{0.5}}{2(-5,000)}$$

$$= \frac{-4,000 \pm 2,449.49}{-10,000}$$

The solution values are

$$\left(\frac{1}{1+IRR}\right)_1 = \frac{-4,000 + 2,449.49}{-10,000} = 0.16$$

$$(1+IRR)_1 = 6.25$$

$$IRR_1 = 5.25, \text{ or } 525\%$$

$$\left(\frac{1}{1+IRR}\right)_2 = \frac{-4,000 - 2,449.49}{-10,000} = 0.64$$

$$(1+IRR)_2 = 1.56$$

$$IRR_2 = 0.56, \text{ or } 56\%$$

Project X has internal rates of return of both 56 and 525%.
c. Figure 12.19 shows the NPV profile for Project A.

MODIFIED INTERNAL RATE OF RETURN (MIRR) METHOD

Earlier we compared the NPV and IRR methods for evaluating independent and mutually exclusive investment projects. We found that for independent projects, both the NPV and the IRR methods will yield the same accept/reject decision rules. We also found that for mutually exclusive

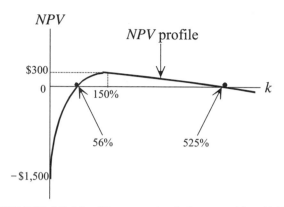

FIGURE 12.19 Diagrammatic solution to problem 12.19.

capital investment projects the *NPV* and the *IRR* methods could result in conflicting accept/reject decision rules.

It was noted that when the net present value profiles of two mutually exclusive projects intersect, the choice of projects should be based on the *NPV* method. This is because the *NPV* method implicitly assumes that net cash inflows are reinvested at the cost of capital, whereas the *IRR* method implicitly assumes that net cash inflows are reinvested at the internal rate of return. In view of its widespread practical application, is it possible to modify the *IRR* method by incorporating into the calculation the assumption that net cash flows are reinvested at the cost of capital? Happily, the answer to this question is yes. What is more, this method also overcomes the problem of multiple internal rates of return.

The *modified internal rate of return (MIRR)* method for evaluating capital investment projects is similar to the *IRR* method in that it generates accept/reject decision rules based on interest rate comparisons. But unlike the *IRR* method, the *MIRR* method assumes that cash flows are reinvested at the cost of capital and avoids some of the problems associated with multiple internal rates of return. The modified internal rate of return for a capital investment project may be calculated by using Equation (12.30)

$$\frac{\Sigma_{t=1 \to n} O_t}{(1+k)^t} = \frac{\Sigma_{t=1 \to n} R_t (1+k)^{n-t}}{(1+MIRR)^n} \tag{12.30}$$

where O_t represents cash outflows (costs), R_t represents the project's cash inflows (revenues), and k is the firm's cost of capital.

The term on the left hand side of Equation (12.30) is simply the present value of the firm's investment outlays *discounted at the firm's cost of capital.* The numerator on the right side of Equation (12.30) is the future value of the project's cash inflows *reinvested at the firm's cost of capital.* The future value of a project's cash inflows is sometimes referred to as the *terminal value* (*TV*) of the project. The modified internal rate of return is defined as the discount rate that equates the present value of cash outflows with the present value of the project's terminal value.

Definition: A project's terminal value is the future value of cash inflows compounded at the firm's cost of capital.

Definition: The modified internal rate of return is the discount rate that equates the present value of a project's cash outflows with the present value of the project's terminal value.

Consider, again, the net cash flows summarized in Table 12.1. Assuming a cost of capital of 10%, and substituting the cash flows in Table 12.1 into Equation (12.30), the *MIRR* for project *A* is

$$\frac{\Sigma_{t=1 \to n} O_t}{(1+k)^t} = \frac{\Sigma_{t=1 \to n} R_t (1+k)^{n-t}}{(1+MIRR_A)^n}$$

$$\frac{\$25,000}{(1.10)^0} = \frac{\$10,000(1.10)^4 + \$8,000(1.10)^3 + \$6,000(1.10)^2}{+\$5,000(1.10)^1 + \$4,000(1.10)^0}$$

$$= \frac{\$14,641 + \$10,648 + \$7,260 + \$5,500 + \$4,000}{(1+MIRR_A)^5}$$

$$\$25,000 = \frac{\$42,049}{(1+MIRR_A)^5}$$

$$(1+MIRR_A)^5 = \frac{\$42,049}{25,000} = 1.68196$$

$$1+MIRR_A = 1.1096$$

$$MIRR_A = 0.1096, \text{ or } 10.96\%$$

The calculation of *MIRR* for project *A* is illustrated in Figure 12.20. Likewise, the *MIRR* for project *B* is

$$\frac{\Sigma_{t=1 \to n} O_t}{(1+k)^t} = \frac{\Sigma_{t=1 \to n} R_t (1+k)^{n-t}}{(1+MIRR_B)^n}$$

$$\frac{\$25,000}{(1.10)^0} = \frac{\$3,000(1.10)^4 + \$5,000(1.10)^3 + \$7,000(1.10)^2}{+\$9,000(1.10)^1 + \$11,000(1.10)^0}$$

$$= \frac{\$3,000(1.4641) + \$5,000(1.331) + \$7,000(1.21)}{+\$9,000(1.10) + \$11,000}$$

$$= \frac{\$4,392.30 + \$6,655.00 + \$8,470.00 + \$9,900 + \$11,000}{(1+MIRR_B)^5}$$

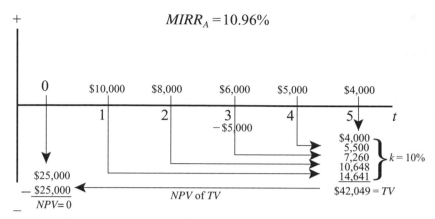

FIGURE 12.20   Modified internal rate of return for project A.

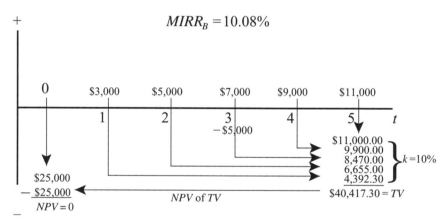

FIGURE 12.21   Modified internal rate of return for project B.

$$\$25,000 = \frac{\$40,417.30}{\left(1 + MIRR_B\right)^5}$$

$$\left(1 + MIRR_B\right)^5 = \frac{\$40,417.30}{\$25,000} = 1.616692$$

$$1 + MIRR_B = 1.1008$$

$$MIRR_A = 0.1008, \text{ or } 10.08\%$$

The calculation of $MIRR$ for project B is illustrated in Figure 12.21.

Based on the foregoing calculations, project A will be preferred to project B because $MIRR_A > MIRR_B$. To reiterate, although the NPV method should be preferred to both the IRR and $MIRR$ methods, the $MIRR$ method is superior to the IRR method for two reasons. Unlike the IRR method, the

MIRR method assumes that cash flows are reinvested at the more defensible cost of capital. Recall that the *IRR* method assumes that cash flows are reinvested at the firm's internal rate of return. Moreover, the *MIRR* method is not plagued by the problem of multiple internal rates of return.

CAPITAL RATIONING

In each of the methods of evaluating capital investment projects discussed thus far it was implicitly assumed that the firm had unfettered access to the funds needed to invest in each and every profitable project. If capital markets are efficient, this assumption is approximately true for large, well-established companies with a good record of performance. For smaller, less well-established companies, however, easy access to finance capital may be limited. In some cases, finance capital may be relatively easy to obtain, but for any of a number of reasons senior management may decide to impose a limit on the company's capital expenditures. Senior management may be reluctant to incur higher levels of debt associated with bank borrowing or with issuing corporate bonds. Alternatively, senior management may be unwilling to issue equity shares (stock) to raise the requisite financing because this will dilute ownership and control. For these and other reasons, senior management may decide to reject potentially profitable projects.

The situation of management-imposed cops on capital expenditures may be generally described as a problem of *capital scarcity*. When finance capital is scarce, the firm's investment alternatives are said to be constrained, in which case whatever finance capital is available should be used as efficiently as possible. The process of allocating scarce finance capital as efficiently as possible is called *capital rationing*.

Definition: Capital rationing refers to the efficient allocation of scarce finance capital.

Although details of the procedures involved in efficiently allocating scarce capital are beyond the scope of the present discussion, a simple example will convey the spirit of the capital rationing process. Assume that senior management has $1,000 to invest in six independent projects, each with a life expectancy of 5 years. Assume also that the firm's cost of capital is 5% per year. Table 12.16 summarizes the net present values of six feasible capital investment projects.

It is readily apparent from Table 12.16 that $1,250 in finance capital will be required for the firm to undertake all six projects for a maximum net present value of $945. The problem, of course, is that the firm only has $1,000 to invest. Given this constraint, which projects should the firm undertake to maximize the net present value of $1,000?

The question confronting senior management is this: Which projects should be selected? Table 12.17 ranks from highest to lowest the alterna-

TABLE 12.16   Net Present Values of Alternative
Capital Investment Projects

Project	Initial outlay	Net present value
1	$400	$250
2	300	150
3	200	140
4	150	140
5	100	135
6	100	130

TABLE 12.17   Investment Alternatives

Option	Projects	Total outlay	Total net present value	Future value of residual earnings	Total net present value
A	2, 3, 4, 5, 6	$850	$695	$191.44	$886.44
B	1, 3, 4, 5, 6	950	795	63.81	858.81
C	1, 2, 5, 6	900	665	127.63	792.63
D	1, 2, 3, 5	1,000	675	0.00	675.00
E	1, 2, 3, 6	1,000	670	0.00	670.00
F	1, 2, 3	950	540	63.81	603.81

tives available to the firm based on total net present value. Table 12.17 assumes that any residual funds not allocated to a project are invested for 5 years at the firm's cost of capital.

For senior management to generate the highest total net present value, the information presented in Table 12.17 points to investments in projects 2, 3, 4, 5, and 6 for a total net present value of $886.44.

THE COST OF CAPITAL

In each of the methods for evaluating capital investment projects discussed thus far the firm's cost of capital was assumed, almost as an afterthought. The firm's cost of capital, however, is a crucial element in the capital budgeting process. Calculation of the firm's cost of capital is a complicated issue, and a detailed discussion of its derivation is beyond the scope of this chapter. Nevertheless, a brief digression into this important concept is fundamental to an understanding of capital budgeting.

To begin with, it must be recognized that the firm has available several financing options. It must decide whether to satisfy its capital financing requirements by assuming long-term debt, by issuing bonds or by commercial bank borrowing, by selling equity shares, which may dilute ownership and control, by issuing preferred stock, or by some combination of these measures. Moreover, the method of financing may affect the profitability of the firm's operations, the public's perception of the riskiness of the method of financing and its impact on the firm's future ability to raise finance capital, and the impact of the method of financing on the future cost of raising finance capital. When the costs of alternative methods of raising finance capital have been considered, the firm must select the debt/equity mix that results in the lowest, risk-adjusted, cost of capital.

WEIGHTED AVERAGE COST OF CAPITAL (WACC)

The firm's cost of capital is generally taken to be some average of the cost of funds acquired from a variety of sources. Generally, firms can raise finance capital by issuing common stock, by issuing preferred stock, or by borrowing from commercial banks or by selling bonds directly to the public.

Definition: Common stock represents a share of equity ownership in a company. Companies that are owned by a large number of investors who are not actively involved in management are referred to as publicly owned or publicly held corporations. Common stockholders earn dividends that are in proportion to the number of shares owned.

Definition: Dividends are payments to corporate stockholders representing a share of the firm's earnings.

Definition: A bond is a long-term debt instrument in which a borrower agrees to make principal and interest payments at specified time intervals to the holder of the bond.

Definition: Preferred stock is a hybrid financial instrument. Preferred stock is similar to a corporate bond in that it has a par value and fixed dividends per share must be paid to the preferred stockholder before common stockholders receive their dividends. On the other hand, a board of directors that opts to forgo paying preferred dividends will not automatically plunge the firm into bankruptcy.

When a firm raises the entire amount of investment capital by issuing *common stock*, the cost of capital is taken to be the firm's required return on equity. In practice, however, firms raise a substantial portion of their finance capital in the form of long-term debt, or by issuing preferred stock. A discussion of the advantages and disadvantages associated with any of these financing methods is clearly beyond the scope of the present discussion.

It may be argued that for any firm there is an optimal mix of debt and preferred and common stock. This optimal mix is sometimes referred to as the firm's *optimal capital structure*. A firm's optimal capital structure is the mix of financing alternatives that maximizes the firm's stock price.

Definition: The optimal capital structure of a firm is the combination of debt and preferred and common stock that maximizes the firm's share values.

The proportion of debt and preferred and common stock, which define the firm's optimal capital structure, may be used to calculate the firm's *weighted average cost of capital* (*WACC*). The weighed average cost of capital may be calculated by using Equation (12.31)

$$WACC = \omega_d k_d (1 - t) + \omega_p k_p + \omega_c k_c \tag{12.31}$$

where ω_d, ω_p, and ω_c are the weights used for the cost of debt, preferred stock, and common stock, respectively.

Definition: The weighted cost of capital is the weighed average of the component sources of capital financing, including common stock, long-term debt, and preferred stock.

The term $\omega_d k_d (1 - t)$ represents the firm's after-tax cost of debt, where t is the firm's marginal tax rate. The after-tax cost of debt recognizes that the financing cost (interest) of debt is tax deductible.

The cost of preferred stock, k_p, is generally taken to be the preferred stock dividend, d_p, divided by the preferred stock price p_p, that is,

$$k_p = \frac{d_p}{p_p} \tag{12.32}$$

In the case of long-term debt and preferred stock, the cost of capital is the rate of return that is required by holders of these securities. As noted earlier, the cost of common stock, k_c, is taken to be the rate of return that stockholders require on the company's common stock. In general, there are two sources of equity capital: retained earnings and capital financing obtained by issuing new shares of common stock.

Corporate profits may be disposed in of in one of two ways. Some or all of the profits may be returned to the owners of the corporation, the stockholders, as distributed corporate profits. Distributed corporate profits are commonly referred to as *dividends*. Corporate profits not returned to the stockholder are referred to as undistributed corporate profits. Undistributed corporate profits are commonly referred to as *retained earnings*.

An important source of finance capital is retained earnings. It is tempting to think of retained earnings as being "free," but this would be a mistake. Retained earnings that are used to finance capital investment projects have opportunity costs. Remember, in the final analysis retained earnings belong to the stockholders but have been held back by senior management to reinvest in the company. Had the stockholders received these undistributed corporate profits, they would have been in a position to reinvest the funds in alternative financial instruments. What then is the cost of funds of retained earnings? This cost should be the rate of return the stockholder could earn on an investment of equivalent risk. In general, a firm that cannot earn at least this equivalent to the rate of return should pay out retained earnings to the stockholders.

CHAPTER REVIEW

Capital budgeting is the application of the principle of profit maximization to multiperiod projects. Capital budgeting involves investment decisions in which expenditures and receipts continue over a significant period of time. In general, capital budgeting projects may be classified into one of several major categories, including *capital expansion, replacement, new product lines, mandated investments,* and *miscellaneous investments.*

Capital budgeting involves the subtraction of cash outflows from cash inflows with adjustments for differences in their values over time. Differences in the values of the flows are based on the *time value of money,* which says that a dollar today is worth more than a dollar tomorrow.

There are five standard methods used to evaluate the value of alternative investment projects: *payback period, discounted payback period, net present value (NPV), internal rate of return (IRR),* and *modified internal rate of return (MIRR).* The payback period is the number of periods required to recover an original investment. In general, risk-averse managers prefer investments with shorter payback periods.

The net present value of a project is calculated by subtracting the discounted present value of all outflows from the discounted present value of all inflows. The discount rate is the interest rate used to evaluate the project and is sometimes referred to as the *cost of capital, hurdle rate, cutoff rate,* or *required rate of return.* If the net present value of an investment is positive (negative), the project is accepted (rejected). If the net present value of an investment is zero, the manager is indifferent to the project.

The internal rate of return is the interest rate that equates the present values of inflows to the present values of outflows; that is, the rate that causes the net present value of the project to equal zero. If the internal rate of return is greater than the cost of capital, the project is accepted.

There are a number of problems associated with using the *IRR* method for evaluating capital investment projects. One problem is the possibility of multiple internal rates of return. Multiple internal rates of return occur when a project that has two or more internal rates of return.

For independent projects both the *NPV* and the *IRR* methods will yield the same accept/reject decision rules. For mutually exclusive capital investment projects, the *NPV* and the *IRR* methods could result in conflicting accept/reject decision rules. This is because the *NPV* method implicitly assumes that net cash inflows are reinvested at the cost of capital, whereas the *IRR* method assumes that net cash inflows are reinvested at the internal rate of return.

The *modified internal rate of return (MIRR)* method for evaluating capital investment projects is similar to the *IRR* method in that it generates accept/reject decision rules based on interest rate comparisons. But unlike the *IRR* method, the *MIRR* method assumes that cash flows are reinvested at the cost of capital and avoids some of the problems associated with multiple internal rates of return.

Categories of cost of capital include the *cost of debt, the cost of equity*, and the *weighted cost of capital*. The cost of debt is the interest rate that must be paid on after-tax debt.

The weighed cost of capital is a measure of the overall cost of capital. It is obtained by weighting the various costs by the relative proportion of each component's value in the total capital structure.

KEY TERMS AND CONCEPTS

Abnormal cash flow   Large cash outflows that occur during or toward the end of the life of a project.

Annuity   A series of equal payments, which are made at fixed intervals for a specified number of periods.

Annuity due   An annuity in which the fixed payments are made at the beginning of each period.

Capital budgeting   The process whereby senior management analyzes the comparative net revenues from alternative investment projects. In capital budgeting future cash inflows and outflows of different capital investment projects are expressed as a single value at a common point in time, usually at the moment the project is undertaken, so that they may be compared.

Capital rationing   The efficient allocation of scarce finance capital.

Cash flow diagram   Illustrates the cash inflows and cash outflows expected to arise from a given investment.

Common stock   A share of equity ownership in a company. Companies that are owned by a large number of investors who are not actively involved in management are referred to as publicly owned or publicly held corporations. Common stockholders earn dividends that are in proportion to the number of shares owned.

Compounding   With an adjective (e.g., annual) indicates how frequently the rate of return on an investment is calculated.

Cost of capital   The cost of acquiring funds to finance a capital investment project. It is the minimum rate of return that must be earned to justify a capital investment. The cost of capital is often referred to as the required rate of return, the cutoff rate, or the hurdle rate.

Cost of debt   The term $\omega_d k_d(1 - t)$ represents the firm's after-tax cost of debt, with t standing for the firm's marginal tax rate. The after-tax cost of debt recognizes that the financing cost (interest) of debt is tax deductible.

Cost of equity   The required rate of return on common stock.

Coupon bond   A debt obligations in which the issuer of the bond promises to pay the bearer of the bond fixed dollar interest payments at regular intervals for a specified period of time.

Crossover rate　The cost of capital at which the net present values of two projects are equal. Diagrammatically, this is the cost of capital at which the net present value profiles of two projects intersect.

Cutoff rate　Another name for the hurdle rate.

Discount rate The rate of interest that is used to discount a cash flow.

Discounted cash flow　The present value of an investment, or series of investments.

Discounted payback period　Similar to the payback period except that the cost of capital is used in discounting cash flows.

Dividends　Payments to corporate stockholders representing a share of the firm's earnings. Commonly referred to as distributed corporate profits.

Future value (FV)　The final accumulated value of a sum of money at some future time period.

Future value of an annuity due ($FVAD$)　The future value of an annuity in which the fixed payments are made at the beginning of each period.

Future value of an ordinary annuity ($FVOA$)　The future value of an annuity in which the fixed payments are made at the end of each period.

Hurdle rate　The cost of capital that must be covered by the internal rate of return if a project is to be undertaken. The hurdle rate is often referred to as the required rate of return or the cutoff rate.

Independent projects　Projects are independent if their cash flows are unrelated.

Internal rate of return (IRR)　The discount rate that equates the present value of a project's cash inflows to the present value of its cash outflows.

Modified internal rate of return ($MIRR$)　The discount rate that equates the present value of a project's cash outflows with the present value of its terminal value.

Multiple internal rates of return　Two or more internal rates of return for the same project.

Mutually exclusive projects　Projects are mutually exclusive if acceptance of one project means rejection of all other projects.

Net present value (NPV)　The present value of future net cash flows discounted at the cost of capital.

Normal cash flow　One or more cash outflows of a project followed by a series of cash inflows.

Ordinary (deferred) annuity　An annuity in which the fixed payments occur at the end of each period.

Operating cash flow　The cash flow generated from a company's operations.

Par value of a bond　The face value of the bond. It is the amount originally borrowed by the issuer.

Payback period   The number of years required to recover the original investment.

Preferred stock   Similar to a corporate bond in that it has a par value and that a fixed amount of dividends per share must be paid to the preferred stockholder before dividends can be distributed to common stockholders. A board of directors that opts to forgo paying preferred dividends will not automatically plunge the firm into bankruptcy.

Present value (*PV*)   The value of a sum of money at some initial time period.

Present value of an annuity   The present value of a series of fixed payments made at fixed intervals for a specified period of time.

Required rate of return   Another name for the hurdle rate or the cutoff rate.

Retained earnings   The portion of corporate profits not returned to the stockholders. Commonly referred to as undistributed corporate profits.

Salvage value   The estimated market value of a capital asset at the end of its life.

Terminal value (*TV*)   The future value of a project's cash inflows compounded at the firm's cost of capital.

Time value of money   Reflects the understanding that a dollar received today is worth more than a dollar received tomorrow.

Weighted average cost of capital   The weighed average of the component sources of capital financing, including common stock, long-term debt, and preferred stock.

Yield to maturity (*YTM*)   The rate of return that is earned on a bond when held to maturity.

CHAPTER QUESTIONS

12.1 Define capital budgeting. What are the four main categories of capital budgeting projects? Briefly explain each.

12.2 Explain why assessing the time value of money is important in capital budgeting.

12.3 A dollar received today will never be worth the same as a dollar received tomorrow. Do you agree? If not, then why not?

12.4 Explain the difference between an ordinary annuity and an annuity due.

12.5 Other things being equal, the future value of an ordinary annuity is greater than the future value of an annuity due. Do you agree with this statement? Explain.

12.6 The more frequent the compounding, the greater the present value of a lump-sum investment. Do you agree? If not, then why not?

12.7 Other things being equal, the present value of an ordinary annuity is greater than the present value of an annuity due. Do you agree with this statement? Explain.

12.8 The smallest interest component of an amortization schedule is paid in at the end of the first year; thereafter, as the amount of the principal outstanding declines, the paid interest component increases. Do you agree or disagree? Explain.

12.9 What is the difference between the payback period and discounted payback period methods of evaluating a capital investment project? Assuming that the projects are mutually exclusive, do the two methods result in the same project rankings? What is the main deficiency of these methods? What is the in primary usefulness?

12.10 If two independent projects have positive net present values, the project with the highest net present value should be adopted. Do you agree? If not, then why not?

12.11 Suppose that two mutually exclusive projects have only cash outflows. The project with the highest net present value should be adopted. Do you agree with this statement? Explain.

12.12 The internal rate of return is the minimum rate of interest an investor will pay to finance a capital investment project. Do you agree? If not, then why not?

12.13 The net present value and internal rate of return methods will always result in the same accept and reject decisions for mutually exclusive projects. Do you agree with this statement?

12.14 What is the relationship between changes in the hurdle rate and changes in the net present value of a project?

12.15 The net present value of a project in which the cash flows are received in the near future will decline at a faster rate than the net present value for projects in which the cash flows are generated in the distant future. Do you agree with this statement?

12.16 Why may the net present value profiles of two projects intersectz. Give two reasons.

12.17 For mutually exclusive projects, when the net present value profiles of two projects intersect, should the net present value method or the internal rate of return method be used for selecting one project over the other?

12.18 What are the maximum possible internal rates of return for a single project?

12.19 Under what circumstances is a project likely to exhibit multiple internal rates of return possible?

12.20 What is the difference between the internal rate of return method and the modified internal rate of return method for evaluating capital investment projects? What problem does the second method overcome?

12.21 The modified internal rate of return method is preferable to the net present value method for evaluating capital investment projects because it assumes that cash flows are reinvested at the cost of capital. Do you agree with this statement?

CHAPTER EXERCISES

12.1 What is the present value of a cash inflow of $100,000 in 5 years if the annual interest rate is 8%? What would the present value be if there was an additional cash inflow of $200,000 in 10 years?

12.2 An drew borrows $20,000 for 3 years at an annual rate of 7% compounded monthly to purchase a new car. The first payment is due at the end of the first month.

   a. What is the amount of Andrew's automobile payments?
   b. What is the total amount of interest paid?

12.3 Suppose that Adam deposits $200,000 in a time deposit that pays 15% interest per year compounded annually. How much will Adam receive when the deposit is redeemed after 7 years? How would your answer have been different for interest compounded quarterly?

12.4 Suppose that Adam borrows $20,000 from the National Central Bank and agrees to repay the loan in 4 years at an interest rate of 8% per year, compounded continuously. How much will Adam have repaid to the bank at the end of 4 years?

12.5 Calculate the future value of a 5-year annuity due with payments of $5,000 a year at 4% compounded semiannually.

12.6 How much should an individual invest today for that investment to be worth $750 in 8 years if the interest rate is 22% per year, compounded annually?

12.7 If the prevailing interest rate on a time deposit is 9% per year compounded annually, how much would Eleanor Rigby have to deposit today to receive $400,000 at the end of 6 years?

12.8 Consider the cash flow diagram in Figure E12.8.

Calculate the terminal value of the cash flow stream at $t = 3$ if interest is compounded quarterly.

12.9 Calculate the present value of $20,000 in 10 years if the interest rate is 7% compounded

   a. Annually
   b. Quarterly
   c. Monthly
   d. Continuously

12.10 If the prevailing interest rate on a time deposit is 9% annually, how much would Sam Orez have to deposit today to receive $400,000 at the end of 6 years if the interest rate were compounded quarterly, monthly, and continuously?

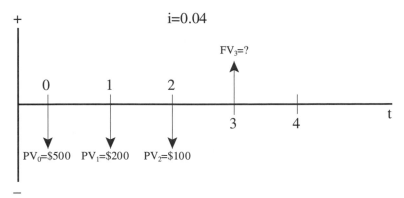

FIGURE E12.8

TABLE E12.12   Net Cash Flows (CF_t)
for Projects A and B

Year, t	Project A	Project B
0	−$20,000	−$20,000
1	10,000	8,000
2	8,000	8,000
3	5,000	8,000
4	3,000	8,000

12.11 Calculate the present value of a 10-year ordinary annuity paying $10,000 a year at 5, 10, and 15%.

12.12 Senior management of Valhaus Entertainment is considering two proposed capital investment projects, A and B. Each project requires an initial cash outlay of $20,000. The projects' cash flows, which have been adjusted to reflect inflation, taxes, depreciation, and salvage values, are summarized in Table E12.12. Use the payback period method to determine, which project should be selected.

12.13 Suppose that the chief financial officer (CFO) of Orange Company is considering two mutually exclusive investment projects. The projected net cash flows for projects X and Y are summarized in Table E12.13.

If the discount rate (cost of capital) is expected to be 15%, which project should be undertaken?

12.14 Senior management of Teal Corporation is considering the projected net cash flows for two mutually exclusive projects, which are provided in Table E12.14.

Determine which project should be adopted if the cost of capital is 6%.

12.15 Suppose that an investment project requires an immediate cash

TABLE E12.13   Net Cash Flows for
Projects X and Y

Year, t	Project X	Project Y
0	-$30,000	-$25,000
1	10,000	6,000
2	12,000	10,000
3	14,000	12,000
4	15,000	12,000
5	8,000	10,000

TABLE E12.14   Net Cash Flows for
Projects Red and Blue

Year, t	Project Red	Project Blue
0	-$5,000	-$10,000
1	3,000	1,000
2	5,500	3,000
3		5,000
4		7,000

outlay of $25,000 and provides for an annual cash inflow of $10,000 for the next 5 years.

a. Estimate the internal rate of return.

b. Should the project be undertaken if the cost of capital (hurdle rate) is 30%?

12.16 Illustrate the net present value profile for alternative interest rates for the cash flow information Projects A and B in Exercise 12.12. Be sure to include in your answer the internal rate of return for each project.

12.17 Red Lion pays a corporate income tax rate of 38%. Red Lion is planning to build a new factory in the country of Paragon to manufacture primary and secondary school supplies. The new factory will require an immediate cash outlay of $4 million but is expected to generate annual profits of $1 million. According to the Paragon Uniform Tax Code, Red Lion may deduct $250,000 annually as a depreciation expense. The life of the new factory is expected to be 10 years. Assuming that the annual interest rate is 20%, should Red Lion build the new factory? Explain.

12.18 Senior management of Vandaley Enterprises is considering two mutually exclusive investment projects. The projected net cash flows for projects A and B are summarized in Table E12.18.

If the discount rate (cost of capital) is expected to be 15%, which project should be undertaken?

TABLE E12.18 Net Cash Flows (CF_t) for Projects A and B

Year, t	Project A	Project B
0	−$27,000	−$21,000
1	8,000	6,500
2	9,000	6,500
3	10,000	6,500
4	10,000	6,500
5	6,000	6,500

TABLE E12.20 Net Cash Flows (CF_t) for Yellow Project

Year, t	CF_t
0	−$1,500
1	500,000
2	−400,000

12.19 Suppose that an investment opportunity, which requires an initial outlay of $100,000, is expected to yield a return of $250,000 after 30 years.

a. Will the investment be profitable if the cost of capital is 7%?

b. Will the investment be profitable if the cost of capital is 2%?

c. At what cost of capital will the investor be indifferent to the investment?

12.20 Consider the net cash flows for Yellow Project given in Table E12.20.

a. What is the net present value profile for Yellow Project at selected costs of capital?

b. Does Yellow Project have multiple internal rate of return? What are they?

c. Diagram your answer.

12.21 Calculate the weighted average cost of capital of a project that is 30% debt and 70% equity. Assume that the firm pays 10% on debt and 25% on equity. Assume that the firm's marginal tax rate is 33%.

SELECTED READINGS

Blank, L. T., and A. J. Tarquin. *Engineering Economy*, 3rd ed. New York: McGraw-Hill, 1989.

Brigham, E. F., and J. F. Houston. *Fundamentals of Financial Management*, 2nd ed. New York: Dryden Press, 1999.

Brigham, E. F., L. C. Gapenski, and M. C. Erhardt. *Financial Management: Theory and Practice*, 9th ed. New York: Dryden Press, 1998.

Palm, T., and A. Qayum. *Private and Public Investment Analysis.* Cincinnati, OH: South-Western Publishing, 1985.

Schall, L. D., and C. W. Haley. *Introduction to Financial Analysis*, 6th ed. New York: McGraw-Hill, 1991.

13

INTRODUCTION TO
GAME THEORY

In Chapter 10 we examined the importance of interdependence among firms in pricing and output decisions in connection with duopolistic and oligopolistic market structure. In particular, we saw how the output and pricing decisions of one firm affect, and are affected by, the pricing and output decisions of other firms in the same industry. Moreover, we saw that this interdependency in the managerial decision-making process tends to become more pronounced the smaller the number of firms in the industry or, which is nearly the same thing, as two or more firms grow large enough to dominate industry supply.

In this chapter we take a closer look at a very important analytical tool that was only briefly examined in our discussion of oligopolistic behavior. This chapter is devoted to a more detailed examination of *game theory*. As we mentioned in Chapter 10, game theory is perhaps the most important tool in the economist's analytical kit for analyzing *strategic behavior*. Strategic behavior is concerned with how individuals make decisions when they recognize that their actions affect, and are affected by, the actions of other individuals or groups. In other words, strategic behavior recognizes that the decision-making process is frequently mutually interdependent.

Definition: Strategic behavior reflects recognition that decisions of competing individuals and groups are mutually interdependent.

As we noted in our discussion of oligopolistic markets in Chapter 10, game theory has numerous and widespread applications for analyzing the managerial decision-making process. It is a topic without which no textbook in managerial economics would be complete.

GAMES AND STRATEGIC BEHAVIOR

Most of our treatment of the behavior of profit-maximizing firms has been rather mechanistic in the sense that managers make pricing and output decisions without regard to the actions of their competitors. While this argument may be more or less correct for firms operating at the extreme end of the competitive spectrum (perfect competition and monopoly), it is far less likely apply to intermediate market structures, such as monopolistic competition, duopoly, and oligopoly. As we noted in Chapter 10, decision making by firms in oligopolistic industries is characterized by strategic behavior: the actions that result because individuals and groups that make decisions recognize that their actions affect, and are affected by, the actions of other individuals or groups.

In many respects, running a business is like playing a game of football or chess. The object of the game is to achieve an optimal outcome. But unlike these games, the "best" outcome does not always mean that your opponent loses. As we will see, the best outcome often results when the players cooperate. When cooperation is not possible, or illegal, then the objective is to win the game. But, victory does not always go to the strongest, or the fastest, or the most talented. Very often, victory belongs to the player who best understands the rules and has the superior game plan. The purpose of this chapter is to learn how to play a good game, regardless of whether cooperation and mutually beneficial outcomes are possible.

What is a game? Most of us think of a game as an activity involving two or more individuals, or teams, hereinafter referred to as players, in competition with each other. In general, the objective is to win the game because "to the winner go the spoils." Sometimes the spoils are little more than "bragging rights," often symbolized by a metal or glass artifact (trophy) of undistinguished design. Sometimes the spoils are monetary. Sometimes the winner wins both cash and trinkets—for example, to the owner of the winning team in the Super Bowl is presented the sterling silver Vince Lombardi Trophy and each player receives a gold and diamond ring and a cash award. After winning Super Bowl XXXV, each member of the Baltimore Ravens, received $58,000, while the losing New York Giants, received $34,500 per player. In business, we tend to think of the winning "team" as the firm that earns the greatest profits, or captures the largest market share, or achieves some objective more successfully than its rivals. Unlike football games, however, sometimes it is in the best interest of the teams to cooperate to achieve a mutually advantageous outcome.

In general, all games involve social and economic interactions in which the decisions made by one player affect, and are affected by, the decisions made by other players. It would be foolish for a chess player to make a move without first considering the prior play of his or her opponent. It would not make much business sense for the owner of a gasoline station to set prices for the various grades of gasoline without first considering the prices charged by other gas station owners in the neighborhood. It is this interdependency in the decision-making process that is at the heart of all games.

In game theory, decision makers are called players. Players make decisions based on strategies. These decisions dictate the players' moves. Players with the best strategies very often win the game, although this does not always happen. The rules of the game dictate the manner in which the players move. In a *simultaneous-move game*, it is useful to think of players moving at the same time. Simultaneous-move games are sometimes referred to as *static games*. Examples of simultaneous-move games are the children's games of war and rock–scissors–paper. The distinguishing characteristic of a simultaneous-move game is that no player is aware of the decisions of any other player until after the moves have been made. In a two-player game, player A is unaware of the decisions of player B, and vice versa, until both have moved.

Definition: In a simultaneous-move game the players effectively move at the same time.

In a simultaneous-move game the players are not required to actually move at the same time. In the card game called war, a standard deck of cards is shuffled and dealt out equally between two players. The players then recite the phrase "w-a-r spells war." When they say the word "war," in unison they place a card, face up, on the table. The cards are valued from lowest to highest 2–10, jack, queen, king, ace. Suits (clubs, diamonds, hearts, and spades) in this game are irrelevant. The player who shows the highest valued card wins the other player's card. If both players show a card with the same value the move is repeated until a player wins. The game ends when the deck is exhausted. The player with the greatest number of cards at the end of the game wins.

It is reemphasized that the players of simultaneous-move games are not actually required to move at the same time. "War" could also be played, for example, by isolating the players in separate rooms. Communication between the players is prohibited. A third individual, the referee, asks both players to reveal the top card on their respective portions of the deck and declares a winner accordingly. It is assumed that both players are honest and do not attempt to rearrange the order of the cards in the deck when no one is looking. The essential element of this game is that each player must move without prior knowledge of the move of the other player.

In a *sequential-move game* the players take turns. Sequential-move games are sometimes referred to as *multistage* or *dynamic games*. In a two-player game, player A moves first, followed by player B, followed again by player A, and so on. Unlike a simultaneous-move game, player B's move is based on the knowledge of how player A has already moved. Moreover, player A's next move will be based on the knowledge of how player B

moved in response to player A's last move, and so on. Examples of sequential-move games include most board games, such as chess, checkers, and Monopoly. The model of duopoly developed by Augustin Cournot (1897), which was discussed in Chapter 10, is an example of a sequential-move game. Although Cournot's work was later criticized by Joseph Bertrand in the *Journal des Savants* (September 1883), both models attempt to explain the dynamic interaction of firms in a market setting.

Definition: In a sequential-move game, the players move in turn.

In addition to the manner in which the players move, games are defined by the number of games played. *One-shot games* are played only once. *Repeated games* are played more than once. If, for example, you agree with a friend to play just one game of backgammon, then you are playing a one-shot game. If you agree to play more than one game, then you are playing a repeated game.

Definition: A one-shot game is a game that is played only once.

Definition: A repeated game is a game that is played more than once.

In many ways running a business is like playing a game. In a competitive environment, the objective is to win the game. In the paragraphs that follow we will develop the basic principles of *game theory*. Game theory is the study of how rivals make decisions in situations involving strategic interaction (move and countermove). In other words, game theory refers to process by which the strategic behavior of the players is modeled. The modern version of game theory can be traced to the groundbreaking work of mathematician John von Neumann and economist Oskar Morgenstern in their 1944 classic, *Theory of Games and Economic Behavior*. As we will see, game theory is a very powerful tool for analyzing a wide variety of competitive business situations.

Definition: Game theory is the study of how rivals make decisions in situations involving strategic interaction (i.e., move and countermove) to achieve an optimal outcome.

NONCOOPERATIVE, SIMULTANEOUS-MOVE, ONE-SHOT GAMES

In this section we will examine two-person, noncooperative, non-zero-sum, simultaneous-move, one-shot games. Although the description of games of these types sounds rather daunting, it is the most basic of all game theoretic scenarios. We will begin by assuming that only two players will be playing. We will also assume that the games are noncooperative. In a *noncooperative game* the two players do not engage in collusive behavior. In other words, the two players do not conspire to "rig" the final outcome.

We will also consider non-zero-sum games. A *zero-sum game* is one in which one player's gain is exactly the other player's loss. Poker and lotteries are zero-sum games. We will consider games in which the final solution is mutually advantageous. Each player has one, and only one, move, and both players move simultaneously. The significance of this assumption is that neither player enjoys the benefit of knowing the intentions of the other player, although each player knows the resulting payoffs from any combination of moves by both players. The Prisoners' Dilemma, discussed in Chapter 10, is an example of a two-person, noncooperative, non-zero-sum, simultaneous-move, one-shot game.

Definition: A noncooperative game is one in which the players do not engage in collusive behavior. In other words, the players do not conspire to "rig" the final outcome.

Definition: A zero-sum game is one in which one player's gain is exactly the other player's loss.

Moves are based on strategies. A strategy is a game plan. It is a kind of decision rule that a player will apply to situations in which choices need to be made. Knowledge of a player's strategy should allow us to predict what course of action a player will take when confronted with options.

Definition: A strategy is a game plan. It is decision rule that indicates what action a player will take when confronted with the need to make a decision.

Before presenting an example of a simultaneous-move, one-shot game, it is important to distinguish between *risk takers* and *risk avoiders*. The strategy selected reflects the personality of the player. Gamblers, for example, are risk takers. Risk takers have an "all or nothing" mentality; they prefer situations in which the prospect of winning results in a big payoff, even though the probability of losing is greater, and sometimes considerably so, than the probability of winning. In the parlance of probability theory, individuals are said to be risk takers (sometimes called risk lovers), when they prefer the expected value of a payoff to its certainty equivalent. Risk takers are commonly found Las Vegas, Atlantic City, and the New York Stock Exchange.[1]

Definition: Risk takers are individuals who prefer risky situations in which the expected value of a payoff is preferred to its certainty equivalent.

Risk avoiders, on the other hand, prefer a certain payoff to a risky prospect with the same expected value. Risk-averse individuals seek to minimize uncertainty. Risk avoiders prefer predictable behavior to probabilistic outcomes. When probabilistic outcomes are unavoidable, risk avoiders

---

[1] An expected value is defined as the weighted average of all possible outcomes, with the weights being the probability of each outcome, this is,

$$E(x) = \sum_{i=1 \to n} x_i p_i$$

where x_i is the value of the outcome and p_i is the probability of its occurrence.

will choose the "safer" outcome. Risk avoiders are loss minimizers. Depending of the level of risk aversion, for example, risk avoiders would prefer to invest in a mutual fund rather than in the individual stocks that make up the mutual fund. The reason for this is that although the expected rate of return may be lower, so too is the probability of loss. Of course, risk aversion is a relative concept. For extremely risk-averse individuals, investing in mutual funds may seem like a risky proposition. For these individuals, investing in high-grade corporate bonds or commercial bank certificates of deposits may be the way to go.

Definition: Risk avoiders prefer a certain payoff to a risky prospect with the same expected value. Risk avoiders prefer predictable outcomes to probabilistic expectations.

A player's strategy will reflect the individual's attitude toward risk. Since risk avoidance would appear to be the dominant manifestation of human behavior, we will assume in our game theoretic scenarios that the players are risk avoiders. Consider, for example, the two-player, noncooperative, non-zero-sum, simultaneous-move, one-shot game presented in Figure 13.1.

Figure 13.1 summarizes the players in the game (player A and player B), the possible strategies of each player ($A1$, $A2$, $B1$, and $B2$), and the payoffs to each player from each strategic combination. The list of strategies of each player in a game is referred to as a *strategy profile*. Strategy profiles are often depicted within curly braces. In the game depicted in Figure 13.1 there were four strategy profiles: $\{A1, B1\}$, $\{A1, B2\}$, $\{A2, B1\}$, and $\{A2, B2\}$.

The entries in the cells of the matrix refer to the payoffs to each player from each combination of strategies. The first entry in each cell of the *payoff matrix* refers to the payoff to player A and the second entry refers to the payoff to player B. Payoffs are often depicted in parentheses. We will adopt the convention that the first entry in each cell refers to the payoff to the player indicated on the left of the payoff matrix and the second entry refers in each cell refers to the payoff to the player indicated at the top. There are four payoffs depicted in Figure 13.1: (100, 200), (150, 75), (50, 50), and (100, 100). For example, if player A follows strategy $A1$ while player B follows

		Player B	
		B1	B2
Player A	A1	(100, 200)	(150, 75)
	A2	(50, 50)	(100, 100)

Payoffs: (Player A, Player B)

FIGURE 13.1   Payoff matrix for a two-player, simultaneous-move game.

strategy $B2$, $\{A1, B2\}$, then the payoff to player A is *150* and the payoff to player B is *75*, (150, 75). The representation, which is depicted in Figure 13.1, is referred to as a *normal-form game*.

Definition: A normal-form game summarizes the players, possible strategies, and payoffs from alternative strategies in a simultaneous-move game.

Games such as the one presented in Figure 13.1 can apply to almost any situation involving decisions between two or more "players." In Chapter 10 the Cournot duopoly model was introduced as an example of two firms interacting in a market setting. The Cournot duopoly model is an attempt to explain the process by which two firms decide whether to charge a high price or a low price for its product, and the likely effect on each firm's profits from alternative combinations of strategies. The game might involve two competing firms trying to decide whether to advertise on television or in magazines, to introduce an entirely new product into the market, or to improve on an existing product.

STRICTLY DOMINANT STRATEGY

What is the optimal strategy for each player in the game depicted in Figure 13.1? Consider the strategies open to player A. If player A chooses strategy $A1$, then the payoffs will be 100 if player B chooses strategy $B1$ and 150 if player B chooses strategy $B2$. On the other hand, if player A chooses strategy $A2$, then the payoffs will be 50 if player B chooses strategy $B1$ and 100 if player B chooses $B2$. In this case, there is no question about what player A will do. Since the highest payoff that player A can expect by following strategy $A2$ is the same as the lowest payoff from following strategy $A1$, player A will obviously choose strategy $A1$. Here, strategy $A1$ is referred to as a *strictly dominant strategy* because that strategy will result in the largest payoff for each action that can be taken by player B.

Definition: A strictly dominant strategy is a strategy that results in the largest payoff regardless of the strategy adopted by other players.

What is the optimal strategy for player B? The reader should verify that player B does not have a strictly dominant strategy. Nevertheless, the fact that player A does have a strictly dominant strategy determines player B's next move. Since player A's strictly-dominant strategy is A, the best player B can do is choose strategy $B1$, which yields the largest payoff.

NASH EQUILIBRIUM

The final solution to the game in Figure 13.1 is the strategy profile $\{A1, B1\}$. An interesting aspect of this solution is that even though player A has the strictly dominant strategy, player A does not receive the maximum payoff of 150. Thus, having a dominant strategy does not guarantee that a player will receive the largest payoff. What is more, unless there is a fundamental change in the condition of the game, this solution constitutes equilibrium, at which time the game ends. Why? The answer is that no player can unilaterally improve his or her payoff by changing strategies. In Figure 13.1, if either player A or player B changes strategy, the payoff to both players is reduced. This resolution is called a *Nash equilibrium*, named for John Forbes Nash Jr., who, along with John Harsanyi and Reinhard Selten, received the 1994 Nobel Prize in economics for pioneering work in game theory.

Nash created quite a stir in the economics profession when he first proposed his now famous solution, which he called a "fixed-point equilibrium," in 1950. The reason was that his result often contradicts Adam Smith's famous metaphor of the invisible hand, according to which the welfare of society as a whole is maximized when each individual pursues his or her own private interests. This was illustrated, for example, in the final solution to the pricing game depicted in Figure 10.9. In that case, the strictly-dominant strategy of each firm was to charge a "low" price. The resulting payoff to each firm was $250,000. Yet, the strategy profile {low price, low price} did not result in the largest payoff to both firms. The best outcome would have required both firms to engage in cooperative, or collusive, behavior by charging a "high" price. In that case, the strategy profile {high price, high price} would have resulted in payoffs to both firms of $1,000,000.

Definition: A Nash equilibrium occurs when each player adopts the strategy believed to be the best response to the other player's strategy. When a game is in Nash equilibrium, the players' payoffs cannot be improved by changing strategies.

Nash equilibria are appealing precisely because they are self-fulfilling solutions to a game theoretic problem. In particular, if each player expects the other to adopt a Nash equilibrium strategy, both parties will, in fact, choose a Nash equilibrium strategy. For Nash equilibria, actual and anticipated behavior are one and the same.

EXAMPLE: OIL DRILLING GAME

Bierman and Fernandez (1998, Chapter 1) illustrate the concepts of dominant strategy and Nash equilibrium in the Oil Drilling game. The game begins by assuming that the Clampett Oil Company owns a 2-year lease on land that lies above a 4-million-barrel crude oil deposit with an estimated market value of $80 million, or $20 per barrel. The price per barrel of crude oil is not expected to change in the foreseeable future. To extract the oil, Clampett has the option of drilling a "wide" well or a "narrow" well. If Clampett drills a "wide" well, the entire deposit can be extracted in a year at a profit of $31 million. On the other hand, if Clampett drills a "narrow" well it will take 2 years to extract the oil but the profit will be $44 million.

STRICTLY DOMINANT STRATEGY EQUILIBRIUM

Enter the Texas Exploration Company (TEXplor). TEXplor has purchased a 2-year lease on land adjacent to the land leased by Clampett. The land leased by TEXplor lies above the same crude oil deposit. If both companies sink wells of the same size at the same time, each company will receive half the total crude oil reserve. For example, if both companies sink "wide" wells, each will extract 2 million barrels in 6 months, but each will earn profits of only $1 million. On the other hand, if each company sinks a "narrow" well, it will take a year for Clampett and TEXplor to extract their respective shares, but their profits will be $14 million apiece. Finally, if one company drills a "wide" well while the other company drills a "narrow" well, the first company will extract 3 million barrels and the second company will extract only 1 million barrels. In this case the first company will earn profits of $16 million and the second company will actually lose $1 million. The payoff matrix ($ millions) for this game is illustrated in Figure 13.2.

In the Oil Drilling game, the strategy profiles are {*Narrow, Narrow*}, {*Narrow, Wide*}, {*Wide, Narrow*}, and {*Wide, Wide*}. The respective payoffs from each strategy profile are (14, 14), (−1, 16), (16, −1), and (1, 1). Unlike the game theoretic scenario depicted in Figure 13.1, the payoffs depicted in Figure 13.2 are symmetrical. Which strategy should each player adopt? First consider the decision choices faced by Clampett. Whether Clampett will drill a "narrow" well or a "wide" well depends on the kind of well the firm thinks TEXplor will sink. If Clampett believes that TEXplor will drill a "narrow" well, then Clampett's best strategy is to sink a "wide" well because of its higher payoff. If, on the other hand, Clampett believes that TEXplor will sink a "wide" well, then once again Clampett's best strategy is to sink a "wide" well. In other words, regardless of the decision make by TEXplor, Clampett best strategy is to sink a "wide" well. The Oil Drilling game depicted in Figure 13.2 may look familiar. It is a variation of the Prisoners' Dilemma, which was discussed in Chapter 10. The distinguishing characteristic of both games is that each player has a strictly dominant strategy.

		Clampett	
		Narrow	Wide
TEXplor	Narrow	(14, 14)	(−1, 16)
	Wide	(16, −1)	(1, 1)

Payoffs: (TEXplor, Clampett)

FIGURE 13.2   Payoff matrix with a strictly dominant strategy equilibrium.

Since a "wide" strategy will be chosen by Clampett regardless of the strategy adopted by TEXplor, it may be said that a "wide" strategy *strictly dominates* a "narrow" strategy. Stated differently, a "narrow" strategy is *strictly dominated* by a "wide" strategy. Because of the symmetrical nature of the problem, the same must hold true for TEXplor. In this case, the strategy profile is {*Wide, Wide*} and with payoffs of (1, 1). Since both companies have the same strictly dominant strategy, the Nash equilibrium for this problem is called a *strictly dominant strategy equilibrium*.

Definition: A strictly dominant strategy equilibrium is a Nash equilibrium that results when all players have a strictly dominant strategy.

WEAKLY DOMINANT STRATEGY

Consider the variation of the Oil Drilling game summarized in Figure 13.3 (Bierman and Fernandez, 1998, Chapter 1). In this variation, the reader will quickly verify that if TEXplor chooses a *Wide* strategy, Clampett will be indifferent between a *Narrow* and a *Wide* strategy. In this case, *Wide* is no longer a strictly dominant strategy because both strategies yield a zero profit for Clampett if TEXplor chooses to drill a "wide" well. In this case, *Wide* is referred to as a *weakly dominant strategy*.

Definition: A weakly dominant strategy is a strategy that results in a payoff that is no lower than any other payoff regardless of the strategy adopted by the other player.

A rational player will always play a weakly dominant strategy. In the symmetrical game depicted in Figure 13.3, this means that the *weakly dominant strategy equilibrium* is for both players to drill a wide well. The reason for this is simple. Playing a weakly dominant strategy will never result in a lower payoff, while playing a weakly dominated strategy might. Suppose, for example, that TEXplor chooses to drill a narrow well. By drilling a narrow well, the best that Clampett can expect is a payoff of $14 million. The lowest payoff is $0. On the other hand, by drilling a wide well, Clampett's highest possible payoff is $16 million. The lowest possible payoff is still $0. If Clampett is rational, there is no reason ever to adopt a

		Clampett	
		Narrow	Wide
TEXplor	Narrow	(14, 14)	(0, 16)
	Wide	(16, 0)	(0, 0)

Payoffs: (TEXplor, Clampett)

FIGURE 13.3 Payoff matrix with a weakly dominant strategy ($ millions).

Narrow strategy. Since the game is symmetrical, the same is true for TEXplor. Finally, the reader should note that the strategy profile {*Wide*, *Wide*} is a Nash equilibrium because neither player can improve the payoff by switching strategies.

Definition: A weakly dominant strategy equilibrium is a Nash equilibrium that results when all players have a strictly dominant strategy.

ITERATED STRICTLY DOMINANT STRATEGY

When both players have a strictly dominant strategy, the solution to a noncooperative, simultaneous-move, one-shot game is fairly straightforward. In the following version of the Oil Drilling game, which is also taken from Bierman and Fernandez (1998, Chapter 1), however, neither TEXplor nor Clampett has a strictly dominant strategy.

The payoff matrix in Figure 13.4 introduces a third strategy—*Don't drill*. An examination of the payoff matrix reveals that *Wide* strictly dominates *Don't drill*, but no longer dominates *Narrow*. For example, if TEXplor chooses a *Don't drill* strategy, Clampett should choose *Narrow*. On the other hand, if TEXplor chooses *Narrow* or *Wide*, Clampett should choose *Wide*. Moreover, *Narrow* does not dominate either *Don't drill* or *Wide*. The only thing that is absolutely certain is that Clampett will not adopt a *Don't drill* strategy. *Don't drill* is called a strictly dominated strategy. A strictly dominated strategy is a strategy that is dominated by every other strategy.

Definition: A strictly dominated strategy is a strategy that is dominated by every other strategy and will always result in a lower payoff (i.e., regardless of the strategy adopted by other players).

Since the payoff matrix in Figure 13.4 is symmetrical, the same is true for TEXplor. Since neither TEXplor nor Clampett will ever choose *Don't drill*, this strategy may be eliminated from consideration. The resulting payoff matrix reduces to the two-strategy game in Figure 13.2, which had the strictly dominant strategy equilibrium {*Wide*, *Wide*}. Thus, *Wide* is the solution to the three-strategy game summarized in Figure 13.4. Wide is

		Clampett		
		Don't drill	Narrow	Wide
	Don't drill	(0, 0)	(0, 44)	(0, 31)
TEXplor	Narrow	(44, 0)	(14, 14)	(!1, 16)
	Wide	(31, 0)	(16, −1)	(1, 1)

Payoffs: (TEXplor, Clampett)

FIGURE 13.4 Payoff matrix with a iterated strictly dominant strategy ($ millions).

called an *iterated strictly dominant strategy* because it was obtained after systematically eliminating *Don't drill* from both players' strategy profiles.

Games with a large number of strategies and players may require several iterations before an iterated strictly dominant strategy equilibrium is achieved. As long as each player has a strictly dominant strategy, the order in which strictly dominated strategies are eliminated is irrelevant. We will still end up with a strictly dominant strategy equilibrium. On the other hand, if strictly dominant strategies are replaced by weakly dominant strategies, it may be demonstrated that the order in which weakly dominated strategies are removed could change the outcome of the game.

NON–STRICTLY DOMINANT STRATEGY

Finally, consider yet another variation on the Oil Drilling game, also taken from Bierman and Fernandez (1998, Chapter 1). Suppose that instead of losing $1 million from a {*Narrow, Wide*} strategy Clampett and TEXplor earn a positive profit of $2 million. The revised payoff matrix is illustrated in Figure 13.5.

An examination of the payoff matrix in Figure 13.5 reveals that no strictly dominant strategy exists for either player. The optimal strategy for both players depends on what each player *believes* the other player will do. To see this, suppose that Clampett believes that TEXplor will drill a "narrow" well. Clearly, it will be in Clampett's best interest to drill a "wide" well, since that strategy will generate $16 million in profits, which is greater than $14 million if it drills a narrow well. From Clampett's perspective a {*Narrow, Wide*} strategy is rational. Similarly, if Clampett *believes* that TEXplor intends drill a wide well, Clampett will drill a narrow well and earn only $2 million. In this case, a {*Wide, Narrow*} strategy is rational. Since both Clampett and TEXplor believe that this strategy profile is in their best interest, it will be adopted. Thus, the strategy profile {*Wide, Narrow*} leads to a Nash equilibrium. The important thing is that if either firm believes that the other will adopt a particular strategy, it will be in the best interest of that firm to adopt the same strategy. When this occurs, the strategy profile is said to be *self-confirming*.

		Clampett	
		Narrow	Wide
TEXplor	Narrow	(14, 14)	(2, 16)
	Wide	(16, 2)	(1, 1)

Payoffs: (TEXplor, Clampett)

FIGURE 13.5 Payoff matrix with a non–strictly dominant strategy ($ millions).

Definition: In a two-person game, a non–strictly dominant strategy exists when a strictly dominant strategy does not exist for either player. In this case, the optimal strategy for either player depends on what each player believes to be the strategy of the other player.

Although the concept of a Nash equilibrium is virtually unchallenged as a solution to noncooperative games, it is not without controversy. The reason for this is that Nash equilibria are often not unique. As the reader will readily verify, the strategy profiles {*Narrow*, *Wide*} and {*Wide*, *Narrow*} constitute a Nash equilibrium to the game depicted in Figure 13.5. When there is one than more than Nash equilibrium, it will be difficult to predict the strategies of the other players without more information. In other words, the existence of a Nash equilibrium does not always guarantee a solution to a game. One proposed solution to games involving multiple Nash equilibria is a *focal-point equilibrium*, which will be discussed later in this chapter.

MAXIMIN STRATEGY

In the game depicted in Figure 13.1 we saw that the strictly dominant strategy of player A determined the optimal strategy of player B. But what if neither player has a strictly dominant strategy? Will it still be possible to determine the optimal strategy profile for the game? Will the game still have a Nash equilibrium? If we assume that both players are risk averse, an optimal strategy profile may be determined when both players choose a *maximin strategy*. Sometimes referred to as a *secure strategy*, a maximin strategy selects the highest payoff from the worst possible scenarios.

Definition: A maximin strategy selects the largest payoff from among the worst possible payoffs.

Consider, again, the game depicted in Figure 13.1. Player A has a strictly dominant strategy ($A1$), which determined player B's strategy ($B1$). But suppose that player B had no knowledge of the payoffs to player A. What would have been player B's secure (maximin) strategy? In that game, had player B opted for strategy $B1$, the worst possible payoff would have been 50. Had player B selected strategy $B2$, then the worst possible payoff would have been 75. Thus, player B's maximin strategy would have been strategy $B2$, since it would have resulted in the largest payoff from among the worst possible payoffs. Of course, player B did not play the secure strategy because player A's strictly dominant strategy determined player B's next move.

To underscore the logic underlying a maximin strategy, consider the following variation of the game depicted in Figure 13.1. The reader will immediately verify that neither player A or player B has a dominant strategy. If player A, selects strategy $A1$, then player B will select strategy $B1$. If player A selects strategy $A2$, then player B will select strategy $B2$. On the other

Player *B*

		B1	B2
	A1	(100, 100)	(75, 75)
Player *A*	A2	(−100, 100)	(200, 200)

Payoffs: (Player *A*, Player *B*)

FIGURE 13.6   Payoff matrix and a maximin strategy.

hand, if player *B* selects strategy *B1*, then player *A* will select strategy *A1*. If player *B* selects strategy *B2*, then player *A* will select strategy *A2*. What strategy will players *A* and *B* choose?

Suppose that in the game depicted in Figure 13.6 both players follow a maximin strategy. If player *B* plays strategy *B1*, then the minimum payoff for player *A* is −100 by playing strategy *A2*. If player *B* plays strategy *B2*, then the minimum payoff for player *A* is 75 by playing strategy *A1*. Following a maximin strategy, player *A* will choose the strategy with the largest of the two worst payoffs. In this case, player *A*'s secure strategy is to play strategy *A1*.

What about player *B*? If player *A* plays strategy *A1*, the minimum payoff for player *B* is 75 by choosing strategy *B2*. If player *A* plays strategy *A2*, then the minimum payoff for player *B* is 100 by playing strategy *B1*. The maximin (secure) strategy for player *B* is to play strategy *B1*. Thus, the strategy profile for this game is {*A1*, *B1*}. The reader should verify that this strategy profile constitutes a Nash equilibrium, but not the only Nash equilibrium.

Regrettably, solutions to games using a maximin strategy may not be as simple as they appear. Consider another variation on the game depicted in Figure 13.1. In Figure 13.7 the reader should verify that player *B* has the dominant strategy *B2*. Player *A* knows that player *B* has a dominant strategy and that player *B* is likely to play that strategy. In this case, player *A*'s best move is to play strategy *A2*, which results in a payoff of 200. Thus, the strategy profile in this game is {*A2*, *B2*} for payoffs of (200, 100).

Suppose, however, that in the game depicted in Figure 13.7 player *A* believes that player *B* might not, in fact, play his or her dominant strategy. This possibility might arise if player *B* has a history of making mistakes. When risk and uncertainty are introduced, the game changes. Depending on the level of risk aversion, it might be in player *A*'s best interest to follow a maximin strategy, especially if the potential loss by choosing the wrong strategy is great. In this case, player *A* believes that player *B* might adopt either strategy *B1* or *B2*. If player *B* follows strategy *B1*, the lowest payoff for player *A* will be −1,000 by following strategy *A2*. If player *B* follows strategy *B2*, the lowest payoff to player *A* is 100 by following strategy *A1*.

Player B

		B1	B2
Player A	A1	(100, 0)	(100, 100)
	A2	(−1,000, 0)	(200, 100)

Payoffs: (Player A, Player B)

FIGURE 13.7   Risk aversion and a maximin strategy.

Baltimore Ravens

		Pass	Run
New York Giants	Pass defense	(50, 50)	(40, 60)
	Run defense	(20, 80)	(80, 20)

Payoffs: (New York Giants, Baltimore Ravens)

FIGURE 13.8   Payoff matrix and the Touchdown game.

Being risk averse, player A might decide that a guaranteed payoff of 100 by following a secure (maximin) strategy is preferable to an uncertain payoff of 200, or possible loss of −1,000.

Example: Touchdown Game

Suppose that the New York Giants and the Baltimore Ravens are in the fourth quarter of the Super Bowl with seconds remaining on the clock. It is the last play of the game. The score is Ravens 13 and the Giants 17. The Ravens have the ball on the Giants' 8 yard line. There are no time-outs for either side. A field goal for 3 points will not help Baltimore. To win the game, Baltimore must score a touchdown for 6 points. Both sides must decide on a strategy for the final play of the game. The objective of both teams is to maximize the probability of winning the game. Both head coaches are aware of the strengths and weaknesses of the other team. The probabilities of either team winning the game from alternative offensive and defensive strategies are summarized in Figure 13.8. The student should note that the sum of the probabilities in each cell is 100%.

An examination of the payoff matrix in Figure 13.8 will verify that neither team has a strictly dominant strategy. If the Giants, for example, adopt a pass defense, the best offensive play for the Ravens is to run the ball. If the Giants adopt a run defense, the best offensive play for the Ravens is to pass. On the other hand, if the Ravens decide to pass the ball, the best strategy for the Giants is a pass defense. If the Ravens decide to run the ball, then the best strategy for the Giants is a run defense. The student should also verify that a Nash equilibrium does not exist here because there is no strategy profile for which a change in strategy will result in a lower payoff for either team.

Since neither team has a strictly dominant strategy, what strategy should be adopted by each coach? If we assume that both head coaches are risk averse, both teams should adopt a maximin strategy. If the coach of the New York Giants decides to play a pass defense, the worst the team can do is a 40% probability of winning the game. If the Giants decide to play a run defense, the worst they can do is a 20% chance of winning. Since a 40% probability of winning the game is the largest payoff from among the worst possible scenarios, playing a pass defense is the Giants secure strategy.

Now consider the secure strategy of the Baltimore Ravens. If the Ravens play a pass offense, the worst the team can do is a 50% probability of winning the game. If the Ravens decide to play a run offense, the worst they can do is a 20% probability of winning the game. Since a 50% probability of winning the game is the largest payoff from among the worst possible scenarios, playing a pass offense is the Ravens's secure strategy. Thus, the solution profile for this version of the Touchdown game is {*Pass defense, Pass*}.

Problem 13.1. Suppose that in the Touchdown game the probabilities of either team winning from alternative offensive and defensive strategies are as shown in Figure 13.9.
a. Does either firm have a strictly dominant strategy?
b. Assuming that both coaches are risk averse, what strategy will each coach likely adopt for the last play of the game?
c. Does this game have a Nash equilibrium?

Solution
a. Neither team has a strictly dominant strategy. If the New York Giants adopt a pass defense, the best offensive play for the Baltimore Ravens is to run the ball. If the Giants adopt a run defense, the best offensive play for the Ravens is to pass. On the other hand, if the Ravens decide to pass the ball, the best strategy for the Giants is a pass defense. If the

Baltimore Ravens

		Pass	Run
New York Giants	Pass defense	(70, 30)	(20, 80)
	Run defense	(10, 90)	(50, 50)

Payoffs: (New York Giants, Baltimore Ravens)

FIGURE 13.9   Payoff matrix for problem 13.1.

Ravens decide to run the ball, the best strategy for the Giants is a run defense.

b. Assuming again that both head coaches are risk averse, both teams should adopt a secure strategy. If the coach of the New York Giants decides to play a pass defense, the worst the team can do is a 20% chance of winning the game. If the Giants decide to play a run defense, the worst they can do is a 10% chance of winning the game. Since a 20% probability of winning the game is the larger of the two worst payoffs, the Giants' secure strategy is to play a pass defense.

Now consider the secure strategy of the Baltimore Ravens. If the Ravens play a pass offense, the worst the team can do is a 30% chance of winning. If the Ravens decide to play a run offense, the worst they can do is a 50% chance of winning. Since a 50% chance of winning is the larger of the two worst payoffs, the Ravens's secure strategy is to run the ball. Thus, the solution profile for this version of the Touchdown game is {*Pass defense, Run*}. The reader should verify once again that this strategy profile does not constitute a Nash equilibrium.

c. A Nash equilibrium does not exist for this game. Either team can improve its payoff by switching strategies.

Problem 13.2. The two leading firms in the highly competitive running shoe industry, Treebark and Adios, are considering an increase in advertising expenditures. Both companies are considering buying advertising space in *Joggers World*, the leading national magazine about recreational, long-distance running, or buying air time with KNUT, an all-talk, all-sports, all-the-time radio station. Figure 13.10 summarizes the payoffs associated with the advertizing strategy of each firm.

a. Do either Treebark or Adios have a dominant strategy?
b. Based on your answer to part a, what is the strategy of the other firm?
c. What is the Nash equilibrium for this problem?

Solution
a. While Treebark has a dominant strategy, which is to advertise in *Joggers World*, Adios does not. To see this, suppose that Adios advertises in

		Treebark	
		Joggers World	KNUT
Adios	Joggers World	($1,000,000, $2,000,000)	($300,000, $350,000)
	KNUT	($750,000, $750,000)	($2,500,000, $500,000)

Payoffs: (Adios, Treebark)

FIGURE 13.10   Payoff matrix for problem 13.2.

Joggers World, Treebark's best response is to advertise in *Joggers World* as well. If Adios advertises on KNUT, again Treebark's best response is to advertise in *Joggers World*. In both instances, Treebark should advertise in *Joggers World*.

b. Adios does not have a dominant strategy. As can be seen from Figure 13.10, if Treebark advertises in *Joggers World*, then Adios's best response is to advertise in *Joggers World*. On the other hand, if Treebark advertises on KNUT, Adios's best strategy is to advertise on KNUT. In other words, Adios's strategy will depend on what it thinks Treebark will do. This is not the case for Treebark, which will advertise in *Joggers World* regardless of the strategy adopted by Adios. Since Treebark will advertise in Joggers World regardless of the strategy adopted by Adios, then it will be in the best interest of Adios to advertise in Joggers World as well. Thus, the solution profile for this game is {Joggers World, Joggers World} with payoffs to Adios and Treebark of $1,000,000 and $2,000,000, respectively.

c. A Nash equilibrium occurs when both Treebark and Adios advertise in *Joggers World*. The reason for this is that if Treebark changes its strategy to buying air time on KNUT, its payoff falls to $350,000. If Adios changes its strategy to buying air time on KNUT, its payoff falls to $750,000. This is a Nash equilibrium, since neither player can unilaterally improve its payoff by changing strategies.

COOPERATIVE, SIMULTANEOUS-MOVE, INFINITELY REPEATED GAMES

Consider, again, the duopoly problem discussed in Chapter 10 in which firms *A* and *B* are confronted with the decision to charge a "high" price or a "low" price for their product. The payoff matrix for that problem, Figure 10.9, is reproduced here.

We saw in this game that the strictly dominant strategy of both firm *A* and firm *B* was to charge a "low" price. The reason is that if firm *B* chooses

Firm B

		High price	Low price
	High price	($1,000,000, $1,000,000)	($1,000,000, $5,000,000)
Firm A			
	Low price	($6,000,000 $100,000)	($250,000, $250,000)

Payoffs: (Player *A*, Player *B*)

FIGURE 10.9   Game theory and interdependent pricing behavior.

a "low" price with a payoff of $5,000,000, then, from firm B's perspective, it will be rational for firm A to choose a "high" price, where the payoff is $1,000,000. From firm B's perspective the rational combination of strategies is (Low, $High$). Since the payoff matrix is symmetrical, the same reasoning pertains to firm A. From firm B's perspective the rational combination of strategies is also (Low, $High$). The result, however, is an "irrational" (Low, Low) combination of strategies in which firms A and B earn profits of $250,000. This is a Nash equilibrium because neither player can unilaterally improve its payoff by changing strategies. For example, if firm A were to switch to a "high" price strategy while firm B continues to charge a "low" price, firm B's profits will drop to $100,000, while firm A's profits will increase to $5,000,000. Precisely the same thing would occur should firm B attempt to switch to a "high" price strategy while firm A continued to charge a "low" price.

The problem summarized in Figure 10.9 illustrates the Bertrand duopoly pricing model discussed in Chapter 10. The reader will recall that in the Bertrand model each firm will set the price of its product duopoly to maximize profits while ignoring its rival's output level. In the problem, both firms can clearly maximize profits by agreeing to charge a "high" price for their product. For this to occur, however, both firms must agree to collude on their pricing decisions (see Chapter 10). The problem with collusive behavior, however, is that for a two-person, non-zero-sum, simultaneous-move, one-shot game, there is an incentive for either firm to "cheat." In other words, it is in the best interest to either firm to violate any formal pricing agreement by charging a low price at the expense of its rival.

The game theoretic scenario summarized in Figure 10.9 illustrates the fragile nature of collusion in a two-person, non-zero-sum, simultaneous-move, one-shot game. It was demonstrated that in the absence of a cooperative pricing strategy, a Nash equilibrium occurs when both firms charged a "low" price, with each firm earning $250,000 in profits. On the other hand, if the firms collude, both will charge a "high" price and each will earn $1,000,000 in profits. In a one-time game, however, if firm A were to violate the agreement and charge a "low" price, many consumers would switch their purchases away from firm B. Firm A's profit would soar from $250,000 to $5,000,000, while firm B's profits would fall from $250,000 to $100,000. The result would be precisely the same if firm B violated the agreement.

The duopoly problem illustrates the situation in which, in the absence of collusion, a Nash equilibrium results in an inferior solution. Why, then, will the two firms not engage in collusive behavior? For one thing, collusion is illegal in the United States. For another, in a two-person, non-zero-sum, simultaneous-move, one-shot game, the incentive to cheat will ultimately undermine any such agreement. In fact, since both firms are aware of the inherent weakness of collusive behavior, it is unlikely that the cooperative pricing arrangement would have been entered into in the first place.

A cartel is an example of a collusive arrangement. A cartel is a formal agreement among firms in oligopolistic industries to allocate market share and/or industry profits. To take perhaps the most famous example, the members of the Organization of Petroleum Exporting Countries are able to influence world oil prices by jointly agreeing on production levels. For the reasons cited, however, cartel arrangements have historically proven to be very short-lived precisely because of the sometimes irresistible temptation to cheat. In the case of OPEC, Venezuela has repeatedly cheated on almost every production agreement it has entered into. The government in Caracas would encourage OPEC members, especially the cartel's "swing" producer, Saudi Arabia, to restrict output to raise oil prices, after which it would increase its own production levels to bolster profits.

Is "cheating" inevitable? Under the appropriate conditions, for a two-person, non-zero-sum, simultaneous-move, one-shot game, the answer is more than likely to be yes. But, what if the game were played more than once? What if the game were infinitely repeated, as is seemingly the case with OPEC production agreements? As we will see, naughty behavior may be punishable, which may affect the manner in which the players play future games. It is this possibility that we will consider in the next section.

In our discussion of two-person, non-zero-sum, simultaneous-move, one-shot games, we observed that collusive behavior among the players was inherently unstable because of the incentive to cheat. Does this conclusion hold, however, if the game infinitely repeated? In this section we will consider the game theoretic scenario of two cooperating players engaged in a simultaneous, non-zero-sum game, which is played over and over again. As the reader may have guessed, with infinitely repeated games, cheating may have consequences for how future games are played.

Definition: Infinitely repeated games are games that are played over and over again with no end.

Suppose that instead of the game being played just once, it is infinitely repeated. Do the conclusions reached with respect to the infeasibility of collusive behavior for two-person, non-zero-sum, simultaneous-move, one-shot games continue to hold? Maybe not. Past naughty behavior by one player may cause the other player to adopt a different strategy for future play. Such contingent game plans are referred to as *trigger strategies*. A trigger strategy is a game plan that is adopted by one player in response to unanticipated moves by the other player. Once adopted, a trigger strategy will continue to be used until the other player initiates yet another unanticipated move.

Definition: A trigger strategy is a game plan that is adopted by one player in response to unanticipated moves by the other player. A trigger strategy will continue to be used until the other player initiates yet another unanticipated move.

For two-person, cooperative, non-zero-sum, simultaneous-move, infinitely repeated games, trigger strategies may, in fact, introduce stability into collusive arrangements. The reason for this is the so-called *credible threat*. To see what is involved, consider again the game theoretic scenario summarized in Figure 10.9. Suppose that firms A and B agree, perhaps illegally, to charge a "high" price for their products. Unlike the one-shot game, if either player "cheats," future game plays will be changed. If firm A were to charge a "low" price in violation of its agreement, firm B might seek to punish firm A by ruling out any future cooperation. In other words, a violation of firm A's agreement with firm B could "trigger" a strategy change by firm B. Firm B's promise to retaliate may prevent firm A from violating the agreement, but only if this threat is considered to be credible. A threat is credible only if it is in the best interest of the player making the threat to follow through when the trigger situation presents itself.

Definition: A threat is credible only if it is in a player's best interest to follow through with the threat.

Does the knowledge that naughty behavior will result in punishment eliminate the possibility of cheating? Not necessarily. To begin with, if the threat of retaliation is not credible, it will be ignored. Moreover, even if threats are credible, cheating may still occur in infinitely repeated games if naughty behavior (cheating) is more profitable than honest behavior. To see this, it is necessary to compare the present value of the stream of profits resulting from cheating to the present value of profits earned by adhering to the agreement.

Recall from Chapter 12 the present value of an annuity due ($PVAD$), which is summarized in Equation (12.21). If we assume that the profits earned by a firm are the same in each period, then Equation (12.21) may be rewritten as

$$PVAD = \frac{\pi}{(1+i)^{n-1}} + \frac{\pi}{(1+i)^{n-2}} + \dots + \frac{\pi}{(1+i)^{0}}$$
$$= \sum_{t=0 \to n} \left(\frac{1}{1+i}\right)^{n-1} \tag{13.1}$$

where $PVAD$ is the present value of an annuity due and i is the nominal (market) interest rate. For infinitely repeated games ($n = \infty$), it can be easily demonstrated that

$$PVAD = \frac{\pi(1+i)}{i} \tag{13.2}$$

since Equation (13.2) is the sum of a geometric progression (see Chapter 2).[2]

COLLUSION

Consider, once again, the simultaneous-move game summarized in Figure 10.9. We saw that in a one-shot game the Nash equilibrium was reached when both firms charged a "low" price. Now suppose that firms A and B collude, perhaps illegally, to charge a "high" price. Suppose, further, that cheating by one firm "triggers" a change in strategy by the other firm. In particular, suppose that firm B violates the agreement by charging a "high" price. This action would cause firm A to punish firm B by charging a "low" price in all future periods. If both firms adopt the same trigger strategy, will the cartel hold together? The answer to this question depends on a comparison of the economic incentives to cheat and to maintain the agreement.

The economic benefit of maintaining the agreement is the present value of all future profits earned by remaining "honest" ($PVAD_H$) to the terms of the agreement, which is given by the Equation (13.3).

---

[2] Equation (13.1) may be rewritten as

$$
\begin{aligned}
PVAD &= \pi + \pi \left[\frac{\pi}{1+i} + \frac{1}{(1+i)^2} + \frac{1}{(1+i)^3} + \ldots \right] \\
&= \pi \left[\frac{1+1}{1+i} + \frac{1}{(1+i)^2} + \frac{1}{(1+i)^3} + \ldots \right] \\
&= \pi S
\end{aligned}
\tag{F13.1}
$$

where

$$
S = \frac{1+1}{1+i} + \frac{1}{(1+i)^2} + \frac{1}{(1+i)^3} + \ldots
\tag{F13.2}
$$

After multiplying both sides of Equation (F13.2) by $1/(1 + i)$, we get

$$
S\left(\frac{1}{1+i}\right) = \frac{1}{1+i} + \frac{1}{(1+i)^2} + \frac{1}{(1+i)^3} + \frac{1}{(1+i)^4} + \ldots
\tag{F13.3}
$$

Subtracting Equation (F13.3) from Equation (F13.2) yields

$$
S - S\frac{1}{1+i} = 1
$$

which simplifies to

$$
S = \frac{1+i}{i}
\tag{F13.4}
$$

Subtracting Equation (F13.3) from Equation (F13.2) yields

$$
PVAD = \frac{\pi(1+i)}{i} \qquad \text{Q.E.D.}
$$

$$PVAD_H = \frac{\pi_H(1+i)}{i} \tag{13.3}$$

If, on the other hand, a firm were to violate the agreement, the economic benefit would be the immediate (one-shot) gain from cheating (π_C) plus the present value of the per-period profits (π_N) earned in the absence of a collusive agreement ($PVAD_N$). The economic benefit of violating the agreement is summarized in Equation (13.4).

$$\pi_C + PVAD_N = \pi_C + \frac{\pi_N(1+i)}{i} \tag{13.4}$$

When will it pay to cheat? Cheating will occur when the present value of violating the agreement is greater than the present value of remaining "honest." This condition is summarized in the inequality (13.5):

$$\pi_C + PVAD_N > PVAD_H$$

or

$$\pi_C + \pi_N \frac{(1+i)}{i} > \frac{\pi_H(1+i)}{i} \tag{13.5}$$

Problem 13.3. Consider, again, the payoff matrix summarized in Figure 10.9. Suppose, further, that this is an infinitely repeated game and that the interest rate at which profits may be reinvested is 5%.

a. What is the economic benefit to firm A and firm B from a Nash equilibrium (no collusion) in an infinitely repeated game?

b. What is the economic benefit to firm A and to firm B from a collusive agreement?

c. What is the economic benefit to firm A or firm B from violating (cheating) the agreement?

d. Based on your answers to parts a and b, is the collusive agreement stable? That is, is the cartel likely to last?

Solution

a. A Nash equilibrium occurs when both firms A and B charge a "low" price. From Equation (13.5), the economic benefit of a Nash equilibrium for an infinitely repeated game is

$$\frac{\pi_N(1+i)}{i} = \frac{\$250,000(1.05)}{0.05} = \$250,000(21) = \$5,250,000$$

b. In a collusive agreement, both firms will charge a "high" price. From Equation (13.3), the economic benefit of charging a "high" price in an infinitely repeated game, and remaining "honest" to the agreement is

$$\frac{\pi_H(1+i)}{i} = \frac{\$1,000,000(1.05)}{0.05} = \$1,000,000(21) = \$21,000,000$$

c. From Equation (13.5), the economic benefit from violating the agreement is the immediate (one-shot) gain from cheating (π_C) plus the present value of all profits that will be earned from the Nash equilibrium ($PVAD_N$) thereafter:

$$\pi_C + \frac{\pi_N(1+i)}{i} = \$5,000,000 + \$5,250,000 = \$10,250,000$$

d. Since $\pi_C + \pi_N(1+i)/i < \pi_H(1+i)/i$, there is no incentive to cheat. In other words, since the economic benefit to both firms to remain "honest" is greater than the economic benefit to either firm of cheating ($21,000,000 > \$10,250,000$), there is no incentive for either firm to cheat.

Problem 13.4. Suppose that in Problem the interest rate is 20%.
a. What is the economic benefit to both firms from a Nash equilibrium in an infinitely repeated game?
b. What is the economic benefit to both firms from a collusive agreement?
c. What is the economic benefit to either firm of cheating?
d. Based on your answers to parts a and b, is the collusive agreement stable?

Solution
a. From Equation (13.5), the economic benefit of a Nash equilibrium for an infinitely repeated game is

$$\frac{\pi_N(1+i)}{i} = \frac{\$250,000(1.20)}{0.20} = \$250,000(6) = \$1,500,000$$

b. In a collusive agreement, both firms will charge a "high" price. From Equation (13.3), the economic benefit of charging a "high" price in an infinitely repeated game, and remaining "honest" with respect to the agreement is

$$\frac{\pi_H(1+i)}{i} = \frac{\$1,000,000(1.20)}{0.20} = \$1,000,000(6) = \$6,000,000$$

c. From Equation (13.4), the economic benefit from violating the agreement is the immediate (one-shot) gain from cheating (π_C) plus the present value of all profits that will be earned from the Nash equilibrium ($PVAD_N$) thereafter:

$$\pi_C + \frac{\pi_N(1+i)}{i} = \$5,000,000 + \$1,500,000 = \$6,500,000$$

d. Since $\pi_C + \pi_N(1 + i)/i > \pi_H(1 + i)/i$ (i.e., \$6,500,000 > \$6,000,000), there is an incentive to cheat. In other words, the cartel is unstable and the collusive agreement is likely to break down.

CHEATING RULE FOR INFINITELY-REPEATED GAMES

Admittedly, the foregoing assumptions of unchanged profits and interest rates for a two-person, cooperative, non-zero-sum, simultaneous-move, infinitely repeated game are simplistic. Nevertheless, with these assumptions it is possible to summarize the conditions under which a cartel is likely to be unstable. Inequality (13.5) may be rearranged to yield

$$\frac{\pi_H - \pi_N}{\pi_C + \pi_N - \pi_H} < i \tag{13.6}$$

Inequality (13.6) admits to a straightforward interpretation. If the net rate of return from adhering to the collusive agreement relative to the net rate of return from cheating is less than the prevailing rate of interest, there is an incentive to violate the agreement. If the inequality (13.6) is satisfied, the cartel will be unstable, since the incentive to "cheat" is greater than the incentive to be "honest." If the inequality (13.6) is not satisfied—that is, if $(\pi_H - \pi_N)/(\pi_C + \pi_N - \pi_H) > i$, then a trigger strategy by one firm that punishes the cheater by refusing to enter into future collusive agreements will be sufficient to hold the cartel together. Finally, if $(\pi_H - \pi_N)/(\pi_C + \pi_N - \pi_H)/i$, then, *ceteris paribus*, each firm will be indifferent between cheating and remaining honest.

Problem 13.5. Consider, again, the payoff matrix summarized in Figure 10.9. Suppose that each firm adopts the trigger strategy such that it will respond to cheating by the other firm by choosing a one-shot Nash equilibrium for all future plays. Assuming that the payoffs in Figure 10.9 are expected to be infinitely repeated, below what interest rate can we expect the cartel to break down?

Solution. Substituting the data from Figure 10.9 into the left-hand side of inequality (13.6) yields

$$\frac{\pi_H - \pi_N}{\pi_C + \pi_N - \pi_H} = \frac{\$1,000,000 - \$250,000}{\$5,000,000 - \$250,000 - \$1,000,000}$$

$$= \frac{\$750,000}{\$4,750,000} = 0.1765$$

Thus, from inequality (13.6), if the prevailing rate of interest is greater than 17.65%, each firm will have an incentive to violate the collusive agreement, rendering the cartel unstable. If the rate of interest is less than

17.65%, then it will be in the best interest for both firms to honor the agreement and the cartel will be stable. Finally, if the interest rate is exactly 17.65%, then, *ceteris paribus*, each firm will be indifferent between cheating and remaining honest.

Problem 13.6. Consider the payoff matrix in Figure 13.11: two firms that must decide whether to charge $30 or $50 for their product. The first entry in each cell of the matrix represents the profit earned by firm *a* and the second entry represents the profit earned by firm *B*. Thus, if firm *A* charges $30 while firm *B* charges $50, the first firm's profit is $100,000 and the second firm will get $30,000.

a. For a noncooperative, simultaneous-move, one-shot game, does either firm have a dominant strategy? If not, what is each firm's secure strategy? What is the Nash equilibrium for this problem? Why?

b. If this were a cooperative, simultaneous-move, one-shot game, what price should each firm charge? Why?

c. Suppose that the interest on reinvested profits is 20%. What is the economic benefit to firm *A* and to firm *B* from a Nash equilibrium (no collusion) in an infinitely repeated game?

d. Find the economic benefit to firm *A* and to firm *B* from a collusive agreement.

e. Find the economic benefit to firm *A* or firm *B* from violating (cheating) the agreement.

f. Based on your answers to parts a and b, is the collusive agreement stable? That is, is the cartel likely to last?

g. Suppose that the interest rate was 30%. Is the collusive agreement stable?

h. Suppose that each firm adopts the trigger strategy such that it will respond to cheating by the other firm by choosing a one-shot Nash equilibrium for all future plays. Above what interest rate can we expect the cartel to break down?

Solution

a. The dominant strategy of both firms is to charge $30 for their product. The strategy profile {$30, $30} is a strictly dominant strategy equilibrium,

Firm B

		$30	$50
Firm A	$30	($60,000, $60,000)	($100,000, $30,000)
	$50	($30,000, $100,000)	($80,000, $80,000)

Payoffs: (Player A, Player B)

FIGURE 13.11 Payoff matrix for problem 13.6.

which is a Nash equilibrium because neither player can improve its payoff by switching strategies.

b. If this was a cooperative, simultaneous-move, one-shot game, it would pay for firm A and firm B to enter into a collusive agreement and charge $50, since each firm would earn profits of $80,000.

c. From Equation (13.5), the economic benefit of a Nash equilibrium for an infinitely repeated game is

$$\frac{\pi_N(1+i)}{i} = \frac{\$60,000(1.20)}{0.20} = \$60,000(6) = \$360,000$$

d. In a collusive agreement, both firms will charge $50. From Equation (13.3), the economic benefit is

$$\frac{\pi_H(1+i)}{i} = \frac{\$80,000(1.20)}{0.20} = \$80,000(6) = \$480,000$$

e. From Equation (13.4), the economic benefit from violating the agreement is

$$\frac{\pi_C + \pi_N(1+i)}{i} = \$100,000 + \$360,000 = \$460,000$$

f. Since $\pi_C + \pi_N(1+i)/i > \pi_H(1+i)/i$, (i.e., $460,000 > $480,000), there is no incentive to cheat. In other words, the cartel is stable and the collusive agreement is not likely to break down.

g.
$$\frac{\pi_N(1+i)}{i} = \frac{\$60,000(1.30)}{0.30} = \$60,000(4.33) = \$260,000$$

$$\frac{\pi_H(1+i)}{i} = \frac{\$80,000(1.30)}{0.30} = \$80,000(4.33) = \$346,666.67$$

$$\pi_C = \$100,000$$

Since $\pi_C + \pi_N(1+i)/i > \pi_H(1+i)/i$ ($360,000 > $346,666.67), then there is an incentive to cheat and the cartel is unstable. The collusive agreement is likely to break down.

h. Substituting the information in the payoff matrix into the left-hand side of inequality (13.6) yields

$$\frac{\pi_H - \pi_N}{\pi_C + \pi_N - \pi_H} = \frac{\$80,000 - \$60,000}{\$100,000 + \$60,000 - \$80,000}$$
$$= \frac{\$20,000}{\$80,000} = 0.25$$

Thus, from inequality (13.6), if the rate of return of 25% from remaining "honest" is less than the prevailing rate of interest, there will be an incentive to violate the collusive agreement and the cartel will be unstable. If the rate of return of 25% is greater than the prevailing rate of interest, it will be in the best interest for both firms to honor the agreement, in which case the cartel will be stable. These conclusions were verified by the answers to parts f and g.

Finally, if the interest rate is exactly 25%, then, *ceteris paribus*, each firm will be indifferent between cheating and remaining honest. This result may be verified by substituting 25% into the following expressions:

$$\frac{\pi_N(1+i)}{i} = \frac{\$60,000(1.25)}{0.25} = \$60,000(5) = \$300,000$$

$$\frac{\pi_H(1+i)}{i} = \frac{\$80,000(1.25)}{0.25} = \$80,000(5) = \$400,000$$

$$\pi_C = \$100,000$$

Since $\pi_C + \pi_N(1 + i)/i = \pi_H(1 + i)/i$ (i.e., \$400,000 = \$400,000), then, other things equal, each firm will be indifferent between cheating and remaining honest.

DETERMINANTS OF COLLUSIVE AGREEMENTS

The collusive agreements discussed thus for involved only two firms. The success of the collusion depended on the economic benefit of violating the agreement. If the economic benefit of violating the agreement is greater than the economic benefit of remaining faithful to the agreement, the cartel is likely to collapse. If the economic benefit of violating the agreement is less than the economic benefit of adhering to the collusive agreement, the viability of the cartel will depend on the existence of an effective trigger strategy to punish the cheater. Thus it would be useful to be ask to determine, in general, when collusive agreements are likely to be entered into and under what circumstances they are likely to succeed.

Number of Firms

Collusive agreements are more likely when the number of firms with similar interests and objectives is small. Collusive agreements are difficult to achieve among a large number of firms with widely divergent interests. Nevertheless, similarity of interests is no guarantee of success. In fact, as the number of firms that are party to the agreement increases, the probability of its success declines.

As the membership of a collusive agreement increases, it becomes increasingly difficult to monitor the behavior of each member. To see this, suppose that there are n parties to the agreement. Each member of the cartel must monitor the behavior of the other $(n-1)$ members. Thus, the total number of monitoring arrangements necessary to police the cartel is $n(n-1)$. In the two-firm case, only $2(2-1) = 2$ monitoring arrangements were needed to police the cartel. In the case of OPEC, which has 11 members (Algeria, Indonesia, Iran, Iraq, Kuwait, Libya, Nigeria, Qatar, Saudi Arabia, the United Arab Emirates, and Venezuela), 110 monitoring arrangements are necessary to police compliance. Policing is made more difficult in the case of OPEC because of the widely divergent cultural, economic, and political characteristics of the members. Is it any wonder the membership of OPEC meets as frequently as it does to hammer out new production agreements? The incentive to cheat, especially by members with low production quotas, is very strong.

In addition to the difficulty of forming a collusive agreement, as the number of parties to the agreement increases, rising monitoring costs may make continuation of the cartel impractical. Under these circumstances the threat of sanctions being levied against the offending member is an empty one, and the cartel is likely to break down.

Firm Size

Economies of scale exist in the monitoring and policing of cartel arrangements. It is relatively less expensive for large firms to monitor the behavior of a relatively small number of large rivals, or a large number of relatively small rivals, than it is for small firms to monitor the behavior of a relatively large number of small rivals, or a small number of large rivals.

Explicit Versus Tacit Collusion

An important factor determining the existence and durability of collusive agreements is the manner in which such arrangements are entered into. Collusions may be either explicit or tacit. If a collusive agreement is explicit, the firms actually meet to hammer out details. An explicit collusive agreement will specify the responsibilities of each member. For example, explicit collusive agreements will specify production quotas for each member, collective pricing policies, and market shares. Moreover, to be effective, the collusive agreement will also specify the penalties for violating the agreement.

When an explicit agreement is not possible, perhaps because such an arrangement is illegal, firms may engage in tacit collusion. Tacit collusion occurs when firms do not explicitly conspire but, instead, come to an agreement indirectly. Such implicit agreements are possible only when firms in an industry develop an understanding of how the game is played. Firms develop this understanding by observing the behavior of rivals over time.

In the case of tacit collusions, firms also learn the most likely penalties levied for violating such "gentlemen's agreement". The reader might recall the "kinked" demand curve model of oligopolistic behavior discussed in Chapter 10. A central feature of that model was the anticipated reaction of firms to a price change by a rival. In the model, if a maverick firm lowered the price of its product to increase its market share, the price reduction would be matched by other firms in the industry, thereby thwarting the intentions of the initiator of the "price war." On the other hand, if a firm raised the price of its product, that increase would not be matched by its rivals, and the maverick firm would lose market share. This, of course, does not mean that prices are never raised or lowered. In the "kinked" demand curve model, for example, changes in collective price and output policy occurred only after changes in market and cost conditions common to all firms indicated that such changes were appropriate.

Finally, the threat of punishment for violating a collusive agreement will be meaningful only if threats are actually carried out. If member firms are unwilling or unable to punish violators, explicit and implicit collusions will be unstable and will ultimately break down. On the other hand, if the threat of sure, swift punishment is credible, collusive agreements will be stable.

Discriminatory Pricing

In the case of the "kinked" demand curve model, it was assumed that all firms in the industry charged customers the same price. Thus effective punishment of attempts by one firm to capture a larger market share by lowering price requires all firms in the industry to lower their prices as well. Clearly, in this case the cost of policing a collusive agreement will be quite high. On the other hand, if the industry is characterized by discriminatory pricing (i.e., charging a different price to different customers), member firms can punish violators by charging the lower price to the rival's customers while continuing to charge the higher price to its own customers. In this case, the cost of policing a collusive agreement is considerably reduced.

COOPERATIVE, SIMULTANEOUS-MOVE, FINITELY REPEATED GAMES

We have thus far considered games played only once and games played an infinite number of times. In this section we will examine games that are repeated a finite number of times.

Definition: A finitely repeated game is a game that is repeated a limited number of times.

There are two classes of finitely repeated games: those in which the players are uncertain about when the game will end and those in which the last play of the game is known to each player.

FINITELY REPEATED GAMES WITH AN UNCERTAIN END

Analytically, the only difference between infinitely repeated games and finitely repeated games with an uncertain end is the probability that the game will end after each play is $0 < \theta < 1$. Thus, the undiscounted, expected profit stream may be written as

$$E(\pi) = \pi + (1-\theta)\pi + (1-\theta)^2\pi + (1-\theta)^3\pi + \cdots$$

Thus, the discounted value of the expected profit stream may be written as

$$PVAD = \pi\frac{1-\theta}{(1+i)^{n-1}} + \pi\frac{1-\theta}{(1+i)^{n-2}} + \cdots + \pi\frac{(1-\theta)^0}{(1+i)^0}$$

$$= \sum_{t=1\to n} \pi\left(\frac{1-\theta}{1+i}\right)^{n-1} \tag{13.7}$$

where $PVAD$ is the present value of an annuity due, i is the nominal (market) interest rate, and θ is the probability that the game will end. For infinitely repeated games $(n = \infty)$, it can be demonstrated that

$$PVAD = \frac{\pi(1+i)}{1+\theta} \tag{13.8}$$

The economic benefit of maintaining the agreement is the present value of all expected future profits earned by remaining "honest" ($PVAD_H$) with respect to the terms of the agreement, which is given by

$$PVAD_H = \frac{\pi_H(1+i)}{1+\theta} \tag{13.9}$$

If, on the other hand, a firm were to violate the agreement, the economic benefit is the immediate (one-shot) gain from cheating (π_C) plus the present value of all expected profits that will be earned from the Nash equilibrium ($PVAD_N$), that is, the profits earned in the absence of a collusive agreement (π_N). The economic benefit of violating the agreement is summarized as follows:

$$\pi_C + PVAD_N = \pi_C + \frac{\pi_N(1+i)}{1+\theta} \tag{13.10}$$

When will it pay to cheat for finitely repeated games? Cheating will occur when the expected present value of violating the agreement is greater than the expected present value of remaining "honest." This condition is summarized in the following inequality:

$$\pi_C + PVAD_N > PVAD_H$$

or

$$\pi_C + \frac{\pi_N(1+i)}{i+\theta} > \frac{\pi_H(1+i)}{1+\theta} \tag{13.11}$$

CHEATING RULE FOR FINITELY REPEATED
GAMES WITH AN UNCERTAIN END

Inequality (13.11) may be rearranged to yield the cheating rule for finitely repeated games with an uncertain end. The interpretation of inequality (13.12) is similar to the interpretation of inequality (13.6). If the expected rate of return from adhering to the collusive agreement is less than the prevailing rate of interest, there will be an incentive to cheat and the cartel will break down.

$$\frac{\pi_H - \pi_N - \theta\pi_C}{\pi_C + \pi_N - \pi_H} < i \tag{13.12}$$

It should also be noted that inequality (13.12) differs from inequality (13.6) by the addition of $-\theta\pi_c$ in the numerator. This indicates that in the presence of uncertainty about the duration of the game, the threshold for violating the agreement is lowered. In other words, in the presence of uncertainty about the duration of the game, the likelihood that a player will violate the agreement will be greater than for an infinitely repeated game.

The reader should note that when the probability that a game will end is zero, the solution to inequality (13.12) is identical to that of inequality (13.6). Finally, it is interesting to ask at what probability any positive interest rate will result in a breakdown of the collusive agreement. This probability may be determined by setting the left-hand side of inequality (13.12) equal to zero and solving for θ:

$$\frac{\pi_H - \pi_N - \theta\pi_C}{\pi_C + \pi_N - \pi_H} = 0 \tag{13.13}$$

Assuming that the denominator of Equation (13.13) is nontrivial, then this reduces to

$$\pi_H - \pi_N - \theta\pi_C = 0$$

or

$$\theta = \frac{\pi_H - \pi_N}{\pi_C} \tag{13.14}$$

Problem 13.7. Consider once again, the payoff matrix summarized in Figure 10.9.
a. Suppose that the probability that will the game end after each play is *0.1*. Above what interest rate can we expect the cartel to break down?
b. Above what probability will the game end on the next play for any positive interest rate result if at least one player violates the collusive agreement?

Solution

a. Substituting the data from Figure 10.9 into the left-hand side of inequality (13.12) yields

$$\frac{\pi_H - \pi_N - \theta\pi_C}{\pi_C + \pi_N - \pi_H} = \frac{\$1,000,000 - \$250,000 - 0.1(\$5,000,000)}{\$5,000,000 - \$250,000 - \$1,000,000}$$

$$= \frac{\$250,000}{\$4,750,000} = 0.0526$$

Thus, from inequality (13.6), if the prevailing rate of interest is greater than 5.26%, each firm will have an incentive to violate the collusive agreement, in which case the cartel will be unstable. If the rate of interest is less than 5.26%, it will be in the best interest for both firms to honor the agreement and the cartel will be stable. Finally, if the interest rate is exactly 5.26%, then *ceteris paribus*, each firm will be indifferent between cheating and remaining honest.

b. Substituting the data from Figure 10.9 into the right-hand side of Equation (13.14) yields

$$\theta = \frac{\pi_H - \pi_N}{\pi_C} = \frac{\$1,000,000 - \$250,000}{\$5,000,000}$$

$$= \frac{\$750,000}{\$5,000,000} = 0.15$$

That is, if the probability that the game will end on the next play is 15% or greater, any positive interest rate will result in cheating. To verify this result, substitute $\theta = 0.15$ into the left-hand side of inequality (13.12). This yields

$$\frac{\pi_H - \pi_N - \theta\pi_C}{\pi_C + \pi_N - \pi_H} = \frac{\$1,000,000 - \$250,000 - 0.15(\$5,000,000)}{\$5,000,000 - \$250,000 - \$1,000,000}$$

$$= \frac{\$0}{\$4,750,000} = 0.0$$

FINITELY REPEATED GAMES WITH A CERTAIN END

Surprisingly, when a finitely repeated game has a certain end, the solution collapses into a series of noncooperative one-shot games. To see this, consider once again the game in Figure 10.9. Let us assume initially that this game is played just twice. Suppose, further, that firms A and B agree to charge a "high" price for their product. In an infinitely repeated game, violation of the agreement by either player will alter future game plays. For example, if firm A were to charge a "low" price in violation of its agreement, firm B, might seek to punish firm A by ruling out any future cooperation. In other words, a violation of firm A's agreement with firm B could "trigger" a strategy change by firm B.

With a finitely repeated game with a certain end, however, the use of trigger strategies to enforce a collusive agreement will fail. The reason for this is relatively straightforward. Since each player realizes that there can be no punishment for "dishonest" actions in subsequent periods, each has the incentive to adopt a strategy that is consistent with a one-shot noncooperative game. This is known as the end-of-period problem. In the game depicted in Figure 10.9, the end-of-period problem means that each player will adopt a "low" price strategy in the second period. Even if firm A believed that firm B would continue to charge a "high" price, it would be in firm A's best interest to charge a "low" price because there is nothing firm B can do to punish firm A for deviant behavior. The same line of reasoning, of course, holds true for firm B. This result is not surprising, nor is it particularly interesting. What is interesting, however, is how the play in the second period affects the play in the first period.

In the game depicted in Figure 10.9, since each firms realizes that its rival will charge a "low" price in the second period, the first period, in effect, becomes the last period, in which case both firms again have an incentive to adopt the same strategy as in a one-shot game! In terms of the game in Figure 10.9, each firm will charge a "low" price in the first period as well. In other words, the Nash equilibrium for both periods is for both firms to charge a "low" price, with each player earning profits of $250,000.

What is remarkable about finitely repeated games with a certain end is that regardless of the number of periods, the process reduces to a series of noncooperative one-shot games. In other words, once the last period has been identified, each player has an incentive to view the next-to-the-last period as a one-shot game, which transforms that period into the last period, and so on. This process, which has been described as "backward unraveling," effectively renders collusive agreements unworkable.

Definition: The end-of-period problem arises in a finitely repeated game with a certain end because each period effectively becomes the final period, in which case the game reduces to a series of noncooperative one-shot games.

Two interesting examples of the end-of-game problem may be found in Baye and Beil (1994, Chapter 10). In the first, a worker announces the intention to quit on a specified date. In general, it is reasonable to assume that at least one reason people work hard is the fear of being fired if they are caught "goofing off." In fact, if the net benefit of being diligent is greater than the net benefit of being a "gold brick," workers will find it in their best interest to do a good job.

Now, suppose that a worker announces on Monday the intention quit on Tuesday. How seriously will the worker take his or her job on Tuesday?

Probably not very seriously. Why? Since the worker has no intention of showing up on Wednesday, any threat by management to "fire" the employee on Tuesday is meaningless. In terms of the preceding discussion, the worker's choice of working hard or goofing off reduces to a noncooperative, one-shot game. Since the threat of being fired no longer has any meaning, the net benefit of working hard is considerably reduced, suggesting that it may be in the worker's best interest to goof off on Tuesday.

Will the employee's attitude toward work on Monday be affected by the decision to quit on Tuesday? Probably, yes. As noted earlier, since the worker has identified Tuesday as the final period, there is an incentive to view Monday as a one-shot game as well, which suggests that the worker will goof off on Monday. Even if the employee had given 2 weeks notice, the remaining days on the job will collapse into a series of noncooperative, one-shot games. Does this scenario sound unrealistic? If it does, consider how your attitude toward work might change if you handed in your 2-week notice. Would you be disposed to work just as hard as before, or would you instead "take it easy" while counting down your final days?

What, if anything, should management do under these circumstances? Management could, of course, fire the worker immediately upon learning of the worker's intention to quit, but such a move would be counterproductive. The reason for this is that workers would change their strategy of giving "2 weeks notice" to a strategy of advising management at the close of business on the day of the planned resignation. This would present management with the extremely difficult task of finding replacement workers at short notice without disrupting the production process.

On discussion of a finitely repeated game with a certain end, however, suggests a possible solution to management's dilemma. The answer lies in extending the game beyond the resignation date. For example, management could offer the employee assistance in identifying new employment opportunities, or perhaps provide letters of recommendation to potential future employers. By extending the game into the future, it will be in the worker's best interest to avoid "burning bridges" by goofing off during the final days of employment.

Baye and Beil's second example of the end-of-game problem deals with the so-called snake oil salesman. During the American westward expansion of the late nineteenth century, "snake oil" salesmen traveled from frontier town to frontier town selling bottles of elixirs promising everything from a cure for toothaches to a remedy for baldness. Of course, these claims were bogus, but by the time customers realized that they had been "had," the salesman would be long gone. By contrast, had a local merchant attempted to pull a similar scam, there was a very good chance that the merchant would soon be decorating the nearest tree—from the neck! In fact, it is precisely because the local merchant is playing a finitely repeated game (assuming that he or she does not live forever) with an uncertain future that the threat of punishment for unethical behavior ensures that the person sells products of reliable quality. For the snake oil salesman there is no tomorrow, and so the transaction is played as a noncooperative, one-shot game.

FOCAL-POINT EQUILIBRIUM

As the preceding paragraphs testify, the idea of a Nash equilibrium is a very powerful concept. Unfortunately, the existence of a Nash equilibrium does not guarantee that solutions to game-theoretic problems will be unique. The game summarized earlier in Figure 13.5 is one such example. Although it was argued that TEXplor and Clampett acted rationally by adopting the strategy profile {Wide, Narrow}, the result was an "irrational" {Wide, Wide} strategy profile, which was nonetheless a Nash equilibrium. The strategy profile {Wide, Wide} is a Nash equilibrium because neither firm can improve its payoff by switching strategies. It can be readily verified, however, that if the firms had adopted a {Narrow, Wide} strategy profile, the result would have been a {Narrow, Narrow} Nash equilibrium.

In general, it may be demonstrated that if both players have a strictly dominant strategy, the result will be a strictly dominant strategy equilibrium, in which case there is a unique Nash equilibrium. If neither player has a strictly dominant strategy, or if the strategy profile results in a weakly dominant strategy equilibrium, then the Nash equilibrium may not be unique. When there are multiple Nash equilibria, then without additional information regarding the terms of the game, it will be difficult to predict the strategy profiles that will be adopted by players, the context within which the game is being played, or the interactions between players. One possible solution to a game theoretic problem in the presence of multiple Nash equilibria is the *focal-point equilibrium*, suggested by Thomas Schelling (1960). Schelling has suggested that in the presence of multiple Nash equilibria, a single solution may "stand out" because the players share a common "understanding" of the problem.

Definition: A focal-point equilibrium may exist in the presence of multiple Nash equilibria when a single solution "stands out" because the players share a common "understanding" of the problem.

To illustrate the concept of a focal-point equilibrium, suppose that a father and his son become separated in an amusement park, and no prior arrangement had been made to set a place to meet in the event that this happened. Is it not likely, however, that in the event of separation both would think of the same place to try and find the other, such as the park's main gate or the office of park security? Bierman and Fernandez (1998,

Chapter 1) referred to this common understanding of the problem as "conventional wisdom." Shelling illustrated the concept of focal-point equilibria with the following "abstract puzzles."

1. A coin is flipped and two players are instructed to call "heads" or "tails." If both players call "heads," or both call "tails," then both win a prize. If one player calls "heads" and the other calls "tails," then neither wins a prize.

2. A player is asked to circle one of the following six numbers: 7, 100, 13, 261, 99, and 555. If all of the players circle the same number, then each wins a prize; otherwise no one wins anything.

3. A player is asked to put a check mark in one sixteen squares, arranged as shown. If all the players check the same square, each wins a prize; otherwise no one wins anything.

4. Two players are told to meet somewhere in New York City, but neither player has been told where the meeting is to occur. Neither player has ever been placed in this situation before, and the two are not permitted to communicate with each other. Each player must guess the other's probable location.

5. In the preceding scenario each player is told the date, but not the time, of the meeting. Each player must guess the exact time that the meeting is to take place.

6. A player is told to write down a positive number. If all players write the same number, each player wins a prize; otherwise no one wins anything.

7. A player is told to name an amount of money. If all players name the same amount, each wins that amount.

8. A player is asked to divide $100 into two piles labeled pile *A* and pile *B*. Another player is asked to do the same. If the amounts in all four piles coincide, player each receives $100, otherwise, neither player wins anything.

9. The results of a first ballot in an election were tabulated as follows:

Smith	19 votes
Jones	28 votes
Brown	15 votes
Robinson	29 votes
White	9 votes

A second ballot is to be taken. A player is asked to predict which candidate will receive a majority of votes on the second ballot. The player has no interest in the outcome of the second ballot. The player who correctly predicts the candidate receiving the majority of votes will win a prize, and everyone knows that a correct prediction is in everyone's best interest. If the player incorrectly predicts the "winner" of the second ballot, he or she will win nothing.

In each of these nine scenarios there are multiple Nash equilibria. Schelling found, however, that in an "unscientific sample of respondents," people tended to focus (i.e., to use focal points) on just a few such equilibria. Schelling found, for example, that 86% of the respondents chose "heads" in problem 1. In problem 2 the first three numbers received 90% of the votes, with the number 7 leading the number 100 by a slight margin and the number 13 in third place. In problem 4, an absolute majority of the respondents, who were sampled in New Haven, Connecticut, proposed meeting at the information booth in Grand Central Station, and virtually all of them agreed to meet at 12 noon. In problem 6, two-fifths of all respondents chose the number 1. In problem 7, 29% of the respondents chose $1 million, and only 7 percent chose cash amounts that were not multiples of 10. In problem 8, 88% of the respondents put $50 into each pile. Finally, in problem 9, 91% of the respondents chose Robinson.

Schelling also found that the respondents chose focal points even when these choices where not in their best interest. For example, consider the following variation of problem 1. Players A and B are asked to call "heads" or "tails." The players are not permitted to communicate with each other. If both players call "heads," player A gets $3 and player B gets $2. If both players call "tails," then player A gets $2 and player B gets $3. Again, if one player calls "heads" and the other calls "tails," neither player wins a prize. In this scenario Schelling found that 73% of respondents chose "heads" when given the role of player A. More surprising is that 68% of respondents in the role of player B still chose "heads" in spite of the bias against player B. The reader should verify that if both players attempt to win $3, neither one will win anything.

The economic significance of focal-point equilibria becomes readily apparent when we consider cooperative, non-zero-sum, simultaneous-move, infinitely repeated games. Where explicit collusive agreements are prohibited, the existence of focal-point equilibria suggests that tacit collusion, coupled with the policing mechanism of trigger strategies, may be possible. A fuller discussion of these, and other related matters, is deferred to the next section.

MULTISTAGE GAMES

The final scenario we will consider in this brief introduction to game theory is that of the multistage game. Multistage games differ from the games considered earlier in that play is sequential, rather than simultaneous. Figure 13.12, which is an example of an *extensive-form game*, summarizes the players, the information available to each player at each stage, the order of the moves, and the payoffs from alternative strategies of a multistage game.

Definition: An extensive-form game is a representation of a multistage game that summarizes the players, the stages of the game, the information available to each player at each stage, player strategies, the order of the moves, and the payoffs from alternative strategies.

The extensive-form game depicted in Figure 13.12 has 2 players: player *A* and player *B*. The boxes in the figure are called *decision nodes*. Inside each box is the name of the player who is to move at that decision node. At each decision node the designated player must decide on a strategy, which is represented by a *branch*, which represents a possible move by a player. The arrow indicates the direction of the move. The collection of decision nodes and branches is called a *game tree*. The first decision node is called the *root* of the game tree. In the game depicted in Figure 13.12, player *A* moves first. Player *A*'s move represents the first stage of the game. Player *A*, who is at the root of the game tree, must decide whether to adopt a *Yes* or a *No* strategy. After player *A* has decided on a strategy, player *B* must

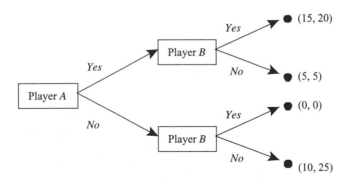

Payoffs: (Player *A*, Player *B*)

FIGURE 13.12   Extensive-form game.

decide how to respond in the second stage of the game. For example, if player A's strategy is *Yes*, then player B must decide whether to respond with a *Yes* or a *No*.

At the end of each arrow are small circles called *terminal nodes*. The game ends at the terminal nodes. To the right of the terminal notes are the payoffs. In Figure 13.12, the first entry in parenthses is the payoff to player A and the second entry is the payoff to player B. If player B adopts a *Yes* strategy, the payoff for player A is 15 and the payoff for player B is 20. In summary, an extensive-form game is made up of a game tree, terminal nodes, and payoffs.

As with simultaneous-move games, the eventual payoffs depend on the strategies adopted by each player. Unlike simultaneous-move games, in multistage games the players move sequentially. In the game depicted in Figure 13.12, player A moves without prior knowledge of player B's intended response. player B's move, on the other hand, is conditional on the move of player A. In other words, while player B moves with the knowledge of player A's move, player A can only anticipate how player B will react. The ideal strategy profile for player A is {*Yes*, *Yes*}, which yields payoffs of (15, 20). For player B, the ideal strategy profile is {*No*, *No*}, which yields payoffs of (10, 25). The challenge confronting player B is to get player A to say *No* on the first move. As we will see, the solution is for player B to convince player A that regardless of what player A says, player B will say *No*. To see this, consider the following scenario.

Suppose that player B announces that he or she has adopted the following strategy: if player A says *Yes*, then player B will say *No*; if player A says *No*, player B will also say *No*. With the first strategy profile {*Yes*, *No*} the payoffs are (5, 5). With the second strategy profile the payoffs are (10, 25). In this case, it would be in player A's best interest to say *No*. Of course, the choice of strategies is a "no brainer" if player A believes that player B will follow through on his or her "threat." player A's first move will be *No* because the payoff to player A from a {*No*, *No*} strategy is greater than from a {*Yes*, *No*} strategy. In fact, the strategy profile {*No*, *No*} is a Nash equilibrium. Why? If player B's threat to always say *No* is credible, then player A cannot improve his or her payoff by changing strategies.

As the reader may have already surmised, the final outcome of this game depends crucially on whether player A believes that player B's threat to always say *No* is credible. Is there a reason to believe that this is so? Probably not. To see this, assume again that the optimal strategy profile for player A is {*Yes*, *Yes*}, which yields the payoff (15, 20). If player A says *Yes*, the payoff to player B from saying *No* is 5, but the payoff for saying *Yes* is 20. Thus, if player B is rational, the threat to say *No* lacks credibility and the resulting strategy profile is {*Yes*, *Yes*}.

Note that strategy profile {*Yes*, *Yes*} is also a Nash equilibrium. Neither player can improve his or her payoff by switching strategies. In particular, if player B's strategy was to say *Yes* if player A says *Yes* and say *No* if player A says *No*, then player A's payoff is 15 by saying *Yes* and 10 by saying *No*. Clearly, player A's best strategy, given player B's move, is to say *Yes*.

We now have two Nash equilibria. Which one is the more reasonable? It is the Nash equilibrium corresponding to the strategy profile {*Yes*, *Yes*} because player B has no incentive to carry through with the threat to say *No*. The Nash equilibrium corresponding to the strategy profile {*Yes*, *Yes*} is referred to as a *subgame perfect equilibrium* because no player is able to improve on his or her payoff at any stage (decision node) of the game by switching strategies. In a subgame perfect equilibrium, each player chooses at each stage of the game an optimal move that will ultimately result in optimal solution for the entire game. Moreover, each player believes that all the other players will behave in the same way.

Definition: A strategy profile is a subgame perfect equilibrium if it is a Nash equilibrium and allows no player to improve on his or her payoff by switching strategies at any stage of a dynamic game.

The idea of a subgame perfect equilibrium may be attributed to Reinhard Selten (1975). Selten formalized the idea that a Nash equilibrium with incredible threats is a poor predictor of human behavior by introducing the concept of the *subgame*. In a game with perfect information, a subgame is any subset of branches and decision nodes of the original multistage game that constitutes a game in itself. The unique initial node of a subgame is called a *subroot* of the larger multistage game. Selten's essential contribution is that once a player begins to play a subgame, that player will continue to play the subgame until the end of the game. That is, once a player begins a subgame, the player will not exit the subgame in search of an alternative solution. To see this, consider Figure 13.13, which recreates Figure 13.12.

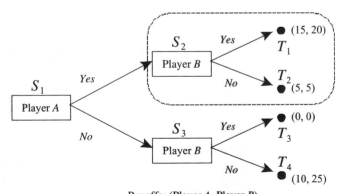

Payoffs: (Player A, Player B)

FIGURE 13.13   A subgame.

Figure 13.13 is a multistage game consisting of two subgames. The multistage game itself begins at the initial node, S_1. The two subgames begin at subroots S_2 and S_3. The subgame that begins at subroot S_2, which is highlighted by the dashed, rounded rectangle, has two terminal nodes, T_1 and T_2, with payoffs of (15, 20) and (5, 5), respectively. In games with perfect information, every decision node is the subroot of a larger game. A player who begins a subgame is common knowledge to all the other players. The student should verify that this subgame has a unique Nash equilibrium. At this Nash equilibrium player B says *Yes*. The reader should also verify that the subgame with subroot S_3 also has a unique Nash equilibrium.

As we have seen, the final outcome of the multistage game depicted in Figure 13.12 depends on whether player A believes that player B's threat to say *No* is credible. If player B is rational, the threat to say *No* lacks credibility and the resulting strategy profile is {*Yes, Yes*}. Thus, the nonoptimality of the strategy profile {*No, No*} makes player B's threat incredible. Thus, this strategy profile is eliminated by the requirement that Nash equilibrium strategies remain when applied to any subgame. A Nash equilibrium with this property is called a *subgame perfect equilibrium*. The Nash equilibrium corresponding to the strategy profile {*Yes, Yes*} is referred to as a subgame perfect equilibrium because no player is able to improve on his or her payoff at any stage (decision node) of the game by switching strategies. As we will soon see, the concept of a subgame perfect equilibrium is essential element of the backward induction solution algorithm.

EXAMPLE: SOFTWARE GAME

As we have already seen, one of the problems with multistage games is the selection of an optimal strategy profile in the presence of multiple Nash equilibria. This issue will be addressed in later sections. For now, consider the following example of a subgame perfect equilibrium, which comes directly from Bierman and Fernandez (1998, Chapter 6).

Macrosoft Corporation is a computer software company that is planning to introduce a new computer game into the market. Macrosoft's management is considering two marketing approaches. The first approach involves a "Madison Avenue" type of advertising campaign, while the second approach emphasizes word of mouth. Bierman and Fernandez described the first approach as "slick" and the second approach as "simple."

The timing involved in both approaches is all-important in this example. Although expensive, the "slick" approach will result in a high volume of sales in the first year, while sales in the second year are expected to decline dramatically as the market becomes saturated. The inexpensive "simple" approach, on the other hand, is expected to result in relatively low sales volume in the first year, but much higher sales volume in the second year as "word gets around." Regardless of the promotional campaign adopted,

TABLE 13.1   Macrosoft's Profits if Microcorp Does Not Enter the Market

	Slick	Simple
Gross profit in year 1	$900,000	$200,000
Gross profit in year 2	$100,000	$800,000
Total gross profit	$1,000,000	$1,000,000
Advertising cost	−$570,000	−$200,000
Total net profit	$430,000	$800,000

TABLE 13.2   Macrosoft's Profits if Microcorp Enters the Market

	Slick	Simple
Gross profit in year 1	$900,000	$200,000
Gross profit in year 2	$50,000	$400,000
Total gross profit	$950,000	$600,000
Advertising cost	−$570,000	−$200,000
Total net profit	$380,000	$400,000

no significant sales are anticipated after the second year. Macrosoft's net profits from both campaigns are summarized in Table 13.1.

The data presented in Table 13.1 suggest that Macrosoft should adopt the inexpensive "simple" approach because of the resulting larger total net profits. The problem for Macrosoft, however, is the threat of a "legal clone," that is, a competing computer game manufactured by another firm, Microcorp, that is, to all outward appearances, a close substitute for original. The difference between the two computer games is in the underlying programming code, which is sufficiently different to keep the "copycat" firm from being successfully sued for copyright infringement. In this example, Microcorp is able to clone Macrosoft's computer game within a year at a cost of $300,000. If Microcorp decides to produce the clone and enter the market, the two firms will split the market for the computer game in the second year. The payoffs to both companies in years 1 and 2 are summarized in Tables 13.2 and 13.3.

Given the information provided in Tables 13.2 and 13.3 what is the optimal marketing strategy for each player, Macrosoft and Microcorp? Since the decisions of both companies are interdependent and sequential the problem may be represented as the extensive-form game in Figure 13.14.

It should be obvious from Figure 13.14 that Macrosoft moves first and has just one decision node. The choices facing Macrosoft consist of "slick"

TABLE 13.3   Microcorp's Profits after Entering the
Market

	Slick	Simple
Gross profit in year 1	$0	$0
Gross profit in year 2	$50,000	$400,000
Total gross profit	$50,000	$400,000
Cloning cost	−$300,000	−$300,000
Total net profit	$250,000	$100,000

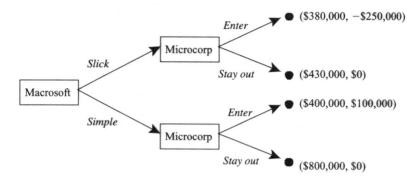

Payoffs: (Macrosoft, Microcorp)

FIGURE 13.14   The software game.

and "simple." Microcorp, on the other hand, has two decision nodes. Microcorp's strategy is conditional on Macrosoft's decision of a promotional
campaign. For example, if Macrosoft decides upon a "slick" campaign,
Microcorp might decide to "stay out" of the market. On the other hand, if
Macrosoft decides on a "simple" campaign, Microcorp might decide that its
best move is to "enter" the market. This strategy profile for Microcorp might
be written {Stay out, Enter}. As the reader will readily verify, there are four
possible strategy profiles available to Microcorp. These strategy profiles
represent Microcorp's contingency plans. Which strategy is adopted will
depend on Macrosoft's actions. Since different strategies will often result in
the same sequence of moves, it is important not to confuse strategies with
actual moves.

NASH EQUILIBRIUM AND BACKWARD
INDUCTION

At this point we naturally are interested in the strategic choices of each
player. As we will soon see, finding an optimal solution for multistage games

Macrosoft

		Slick	Simple
Microcorp	Enter	(−$250,000, $380,000)	($100,000, $400,000)
	Stay out	($0, $430,000)	($0, $800,000)

Payoffs: (Microcorp, Macrosoft)

FIGURE 13.15   Payoff matrix for a two-player, simultaneous-move game.

is not nearly as simple as it might seem at first glance. This is because multistage noncooperative games are often plagued with multiple Nash equilibria. A *solution concept* is a methodology for finding solutions to multistage games. There is no universally accepted solution concept that can be applied to every game. Bierman and Fernandez (1998, Chapter 6) have proposed the *backward induction* concept for finding optimal solutions to multistage games involving multiple Nash equilibria. The backward induction method is sometimes referred to as the *fold-back method*.

Definition: Backward induction is a methodology for finding optimal solutions to multistage games involving multiple Nash equilibria.

The solution concept of backward induction will be applied to the multistage game depicted in Figure 13.14, which assumes that Macrosoft and Microcorp have *perfect information*. Perfect information consists of player awareness of his or her position on the game tree whenever it is time to move. Before discussing the backward induction methodology, consider again the payoffs (in $000's) in Figure 13.14, which is summarized as the normal-form game in Figure 13.15.

Now consider the noncooperative solution to the game depicted in Figure 13.15. The reader should verify that a Nash equilibrium to this game is the strategy profile {*Enter, Simple*}. It will be recalled that in a Nash equilibrium, each player adopts a strategy it believes is the best response to the other player's strategy and neither player's payoff can be improved by changing strategies.

The limitation of a Nash equilibrium as a solution concept is that changing the strategy of any single player may result in a new Nash equilibrium, which may be not be an optimal solution. To see this, consider Figure 13.16, which is the *strategic form* of the multistage game in Figure 13.14. Strategic-form games illustrate the payoffs to each player from every possible strategy profile. Macrosoft, for example, may adopt one of two promotional campaigns—*Slick* or *Simple*. Microcorp, on the other hand, may adopt one of four strategic responses: (*Enter, Enter*), (*Enter, Stay out*), (*Stay out, Enter*), or (*Stay out, Stay out*).

Definition: The strategic form of a game summarizes the payoffs to each player arising from every possible strategy profile.

Macrosoft

	Slick	Simple
(Enter, Enter)	(−$250,000, $380,000)	**($100,000, $400,000)**
(Enter, Stay out)	(−$250,000, $380,000)	($0, 800,000)
(Stay out, Enter)	**($0, $430,000)**	($100,000 $400,000
(Stay out, Stay out)	($0, $430,000)	($0, $800,000

Microcorp (label at left spanning rows)

Payoffs: (Microcorp, Macrosoft)

FIGURE 13.16   Payoff matrix for a strategic-form game.

The cells in Figure 13.16 summarize the payoffs from all possible strategic combinations. For example, suppose that Microcorp decides to "enter" regardless of the promotional campaign adopted by Macrosoft. In this case, Macrosoft will select a "simple" campaign, which is the Nash equilibrium of the normal-form game illustrated in Figure 13.15. The strategy profile for this game may be written {*Simple*, (*Enter*, *Enter*)}. On the other hand, if Macrosoft adopts a "slick" strategy, Microcorp can do no better than to adopt the strategy (*Stay out*, *Enter*). The strategy profile for this game may be written {*Slick*, (*Stay out*, *Enter*)}. This is a Nash equilibrium for the strategic-form game in Figure 13.16 but is not a Nash equilibrium for the normal-form game in Figure 13.15!

Finding an optimal solution to a multistage game using the backward induction methodology involves five steps:

1. Start at the terminal nodes. Trace each node to its immediate predecessor node. The decisions at each node may be described as "basic," "trivial," or "complex." Basic decision nodes have branches that lead to exactly one terminal node. Basic decision nodes are trivial if they have only one branch. A decision node is complex if it is not basic, that is, if at least one branch leads to more than one terminal node. If a trivial decision node is reached, continue to move up the decision tree until a complex or a nontrivial decision node is reached.

2. Determine the optimal move at each basic decision node reached in step 1. A move is optimal if it leads to the highest payoff.

3. Disregard all nonoptimal branches from decision nodes reached in step 2. With the nonoptimal branches disregarded, these decision nodes become trivial (i.e., they now have only one branch). The resulting game tree is simpler than the original game tree.

4. If the root of the game tree has been reached, then stop. If not, repeat steps 1–3. Continue in this manner until the root of the tree has been reached.

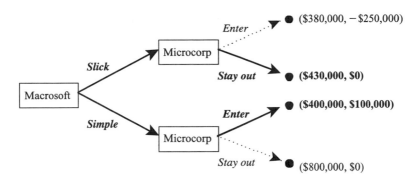

Payoffs: (Macrosoft, Microcorp)

FIGURE 13.17   Using backward induction to find a Nash equilibrium.

5. After the root of the game tree has been reached, collect the optimal decisions at each player's decision nodes. This collection of decisions comprises the players' optimal strategies.

The backward induction solution concept will now be applied to the multistage game depicted in Figure 13.14. From each terminal node, move to the two Microcorp decision nodes. Each of these decision nodes is basic, since the branches lead to exactly one terminal node. If Macrosoft chooses a "slick" campaign, the optimal move for Microcorp is to stay out, since the payoff is $0 compared with a payoff of –$250,000 by entering. The "enter" branch should be disregarded in future moves. If Macrosoft chooses a "simple" campaign, the optimal move for Microcorp is to enter, since the payoff is $100,000 compared with a payoff of $0 by staying out. This "stay out" branch should be disregarded in future moves. The resulting extensive-form game is illustrated in Figure 13.17.

An examination of Figure 13.17 will reveal that the optimal strategy for Microcorp is (*Stay out, Enter*). The final optimal strategy profile is {*Slick*, (*Stay out, Enter*)}, which yields payoffs of $430,000 for Macrosoft and $0 for Microcorp. The reader should note that the choice of this Nash equilibrium ($0, $430,000) from Figure 13.16 differs from the Nash equilibrium ($100,000, $400,000) in Figure 13.12. The implication of the backward induction method is straightforward. By taking Microcorp's entry decision into account, Macrosoft avoided making a strategy decision that would have cost it $30,000.

Problem 13.8. Consider, again, the strategy for the software game summarized in Figure 13.17. Suppose that the cost of cloning Macrosoft's computer game is $10,000 instead of $300,000.

TABLE 13.4   Microcorp's Profits after Entering the
Market

	Slick	Simple
Gross profit in year 1	$0	$0
Gross profit in year 2	$50,000	$400,000
Total gross profit	$50,000	$400,000
Cloning cost	–$10,000	–$10,000
Total net profit	$40,000	$390,000

a. Diagram the new extensive-form for this multistage game.
b. Use the backward induction solution concept to determine the new
   optimal strategy profile for this game. Illustrate your answer.

Solution

a. Microcorp's profits at the lower cost of cloning Macrosoft's computer
   game and entering the market are presented in Table 13.4.
   Assuming that Macrosoft's net profits remain unchanged, the extensive
   form of this game is as shown in Figure 13.18.
b. Using the backward induction solution methodology, from each terminal node move to Microcorp's two decision nodes. Each of these decision nodes is basic. If Macrosoft chooses a *Slick* campaign, the optimal
   move for Microcorp is to *Enter*, since the payoff is $40,000 compared
   with a payoff of $0 by staying out. The *Stay out* branch should be disre-
   garded in future moves. If Macrosoft chooses a *Simple* campaign, the
   optimal move for Microcorp is to Enter, since the payoff is $390,000 com-
   pared with a payoff of $0 if it adopts a *Stay out* strategy. The *Stay out*
   branch should be disregarded in future moves. In the resulting extensive-
   form game, diagrammed in Figure 13.19, we see that the optimal strategy for Microcorp is (*Enter*, *Enter*). The final optimal strategy profile is
   {*Simple*, (*Enter*, *Enter*)}, which yields payoffs of $400,000 for Macrosoft
   and $390,000 for Microcorp.

Problem 13.9. Suppose that in Problem 13.8 the cost of cloning
Macrosoft's computer game is $500,000 instead of $300,000.
a. Diagram the new extensive-form for this multistage game.
b. Use the backward induction solution concept to determine the new
   optimal strategy profile for this game. Illustrate your answer.

Solution

a. Microcorp's profits at the higher cost of cloning Macrosoft's computer
   game and entering the market are presented in Table 13.5.
   The extensive form of this game, assuming that Macrosoft's net profits
   remain unchanged, is diagrammed in Figure 13.20.

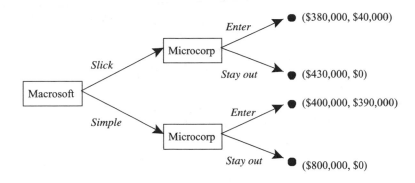

Payoffs: (Macrosoft, Microcorp)

FIGURE 13.18 Game tree for problem 13.8.

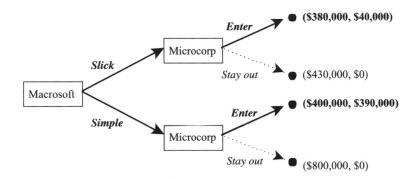

Payoffs: (Macrosoft, Microcorp)

FIGURE 13.19 Solution to problem 13.8 using backward induction.

TABLE 13.5 Microcorp's Profits after Entering the Market

	Slick	Simple
Gross profit in year 1	$0	$0
Gross profit in year 2	$50,000	$400,000
Total gross profit	$50,000	$400,000
Cloning cost	$500,000	$500,000
Total net profit	−$450,000	−$100,000

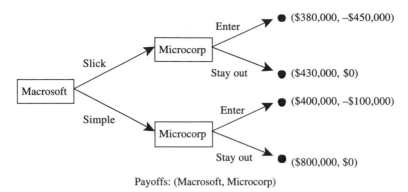

FIGURE 13.20   Game tree for problem 13.9.

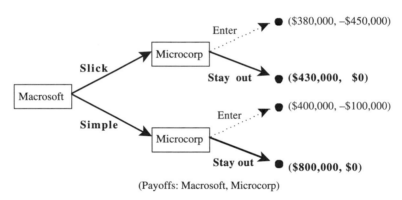

FIGURE 13.21   Solution to problem 13.9 using backward induction.

b. Using the backward induction solution concept, from each terminal node move to Microcorp's two decision nodes. Each of these decision nodes is basic. If Macrosoft chooses a "slick" campaign, the optimal move for Microcorp is to stay out, since the payoff is $0 compared with a payoff of −$450,000 by entering. The "enter" branch should be disregarded in future moves. If Macrosoft chooses a "simple" campaign, again the optimal move for Microcorp is to stay out, since the payoff is $0 compared with a payoff of −$100,000. The "enter" branch should be disregarded in future moves. In the resulting extensive-form game, diagrammed in Figure 13.21, we see that the optimal strategy for Microcorp is (*Stay out, Stay out*). The final optimal strategy profile is {*Simple*, (*Stay out, Stay out*)}, which yields payoffs of $800,000 for Macrosoft and $0 for Microcorp.

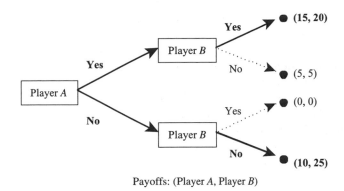

Payoffs: (Player A, Player B)

FIGURE 13.22 Solution to problem 13.10 using backward induction.

Problem 13.10. Consider again the multistage game in Figure 13.12. Use the backward induction solution concept to determine the optimal strategy profile for this game. Illustrate your answer.

Solution. Using the backward induction solution concept, from each terminal node move to the two Microcorp decision nodes. Each of these decision nodes is basic. If player A says "yes," the optimal move for player B is to say "yes," since the payoff is $20 compared with $5 by saying "no." Thus, the "no" branch should be disregarded in future moves. If player A says "no," the optimal move for player B is to say "no" since the payoff is $25 compared with $0 by saying "yes." The "yes" branch should be disregarded in future moves. In the resulting extensive-form game, diagrammed in Figure 13.22, we see that the optimal strategy for player B is (Yes, No). The final optimal strategy profile is $\{Yes, (Yes, No)\}$, which yields payoffs of 15 for player A and 20 for player B. The student is encouraged to compare this result with the earlier discussion of the selection of Nash equilibria with credible threats.

BARGAINING

In Chapter 8, perfectly competitive markets were characterized by large numbers of buyers and sellers. Firms in perfectly competitive industries were described as "price takers" because of their inability in influence the market price through individual production decisions. Consumers in such markets may similarly be described as price takers because they are individually incapable of extracting discounts or better terms from sellers. Since neither the buyer nor seller has "market power," the theoretical ability to "haggle" over the terms of the sale, or product content, is nonexistent. In the case of a monopolist selling to many small buyers, which was also discussed in Chapter 8, it was assumed that firms set the selling price of the product, and buyers, having no place else to go, accept that price without question. Even when of a neither the buyer or the seller may be thought of as a "price taker," such as the case monopsonist selling to an oligopolist, economists have had little to say about the possibility of negotiating, or "bargaining" over the contract terms.

Yet, bargaining is a fact of life. Whether bargaining with the boss for an increase in wages and benefits or haggling over the price of a new car, such interactions between buyer and seller are commonplace. In many instances, contract negotiations between producer and supplier, contractor and subcontractor, wholesaler and distributor, retailer and wholesaler, and so on, are the norm, rather than the exception. As an exercise, the reader is asked to consider why market power and the ability to bargain with product suppliers allow large retail outlets, such as Home Depot, Sports Authority, or Costco, to offer prices that are generally lower than those featured at the local hardware store, sporting goods store, or other retailer. Even in markets characterized by many buyers and sellers, it is often possible to find "pockets" of local monopoly or monopsony power that permits limited bargaining over contract terms to take place. Game theory is a useful tool for analyzing and understanding the dynamics of the bargaining process.

BARGAINING WITHOUT IMPATIENCE

We will begin our discussion of the bargaining process by considering the following scenario. Suppose that Andrew wishes to purchase an annual service contract from Adam. It is known by both parties that Andrew is willing to pay up to $100 for the service contract and that Adam will not accept any offer below $50. The maximum price that Andrew is willing to pay is called the *buyer's reservation price* and the minimum price that Adam is willing to accept is called the *seller's reservation price*. If Andrew and Adam can come to an agreement, the gain to both will add up to the difference between the buyer's and the seller's reservation prices, which in this case is $50.

Negotiations between Andrew and Adam may be modeled as the extensive-form game illustrated in Figure 13.23. We will assume for simplicity that negotiations involve only two offers and that Andrew makes the first offer, which is denoted as P_1. This is indicated as the first branch of the decision tree. After Andrew has made the offer, Adam can either accept or reject it. If Adam accepts the offer, the bargaining process is completed and the payoffs for Andrew and Adam are $(100 - P_1, P_1 - 50)$, respectively. For example, if Adam accepts Andrew's offer of, say, $80, then Andrew's gain from trade is $20 and Adam's gain from trade is $30, which sum to the difference between the respective parties' reservation prices. If Adam

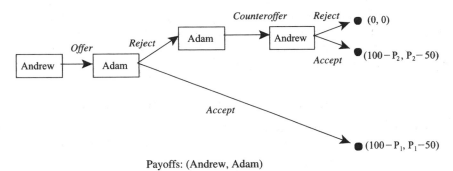

Payoffs: (Andrew, Adam)

FIGURE 13.23 Bargaining without impatience.

rejects Andrew's offer, Adam can come back with a counteroffer, which is denoted as P_2. If Andrew accepts Adam's counteroffer, the payoffs to Andrew and Adam are $(100 - P_2, P_2 - 50)$, respectively. If, on the other hand, Andrew rejects Adam's counteroffer, this game comes to an end and no agreement is reached, in which case the payoffs are $(0, 0)$.

Earlier we discussed the procedure of backward induction for finding solution values to multistage games with multiple equilibria. Applying this approach to the present bargaining game, it is easy to see that as long as Adam's counteroffer is not greater than $100, Andrew will accept. The reason for this is that Andrew cannot do any better than to accept an offer that does not exceed $100. Moving up the game tree to another node, it is equally apparent that Adam will reject any offer by Andrew that is less than $100. Moreover, accepting the offer ignores the fact that Adam has the ability to make a more advantageous (to him) counteroffer in the next round of negotiations. What all this means is that no matter what Andrew's initial offer was, he will end up paying Adam $100. In other words, as long as Adam has the ability to make a counteroffer, Adam will never accept Andrew's offer as final! Thus, in the two rounds of negotiation in this game, since Adam has the last move, then Adam "holds all the cards." The ability of Adam to dictate the final terms of the negotiations is referred to as the *last-mover's advantage*. Andrew might just as well save his breath and offer Adam $100 at the outset of the bargaining process.

As the scenario illustrates, the final outcome of this class of bargaining processes depends crucially on who makes the first offer, and on the number of rounds of offers. The reader can verify, for instance, that if Andrew makes the first offer, and there are an odd number of rounds of negotiations, Andrew has the last-mover's advantage, in which case Andrew will be able to extract the entire surplus of $50. If such is the case, it will be in both parties' best interest for Adam to accept Andrew's initial offer of $50, thereby saving both individuals the time, effort, and aggravation of an extended bargaining process. Similarly, if Adam has the first move and there are an even number of rounds of negotiations, it will in both parties' interest for Andrew to accept Adam's initial offer $100. In this case, Adam will extract the entire surplus of $50.

BARGAINING WITH SYMMETRIC IMPATIENCE

If negotiations of the type just described were that simple, bargaining would never take place. Of course, bargaining is a fact of life, so something must be missing. In this section we will make the underlying conditions of the bargaining process somewhat more realistic by assuming that there are multiple rounds of offers and counteroffers and costs associated with not immediately reaching an agreement. In the terminology of capital budgeting, this section will introduce the time value of money by discounting to the present future payoffs from negotiations.

In the example of bargaining without impatience, it was assumed that there were only two rounds of bargaining. In fact, the bargaining process is likely to involve multiple rounds of offer and counteroffer lasting days, weeks, or months. Failure to reach an agreement immediately may impose considerable costs on the bargainers. Consider, for example, the rather large opportunity costs incurred by a person who discovers that his or her car has been stolen. It is Saturday and the person needs to be able to drive to work on Monday. Although the stolen car was old, and the person was planning to buy another car anyway, the theft has the introduced a higher than usual level of anxiety into the situation. Failure to quickly come to terms on the purchase price of a replacement car may result not only in high psychological opportunity costs but in lost income, as well.

In this scenario, the buyer can take one of two possible approaches in negotiations with the used-car salesman. On the one hand, the buyer can withhold from the seller the details of his or her ill fortune and negotiate with a "cool head." Alternatively, the buyer may be unable, or unwilling, to withhold knowledge of the theft, preferring to attempt to garner understanding and sympathy. As we will soon see, sympathy in the bargaining process is not without cost: when one person's gain is another's loss, a buyer seeking sympathy will be better off visiting a psychiatrist, not a used-car salesman. To see this, let us consider the situation in which the buyer and the seller enter into negotiations without any knowledge of the opportunity costs that may be imposed on the other because of a failure to immediately reach an agreement. This situation is equivalent to the situation of the buyer who negotiates with the used-car salesperson with a "cool head."

Suppose, once again, that Andrew wishes to purchase an annual service contract from Adam, that Andrew is willing to pay up to $100 for the service contract and that Adam will not accept any offer below $50. Instead of only two negotiating rounds, however, suppose that there are 50 offer-

TABLE 13.6 Nash Equilibrium with Symmetric Impatience

Round	Offer maker	Offer price	Adam's surplus	Andrew's surplus
50	Seller	$100.00	$50.00	$0.00
49	Buyer	$97.50	$47.50	$2.50
48	Seller	$97.62	$47.62	$2.38
47	Buyer	$95.24	$45.24	$4.76
46	Seller	$95.48	$45.48	$4.52
:	:	:	:	:
5	Buyer	$76.78	$26.78	$23.22
4	Seller	$77.94	$27.94	$22.06
3	Buyer	$76.55	$26.55	$23.46
2	Seller	$77.72	$27.72	$22.28
1	Buyer	$76.33	$26.33	$23.67

counteroffer rounds. Since neither Andrew nor Adam knows anything about the other's personal circumstances, let us further assume that any delay in reaching an agreement reduces the gains from trade to both by 5% per round. This assumption is equivalent to assuming that both players have *symmetric patience*. We will assume that both players are aware of the cost imposed on the other by failing to come to an agreement immediately. With 50 rounds of negotiations, it is impractical to illustrate the bargaining process as an extensive-form game. Nevertheless, it is still possible to use backward induction to determine Andrew's and Adam's negotiating strategies. Consider the information summarized in Table 13.6.

We know that since Andrew makes the first offer and there are an even number of negotiating rounds, Adam has the last-mover's advantage. Thus, if negotiations drag on to the 50th round, Adam will sell the service contract for $100 and extract the entire surplus of $50. Andrew, of course, knows this. Andrew also knows that Adam will be indifferent between receiving $100 in the 50th round and receiving the entire surplus of $50, or receiving $97.50 in the 49th round because delays in reaching an agreement reduce Adam's gain by 5% per round. Thus, Adam will accept any offer from Andrew of $97.50 or more in the 49th round, which results in a surplus of $47.50, and reject any offer that is less than that. In capital budgeting terminology, the time value of $97.50 in the 49th round for Adam is the same as the time value of $100 in the 50th round. But this is not the end of the game.

Adam also knows that delays in reaching an agreement will reduce Andrew's gain from trade by 5% per round. Thus, Andrew is indifferent between receiving a surplus of $2.50 in the 49th round or receiving 5% less ($2.38) in the 48th round. Thus, Adam should offer to sell the service contract for $97.62 in the 48th round, thereby receiving a surplus of $47.62.

Once again, Andrew knows that Adam is indifferent between a price of $97.62 in the 48th round and $95.24 in the 47th round, which reduces Adam's surplus by 5%, to $45.24. Andrew's surplus, on the other hand, will increase to $4.76. Continuing in the same manner, the reader can verify through the use of backward induction that Andrew's best offer in the first round is $76.33, which Adam should accept. Adam's and Andrew's gains from trade are $26.33 and $23.67, respectively. The reader might suspect that if this process is continued, eventually Andrew and Adam will evenly divide the surplus; but as long as Adam moves last, he will enjoy an advantage, however slight, over Andrew.

BARGAINING WITH ASYMMETRIC IMPATIENCE

Suppose that instead of maintaining an "even keel" the buyer reveals to the used-car salesman the importance of quickly replacing the stolen car. The used-car salesman will immediately recognize the higher opportunity cost to the buyer from delaying a final agreement. To demonstrate the impact that his knowledge has on the bargaining process, consider again the negotiations between Andrews and Adam. We will continue to assume that there are 50 rounds of negotiations, but that the opportunity cost to Andrew from delaying an agreement reduces the gain from trade by 10% per round, while the opportunity cost to Adam continues to be 5% per round. Proceeding as before, the information in Table 13.7 summarizes the gains from trade to both Andrew and Adam that result from bargaining in the presence of asymmetric impatience (i.e., different opportunity costs for each player).

Utilizing backward induction, the reader will readily verify from Table 13.7 that Andrew's best first round offer is $83.10. This will result in a

TABLE 13.7 Nash Equilibrium with Asymmetric Impatience

Round	Offer maker	Offer price	Adam's surplus	Andrew's surplus
50	Seller	$100.00	$50.00	$0.00
49	Buyer	$97.50	$47.50	$2.50
48	Seller	$97.75	$47.75	$2.25
47	Buyer	$95.36	$45.36	$4.64
46	Seller	$95.83	$45.83	$4.17
⋮	⋮	⋮	⋮	⋮
5	Buyer			
4	Seller	$84.91	$34.91	$15.09
3	Buyer	$83.16	$33.16	$16.84
2	Seller	$84.84	$34.84	$15.16
1	Buyer	$83.10	$33.10	$16.90

surplus to Adam of $33.10, which is nearly twice the gain from trade enjoyed by Andrew. The results presented in Table 13.7 demonstrate that the negotiating party with the lowest opportunity cost has the clearest advantage in the negotiating process. Within the context of the stolen car example, clearly patience and secrecy are virtues. By "crying the blues" to the used-car salesman, the buyer placed himself or herself at a bargaining disadvantage. Unless the buyer is dealing with a paragon of rectitude and virtue, looking for sympathy from a rival during negotiations will clearly result in a disadvantageous division of the gains from trade.

If effect, impatience has been used as the discount rate for finding the present value of gains from trade in bargaining. The greater the players' impatience (the higher the discount rate), the less advantageous will be the gains from bargaining. Ariel Rubinstein (1982) has demonstrated that in this type of two-player bargaining game there exists a unique subgame perfect equilibrium. Assume that, player A and player B are bargaining over the division of a surplus and player B makes the first offer. Assume further that there is no limit to the number of rounds of offer and counteroffer and that both players accept offers when indifferent between accepting and rejecting the offer. Denote player A's discount rate as δ_A and Player B's discount rate as δ_B. A bargaining game has a unique subgame perfect equilibrium if in the first round player B offers player A

$$\omega_A = \frac{\theta_A(1-\theta_B)}{1-\theta_A\theta_B} \qquad (13.15)$$

as a share of the surplus, where $\theta_A = 1 - \delta_A$ and $\theta_B = 1 - \delta_B$. Player B's share of the surplus is

$$\omega_B = \frac{1-\theta_A}{1-\theta_A\theta_B} \qquad (13.16)$$

Problem 13.11. Andrew and Adam are bargaining over a surplus of $50. Assume that there is no limit to the number of rounds of offer and counteroffer, and that the discount rates for both players are $\delta_A = 0.05$ and $\delta_B = 0.05$.

a. For a subgame perfect equilibrium to exist, what portion of the surplus should Adam offer Andrew in the first round? What portion of the surplus should Adam keep for himself?

b. Suppose that Adam's discount rate is $\delta_A = 0.05$ and Andrew's discount rate is $\delta_B = 0.10$. What portion of the surplus should Adam offer Andrew in the first round and what portion should he keep for himself?

Solution

a. $\theta_A = 1 - \delta_A = 0.95$; $\theta_B = 1 - \delta_B = 0.95$. Substituting these values into expression (13.15) we obtain

$$\omega_A = \frac{\omega_A(1-\theta_B)}{1-\theta_A\theta_B} = \frac{(0.95)(1-0.95)}{1-0.9025} = \frac{0.0475}{0.0975} = 0.4872$$

The amount of the surplus that Adam should offer Andrew is

$$\omega_A(\$50) = 0.4872(\$50) = \$24.36$$

From equation (3.16) we obtain,

$$\omega_B = \frac{1-\theta_A}{1-\theta_A\theta_B} = \frac{(1-0.95)}{1-(0.95)(0.95)} = \frac{0.05}{0.0975} = 0.5128$$

The share of the surplus that Adam should keep is, therefore,

$$\omega_B(\$50) = 0.5128(\$50) = \$25.64$$

Of course, the sum of the shared surpluses is \$50. The student should note that as the last mover, Adam earns slightly more of the surplus than Andrew. The student is urged to compare these results with those found in Table 13.6. For the same discount rates and 50 negotiating rounds Adam received \$26.33 and Andrew received \$23.67.

b. $\theta_A = 1 - \delta_A = 0.90; \theta_B = 1 - \delta_B = 0.95$. Substituting these values into expression (13.15) we obtain

$$\omega_A = \frac{\omega_A(1-\theta_B)}{1-\theta_A\theta_B} = \frac{(0.90)(1-0.95)}{1-(0.90)(0.95)} = \frac{0.045}{0.145} = 0.3103$$

The amount of the surplus that Adam should offer Andrew is

$$0.3103(\$50) = \$15.52$$

The share of the surplus that Adam should keep for himself can be found by first substituting the information provided into expression (13.16), or

$$\omega_B = \frac{1-\theta_A}{1-\theta_A\theta_B} = \frac{1-0.90}{1-(0.90)(0.95)} = \frac{0.10}{0.145} = 0.6897$$

The share of the surplus that Adam should keep is, therefore,

$$\omega_B = 0.6897(\$50) = \$34.48$$

Once again, the sum of the shared surpluses is \$50. The student should note that, as the last mover, Adam retains more of the surplus then Andrew.

CHAPTER REVIEW

Game theory is the study of the strategic behavior involving the interaction of two or more individuals, teams, or firms, usually referred to as players. Two game theoretic scenarios were examined in this chapter: *simultaneous-move* and *multistage* games. In simultaneous-move games the players effectively move at the same time. A *normal-form game* summarizes the players' possible strategies and payoffs from alternative strategies in a simultaneous-move game.

Simultaneous-move games may be either *noncooperative* or *cooperative*. In contrast to noncooperative games, players of cooperative games engage in collusive behavior (i.e., they conspire to "rig" the final outcome). A *Nash equilibrium*, which is a solution to a problem in game theory, occurs when the players' payoffs cannot be improved by changing strategies.

Simultaneous-move games may be either *one-shot* or *repeated games*. One-shot games are played only once. Repeated games are played more than once. *Infinitely repeated games* are played over and over again without end. *Finitely repeated games* are played a limited number of times. Finitely repeated games can have certain or uncertain ends.

Analytically, there is little difference between infinitely repeated games and finitely repeated games with an uncertain end. With infinitely repeated games and finitely repeated games with an uncertain end, collusive agreements between and among the players are possible, although not necessarily stable. The solution to a finitely repeated game with a certain end collapses into a series of noncooperative, one-shot games. Collusive agreements between and among players of finitely repeated games are inherently unstable.

Multistage games differ from simultaneous-move games in that the play is sequential. An *extensive-form game* summarizes the players, the information available to each player at each stage, the order of the moves, and the payoffs from alternative strategies of a multistage game. A Nash equilibrium in a multistage game is a *subgame perfect equilibrium*. In this case, no player is able to improve on his or her payoff at any stage of the game by switching strategies. *Backward induction* is a solution concept proposed by Bierman and Fernandez for finding optimal solutions to multistage games involving multiple Nash equilibria.

Bargaining is a version of a multistage game. In *bargaining without impatience*, players assume that negotiators incur no costs by not immediately reaching an agreement. To use capital budgeting terminology, the discount rate for finding the present value of future payoffs is zero. The final outcome of this class of bargaining processes depends crucially on who makes the first offer, and on the number of rounds of offers. Players who make the final offer in negotiations have *last-mover's advantage* and are able to extract the entire gains from trade.

In *bargaining with impatience*, players assume that negotiators do incur costs when agreements are not immediately reached. Impatience may be symmetric or asymmetric. In *symmetric impatience*, players assume that the costs to the negotiators from not immediately reaching an agreement are identical. In this case, the discount rate for finding the present value of a future settlement is the same for both players. In *asymmetric impatience*, players assume that this discount rate is different for each player. Players with greater patience (lower discount rate) have the advantage in the negotiating process. In both cases, the player with the final move will receive most of the gains from trade. The extent of this gain will depend on the relative degrees of impatience of the negotiators. The greater a negotiator's patience, the larger will be that player's gain from trade.

KEY TERMS AND CONCEPTS

Backward induction   A methodology for finding optimal solutions to multistage games involving multiple Nash equilibria.

Cheating rule for infinitely repeated games   For a two-person, cooperative, non-zero-sum, simultaneous-move, infinitely repeated game, where future payoffs and interest rates are assumed to be unchanged, a collusive agreement will be unstable if $(\pi_H - \pi_N)/(\pi_C + \pi_N - \pi_H) < i$, where π_H is the one-period payoff from adhering to the agreement, π_C is the first-period payoff from violating a collusive agreement, π_N is the per-period payoff in the absence of a collusive agreement, and i is the market interest rate. For a two-person, cooperative, non-zero-sum, simultaneous-move, finitely repeated game with an uncertain end, a collusive agreement will be unstable if $(\pi_H - \pi_N - \theta\pi_C)/(\pi_C + \pi_N - \pi_H) < i$, where $0 < \theta < 1$ is the probability that the game will end after each play.

Cooperative game   A game in which the players engage in collusive behavior to "rig" the final outcome.

Credible threat   A threat is credible only if it is in a player's best interest to follow through with the threat when the situation presents itself.

Decision node   A point in a multistage game at which a player must decide upon a strategy.

End-of-period problem   For finitely repeated games with a certain end, each period effectively becomes the final period, in which case the game reduces to a series of noncooperative one-shot games.

Finitely repeated game   A game that is repeated a limited number of times.

Focal-point equilibrium   When a single solution to a problem involving multiple Nash equilibria "stands out" because the players share a common "understanding" of the problem, focal-point equilibrium has been achieved.

Game theory   The study of how rivals make decisions in situations involving strategic interaction (i.e., move and countermove) to achieve an optimal outcome.

Infinitely repeated game A game that is played over and over again without end.

Maximin strategy A strategy that selects the largest payoff from among the worst possible payoffs.

Nash equilibrium Is reached when each player adopts a strategy it believes to be the best response to the other players' strategy. When a game is in a Nash equilibrium, the players' payoffs cannot be improved by changing strategies.

Noncooperative game A game in which the players do not engage in collusive behavior. In other words, the players do not conspire to "rig" the final outcome.

Non–strictly dominant strategy When a strictly dominant strategy does not exist for either player and the optimal strategy for either player depends on what each player believes to be the strategy of the other players, the result is a non–strictly dominant strategy.

Normal-form game A game in which each player is aware of the strategy of every other player as well as the possible payoffs resulting from alternative combinations of strategies.

One-shot game A game that is played only once.

Repeated game A game that is played more than once.

Risk avoider An individual who prefers a certain payoff to a risky prospect with the same expected value. A risk avoider prefers predictable outcomes to probabilistic expectations.

Risk taker An individual who prefers a risky situations in which the expected value of a payoff is preferred to its certainty equivalent.

Sequential-move game A game in which the players move in turn.

Simultaneous-move game A game in which the players move at the same time.

Strategic behavior The actions of those who recognize that the behavior of an individual or group affect, and are affected by, the actions of other individuals or groups.

Strategic form of a game A summary of the payoffs to each player arising from every possible strategy profile.

Strategy A game plan or a decision rule that indicates what action a player will take when confronted with the need to make a decision.

Strictly dominant strategy A strategy that results in the largest payoff regardless of the strategy adopted by another player.

Strictly dominant strategy equilibrium A Nash equilibrium that results when all players have a strictly dominant strategy.

Subgame perfect equilibrium A strategy profile in a multistage game that is a Nash equilibrium and allows no player to improve on his or her payoff by switching strategies at any stage of the game.

Trigger strategy A game plan that is adopted by one player in response to unanticipated moves by the other player. A trigger strategy will continue to be used until the other player initiates yet another unanticipated move.

Weakly dominant strategy   A strategy that results in a payoff that is no lower than any other payoff regardless of the strategy adopted by the other players.

Zero-sum game   A game in which one player's gain is exactly the other player's loss.

CHAPTER QUESTIONS

13.1 In the game "rock–scissors–paper" two players in unison show a fist (rock), two fingers (scissors), or an open hand (paper). The winner of each round is determined by what hand signals the players shows. If one player shows a fist, while another shows two fingers, the first player wins because "rocks break scissors." If, on the other hand, the second player shows an open hand, then that player wins because "paper covers rock." Finally, if one player shows two fingers and the other player shows an open hand, then the second player wins because "scissors cut paper," and so on. An alternative way to play this game is to isolate the players in separate rooms, prohibiting communication between them. A third individual, the referee, goes to each room and asks the player to reveal his or her hand. After inspecting the hand of each player, the referee declares a winner. Both versions of this game may be called simultaneous-move games. Do you agree? If not, then why not?

13.2 A subgame perfect equilibrium is impossible in a game with multiple Nash equilibria. Do you agree or disagree? Explain.

13.3 Explain the difference between moves and strategies.

13.4 Suppose you and a group of your coworkers have decided to have lunch at a Japanese restaurant. It has been decided in advance that the lunch bill will be divided equally. Each person in the group is concerned about his or her share of the bill. Without explicitly agreeing to do so, each person will order from among the least expensive items on the menu. Comment.

13.5 Explain the difference between a strictly dominant strategy and a non–strictly dominant strategy equilibrium. Under what circumstances will a strictly dominant strategy lead to a non–strictly dominant strategy equilibrium?

13.6 The existence of a Nash equilibrium confirms Adam Smith's famous metaphor of the invisible hand. Do you agree with this statement? If not, then why not?

13.7 Explain the difference between a strictly dominant strategy and an iterated strictly dominant strategy.

13.8 In a two-player, simultaneous-move game with a strictly dominant strategy equilibrium, at least one of the players will adopt a secure strategy. Do you agree? If not, why not?

13.9 Explain the difference between a strictly dominant strategy and a weakly dominated strategy.

13.10 It is not possible to have multiple Nash equilibria in the presence of a subgame perfect equilibrium. Do you agree with this statement? If not, why not?

13.11 In a two-player, one-shot game, if one player has a dominant strategy, the second player will never adopt a maximin strategy. Do you agree? Explain.

13.12 Explain the difference between a strictly dominant strategy and a weakly dominant strategy.

13.13 If neither player in a noncooperative, one-shot game has a strictly dominant strategy, or if the strategy results in a weakly dominant strategy equilibrium, explain how the concept of a focal-point equilibrium might lead to a solution in game theory.

13.14 Under what conditions will trigger strategies be successful in maintaining the integrity of a collusive agreement?

13.15 The existence of a trigger strategy that punishes a violator of a cooperative agreement will eliminate the problem of cheating in a simultaneous-move, infinitely repeated game. Do you agree? Explain.

CHAPTER EXERCISES

13.1 Argon Airlines and Boron Airways are two equal-sized commercial air carriers that compete for passengers along the lucrative Boston–Albany–Buffalo route. Both firms are considering offering discount air fares during the traditionally slow month of February. The payoff matrix ($ millions) for this game is illustrated in Figure E13.1.

a. Does either firm have a strictly dominant strategy?

b. What is the Nash equilibrium for this game?

		Boron	
		Discount	No discount
Argon	Discount	(2, 3)	(7.5, 1)
	No discount	(1.5, 6)	(3, 2)

Payoffs: (Argon, Boron)

FIGURE E13.1   Payoff matrix for chapter excercise 13.1.

Firm B

	Don't cheat	Cheat
Firm A Don't cheat	(10, 10)	(−5, 20)
Cheat	(20, −5)	(5, 5)

Payoffs: (Firm A, Firm B)

FIGURE E13.2   Payoff matrix for chapter excercise 13.2.

Firm *B*

	High price	Low price
Firm *A* High price	(10, 10)	(−5, 20)
Low price	(20, −5)	(5, 5)

Payoffs: (Firm *A*, Firm *B*)

FIGURE E13.3   Payoff matrix for chapter exercise 13.3.

13.2 Consider the normal-form, one-shot game shown in Figure E13.2, involving two firms that have entered into a collusive agreement. The payoffs in the parentheses are in millions of dollars. Having entered into the agreement, both firms must decide whether to remain faithful to the agreement (*Don't cheat*) or to violate the agreement (*Cheat*).
  a. Does either firm have a dominant strategy?
  b. If both firms follow a maximin strategy, what is the strategy profile for this game? Is this strategy profile a Nash equilibrium?
  c. Suppose that firm *B* were to cheat on the agreement. What would firm *A* do?
  d. How might your answer be different if this were an infinitely repeated game? What factors not presented here must be considered?
13.3 Consider the two-person, noncooperative, non-zero-sum, simultaneous-move, one-shot pricing game shown in Figure E13.3. The numbers in the parentheses are in millions of dollars.
  a. Does either player have a strictly dominant strategy? If so, what is the dominant strategy equilibrium? Is this a Nash equilibrium?
  b. If this game were repeated an infinite number of times, would either player change strategies?
13.4 Consider Figure E13.4, a normal-form game describing the interaction between labor and management. The payoff matrix reflects management's desire for labor to work hard and labor's desire to take it easy. Management has two options. Managers can either secretly monitor

Labor

		Work hard	Goof off
Management	Observe	(–1, 1)	(1, –1)
	Don't observe	(1, –1)	(–1, 1)

Payoffs: (Management, Labor)

FIGURE E13.4   Payoff matrix for chapter exercise 13.4.

worker performance or they can trust employees to work hard on their own. Labor also has two options: to work or to goof off. The payoff matrix may be read as follows. If management secretly observes labor, management "loses" because of the time spent monitoring workers already working. Presumably labor "wins" because hard work will be rewarded with extra pay, benefits, and so on. In this case, the strategy profile {*Observe, Work hard*} has a payoff of (–1, 1). Note that the payoff is the same for the strategy profile {*Don't observe, Goof off*} because management continues to employ a "goldbrick" while the workers gain leisure time. When the strategy profile is {*Don't observe, Work hard*}, management wins because it did not incur the expense of monitoring the performance of a hard-working employee, while the worker loses because he or she could have goofed off without penalty. Finally, the strategy profile {*Observe, Goof off*} has a payoff of (1, –1) because management discovers, and presumable fires, the shirker.

    a. Does either player in this game have a dominant strategy? Explain.

    b. Does this game have a Nash equilibrium? If not, then why not?

    c. What would the absence of a Nash equilibrium suggest for optimal management–employee relations in the present context?

13.5 Consider the normal-form, simultaneous-move, one-shot game shown in Figure E13.5. Suppose that an industry consists of two firms, Magna Company and Summa Corporation. The firms produce identical products. Magna and Summa are trying to decide whether to expand (*Expand*) or not to expand (*None*) production capacity for the next operating period. Assume that each firm produces at full capacity. The trade-off facing each firm is that expansion will result in a larger market share, but increased output will put downward pressure on price. Expected profits are summarized in Figure E13.5, when the numbers in the parentheses are in millions of dollars. The first payoff is Magna's.

    a. Does either firm have a dominant strategy?

    b. What is the Nash equilibrium for this game?

13.6 Suppose that in Exercise 13.5 Magna and Summa have three options: no expansion (*None*), moderate expansion (*Moderate*), and extensive expansion (*Extensive*). Expected profits are summarized in the normal-

Summma

		None	Expand
Magna	None	(25, 25)	(15, 30)
	Expand	(30, 15)	(20, 20)

Payoffs: (Magna, Summa)

FIGURE E13.5   Payoff matrix for chapter exercise 13.5.

Summa

		None	Moderate	Extensive
	None	(25, 25)	(15, 30)	(10, 25)
Magna	Moderate	(30, 15)	(20, 20)	(8, 13)
	Extensive	(25, 10)	(12, 8)	(0, 0)

Payoffs: (Magna, Summa)

FIGURE E13.6   Payoff matrix for chapter exercise 13.6.

form game shown in Figure E13.6. What is the Nash equilibrium for this game?

13.7 Suppose that the simultaneous move game in Exercise 13.6 was modeled as a sequential-move game, with Magna moving first.

a. Illustrate the extensive form of this game.
b. What are the subgames for this game?
c. What is the Nash equilibrium for each subgame?
d. Use backward induction to find the subgame perfect equilibrium.

13.8 Consider the simultaneous-move, one-shot game shown in Figure E13.8.

a. If player B believes that player A will play strategy A, what strategy should player B adopt?
b. If player B believes that player A will play strategy B, what strategy should player B adopt?
c. Does this game have a Nash equilibrium?
d. Does this game have a unique solution?

13.9 Tom Teetotaler and Brandy Merrybuck are tobacconists specializing in three brands of pipe-weed: Barnacle Bottom, Old Toby, and Southern Star. Both Teetotaler and Merrybuck are trying to decide what brands to carry in their shops, Red Pony and Blue Dragon, respectively. Expected earnings in this simultaneous, one-shot game are summarized in the normal-form game shown in Figure E13.9.

Player B

		Strategy A	Strategy B
Player A	Strategy A	(20, 20)	(5, 25)
	Strategy B	(25, 5)	(2, 2)

Payoffs: (Player A, Player B)

FIGURE E13.8   Payoff matrix for chapter exercise 13.8.

Blue Dragon

		Narrow	Medium	Wide
	Narrow	(150, 150)	(100, 200)	(50, 250)
Red Pony	Medium	(200, 100)	(200, 200)	(150, 300)
	Wide	(250, 50)	(300, 150)	(300, 300)

Payoffs: (Red Pony, Blue Dragon)

FIGURE E13.9   Payoff matrix for chapter exercise 13.9.

Blue Dragon

		Narrow	Medium	Wide
	Narrow	(150, 150)	(200, 250)	(250, 350)
Red Pony	Medium	(250, 125)	(175, 200)	(270, 245)
	Wide	(350, 250)	(150, 275)	(200, 300)

Payoffs: (Red Pony, Blue Dragon)

FIGURE E13.10   Payoff matrix for chapter exercise 13.10.

a. What is the solution to this game?

b. Is this solution a Nash equilibrium?

13.10 Suppose that the payoffs for the game in Exercise 13.9 were as shown in Figure E13.10.

a. Does either firm have a strictly dominant strategy?

b. Is the solution for this game a Nash equilibrium?

13.11 Suppose that the simultaneous-move game in Exercise 13.10 was modeled as a sequential-move game with Red Pony moving first.

a. Illustrate the extensive form of this game.

b. What are the subgames for this game?

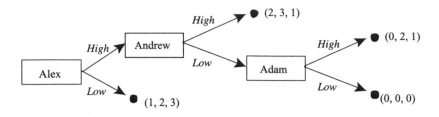

Payoffs: (Alex, Andrew, Adam)

FIGURE E13.12   Game tree for chapter exercise 13.12.

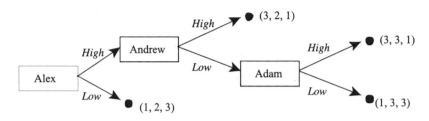

Payoffs: (Alex, Andrew, Adam)

FIGURE E13.13   Game tree for chapter exercise 13.13.

  c. What is the Nash equilibrium for each subgame?

  d. Use backward induction to find the subgame perfect equilibrium.

  13.12 Alex, Andrew, and Adam are playing the multistage game shown in Figure E13.12.

  a. What are the subgames for this game?

  b. What is the Nash equilibrium for each subgame?

  c. Use backward induction to find the subgame perfect equilibrium.

  13.13 Suppose that the multistage game for Alex, Andrew, and Adam is as shown in Figure E13.13.

  a. What are the subgames for this game?

  b. What is the Nash equilibrium for each subgame?

  c. Use backward induction to find the subgame perfect equilibrium.

  13.14 At the Hemlock Bush Tavern, Jethro (Jellyroll) Bottom announces that he will auction off an envelope containing $35. Clem and Heathcliff are the only two bidders, and each has $40. The rules of the auction are as follows:

  (1) The bidders take turns. After a bid is made, the next bidder can make either another bid or pass. The opening bid must be $10.

  (2) Succeeding bids must be in $10 increments.

  (3) Bidders cannot bid against themselves.

(4) The bidding comes to an end when either bidder passes, except on the first bid. If the first bidder passes, the second bidder is given the option of accepting the bid.

(5) The highest bidder wins.

(6) All bidders must pay Jethro the amount of their last bid.

(7) Assume that Clem bids first.

    a. Diagram the game tree for this game.

    b. Determine the subgame perfect equilibrium strategies for Clem and Heathcliff using the method of backward induction.

    c. What is the outcome of the auction?

SELECTED READINGS

Axelrod, R. *The Evolution of Cooperation.* New York: Basic Books, 1984.

Baye, M. R., and R. O. Beil. *Managerial Economics and Business Strategy.* Boston: Richard D. Irwin, 1994.

Besanko, D., D. Dranove, and M. Shanley. *Economics of Strategy,* 2nd ed. New York: John Wiley & Sons, 2000.

Bierman, H. S., and L. Fernandez. *Game Theory with Economic Applications,* 2nd ed. New York: Addison-Wesley, 1998.

Brams, S., and M. Kilgour. *Game Theory and National Security.* Oxford: Basil Blackwell, 1988.

Cournot, A. *Researches into the Mathematical Principles of the Theory of Wealth,* translated Nathaniel T. Bacon. New York: Macmillan, 1897.

Davis, O., and A. Whinston. "Externalities, Welfare, and the Theory of Games." *Journal of Political Economy,* 70 (June 1962), pp. 241–262.

de Fraja, G., and F. Delbono. "Game Theoretic Models of Mixed Oligopoly." *Economic Surveys,* 4 (1990), pp. 1–17.

Dixit, A., and B. Nalebuff. *Thinking Strategically.* New York: W. W. Norton, 1991.

Horowitz, I. "On the Effects of Cournot Rivalry between Entrepreneurial and Cooperative Firms." *Journal of Comparative Economics,* 15 (March 1991), pp. 115–211.

Luce, D. R., and H. Raiffa. *Games and Decisions: Introduction and Critical Survey.* New York: John Wiley & Sons, 1957.

Nash, J. "The Bargaining Problem." *Econometrica,* 18 (1950a), pp. 155–162.

———. "Equilibrium Points in *n*-Person Games." *Proceedings of the National Academy of Sciences, USA,* 36 (1950b), pp. 48–49.

———. "A Simple Three-Person Poker Game" (with Lloyd S. Shapley). *Annals of Mathematics Study,* 24 (1950c).

———. "Noncooperative Games." *Annals of Mathematics,* 51 (1951), pp. 286–295.

———. "A Comparison of Treatments of a Duopoly Situation" (with J. P. Mayberry and M. Shubik). *Econometrica,* 21 (1953a), pp. 141–154.

———. "Two-Person Cooperative Games." Econometrica, 21 (1953b), pp. 405–421.

Nasar, S. *A Beautiful Mind.* New York: Simon & Schuster, 1998.

Poundstone, W. *Prisoners' Dilemma.* New York: Doubleday, 1992.

Rasmusen, E. *Games and Information: An Introduction to Game Theory.* New York: Basil Blackwell, 1989.

Rubinstein, A. "Perfect Equilibrium in a Bargaining Model." *Econometrica,* 61 (1) (1982), pp. 97–109.

Schelling, T. *The Strategy of Conflict.* London: Oxford University Press, 1960.

Schotter, A. *Free Market Economics: A Critical Appraisal.* New York: St. Martin's Press, 1985.

————. Microeconomics: A Modern Approach. New York: Addison-Wesley, 1998.

Selten, R. "Reexamination of the Perfectness Concept for Equilibrium Points in Extensive Games." *International Journal of Game Theory*, 4 (1975), pp. 25–55.

Von Neumann, J., and O. Morgenstern. *Theory of Games and Economic Behavior.* New York: John Wiley & Sons, 1944.

14

RISK AND UNCERTAINTY

We have assumed throughout most of this book that the economic decisions were made under conditions of complete certainty. It was assumed that the decisions of both consumers and producers were based on complete and accurate knowledge of consumer, firm, and market conditions. In fact, however, most economic decisions are made with something less than perfect information, and the consequences of these decisions cannot, therefore, be known beforehand with any degree of precision. A manager cannot know, for example, whether the introduction of a new product will be profitable because of the uncertainty of macroeconomic conditions, consumer tastes, reactions by competitors, resource availability, input prices, labor unrest, political instability, and so forth.

In addition to the uncertainty associated with decisions made at any point in time, the uncertainty of outcomes associated with those decisions tends to increase the further we project into the future. An automobile company that plans to introduce a new model within 2 years is more likely to successfully satisfy prevailing consumer tastes in terms of styling and options, and therefore to be better able to capture a significant market share, than a company that takes 5 years to bring a new product to market. After 5 years, consumer tastes could significantly change, reducing the probability of the product's success.

A formal treatment of the decision-making process under conditions of uncertainty is well beyond the scope of this book. Nevertheless, this chapter will introduce some of the more essential elements of decision making in the absence of complete information. We begin with a formal distinction between *risk* and *uncertainty* and move on to a discussion of decision making with uncertain and risky outcomes.

RISK AND UNCERTAINTY

When one is examining the decision-making process under conditions of imperfect information, it is important to distinguish between the closely related concepts of risk and uncertainty. Risky situations involve multiple outcomes (or payoffs), where the probability of each outcome is known or can be estimated. An example of a risky situation is the flipping of a fair coin. The probability that either a head or a tail will result from flipping a fair coin is 50%. Investing in the stock market is another risky situation. While the investor cannot know with certainty the rate of return on the investment, it is possible to estimate an expected rate of return based on a company's past performance.

Definition: Risk involves choices involving multiple possible outcomes in which the probability of each outcome is known or may be estimated.

Uncertainty also involves multiple-outcomes situations. What distinguishes risk from uncertainty, however, is that with uncertainty the probability of each outcome is unknown and cannot be estimated. In many cases, these probabilities cannot be estimated because of the absence of historical evidence about the event. Nevertheless, there is a fine line between decision making under conditions of risk and of uncertainty.

Definition: Uncertainty involves choices involving multiple possible outcomes in which the probability of each outcome is unknown and cannot be estimated.

When one is considering the different ways in which managers deal with uncertain outcomes it is important to distinguish between two types of uncertainty. In situations of *complete ignorance*, the decision maker is unable to make any assumptions about the probabilities of alternative outcomes under different states of nature. In these situations, the decision maker may adopt any of a number of rational criteria to facilitate the decision-making process.

Situations involving partial ignorance, on the other hand, assume that the decision maker is able to assign subjective probabilities to multiple outcomes. Whenever the decision maker is able to use personal knowledge, intuition, and experience to assign subjective probabilities to outcomes, then decision making under uncertainty is effectively transformed into decision making under risk. In the next section, we will examine the most commonly used statistical measures of risk.

Much of the discussion that follows will deal with decision making under risk, uncertainty involving partial ignorance, or uncertainty involving complete ignorance. While the procedures for evaluating outcomes of decisions made under conditions of risk, or uncertainty involving partial ignorance, are identical, the process of evaluating outcomes under conditions of complete ignorance requires alternative approaches to the decision-making process. In spite of these distinctions, we will refer to all situations in which the probability of each outcome is not known and cannot be estimated as conditions of uncertainty. It will be clear from the context of each situation whether this involves risk or uncertainty from partial or complete ignorance.

MEASURING RISK: MEAN AND VARIANCE

MEAN (EXPECTED VALUE)

The most commonly used summary measures of risky, random payoffs are the *mean* and the *variance*. These random payoffs may refer to profits, capital gains, prices, unit sales, and so on. In risky situations, the expected value of these random payoffs is called the mean. The mean is the weighted average of all possible random outcomes, with the weights being the probability of each outcome. For discrete random variables, the expected value may be calculated using Equation (14.1)

$$E(x) = \mu = \sum_{i=1 \to n} x_i p_i \qquad (14.1)$$

where x_i is the value of the outcome, p_i is the probability of its occurrence, and $\sum_{i=1 \to n} p_i = 1$.

When the probability of each outcome is the same as the probability of every other outcome, then the expected value is the sum of the outcomes divided by the number of observations. In this case, the expected value of a set of uncertain outcomes may be calculated using Equation (14.2)

$$E(x) = \mu = \left(\frac{1}{n}\right) \sum_{i=1 \to n} x_i \qquad (14.2)$$

Definition: The mean is the expected value of a set of random outcomes. The mean is the sum of the products of each outcome and the probability of its occurrence. When the probability of the occurrence of each outcome is the same as the probability of every other outcome, the mean is the sum of the outcomes divided by the number of observations.

Problem 14.1. Suppose that the chief economist of Silver Zephyr Ltd. believes that there is a 40% ($p_1 = 0.4$) probability of a recession in the next operating period and a 60% ($p_2 = 0.6$) probability that a recession will not occur. The COO of Silver Zephyr believes that the firm will earn profits of $\pi_1 = \$100$ in the event of a recession and $\pi_2 = \$1{,}000$ otherwise. What are Silver Zephyr's expected profits?

Solution. Silver Zephyr's expected profits are

$$E(\pi) = \sum_{i=1 \to 2} \pi_i p_i = \pi_1 p_1 + \pi_2 p_2$$
$$= 0.4(100) + 0.6(1,000)$$
$$= 40 + 600 = \$640$$

Thus, Silver Zephyr's expected profits for the next operating period are $640.

Problem 14.2. Suppose that Bob mates his brother Nob the following offer. For a payment of $3.50, Bob will pay Nob the dollar value of any roll, v, of a fair die. For example, for a roll of 1, Bob will pay Nob $1. For a roll of 6, Bob will pay Nob $6. How much can Nob expect to earn if he accepts Bob's offer?

Solution. Since the probability of any number between 1 and 6 is 1/6, then Bob's expected payout is

$$E(v) = \left(\frac{1}{n}\right) \sum_{i=1 \to n} v_i$$
$$= \left(\frac{1}{6}\right)(1+2+3+4+5+6) = \left(\frac{1}{6}\right)(21) = \$3.50$$

Since it will cost $3.50 to play this game, Nob's can expect to earn $E(v) - 3.50 = \$0$. Whether Nob should accept Bob's offer will depend on Nob's attitude toward risk. An individual's attitude toward risk will be discussed in the paragraphs to follow.

VARIANCE

The strength of the mean is its simplicity. In a single number, the mean (expected value) summarizes important information about the most likely outcome of a set of random payoffs. Unfortunately, this strength hides other important information that is valuable to the decision maker. For example, suppose that an individual is offered the following fair wager. If the individual flips a coin and it comes up heads, then the individual wins $10. On the other hand, if the coin comes up tails, then the individual loses $10. The reader should verify that the expected value of the wager is $0. Suppose, on the other hand the payoffs were $1,000 and −$1,000 for a head and tail, respectively. Once again, the reader will verify that the expected value of the wager is $0. While the expected values of the two wagers are the same, clearly the wagers themselves are different. While the potential payoff is much greater than in the second scenario, so too is the potential loss. While the individual may be prepared to accept the first bet, that person may not be willing to accept the second because the possibility of such a large loss may be unacceptable. For this individual, the second wager may simply be too risky.

The second wager is riskier because the spread, or dispersion, of the possible payoffs is greater. Each has the same expected value, but the swing between a gain and a loss is considerably greater. It is this dispersion in the possible payoffs that is the distinguishing characteristic of risk. The most commonly used measure of the dispersion of a set of random outcomes is the variance. The variance is the weighed average of the squared deviations of all possible random outcomes from its mean, with the weights being the probability of each outcome. The variance of a set of random payoffs may be calculated by using Equation (14.3).

$$E\left[(x-\mu)^2\right] = \sigma^2 = \sum_{i=1 \to n} (x_i - \mu)^2 p_i \qquad (14.3)$$

When the probability of each outcome is the same, then the variance is simply the sum of the squared deviations divided by the number of outcomes.

$$E\left[(x-\mu)^2\right] = \sigma^2 = \left(\frac{1}{n}\right) \sum_{i=1 \to n} (x_i - \mu)^2 \qquad (14.4)$$

Definition: The variance of a set of random outcomes is the expected value of the squared deviations of an outcome from its mean. The variance is a measure of the dispersion of a data series around its expected value. The greater this dispersion, the greater the value of the variance. The variance is the sum of the products of the square of the deviation of each outcome from its mean and the probability of the occurrence of the outcome. When the probability of the occurrence of each outcome is the same as the probability of the occurrence of every other outcome, the mean is the sum of the squared deviations divided by the number of outcomes.

Denoting a win and a loss as x_1 and x_2, respectively, the variances of the two wagers, σ_1^2 and σ_2^2 are

$$\sigma_1^2 = \sum_{i=1 \to n} (x_i - \mu)^2 p_i = 0.5(10-0)^2 + 0.5(-10-0)^2$$
$$= 0.5(100) + 0.5(100) = 50 + 50 = 100$$

$$\sigma_1^2 = \sum_{i=1 \to n} (x_i - \mu)^2 p_i = 0.5(1,000-0)^2 + 0.5(-1,000-0)^2$$
$$= 0.5(1,000,000) + 0.5(1,000,000) = 500,000 + 500,000 = 1,000,000$$

Since $\sigma_2^2 > \sigma_1^2$, then the second wager is riskier than the first.

An alternative way to express the riskiness of a set of random outcomes is the *standard deviation*. The standard deviation is simply the square root of the variance, σ.

$$\sigma = \sqrt{\sigma^2} \qquad (14.5)$$

Definition: The standard deviation is the square root of the variance.

For the foregoing wagers the standard deviations are $\sigma_1 = \sqrt{\sigma_1^2} = \sqrt{100} = 10$ and $\sigma_2 = \sqrt{\sigma_2^2} = \sqrt{1,000,000} = 1,000$. Since the standard deviation is a monotonic transformation of the variance, the ordering of relative risks of the wagers is preserved. Thus, since $\sigma_2 > \sigma_1$ the second wager is riskier than the first.

Problem 14.3. Using the information provided in Problem 14.1, calculate the variance and the standard deviation of Silver Zephyr's expected profits.

Solution. From Problem 14.1, expected profits are $640. The variance of Silver Zephyr's expected profits is

$$
E\{[\pi - E(\pi)]^2\} = \sum_{i=1 \to 2} [\pi_i - E(\pi)]^2 \, p_i = \sigma^2
$$

$$
= [\pi_1 - E(\pi)]^2 \, p_1 + [\pi_2 - E(\pi)]^2 \, p_2
$$

$$
= 0.4(100 - 640)^2 + 0.6(1,000 - 640)^2
$$

$$
= 0.4(-540)^2 + 0.6(360)^2 = 0.4(291,600) + 0.6(129,600)
$$

$$
= 116,640 + 77,760 = \$194,400
$$

The standard deviation is

$$
\sigma = \sqrt{\sigma^2} = \sqrt{194,400} = \$440.91
$$

Problem 14.4. From Problem 14.2, calculate the variance and standard deviation of Bob's expected payout.

Solution. Since the probability of any number between 1 and 6 is 1/6, then Bob's expected payout is

$$
E\{[v - E(v)]^2\} = \left(\frac{1}{n}\right) \sum_{i=1 \to 2} [v - E(v)]^2 = \sigma^2
$$

$$
= \left(\frac{1}{n}\right)\{[v_1 - E(v)]^2 + [v_2 - E(v)]^2 + \ldots + [v_6 - E(v)]^2
$$

$$
= \left(\frac{1}{6}\right)[(1 - 3.5)^2 + (2 - 3.5)^2 + (3 - 3.5)^2 + (4 - 3.5)^2
$$

$$
+ (5 - 3.5)^2 + (6 - 3.5)^2]
$$

$$
= \left(\frac{1}{6}\right)[(-2.5)^2 + (-1.5)^2 + (-0.5)^2 + (0.5)^2 + (-1.5)^2 + (-2.5)^2]
$$

$$
= \left(\frac{1}{6}\right)[6.25 + 2.25 + 0.25 + 0.25 + 2.25 + 6.25] = \left(\frac{1}{6}\right)(17.5)
$$

$$
= \$2.92
$$

The standard deviation is

$$
\sigma = \sqrt{\sigma^2} = \sqrt{2.92} = \$1.71
$$

COEFFICIENT OF VARIATION

Unfortunately, neither the variance nor the standard deviation can be used to compare the riskiness involving two or more risky situations with different expected values. The reason for this is that neither measure is independent of the units of measurement. To measure the relative riskiness of two or more outcomes, we may use the coefficient of variation, which may be calculated by using Equation (14.6). The coefficient of variation allows us to compare the riskiness of alternative projects by "normalizing" the standard deviation of each by its expected value.

$$CV = \frac{\sigma}{\mu} \qquad (14.6)$$

Definition: The coefficient of variation is a dimensionless number that is used to compare risk involving two or more outcomes involving different expected values. It is calculated as the ratio of the standard deviation to the mean.

Problem 14.5. Suppose that capital investment project A has an expected value of $\mu_A = \$100,000$ and a standard deviation of $\sigma_A = \$30,000$. Additionally, suppose that project B has an expected value $\mu_B = \$150,000$ and a standard deviation of $\sigma_B = \$40,000$. Which is the relatively riskier project?

Solution. From Equation (14.6) the relative riskiness of projects A and B are

$$CV_A = \frac{\sigma_A}{\mu_A} = \frac{30,000}{100,000} = 0.300$$

$$CV_B = \frac{\sigma_B}{\mu_B} = \frac{40,000}{150,000} = 0.267$$

Thus, although project B has the larger standard deviation, it is the relatively less risky project.

CONSUMER BEHAVIOR AND RISK AVERSION

Suppose that a manager is confronted with the choice of two investment projects with the same expected rate of return. Which project will the manager choose? Most managers will select the project with the lowest risk, that is, the one with the smallest standard deviation. These managers are said to be *risk averse*. On the other hand, *risk-loving* managers would choose the riskier project. Managers who are indifferent to risk are said to be *risk neutral*. The reason for these differences in managers' behavior toward risk may be explained in terms of the *marginal utility of money*.

In Figure 14.1, which illustrates three total utility of money functions, money income or wealth is measured along the horizontal axis, and a car-

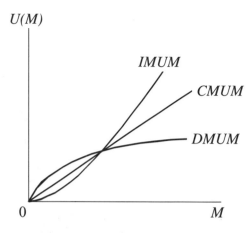

FIGURE 14.1 Increasing, constant, and diminishing marginal utility of money.

dinal index of the utility (satisfaction) of money is measured along the vertical axis. The three total utility of money functions in Figure 14.1 illustrate the concepts of constant marginal utility of money (*CMUM*), increasing marginal utility of money (*IMUM*), and diminishing marginal utility of money (*DMUM*). When conditions of increasing marginal utility of money exist, as more money income is received, the total utility of money increases at an increasing rate. Similarly, constant marginal utility of money means that the total utility of money increases at a constant rate. Finally, decreasing marginal utility of money means that the total utility of money increases at a decreasing rate.

Most individuals are risk averse because their total utility of money function exhibits decreasing marginal utility. To see this, consider an individual who offers the following wager. If the individual flips a coin that comes up "heads," then the individual wins $1,000. On the other hand, if the individual flips a coin that comes up "tails," then the individual loses $1,000. The coin is assumed to be "fair" so there is an even chance of flipping either "heads" or "tails." If we denote the value of the wager as M, the expected value of this wager is $E(M) = 0.5(-\$1,000) + 0.5(\$1,000) = -\$5,000 + \$5,000 = 0$. This wager is sometimes referred to as a *fair gamble* because the expected value of the payoff is zero.

Definition: A fair gamble is one in which the expected value of the payoff is zero.

Problem 14.6. Lugg Hammerhands has been offered the following wager (*M*). Blindfolded, Lugg may draw a single marble from an urn containing 10 marbles that are perfectly identical in terms of size, shape, and weight. Nine of the marbles in the urn are green and one marble is red. If Lugg draws a green marble, then he loses $50. If Lugg draws the red marble, wins $450. Is this a fair gamble?

Solution. The expected value of the wager is

$$E(M) = 0.9(-\$50) + 0.1(\$450) = -\$45 + \$45 = 0$$

Since the expected value of the wager is zero, then this is a fair gamble.

Problem 14.7. In the United States, many state governments sponsor lotteries to support of public education. In New York State, for example, $1 purchases two games of Lotto. Each game involves selecting six of 59 numbers. The New York State Lottery Commission randomly draws six numbers, and whoever has selected the correct combination wins, or shares, the top prize, which is in the millions of dollars. According to the New York State Lottery Commission, the odds of winning the top prize on a $1 bet are 1 in 22,528,737. Suppose, for example, that the top prize is $20 million. Is this a fair gamble?

Solution. Denoting a $1 wager as M, the expected value of one player winning the top prize is

$$E(M) = \left(\frac{1}{22{,}528{,}737}\right)(20{,}000{,}000) + \left(\frac{22{,}528{,}736}{22{,}528{,}737}\right)(-1) = -0.11$$

Since the expected value is negative, then this game of Lotto is an unfair gamble.

More formally, the utility of money function may be written as

$$U = U(M) \tag{14.7}$$

Utility is assumed to be an increasing function of money, that is, $dU/dM > 0$. Constant marginal utility of money requires that $d^2U/dM^2 = 0$. Increasing marginal utility of money requires that $d^2U/dM^2 > 0$. Diminishing marginal utility of money requires that $d^2U/dM^2 < 0$. The utility of money function of risk-averse individuals exhibits diminishing marginal utility of money (i.e., the total utility of money increases at a decreasing rate). The reason for this is that a risk-averse individual will experience a greater loss of utility by losing $1,000 than he or she would gain by winning $1,000. To see this, consider once again the fair gamble of winning or losing $1,000 on the flip of a coin.

Suppose that the individual's utility of money function is $U = 100M^{0.5}$. The reader will readily verify that this total utility of money function exhibits diminishing marginal utility of money, since $dU/dM = 50M^{-0.5} > 0$ and $d^2U/dM^2 = -25M^{-1.5} < 0$. As we saw earlier, this is a fair gamble because $E(M) = (1,000)0.5 + (-1,000)0.5 = 0$. Even though this is a fair gamble, a risk-averse individual would not accept the wager. To see this, suppose that the individual's initial money wealth is $M = \$50,000$. The utility of money for this individual is $U = 100(50,000)^{0.5} = 22,361$ units. Now, suppose that the individual flips "heads" and wins $1,000. The individual's new money wealth is $M' = \$51,000$. The individual's total utility of money is $U = 100(51,000)^{0.5}$

= 22,583 units. That is, the individual gains 222 utility units. Suppose, on the other hand, that the individual flips "tails" and loses $1,000. The individual's new money wealth is now $49,000. The individual's total utility of money is $U = 100(49,000)^{0.5} = 22,136$ units. In this case, the individual's utility index falls by 225. The expected change in utility from the bet is

$$E(\Delta U) = \sum_{i=1 \to n} (\Delta U_i)p_i = (\Delta U_1)p_1 + (\Delta U_2)p_2$$
$$= (222)0.5 + (-225)0.5 = -15 \text{ units}$$

Since the expected utility change is negative, this individual will not accept this fair gamble.

There is yet another way to interpret risk-averse behavior. In the example just given, a risk-averse individual would prefer not to bet, a sure amount of zero than to wager $1,000 with an expected value of zero. In other words, a risk-averse individual will not accept a fair gamble. Denoting the sure amount as M, a risk-averse individual will prefer a sure amount to its expected value, that is, $M > E(M)$. An individual is said to be risk loving if the reverse is true; that is, the expected value of a payoff is preferred to its certainty equivalent, or $E(M) > M$. Finally, an individual who is indifferent between a certain payoff and its expected value, that is, $M \approx E(M)$, is said to be risk neutral.

It should be noted that while most individuals are risk averse most of the time, under certain circumstances they may be risk loving. In particular, many risk-averse individuals are risk loving for small gambles. An individual who, for example, is willing to wager $1.00 on the flip of a coin may would not be willing to wager $1,000. In the first instance $E(M) > M$, but in the second instance $M > E(M)$. In Problem 14.7, we saw that playing Lotto is an unfair gamble. Yet, risk-averse individuals frequently play Lotto because it involves a very small wager and a potentially very large payoff.

Definition: An individual is risk averse if he or she prefers a sure amount to a risky payoff with the same expected value.

Definition: An individual is risk loving when the expected value of a risky payoff is preferred to a sure amount of the same value.

Definition: An individual is risk neutral when the individual is indifferent between a sure amount and a risky payoff with the same expected value.

Problem 14.8. Suppose that an individual is offered the fair gamble of receiving $1,000 on the flip of a coin showing heads and losing $1,000 on the flip of a fair coin showing tails. Suppose further that the individual's utility of money function is

$$U = M^{1.1}$$

a. For positive money income, what is this individual's attitude toward risk?
b. If the individual's initial money income is $50,000, will he or she accept this bet? Explain.

Solution

a. The first derivative of the utility function with respect to money income is

$$\frac{dU}{dM} = (1.1)M^{0.1} > 0$$

That is, the individual's utility is an increasing function of money income. The second derivative of the utility function with respect to money income is

$$\frac{d^2U}{dM^2} = (0.1)(1.1)M^{-0.9} > 0$$

Since the second derivative of the utility function with respect to money income is positive, this individual is a risk lover.

b. Suppose, for example, that the individual's initial money income is $M = \$50,000$. At this level of money income the index of the utility of money is

$$U = (50,000)^{1.1} = 147,525.47$$

If the individual wins $1,000, then the corresponding utility index is

$$U = (51,000)^{1.1} = 150,774.26$$

That is, $\Delta U_1 = 3,248.79$.

If the individual's loses $1,000, then the corresponding utility index is

$$U = (49,000)^{1.1} = 144,283.17$$

That is, $\Delta U_2 = -3,242.30$.

The expected utility of the bet is given as

$$E(\Delta U) = \sum_{i=1 \to n} (\Delta U_i)p_i = (\Delta U_1)p_1 + (\Delta U_2)p_2$$
$$= (3,248.79)0.5 + (-3,241.70)0.5 = 3.55$$

Since the expected utility change from the bet is positive, this risk-loving individual will accept this fair bet.

EXAMPLES OF RISK-AVERSE
CONSUMER BEHAVIOR

Knowledge of risk-averse behavior by consumers has a wide range of applications in managerial decision making. Suppose, for example, that a firm plans to introduce a new brand of coffee. Suppose further that the new brand has only one competitor. Will knowledge of risk-averse behavior by consumers influence the firm's marketing strategy? The challenge to the firm is to persuade consumers to give the new brand of coffee a try. If both brands cost the same, then a risk-averse consumer will tend to stay with the old brand rather than switch to the new brand with an uncertain outcome. This, of course, suggests two possible marketing strategies. Either the firm can offer the product, at least initially, at a lower price to compensate the consumer for the risk of trying the new brand, or the firm can adopt an advertising campaign designed to convince the consumer that the new brand is superior. Either marketing strategy will raise the expected value to the consumer of trying the new brand.

Another example of the consequences of risk-averse behavior relates to the benefits enjoyed by chain stores and franchise operations over independently owned and operated retail operations. A risk-averse American tourist visiting, say, Athens, Greece, for the first time is more likely to have his or her first meal at McDonald's or Burger King rather than sample native victuals at a neighborhood bistro. The reason for this is that the risk-averse tourist may initially prefer a familiar meal of predictable quality to exotic menus of unpredictable quality. Of course, this will very likely change as the tourist over time becomes familiar with the indigenous cuisine and the reputation of local dining establishments. It is left as an exercise for the student to explain why large retail chain stores or franchise operations are typically found in areas in which there are a relatively large number of out-of-town visitors.

Perhaps the most familiar example of risk-averse behavior relates to the purchase of insurance. People purchase insurance, which typically involves small premium payments (relative to the potential loss), to protect themselves against the possibility of catastrophic financial loss. Many homeowners, for example, purchase fire insurance in the unlikely event that their house will burn down. If the insurance premiums for given level of financial protection are equal to the expected value of financial loss resulting from a fire, then this may be viewed as a fair gamble. For a fair gamble, a risk-averse homeowner will purchase fire insurance because he or she prefers a sure outcome to a risky prospect of equal expected value. Because of the difficulties associated with estimating the probability of catastrophic loss, it should not be surprising that insurance companies employ actuaries to determine insurance premiums.

FIRM BEHAVIOR AND RISK AVERSION

As the examples thus for illustrate, an understanding of consumer behavior in situations of risk and uncertainty is an important element in the pricing and output decisions of firms. Risk and uncertainty also have important implications for the firm's investment and production decisions. The concepts introduced in the foregoing discussion of decision making by consumers under conditions of risk are directly applicable to decision making by managers.

RISK-ADJUSTED DISCOUNT RATES

Chapter 12 introduced the concept of the net present value of a capital investment project. The reader will recall that the net present value of a capital project is the difference between the net present value of cash inflows and cash outflows. If the net present value of a project is negative, then it should be rejected. If the net present value of a project is positive, then the project should be considered for adoption. It was demonstrated that the net present value method could be used to evaluate projects of equal or equivalently equal lives. In general, when this method is used, projects with higher net present values are preferred to projects with lower net present values. Equation (12.26) summarizes the net present value of a project as the difference between cash inflows (revenues), R_t, and cash outflows, O_t.

$$NPV = \frac{\sum_{t=1 \to n} R_t}{(1+K)^t} - \frac{\sum_{t=1 \to n} O_t}{(1+k)^t} \qquad (12.26)$$

where k is the appropriate discount rate. Recall from Chapter 12 that the rate of interest used to discount a cash flow is called the *discount rate*. The reader will immediately recognize that calculations of net present value by means of Equation (12.26) are made under conditions of certainty. No mention was made of the potential the riskiness of alternative capital investment projects under consideration.

The use of risk-adjusted discount rates introduces the investor's attitude toward risk directly into the manager's net present value calculations. In Figure 14.2, which illustrates three possible risk–return trade-off functions, the riskiness of a capital investment project, measured as the standard deviation of the expected rate of return, is measured along the horizontal axis, and the discount rate (k), interpreted as the expected rate of return on an investment, or portfolio of investments, is measured along the vertical axis.

The risk–return trade-offs illustrated in Figure 14.2 are called investor *indifference curves*. These indifference curves summarize the expected rates of return that an investor must receive in excess of the expected rate of return from risk-free investment to compensate for the risk associated with a particular investment project. Risk–return indifference curves also reflect the investor's different attitudes toward risk. To see this, consider a risk-free investment where $\sigma = 0$. Here, the risk-free rate of return for each investor is k_{rf}. For a risky investment in which $\sigma > 0$, however, the investor must be compensated with a *risk premium*.

Definition: Investor indifference curves summarize the combinations of risk and expected rate of return for which the investor will be indifferent between a risky and a risk-free investment.

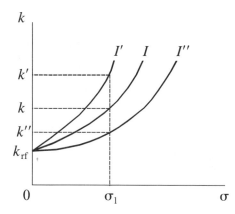

FIGURE 14.2 Investor risk–return indifference curves.

The risk premium on an investment is the difference between the expected rate of return on a risky investment and the expected rate of return on a risk-free investment. The size of the risk premium will depend on the investor's attitude toward risk. Consider, for example, the investor's indifference curve I in Figure 14.2. In this case, a risk premium of $k - k_{rf}$ is required to make this investor indifferent between an investment with risk $\sigma_1 > 0$ and a risk-free investment, $\sigma = 0$. On the other hand, the indifference curve labeled I' illustrates the risk–return trade-offs of a more risk-averse investor. In this case, the investor will require a larger risk premium, $(k' - k_{rf}) > (k - k_{rf})$ as compensation for the same level of risk incurred. Similarly, the indifference curve labeled I'' summarizes the risk–return trade-offs for a less risk-averse investor. Here, a risk premium of $(k'' - k_{rf}) < (k - k_{rf})$ is required to make this investor indifferent to a risk-free investment.

Definition: A risk premium is the difference between the expected rate of return on a risky investment and the expected rate of return on a risk-free investment.

The risk–return indifference curves may be used to evaluate *mutually exclusive* and *independent* investment projects. The reader may recall from Chapter 12 that projects are mutually exclusive if acceptance of one project means rejection of all other projects. Projects are said to be independent if the cash flows from alternative projects are unrelated to each other. Figure 14.3 illustrates management's risk–return indifference curve and three mutually exclusive investment opportunities. As measured by the standard deviation of the expected rates of return, projects A, B, and C are assumed to be equally risky.

The reader may well question the usefulness of proceeding in this manner. After all, when confronted with alternative, mutually exclusive investment projects of equivalent risk, is it not logical to presume that management would choose the project with the highest rate of return? The

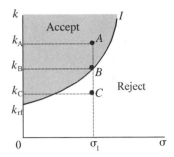

FIGURE 14.3 Risk–return indifference curve and alternative investment projects.

answer to this question is yes, but only if the investment project with the highest expected rate of return is acceptable. It should be readily apparent from Figure 14.3 that only risk–return combinations in the shaded region, such as project A, represent acceptable investments. The reason for this is that expected rate of return from project A (k_A) is greater than the expected rate of return required to make management indifferent between accepting or rejecting the project (k_B). By contrast, the rate of return from project B (k_B) is just sufficient to compensate management for the risk incurred. Clearly, if the projects are mutually exclusive, the investor will prefer project A to project B. On the other hand, project C is unacceptable and will be rejected outright because the rate of return (k_C) is not sufficient to compensate the investor for the risk incurred. Thus, any risk–return combination in the unshaded region will be rejected by a risk-averse investor. By contrast, if the projects under consideration are independent, then the investor will choose project A and may choose project B, but will reject project C.

We have suggested that knowledge of the expected rate of return and of the riskiness of a project, as measured by the standard deviation, is not sufficient to identify the manager's optimal investment strategy. It is also necessary to know the investor's attitude toward risk, which is summarized in the investor's risk–return indifference curve. To amplify this point, consider the situation depicted in Figure 14.4.

The reader will visually verify from Figure 14.4 that the expected rate of return from project C is greater than that from project D, which is greater than the expected rate of return from project A. Finally, project B has the lowest expected rate of return. On the other hand, as measured by the standard deviation of the expected rates of return, project C is the riskiest of the four projects, while project B is the least risky. It should be clear from Figure 14.4 that if projects A, B, and C are independent, then management will accept projects B and D, but will reject project C. Since point A lies on the risk–return indifference curve, the investor is indifferent between accepting or rejecting project A. On the other hand, if the projects are mutu-

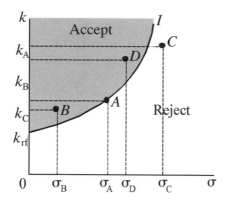

FIGURE 14.4 Risk-indifference curve and alternative investment projects.

ally exclusive, should management will accept project B or project D? The answer to this question will be addressed in the next section.

RISK–RETURN INDIFFERENCE MAP

We saw in the preceding section that knowledge of the expected rates of return and standard deviations of alternative investment projects is not sufficient to determine the investor's optimal investment strategy. An understanding of the individual's attitude toward risk is absolutely essential for determining the optimal investment strategy. We also saw that an investor's indifference curve summarizes the combinations of risk and return at which the investor will be indifferent between a risky and a risk-free investment. Each investor has a "map" of such risk–return indifference curves. Consider the investor's indifference map in Figure 14.5.

The concept of an investor indifference curve is similar to that of the consumer's indifference curve of utility theory (see Appendix 3′A). The higher the risk–return indifference curve, the greater the investor's level of utility (satisfaction). In Figure 14.5, for example, the risk–return combinations summarized by indifference curve I_3 are preferred to those of I_2 because for any given level of risk, the investor receives a higher expected rate of return. Each investor has an infinite number of such risk–return indifference curves, and each investor has a unique indifference map. Return again to Figure 14.4. Will the investor choose project A or project B? If project B lies on a higher risk–return indifference curve, which seems likely, then project B will be preferred to project A.

EQUILIBRIUM

Suppose that an investor is considering investing a certain amount in both a risky asset and a risk-free asset. If the investor invests the entire

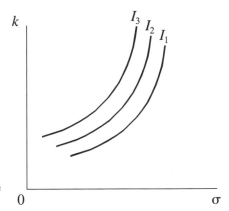

FIGURE 14.5 Investor's indifference map.

amount in the risk-free asset, he or she will earn the expected risk-free rate of return, k_{rf}. If the investor's portfolio includes a combination of the risky and risk-free assets, the expected rate of return from the combination of risky and risk-free assets is

$$k_p = \theta k_{rf} + (1 - \theta)k_r \qquad (14.8)$$

where k_p is expected return from the portfolio of assets, θ is the percentage of the portfolio comprising the risk-free asset, and $(1 - \theta)$ is the percentage of the portfolio made up of the risky asset, k_r. Equation (14.8) is simply a weighted average of the expected return from the individual assets in the portfolio.

The relationship between the expected rate of return and riskiness of the portfolio consisting of risky and risk-free assets is called the *capital market line*. Figure 14.6 illustrates two capital market lines, M_0 and M_1. The equation of the capital market line is

$$k_p = k_{rf} + \left(\frac{k_r - k_{rf}}{\sigma_r} \right) \sigma_p \qquad (14.9)$$

where k_p is the expected rate of return, σ_p is the standard deviation of returns on the portfolio, and σ_r is the standard deviation of returns on the risky assets.[1]

Definition: The capital market line summarizes the market opportunities available to an investor from a portfolio consisting of alternative combinations of risky and risk-free investments.

The slope of the capital market line is the difference between the expected rate of return from the risky asset and the expected rate of return

---

[1] The slope of the linear capital market line is $\Delta k_p / \Delta \sigma_p$. Starting at the vertical axis, $\Delta \sigma_p = \sigma_r - \sigma_p = \sigma_r - 0 = \sigma_r$ and $\Delta k_p = k^r - k^{rf}$. Thus, the slope of the capital market line is $(k^r - k^{rf})/\sigma_r$.

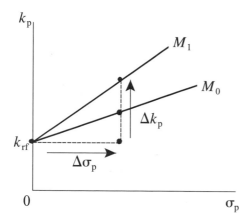

FIGURE 14.6 Investor's opportunity set.

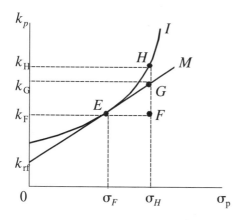

FIGURE 14.7 Investor equilibrium.

from the risk-free asset, divided by the standard deviation of the risky asset, $(k_r - k_{rf})/\sigma_r$, which is called the *market risk premium*. The slope of the capital market line is the expected return on a portfolio of risky and risk-free assets. The steeper the slope of the capital market line, the greater the additional expected rate of return from higher levels of risk associated with holding a greater percentage of the risky asset. In Figure 14.6, the capital market line M_1 represents the higher expected rate of return that is required to compensate the investor for any given level of additional risk incurred.

In Figure 14.7, point E represents the highest risk–return indifference curve that this investor can attain given the capital market line M. At point E, the slope of the risk–return indifference curve is equal to the slope of the capital market line. Equilibrium requires that the expected rate of return on an efficient portfolio of risky and risk-free assets be equal to the expected rate of return at which the investor is indifferent between a risky and a risk-free investment.

There are, of course, other portfolios with equivalent risk–return trade-offs, such as point H in Figure 14.7, that are equally preferred to portfolio E, but these portfolios are not attainable given the amount of the invest-ment and the expected rates of return on risky and risk-free assets. Portfo-lio H, for example, has a higher level of risk, σ_H, than portfolio E. For the investor to assume this higher level of risk, he or she would have to be com-pensated with the additional expected rate of return, $k_H - k_F$, which is not possible. An increase in the expected risk-free rate of return or an increase in the market risk premium, $(k_r - k_{rf})/\sigma_r$, would enable the investor to pur-chase portfolio H by moving the investor to a higher risk–return indiffer-ence curve.

Problem 14.9. Webb Ungoliant has just won \$1,000,000 in the state lottery. Webb has decided to invest his winnings in either U.S. Treasury bills that yield a risk-free expected rate of return of 5%, or risky equity shares in the Lugburz Corporation, which has an expected rate of return of 11%. Webb has analyzed the company's past performance and has determined that the standard deviation of returns is \$3 per share. Suppose that Webb's invest-ment utility function is

$$U = k_p - \sigma_p^2$$

where k_p and σ_p are the portfolio's expected return and standard deviation on the portfolio, respectively. How should Webb's investment be divided between risk-free U.S. Treasury bonds and risky Lugburz shares?

Solution. From Equation (14.9), the capital market line is

$$k_p = k_{rf} + \left(\frac{k_r - k_{rf}}{\sigma_r}\right)\sigma_p = 5 + \left(\frac{11-5}{3}\right)\sigma_p = 5 + 2\sigma_p$$

The problem confronting Webb Ungoliant is to create a portfolio of U.S. Treasury bonds and Lugburz shares that maximizes his investment utility subject to a fixed investment of \$1,000,000. This problem may be conve-niently expressed as the constrained maximization problem

$$\text{Maximize:} \quad U(k_p, \sigma_p) = k_p - \sigma_p^2$$

$$\text{Subject to:} \quad k_p = 5 + 2\sigma_p$$

There are at least two solution methods to this problem, which were dis-cussed in Chapter 2. One approach to this constrained profit maximization problem is the substitution method. Substituting the capital market line into the objective function yields

$$U = k_p - \sigma_p^2 = 5 + 2\sigma_p - \sigma_p^2$$

The first-order condition for maximizing this equation with respect to σ_p is

$$\frac{dU}{d\sigma_p} = 2 - 2\sigma_p = 0$$

which yields the solution value

$$2\sigma_p = 2$$

$$\sigma_p{}^* = 1\%$$

Note that $d^2U/d\sigma_p{}^2 = -2 < 0$, which is the second-order condition for utility maximization. Substituting this solution value into the equation for the capital market line results in the expected return from the portfolio:

$$k_p{}^* = 5 + 2(1) = 7\%$$

The composition of Webb's portfolio is

$$k_p = \theta k_{rf} + (1 - \theta)k_r$$

where k_p is expected return from the portfolio of the risky and risk-free assets, p is the percentage of the portfolio consisting of the risk-free asset, and $(1 - p)$ is the percentage of the portfolio consisting of the risky asset. Substituting yields

$$7 = \theta(5) + (1 - \theta)11$$

$$\theta = 0.6667$$

or 66.67% of Webb Ungoliant's portfolio consists of U.S. Treasury bills and $(1 - \theta) = 0.3333$, or 33.33% consists of Lugburz shares.

An alternative solution to this problem is the Lagrange multiplier method. The first step in the Lagrange multiplier method is to bring all terms to left side of the constraint.

$$k_p - 5 - 2\sigma_p = 0$$

The resulting Lagrange function may be written as

$$\mathcal{L}(k_p, \sigma_p, \lambda) = k_p - \sigma_p{}^2 + \lambda(k_p - 5 - 2\sigma_p)$$

The first-order conditions for a maximum are

$$\frac{\partial \mathcal{L}}{\partial k_p} = 1 + \lambda = 0$$

$$\frac{\partial \mathcal{L}}{\partial \sigma_p} = -2\sigma_p - 2\lambda = 0$$

$$\frac{\partial \mathcal{L}}{\partial \lambda} = k_p - 5 - 2\sigma_p = 0$$

Assuming that the second-order conditions for a maximum are satisfied, the simultaneous solution of this system of equations yields the solution values

$$K_p{}^* = 7\%; \sigma_p{}^* = 1\%; \lambda^* = -1$$

As demonstrated in Chapter 2, the Lagrange multiplier is the marginal change in the maximum value of the objective function with respect to a parametric change in the value of the constraint. In the present example, the constraint is the expected rate of return on the portfolio. The value of the Lagrange multiplier is

$$\lambda^* = \frac{\partial \mathscr{L}}{\partial k_p} = \frac{\partial U^*}{\partial k_p} = -1$$

From the value of the Lagrange multiplier, we can say that in the limit, an increase of 1% in expected portfolio rate or return will reduce the maximum value Webb's investment utility index by 1 unit. By construction, the optimization procedure guarantees that Webb's investment utility function will always be maximized subject to the capital market line. Altering the expected rate of return on the portfolio will simply change the maximum value of U^*.

Our discussion of the selection of an optimal portfolio was very simple. It was restricted to the choice of the optimal combination of a single risk-free and a single risky asset. A more realistic discussion of the selection of an optimal portfolio must include the possibility of multiple risk-free and risky asset holdings. Although a more extensive treatment of optimal portfolio selection is beyond the scope of this book, the preceding discussion underscores the importance of identifying the investor's behavior toward risk when constraints on alternative investment opportunities are under consideration. For a more detailed treatment of this and related topics dealing with portfolio optimization, the reader is encouraged to consult a text on financial management, such as Brigham, Gapenski, and Ehrhardt (1998).

In Chapter 12 we considered the net present value method for evaluating alternative capital investment projects. We are now in a position to adjust the net present value method to explicitly consider the relative riskiness of the alternative capital projects. We will begin the discussion by rewriting Equation (12.26) as

$$NPV = \frac{\sum\limits_{t=1 \to n} (R_t - O_t)}{(1+k)^t} \tag{14.10}$$

where $(R_t - O_t)$ represents the firm's net revenues on an investment and k is the discount rate. Suppose, for example, that a firm is considering investing in a project that promises annual net revenues of $100,000 for the next

5 years. If the risk-free discount rate is 10%, then the net present value of this investment project is

$$NPV = \frac{\sum_{t=1\to5} (\$100,000)}{(1.10)^t} = \$100,000 \sum_{t=1\to5} \left(\frac{1}{1.10}\right)^t$$

$$= \$100,000 \left[\left(\frac{1}{1.10}\right)^1 + \left(\frac{1}{1.10}\right)^2 + \left(\frac{1}{1.10}\right)^3 + \left(\frac{1}{1.10}\right)^4 + \left(\frac{1}{1.10}\right)^5 \right]$$

$$= \$100,000(0.91 + 0.83 + 0.75 + 0.68 + 0.62) = \$379,000$$

Suppose, on the other hand, the investor perceives the project as risky and uses a risk-adjusted discount rate of 20%. The net present value of the project is

$$NPV = \frac{\sum_{t=1\to5} (\$100,000)}{(1.20)^t} = \$100,000 \sum_{t=1\to5} \left(\frac{1}{1.10}\right)^t$$

$$= \$100,000 \left[\left(\frac{1}{1.20}\right)^1 + \left(\frac{1}{1.20}\right)^2 + \left(\frac{1}{1.20}\right)^3 + \left(\frac{1}{1.20}\right)^4 + \left(\frac{1}{1.20}\right)^5 \right]$$

$$= \$100,000(0.83 + 0.69 + 0.58 + 0.48 + 0.40) = \$298,000$$

Since the net present value of the investment is positive, the project will be considered for adoption. On the other hand, it should be clear from the example that, *ceteris paribus*, riskier investment projects are less preferred.

Definition: Risk-adjusted discount rates are used when one is calculating net present values to compensate for the perceived riskiness of an investment. The greater the perceived risk, the higher will be the discount rate used to calculate the net present value.

Problem 14.10. Suppose that the Orcrist Sword and Blade Company is considering an expansion of its production capability by purchasing a new grinding and polishing machine. While the cost of the investment is known with certainty, the cash inflows are not. The cost of the machine is $100,000 and the expected annual cash inflows are $40,000 annually for 5 years.

a. Should Orcrist consider the investment if the discount rate is 10%?

b. Suppose that the riskiness of expected cash inflows is such that management requires a 30% rate of return. Should Orcrist consider this investment?

Solution

a. At a discount rate of 10%, the net present value of this investment project is

$$NPV = \sum_{t=1 \to n}\left[\frac{R_t}{(1+k)^t}\right] - O_0 = \frac{\sum\limits_{t=1 \to 5}(\$40,000)}{(1.10)^t} - \$100,000$$

$$= \$400,000\sum_{t=1 \to 5}\left(\frac{1}{1.10}\right)^t - \$100,000$$

$$= \$400,000\left[\left(\frac{1}{1.10}\right)^1 + \left(\frac{1}{1.10}\right)^2 + \left(\frac{1}{1.10}\right)^3 + \left(\frac{1}{1.10}\right)^4 + \left(\frac{1}{1.10}\right)^5\right]$$

$$-\$100,000$$

$$= \$40,000(0.83 + 0.69 + 0.58 + 0.48 + 0.40) - \$100,000$$

$$= \$51,600$$

Since the net present value of the investment project is positive, Orcrist should undertake the investment.

b. At a risk-adjusted discount rate of 30%, the net present value of this investment project is

$$NPV = \sum_{t=1 \to n}\left[\frac{R_t}{(1+k)^t}\right] - O_0$$

$$= \frac{\sum\limits_{t=1 \to 5}(\$40,000)}{(1.30)^t} - \$100,000 = \$400,000\sum_{t=1 \to 5}\left(\frac{1}{1.30}\right)^t - \$100,000$$

$$= \$40,000\left[\left(\frac{1}{1.30}\right)^1 + \left(\frac{1}{1.30}\right)^2 + \left(\frac{1}{1.30}\right)^3 + \left(\frac{1}{1.30}\right)^4 + \left(\frac{1}{1.30}\right)^5\right]$$

$$-\$100,000$$

$$= \$40,000(0.77 + 0.59 + 0.46 + 0.35 + 0.27) - \$100,000$$

$$= \$2,400$$

Since the net present value of the risk-adjusted investment project is negative, Orcrist should not undertake the expansion.

Although the foregoing examples highlight the importance of considering the potential riskiness of investment projects, they suffer from at least two shortcomings. The first deals with the subjective selection of the risk-adjusted discount rate. In general, it will not be possible to consistently and objectively determine the risk-adjusted discount rate, especially in the absence of historical data. Another, more conceptual, shortcoming is that the risk-adjusted discount rate approach does not explicitly consider the investor's attitude toward risk. While the first shortcoming is problematic, it is possible to compensate for the second shortcoming by evaluating potential investments by using the *certainty-equivalent approach*.

CERTAINTY-EQUIVALENT APPROACH

Earlier, the perceived riskiness of an investment was incorporated into the net present value method by raising the discount rate. Recall from Chapter 12 that the net present value of a project may be calculated as

$$NPV = CF_0 + \frac{CF_1}{(1+k)^1} + \frac{CF_2}{(1+k)^2} + \ldots + \frac{CF_n}{(1+k)^n}$$

$$= \frac{\sum_{t=0 \to n} CF_t}{(1+k)^t} \tag{12.25}$$

where CF_t is the expected net cash flow in period t, k is the cost of capital, and n is the life of the project. Net cash flows are defined as the difference between cash inflows (revenues), R_t, and cash outflows, O_t. Thus, Equation (12.25) was rewritten as

$$NPV = \frac{\sum_{t=0 \to n} R_t}{(1+k)^t} - \frac{\sum_{t=0 \to n} O_t}{(1+k)^t}$$

$$= \frac{\sum_{t=1 \to n} (R_t - O_t)}{(1+k)^t} \tag{12.26}$$

By contrast, the certainty-equivalent approach incorporates risk into the net present value method by multiplying expected net cash flows by the term α_t, which is called the *certainty-equivalent coefficient*. The new expression is

$$NPV = \frac{\sum_{t=1 \to n} \alpha_t(R_t - O_t)}{(1+k)^t} = \frac{\sum_{t=1 \to n} \alpha_t CF_t}{(1+k)^t} \tag{14.11}$$

The certainty-equivalent coefficient is defined as the ratio of a risk-free net cash flow to its equivalent risky cash flow

$$\alpha_t = \frac{CF_t^*}{CF_t} \tag{14.12}$$

where CF_t^* is the risk-free cash flow and CF_t is the actual, risky cash flow that is considered to be equivalent to CF_t^*. Since $CF_t^* \leq CF_t$, then $0 \leq \alpha_t \leq 1$. When $CF_t^* = CF_t$, then $\alpha_t = 1$, in which case the investment is considered to be risk free. On the other hand, when the risky cash flow that is considered to be equivalent to the risk-free cash flow is infinitely large (i.e., $CF_t = \infty$), then $\alpha_t = 0$, in which case the project should be rejected out of hand.

Definition: The certainty-equivalent approach modifies the net present value approach to evaluating capital investment projects by incorporating risk directly into expected cash flows by means of a certainty-equivalent coefficient.

Definition: The certainty-equivalent coefficient is the ratio of a risk-free net cash flow to its equivalent risky cash flow. The smaller the coefficient, the greater the perceived riskiness of an investment.

To illustrate the certainty-equivalent approach, suppose that a firm is considering an investment with expected net revenues of $100,000 for the next 5 years. Suppose, further, that management believes that the risk of future cash-flow receipts will increase over time. Thus, management has subjectively determined that $\alpha_1 = 0.9$, $\alpha_2 = 0.8$, $\alpha_3 = 0.7$, $\alpha_4 = 0.6$, and $\alpha_5 = 0.5$. The risk-free discount rate is assumed to be 10%. Using the certainty-equivalent approach, the risk-adjusted net present value of this investment project is

$$NPV = \frac{\sum_{t=1 \to n} \alpha_t CF_t}{(1+k)^t}$$

$$= \left[0.9(\$100,000)\left(\frac{1}{1.10}\right)^1 + 0.8(\$100,000)\left(\frac{1}{1.10}\right)^2 \right.$$

$$+ 0.7(\$100,000)\left(\frac{1}{1.10}\right)^3 + 0.6(\$100,000)\left(\frac{1}{1.10}\right)^4$$

$$\left. + 0.5(\$100,000)\left(\frac{1}{1.10}\right)^5 \right] = \$272,600$$

Of course, since the net present value of the investment is positive, the firm will consider the project for adoption. The reader should verify that riskier projects with lower certainty-equivalent coefficients will result in lower risk-adjusted net present values.

As with the risk-adjusted discount rate approach, the certainty-equivalent method suffers from the shortcoming of the subjective determination of the certainty equivalent cash flow (CF_t) in Equations (14.11) and (14.12). On the other hand, the certainty-equivalent approach is conceptually superior to the risk-adjusted discount rate approach in that it explicitly considers the investor's attitude toward risk.

COST OF EQUITY CAPITAL: CAPITAL ASSET PRICING MODEL (CAPM)

Earlier, we defined the cost of common stock, k_c, as the stockholder's required rate of return on common stock. It was also noted that there are two sources of equity capital: retained earnings and capital financing obtained by issuing new shares of common stock. What is the *required rate of return*? It may be argued that investors expect to receive the stock's dividend yield plus its expected growth rate, g. If we denote the dividend payout at time t as D_t and the share price at the time of purchase as S_0, we may write the expected rate of return as $D_t/S_0 + g$. Alternatively, the required rate of return may be interpreted as the rate of return on a risk-free investment, say the short-term (30-day) U.S. Treasury bill rate, k_{rf}, plus a risk premium, rp. The risk premium may be taken to be the difference between the expected rate of return from a "market" investment, k_m (i.e., the rate of return on an "average" investment) and k_{rf}. Thus, the required rate of return may be defined as

$$k_c = k_{rf} + rp = \frac{D_t}{S_0} + g \qquad (14.13)$$

One approach for estimating the cost of common stock by means of the concepts just introduced is to use the *capital asset pricing model*, or *CAPM*. The *CAPM* model is summarized in Equation (14.14).

$$k_c = k_{rf} + \beta_i(k_m - k_{rf}) \qquad (14.14)$$

The capital asset pricing model is used to analyze the relationship between the risk associated with the purchase of a stock and its rate of return. The *beta coefficient*, β_i, is one measure of this risk. The beta coefficient is a measure of the tendency of stock prices for company i to move up and down with "average" stock prices as measured by some market index, such as the S&P 500, the New York Stock Exchange Index, or the Dow Jones Industrial Average. Stock prices that move in step with the market average have a beta coefficient equal to unity ($\beta_i = 1$). Stocks that exaggerate fluctuations in the market—that is, stock prices exhibiting more than the average price fluctuations—have beta coefficients greater than unity ($\beta_i > 1$), while stock prices that are less volatile have positive beta coefficients less than unity ($0 < \beta_i < 1$).

Definition: The capital asset pricing model (CAPM) establishes a relationship between the risk associated with the purchase of a stock and its rate of return. CAPM asserts that the required return on a company's stock is equal to the risk-free rate of return plus a risk premium.

Definition: The beta coefficient measures the price volatility of a given stock with the price volatility of "average" stock prices.

Equation (14.14) admits to several interesting relationships. Taking the first partial derivatives of k_c with respect to k_{rf}, k_m, and β_i yields

$$\frac{\partial k_c}{\partial k_{rf}} = 1 - \beta_i \qquad (14.15)$$

$$\frac{\partial k_c}{\partial k_m} = \beta_i \qquad (14.16)$$

$$\frac{\partial k_c}{\partial \beta_i} = k_m - k_{rf} \qquad (14.17)$$

Equation (14.15) says that the required rate of return varies directly or inversely with the risk-free rate of return depending upon the value of β_i. When the rate of return on a company's stock is more volatile than the market average ($\beta_i > 1$), then an increase in the risk-free rate results in a decline in the required rate of return, and vice versa. On the other hand, when the rate of return on a company's stock price is less volatile than the market average ($0 < \beta_i < 1$), an increase in the risk-free rate will result in an increase in the required rate of return.

Equation (14.16) says that the required rate of return varies directly with the market rate of return, which is the value of the beta coefficient. Finally, Equation (14.17) says that as long as the market rate of return is greater than the risk-free rate, the more volatile the stock, the greater the required rate of return.

The procedure for estimating the cost of common stock using the CAPM approach is straightforward. The procedure begins with selecting some risk-free rate, k_{rf}, which is usually taken to be the return on a U.S. government security. Next, estimate β_i, which may be accomplished by "regressing" the historic realized returns on a company's stock, k_c, against the historic realized returns on average stock prices, k_m, using some market index as a proxy (see, e.g., Greene, 1997). These values may be substituted into Equation (14.14) to determine a "risk-adjusted" cost of capital stock.

Problem 14.11. Suppose that the rate of return on 3-month U.S. Treasury bills is 7% and the market rate of return is 10%.
a. If $\beta_i = 1.5$, what is a company's required rate of return? What is the required rate of return if $\beta_i = 0.75$?
b. Suppose that $\beta_i = 1.5$. If the rate of return on 3-month U.S. Treasury bills rises to 8%, what is the company's required rate of return?

Solution
a. According to the capital asset pricing model, the required rate of return on an individual stock is calculated as

$$k_c = k_{rf} + \beta_i(k_m - k_{rf})$$

where k_c is the required rate of return on stock i, k_{rf} is the risk-free rate of return, and k_m is the market rate of return. Substituting into this expression the values given in the problem yields

$$k_c = 7 + 1.5(10 - 7) = 11.5\%$$

Thus, the required rate of return is 11.5%.
   When $\beta_i = 0.75$, then

$$k_c = 7 + 0.75(10 - 7) = 9.25\%$$

b. When $k_{rf} = 8$ and $\beta_i = 1.5$, then

$$k_c = 8 + 1.5(10 - 8) = 11.0\%$$

GAME THEORY AND UNCERTAINTY

In Chapter 13 we introduced non cooperative, simultaneous, one-shot, finitely and infinitely repeated games with known payoffs. The focus of those discussions was decision making that involves the strategic interaction (move and countermove) of players. How might the implications of game theory be modified in circumstances in which the payoffs are uncertain? To illustrate, consider the following variation of the Prisoners' Dilemma, called the Slumlords' Dilemma, which was first discussed by Davis and Whinston (1962).

SLUMLORDS' DILEMMA

Suppose that there are two owners of adjacent slum tenements: Slumlord Larry and Slumlady Sally. Both Slumlord Larry and Slumlady Sally are considering investing $100,000 to renovate their apartment buildings. If both individuals invest in their properties, they will have the most appealing low-rent apartments in the area and can expect higher profits. If Slumlady Sally invests but Slumlord Larry does not, then Slumlord Sally will lose money while Slumlord Larry will earn positive profits.

The reason for these outcomes is that this type of investment involves externalities. Slumlady Sally will experience only a small increase in the demand for her apartments because of the negative externality of being located near Slumlord Larry's run-down tenement. Slumlord Larry, on the other hand, will find a sharp increase in the demand for his apartments because of the positive effect on the neighborhood from Slumlady Sally's investment. The opposite result would occur if Larry invested and Sally did not. Finally, if neither invests, the economic profits of both will be zero. This normal-form game is depicted in Figure 14.8.

The reader will readily verify that if Slumlord Larry and Slumlady Sally do not cooperate, the solution to the Slumlords' Dilemma will be the strategy profile {Don't invest, Don't invest}. That is, in the absence of an agreement between Larry and Sally, it will be in both individuals' interest not to invest in their properties. The reason for this is that both players have a strictly dominant strategy. For example, regardless of whether Slumlady Sally invests, it will be in Slumlord Larry's best interest not to invest because not investing will result in the highest profit. The same is true

Slumlady Sally

		Invest	Don't invest
Slumlord Larry	Invest	($5,000, $5,000)	(–$3,000, $7,500)
	Don't invest	($7,500, –$3,000)	($0, $0)

Payoffs: (Slumlord Larry, Slumlady Sally)

FIGURE 14.8   Slumlords' Dilemma.

for Slumlady Larry regardless of whether Slumlord Larry invests or does not invest. Moreover, this solution constitutes a Nash equilibrium, since neither player will be able to increase profits by unilaterally switching strategies.

It is obvious that it will be in the best interest of both Slumlord Larry and Slumlady Sally to cooperate and agree to invest in their properties. If both tenement owners trust each other to keep the agreement, then the strategy profile {*Invest, Invest*} will result in a mutually beneficial outcome for both players. But since there is an obvious incentive for Slumlord Larry and Slumlady Sally to mislead each other, neither one will be certain whether the other will actually invest in spite of the agreement to do so. Now, magnify this scenario into a more realistic situation involving three or more tenement owners in which the decision by one owner to invest depends on the investment decisions of each of several others. As difficult as it may be for Slumlord Larry and Slumlady Sally to trust each other, imagine the implausibility of simultaneous trust among three or more tenement owners, even though investment in their properties would be in the best interest of owners and residents alike. This inability of tenement owners to trust one another will result in the perpetuation of uneconomic slum conditions.

In this and other cases involving externalities, the solution to the problem is found by internalizing these third-party effects. In this case, the problem is the uncertainty arising from a lack of trust among the participants. This problem would be eliminated if there was only one owner of all the tenements in the area. If there are only two owners, as in the situation depicted in Figure 14.8, it might be possible to, say, persuade Slumlord Larry to sell out to Slumlady Sally. When there are three or more owners, however, the likelihood that one owner will be able to buy out the others diminishes as the number of owners increases. One public policy solution to this problem is for local government to exercise the power of eminent domain and purchase the run-down properties. The government might redevelop the properties on its own, or sell them to a single developer who will agree to do so. This process is commonly known as urban renewal.

		State A	State B
	Invest	$5,000	–$1,000
Slumlord Larry	Don't invest	$3,000	$0

FIGURE 14.9   The Slumlords' Dilemma under alternative states of nature.

The Slumlords' Dilemma is typical of the simultaneous move, one-shot games discussed in Chapter 13 in which the outcomes of the combined strategies are known with certainty. The nature of the game fundamentally changes, however, if uncertainty is explicitly introduced into the deliberations. To see this, consider Figure 14.9, which summarizes the revised possible outcomes confronting Slumlord Larry under alternative states of nature.

The reader will immediately recognize from Figure 14.9 that Slumlord Larry no longer has a dominant strategy. The payoff to Slumlord Larry is greater by investing in state A and by not investing in state B. Now, suppose that Slumlord Larry believes that the state of nature is determined by Slumlady Sally, and that state A is to invest and state B is not to invest. In this case, Slumlord Larry recognizes that Slumlady Sally has a dominant strategy not to invest. If Slumlady Sally invests, then it is in Slumlord Larry's best interest to invest, and if Slumlady Sally does not invest, then it is in Slumlord Larry's best interest not to invest. Thus, if Slumlord Larry and Slumlady Sally do not cooperate, the strategy profile {*Don't invest, Don't invest*}, which still constitutes a Nash equilibrium.

Suppose, now, that the states of nature depicted in Figure 14.9 no longer represent Slumlady Sally's investment decisions. Instead, suppose the states of nature represent circumstances outside either player's control, which nevertheless affect the likelihood of the outcomes. For example, suppose that Slumlord Larry's tenement is located in an area of the city known for its high arson rate. Suppose that it is commonly known that state *B* represents a 20% probability that the tenement will be "torched." The expected payoffs of investing and not investing given these states of nature are $0.8(\$5,000) + 0.2(-\$1,000) = \$3,800$ and $0.8(\$3,000) - 0.2(\$0) = \$2,400$, respectively.

With expected values of the outcomes, Slumlord Larry's optimal strategy is to invest because of the greater expected value, regardless of what Slumlady Sally decides to do. A shortcoming of this solution is that in the presence of uncertain outcomes it does not explicitly consider Slumlord Larry's attitudes toward risk. In other cases, the probabilities of the different states of nature are not known, nor can they be inferred, in which case some other decision rule must be used to determine the player's optimal strategy. These situations will be considered in the next section.

GAME TREES

In Chapter 13 we introduced the concept of the extensive form of multistage games. Multistage games differ from simultaneous-move games in that the players' moves are sequential. An extensive-form game summarizes the players, game stages, information set, strategies, order of the moves, and payoffs from alternative strategies. The collection of decision nodes and branches that characterize the extensive for of multistage games was referred to as a *game tree*. The game trees presented in Chapter 13 were used to analyze certain outcomes from alternative strategies. In this section, we will use game trees to analyze expected (risky) outcomes from alternative strategies.

Definition: Game trees are used to analyze outcomes from alternative strategies in multistage (sequential move) games. Game trees are made up of decision nodes and branches. At each decision node a decision maker must choose from among alternative moves. The first decision node is called the root of the game tree. Each move is represented by a branch. A game tree is used to determine a decision maker's optimal strategy. A strategy is the decision maker's game plan under all eventualities.

To illustrate how game trees may be used in the decision-making process, consider the following multistage game involving the management of two firms deciding whether to adopt a high-price or a low-price strategy. This is a sequential-move game in that firm *A* must first decide whether to charge a high price or a low price without having the luxury of knowing how firm *B* will respond. The players, strategies, and profits of this game are summarized in Figure 14.10.

According to the backward induction solution methodology discussed in Chapter 13, if firm *A* adopts a "high-price" strategy, then firm *B*'s best move

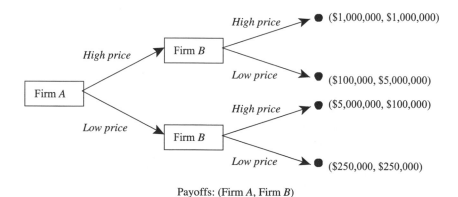

Payoffs: (Firm *A*, Firm *B*)

FIGURE 14.10 Game tree for a multistage game.

is to adopt a "low-price" strategy, since the profit is $5,000,000 compared with a profit of $1,000,000 by charging a high price. Thus, the "high-price" branch from the firm B decision node should be disregarded. On the other hand, if firm A adopts a "low-price" strategy, firm B's optimal strategy is to charge a low price because the resulting profit is $250,000 compared with a profit of $100,000.

An examination of Figure 14.10 readily reveals that the optimal strategy for firm B is to charge a low price if firm A charges a high price, or to charge a low price if firm A charges a low price. Firm B's optimal strategy may be summarized as *(Low price, Low price)*. It is clear from the extensive-form game in Figure 14.10 that the optimal strategy for firm A is to charge a low price, which will result in a profit of $250,000, compared with a profit of $100,000 if it adopts a high-price strategy. Thus, the final optimal strategy profile for this game is {*Low price*, (*Low price, Low price*)}, which yields profits of $250,000 for both firm A and firm B.

We will now modify the game depicted in Figure 14.10 by introducing risk into the decision-making process. Suppose, for example, that firm A believes that by adopting a high-price strategy there is a 40% probability that firm B will charge a high price and a 60% probability that its rival will change a low price. Similarly, if firm A believes that by adopting a low strategy there is an 80% probability that firm B will charge a high price and a 20% probability of a low price. The resulting extensive form for this multi-stage game is illustrated in Figure 14.11.

In Figure 14.11, the first entry in the parentheses at the terminal nodes indicates the expected profit to firm A. The second entry indicates a certain profit to firm B. The reason for this is that firm A is uncertain whether firm B will adopt a "high-price" or a "low-price" strategy. On the other hand, once firm A has decided on its strategy, firm B's strategy is certain. Once again, using the technique of backward induction introduced in Chapter 13,

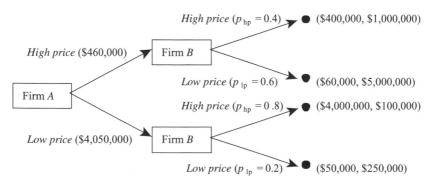

Payoffs: (Firm A, Firm B)

FIGURE 14.11   Game tree for an extensive-form game.

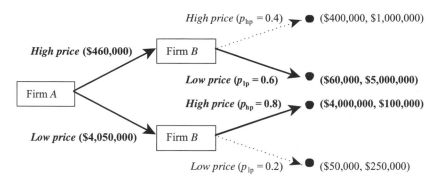

Payoffs: (Firm A, Firm B)

FIGURE 14.12 Using backward induction with probabilistic payoffs to find a Nash equilibrium.

if firm A adopts a "high-price" strategy, then firm B's best move is to adopt a "low-price" strategy. If firm A adopts a "low-price" strategy, then firm B's best move is to charge a "high price." The resulting extensive-form game is illustrated in Figure 14.12.

Once again, an examination of Figure 14.10 reveals that the optimal strategy for firm B is to charge a low price if firm A charges a high price, or to charge a low price if firm A charges a low price. As before, the optimal strategy for firm B is to charge a low price. In the situation depicted in Figure 14.12, however, the optimal strategy of firm A is based on the expected profit from a "high-price" strategy versus the expected profit from a "low-price" strategy. If firm A adopts a "high-price" strategy, the expected profit is $\pi_{hp} = 0.4(\$1,000,000) + 0.6(\$100,000) = \$460,000$. If firm A adopts a "low-price" strategy, the expected profit is $\pi_{lp} = 0.8(\$5,000,000) + 0.2(\$250,000) = \$4,050,000$. But should firm A adopt a "low-price" strategy simply because of its higher expected profit?

Whether firm A adopts a "high-price" strategy or a "low-price" strategy will depend on management's attitude toward risk. To see this, let us calculate the standard deviation of expected profit from each strategy. The standard deviation of firm A's expected profit from a "high-price" strategy is

$$\sigma_{hp} = (\sigma^2)^{0.5} = \left\{ [\pi_{hp} - E(\pi)]^2 p_{hp} + [\pi_{lp} - E(\pi)]^2 p_{lp} \right\}^{0.5}$$

$$= \left\{ 0.4(1,000,000 - 460,000)^2 + 0.6(100,000 - 460,000)^2 \right\}^{0.5}$$

$$= \left\{ 0.4(540,000)^2 + 0.6(-360,000)^2 \right\}^{0.5} = 440,908$$

The standard deviation of firm A's expected profit from a "low-price" strategy is

$$\sigma_{lp} = (\sigma^2)^{0.5} = \left\{ [\pi_{hp} - E(\pi)]^2 \, p_{hp} + [\pi_{lp} - E(\pi)]^2 \, p_{lp} \right\}^{0.5}$$

$$= \left\{ 0.8(5,000,000 - 4,050,000)^2 + 0.2(250,000 - 4,050,000)^2 \right\}^{0.5}$$

$$= \left\{ 0.8(950,000)^2 + 0.2(-3,800,000)^2 \right\}^{0.5} = 1,900,000$$

These calculations indicate that the higher expected profit from a "low-price" strategy is relatively less risky than the lower expected profit from a "high-price" strategy. These results suggest that the optimal pricing strategy for firm A is to charge a low price. Before concluding that the optimal strategy profile for this game is {*Low price*, (*Low price*, *Low price*)}, it is important to consider management's attitude toward risk. Although a "low-price" strategy has the highest expected return and the lowest risk, if the expected rate of return is insufficient to compensate the investor for the associated riskiness of the project (i.e., the risk–return combination is in the unshaded region of Figure 14.3), then even this investment opportunity will be rejected.

Problem 14.12. Consider the extensive-form game in Figure 14.10. Suppose that firm A believes that adopting a high-price strategy will result in a 95% probability that firm B will charge a high price and a 5% probability that it will charge a low price. Similarly, firm A believes that a low-price strategy will result in a 2% probability that firm B will charge a high price and a 98% probability of a low price. What is the optimal strategy profile for this game?

Solution. The revised extensive form of this game is illustrated in Figure 14.13, which indicates that the optimal strategy for firm B is to charge a low price if firm A charges a high price, or to charge a low price if firm A charges a low price. Thus, firm B's optimal strategy may be summarized as (*Low price, Low price*). Firm A's optimal strategy is based on the expected profit from charging a high price versus the expected profit from charging a low price. If firm A adopts a "high-price" strategy, the expected profit is $0.95(\$1,000,000) + 0.05(\$100,000) = \$955,000$. If firm A adopts a "low-price" strategy, the expected profit is $0.02(\$5,000,000) + 0.98(\$250,000) = \$345,000$. Although firm A's expected profit is greater for a "high-price" strategy, the firm's strategy will depend on management's attitude toward risk. To determine the riskiness of each strategy, calculate the standard deviations of the expected payoffs.

$$\sigma_{hp} = (\sigma^2)^{0.5} = \left\{ [\pi_{hp} - E(\pi)]^2 \, p_{hp} + [\pi_{lp} - E(\pi)]^2 \, p_{lp} \right\}^{0.5}$$

$$= \left\{ 0.95(1,000,000 - 955,000)^2 + 0.05(100,000 - 955,000)^2 \right\}^{0.5}$$

$$= \left\{ 0.95(45,000)^2 + 0.05(-855,000)^2 \right\}^{0.5} = 196,150$$

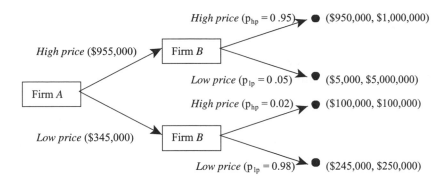

Payoffs: (Firm *A*, Firm *B*)

FIGURE 14.13   Game tree for problem 14.12.

The standard deviation of firm *A*'s expected profits from a "low-price" strategy is

$$\sigma_{lp} = (\sigma^2)^{0.5} = \left\{ [\pi_{hp} - E(\pi)]^2 p_{hp} + [\pi_{lp} - E(\pi)]^2 p_{lp} \right\}^{0.5}$$

$$= \left\{ 0.02(5,000,000 - 345,000)^2 + 0.98(250,000 - 345,000)^2 \right\}^{0.5}$$

$$= \left\{ 0.02(4655,000)^2 + 0.98(-95,000)^2 \right\}^{0.5} = 665,000$$

The standard deviations of expected profits suggest that the "high-price" strategy is also the less risky. Since the 'high-price" strategy also has the higher expected profit, then the optimal pricing strategy for firm *A* is to charge a high price. Thus, the optimal strategy profile for this game is {*High price, (Low price, low price)*}.

In the preceding examples, we assumed that firm *A* would select that strategy with the highest expected profit and the lowest risk. Although this may appear quite logical, it fails to explicitly consider management's attitude toward risk. This is important because it might very well be that neither strategy is acceptable, in which case the firm might consider a third, "no change," price strategy. To amplify this point, suppose that a "high-price" strategy had the highest expected profit and was most risky, while the "low-price" strategy had the lowest expected profit and was the least risky. In this case, a risk-loving management might prefer a "high-price" strategy, whereas a risk-averse management might prefer the "low-price" strategy. It is important to recognize that while game trees are useful analytical devices for evaluating sequential managerial decisions, the selection of optimal strategies should also take into account management attitudes toward risk.

DECISION MAKING UNDER UNCERTAINTY
WITH COMPLETE IGNORANCE

It was mentioned earlier that whenever the decision maker is able to use personal knowledge, intuition, and experience to assign subjective probabilities to outcomes, decision making under uncertainty is transformed into decision making under risk. These situations were described as decision making under conditions of uncertainty with partial ignorance. When managers are unable to assign probabilities to alternative outcomes, some other rational decision-making criteria must be used. As mentioned earlier, this is referred to as decision making under conditions of uncertainty with complete ignorance. In this section we will examine four such rational decision criteria: the *Laplace criterion*, the *Wald (maximin) criterion*, the *Hurwicz criterion*, and the *Savage (minimax regret) criterion*. No single decision rule is appropriate for all decision-making situations. The choice of the criterion should be appropriate to the circumstances and consistent with organizational objectives and philosophy.

LAPLACE DECISION CRITERION

Before examining in detail the Laplace decision criterion for selecting among alternative strategies under conditions of complete ignorance, consider the situation depicted in Figure 14.14. This figure summarizes the payoffs from three possible pricing strategies given three different states of the economy: economic expansion, stability, and contraction. The payoffs in the matrix represent the firm's expected rates of return.

Under conditions of risk or partial ignorance, however, the decision maker may be able to assign objective or subjective probabilities to the different states of the economy. These probabilities (in parentheses), and the expected values of the payoffs from each strategy, $E(S_i) = \mu_i$, are summarized in Figure 14.15. As in the Slumlords' Dilemma, if management decides to adopt the pricing strategy with the highest expected rate of return, then the best strategy is to "raise price." The most significant draw-

		Economy		
		Expansion	Stability	Contraction
	Raise price	25	15	−10
Strategy	No change	15	20	−5
	Lower price	15	0	5

FIGURE 14.14   Payoff matrix for pricing strategies under alternative states of nature.

Economy

		Expansion	Stability	Contraction	μ_i	σ_i
	Raise price	25(0.35)	15(0.5)	−10(0.15)	14.75	11.34
Strategy	No change	15(0.35)	20(0.5)	−5(0.15)	9.5	9.86
	Lower price	15(0.35)	0(0.5)	5(0.15)	6	6.8

FIGURE 14.15 Decision making under risk: expected values and standard deviations of returns for each pricing strategy with different probabilistic outcomes.

back of this decision is that it fails to consider management's attitude toward risk.

A more complete examination of the alternative strategies under different states of nature requires an examination of the risk associated with each strategy. In addition to the expected rates of return from each strategy, Figure 14.15 summarizes the standard deviations of the expected rates of return as a measure of the riskiness of each strategy. An examination of the payoff matrix reveals that while a "raise price" strategy has the greatest expected rate of return, it is also the most risky as measured by the standard deviation. By contrast, a "lower price" strategy is the least risky, but it also has the lowest expected rate of return. Clearly, the selection of the optimal strategy cannot be determined on the basis of a comparison of the expected rates of return and risk alone. In this and many similar situations, it is necessary to examine management's attitude toward risk before determining management's optimal strategy, as the following problem illustrates.

Problem 14.13. Consider again the payoff matrix from three possible pricing strategies given three different states of nature in Figure 14.15. The payoffs in the matrix represent the firm's expected rate of return from each strategy. Suppose that management requires at least the equivalent of a 7% risk-free rate of return. Management's attitude toward risk is summarized by the risk–return indifference curve

$$\mu_i = 6 + 2^{\sigma_i}$$

where μ_i represents the expected rate of return and σ_i is the standard deviation of the expected rates or return. In this case, management's risk–return indifference curve summarizes the different combinations of expected rates of return and standard deviations for which management is indifferent between accepting and rejecting a particular price strategy.

a. Verify that management's risk-free rate of return is 7%.
b. On the basis management's risk–return indifference curve, determine the firm's most preferred pricing strategy.

Solution

a. A strategy with zero risk requires that $\sigma_i = 0$. Thus, the risk-free rate of return is

$$\mu_i = 6 + 1.2^{\sigma_i} = 6 + 1.2^0 = 6 + 1 = 7\%$$

For a risk-free strategy, management will accept any strategy with an expected rate of return greater than 7% and will reject any strategy with an expected rate of return less than 7%. Management will be indifferent between accepting and rejecting any pricing strategy that promises an expected rate of return of exactly 7%.

b. To determine the optimal pricing strategy for this firm, consider the rates of return for which the firm would be indifferent accepting or rejecting a particular pricing strategy.

$$\mu_{\text{Raise price}} = 6 + 1.2^{\sigma_i} = 6 + 1.2^{11.34} = 6 + 7.91 = 13.91\%$$

$$\mu_{\text{No change}} = 6 + 1.2^{\sigma_i} = 6 + 1.2^{9.86} = 6 + 6.04 = 12.04\%$$

$$\mu_{\text{Lower price}} = 6 + 1.2^{\sigma_i} = 6 + 1.2^{6.8} = 6 + 3.45 = 9.45\%$$

Management will reject both the "no change" and "lower price" strategies because the respective risk–indifferent rates of return (12.04 and 9.45%) are greater than the respective expected rate of return (9.5 and 6%). On the other hand, management will accept the "raise price" strategy because the risk-indifferent rate of return (13.91%) is less than the expected rate of return (14.75%). These solutions are illustrated in Figure 14.16.

The shaded area in Figure 14.16 indicates the combinations of expected rates of return at alternative standard deviations for which the pricing strategy is acceptable. Strategies with expected rates of return in the unshaded region are rejected. The reader will verify that only the

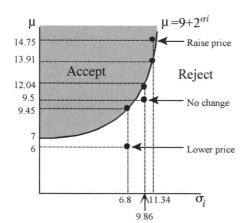

FIGURE 14.16 Diagrammatic solution to problem 14.13.

expected rate of return from the "raise price" strategy is located in the shaded region.

The situations considered thus far have assumed that probabilities could be objectively or subjectively assigned to each outcome from alternative strategies under alternative states of nature. It was also demonstrated that it is not sufficient to determine an optimal strategy based solely on expected values of the outcomes. It is necessary to consider not only the relative risk of each strategy, but also the decision maker's attitude toward risk. But what if it is not possible to assign probabilities to alternative outcomes? What other rational decision criteria are available to the manager in the presence of complete ignorance?

The Laplace decision criterion requires only a minor conceptual modification to the procedure just outlined. Decision making under conditions of complete ignorance assumes that the probabilities of the possible outcomes are not known, nor can they be inferred. The Laplace decision criterion asserts that since the probabilities of the outcomes are unknown, all possible outcomes must be assumed to be equally likely. This assumption effectively transforms the problem of decision making under uncertainty into decision making under risk. Consider again the situation depicted in Figure 14.15. The Laplace decision criterion assumes that the probability of each of these payoffs is one-third. The revised expected values and coefficients of variation from each strategy are summarized in Figure 14.17.

Of course, assuming equal probabilities for each outcome under the alternative states of the economy is equivalent to asserting that the expected value of the payoffs is a simple average of the outcomes. The information summarized in Figure 14.17 indicates that a "no change" strategy has the same expected return as a "raise price" strategy, but is less risky. A "lower price" strategy is the least risky, but also has the lowest expected rate of return. To determine which strategy will be adopted, it is necessary to consider the manager's attitude toward risk.

Definition: The Laplace decision criterion transforms decision making under complete ignorance to decision making under risk by assuming that all possible outcomes are equally likely.

Economy

		Expansion	Stability	Contraction	μ_i	σ_i
	Raise price	25(0.333)	15(0.333)	−10(0.333)	10	14.71
Strategy	No change	15(0.333)	20(0.333)	−5(0.333)	10	10.79
	Lower price	15(0.333)	0(0.333)	5(0.333)	6.67	6.23

FIGURE 14.17 Laplace decision criterion: expected values and coefficients of variation for each pricing strategy assuming equal probabilistic outcomes.

The primary deficiency of the Laplace decision criterion is the rather arbitrary manner in which the outcomes are assumed to be equally likely. The assumption of equiprobability of the different states of nature is especially problematic in the short run because it is oblivious to current conditions and known circumstances. Because of this, the Laplace decision criterion is more appropriate for strategic decisions, especially by larger firms that are better able to afford the cost of selecting a nonoptimal strategy.

WALD DECISION CRITERION

The Wald decision criterion is yet another rational approach to decision making under conditions of complete ignorance. The Wald decision criterion is analogous to the maximin, or secure, strategy for one-shot, simultaneous-move games as discussed in Chapter 13. The Wald decision criterion has also been called the strategy of extreme pessimism. A manager who employs the Wald (maximin) decision criterion will examine all possible payoffs associated with alternative strategies under different states of nature and will choose the strategy that results in the largest payoff from among the worst possible payoffs.

Definition: The Wald (maximin) decision criterion is a decision-making approach in the presence of complete ignorance that involves the selection of the largest payoff from among the worst possible payoffs.

Application of the Wald decision criterion is illustrated in Figure 14.18, which replicates the strategies and payoffs summarized in Figure 14.12. Figure 14.15 also summarizes the minimum (m) and maximum (M) payoffs from each strategy. The best of the worst (maximin) payoffs and the best of the best (maximax) payoffs are identified with asterisks (*). The maximax payoff is also identified because it will serve as a useful counterpoint to the maximin payoff in the subsequent discussion of the *Hurwicz decision criterion*.

The Wald decision criterion represents an extremely risk-averse approach to decision making in the presence of complete ignorance. In essence, the Wald decision criterion attempts to maximize management's

		Economy				
		Expansion	Stability	Contraction	**m**	**M**
	Raise price	25	15	−10	−10	25*
Strategy	No change	15	20	−5	−5	20
	Lower price	15	0	5	0*	15

FIGURE 14.18   Wald (maximin) decision criterion.

feelings of security; in Figure 14.18 the indicated solution is a "lower price" strategy with a maximin payoff of 0, which stands in contrast to the selection of a "no change" pricing strategy obtained by using the Laplace decision criterion.

How are we to assess the wisdom of a maximin approach to the decision-making process? What are the benefits and drawbacks of adopting such a conservative approach? As with other decision criteria considered, the answer ultimately turns on management's attitudes toward risk. In the situation depicted in Figure 14.18, only a "lower price" strategy avoids an economic loss in the event of an economic contraction. For any other state of the economy, however, a "lower price" strategy results in the lowest of all possible payoffs. In the end, only management can decide whether a low rate of return under the best economic conditions is worth the feeling of financial security that comes with the knowledge that the firm will be able to weather an economic downturn. The managements of what types of firm are most likely to adopt the Wald decision criterion? Most likely, the firms that are least able to weather financial reversals, such as small, start-up companies whose very survival will often depend on management's ability to avoid losses.

While the maximin strategy represents an extremely pessimistic approach to the decision-making process, a maximax strategy by contrast is extremely optimistic. Managers who use this approach will select as optimal that strategy that promises the best of the best of all possible outcomes. In the situation depicted in Figure 14.18, the decision to raise price represents one such maximax strategy. But, how likely is it that this, or any, firm would knowingly adopt such a strategy? The selection of a maximax strategy suggests that managers are risk lovers who are willing to gamble with the firm's assets in the hope of a big payoff, which in Figure 14.18 occurs with economic expansion. Under the other two phases of the business cycle, this firm will earn the lowest possible payoff. Since managers are ultimately responsible to the shareholders, it is very unlikely that such a strategy would ever be adopted. So why is it presented here? Minimax and maximax decision criteria are two extreme examples of the Hurwicz decision criteria.

HURWICZ DECISION CRITERION

We introduced the Wald decision criterion as a rather mechanistic approach to the selection of an optimal strategy by extremely risk-averse managers under conditions of complete ignorance. The manager using the maximin approach will select the strategy that results in the best of the worst possible outcomes. Unfortunately, the Wald approach makes no effort to explicitly incorporate management's attitude toward risk when it is not possible to assign probabilities to each outcome.

Although it is not possible to estimate the probabilities of all possible outcomes, the Hurwicz decision criterion is an attempt to incorporate the decision maker's attitude toward risk into the Wald decision criterion by creating a decision index for each strategy. This index is a weighted average of the maximum and minimum payoff from each strategy. These weights are called *coefficients of optimism*. The equation for estimating the Hurwicz decision index for each strategy is

$$D_i = \alpha M_i + (1 - \alpha) m_i \tag{14.18}$$

where D_i is the decision index, M_i is the maximum payoff from each strategy, m_i is the minimum payoff from each strategy, and α is the coefficient of optimism. The optimal strategy using the Hurwicz decision criterion has the highest value for D_i.

Definition: The Hurwicz decision criterion is a decision-making approach in the presence of complete ignorance in which the optimal strategy is selected based on a decision index calculated from a weighted average of the maximum and minimum payoff of each strategy. The weights, which are called coefficients of optimism, are measures of the decision maker's attitude toward risk.

The value of the coefficient of optimism, which ranges in value from 0 to 1, represents management's subjective attitude toward risk. When $\alpha = 0$, the decision maker is completely pessimistic about the outcomes. When $\alpha = 1$, the decision maker is completely optimistic about the outcomes. Figure 14.19 summarizes the estimated values of the Hurwicz indices for selected values of α between 0 and 1. Consider, for example, a relatively pessimistic manager with a coefficient of optimism of $\alpha = 0.3$. From the maximum and minimum payoffs summarized in Figure 14.12, the Hurwicz decision index for a "raise price" strategy is

$$D_i = \alpha M_i + (1 - \alpha) m_i$$
$$= 0.3(25) + (1 - 0.3)(-10) = 0.5$$

The reader should verify that when $\alpha = 0$ the optimal strategy under the Hurwicz decision is identical to the optimal strategy that would be selected by using the extremely pessimistic Wald (maximin) decision criterion. Moreover, when $\alpha = 1$, the optimal strategy under the Hurwicz decision criterion is identical to the optimal strategy obtained by using the maximax decision criterion. Figure 14.19 identifies the optimal strategies from the highest values for D_i with an asterisk. For values for $\alpha < 0.5$, the optimal (risk-averse) decision criterion is the "lower price" strategy. For values of $\alpha > 0.5$, the optimal (risk-loving) decision criterion is a "raise price" strategy. When $\alpha = 0.5$, the decision maker is indifferent to the different pricing strategies.

The Hurwicz decision criterion is superior to the Wald decision criterion because it forces managers to confront their attitudes toward risk. More-

α =	0.0	0.1	0.2	0.3	0.4	0.5	0.6	0.7	0.8	0.9	1.0
Raise price	−10	−6.5	!3	0.5	4	7.5*	11*	14.5*	18*	21.5*	25*
No change	−5	−2.5	0	2.5	5	7.5*	10	12.5	15	17.5	20
Lower price	0*	1.5*	3*	4.5*	6*	7.5*	9	10.5	12	13.5	15

FIGURE 14.19 Estimated Hurwicz D values for selected values of α, the coefficient of optimism.

over, it forces managers to be consistent when they are considering the relative merits of alternative strategies. Of course, one drawback to this approach is the possible negative impact on company earnings should management's sense of optimism prove to be misplaced. Of course, this criticism might be leveled at any decision criterion that involves the subjective determination of probabilistic outcomes. In spite of this, the Hurwicz decision criterion does represent a conceptual improvement over the somewhat arbitrary Wald decision criterion.

SAVAGE DECISION CRITERION

The Savage decision criterion, which is sometimes referred to as the *minimax regret criterion*, is based on the opportunity cost (or regret) of selecting an incorrect strategy. In this instance, opportunity costs are measured as the absolute difference between the payoff for each strategy and the strategy that yields the highest payoff from each state of nature. Once these opportunity costs have been estimated, the manager will select the strategy that results in the minimum of all maximum opportunity costs.

Definition: The Savage decision criterion is used to determine the strategy that results in the minimum of all maximum opportunity costs associated with the selection of an incorrect strategy.

Figure 14.20 illustrates the calculations of the opportunity costs for the payoffs summarized in Figure 14.12. For example, the maximum possible payoff during an economic expansion is 25 for a "raise price" strategy. The absolute difference between the maximum payoff and the payoffs from each strategy during an economic expansion are calculated and summarized in each cell of the matrix. Figure 14.20 summarizes the maximum regret (opportunity cost) from each strategy. The minimum of these maximum opportunity costs, which is identified with an asterisk, is the strategy that will be selected by means of the Savage decision criterion.

Neither overly optimistic nor overly pessimistic, the Savage decision criterion is most appropriate when management is interested in earning a satisfactory rate of return with moderate levels of risk over the long term. Thus, the Savage decision criterion may be more appropriate for long-term capital investment projects.

Economy

		Expansion	Stability	Contraction	*Maximum regret*
	Raise price	$\lvert 25 - 25\rvert = 0$	$\lvert 15 - 20\rvert = 5$	$\lvert -10 - 5\rvert = 15$	15
Strategy	No change	$\lvert 15 - 25\rvert = 10$	$\lvert 20 - 20\rvert = 0$	$\lvert -5 - 5\rvert = 10$	10*
	Lower price	$\lvert 15 - 25\rvert = 10$	$\lvert 0 - 20\rvert = 20$	$\lvert 5 - 5\rvert = 0$	20

FIGURE 14.20   Savage regret matrix.

MARKET UNCERTAINTY AND INSURANCE

Markets operate best when all parties have equal access to all information regarding the potential costs and benefits associated with an exchange of goods or services. When this condition is not satisfied, then uncertainty exists and either the buyer or the seller may be harmed, which will result in an inefficient allocation of resources. In this section, we will examine some of the problems that arise in the presence of market uncertainty.

ASYMMETRIC INFORMATION

For markets to operate efficiently, both the buyer and the seller must have complete and accurate information about the quantity, quality, and price of the good or service being exchanged. When uncertainty is present, market participants can, and often do, make mistakes. An important cause of market uncertainty is *asymmetric information*. Asymmetric information exists when some market participants have more and better information than others about the goods and services being exchanged. An extreme example of the problems that might arise in the presence of asymmetric information is fraud. The reader will recall from Chapter 13 the discussion of the "snake oil" salesman, who traveled from frontier town to frontier town in the American West selling bottles of elixirs promising everything from a cure for toothaches to a remedy for baldness. Of course, these claims were bogus, but by the time customers realized that they had been "had" the snake oil salesman was long gone. Had the customer known that the elixir was worthless, the transaction would never have taken place.

In the extreme case, the knowledge that, some market participants had improperly exploited their access to privileged information could result in a complete breakdown of the market. In insider trading, for example, some market participants have access to classified information about a firm whose shares are publicly traded. Thus an executive who discovers that senior management of his firm plans to merge with a competitor, which will result in an increase in the firm's stock price, might act on this information by buying shares of stock in his own company. This person is guilty of insider trading. When insider trading is pervasive, rational investors who are not privy to privileged information may choose not to participate at all, rather than to put themselves at risk of buying or selling shares at the wrong price.

The uncertainty arising from asymmetric information affects managerial decisions as well. The reader will recall from Chapter 7, for example, that a profit-maximizing competitive firm will hire additional workers as long as the additional revenue generated from sale of the increased output (the marginal revenue product of labor) is greater than the wage rate. The marginal revenue product of labor is defined as the price of the product times the marginal product of labor, $P \times MP_L$. But how is the manager to know the potential productivity of a prospective job applicant? This is a classic example of asymmetric information. The prospective job applicant has much better information than the manager about his or her skills, capabilities, integrity, and attitude toward work. Since the potential cost to the firm of hiring an unproductive worker may be very high, managers will take whatever reasonable measures are necessary to rectify this asymmetry. This is why firms require job applicants to submit résumés, college transcripts, letters of recommendations, and so on. The firm's human resources officer may require job applicants to be interviewed by responsible professionals within the firm. Firms may also conduct background and credit checks, require applicants to sit for examinations to evaluate job skills, mandate probationary periods prior to full employment, and so forth.

ADVERSE SELECTION

The problem of *adverse selection* arises whenever there is asymmetric information. The classic example of adverse selection is the used-car market (Akerlof, 1970). A person with a used car to sell has the option of selling the vehicle to a used-car dealer or selling it privately. For simplicity, assume that all the used cars for sale are similar in every respect (age, features, etc.) except that half are "lemons" (bad cars) and the others are plums (good cars). Finally, suppose that potential buyers are willing to pay $5,000 for a plum and only $1,000 for a lemon.

Potential buyers have no way of distinguishing between lemons and plums. Since there is a fifty-fifty chance of getting a lemon, the expected market price of the used car is $3,000. Since only the sellers know whether their cars are lemons, there is a problem of asymmetric information. The seller has the option of selling to a used-car dealer or selling privately. If a lemon is sold to the used-car dealer for $3,000, then the seller will extract $2,000 at the expense of the buyer, while if a plum sells for $3,000, then the buyer will extract $2,000 at the expense of the seller. Thus, it is in the best interest of lemon owners to sell to used-car dealers, while it is in the best interest of plum owners to sell privately.

Buyers of used cars have the choice of buying from a used-car dealer or buying directly from an owner. Of course, buyers come to realize that probability of buying a lemon from a used-car dealer is greater than from buying from the owner directly. Thus, the used-car dealer price will fall. This will further exacerbate matters, since it will create an even greater incentive for plum owners to avoid the used-car market and sell privately. In the end, only lemons will be available from used-car dealers. In this case, the lemons drive the plums out of the market. This is an example of adverse selection. Here, the market has adversely selected the product of inferior quality because of the presence of asymmetric information.

Definition: In the presence of asymmetric information, adverse selection refers to the process in which goods, services, and individuals with economically undesirable characteristics tend to drive out of the market goods, services, and individuals with economically desirable characteristics.

The problem of adverse selection is particularly problematic in the market for insurance. As discussed earlier, risk-averse individuals purchase insurance to eliminate the risk of catastrophic financial loss in exchange for premium payments that are small relative to the potential loss. The problem confronting an insurance company is that it is difficult to distinguish high-risk from low-risk individuals. One possible solution would be for insurance companies to charge an insurance premium that is a weighted average of the premiums charged to individuals falling into different risk categories. In this case, high-risk individuals will purchase insurance policies while low-risk individuals will not. As a result, the insurance company will have to revise upward its insurance premium just to break even.

As an illustration of adverse selection in the insurance market, consider a firm that sells automobile collision insurance to residents of a particular area. The insurance company has identified two, equal-sized groups of high-risk and low-risk individuals. The insurance company has decided that the probability of an automobile accident is $p = 0.1$ for a member of the high-risk group and only $p = 0.01$ for a member of the low-risk group. If there are 100 people in each group, this is tantamount to an average of 10 automobile accidents per year for the high-risk group compared with one for the low-risk group. Suppose that the average repair bill per automobile accident is $1,000. If the insurance premium charged is the expected average repair bill loss, then the firm should charge the high-risk group 0.1($1,000) = $100 per year and the low-risk group 0.01($1,000) = $10 per year. If it is not possible for the insurance company to identify the members of each group, then the insurance company could decide to charge a premium based on the average risk, that is, 0.5($100) + 0.5($10) = $55.

The situation just described gives rise to the problem of adverse selection. If the insurance company charges a premium of $55, then some members of the low-risk group will opt not to purchase insurance. If 50 members of the low-risk group decide to withdraw from the insurance

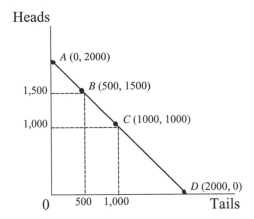

FIGURE 14.21   Fair-odds line for different states of nature.

market, then the total pool of individuals buying insurance falls from 200 to 150. As a result, the premium charged will increase to 0.67($100) + 0.33($10) = $70.3. Of course, some of the remaining individuals in the low-risk group will find that this premium is too high and will, in turn, withdraw from the insurance market. This process will continue until, in the end, only the most risk-averse individuals continue to buy insurance or, which is more likely, only members of the high-risk group remain.

FAIR-ODDS LINE

It is possible to analyze the problem of adverse selection by recasting individuals' attitudes toward risk within the framework of state-dependent indifference curves.[1] Consider again the situation in which an individual is offered a fair gamble on the flip of a coin. Suppose that the individual has $1,000. The person can bet all or part of this amount on the flip of a coin. If the coin comes up "heads," then the individual wins $1 for every $1 wagered. If the coin comes up "tails," then the individual loses $1 for every $1 wagered. Figure 14.21 illustrates the results of alternative wagers from this fair gamble. The horizontal axis represents the individual's money holdings if the coin comes up tails, while the vertical axis represents the individual's money holdings if the coin comes up heads. In a broader sense, the horizontal and vertical axes of Figure 14.21 may be thought of as the outcomes of two probabilistic states of nature. Point C in Figure 14.21 identifies the individual's money holdings on a decision not to bet. That is, regardless of the results of the flip of the coin, the individual will still have a cash "endowment" of $1,000, since no amount was placed at risk.

[1] For a detailed discussion of indifference curves see, for example, Walter Nicholson, Microeconomic Theory: Basic Principles and Extensions, 6th ed. (Font Worth: The Dryden Press, 1995), Chapter 3.

Suppose that the individual decides to wager $500 on the flip of the coin. If the coin comes up heads, then the individual wins $500. If the coin comes up tails, then the individual loses $500. Point B in Figure 14.21 illustrates the possible outcomes of this bet. If the individual loses the wager, then his or her endowment is reduced to $500. On the other hand, if the individual wins the wager, his or her endowment is increased to $1,500. This combination of outcomes is identified in the parentheses at point B. Alternatively, if the individual wagers the entire $1,000, then the possible combination of outcomes corresponds to point A, where the individual is left penniless if the coin comes up tail but has an endowment of $2,000 if the coin comes up heads. What about the points in Figure 14.21 below C, such as point D? Points below point C represent a reversal of the terms of the wager (i.e., tails wins and heads loses).

The situation depicted in Figure 14.21 is analogous to the budget constraint introduced in Chapter 7 in that the endowments define the individual's consumption possibilities. Figure 14.21 is referred to as the individual's *fair-odds line*. In general, whenever the expected value of a wager is zero, then the gamble is said to be actuarially fair. A gamble is said to be fair if its expected value is zero. In the foregoing example, if the individual decides not to wager any amount, he or she is left with the initial endowment of $1,000. If the individual decides to wager some amount, the expected value of the bet is zero, in which case the expected value of the endowment is still $1,000.

The fair-odds line in Figure 14.21 is summarized in Equation (14.19), which represents an actually fair gamble where p is the probability of a monetary gain if the individual wins the bet and $(1 - p)$ is the probability of a monetary loss if the individual loses the bet.

$$pW + (1 - p)L = 0 \tag{14.19}$$

The slope of the fair-odds line is given as the monetary gain divided by the monetary loss from a fair gamble. Suppose, for example, that the individual places a wager of $500. If the individual wins the bet, his or her endowment will increase to $1,500 (i.e., the amount of the gain is $W = \$500$). On the other hand, if the individual loses the bet, his or her endowment is reduced to $500 (i.e., $L = -\$500$). This is illustrated as a move from point C to point B in Figure 14.21. Solving Equation (14.19), we obtain

$$\frac{W}{L} = \frac{1 - p}{p} \tag{14.20}$$

The reader should verify that the budget constraint depicted in Figure 14.21 had a slope of -1. The reader should also verify that, in general, an increase in the probability of winning means that for the gamble to remain fair, the amount of the win will have to decrease. For example, when $p = 0.5$, then $W/L = -(1 - 0.5)/0.5 = -1$. If the probability of winning increases

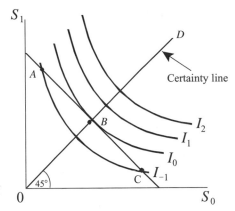

FIGURE 14.22 Indifference map of risk-averse preferences.

to $p = 0.75$, then $W/L = -(1 - 0.75)/0.75 = -0.25/0.75 = -0.33$. Similarly, if the probability of losing increases, the amount of the win will have to increase for the gamble to remain fair. These three situations are illustrated in Figure 14.22.

STATE PREFERENCES

The indifference curve framework can also be used to identify an individual's attitudes toward risk. In this case, however, the two goods that are normally identified along the horizontal and vertical axes are replaced with different combinations of state-dependent consumption levels that yield equal levels of utility. The shapes of these indifference curves reflect the individual's behavior when confronted with risky situations.

In Figure 14.22, which illustrates the case of an individual with risk-averse preferences, S_1 and S_0 represent two different states of nature. It will be recalled that an individual with risk-averse preferences will never accept a fair gamble with an expected value equal to zero. This is because a risk-averse individual will always prefer a certain sum to an uncertain sum with the same expected value. Thus, the indifference curves of an individual with risk-averse preferences are convex with respect to the origin.

The individual described in Figure 14.22 will prefer a consumption level corresponding to point B to any other point on the fair-odds line. Consumption levels that correspond to points A and C are found on an indifference curve that is closer to the origin, which yields a lower level of utility. The point of tangency between the fair-odds line and the indifference curve I_0 at point B represents the highest level of utility that this individual can attain with a given endowment. At point B the slope of the indifference curve is $-(1 - p)/p$. Line $0D$, which represents the locus of all such fair-odds tangency points at fair odds, is called the *certainty line*, which is analytically equivalent to the income consumption curve in utility theory and the expansion path in production theory. The certainty line represents equal consumption in either state of nature.

The choices confronting a person with risk-neutral preferences are illustrated in Figure 14.23. Points A, B, and C all yield the same level of utility, since the indifference curve I_0 corresponds to the fair-odds line. A risk-neutral individual is indifferent between a certain sum and an uncertain sum with the same expected value. Finally Figure 14.24 illustrates the case of a risk-loving individual. A risk lover will always accept a fair gamble with an expected value equal to zero. Risk lovers have indifference curves that are concave with respect to the origin. Accepting a fair gamble will move the individual away from point B and result in a higher level of utility. In fact, concave indifference curves will invariably result in a corner solution, such as points A and C, in which the individual will gamble the total amount of his or her endowment.

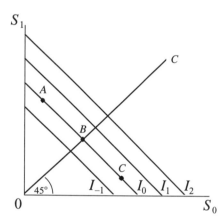

FIGURE 14.23 Indifference map of risk-neutral preferences.

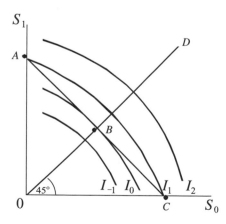

FIGURE 14.24 Indifference map of risk-loving preferences.

INSURANCE PREMIUMS

The state preferences model just presented can be used to analyze the demand for insurance. We will initially assume that insurance is provided at zero administrative cost. We will also assume that insurance is offered at actuarially fair terms. In the event of an adverse state of nature, the insurance company agrees to pay out the full amount of the loss, while in a favorable state of nature the insurance company pays nothing. The insurance premium is equal to the expected value of the payout, that is,

$$P = pL \qquad (14.21)$$

where $(1 - p)$ is the probability of an adverse state of nature, such as the financial loss arising from an accident (L), and p is the probability of a favorable state of nature. In our example of automobile collision insurance, if the insurance policy provides \$1,000 annual coverage and the probability of an automobile is 10%, then an actuarially fair premium is \$100 per year. For each additional \$100 of coverage the additional premium will be \$10. Figure 14.25 illustrates the situation of an individual buying fair insurance.

In Figure 14.25 the individual's endowment is at point A. Suppose that the individual wishes to equalize his or her consumption in either state of nature. This will involve moving along the fair-odds line from point A to point B on the full insurance line $0D$. This will involve the payment of an insurance premium AC in exchange for an insurance payout of CB should the adverse event occur. In general, risk-averse individuals will purchase full insurance offered at fair odds. But what if insurance is offered at unfair odds? This situation is depicted in Figure 14.26.

Thus far we have assumed that insurance companies operate at zero cost. This assumption allowed us to assume that insurance companies are able to provide insurance at actuarially fair terms. This assumption is obviously

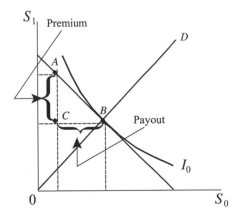

FIGURE 14.25 Full insurance at fair odds.

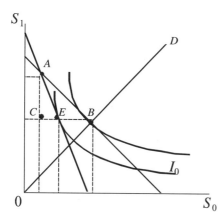

FIGURE 14.26 Partial insurance at unfair odds.

unrealistic, since insurance companies are analytically subject to the same long-run and short-run production considerations faced by any other firm. Thus, since the provision of insurance, or any other good or service, is not free, we must modify our analysis to recognize that the premium charged is not equal to the expected payout. When insurance is not provided at fair odds, the fair-odds line will pivot in a clockwise direction around the individual's initial endowment. In Figure 14.26, this is illustrated by the individual's new budget line that passes through points A and E.

Inspection of Figure 14.26 reveals that when insurance is not provided at actuarially fair terms, the individual will purchase partial insurance $CB - EB$ for the same insurance premium AC. In other words, when insurance is not provided at actuarially fair terms, a risk-averse individual will nonetheless purchase partial coverage even though the premium payments are greater than the expected loss. It is evident from Figure 14.26 that insurance provided at unfair odds will move the individual's consumption level in either state of nature to a lower indifference curve than would be the case if insurance were provided at fair odds. As before, in equilibrium the individual's marginal rate of substitution between the state-dependent consumption levels is equal to the slope of the fair-odds (budget) constraint, although consumption levels will obviously be less than in a favorable state of nature.

We are now in a position to formally analyze the problem of adverse selection arising from asymmetric information. Recall from the automobile collision insurance example that the problem of adverse selection arises when the insurance company is unable to distinguish individuals belonging to the high- and low-risk groups. In terms of the state preference model, Figure 14.27 illustrates the fair-odds lines of the high-risk group, the low-risk group, and the average market risk.

In Figure 14.27, the fair-odds lines of the high- and low-risk groups are F_H and F_L, respectively. The average-market fair-odds line is F_M. Figure 14.27

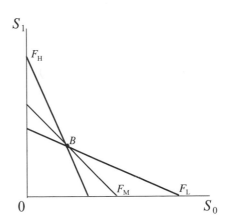

FIGURE 14.27 High-risk, low-risk, and average-market fair-odds lines.

assumes that both the high- and low-risk groups have the same initial endowment, with is indicated at point B. The different risks associated with each group are reflected in the slopes of the fair-odds lines, that is, $[-(1 - p_H)/p_H] < [-(1 - p_L)/p_L]$. This is because the probability that an individual in the high-risk group will have an accident $(1 - p_H)$ is greater than the probability that an individual in the low-risk group will have an accident $(1 - p_L)$.

The different risks faced by individuals in both groups are also reflected in the slopes of the indifference curves. Figure 14.28 illustrates the indifference curves for the high- and low-risk groups. Individuals belonging to the low-risk group are less likely to make a claim under an insurance policy than individuals belonging to the high-risk group. Thus, low-risk individuals will require greater compensation for a given reduction in consumption in a favorable state of nature. In Figure 14.28, low-risk individuals making a claim will require an additional amount AE in state of nature S_0, while high-risk individuals will require $AC < AE$. Thus, the indifference curve for the low-risk individual (I_L) is flatter than the indifference curve for the high-risk group (I_H).

The problem of adverse selection is illustrated in Figure 14.29. Note that the slope of the low-risk individual's indifference curve is flatter than the market-average fair-odds line, F_M, at the initial endowment point B. In exchange for a sure amount in a favorable state of nature, AB, the individual is able to obtain only AC coverage in an adverse state of nature. But, to be as well off as at point B, the low-risk individual would require an additional amount CE in an adverse state of nature. Thus, the low-risk individual would be better off with no insurance at all.

In general, adverse selection is more likely to be a problem when the market consists of a high proportion of high-risk individuals, which has the effect of moving the average-market fair-odds line closer to the fair-odds

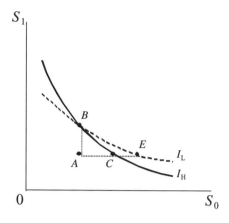

FIGURE 14.28 The indifference curve of a low-risk individual is flatter than the indifference curve of a high-risk individual.

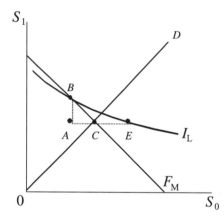

FIGURE 14.29 Adverse selection: low-risk individuals choose not to purchase insurance.

line for the high-risk group (F_H) in Figure 14.27. Adverse selection is also more likely to be a problem if there is a large gap in the perceptions toward risk of the high- and low-risk groups. Adverse selection will be less a problematic if some individuals are extremely risk averse. In practice, it is common for insurance companies to differentiate candidates for insurance to capture different attitudes toward risk. Thus, differential premiums based on age, sex, occupation, lifestyle, and domicile are a commonly found in the insurance industry.

MORAL HAZARD

Another problem that arises in the presence of asymmetric information is the problem of *moral hazard*. We saw earlier that risk-averse individuals will purchase insurance to protect themselves against catastrophic financial losses. Of course, the probability that such catastrophic losses will occur is inversely related to individual efforts to avoid such losses. For example, the probability of having an automobile accident depends on how carefully one drives. Other things being equal, individuals tend to be more careful behind the wheel if they are not insured than when they are fully insured. The reason for this is that the insured knows that he or she will be fully compensated for damages incurred as a result of an accident. If an insured individual has a reduced incentive to be careful, a moral hazard is said to exist. Other examples of moral hazard include individuals who lead less-than-healthy lifestyles after obtaining health insurance, or doctors who are less than conscientious about administering medical care after obtaining medical malpractice insurance.

Definition: A moral hazard exists when insurance coverage causes an individual to behave in such a way that changes the probability of incurring a loss.

In general, a moral hazard exists when an individual can determine the probability of an undesirable outcome. To see this, consider the case of an insurance company that has estimated that the probability p that an automobile will be stolen. Ignoring administrative costs, the insurance company will provide coverage against automobile theft for the premium payment P in Equation (14.21). Now, suppose that an insured individual can determine the probability that his or her car will be stolen. Suppose, for example, that the insured is able to set $p = 1$. In this case, the insured individual is effectively attempting to use the insurance policy to obtain the price of a new car. Of course, if the insurance company knows this, automobile theft insurance will not be offered. In this case, a moral hazard exists because the insurance company does not, indeed cannot, know the probability that the insured will submit a claim.

The problem of moral hazard may be represented diagrammatically by means of the state preferences model. Figure 14.30 illustrates the amount of care that an individual exercises to avoid the probability of an adverse state of nature. The flatter the indifference curve, the greater the care an individual takes to avoid a loss. The indifference curves in Figure 14.30 associated with low and high probabilities of an adverse state of nature are identified as I_L and I_H, respectively. To understand why this is the case, we can ask ourselves the following question: How much will an individual be willing to sacrifice in an adverse state of nature to obtain a given amount in a favorable state of nature?

The answer to this question depends on how likely it is that the individual will experience the adverse state of nature, which, of course, depends on the actions of the individual. In Figure 14.30, for an extra amount of consumption in a favorable state of nature, AB, the careful individual is willing to sacrifice a larger amount in the adverse state of nature than would the careless individual. The reason for this is that the probability that an adverse

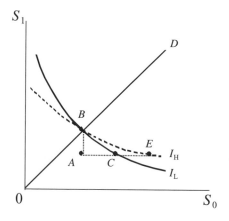

FIGURE 14.30 The slope of the state preference indifference curve is flatter when more care is taken to avoid an adverse state of nature.

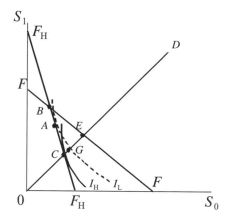

FIGURE 14.31 Moral hazard and partial insurance.

state of nature will occur is less because of the greater care exercised. The additional amount that the high-care individual is willing to sacrifice is given by the distance CE. Thus, the indifference curve I_H reflects the greater care that an individual takes to avoid a loss, compared with individuals who are less careful and are willing to sacrifice only AC.

Figure 14.31 illustrates the situation in which the individual's initial endowment is given at point B and the fair-odds line is given as FF. If an insured individual is able to increase the probability of an adverse state of nature by exercising less care, then the fair-odds line will pivot clockwise around point B. This is illustrated in Figure 14.31 as $F_H F_H$. Point E on the fair-odds line FF is no longer an equilibrium in the presence of a moral hazard, since no insurance company would offer such coverage at the premium pL.

In Figure 14.31 the new equilibrium at point C represents the individual's behavior along the new fair-odd line $F_H F_H$ associated with the higher probability that the adverse state of nature will occur. An individual offered insurance along the new fair-odds line might obtain a higher level of utility by exercising greater care and purchasing partial insurance coverage. This situation is depicted at point A because I_L passes through the certainty equivalent (full insurance) line $0D$ at point G, which is above point C. The insured individual will be better off paying the amount CG, provided it does not represent a cost greater than the cost associated with exercising greater care to avoid the adverse state of nature.

Insurance companies attempt to reduce the problem of moral hazard by requiring insured individuals to share the losses that arise from an adverse state of nature by applying a deductible on all insurance claims. To be effective, the amount of the deductible should be no greater than the distance CG in Figure 14.31. Provided the deductible is not too large, an insured individual is likely to drive more carefully or choose a more healthy lifestyle when he or she is required to share the cost of an accident or illness.

CHAPTER REVIEW

Most economic decisions are made with something less than perfect information, and the consequences of these decisions cannot be known with any degree of precision. Moreover, the uncertainty of outcomes associated with those decisions increases with time. Most economic decisions are made under conditions of *risk* and *uncertainty*.

Risk involves choices with multiple outcomes in which the probability of each outcome is known or can be estimated. Uncertainty, on the other hand, involves multiple outcomes in which the probability of each one is unknown or cannot be estimated.

There are two sources of uncertainty. Uncertainty with *complete ignorance* refers to situations in which no assumptions can be made about the probabilities of alternative outcomes under different states of nature. Uncertainty with *partial ignorance* refers to situations in which the decision maker is able to assign subjective probabilities to possible outcomes. These subjective probabilities may be based on personal knowledge, intuition, or experience. Decision making under conditions of partial ignorance is effectively the same as decision making under risk. Uncertainty with complete ignorance requires alternative approaches to the decision-making process.

The most commonly used summary measures of uncertain, random outcomes are the *mean* and the *variance*. The expected value of random outcomes, such as profits, capital gains, prices, and unit sales, is called the *mean*. The mean is the weighted average of all possible random outcomes, where the weights are the probabilities of each outcome.

Risk may be measured as the dispersion of all possible payoffs. The most commonly used measure of the dispersion of possible outcomes is the *vari-*

ance. The variance is the weighed average of the squared deviations of all possible random outcomes from its mean, where the weights are the probabilities of each outcome. An alternative way to express the riskiness of a set of random outcomes is the *standard deviation*, which is the square root of the variance.

Neither the variance nor the standard deviation can be used to compare risk when there are two or more risky situations involving different expected values. The *coefficient of variation* is used to compare the relative riskiness of alternative outcomes. The project with the lowest coefficient of variation is the least risky.

Whether an individual undertakes a risky project will depend on the individual's attitude toward risk. An individual who prefers a certain payoff to a risky prospect with the same expected value is said to be *risk averse*. An individual who prefers the expected value of a risky prospect to its certainty equivalent is said to be a *risk lover*. Finally, an individual who is indifferent between a certain payoff and its expected value is *risk neutral*.

Generally speaking, most individuals are risk averse in accordance with the principle of the *diminishing marginal utility of money*. Most individuals, however, are not risk averse under all circumstances. It is not unusual to find that even extremely risk-averse individuals become risk lovers for "small" gambles, such as buying a lottery that costs far less than the expected value of winning.

Managers often evaluate equal or, equivalently, equal-lived capital investment projects, by calculating the net present values of net cash flows. *Risk-adjusted discount rates* are used in the calculation of net present values to compensate for the perceived riskiness of alternative capital investment projects. The greater the perceived risk, the higher will be the discount rate that will be used to calculate the net present value. The difference between the risk-free discount rate and the risk-adjusted discount rate is called the *risk premium*. The size of the risk premium will depend on the investor's attitude toward risk.

An alternative to the use of risk-adjusted discount rates for assessing capital investment projects is the *certainty-equivalent approach*. The certainty-equivalent approach incorporates risk directly into the net present value method by using the *certainty-equivalent coefficient* to modify expected net cash flows. As with the risk-adjusted discount rate approach, however, the certainty-equivalent method suffers from the shortcoming of the subjective determination of the certainty-equivalent cash flow. It is conceptually superior to the risk-adjusted discount rate approach, however, in that it explicitly considers the investor's attitude toward risk.

Decision making under conditions of uncertainty with complete ignorance requires rational decision-making criteria that do not rely on probabilistic outcomes. Four such rational decision criteria include the *Laplace criterion*, the *Wald (maximin) criterion*, the *Hurwicz criterion*, and the *Savage (minimax regret) criterion*.

The Laplace decision criterion transforms decision making under complete ignorance to decision making under risk by assuming that all possible outcomes are equally likely. The Wald (maximin) decision criterion selects the largest of the worst possible payoffs. The Hurwicz decision criterion involves the selection of an optimal strategy based on a decision index calculated from a weighted average of the maximum and minimum payoffs of each strategy. The weights, which are called coefficients of optimism, are measures of the decision maker's attitude toward risk. Finally, the Savage decision criterion is used to select a strategy that results in the minimum of all maximum opportunity costs associated with the selection of an incorrect strategy.

For markets to operate efficiently, both buyers and sellers must have complete and accurate information about the quantity, quality, and price of the good or service being exchanged. When uncertainty is present, market participants can, and often do, make mistakes. An important cause of market uncertainty is *asymmetric information*. Asymmetric information exists when some market participants have more and better information about the goods and services being exchanged. The problem of *adverse selection* arises whenever there is asymmetric information. In adverse selection, the interaction of buyers and sellers results in the market provision of goods and services with undesirable characteristics.

Another problem that arises in the presence of asymmetric information is called *moral hazard*. When obtaining information is costly, monitoring the behavior of the parties to a transaction becomes difficult. When the parties to a contract have an incentive alter their behavior from what was anticipated when the contract was entered into, a moral hazard exists.

KEY TERMS AND CONCEPTS

Adverse selection The process whereby, in the presence of asymmetric information, goods, services, and individuals with economically undesirable characteristics tend to drive out of the market goods, services, and individuals having economically desirable characteristics.

Beta coefficient (β) A measure of the price volatility of a given stock versus the price volatility of "average" stock prices.

Capital asset pricing model (CAPM) Establishes a relationship between the risk associated with the purchase of a stock and its rate of return. CAPM asserts that the required return on a company's stock is equal to the risk-free rate of return plus a risk premium.

Capital market line   Summarizes the market opportunities available to an investor from a portfolio consisting of alternative combinations of risky and risk-free investments.

Certainty-equivalent approach   Modifies the net present value approach to evaluating capital investment projects by incorporating risk directly into expected cash flows by means of a certainty-equivalent coefficient.

Certainty-equivalent coefficient   The ratio of a risk-free net cash flow to its equivalent risky cash flow. The smaller the coefficient, the greater the perceived riskiness of an investment.

Coefficient of variation   A measure used to compare risk of two or more outcomes when there are different expected values. It is calculated as the ratio of the standard deviation to the mean.

Fair gamble   A gamble in which the expected value of the payoff is zero.

Hurwicz decision criterion   A decision-making approach in the presence of complete ignorance an optimal strategy in which is selected based on a decision index calculated from a weighted average of the maximum and minimum payoff of each strategy. The weights, which are called coefficients of optimism, are measures of the decision maker's attitude toward risk.

Investor indifference curve   Summarizes the combinations of risk and expected return in which the investor will be indifferent between a risky and a risk-free investment.

Laplace decision criterion   A decision-making approach that transforms decision making under complete ignorance to decision making under risk by assuming that all possible outcomes are equally likely.

Mean   The expected value of a set of random outcomes. The mean is the sum of the products of each outcome and the probability of its occurrence.

Moral hazard   Exists when insurance coverage causes an individual to behave in such a way that change the probability of incurring a loss.

Risk   The existence of choices involving multiple possible outcomes in which the probability of each outcome is known or may be estimated.

Risk-adjusted discount rate   The discount rate used to calculate net present values to compensate for the perceived riskiness of an investment. The greater the perceived risk, the higher will be the discount rate that is used to calculate the net present value.

Risk aversion   An individual who prefers a certain payoff to a risky prospect with the same expected value is said to be risk averse.

Risk loving   Preferring the expected value of a payoff to its certainty equivalent.

Risk neutrality   Indifference between a certain payoff and its expected value.

Savage decision criterion   A decision-making approach in the presence of complete ignorance that involves the selection of the strategy that results in the minimum of all maximum opportunity costs. Opportunity costs are measured as the absolute difference between the payoff for each strategy and the strategy that yields the highest payoff for each state of nature.

Standard deviation   The square root of the variance.

Uncertainty   The existence of choices involving multiple possible outcomes in which the probability of each outcome is unknown and cannot be estimated.

Variance   A measure of the dispersion of a set of random outcomes. It is the sum of the products of the squared deviations of each outcome from its mean and the probability of each outcome.

Wald (maximin) decision criterion   A decision-making approach in the presence of complete ignorance in which one selects the largest from among the worst possible payoffs.

CHAPTER QUESTIONS

14.1 What is the difference between risk and uncertainty?

14.2 What are the most commonly used measures of risk?

14.3 Can uncertainty be estimated? If not, then why not? Explain.

14.4 When is the process of decision making under conditions of risk the same as the process of decision making under conditions of uncertainty?

14.5 Decision making under conditions of uncertainty with complete ignorance is never the same as decision making under conditions of uncertainty under partial ignorance. Do you agree? Explain.

14.6 What is the difference between the standard deviation and the coefficient of variation as a measure of risk? When would it be appropriate to use each one?

14.7 Risk-averse individuals will always reject a fair gamble. Do you agree? Explain.

14.8 Can the internal rate of return method discussed in Chapter 12 be used to determine the risk-adjusted discount rate?

14.9 Explain why many life insurance policies contain clauses stipulating that benefits will not to the heirs of a policyholder who commits suicide.

14.10 Explain why insurance companies charge higher premiums to male drivers between 18 and 25 years of age than for all other drivers.

14.11 What risk preferences are described by L-shaped indifference curves?

14.12 An individual with L-shaped indifference curves is indifferent to insurance offered at fair or unfair odds. Do you agree with this statement? Explain.

14.13 Briefly explain the following decision criteria and the conditions under which each might be used:

a. Laplace criterion
b. Wald (maximin) criterion
c. Hurwicz criterion
d. Savage criterion

14.14 Insurance companies require a deductible on all insurance claims to reduce costs and bolster profits. Do you agree? Explain.

14.15 Define adverse selection. Give an example.

14.16 Define moral hazard. Give an example.

14.17 How do deductibles on insurance claims address the problem of moral hazard?

CHAPTER EXERCISES

14.1 Illustrate, with the use of investor indifference curves, that project A is the most preferred project when the expected rates of return from the investment projects are $k_C > k_A > k_B$ and the risks associated with each project are $\sigma_C > \sigma_A > \sigma_B$.

14.2 Illustrate, with the use of investor indifference curves, that project A is the most preferred project when the expected rates of return from the investment projects are $k_A > k_B > k_C$ and the risks associated with each project are $\sigma_C > \sigma_A > \sigma_B$.

14.3 Rosie Hemlock offers Robin Nightshade the following wager. For a payment of $10, Rosie will pay Robin the dollar value of any card drawn from a standard deck of 52 cards. For example, for an ace of any suit Rosie will pay Robin $1. For an 8 of any suit Rosie will pay Robin $8. A ten or picture card of any suit is worth $10.

a. What is the expected value of Rosie's offer?
b. Should Robin accept Rosie's offer?

14.4 Suppose that capital investment project X has an expected value of $\mu_X = \$1,000$ and a standard deviation of $\sigma_X = \$500$. Suppose, also, that project Y has an expected value $\mu_Y = \$1,500$ and a standard deviation of $\sigma_Y = \$750$. Which is the relatively riskier project?

14.5 The management of Rubicon & Styx is trying to decide whether to advertise its world-famous hot sauce Sergeant Garcia's Revenge on television (campaign A) or in magazines (campaign B). The marketing department of Rubicon & Styx has estimated the probabilities of alternative sales revenues (net of advertising costs) using each of the two media outlets, summarized in Table E14.5.

a. Calculate the expected revenues from sales of Sergeant Garcia's Revenue from each advertising campaign.
b. What is the standard deviation of the distribution of profits from each advertising campaign?
c. Which advertising campaign appears relatively riskier?
d. Which advertising campaign should Rubicon & Styx select?

TABLE E14.5 Probabilities of alternative sales revenues for chapter exercise 14.5

Campaign A (television)		Campaign B (magazines)	
Sales, S_i	Probability	Sales, S_i	Probability
$5,000	0.20	$6,000	0.15
$8,000	0.30	$8,000	0.35
$11,000	0.30	$10,000	0.35
$14,000	0.20	$12,000	0.15

14.6 Suppose that Ted Sillywalk offers Will Wobble the fair gamble of receiving $500 on the flip of a coin showing heads and losing $500 on the flip of a fair coin showing tails. Suppose further that Will's utility of money function is

$$U = M^{1.2}$$

a. For positive money income, what is Will's attitude toward risk?
b. If Will's current income is $5,000, will he accept Ted's offer? Explain.

14.7 Mat Heathertoes has just inherited $10,000 from his Aunt Lobelia. Mat has decided to invest his inheritance either in 3-month Treasury bills, which yield a risk-free expected rate of return of 8%, or in shares of Hardbottle Company, which have an expected rate of return of 15%. Mat has analyzed Hardbottle's past performance and has determined that the standard deviation of returns is $3.50 per share. Mat's investment utility equation is

$$U = k_p - 100\sigma_p^{2}$$

where k_p and σ_p are the portfolio's expected return and standard deviation, respectively. How should Mat's investment be divided between 3-month Treasury bills and Hardbottle shares?

14.8 Harry Frogfoot is the proprietor of The Floating Log restaurant, which is located on the Delaware River near Frenchtown. Harry is considering expanding the dining area of his restaurant. The $150,000 cost of the investment is known with certainty. Harry has estimated that the expected cash inflows are $50,000 per year for the next 5 years.

a. Should Harry consider the investment if the discount rate is 8%?
b. Suppose that the riskiness of expected cash inflows was such that management requires a 25% rate of return. Should Harry consider this investment?

14.9 Suppose that you are given the information in Table E14.9 on cash flows and their probabilities for a proposed project.

If the discount rate is 0.0%, what is the expected value of the cash flows?

14.10 Suppose that the discount rate in Exercise 14.9 is 10.0%.

TABLE E14.9   Cash flows and probabilities for chapter exercise 14.9

Period 1		Period 2	
Probability	Cash flow	Probability	Cash flow
0.20	500	0.15	250
0.60	750	0.70	500
0.20	1,000	0.15	750

TABLE E14.11   Sales revenue expectations and probabilities for chapter exercise 14.11

Sales ($000s)	Probabilities
100	0.05
120	0.15
140	0.30
160	0.30
180	0.15
200	0.05

a. What is the expected value of the project?

b. If the initial investment was $1,000, what is net present value of this project?

14.11 Consider the sales revenue expectations and probabilities given in Table E14.11.

a. Calculate expected sales revenues.

b. Calculate the standard deviation of expected sales revenues.

c. Calculate the coefficient of variation.

14.12 Suppose that the equation for the risk–return indifference curve in Exercise 14.13 is

$$\mu_i = 3 + 2^{\sigma_i}$$

a. What is the new required risk-free rate of return?

b. What is the firm's optimal pricing strategy?

14.13 Suppose that the senior management of Red Wraith Enterprises is provided with the data for a proposed capital investment project given in Table E14.13.

a. Calculate the net present value of the proposed capital investment project if the risk-free discount rate is 10%.

b. On the basis of your answer to part a, should senior management of Red Wraith invest in this project?

TABLE E14.13   Data for proposed capital investment
project for chapter exercise 14.13

Year	Cash flow	Certainty-equivalent coefficient
0	-$65,000	1.00
1	10,000	0.95
2	15,000	0.90
3	20,000	0.85
4	25,000	0.80
5	30,000	0.75

SELECTED READINGS

Akerlof, G. "The Market for Lemons: Qualitative Uncertainty and the Market Mechanism." *Quarterly Journal of Economics*, 84 (1970), pp. 488–500.

Baumol, W. J. *Economic Theory and Operations Analysis*, 4th ed. Englewood Cliffs, NJ: Prentice Hall, 1977.

Bierman, H. S., and L. Fernandez. *Game Theory with Economic Applications*, 2nd ed. New York: Addison-Wesley, 1998.

Brigham, E. F., L. C. Gapenski, and M. C. Erhardt. *Financial Management: Theory and Practice*, 9th ed. New York: Dryden Press, 1998.

Davis, O., and A. Whinston. "Externalities, Welfare, and the Theory of Games." *Journal of Political Economy*, 70 (June 1962), pp. 241–262.

Dreze, J. "Axiomatic Theories of Choice, Cardinal Utility and Subjective Utility: A Review." In P. Diamond and M. Rothschild, eds., *Uncertainty in Economics*. New York: Academic Press, 1978, pp. 37–57.

Friedman, L. *Microeconomic Policy Analysis*. New York: McGraw-Hill, 1984.

Friedman, M., and L. Savage. "The Utility Analysis of Choices Involving Risk." *Journal of Political Economy*, 56 (August 1948), pp. 279–304.

Greene, W. H. *Econometric Analysis*, 3rd ed. Upper Saddle River, NJ: Prentice Hall, 1997.

Hirshleifer, J., and J. Riley. "The Analytics of Uncertainty and Information—An Expository Survey." *Journal of Economic Literature*, 57(4) (December 1979), pp. 1375–1421.

Hope, S. *Applied Microeconomics*. New York: John Wiley & Sons, 1999.

Knight, F. H. *Risk, Uncertainty, and Profit*. Boston: Houghton Mifflin, 1921.

Kunreuther, H. "Limited Knowledge and Insurance Protection." *Public Policy*, 24(2) (Spring 1976), pp. 227–261.

Pauly, M. "The Economics of Moral Hazard." *American Economic Review*, 58 (1968), pp. 531–537.

Schotter, A. *Free Market Economics: A Critical Appraisal*. (New York: St. Martin's Press, 1985).

Silberberg, E. *The Structure of Economics: A Mathematical Analysis*, 2nd ed. New York: McGraw-Hill, 1990.

Simon, H. "Theories of Decision-Making in Economics and Behavioral Science." American Economic Review, 49 (1959), pp. 253–283.

Varian, H. *Microeconomic Analysis*, 2nd ed. New York: W. W. Norton, 1984.

15

MARKET FAILURE AND GOVERNMENT INTERVENTION

Thus far, we have generally assumed that market transactions were, for the most part, free of government interference. In reality, however, government intervention in private transactions in the form of taxes and regulations is pervasive. Why? The cynical response to this question might be that legislators are more concerned with generating tax revenues to subsidize pork-barrel projects to curry the favor of one particular group of voters over another, or to attract the political and monetary support of special interest groups. While these explanations may be valid, the fact is that government intervention is often motivated by the failure of free markets to provide a socially optimal mix of goods and services. A socially optimal mix of goods and services may be defined as one in which the collective welfare of society has been maximized. Maximizing social welfare requires not only that the economy be producing efficiently given the productive resources available to it, but also that it be consuming efficiently. By this we mean that economy needs to be producing the goods and services that are most in demand by society.

Definition: Market failure occurs when private transactions result in a socially inefficient allocation of goods, services, and productive resources.

This chapter will examine three sources of market failure: market power, externalities, and public goods. Another source of market failure, asymmetric information, was discussed in Chapter 14. While the problems and potential solutions to the problems of market failure were touched on in earlier chapters, this chapter will focus on specific government remedies to problems arising from production and allocation inefficiencies.

MARKET POWER

We saw in Chapter 8 that a firm has market power when a firm's selling price exceeds the marginal cost of production. Consider, again, Figure 8.10, which depicts the situation of equilibrium in a perfectly competitive market. The shaded area $0AEQ*$ represents the total benefits derived by consumers in competitive equilibrium. Total expenditures for $Q*$ units of output is given by the area $0P*EQ*$. The difference between the total net benefits received from the consumption of $Q*$ units of output and total expenditures on $Q*$ units of output is given by the shaded area $0AEQ* - 0P*EQ*$ $= P*AE$. The area $P*AE$, which is called the *consumer surplus*, is the difference between what consumers would be prepared to pay for a given quantity of a good or service and the amount they actually pay.

Definition: Consumer surplus is the difference between what consumers are willing to pay for a given quantity of a good or service and the amount they actually pay.

Figure 8.10 also illustrates the concept of producer surplus. In the figure, the total cost of producing $Q*$ units of output is given by the area $0BEQ*$. Total revenues (consumer expenditures) earned from the sale of $Q*$ units of output is given by the area $0P*EQ*$. The difference between the total revenues from the sale of $Q*$ and the total cost of producing $Q*$ (total economic profit) is given by the shaded area $0BEQ* - 0P*EQ* = BP*E$. The shaded area $BP*E$ is referred to as *producer surplus*. Producer surplus is the difference between the total revenues earned from the production and sale of a given quantity of output and what the firm would have been willing to accept for the production and sale of that quantity of output.

Definition: Producer surplus is the difference between the total revenues earned from the production and sale of a given quantity of output and what the firm would have been willing to accept for the production and sale of that quantity of output.

Perfect competition represents an ideal market structure in the sense that it guarantees a socially optimal level of goods and services. This occurs because profit-maximizing firms produce up to the point where the market-

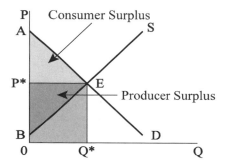

FIGURE 8.10. Consumer and producer surplus.

determined price (marginal revenue) equals the marginal cost of production. In perfectly competitive markets, output will expand up to the point where the marginal benefit derived by consumers, as evaluated along the demand function, is just equal to the marginal opportunity cost to society of producing the last unit of output. This is illustrated at point E in Figure 8.10. Total social benefits will be maximized because voluntary exchanges between buyers and sellers will continue only so long as both parties benefit from the transaction. Moreover, in the long run, perfect competition guarantees that productive resources are efficiently allocated and that production occurs at minimum cost. It should be readily apparent that at point E in Figure 8.10 consumer and producer surplus is maximized. Perfect competition is considered a superior market structure precisely because perfect competition maximizes total societal benefits.

Contrast the situation depicted in Figure 8.10 with that of a profit-maximizing monopolist depicted in Figure 8.11. A monopolist may be a single firm that is the sole producer of a good or service, or a group of firms engaged in collusive output and pricing behavior. A monopolist will maximize profits by producing at the output level where $MR = MC$. This occurs at an output level of Q_m. The profit-maximizing price charged by the monopolist is P_m. It is clear from the figure that under monopoly the consumer is paying a higher price for less output. The reader will also verify that consumer surplus has been reduced from $P*AE$ to P_mAC. The consumer is made worse off by the area $P*P_mCE$.

Figure 8.11 also illustrates the extent to which the monopolist has benefitted at the expense of the consumer. Compared with perfect competition, producer surplus has changed from the area $BP*E$ to BP_mCF. The net change in producer surplus is $P*P_mCG - FGE$. The portion of lost consumer surplus $P*P_mCE$ captured by the monopolist ($P*P_mCE$) represents an income transfer from consumer to producer. If the net change in producer surplus is positive, then the producer has been made better off as a result of the monopolization of the industry.

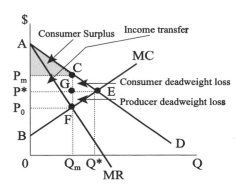

FIGURE 8.11. Consumer and producer deadweight loss.

Is society better off or worse off under monopoly as compared with perfect competition? Referring again to Figure 8.11, the reader will verify that under perfect competition the net benefits to society are given by the sum of consumer and producer surplus, $P*AE + BP*E = BAE$. Under monopoly, however, the net benefits to society are given by the sum of consumer and producer surplus $P_mAC + BP_mCF = BACF$. Since $BACF < BAE$, then society has been made worse off as a result of monopolization of the industry. The lost consumer and producer surplus is given by the area $GCE + FGE = FCE$. The area FCE is referred to as *total deadweight loss*. The area GCE is referred to as the *consumers' deadweight loss*, which represents the reduction in consumer surplus that is not captured by the monopolist. The area FGE is referred to as *producers' deadweight loss*. Since the monopolist is not producing at minimum per unit cost, producer deadweight loss represents the loss to society from the inefficient allocation of productive resources.

Definition: Total deadweight loss is the loss of consumption and production efficiency arising from monopolistic market structures. It is the loss of consumer and producer surplus when a monopolist charges a price that is greater than the marginal cost of production.

Governments can attempt to reduce or eliminate total deadweight loss by making it illegal for a firm or group of firms to exercise or acquire market power. *Antitrust legislation* represents an attempt by government to move industries closer to the "ideal" price and output conditions that would prevail under a perfectly competitive market structure.

Definition: Antitrust legislation represents government intervention in the marketplace, such as making it illegal for firms in an industry to engage in collusive pricing and output practices, to prevent industry abuse of market power.

LANDMARK U.S. ANTITRUST LEGISLATION

As we have already seen, a perfectly competitive market structure provides a model for evaluating economic efficiency. As we have seen in Chapter 8 and elsewhere, perfectly competition is defined by a number of important requirements, including a large number of buyers and sellers, homogeneous goods and services, perfect information, easy entry into and exit from the industry by approximately identical firms, and the absence economies of scale. Also characteristic of perfectly competitive markets is the principle of *laissez-faire*, or nonintervention by government in the marketplace.

The conditions that define perfectly competitive market structures, however, are rarely satisfied in practice. The output of different firms, for example, are typically differentiated; buyers and sellers rarely have complete information about the goods and services being transacted; and entry into and exit from the market by potential competitors are frequently inhibited. Moreover, many industries are dominated by large firms that have engaged in monopolistic pricing practices, stifled competition, and inhibited product innovation and new product development. This exercise of market power often causes the market to fail, which means in turn that free markets have failed to provide a socially optimal mix of goods and services.

Since 1890, the U.S. government has endeavored to prevent monopolistic pricing and output behavior to promote competition by promulgating a host of antitrust legislation. The most important of these pieces of antitrust legislation are the Sherman Act (1890), the Clayton Act (1914), the Federal Trade Commission Act (1914), the Willis–Graham Act (1921), the Robinson–Patman Act (1936), the Wheeler–Lea Act (1938), the Celler–Kefauver Act (1950), and the Hart–Scott–Rodino Act (1980). The most significant elements of these antitrust laws are outlined next.

SHERMAN ACT (1890)

The Sherman Act, which was the first major piece of antitrust legislation passed by Congress, was designed to prevent the growth and exercise of monopoly power. The substance of the Sherman Act is contained in its first two sections:

> Section 1. Every contract, combination in the form of trust or otherwise, or conspiracy, in restraint of trade or commerce among the several States, or with foreign nations, is hereby declared illegal. . . .
>
> Section 2. Every person who shall monopolize, or attempt to monopolize, or combine or conspire with any other person or persons, to monopolize any part of the trade or commerce among the several States, or with foreign nations, shall be deemed guilty of a misdemeanor, and, on conviction thereof, shall be punished by a fine not exceeding five thousand dollars, or by imprisonment not exceeding one year, or by both said punishments, in the discretion of the court.

The Sherman Act had a number of shortcomings. To begin with, while it declared monopolistic structures and certain kinds of monopolistic behavior as illegal, the acts that constituted a "restraint of trade" were not clearly specified. Moreover, there was no specific agency designated to enforce the provisions of the Sherman Act. This shortcoming was rectified in 1903 with the creation of the Antitrust Division of the U.S. Department of Justice.

In 1911, two major antitrust cases were brought before the Supreme Court. The plaintiffs were the Standard Oil Company, which controlled about 91% of the petroleum refining industry, and the American Tobacco Company, which controlled between 75 and 90% of the market for tobacco products except cigars. Both companies employed ruthless tactics to acquire competing firms or drive them out of business. The Supreme Court found both companies guilty of violating Sections 1 and 2 of the Sherman Act and ordered each one to divest itself of large holdings in other companies. In its ruling, however, the court indicated that not all actions that seemed to restrain trade violated the Sherman Act. In enunciating its "rule of reason," the court said that violations of the Sherman Act included only those actions that seemed "unreasonable." Thus, it would be possible for a near-monopoly to be in conformity with the Sherman Act as long as it had used reasonable tactics to obtain its market share.

In the subsequent decade, the Justice Department brought antitrust cases against Eastman Kodak, International Harvester, United Shoe Machinery, and United States Steel. While each of these companies controlled a significant share of its market, all four cases were dismissed on the grounds that there was no evidence of "unreasonable conduct." Regrettably, the "rule of reason" did little to clarify the wording of the Sherman Act, a drawback that ultimately led to the drafting of another antitrust law.

CLAYTON ACT (1914)

Enacted by Congress to strengthen the Sherman Act and to clarify the rule of reason, the Clayton Act made a number of specific practices illegal if these practices substantially lessened competition or tended to create a monopoly.

The practices outlawed by the Clayton Act include *price discrimination*, *exclusive contracts*, *tying contracts*, *intercorporate stockholdings*, and *interlocking directorates*. As defined by the legislation, price discrimination is the practice of charging different customers different prices provided these differences were not the result of grade, quality, or quantity of the product sold, where lower prices resulted from cost differences, or where lower prices were offered to match competitors' prices.

Definition: Exclusive contracts were used to force customers to purchase one product as a precondition for obtaining some other product.

Definition: A tying contract makes the purchase of one or more goods or services from one firm contingent on the customer's refusal to purchase other goods and services from competing firms.

Definition: An intercorporate stockholding is the practice of one corporation acquiring shares in a competing corporation.

Definition: An interlocking directorate exists when the same individual sits on the board of directors of two or more competing corporations.

FEDERAL TRADE COMMISSION ACT (1914)

The Federal Trade Commission Act created the Federal Trade Commission (FTC). The FTC was established to investigate "the organization, business conduct, practices and management" of companies engaged in interstate commerce. Unfortunately, the Federal Trade Commission Act also contributed to uncertainty in antitrust legislation by declaring unlawful "unfair methods of competition in commerce." The determination of what constituted unfair methods of competition was left to the FTC. The FTC was also given the authority to issue "cease-and-desist" orders in cases of violations of the Sherman and Clayton Acts. Thus, the Federal Trade Commission could proactively safeguard the public from unfair or misleading business practices. Under the Federal Trade Commission Act it was no longer necessary for the government to await private law suits before prosecuting firms engaged in unfair business practices.

WILLIS–GRAHAM ACT (1921)

The Willis–Graham Act exempted telephone mergers from antitrust review. The reason for this was that the government determined that the telephone industry, which was dominated by the American Telephone & Telegraph Company (AT&T), was a natural monopoly. The reader will recall from Chapter 8 that a natural monopoly may occur when a firm exhibits substantial economies of scale in production. In this case, a single firm may be able to supply the output for the entire market more efficiently than a number of smaller firms. Because AT&T was able to provide telephone service at lower per-unit cost than a large number of smaller utilities, it was believed to be in the public's best interest to regulate, rather than to break up, the telephone industry. The issues involved in optimal price regulation will be discussed shortly.

ROBINSON–PATMAN ACT (1936)

The Robinson–Patman Act was enacted to protect to independent retailers and wholesalers from unfair discrimination by large sellers exercising purchasing power. Often referred to as the Chain Store Act, this legislation amended Section 2 of the Clayton Act dealing with price discrimination. The Robinson–Patman Act outlawed the following practices:

Charging different prices to different customers on identical sales
Selling at different prices in different parts of the country "for the purpose of destroying competition or eliminating a competitor"
Selling at "unreasonably low prices" to eliminate competition or a competitor
Price discrimination
Paying brokerage commissions to buyers, or to intermediaries under their control
Granting allowances, services, or other accommodations to sellers by buyers, regardless of whether the services are provided by the buyer or not, which are "not accorded to all purchasers on proportionally equal terms"

WHEELER–LEA ACT (1938)

The Wheeler–Lea Act extended the language of the Federal Trade Commission Act to protect consumers against "unfair and deceptive acts or practices" in interstate commerce. Wheeler–Lea gave the FTC authority to prosecute companies engaged in false and deceptive advertising. The act defines "false advertising" as "an advertisement other than labeling which is misleading in a material respect." The Wheeler–Lea Act is significant because it gave consumers an equal footing with producers who may have been materially harmed as a result of unfair competition.

CELLER–KEFAUVER ACT (1950)

THE Celler–Kefauver Act extended Section 7 of the Clayton Act, which made it illegal for companies to acquire shareholdings in competing corporations. The Clayton Act outlawed only *horizontal mergers* (mergers of firms producing the same product). The Celler–Kefauver Act closed this loophole by giving the government the authority to prohibit *vertical mergers* (mergers of firms at various stages of the production process) and *conglomerate mergers* (mergers of firms producing unrelated products), provided it can be shown that such mergers substantially reduced competition or tended to result in monopolies.

Definition: A horizontal merger is a merger of firms producing the same product.

Definition: A vertical merger is a merger of firms at various stages of the production process.

Definition: A conglomerate merger is a merger of firms producing unrelated products.

The Celler–Kefauver Act was intended to maintain and promote competition. This legislation applied mainly to mergers among large firms, or mergers of large firms with small firms. The Celler–Kefauver Act was not intended to prevent mergers among small firms that tended to strengthen the competitive position in the market of the new company.

HART–SCOTT–RODINO ACT (1980)

Before the Hart–Scott–Rodino Act, antitrust legislation was directed toward the business practices of corporations. Many large companies, such as law and accounting firms, however, are not corporations but partnerships. The Hart–Scott–Rodino Act extended antitrust legislation to include proprietorships and partnerships. The act also required that proposed mergers between, and among, proprietorships and partnerships be reported to the Antitrust Division of the U.S. Department of Justice.

MERGER REGULATION

Although the Clayton Act (1914) and the Celler–Kefauver Act (1950) gave the federal government the authority to dissolve mergers that "substantially lessen competition," it was not until 1968 that the Antitrust Division of the U.S. Department of Justice issued its first guidelines to reduce uncertainty about the kinds of merger it found unacceptable. These guidelines stated that if the largest four firms in an industry controlled 75% or more of the market, the merger of a firm with 15% or more market share with another firm controlling as little as 1% market share would be challenged in the courts. In 1982 the Justice Department issued a new set of more lenient guidelines. These guidelines were amended in 1984 and remain in effect today. The new guidelines were based on the Herfindahl–Hirschman Index (HHI), which was discussed in Chapter 10. The Herfindahl–Hirschman Index ranges in value from zero to 10,000. According to the guidelines, the Justice Department views any industry with an HHI of 1,000 or less as being "unconcentrated." Mergers in unconcentrated industries will go unchallenged. If the index is between 1,000 and 1,800, however, then a proposed merger will be challenged if, as a result of the merger, the index rises by more than 100 points. Finally, if the HHI is greater than 1,800, proposed mergers will be challenged if the index increases by more than 50 points.

PRICE REGULATION

While antitrust laws attempt to prevent a firm or group of firms from exercising market power to the detriment of consumers, not all anticompetitive arrangements are necessarily undesirable. The production of some goods and services can generate substantial economies of scale. As mentioned in earlier and in Chapter 8, utility companies and other such firms are called natural monopolies, and the government may determine that it is in the public's best interest to allow such monopolies to exist. In return for this privileged market position, however, government authorities often will reserve the right to regulate product prices at socially optimal levels. In principle, the objective of price regulation is to eliminate the deadweight loss associated with monopolistic market structures. This situation is illustrated in Figure 15.1.

Unregulated, profit-maximizing monopolists will produce at the output level at which marginal cost equals marginal revenue. In Figure 15.1, the profit-maximizing monopolist will produce Q_m units of output at a price of P_{pc}. A perfectly competitive industry, on the other hand, will produce at the levels at which supply (marginal cost) equals demand. In Figure 15.1 this occurs at the output level Q_{pc} at a price of P_{pc}. If the government believes

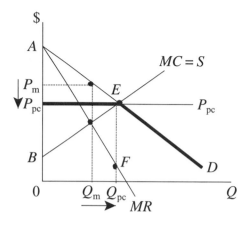

FIGURE 15.1 Regulating price at the perfectly competitive level to eliminate deadweight loss.

that it is in the best interest of society to allow a single firm to produce the industry's output, but wishes to eliminate the deadweight loss associated with monopolistic market structures, then regulatory authorities will mandate that the firm charge a price that is no higher than P_{pc}.

When the price is regulated at P_{pc}, the monopolist's effective demand curve in Figure 15.1 is given by the heavy-line segment $P_{pc}ED$. The firm's new marginal revenue curve is given by the narrow line segments $E(P_{pc})$ and $F(MR)$. A profit-maximizing monopolist will produce at the output level at which $MC = MR$, which occurs at the perfectly competitive output level, Q_{pc}. At this output level the selling price of the good or service will be at the perfectly competitive price, P_{pc}.

By regulating the selling price of the product at P_{pc}, which is less than P_m, the government has effectively eliminated the deadweight loss associated with the monopolist's market power. In the situation depicted Figure 15.1, the result of price regulation at the perfectly competitive level is to reduce monopoly profits but to increase the total societal benefits. The net benefit to society is positive because the loss of producer surplus resulting from regulating price at the perfectly competitive level is less than the increase in consumer surplus.

Our analysis suggests that price regulation is an effective method for inducing profit-maximizing monopolists to produce at socially optimal levels. Unfortunately, while this may be true in principle, reality is quite another matter. Assuming that regulators have the best interests of society as a whole in mind, which may not be the case, government efforts to increase the total societal benefits may be thwarted by an inability to accurately determine the market supply and demand conditions. In fact, the lack of complete or accurate information may set a price that is socially detrimental. To see this, consider the situation depicted in Figure 15.2.

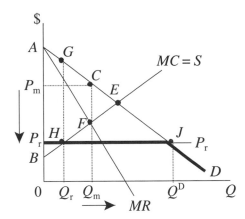

FIGURE 15.2 Regulating price at a
socially detrimental level.

We saw in Figure 8.11 that setting the price at P_m results in a total dead-weight loss to society corresponding to the area of the triangle FCE. From Figure 15.1 we saw that this deadweight loss can be eliminated by regulating price at its perfectly competitive level, P_{pc}. What happens, however, if regulators miscalculate and set the price at P_r in Figure 15.2? As before, a profit-maximizing monopolist will produce at the output level, Q_r, where $MC = MR$. The reader should verify that at a price of P_r, the quantity demand of the product is Q_D, which is greater than the quantity that the monopolist is willing to supply at that price, Q_r. In this case, regulators have caused a shortage of the product. Moreover, regulating the price at P_r has resulted in a total deadweight loss to society that is, in fact, greater than would have occurred in an unregulated market. It is somewhat paradoxical, therefore, that when government regulators succumb to popular pressure for unjustifiably low prices, the result might be socially detrimental levels of essential goods and services, such as is often the case with public utilities or transportation services.

Problem 15.1. Suppose that a monopolist's market demand and total cost equations are

$$Q = 2,000 - 5P$$

$$TC = 100 + 4Q + 0.4Q^2$$

a. Find the monopolist's profit-maximizing price and output.
b. What is the value of consumer deadweight loss? What is the value of producer deadweight loss? Calculate the value of total deadweight loss to society.
c. At what price should the government regulate the monopolist's product to eliminate total deadweight loss?
d. At what output level should the profit-maximizing firm produce at the regulated price?

e. Suppose that government regulates the price of the monopolist's product at $P = \$250$. Has society been made better off or worse off as a result of government intervention?

Solution

a. Solving the demand equation for price yields

$$P = 400 - 0.2Q$$

The monopolist's total and marginal revenue equations are

$$TR = PQ = 400Q - 0.2Q^2$$

$$MR = \frac{dTR}{dQ} = 400 - 0.4Q$$

The monopolist's marginal cost equation is

$$MC = \frac{dTC}{dQ} = 4 + 0.8Q$$

To obtain the monopolist's profit-maximizing level of output, equate marginal cost with marginal revenue, that is,

$$MC = MR$$

$$4 + 0.8Q = 400 - 0.4Q$$

$$Q_m = 330$$

The profit-maximizing price is

$$P_m = 400 - 0.2(330) = \$334$$

b. The solution to part a is illustrated in Figure 15.3.

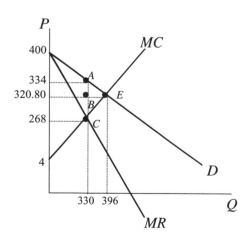

FIGURE 15.3 Diagrammatic solution to problem 15.1, part a.

The value of consumer deadweight loss is given by the area of the triangle ABE, that is,

$$\text{Area } ABE = \frac{1}{2}(334 - 320.80)(396 - 330) = \frac{1}{2}(13.2)(66) = \$435.60$$

The value of producer deadweight loss is given by the area of the triangle BCE, that is,

$$\text{Area } BCE = \frac{1}{2}(320.80 - 268)(396 - 330) = \frac{1}{2}(52.8)(66) = \$1,742.40$$

Total deadweight loss, which is the sum of consumer deadweight loss and producer deadweight loss, is given by the area of the triangle ACE.

$$\text{Total deadweight loss} = \text{area } ABE + \text{area } BCE = \text{area } ACE$$

$$= \frac{1}{2}(334 - 268)(396 - 330) = \$2,178$$

c. To eliminate total deadweight loss, the government should regulate the price of the monopolist's product at its perfectly competitive level, which occurs where supply $(= MC)$ equals demand. This occurs at $P_{pc} = \$320.80$.

d. The profit-maximizing monopolist will produce at the output level at which $MC = MR$. The monopolist's marginal revenue from $Q = 0$ to $Q = 396$ is the regulated price $P = \$320.80$. Thus, the monopolist's profit-maximizing output level is $Q = 396$, which is the perfectly competitive outcome.

e. Consider Figure 15.4, which illustrates the effect of the government regulated price $P = \$250$.
The profit-maximizing monopolist will produce at the level at which

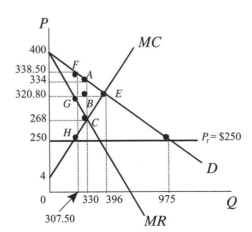

FIGURE 15.4 Diagrammatic solution to problem 15.1, part e.

$$MC = MR$$

$$4 + 0.8Q = 250$$

$$Q = 307.50$$

The value of consumer deadweight loss is given by the area of the triangle FGE, that is,

$$\text{Area } FGE = \frac{1}{2}(338.50 - 320.80)(396 - 307.50) = \$783.225$$

The value of producer deadweight loss is given by the area of the triangle GHE, that is,

$$\text{Area } GHE = \frac{1}{2}(320.8 - 250)(396 - 307.50) = \frac{1}{2}(70.8)(88.5) = \$3,132.90$$

Total deadweight loss, which is the sum of consumer deadweight loss and producer deadweight loss, is given by the area of the triangle FHE:

$$\text{Total deadweight loss} = \text{area } FGE + \text{area } GHE = \text{area } FHE$$

$$= \frac{1}{2}(338.50 - 250)(396 - 307.50) = \$3,916.125$$

Regulating the price of the monopolist's product at \$250 has resulted in an increase in both consumer and producer deadweight loss compared with the situation under monopoly. Moreover, the regulated price of \$250 has resulted in shortage of $975 - 307.50 = 667.50$. Thus, society has clearly been made worse off as a result of government intervention.

There is another issue relating to the price regulation of firms with market power that has not yet been addressed. This is the issue of firm profits in an environment of price regulation. To see this, consider Figure 15.5, which essentially replicates Figure 15.1 but also includes the firm's average total cost curve.

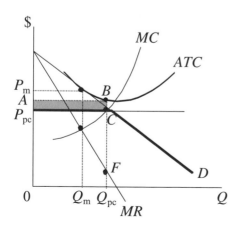

FIGURE 15.5 Regulated price at the perfectly competitive level, at which, however, the monopolist earns an economic loss.

In an unregulated environment the profit-maximizing monopolist in Figure 15.5 will produce Q_m units of output and charge a price of P_m. Since the firm is just earning a normal rate of return, the firm will continue to operate in the long run unless changed circumstances dictate otherwise. Suppose, however, that price is regulated at its perfectly competitive level. To maximize profits, the firm will produce at the output level Q_{pc}. At this output level, since $ATC > P_{pc}$ the firm generates an economic loss of $ABCP_{pc}$. In the long run, this firm will exit the industry. What can the government do to prevent this?

EXTERNALITIES

Market failure also occurs when third parties are positively or negatively affected by a market transaction. These third-party effects are called *externalities*. Externalities may affect either consumers or producers. The discussion that follows will focus on the situation in which production by one firm imposes costs on another firm in an unrelated industry. These costs are referred to as *negative externalities* in production. The most common example of a negative externality in production is pollution.

Definition: An externality is a cost or benefit resulting from a market transaction that is imposed upon third parties.

To make the discussion of negative externalities more concrete, consider the overly simplified example of a fertilizer plant that uses clean water from a nearby river in its production process. After production, the plant discharges its industrial waste further downstream. The amount of fertilizer produced is the result of the interaction of supply and demand in an unregulated fertilizer market. Downstream from the fertilizer plant is a brewery that uses water from the river to produce beer. To meet federal and state health and safety standards, the brewery must purify the river water before using it in the beer. Although the brewery is not a direct participant in fertilizer transactions, the company is indirectly affected because its total cost of producing beer is higher as a result of the need to purify the water polluted by the fertilizer plant. Alternatively, the fertilizer plant's production costs are lower than would be the case if it were required to clean up its effluents. To see the effects of negative externalities in a perfectly competitive industry, consider Figures 15.6.

Figure 15.6 illustrates the situation of a perfectly competitive firm, while Figure 15.7 illustrates the industry in which the firm operates. Suppose initially that the firms in this industry produce no negative externalities, such as pollution. The selling price of the firm's product is P_0, which is determined in the market as the intersection of the market demand and supply curves. In Figure 15.6, MPC^f represents the marginal private cost curve of the firm. Since all costs of production are incurred by the firm, the marginal

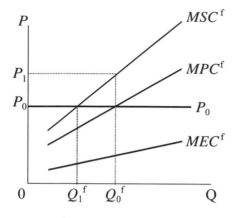

FIGURE 15.6 Negative externality in production for the firm.

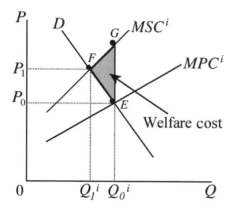

FIGURE 15.7 Negative externality in production for the industry.

private cost curve is identical to the firm's marginal cost curve (i.e., MPC^f = MC). In Figure 15.7, MPC^i represents the industry supply curve, which is simply the sum of all the MPC^f curves.

Now, suppose that the firm depicted in Figure 15.6 is responsible for discharging into the environment pollutants such as fertilizer plant effluents. This is represented by the marginal external cost curve (MEC^f) in Figure 15.6. The MEC^f curve summarizes the additional cost to others, such as the brewery, from an additional unit of output. In particular, MEC^f represents the cost to the brewery of cleaning up the fertilizer plant's effluents to make the water suitable for beer production. The environmental costs of pollution may also take the form of increased health expenditures by users of dirtier water. In either case, the fertilizer plant has imposed costs on third parties who are not directly involved in fertilizer transactions.

The MSC^f curve in Figure 15.6 represents the firm's marginal social cost of production and includes both the marginal private and marginal externality cost (i.e., $MSC^f = MPC^f + MEC^f$). The vertical distance between the MPC^f and MSC^f curves is the marginal externality cost of producing the good. If the externality cost of the firm depicted in Figure 15.6 is typical of all firms in the industry, then the MSC^i curve in Figure 15.7 lies above the MPC^i curve.

The socially efficient level of output occurs when each firm in the industry incurs the full costs of producing the product. This is illustrated in Figure 15.7 at the output level Q_1^i, where the MSC^i curve intersects the industry demand curve, DD. The socially efficient price is P_1. It is apparent from Figures 15.6 and 15.7 that when firms ignore externality costs, there is an inefficiently high level of production. The oversupply of the product is illustrated in Figure 15.7 as the distance $Q_0^i - Q_1^i$. The welfare cost to society is also illustrated in Figure 15.7. This cost is given by the shaded area FGE, which measures the difference between the marginal social cost and marginal social benefit for each unit of overproduction.

Problem 15.2. Suppose that the marginal private cost of producing fertilizer is

$$MPC = 4Q$$

Suppose further that the marginal externality cost of the pollution emitted is

$$MEC = 2Q$$

Finally, suppose that market demand for fertilizer is given as

$$Q = 50 - 0.25P$$

a. Find the perfectly competitive price and output level.
b. If this industry were dominated by a single firm, what would be the profit-maximizing price and output level?
c. Find the socially optimal price and output level.

Solution
a. A perfectly competitive industry will produce at an output level at which marginal private cost equals price, $MPC = P$. Solving the demand equation for price yields

$$P = 200 - 4Q$$

Substituting

$$MPC = P$$

$$4Q = 200 - 4Q$$

$$Q^* = 25$$

$$P^* = 200 - 4(25) = \$100$$

b. A monopolist maximizes profit by producing at an output level at which marginal private cost equals marginal revenue, $MPC = MR$. The monopolist's total revenue equation is

$$TR = PQ = (200 - 4Q)Q = 200Q - 4Q^2$$

$$MR = \frac{dTR}{dQ} = 200 - 8Q$$

$$MPC = MR$$

$$4Q = 200 - 8Q$$

$$Q^* = 16.67$$

$$P^* = 200 - 4(16.67) = \$133.33$$

c. The socially optimal level of output occurs at an output level at which marginal social cost equals price, $MSC = P$. Marginal social cost equals the sum of marginal private and marginal externality costs, $MSC = MPC + MEC$. Thus, the socially optimal level of output is

$$MPC + MEC = P$$

$$4Q + 2Q = 200 - 4Q$$

$$Q^* = 20$$

$$P^* = 200 - 4(20) = \$120$$

COASE THEOREM

The presence of negative externalities is a strong argument in favor of government intervention in the marketplace. In principle, there are at least two ways in which the government can intercede in the market to promote a more socially beneficial outcome. On the one hand, the government can directly involve itself in the market process by, say, requiring producers to directly absorb the cleanup costs of the pollution rather than allowing these costs to be absorbed by witting or unwitting third parties. This approach falls under the general rubric of government regulation. By contrast, the government can try to establish conditions under which the market determines an efficient solution to the externality problem. A theoretical justification for this market approach can be found in the Coase theorem (see Coase, 1960).

To understand the rationale underlying the Coase theorem, it will be useful to view negative externalities as the result of a "missing" market. More specifically, the fertilizer plant discussed earlier has unrestricted access to clean water. Because clean water is free, the total cost of producing fertilizer is less than it would be if the firm had to pay for clean water.

Suppose, on the other hand, that there existed a market for clean water and the fertilizer plant had to pay a positive price per unit of clean water used. In general, the market price for a good or service is determined where the marginal private benefit (demand) curve for clean water intersects the marginal private cost (supply) curve. Since clean water is a scarce resource, the firm would undoubtedly have to pay a positive price for clean water. Thus, the firm's marginal production cost would be higher, its output lower, and the price of fertilizer higher, than would be the case if it obtained clean water for free.

In most cases, however, markets for clean water or clean air do not exist. Why? The reason is that no one "owns" the property (ownership) rights to these resources. Without well-defined property rights, there can be no market for the purchase and sale of, say, clean water, and, therefore, no market price. The result is an inefficient (excessive) use of this clean water. In other words, in the absence of well-defined property rights, there is an incentive for the fertilizer company to "overproduce" and, consequently, to "overpollute." What this suggests, of course, is that one possible way to solve the problems caused by negative externalities is for the government to assign private property (ownership) rights for these resources.

To see how the assignment of property rights will lead to a socially efficient use of clean water, suppose that the government gives the fertilizer plant ownership of the clean water. The profit-maximizing fertilizer plant will now base its output decisions not only on the market for fertilizer but on the market for clean water as well. More specifically, the fertilizer plant must also consider the possible trade-off of reduced profit from lower fertilizer production and income earned from selling clean water to the downriver brewery. If the increase profits earned from the sale of clean water are greater than the reduced profits from lower fertilizer production, then it will be in the fertilizer company's best interest to reduce fertilizer output and, consequently, pollution. This situation is illustrated in Figure 15.6.

The maximum amount the brewery is willing to pay the fertilizer company to reduce its level of output, and thus the level of pollutants discharged, is measured by the vertical difference between the MPC^f and MSC^f curves. The fertilizer company's lost profit from a reduction in output is the vertical difference between the firm's marginal revenue (price) and marginal private cost (MPC^f) curves.

Prior to being assigned the property rights to clean water, the fertilizer company maximized its profit by producing at output level Q_0^f, where $P = MPC^f$. With ownership of clean water property rights, the fertilizer company should be willing to reduce its output as long as the amount of compensation from the brewery is greater than the loss in profits. Assuming that there are no transaction or bargaining costs, it should be obvious from Figure 15.6 that for any output level less than Q_1^f the compensation from the brewery is less than the additional profit from increasing output. Thus, the fertilizer company will expand output to at least Q_0^f. For any output level greater than Q_1^f but less than Q_0^f it will pay for the fertilizer plant to reduce its output. Thus, if the polluting fertilizer company is given the ownership rights to the clean water, then the result will be a socially optimal level of output.

Theorem: The assignment of well-defined private property rights will result in a socially efficient allocation of productive resources and a socially optimal, market-determined level of goods and services.

Of course, the reader might complain that this outcome is "unfair": the perpetrator of pollution damage was assigned the property rights and may be unduly enriched regardless of the outcome. How the fertilizer plant came to possess the property rights to clean water in the first place is an interesting question in its own right, and may be related to political rent-seeking activities on the part of the firm. We will return to this important issue later. For now, however, it is important to recognize that the fundamental cause of socially undesirable levels of pollution was the fact that the private property rights to clean water were not well defined. Assigning private property rights created a market for pollution, which ultimately resulted in a socially desirable level of fertilizer production and pollution.

Fortunately, socially optimal outcomes do not depend on the assignment of private property rights. To see this, suppose that the brewery, not the fertilizer plant, owns the ownership rights to clean water. The question now is how much will the fertilizer plant be willing to pay to the brewery for the right to pollute the river? The answer, of course, is that the fertilizer plant will be willing to pay for the right to pollute as long as the marginal cost, which includes payment for the right to pollute, is less than the marginal revenue from increased production. To see this, consider Figure 15.8.

Suppose, initially, that the fertilizer company is producing at the output level Q_0^f. Suppose further that an increase in the market demand for fertilizer causes the price of fertilizer to rise from P_0 to P_1. The fertilizer plant

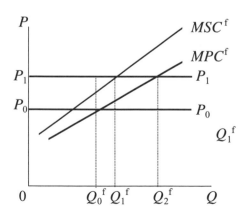

FIGURE 15.8 Negative externality in production where the third party owns the private-property rights.

would like to increase production from Q_0^f to Q_2^f to maximize profits. To increase production, however, the firm must pay the brewery for the right to pollute the river. The compensation paid by the fertilizer company, which reflects the marginal externality cost of pollution, will cause the marginal private cost function of the fertilizer company to increase from MPC^f to MSC^f. How much compensation is the fertilizer company willing to pay? The reader will note that at output level Q_0^f the increase in marginal revenue, $P_1 - P_0$, exceeds the increase in marginal cost, $MSC^f - MPC^f$. Thus, it is in the firm's best interest to increase output up to the socially optimal output level Q_1^f, where $P_1 = MSC^f$.

The Coase theorem is significant because it asserts that the assignment of private property rights will lead to a socially efficient level of production and pollution. The Coase theorem also separates the issue of efficiency from that of equity. Regardless of who owns the private property rights to clean water, a socially efficient level of fertilizer production and pollution results. On the other hand, the assignment of private property rights will determine the distribution of welfare, which may excite controversy about what is considered to be a "fair" outcome.

GOVERNMENT SOLUTIONS: REGULATION

In the absence of well-defined property rights, governments can intervene directly to resolve such problems of negative externalities. In general, governments deal with the social costs arising from environmental problems through the use of regulations, permits, and taxes. In this section we will discuss government regulations in the form of emission standards and penalty fees.

To understand the rationale underlying the use of government regulation to compel firms to produce socially optimal levels of pollution, consider Figure 15.9. To simplify matters, assume initially that the industry

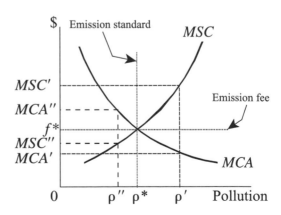

FIGURE 15.9 Emission standards and fees.

depicted in Figure 15.9 consists of a single firm. The total level of pollution emitted by the firm is measured along the horizontal axis, while the unit cost of pollution is measured along the vertical axis. As before, the *MSC* curve represents the marginal social cost of production, which includes both the marginal private and marginal externality cost. We know that marginal social cost is an increasing function of the firm's output level. The marginal social cost curve assumes that the firm is operating with a given level of production technology. Pollution is a by-product of production, and the amount of pollution created is a function of the underlying production technology. We will assume that the level of the pollution created varies directly with the level of the firm's output (i.e., the greater the level of output, the greater the level of pollution created).

On the surface, it may appear that reducing the level of pollution unambiguously benefits society. Unfortunately, nothing could be further from the truth. Pollution is a by-product of production, which generates social benefits. Thus, while reducing pollution lowers marginal social costs, it also results in a reduction of social benefits. This reduction in social benefits may be viewed as the opportunity cost of pollution abatement. This relationship is illustrated in Figure 15.9, where *MCA* represents the firm's marginal cost of pollution abatement.

The position of the *MCA* curve depends on the firm's production technology. If the firm switches to a production technology that results in a lower level of pollution, then the *MCA* curve will shift upward. The marginal private cost of production will also shift upward because of the use of the new, more costly technology, although the marginal social cost curve may be unaffected because of the reduction in negative, third-party effects. It should be clear from Figure 15.9 that with a given production technology, reductions in pollution can be accomplished only through a reduction in output. Contrary to popular belief, therefore, the optimal level of pollution is not zero, since this would imply a zero level of production. This, of course, begs the question: Is there a socially optimal level of pollution?

The optimal level of pollution in Figure 15.9 is ρ^*. To see this, suppose that the firm produced an output level that generated pollution of ρ'. At this level, marginal social cost associated with this level of pollution is MSC'. Reducing production will, of course, reduce the level of production, but at the cost of lower output. As long as the marginal cost of pollution abatement (i.e., the marginal loss of social benefits from production) is less than the marginal cost of pollution, society will be made better off by reducing pollution. On the other hand, if the firm is producing at ρ'', then society will be better off by accepting higher levels of production (and pollution), since the marginal cost of pollution abatement is greater than the marginal social cost of pollution. Clearly, society's welfare will be maximized where the marginal social cost of pollution is equal to the marginal cost of pollution abatement, which in Figure 15.9 occurs at pollution level ρ^*. Of course, there is no *a priori* reason for the firm depicted to produce at this, or any other, level. Unless there is an incentive to do otherwise, the firm depicted in Figure 15.9 will produce at the output level at which marginal revenue equals marginal private cost.

Suppose that the firm depicted in Figure 15.9 maximizes profit by producing at an output level that results in ρ' pollution. Suppose further that the government has determined that the socially optimal level of pollution is ρ^*. What can government do to reduce pollution by the amount $(\rho' - \rho)$? The most obvious solution is for the environmental protection agency of the government to mandate that pollution levels not exceed ρ^*. The firm's management could be discouraged from violating these emission standards by the threat of fines, imprisonment, or some other legal recourse.

Alternatively, government could achieve the same socially optimal level of pollution by imposing an emission penalty fee, a fine levied on the firm per unit of pollution produced. In Figure 15.9, the optimal emission fee is f^*. Whenever the marginal revenue to the firm arising from an increase in production is greater than the emission fee, it will be in the firm's best interest to increase production and pollution until $MCA = f^*$, which would result in the same socially optimal level of pollution ρ^*.

The problem with both emission standards and fees is that these approaches assume that the regulator has complete information about production methods, which is rarely, if ever, the case. To highlight this point, we will relax our earlier assumption that the industry described in Figure 15.8 consists of a single firm. Suppose, instead, that the industry consists of two firms, and each uses a different production technology, which generates different amounts of pollution. This situation is illustrated in Figure 15.10, where firm 1 employs a more environmentally friendly technology than firm 2. For this reason, the MCA_2 curve lies above MCA_1.

Suppose now that the government's environmental protection agency wants to reduce the average level of pollution from each firm to ρ^*. The

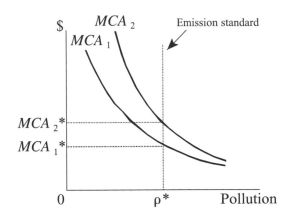

FIGURE 15.10 Emission standards and incomplete information.

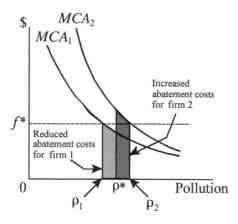

FIGURE 15.11 Emission fees and incomplete information.

government could accomplish this outcome by mandating that each firm's pollution not exceed ρ^*. In the situation depicted in Figure 15.10, both firms reduce the level of pollution to ρ^*, but the marginal cost of abatement for firm 1 is less than the marginal cost of abatement for firm 2. This outcome is not efficient, however, since neither firm minimizes the cost of abatement. A more efficient solution could be accomplished by charging an emission fee. An alternative approach is for the government to impose an emission fee of f^* on both firms. In this way, each firm incurs the same marginal abatement cost, but the levels of pollution produced are different. This outcome is illustrated in Figure 15.11.

Unlike the situation depicted in Figure 15.10, where a mandated emission standard resulted in different marginal abatement costs for the two firms, in this case the marginal abatement costs are the same for both firms, but the amount of pollution is different. As a result of the imposition of the emission fee f^*, firm 1 will reduce the amount of pollution produced to ρ_1 while firm 2 will increase the amount of pollution produced to ρ_2. The average pollution produced by the two firms is the efficient level ρ^*. One advantage of charging an emission fee is that it serves as an incentive for the high-cost firms to adopt production technologies that generate lower levels of pollution.

Unfortunately, incomplete information about the firms' abatement costs could result in large welfare costs to society from incorrectly pricing the emission fee. This situation is illustrated in Figure 15.12, where, because of incomplete information, the government sets the emission fee at $f' < f^*$, and the result of this incorrect pricing is a welfare cost to society equal to the area of the shaded region ABC. When incomplete information about abatement costs threatens to result in large welfare costs to society, setting emissions standards may be superior to charging an emission fee as a solution to the pollution problem.

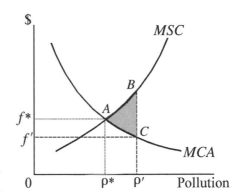

FIGURE 15.12 Incomplete information and welfare costs.

GOVERNMENT SOLUTIONS: PERMITS

An alternative solution to the pollution problem is the sale of transferrable emission permits. The introduction of transferrable emission permits is the distinguishing feature of the Clean Air Act of 1970, as amended in 1990. Firms covered by the Clean Air Act are required by law to purchase from the government permits to emit toxic pollutants into the atmosphere. These permits, which are limited in number, require that firms pay a fee for each unit of pollution emitted. These permits, however, may be bought and sold between firms. Initial purchases of emission permits from the government added to existing firms' total fixed and total variable costs. The addition to fixed cost was the price paid for the permit itself, while the addition to variable cost was the fee paid per unit of pollution. New firms entering an industry are required to adopt or exceed the most efficient pollution reduction methods available. Existing firms are required to do the same within 3 years. New firms can obtain pollution emission permits only by purchasing them from other firms.

The rationale behind this scheme is that a competitive market for emission permits will effectively create a proxy market for pollution. Assuming that the market is efficient, the equilibrium price of the permits will be the marginal cost of pollution abatement. Thus, the officially determined level of pollution emission will be achieved at least cost. To see how this works, consider the situation depicted in Figure 15.13 in which the polluting firm sells its output in a perfectly competitive market.

As mentioned earlier, the purchase of the emission permit causes the firm's fixed and variable costs to increase. The increase in the firm's fixed reflects the price paid by the firm for the permit. The variable cost increases because once the permit has been purchased, the firm must pay a fee for each unit of pollution emitted. This is illustrated in Figure 15.13 by upward shifts of both the average total cost and marginal cost curves. Since a profit-maximizing firm in a perfectly competitive industry will produce at an

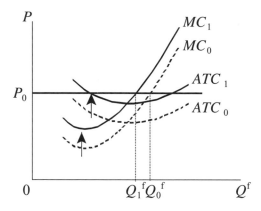

FIGURE 15.13 Effect of the purchase of emission permits on an individual firm's output.

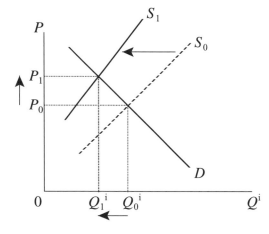

FIGURE 15.14 Effect of the purchase of emission permits on industry price and output.

output level at which the output price is equal to the marginal cost of production, the firm's output level will decline from Q_0^f to Q_1^f, and the firm's per-unit profit will fall from $P_0 - ATC_0$ to $P_0 - ATC_1$. Thus, the result of the Clean Air Act is to compel firms to internalize the cost of pollution generated.

Figure 15.14 illustrates the effect of the sale of emission permits on the market price of the product. Because of the increased marginal cost of production for each firm in the industry, the industry supply curve shifts to the left. The result is that the market equilibrium price rises from P_0 to P_1, and equilibrium industry output level falls from Q_0^i to Q_1^i. The reader will note that the outcome of the market sale of pollution emission permits is the same as outcome depicted in Figure 15.7. The existence of a market for pollution emission permits has two important implications. To begin with, if the market demand for the industry output increases, then new firms will be

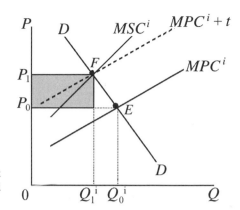

FIGURE 15.15 The use of a per-unit tax to reduce output to a socially optimal level.

able to enter the industry by purchasing permits from firms in nonpolluting industries. Thus, government efforts to control pollution are consistent with competitive market processes.

By contrast, if a market for pollution emission permits did not exist, then the entry of new firms in response to an increase in market demand would not be possible. Another important implication of a market for pollution emission permits is that it encourages firms to develop and install more environmentally friendly production technologies, which will enable innovating firms to recover at least a portion of their development and installation costs by selling emission permits no longer needed.

GOVERNMENT SOLUTIONS: TAXES

The final solution to the pollution problem that will be discussed is a tax levied by the government on the per-unit output of the firm. The rationale behind the use of a per-unit tax is to raise firms' marginal cost of production to reduce industry supply to a socially optimal level of output. To see this, consider Figure 15.15, which modifies Figure 15.17. Recall that the industry supply curve is the sum of the firm's marginal private cost curves. The initial market equilibrium price and quantity is P_0 and Q_0^i, respectively. Now, assume that the socially optimal level of output in Figure 15.15 is Q_1^i. To achieve this level of output, the government imposes a tax that is equivalent to the difference between marginal social cost and marginal private cost at the socially optimal output level. The new marginal private cost curve with the tax is illustrated by the dashed line $MPC^i + t$. The new market equilibrium price and quantity are P_1 and Q_1^i, respectively. The lower level of industry output corresponds to a lower, socially optimal, level of pollution. Government revenues generated by the use of a per-unit tax on output are equal to $(P_1 - P_0) \times Q_1^i$.

Government revenues raised from the per-unit tax (t) on output are illustrated by the shaded rectangle in Figure 15.15. These revenues, which could be used by government to clean up any pollution damage, may or may not equal the total external cost. The reader will recall that marginal externality cost is the difference between marginal social cost and marginal private cost. If marginal external cost is an increasing function of output, then the marginal social cost of production will not be identical to marginal private cost plus the per unit tax. These differences are illustrated in Figure 15.15. Thus, a per-unit tax equal to the marginal external cost at Q_1^i will either underestimate or overestimate pollution damage at any other output level.

Problem 15.3. Suppose as in Problem 15.2 that the marginal private cost and marginal externality cost are

$$MPC = 4Q$$

$$MEC = 2Q$$

As before, the market demand equation is

$$Q = 50 - 0.25P$$

a. At the socially desirable output level, what is the product price?
b. What per-unit tax on output should be levied by the government to achieve a socially desirable output level?
c. What are government revenues at the socially optimal output level?

Solution
a. As we saw earlier, the socially optimal level of output occurs at an output level where marginal social cost equals price, $MSC = P$, where $MSC = MPC + MEC$. Thus, the socially optimal level of output is

$$MPC + MEC = P$$

$$4Q + 2Q = 200 - 4Q$$

$$Q^* = 20$$

At this output level, the marginal private cost of production is

$$MPC = 4Q = 4(20) = \$80$$

The price of the product at this output level is

$$P^* = 200 - 4(20) = \$120$$

b. The per-unit tax on output is

$$t = 120 - 80 = \$40$$

To verify that this tax will result in the socially optimal output level, equate marginal private cost plus the tax to price:

$$MPC + t = P$$

$$4Q + 40 = 200 - 4Q$$

$$Q^* = 20$$

c. Total government revenues at the socially optimal output level are

$$tQ^* = 40(20) = \$800$$

PUBLIC GOODS

There are two characteristics that distinguish public goods from private goods: *nonexcludability* and *nondepletability*. A good or service is nonexcludable if no one can be barred from its consumption. Examples of nonexcludable goods include public street lighting, public radio and television transmissions, national defense, and clean air. By contrast, excludability is a characteristic of most private goods and services. Nonsubscribers, for example, can be denied access to cable television broadcasts.

Definition: A good or service is said to be nonexcludable if it is not possible to prevent nonpayers from consuming it.

A good or service is nondepletable if the consumption of a good or service by one person does not reduce the amount of that good or service available for consumption by some other person. A person listening to a radio program, for example, does not limit the ability of others to listen as well. Other examples of nondepletable goods are public television transmissions, public street lighting, and national defense. By contrast, consumption of a private good reduces the amount of that good that is available to others. For example, when you have eaten a slice of pizza, it is no longer available for anyone else to consume. The reader will note that goods that are excludable are not always depletable. For example, a cable television company may be able to deny nonsubscribers access to its product, but the amount of programming available to one subscriber is not reduced as the number of subscribers increases.

Definition: Goods and services are nondepletable if the amount consumed by one person does not reduce the amount available for consumption by others.

Because of the characteristics of nonexcludability and nondepletability, once a public good has been made available, the marginal cost of consuming that good is zero. For this reason, private markets will not provide efficient levels public goods. Since no one can be denied access to the good, no individual will have an incentive to actually purchase the good. Instead, individuals will rely on others to pay for the good. This is the so-called free-rider problem.

Definition: The free-rider problem occurs when an individual will not contribute to the provision of a public good because of the belief that others will pay for it.

To illustrate, consider the classic example of public street lighting. For a variety of reasons, from reduced automobile accidents to lower incidence of crime, society as a whole benefits from streetlights. Suppose that the residents of a particular community demand streetlights. Unlike the total demand for a private good or service, which is found by summing the individual quantities demanded at each market-determined price, the total demand for a public good is found by summing the amounts each individual is willing to pay at each level of the public good provided. Diagrammatically, the distinction is between horizontally summing individual demand curves for private goods and vertically summing individual demand curves for public goods. The difference is that the quantity supplied of public goods is fixed. What we need to ascertain is how much each individual consumer is willing to contribute.

To illustrate, suppose that three individuals in a particular neighborhood want the municipality to install streetlights. What is the optimal number of streetlights that should be installed? Suppose, for simplicity, that each individual values the amount of public good provided according to the equation

$$P_1 = P_2 = P_3 = 100 - 2Q \tag{15.1}$$

where Q represents the number of streetlights. The total demand for streetlights is the summation of the individual willingness-to-pay demand equations.

$$\begin{aligned} \Sigma_{i=1-3} = P_i = P_1 + P_2 + P_3 = (100 - 2Q) + (100 - 2Q) + (100 - 2Q) \\ = 300 - 6Q \end{aligned} \tag{15.2}$$

Suppose that the cost to the municipality of purchasing a single streetlight is \$90. The socially optimal number of streetlights may be found by equating marginal social benefit to marginal cost, that is,

$$300 - 6Q = 90 \tag{15.3}$$

which results in 35 streetlights. This situation is depicted Figure 15.16.

Note from Figure 15.16 that the cost of a single streetlight is greater than the amount any individual would be willing pay. On the other hand, if each individual pays \$30 per streetlight, then together they will pay \$90 per streetlight, and a socially optimal 35 streetlights will be provided. The problem, of course, is how do you get each individual to pay \$30 per streetlight? Because of the free-rider problem, individuals have an incentive not

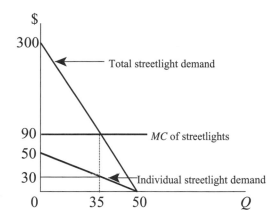

FIGURE 15.16 The optimal provision of a public good.

to reveal their true preferences for streetlights. Since each individual will wait for the someone else to pay for the streetlights, no one will pay. Thus, the market will not provide for any streetlights.

The government can bypass the free-rider problem by providing public goods on behalf of society. The government will finance the provision of public goods by levying taxes, regardless of the true preferences of any individual user. The primary problem with this particular resolution of the free-rider problem is that government probably will not provide a socially efficient amount of the public good. For one thing, the public generally makes its preferences known at the ballot box. But, the democratic process of one-person, one ballot is incapable of revealing the intensity of individual voter preferences. In fact, the government often provides excessive amounts of public goods. The reason for this is that the amount each individual taxpayer contributes is a very small a percentage the total cost of providing the public good. From the point of view of each individual taxpayer, the public good is virtually free. Thus, individual taxpayers tend to overstate their true preferences. In the situation depicted in Figure 15.16, each individual will indicate a preference for 50 streetlights, rather than the socially optimal number of 35 streetlights!

Problem 15.4. Suppose that Mike's demand for a public good is given by the equation

$$Q = 50 - P$$

Ike's demand for the same public good is

$$Q = 20 - 1.25P$$

Suppose that the marginal cost of the public good is \$48.
a. What is the socially efficient amount of the public good?
b. What is the total cost of the socially efficient amount of the public good?

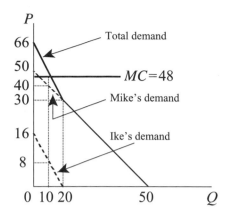

FIGURE 15.17 Diagrammatic solution to problem 15.4, part a.

c. How much should Mike pay for the socially efficient amount of the public good? How much should Ike pay?
d. How much of the public good will actually be provided by the market?
e. Suppose that the government decides to provide the socially efficient amount of the public good. How much in taxes will Mike and Ike have to pay for the socially efficient amount of the public good?

Solution

a. Solving Mike's demand equation for price, which gives the value he places on a unit of the public good provided, yields

$$P = 50 - Q$$

Solving Ike's demand equation for price yields

$$P = 16 - 0.8Q$$

The total demand equation for the public good is $P = 66 - 1.8Q$ for $P = MC > \$30$, and $P = 50 - Q$ for $P = MC < \$30$. Thus, the socially efficient provision of the public good is

$$P = MC$$

$$66 - 1.8Q = 48$$

$$Q^* = 10$$

This solution is illustrated in Figure 15.17.

b. The total cost of the socially efficient amount of the public good is

$$MC \times Q = 48(10) = \$480$$

c. Mike should pay

$$PQ = (50 - Q)Q = (50 - 10)10 = \$400$$

Ike should pay

$$PQ = (16 - 0.8Q)Q = [16 - 0.8(10)]10 = \$80$$

The total amount that Mike and Ike should pay is $480, which is the total cost of providing the public good.

d. Because of the free-rider problem, the market will not provide any amount of the public good. Mike will wait for Ike to pay, and Ike will wait for Mike to pay. The result is that no one will pay, and the public good will not be provided.

e. Because of the free-rider problem, both Mike and Ike have an incentive not to reveal their true preferences for the public good. Thus, the government will finance the provision of the public good by taxing Mike and Ike $240 apiece. Thus Mike gets 10 units of the public good for $160 less than the value he places or them, and Ike pays $200 over his valuation of 10 of these units.

POLITICAL RENT-SEEKING BEHAVIOR

An interesting application of the free-rider problem is political rent-seeking behavior. To see what is involved, consider the Figure 15.18, which illustrates the situation of a profit-maximizing monopolist facing the market demand curve $Q = 22 - P/5$. The reader can verify that for a cost of production is $10Q$, the monopolist will produce 10 units of output, charge a price of $60 per unit, and earn above-normal (economic) profits of $500. Above-normal profits are sometimes referred to as economic rents. The reader should also verify that at the price charged by the monopolist, the amount of consumer surplus is $250.

Now, suppose that a consumer advocacy group mounts a campaign to compel legislators to regulate the price charged by the monopolist at its perfectly competitive level of $10. If the efforts of the consumer advocacy group are successful, then industry output will increase to 20 units, and consumer surplus will increase by $750, while the monopolist will earn zero economic rents. Clearly, it will be in the consumers' best interest to lobby for regulation, while it will be in the monopolist's best interest to lobby against such regulation. How much will consumers be willing to pay to persuade legislators to regulate the industry depicted in Figure 15.18? How much will the monopolist be willing to pay to prevent such regulation?

It would appear that consumers will have the upper hand in their lobbying efforts to regulate the industry. As a group, consumers should be willing to incur up to $750 in lobbying expenses, while the monopolist will be willing to incur no more than $500 to prevent such legislation. Appearances, however, can be deceiving because of the existence of the free-rider problem. From the point of view of the consumer, the gain in consumer

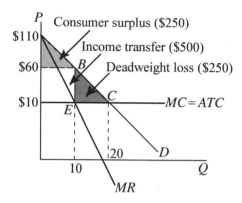

FIGURE 15.18   Rent-seeking behavior.

surplus can be viewed as a public good. The reason for this is that while the increase in consumer surplus for the group is substantial, the gain for any individual consumer may be insignificant. Thus, each individual consumer has an incentive to wait for other individual consumers to underwrite the advocacy group's lobbying efforts. Since are individual consumers can be expected to behave in precisely the same manner, we are confronted by the free-rider problem.

Definition: Political rent seeking occurs when one group attempts to use government to divert consumer or producer surplus away from another group for its own benefit.

No such problem exists for the monopolist. From the point of view of the monopolist, economic profits confer private benefits. Thus, it is in the monopolist's best interest to incur substantial costs in the form of legal fees, campaign contributions, entertainment expenses, and even bribes and under-the-table payments, to prevent price regulation. Such behavior is referred to as *political rent-seeking behavior*.

Problem 15.5. A monopolist faces the following demand equation for its product:

$$Q = 100 - 0.25P$$

The monopolist's total cost equation is

$$TC = 240Q$$

The government is considering legislation that will force the monopolist to charge a perfectly competitive price.

a. How much is the monopolist willing to spend on lobbying efforts to prevent this legislation from being enacted?

b. How much is this legislation worth to consumers?

Solution

a. Solving the demand equation for P yields

$$P = 400 - 4Q$$

The monopolist's total revenue equation is

$$TR = PQ = 400Q - 4Q^2$$

The monopolist's total profit equation is

$$\pi = TR - TC = 400Q - 4Q^2 - 240Q$$

Differentiating the profit equation to Q, setting the result equal to zero, and solving for the profit-maximizing level of output yields

$$\frac{d\pi}{dQ} = 160 - 8Q = 0$$

$$Q_M* = 20$$

The monopolist's economic profits are

$$\pi = 400(20) - 4(20)^2 - 240(20) = \$1,600$$

Thus, the monopolist will be willing to spend up to $1,600 on lobbying efforts to prevent this legislation from being enacted.

b. At the monopolist's profit-maximizing output level, the monopolist will charge

$$P_M = 400 - 4Q_M = 400 - 4(20) = \$320$$

The value of consumer surplus at the monopolist's profit-maximizing price and output level is

$$\text{Consumer surplus} = \frac{1}{2}(400 - P_M)Q_M = \frac{1}{2}(400 - 320)20 = \$800$$

The perfectly competitive price and output level are

$$MC = P$$

$$240 = 400 - 4Q$$

$$Q_{pc} = 40$$

$$P_{pc} = 400 - 4Q_{pc} = 400 - 4(40) = \$240$$

The value of consumer surplus at the perfectly competitive price and output level is

$$\text{Consumer surplus} = \frac{1}{2}(400 - P_{pc})Q_{pc} = \frac{1}{2}(400 - 240)40 = \$3,200$$

To the consumer, the legislation is worth the increase in consumer surplus, which is $3,200 − $800 = $2,400.

CHAPTER REVIEW

This chapter reviewed several reasons for direct government intervention in private markets. In general, government intervention is economically justified when private markets fail to provide socially optimal levels of goods and services. Three important sources of market failure are *market power*, *externalities*, and *public goods*.

Firms, or groups of firms, have market power when they are able to charge a price that exceeds the marginal cost of production. When firms or groups of firms have market power, they are able to earn economic profits by reducing consumer surplus. Not the reduced consumer surplus is captured by firms in the form of higher profits. The loss of consumer surplus not captured by firms is referred to as *consumer deadweight loss*. Moreover, since the firms exercising market power do not produce at minimum per-unit cost, there is a *producer deadweight loss*. This represents the loss to society from the inefficient allocation of productive resources. Total deadweight loss is the sum of the loss of consumer and producer surplus for which there are no offsetting gains to society.

When firms attempt to maximize industry profits by individually or collusively exercising market power, the market has failed to maximize the total benefits to society. Government can reduce or eliminate total deadweight loss by making it illegal for firms to exercise market power. *Antitrust laws* attempt to move industries closer to the "ideal" of perfectly competitive prices and output levels.

Market failure also occurs when third parties are positively or negatively affected by a market transaction. These third-party effects are called *externalities*. In the case of *negative externalities*, too much of a good or service is being produced. In the case of *positive externalities*, too little of a good or service is being produced. This chapter focused on the problems arising from negative externalities, such as environmental pollution.

In the case of negative externalities, there are generally two ways in which the government promotes a more socially beneficial outcome. On the one hand, the government can establish conditions under which the market determines an efficient solution to the externality problem through the assignment of well-defined private property rights. The theoretical justification for this approach to the externality problem is the *Coase theorem*. In the absence of well-defined property rights, governments can intervene directly to resolve the problems of negative externalities through the use of *regulations*, *permits*, and *taxes*.

Governments also intervene in private markets to provide *public goods*. Public goods are distinguished from private goods by the characteristics of *nonexcludability* and *nondepletability*. A good or service is nonexcludable if no one can be barred from its consumption. A good or service is nondepletable if the consumption of a good or service by one person does not reduce the amount of that good or service available for consumption by some other person. Since no one can be prevented from consuming them, individuals will not have an incentive to purchase public goods. Instead, individuals will rely on others to pay for the good. This is the *free-rider* problem.

Governments overcome the free-rider problem by providing public goods on behalf of society. Governments will generally finance the provision of public goods by levying taxes. In general, governments do not provide socially efficient amounts of public goods because of an inability to accurately assess society's preferences for these products.

An interesting application of the free-rider problem is *political rent-seeking* behavior. Political rent seeking occurs when one group attempts to use government to divert consumer or producer surplus away from another group for its own benefit. For example, legislators may attempt to regulate monopoly prices at their perfectly competitive level. From the point of view of the consumer, the potential gain in consumer surplus can be viewed as a public good. While the potential increase in consumer surplus for the group is substantial, the gain to any individual consumer may be insignificant. Thus, each individual consumer has an incentive to wait for others to underwrite the efforts of those lobbying for regulation. On the other hand, economic profits confer private benefits on the monopolist. Thus, it is in the monopolist's best interest to incur substantial costs to prevent price regulation.

KEY TERMS AND CONCEPTS

Antitrust legislation   Government intervention in the marketplace to prevent industry abuse of market power.

Coase theorem   A market-determined solution to the externality problem. The theorem states that the assignment of well-defined private property rights will result in a socially efficient allocation of productive resources and a socially optimal level of goods and services.

Conglomerate merger   A merger of firms producing unrelated products.

Consumer deadweight loss   The reduction in consumer surplus that is not captured as an income transfer to a monopolist.

Consumer surplus   The difference between what consumers are willing to pay for a given quantity of a good or service and the amount they actually pay. Diagrammatically, consumer surplus is illustrated as the area below a downward-sloping demand curve but above the selling price.

Exclusive contract   The practice of forcing customers to purchase one product as a precondition for obtaining some other product.

Externality   A cost or benefit resulting from a market transaction that is imposed on third parties.

Free-rider problem   Occurs when an individual will not contribute to the provision of a public good because of the belief that others will pay for it.

Horizontal merger   A merger of firms producing the same product.

Interlocking directorate   The situation in which the same individual sits on the board of directors of two or more competing corporations.

Interlocking stockholding   The practice of one corporation acquiring shares in a competing corporation.

Market failure   Socially inefficient allocation of goods, services, and productive resources as a result of private transactions.

Nondepletability   Goods and services are nondepletable if the amount consumed by one person does not reduce the amount available for consumption by others.

Nonexcludability   Goods are nonexcludable if no person can be barred from consuming them.

Political rent seeking   Attempts by one group to use government to divert consumer or producer surplus away from another group for its own benefit.

Producer deadweight loss   Arises when society's resources are inefficiently employed because a monopolist does not produce at minimum per-unit cost.

Total deadweight loss   The loss of consumption and production efficiency arising from monopolistic market structures. It is the loss of consumer and producer surplus when a monopolist charges a price that is greater than the marginal cost of production.

Tying contract   The practice of making the purchase of one or more goods or services from one firm contingent on the customer's promise not to purchase other goods and services from competing firms.

Vertical merger   Mergers of firms at various stages of the production process.

CHAPTER QUESTIONS

15.1 Suppose that the firms in a perfectly competitive industry are organized into a profit-maximizing monopoly. The monopolist charges a higher price and produces a lower output level than was the case under perfect competition. The result to a reduction in consumer surplus and an equivalent increase in producer surplus. Thus, while monopolizing the industry is detrimental to consumers, the net effect on society is zero. Do you agree? If not, then why not?

15.2 What is consumer deadweight loss?

15.3 What is producer deadweight loss?

15.4 Explain how the presence of market power results in socially nonoptimal levels of goods and services and a misallocation of productive resources.

15.5 It is always in the public's best interest to regulate prices at levels lower than would be charged by a monopolist. Do you agree? Explain.

15.6 Suppose that the price charged by a monopolist is regulated at its perfectly competitive level. Suppose, however, that at the profit-maximizing level of output $ATC > P_{pc}$. What can the government do to prevent the firm from exiting the industry?

15.7 *Ceteris paribus*, a firm that pollutes a nearby river produces a greater level of output and sells its product at a lower price than a similar firm that cleans up its effluents prior to discharge into the river. Since a lower price and a higher output results in greater consumer surplus, why should the government be so concerned about the problem of pollution?

15.8 Explain how the assignment of private property rights will lead to a socially efficient level of output.

15.9 Suppose that a steel plant discharges significant amounts of air pollution. Residents within a 50-mile radius of the steel plant experience an incidence of lung cancer significantly higher than the national average. A blue-ribbon commission to study the problem determined that there is a direct linkage between air pollution and higher rates of lung cancer. The Coase theorem asserts that the best way to reduce the local incidence of cancer is to assign to the steel plant the private property rights to pollute the atmosphere. In this way, the steel plant can sell clean air to local residents. Will this solution reduce the amount of air pollution emitted by the steel plant? Is this, in fact, the best solution?

15.10 It is reasonable to assert that zero pollution should be the goal of public environmental protection agencies. Do you agree?

15.11 In general, direct government regulation of pollution emissions is superior to charging emission fees because compliance does not depend on the good will of the polluter. Do you agree with this statement? If not, then why not?

15.12 Under what circumstances will setting emissions standards result in a superior solution to the pollution problem than charging emission fees?

15.13 The most important, and unanticipated, shortcoming of the Clean Air Act is that a market for pollution emission permits encourages firms to avoid adopting environmentally friendly production technologies. Do you agree? Explain.

15.14 Explain why private markets will not provide socially efficient levels of public goods?

15.15 What product characteristics cause the free-rider problem?

15.16 Why is it necessary for governments to provide public goods? How do governments finance the provision of public goods? Explain why governments frequently provide socially inefficient amounts of the public goods?

15.17 Explain the importance of the free-rider problem in political rent-seeking activity.

CHAPTER EXERCISES

15.1 Suppose that the demand and supply curves for a perfectly competitive market are given by the following linear equations:

$$Q_D = 200 - 2P$$
$$Q_S = 100 + 4P$$

a. Determine the equilibrium price and output level.
b. At the perfectly competitive equilibrium price and output level, calculate consumer surplus and producer surplus.
c. Suppose that the industry is organized as a monopoly. Assuming that the industry supply curve represents the monopolist's marginal cost of production, determine the profit-maximizing price and output level.
d. Given your answer to part c, calculate consumer surplus and producer surplus.
e. Given your answers to parts b and d, calculate total deadweight loss.

15.2 Suppose that the demand and supply for a product sold in a perfectly competitive market are given by the equations

$$Q = 130 - 2P$$
$$Q = -50 + P$$

a. What are the perfectly competitive equilibrium price and quantity for this product?
b. Suppose the industry that produces this product causes environmental damage valued by the government at 0.5 per unit of output. Determine the socially optimal price and output level for this product.
c. Determine the welfare cost to society when the product is provided at the perfectly competitive price and output level.
d. What tax should the government add to the price of the product to obtain the socially optimal output level?

15.3 Suppose that four individuals have identical demands for a public good, as follows:

$$P_1 = P_2 = P_3 = P_4 = 20 - 2Q$$

Suppose further that the marginal cost of the public good is $40.

    a. What is the socially efficient amount of the public good?

    b. How much should each individual pay for the socially efficient amount of the public good?

    c. How much of the public good will actually be provided by the market?

    d. Suppose that the government decides to provide the socially efficient amount of the public good. How much in taxes will Mike and Ike have to pay?

SELECTED READINGS

Bade, R., and M. Parkin. *Foundations of Microeconomics*. New York: Addison-Wesley, 2002.

Bator, F. M. "The Anatomy of Market Failure." *Quarterly Journal of Economics*, August (1958) pp. 351–379.

Coase, R. H., "The Problem of Social Costs." *Journal of Law and Economics*, 3 (October 1960), pp. 1–44.

Eisner, M. *Antitrust and the Triumph of Economics*. Chapel Hill: University of North Carolina Press, 1991.

Falkinger, J. "On Optimal Public Good Provision with Tax Evasion." *Journal of Public Economics*, 45 (June 1991), pp. 127–133.

Friedman, L. S. *Microeconomic Policy Analysis*. New York: McGraw-Hill, 1984.

Hope, S. *Applied Microeconomics*. New York: John Wiley & Sons, 1999.

Hyman, D. N. *Public Finance: A Contemporary Application of Theory to Policy*, 3rd ed. Hinsdale, IL: Dryden Press, 1990.

Khan, A. E. *The Economics of Regulation*. New York: Wiley, 1971.

Layard, P. R. G., and A. A. Walters. *Microeconomic Theory*. New York: McGraw-Hill, 1978.

Malinvaud, E. *Lectures on Microeconomic Theory*. New York: American Elsevier, 1972.

Nicholson, W. *Microeconomic Theory: Basic Principles and Extensions*, 6th ed. New York: Dryden Press, 1995.

Silberberg, Eugene. *The Structure of Economics: A Mathematical Analysis*, 2nd ed. New York: McGraw-Hill, 1990.

Stiglitz, J. E. *Economics of the Public Sector*, 2nd ed. New York: W. W. Norton, 1988.

INDEX